SUPER**TOKYO**LAND

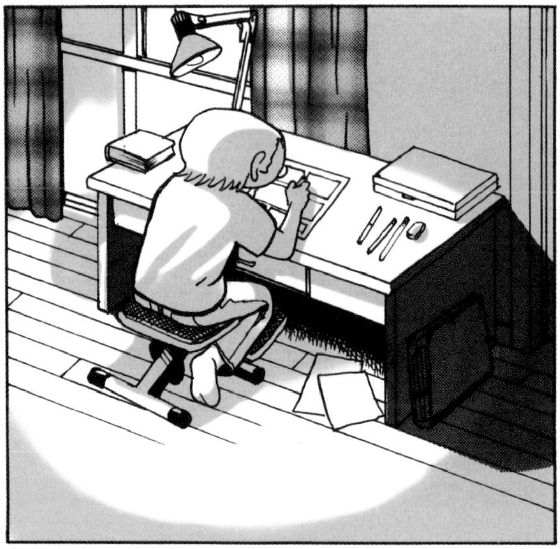

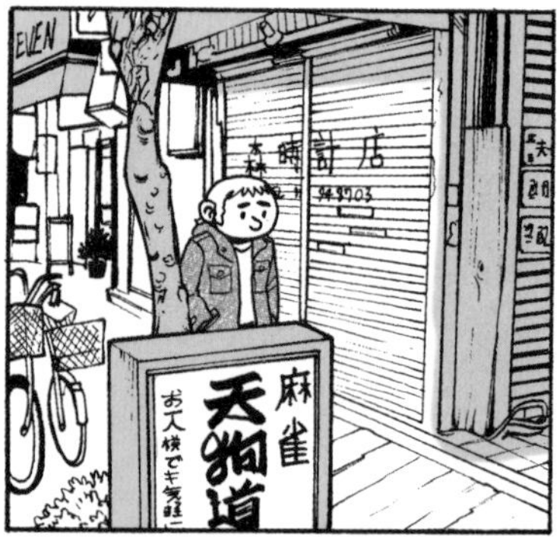
EVEN
森時計店
麻雀
天狗道
お一人様でも気軽

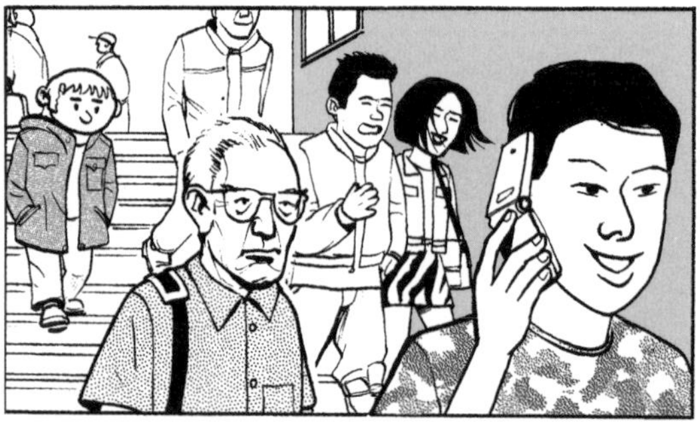

Benjamin Reiss

SUPER TOKYOLAND

TOP SHELF

EDITOR-IN-CHIEF: CHRIS STAROS.

PUBLISHED BY TOP SHELF PRODUCTIONS, PO BOX 1282, MARIETTA, GA 30061-1282, USA. TOP SHELF PRODUCTIONS IS AN IMPRINT OF IDW PUBLISHING, A DIVISION OF IDEA AND DESIGN WORKS, LLC. OFFICES: 2765 TRUXTUN ROAD, SAN DIEGO, CA 92106. TOP SHELF PRODUCTIONS®, THE TOP SHELF LOGO, IDEA AND DESIGN WORKS®, AND THE IDW LOGO ARE REGISTERED TRADEMARKS OF IDEA AND DESIGN WORKS, LLC. ALL RIGHTS RESERVED. WITH THE EXCEPTION OF SMALL EXCERPTS OF ARTWORK USED FOR REVIEW PURPOSES, NONE OF THE CONTENTS OF THIS PUBLICATION MAY BE REPRINTED WITHOUT THE PERMISSION OF IDW PUBLISHING. IDW PUBLISHING DOES NOT READ OR ACCEPT UNSOLICITED SUBMISSIONS OF IDEAS, STORIES, OR ARTWORK.

VISIT OUR ONLINE CATALOG AT WWW.TOPSHELFCOMIX.COM.

ISBN 978-1-60309-418-4

PRINTED IN KOREA.

17 18 19 20 21   5 4 3 2 1

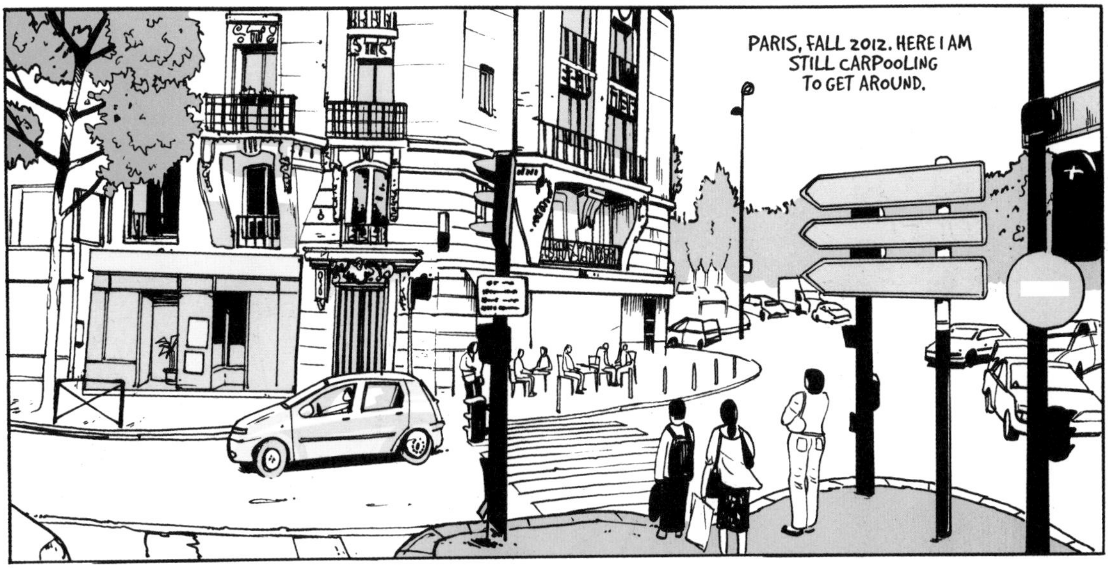
PARIS, FALL 2012. HERE I AM STILL CARPOOLING TO GET AROUND.

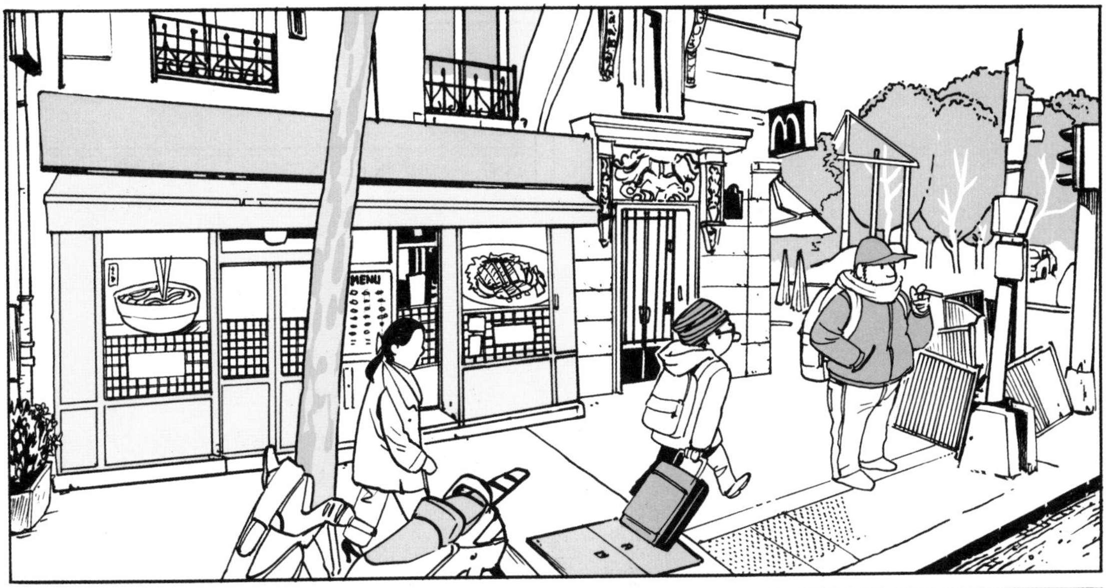
MENU

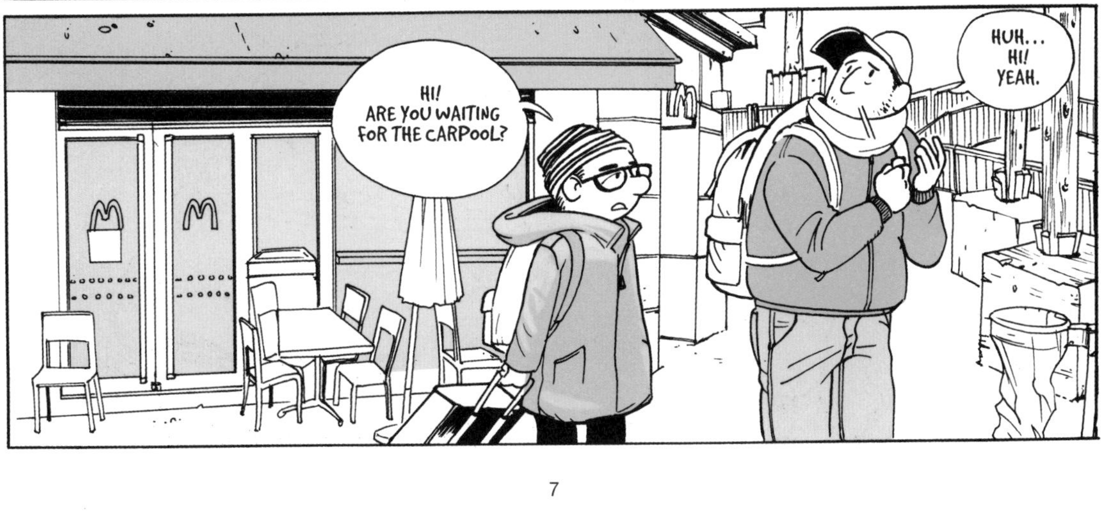
HI! ARE YOU WAITING FOR THE CARPOOL?
HUH... HI! YEAH.

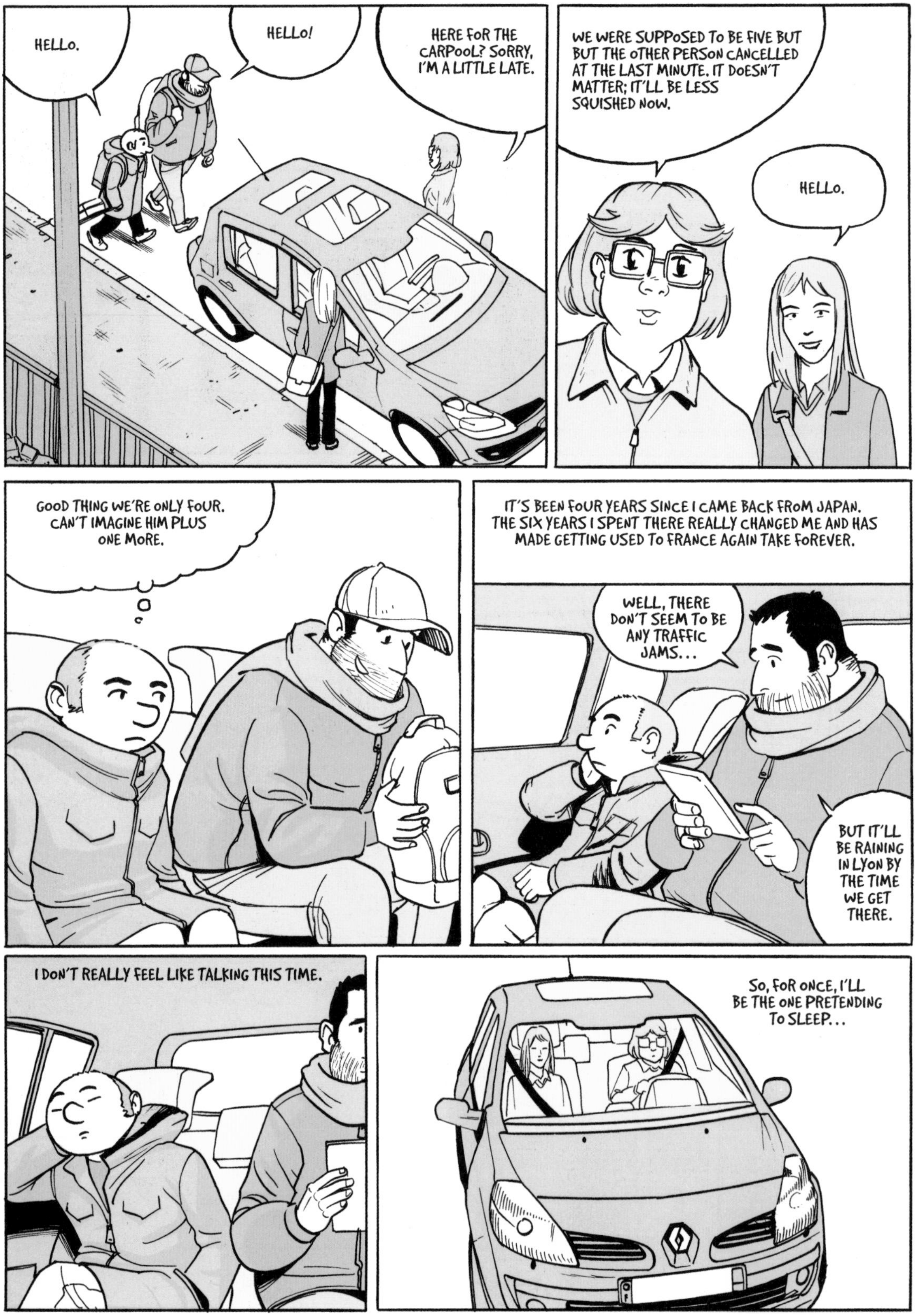
HELLO.
HELLO!
HERE FOR THE CARPOOL? SORRY, I'M A LITTLE LATE.
WE WERE SUPPOSED TO BE FIVE BUT BUT THE OTHER PERSON CANCELLED AT THE LAST MINUTE. IT DOESN'T MATTER; IT'LL BE LESS SQUISHED NOW.
HELLO.
GOOD THING WE'RE ONLY FOUR. CAN'T IMAGINE HIM PLUS ONE MORE.
IT'S BEEN FOUR YEARS SINCE I CAME BACK FROM JAPAN. THE SIX YEARS I SPENT THERE REALLY CHANGED ME AND HAS MADE GETTING USED TO FRANCE AGAIN TAKE FOREVER.
WELL, THERE DON'T SEEM TO BE ANY TRAFFIC JAMS...
BUT IT'LL BE RAINING IN LYON BY THE TIME WE GET THERE.
I DON'T REALLY FEEL LIKE TALKING THIS TIME.
SO, FOR ONCE, I'LL BE THE ONE PRETENDING TO SLEEP...

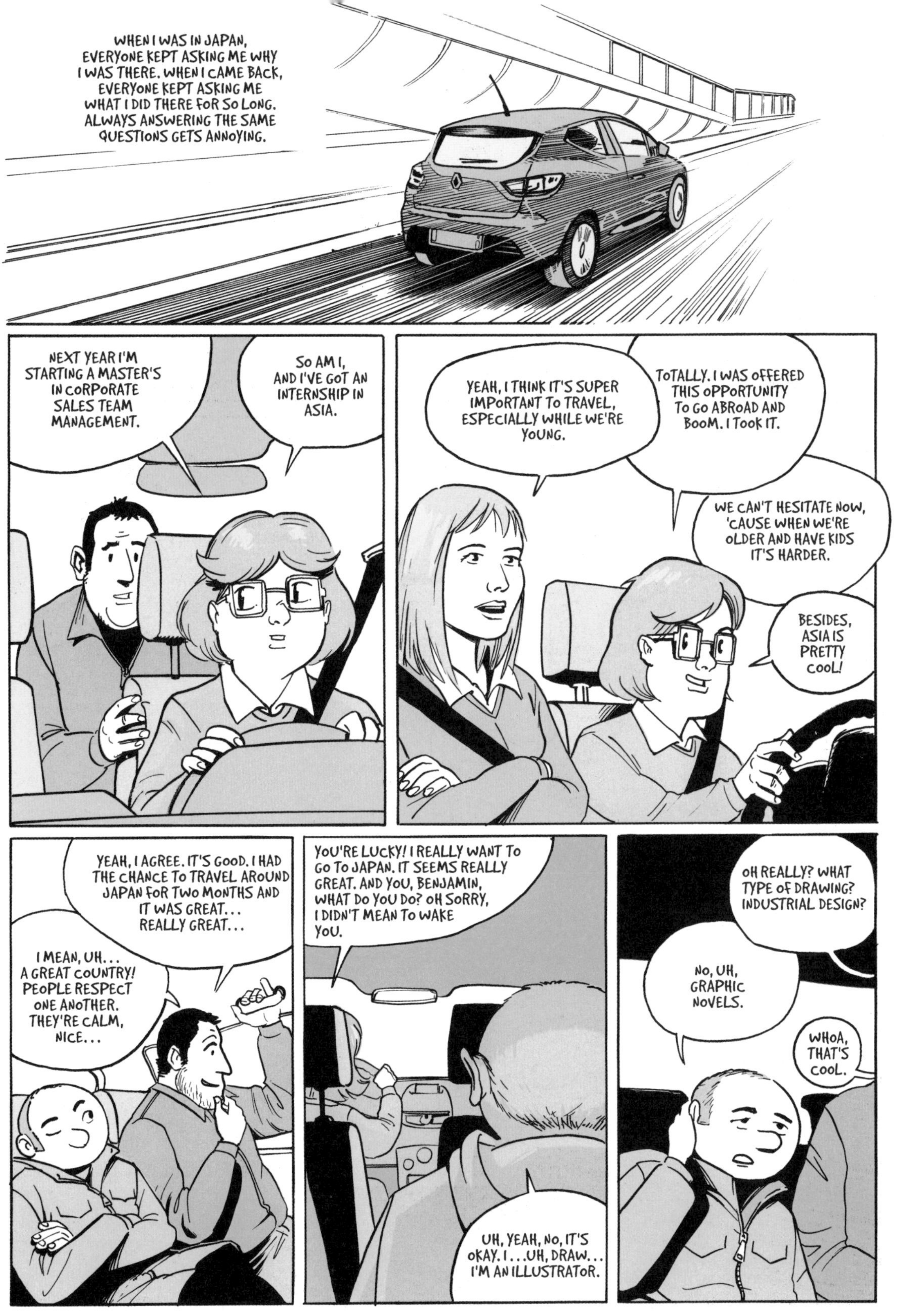
WHEN I WAS IN JAPAN, EVERYONE KEPT ASKING ME WHY I WAS THERE. WHEN I CAME BACK, EVERYONE KEPT ASKING ME WHAT I DID THERE FOR SO LONG. ALWAYS ANSWERING THE SAME QUESTIONS GETS ANNOYING.
NEXT YEAR I'M STARTING A MASTER'S IN CORPORATE SALES TEAM MANAGEMENT.
SO AM I, AND I'VE GOT AN INTERNSHIP IN ASIA.
YEAH, I THINK IT'S SUPER IMPORTANT TO TRAVEL, ESPECIALLY WHILE WE'RE YOUNG.
TOTALLY. I WAS OFFERED THIS OPPORTUNITY TO GO ABROAD AND BOOM. I TOOK IT.
WE CAN'T HESITATE NOW, 'CAUSE WHEN WE'RE OLDER AND HAVE KIDS IT'S HARDER.
BESIDES, ASIA IS PRETTY COOL!
YEAH, I AGREE. IT'S GOOD. I HAD THE CHANCE TO TRAVEL AROUND JAPAN FOR TWO MONTHS AND IT WAS GREAT... REALLY GREAT...
I MEAN, UH... A GREAT COUNTRY! PEOPLE RESPECT ONE ANOTHER. THEY'RE CALM, NICE...
YOU'RE LUCKY! I REALLY WANT TO GO TO JAPAN. IT SEEMS REALLY GREAT. AND YOU, BENJAMIN, WHAT DO YOU DO? OH SORRY, I DIDN'T MEAN TO WAKE YOU.
UH, YEAH, NO, IT'S OKAY. I... UH, DRAW... I'M AN ILLUSTRATOR.
OH REALLY? WHAT TYPE OF DRAWING? INDUSTRIAL DESIGN?
NO, UH, GRAPHIC NOVELS.
WHOA, THAT'S COOL.

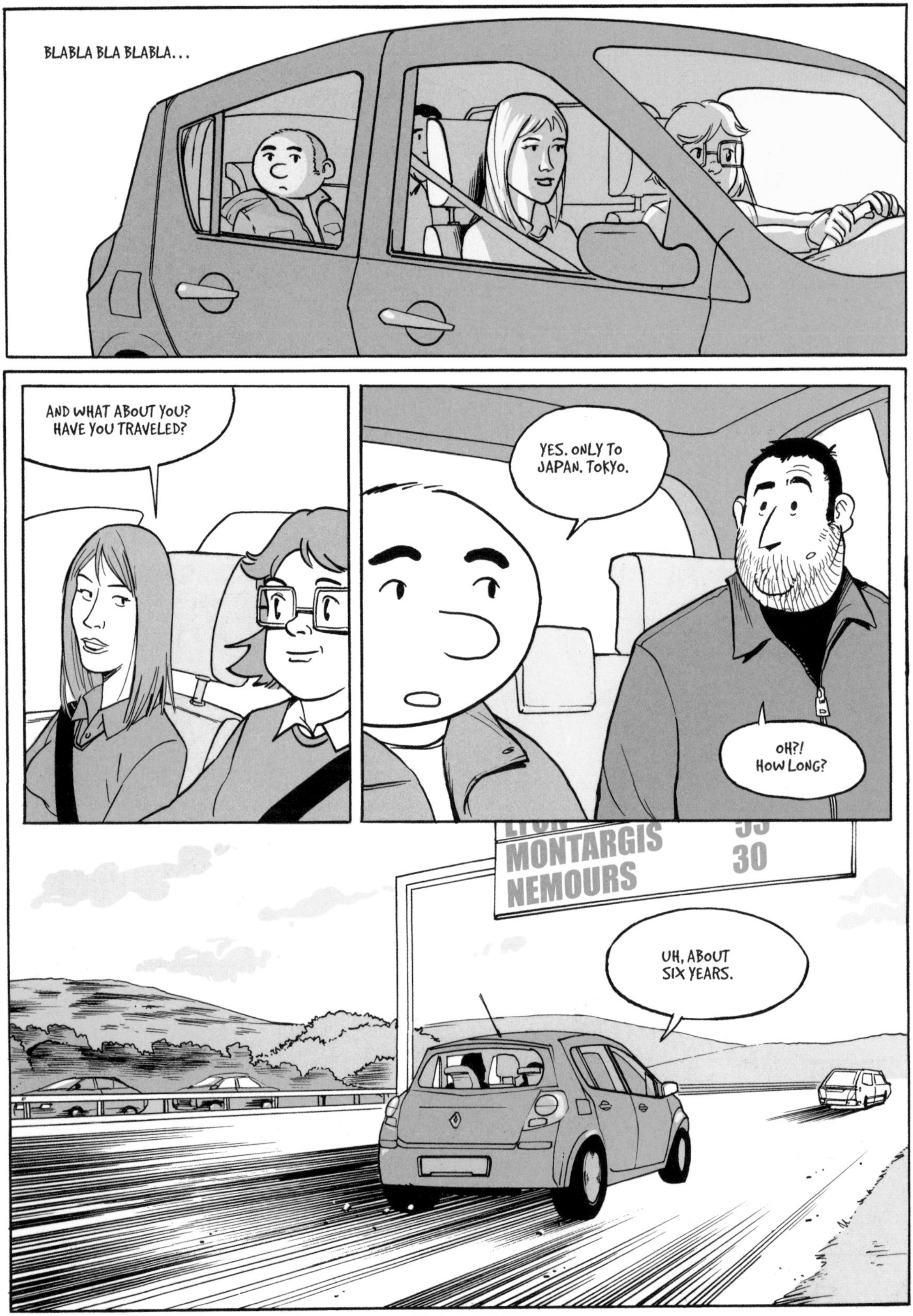
BLABLA BLA BLABLA...
AND WHAT ABOUT YOU? HAVE YOU TRAVELED?
YES. ONLY TO JAPAN. TOKYO.
OH?! HOW LONG?
MONTARGIS 30
NEMOURS
UH, ABOUT SIX YEARS.

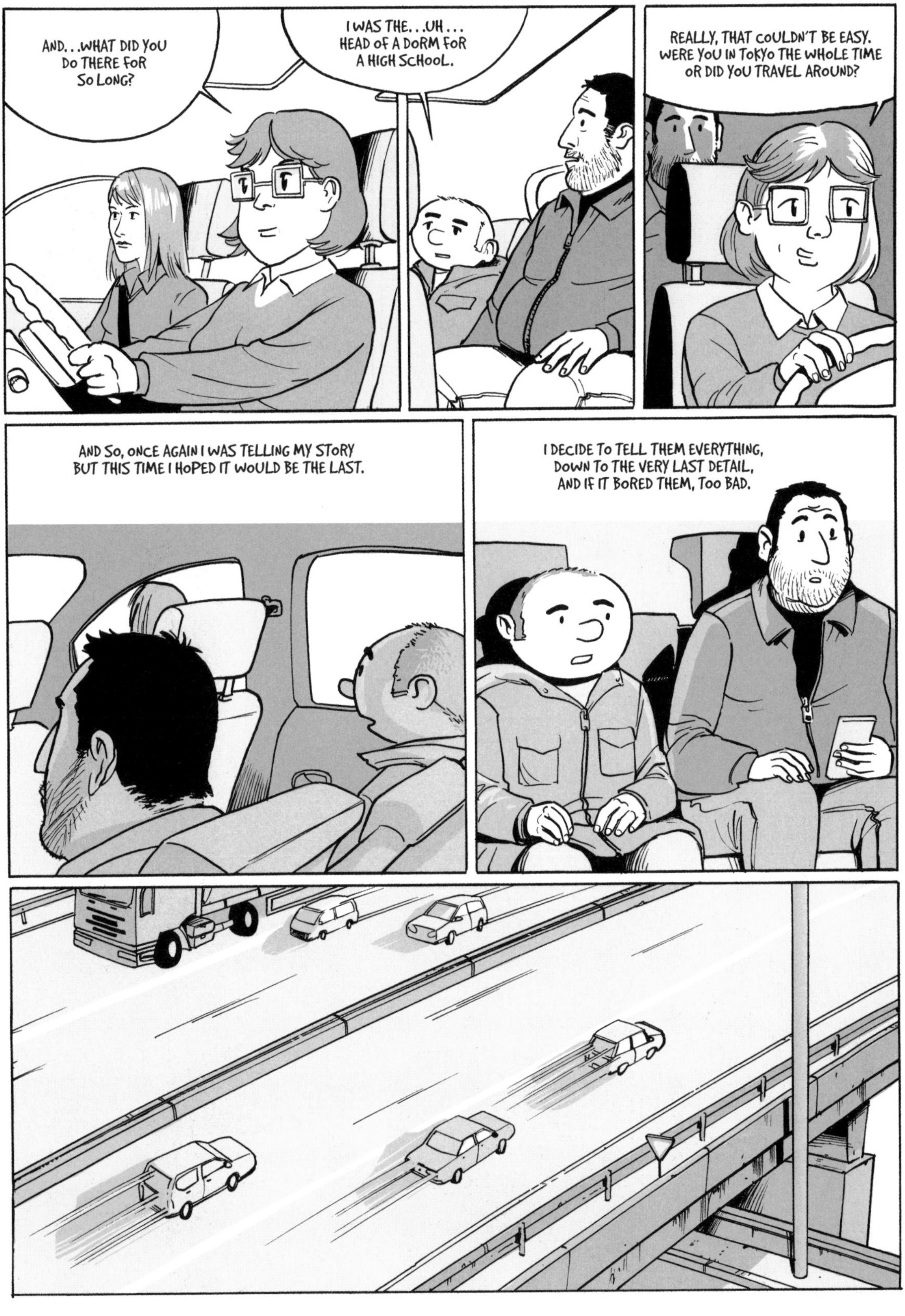
AND...WHAT DID YOU DO THERE FOR SO LONG?
I WAS THE...UH... HEAD OF A DORM FOR A HIGH SCHOOL.
REALLY, THAT COULDN'T BE EASY. WERE YOU IN TOKYO THE WHOLE TIME OR DID YOU TRAVEL AROUND?
AND SO, ONCE AGAIN I WAS TELLING MY STORY BUT THIS TIME I HOPED IT WOULD BE THE LAST.
I DECIDE TO TELL THEM EVERYTHING, DOWN TO THE VERY LAST DETAIL, AND IF IT BORED THEM, TOO BAD.

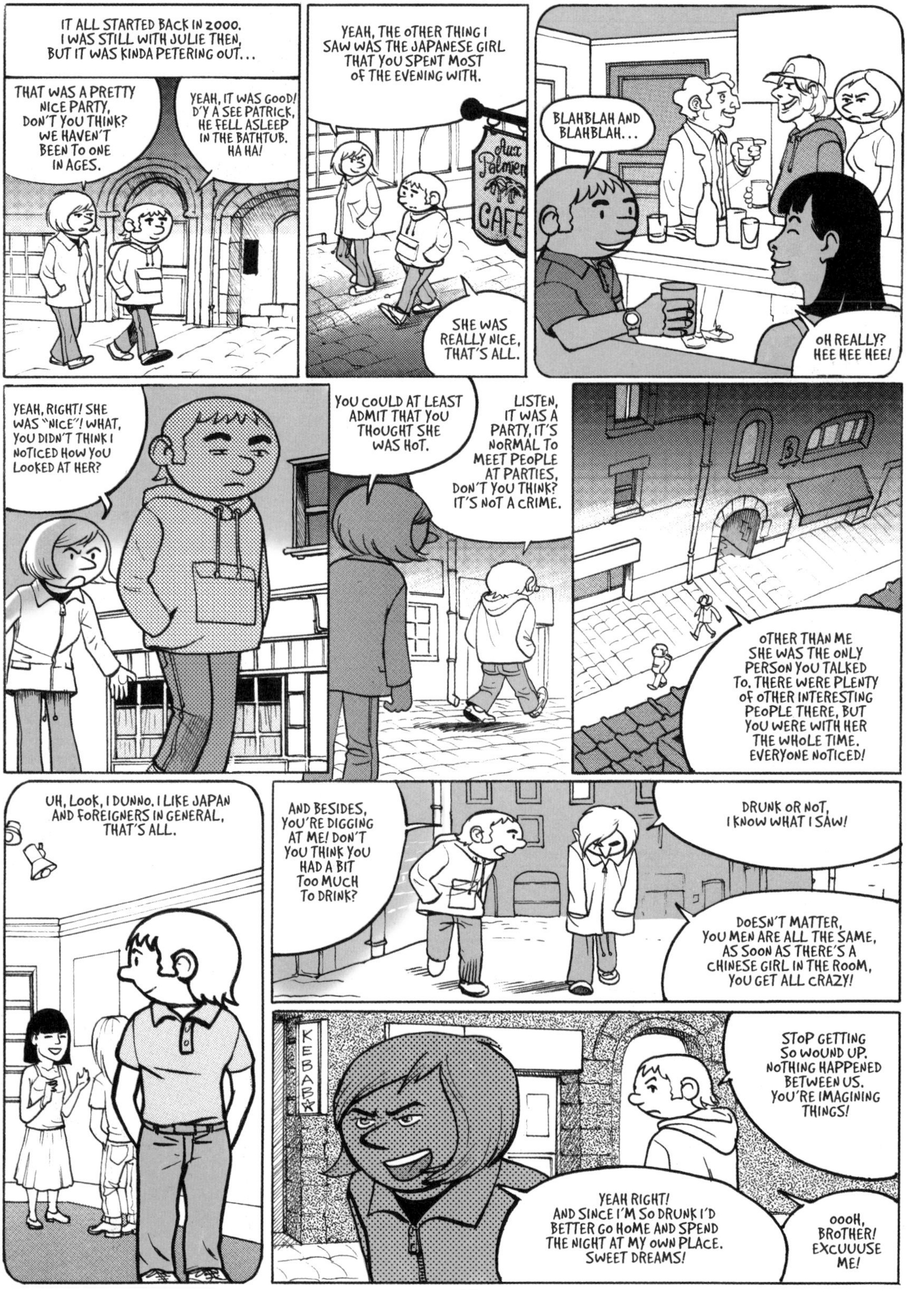

IT ALL STARTED BACK IN 2000. I WAS STILL WITH JULIE THEN, BUT IT WAS KINDA PETERING OUT...
THAT WAS A PRETTY NICE PARTY, DON'T YOU THINK? WE HAVEN'T BEEN TO ONE IN AGES.
YEAH, IT WAS GOOD! D'Y A SEE PATRICK, HE FELL ASLEEP IN THE BATHTUB. HA HA!
YEAH, THE OTHER THING I SAW WAS THE JAPANESE GIRL THAT YOU SPENT MOST OF THE EVENING WITH.
Aux Palmiers
CAFÉ
SHE WAS REALLY NICE, THAT'S ALL.
BLAHBLAH AND BLAHBLAH...
OH REALLY? HEE HEE HEE!
YEAH, RIGHT! SHE WAS "NICE"! WHAT, YOU DIDN'T THINK I NOTICED HOW YOU LOOKED AT HER?
YOU COULD AT LEAST ADMIT THAT YOU THOUGHT SHE WAS HOT.
LISTEN, IT WAS A PARTY, IT'S NORMAL TO MEET PEOPLE AT PARTIES, DON'T YOU THINK? IT'S NOT A CRIME.
OTHER THAN ME SHE WAS THE ONLY PERSON YOU TALKED TO. THERE WERE PLENTY OF OTHER INTERESTING PEOPLE THERE, BUT YOU WERE WITH HER THE WHOLE TIME. EVERYONE NOTICED!
UH, LOOK, I DUNNO. I LIKE JAPAN AND FOREIGNERS IN GENERAL, THAT'S ALL.
AND BESIDES, YOU'RE DIGGING AT ME! DON'T YOU THINK YOU HAD A BIT TOO MUCH TO DRINK?
DRUNK OR NOT, I KNOW WHAT I SAW!
DOESN'T MATTER, YOU MEN ARE ALL THE SAME, AS SOON AS THERE'S A CHINESE GIRL IN THE ROOM, YOU GET ALL CRAZY!
KEBAB
STOP GETTING SO WOUND UP. NOTHING HAPPENED BETWEEN US. YOU'RE IMAGINING THINGS!
YEAH RIGHT! AND SINCE I'M SO DRUNK I'D BETTER GO HOME AND SPEND THE NIGHT AT MY OWN PLACE. SWEET DREAMS!
OOOH, BROTHER! EXCUUUSE ME!

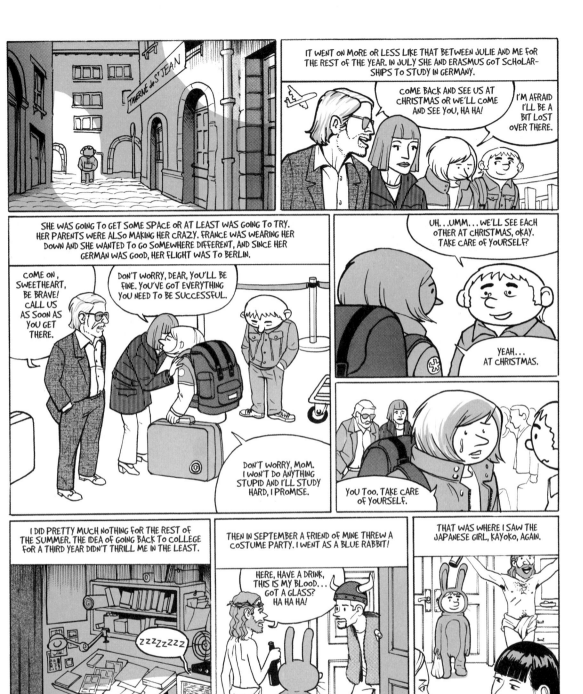

TAVERNE de ST JEAN

IT WENT ON MORE OR LESS LIKE THAT BETWEEN JULIE AND ME FOR THE REST OF THE YEAR. IN JULY SHE AND ERASMUS GOT SCHOLARSHIPS TO STUDY IN GERMANY.

COME BACK AND SEE US AT CHRISTMAS OR WE'LL COME AND SEE YOU, HA HA!

I'M AFRAID I'LL BE A BIT LOST OVER THERE.

SHE WAS GOING TO GET SOME SPACE OR AT LEAST WAS GOING TO TRY. HER PARENTS WERE ALSO MAKING HER CRAZY. FRANCE WAS WEARING HER DOWN AND SHE WANTED TO GO SOMEWHERE DIFFERENT, AND SINCE HER GERMAN WAS GOOD, HER FLIGHT WAS TO BERLIN.

COME ON, SWEETHEART, BE BRAVE! CALL US AS SOON AS YOU GET THERE.

DON'T WORRY, DEAR, YOU'LL BE FINE. YOU'VE GOT EVERYTHING YOU NEED TO BE SUCCESSFUL.

DON'T WORRY, MOM. I WON'T DO ANYTHING STUPID AND I'LL STUDY HARD, I PROMISE.

UH...UMM... WE'LL SEE EACH OTHER AT CHRISTMAS, OKAY. TAKE CARE OF YOURSELF?

YEAH... AT CHRISTMAS.

YOU TOO. TAKE CARE OF YOURSELF.

I DID PRETTY MUCH NOTHING FOR THE REST OF THE SUMMER. THE IDEA OF GOING BACK TO COLLEGE FOR A THIRD YEAR DIDN'T THRILL ME IN THE LEAST.

ZZZZZZZZ

THEN IN SEPTEMBER A FRIEND OF MINE THREW A COSTUME PARTY. I WENT AS A BLUE RABBIT!

HERE, HAVE A DRINK, THIS IS MY BLOOD... GOT A GLASS? HA HA HA!

GREAT COSTUMES, GUYS. COME ON IN! JOIN THE CROWD.

THAT WAS WHERE I SAW THE JAPANESE GIRL, KAYOKO, AGAIN.

13

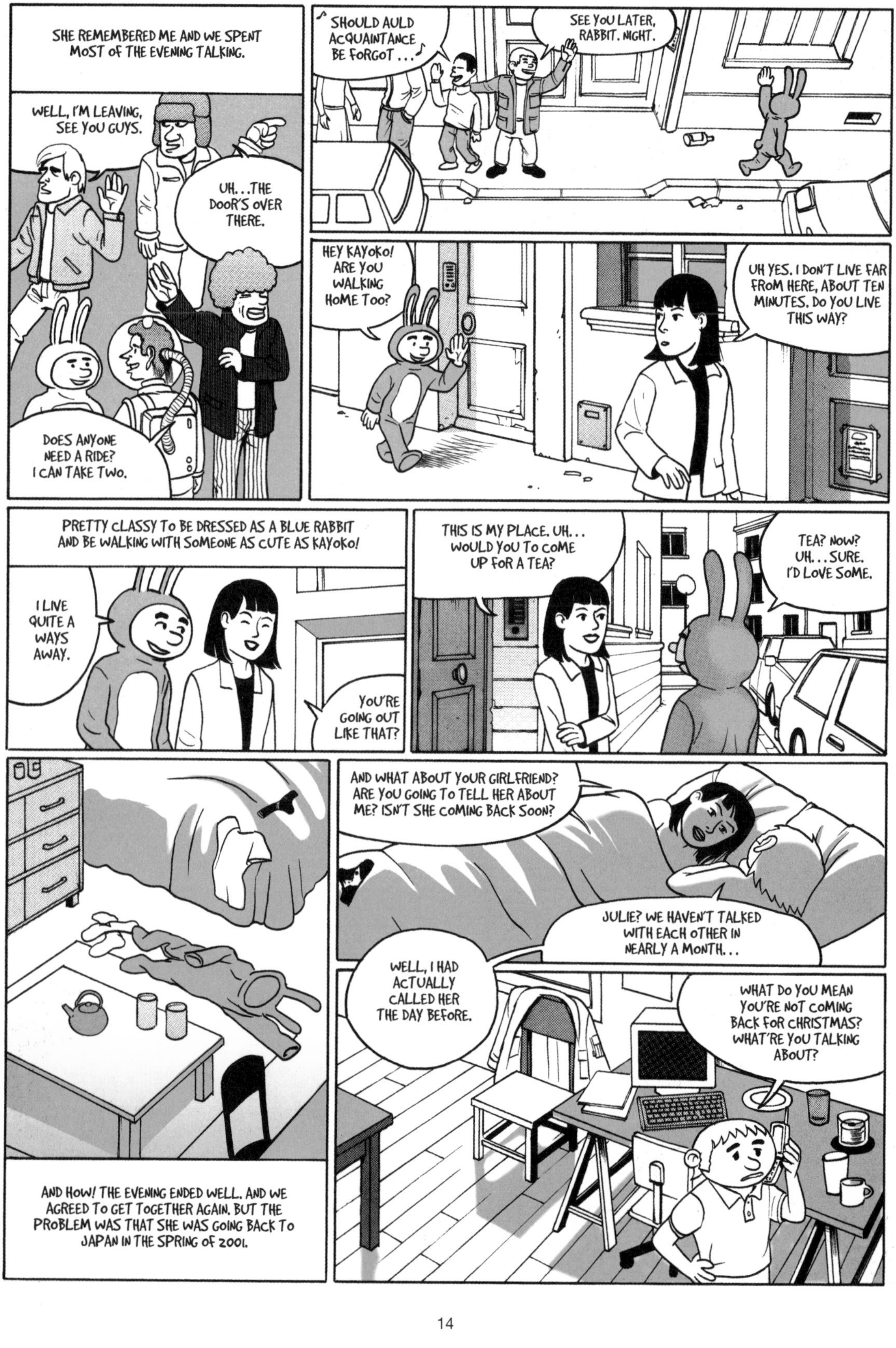
SHE REMEMBERED ME AND WE SPENT MOST OF THE EVENING TALKING.
WELL, I'M LEAVING, SEE YOU GUYS.
UH...THE DOOR'S OVER THERE.
DOES ANYONE NEED A RIDE? I CAN TAKE TWO.
SHOULD AULD ACQUAINTANCE BE FORGOT...
SEE YOU LATER, RABBIT. NIGHT.
HEY KAYOKO! ARE YOU WALKING HOME TOO?
UH YES. I DON'T LIVE FAR FROM HERE, ABOUT TEN MINUTES. DO YOU LIVE THIS WAY?
PRETTY CLASSY TO BE DRESSED AS A BLUE RABBIT AND BE WALKING WITH SOMEONE AS CUTE AS KAYOKO!
I LIVE QUITE A WAYS AWAY.
YOU'RE GOING OUT LIKE THAT?
THIS IS MY PLACE. UH... WOULD YOU TO COME UP FOR A TEA?
TEA? NOW? UH...SURE. I'D LOVE SOME.
AND HOW! THE EVENING ENDED WELL. AND WE AGREED TO GET TOGETHER AGAIN. BUT THE PROBLEM WAS THAT SHE WAS GOING BACK TO JAPAN IN THE SPRING OF 2001.
AND WHAT ABOUT YOUR GIRLFRIEND? ARE YOU GOING TO TELL HER ABOUT ME? ISN'T SHE COMING BACK SOON?
JULIE? WE HAVEN'T TALKED WITH EACH OTHER IN NEARLY A MONTH...
WELL, I HAD ACTUALLY CALLED HER THE DAY BEFORE.
WHAT DO YOU MEAN YOU'RE NOT COMING BACK FOR CHRISTMAS? WHAT'RE YOU TALKING ABOUT?

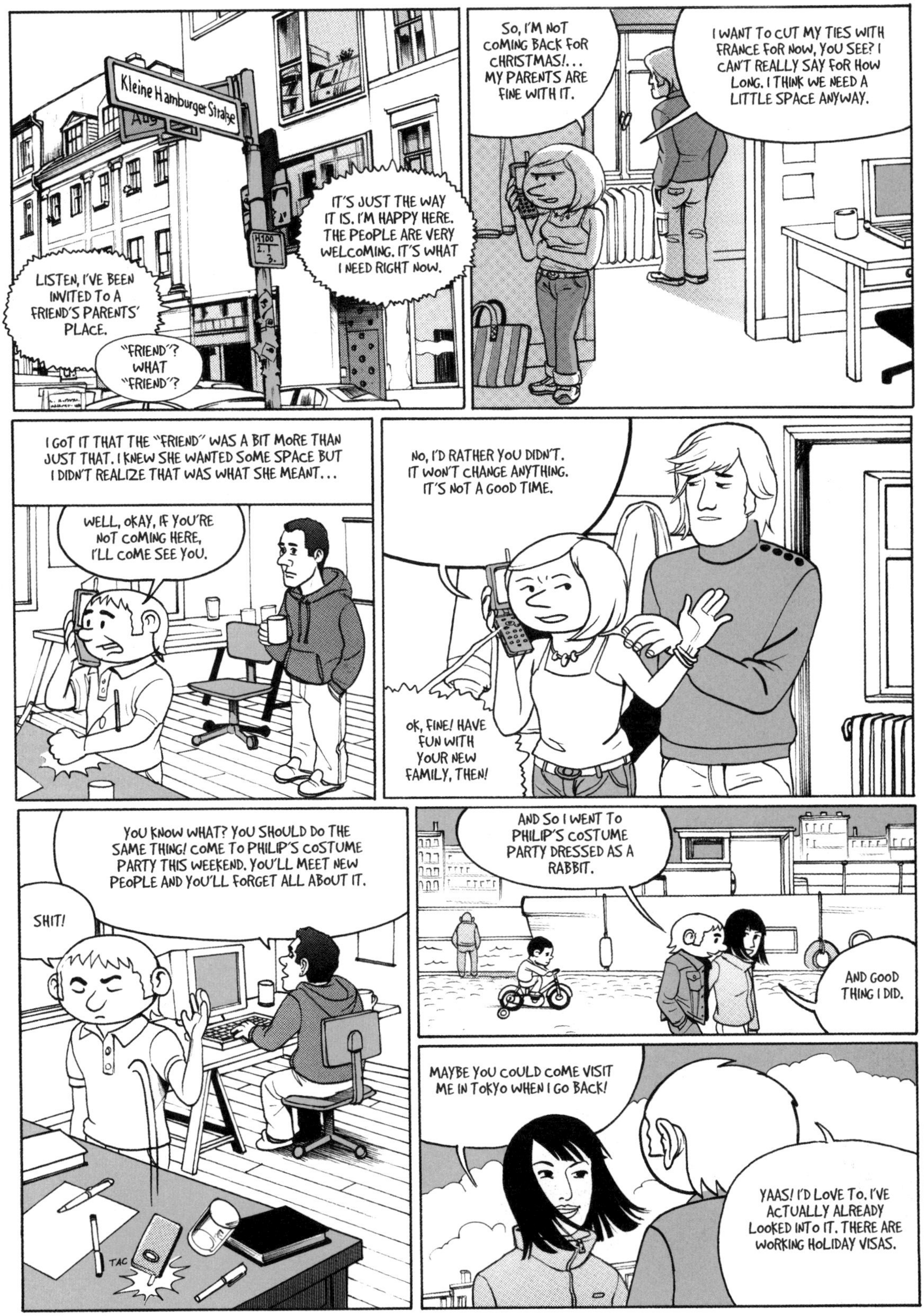
Kleine Hamburger Straße
LISTEN, I'VE BEEN INVITED TO A FRIEND'S PARENTS' PLACE.
"FRIEND"? WHAT "FRIEND"?
IT'S JUST THE WAY IT IS. I'M HAPPY HERE. THE PEOPLE ARE VERY WELCOMING. IT'S WHAT I NEED RIGHT NOW.
SO, I'M NOT COMING BACK FOR CHRISTMAS!... MY PARENTS ARE FINE WITH IT.
I WANT TO CUT MY TIES WITH FRANCE FOR NOW, YOU SEE? I CAN'T REALLY SAY FOR HOW LONG. I THINK WE NEED A LITTLE SPACE ANYWAY.
I GOT IT THAT THE "FRIEND" WAS A BIT MORE THAN JUST THAT. I KNEW SHE WANTED SOME SPACE BUT I DIDN'T REALIZE THAT WAS WHAT SHE MEANT...
WELL, OKAY, IF YOU'RE NOT COMING HERE, I'LL COME SEE YOU.
NO, I'D RATHER YOU DIDN'T. IT WON'T CHANGE ANYTHING. IT'S NOT A GOOD TIME.
OK, FINE! HAVE FUN WITH YOUR NEW FAMILY, THEN!
YOU KNOW WHAT? YOU SHOULD DO THE SAME THING! COME TO PHILIP'S COSTUME PARTY THIS WEEKEND. YOU'LL MEET NEW PEOPLE AND YOU'LL FORGET ALL ABOUT IT.
SHIT!
TAC
AND SO I WENT TO PHILIP'S COSTUME PARTY DRESSED AS A RABBIT.
AND GOOD THING I DID.
MAYBE YOU COULD COME VISIT ME IN TOKYO WHEN I GO BACK!
YAAS! I'D LOVE TO. I'VE ACTUALLY ALREADY LOOKED INTO IT. THERE ARE WORKING HOLIDAY VISAS.

YOU KNOW, BEFORE I CAME TO FRANCE, I HAD A BOYFRIEND... IN TOKYO.

OH REALLY?

YEAH, WE DECIDED TO BREAK UP A MONTH AGO. BASICALLY BECAUSE OF THE DISTANCE.

OUT OF SIGHT, OUT OF MIND.

HOW LONG WERE YOU GUYS TOGETHER?

IT WAS ABOUT TWO YEARS. HE DIDN'T REALLY UNDERSTAND WHY I WANTED TO COME TO FRANCE FOR A YEAR, ALONE. HE NEVER REALLY ACCEPTED IT...

MMM.

BUT HE WAS NICE AND ROMANTIC ABOUT IT. HE EVEN COMPOSED A SONG FOR ME ON THE GUITAR.

CLASSY.

I WOULD NEVER BE ABLE TO DO THAT. HE MUST HAVE REALLY BEEN IN LOVE WITH YOU?

YEAH, I THINK SO, BUT IT WASN'T REALLY WORKING IN THE END.

HA HA HA!

THEY DIDN'T SAY IT WAS GOING TO RAIN TODAY, SHIT!

SO WE TRIED TO MAKE THE MOST OF THE FEW MONTHS WE HAD BEFORE SHE LEFT. SPENDING AS MUCH TIME TOGETHER AS POSSIBLE. WE WENT TO THE MOUNTAINS...

I TOOK HER TO THE PARIS CATACOMBS...

HELLO, THERE, FOLKS!

HELLO!

HI!

WE ALSO SPENT A FEW DAYS AT MY PARENTS' PLACE IN THE COUNTRY.

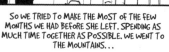

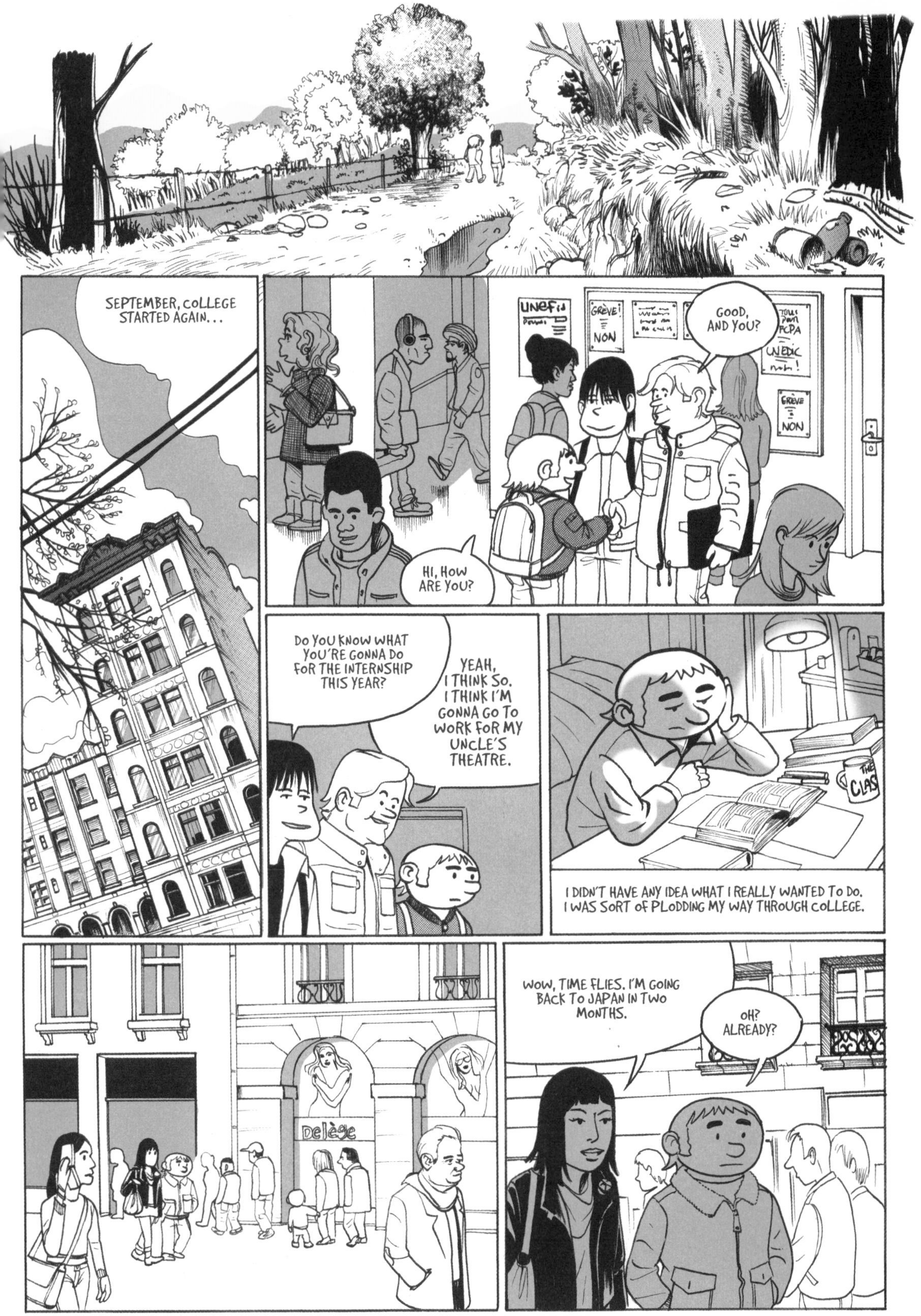

SEPTEMBER, COLLEGE STARTED AGAIN...
HI, HOW ARE YOU?
GOOD, AND YOU?
DO YOU KNOW WHAT YOU'RE GONNA DO FOR THE INTERNSHIP THIS YEAR?
YEAH, I THINK SO. I THINK I'M GONNA GO TO WORK FOR MY UNCLE'S THEATRE.
I DIDN'T HAVE ANY IDEA WHAT I REALLY WANTED TO DO. I WAS SORT OF PLODDING MY WAY THROUGH COLLEGE.
Delège
WOW, TIME FLIES. I'M GOING BACK TO JAPAN IN TWO MONTHS.
OH? ALREADY?

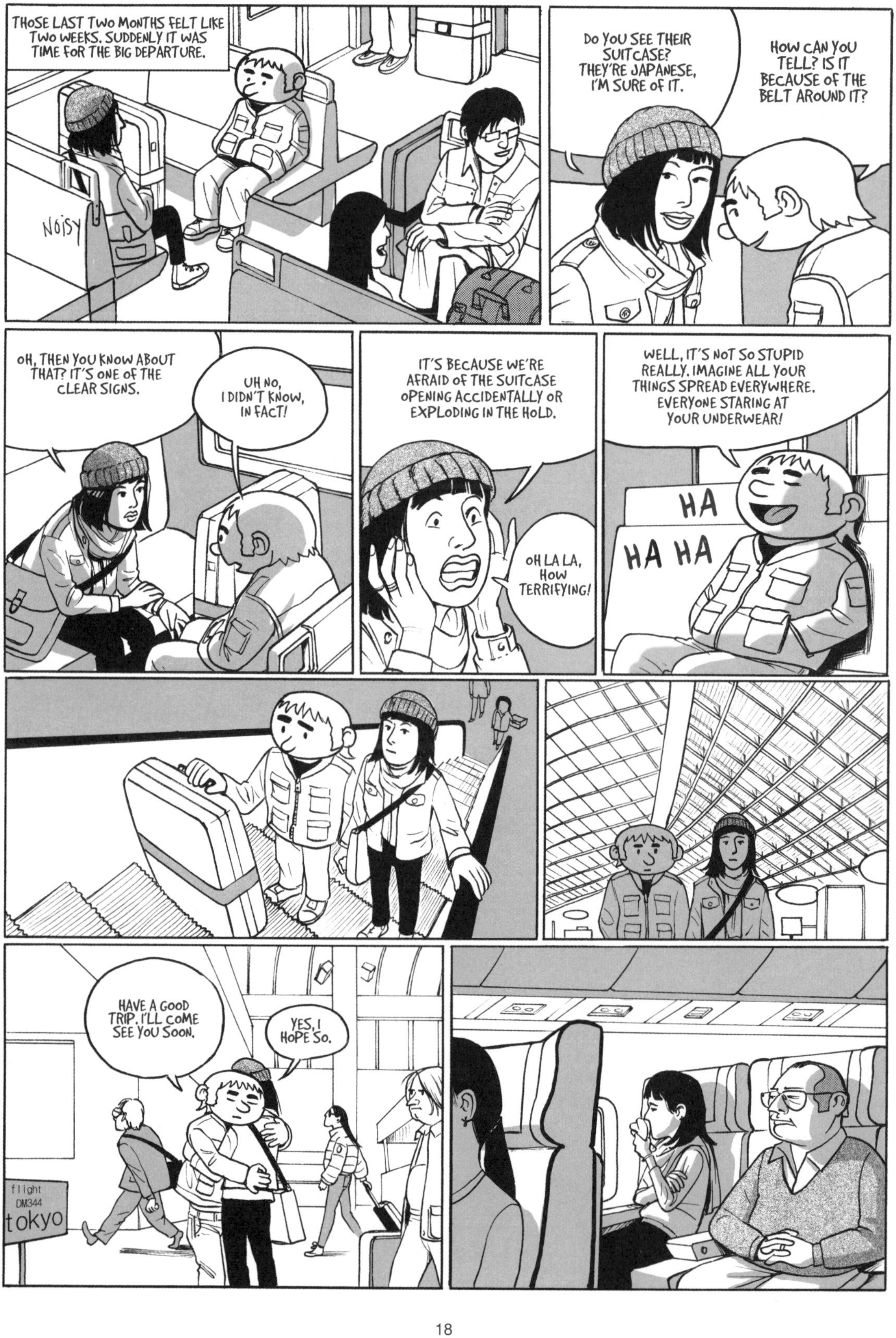
THOSE LAST TWO MONTHS FELT LIKE TWO WEEKS. SUDDENLY IT WAS TIME FOR THE BIG DEPARTURE.
NOISY
DO YOU SEE THEIR SUITCASE? THEY'RE JAPANESE, I'M SURE OF IT.
HOW CAN YOU TELL? IS IT BECAUSE OF THE BELT AROUND IT?
OH, THEN YOU KNOW ABOUT THAT? IT'S ONE OF THE CLEAR SIGNS.
UH NO, I DIDN'T KNOW, IN FACT!
IT'S BECAUSE WE'RE AFRAID OF THE SUITCASE OPENING ACCIDENTALLY OR EXPLODING IN THE HOLD.
OH LA LA, HOW TERRIFYING!
WELL, IT'S NOT SO STUPID REALLY. IMAGINE ALL YOUR THINGS SPREAD EVERYWHERE. EVERYONE STARING AT YOUR UNDERWEAR!
HA
HA HA
HAVE A GOOD TRIP. I'LL COME SEE YOU SOON.
YES, I HOPE SO.
flight
DM344
tokyo

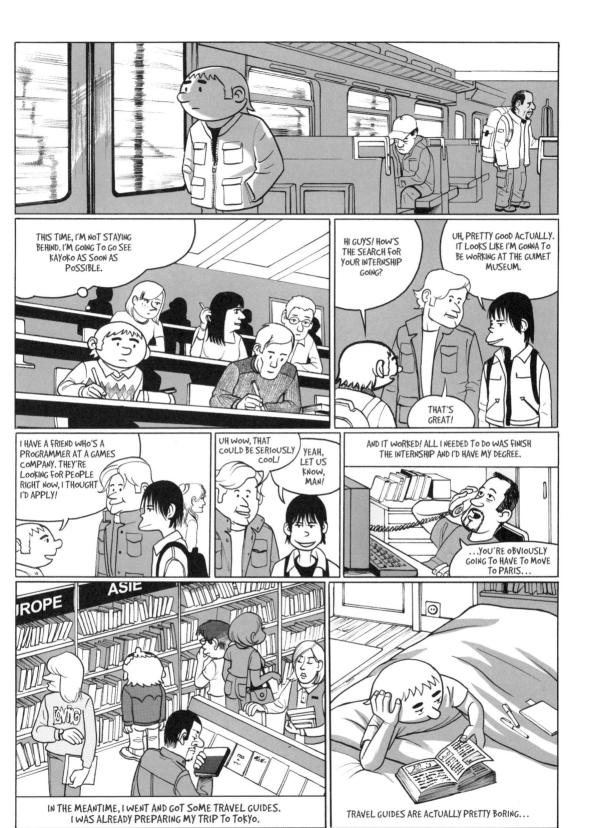

THIS TIME, I'M NOT STAYING BEHIND. I'M GOING TO GO SEE KAYOKO AS SOON AS POSSIBLE.

HI GUYS! HOW'S THE SEARCH FOR YOUR INTERNSHIP GOING?

UH, PRETTY GOOD ACTUALLY. IT LOOKS LIKE I'M GONNA TO BE WORKING AT THE GUIMET MUSEUM.

THAT'S GREAT!

I HAVE A FRIEND WHO'S A PROGRAMMER AT A GAMES COMPANY. THEY'RE LOOKING FOR PEOPLE RIGHT NOW, I THOUGHT I'D APPLY!

UH WOW, THAT COULD BE SERIOUSLY COOL!

YEAH, LET US KNOW, MAN!

AND IT WORKED! ALL I NEEDED TO DO WAS FINISH THE INTERNSHIP AND I'D HAVE MY DEGREE.

...YOU'RE OBVIOUSLY GOING TO HAVE TO MOVE TO PARIS...

IN THE MEANTIME, I WENT AND GOT SOME TRAVEL GUIDES. I WAS ALREADY PREPARING MY TRIP TO TOKYO.

TRAVEL GUIDES ARE ACTUALLY PRETTY BORING...

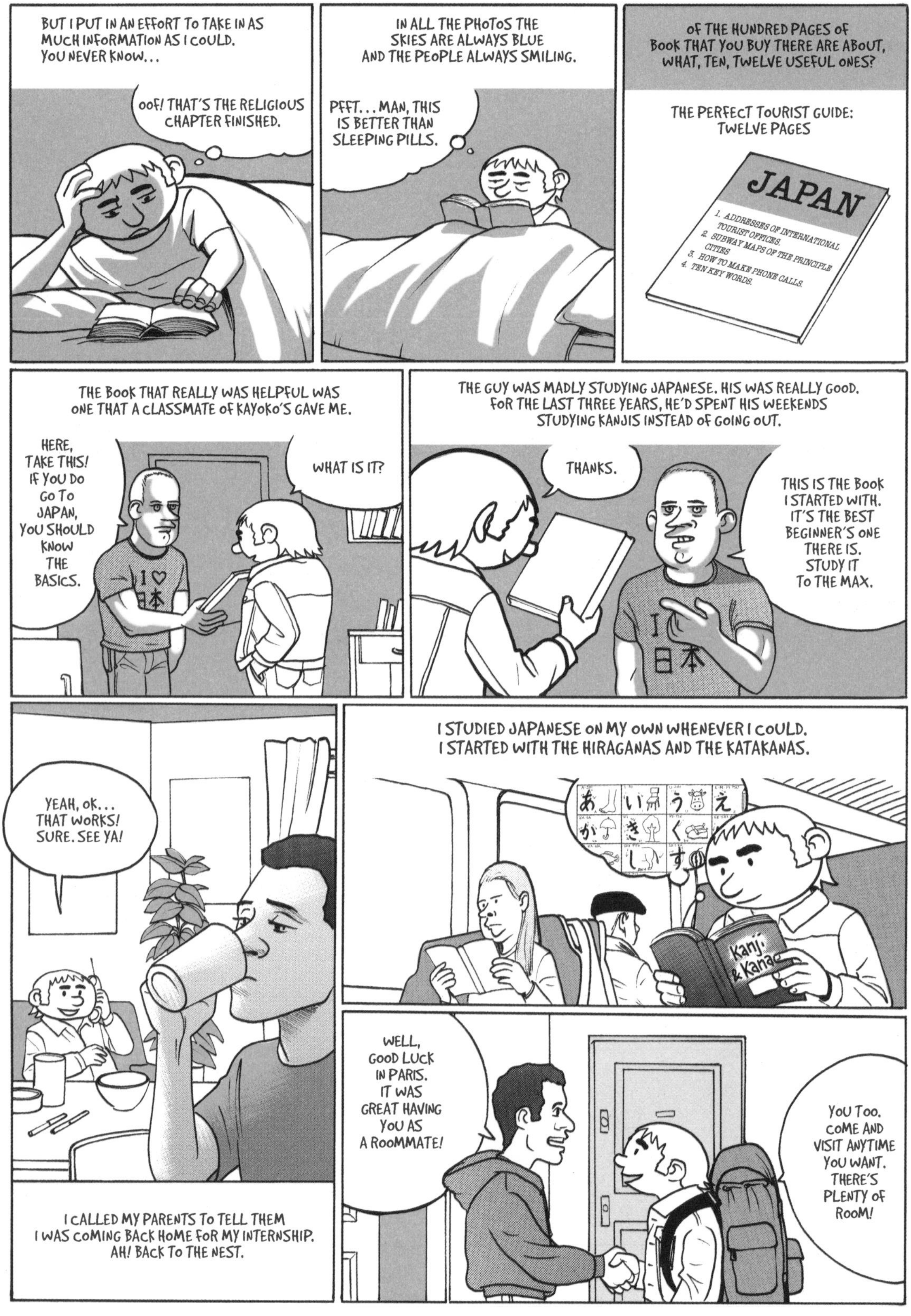
BUT I PUT IN AN EFFORT TO TAKE IN AS MUCH INFORMATION AS I COULD. YOU NEVER KNOW...
OOF! THAT'S THE RELIGIOUS CHAPTER FINISHED.
IN ALL THE PHOTOS THE SKIES ARE ALWAYS BLUE AND THE PEOPLE ALWAYS SMILING.
PFFT... MAN, THIS IS BETTER THAN SLEEPING PILLS.
OF THE HUNDRED PAGES OF BOOK THAT YOU BUY THERE ARE ABOUT, WHAT, TEN, TWELVE USEFUL ONES?
THE PERFECT TOURIST GUIDE: TWELVE PAGES
JAPAN
1. ADDRESSES OF INTERNATIONAL TOURIST OFFICES.
2. SUBWAY MAPS OF THE PRINCIPLE CITIES
3. HOW TO MAKE PHONE CALLS.
4. TEN KEY WORDS.
THE BOOK THAT REALLY WAS HELPFUL WAS ONE THAT A CLASSMATE OF KAYOKO'S GAVE ME.
HERE, TAKE THIS! IF YOU DO GO TO JAPAN, YOU SHOULD KNOW THE BASICS.
WHAT IS IT?
THE GUY WAS MADLY STUDYING JAPANESE. HIS WAS REALLY GOOD. FOR THE LAST THREE YEARS, HE'D SPENT HIS WEEKENDS STUDYING KANJIS INSTEAD OF GOING OUT.
THANKS.
THIS IS THE BOOK I STARTED WITH. IT'S THE BEST BEGINNER'S ONE THERE IS. STUDY IT TO THE MAX.
I ♡ 日本
YEAH, OK... THAT WORKS! SURE. SEE YA!
I CALLED MY PARENTS TO TELL THEM I WAS COMING BACK HOME FOR MY INTERNSHIP. AH! BACK TO THE NEST.
I STUDIED JAPANESE ON MY OWN WHENEVER I COULD. I STARTED WITH THE HIRAGANAS AND THE KATAKANAS.
あ い う え
か き く
し す
WELL, GOOD LUCK IN PARIS. IT WAS GREAT HAVING YOU AS A ROOMMATE!
YOU TOO. COME AND VISIT ANYTIME YOU WANT. THERE'S PLENTY OF ROOM!

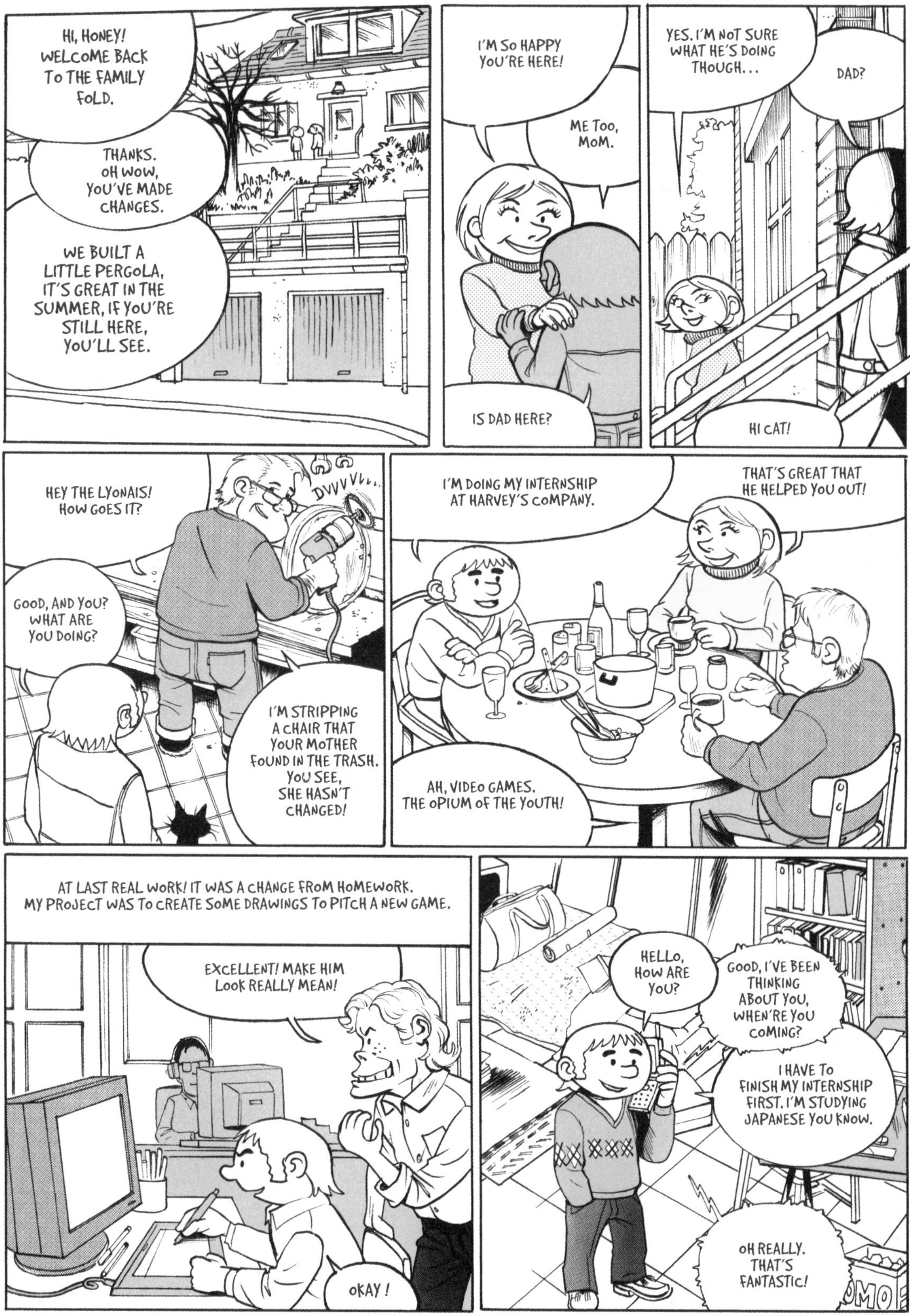
HI, HONEY! WELCOME BACK TO THE FAMILY FOLD.
THANKS. OH WOW, YOU'VE MADE CHANGES.
WE BUILT A LITTLE PERGOLA, IT'S GREAT IN THE SUMMER, IF YOU'RE STILL HERE, YOU'LL SEE.
I'M SO HAPPY YOU'RE HERE!
ME TOO, MOM.
IS DAD HERE?
YES. I'M NOT SURE WHAT HE'S DOING THOUGH...
DAD?
HI CAT!
HEY THE LYONAIS! HOW GOES IT?
DVVVVLLL..
GOOD, AND YOU? WHAT ARE YOU DOING?
I'M STRIPPING A CHAIR THAT YOUR MOTHER FOUND IN THE TRASH. YOU SEE, SHE HASN'T CHANGED!
I'M DOING MY INTERNSHIP AT HARVEY'S COMPANY.
THAT'S GREAT THAT HE HELPED YOU OUT!
AH, VIDEO GAMES. THE OPIUM OF THE YOUTH!
AT LAST REAL WORK! IT WAS A CHANGE FROM HOMEWORK. MY PROJECT WAS TO CREATE SOME DRAWINGS TO PITCH A NEW GAME.
EXCELLENT! MAKE HIM LOOK REALLY MEAN!
OKAY!
HELLO, HOW ARE YOU?
GOOD, I'VE BEEN THINKING ABOUT YOU, WHEN'RE YOU COMING?
I HAVE TO FINISH MY INTERNSHIP FIRST. I'M STUDYING JAPANESE YOU KNOW.
OH REALLY. THAT'S FANTASTIC!

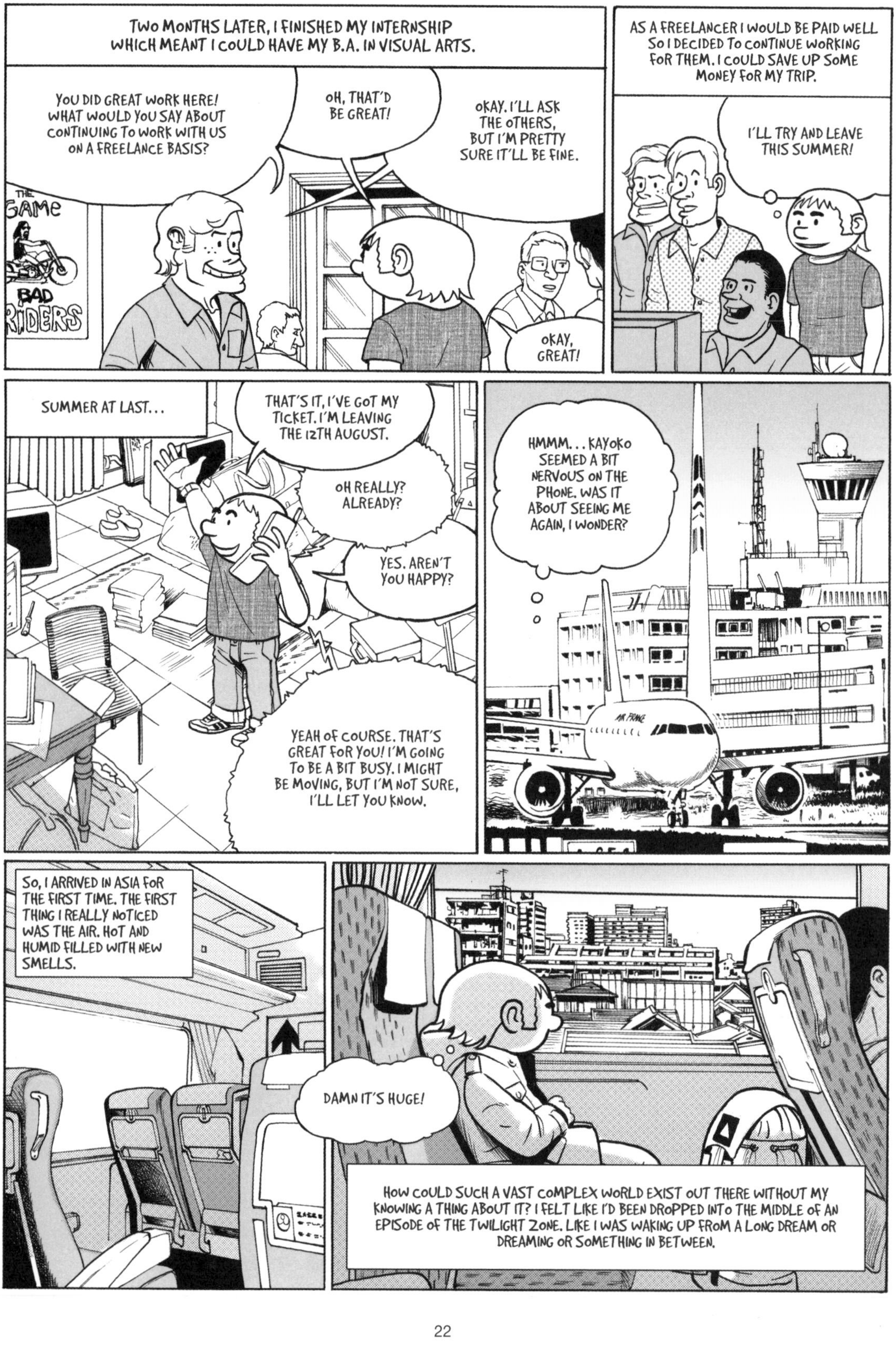

TWO MONTHS LATER, I FINISHED MY INTERNSHIP WHICH MEANT I COULD HAVE MY B.A. IN VISUAL ARTS.
YOU DID GREAT WORK HERE! WHAT WOULD YOU SAY ABOUT CONTINUING TO WORK WITH US ON A FREELANCE BASIS?
OH, THAT'D BE GREAT!
OKAY. I'LL ASK THE OTHERS, BUT I'M PRETTY SURE IT'LL BE FINE.
OKAY, GREAT!
THE GAME
BAD RIDERS
AS A FREELANCER I WOULD BE PAID WELL SO I DECIDED TO CONTINUE WORKING FOR THEM. I COULD SAVE UP SOME MONEY FOR MY TRIP.
I'LL TRY AND LEAVE THIS SUMMER!
SUMMER AT LAST...
THAT'S IT, I'VE GOT MY TICKET. I'M LEAVING THE 12TH AUGUST.
OH REALLY? ALREADY?
YES. AREN'T YOU HAPPY?
YEAH OF COURSE. THAT'S GREAT FOR YOU! I'M GOING TO BE A BIT BUSY. I MIGHT BE MOVING, BUT I'M NOT SURE, I'LL LET YOU KNOW.
HMMM... KAYOKO SEEMED A BIT NERVOUS ON THE PHONE. WAS IT ABOUT SEEING ME AGAIN, I WONDER?
AIR FRANCE
SO, I ARRIVED IN ASIA FOR THE FIRST TIME. THE FIRST THING I REALLY NOTICED WAS THE AIR. HOT AND HUMID FILLED WITH NEW SMELLS.
DAMN IT'S HUGE!
HOW COULD SUCH A VAST COMPLEX WORLD EXIST OUT THERE WITHOUT MY KNOWING A THING ABOUT IT? I FELT LIKE I'D BEEN DROPPED INTO THE MIDDLE OF AN EPISODE OF THE TWILIGHT ZONE. LIKE I WAS WAKING UP FROM A LONG DREAM OR DREAMING OR SOMETHING IN BETWEEN.

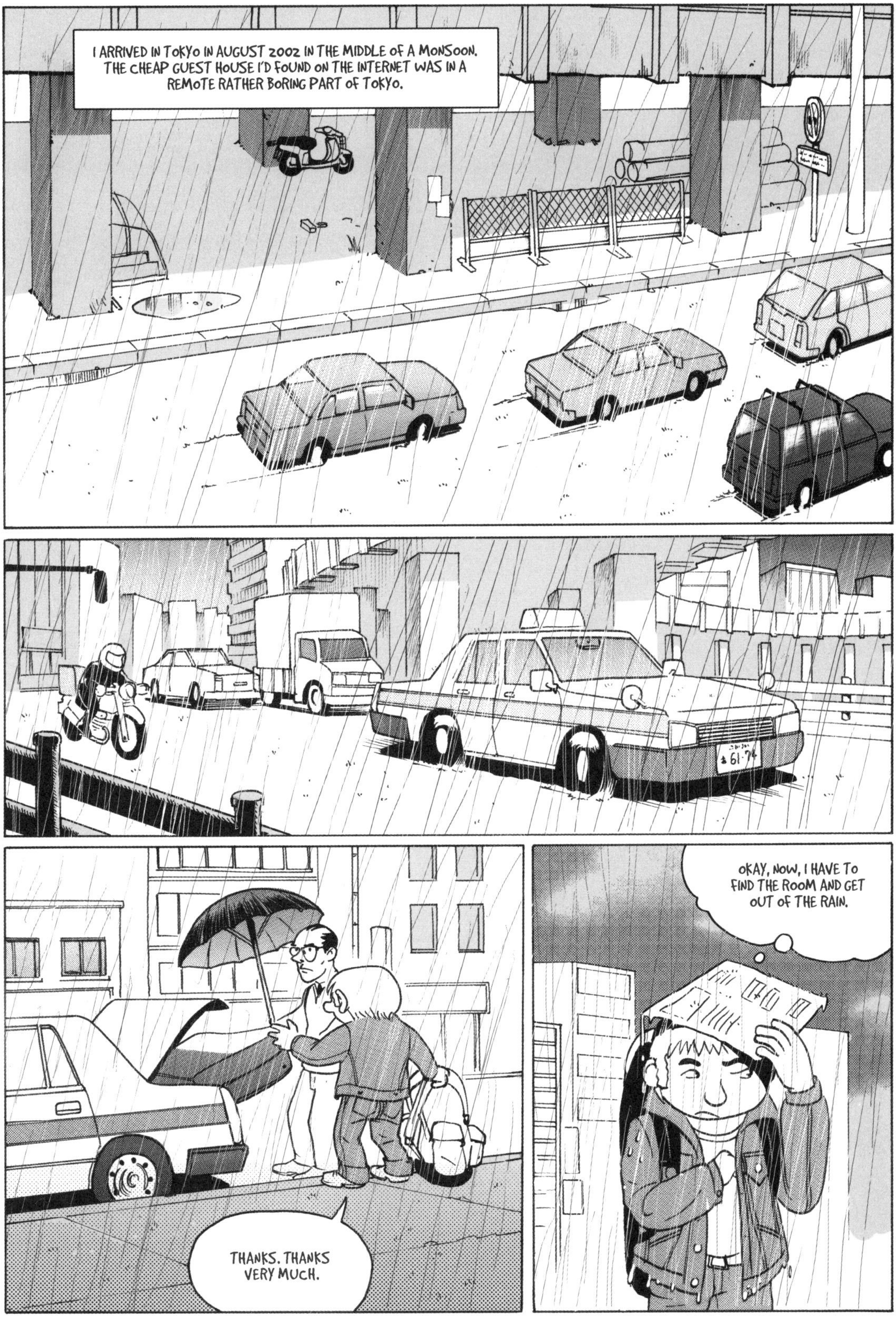
I ARRIVED IN TOKYO IN AUGUST 2002 IN THE MIDDLE OF A MONSOON. THE CHEAP GUEST HOUSE I'D FOUND ON THE INTERNET WAS IN A REMOTE RATHER BORING PART OF TOKYO.
THANKS. THANKS VERY MUCH.
OKAY, NOW, I HAVE TO FIND THE ROOM AND GET OUT OF THE RAIN.

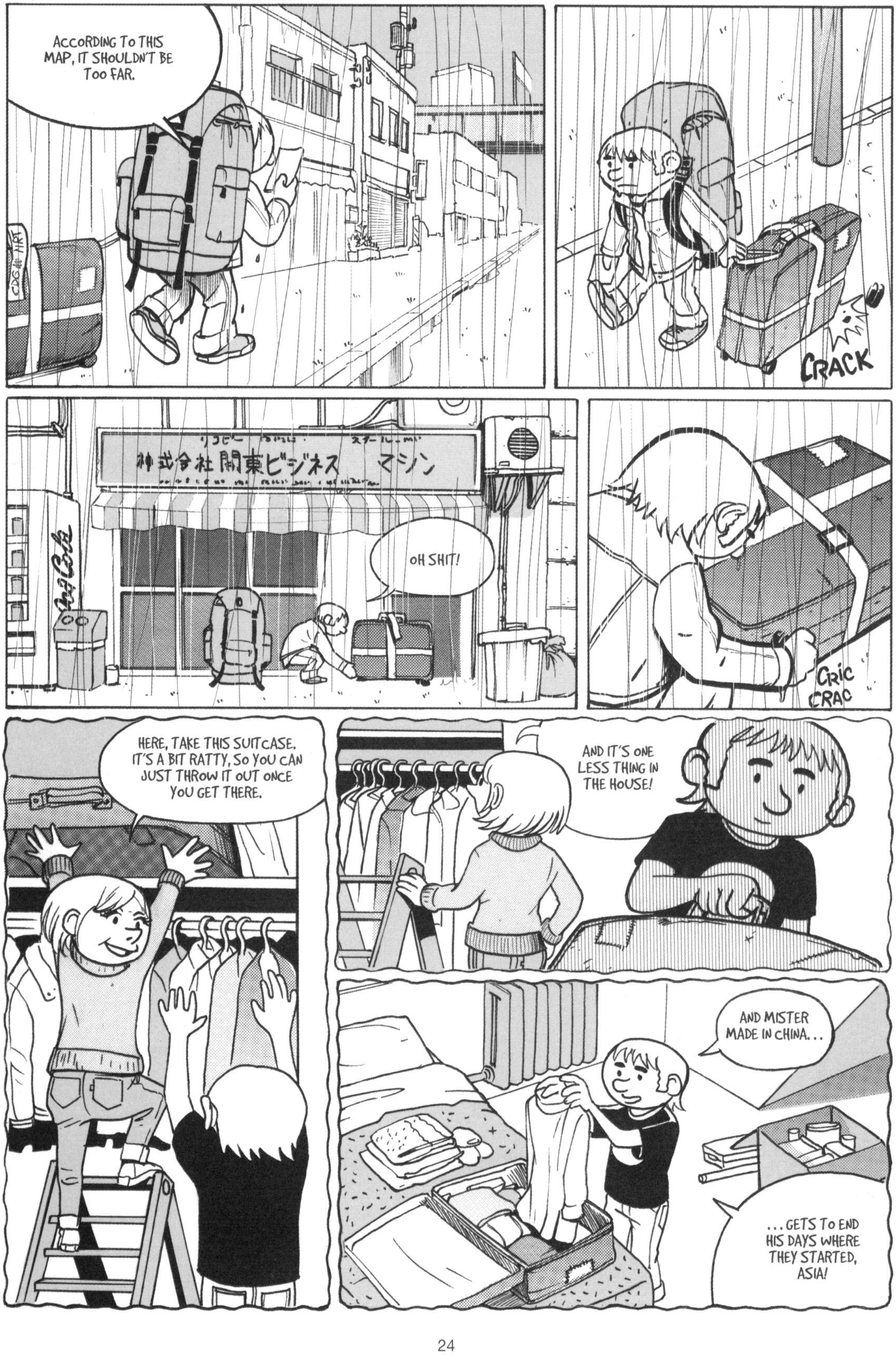
ACCORDING TO THIS MAP, IT SHOULDN'T BE TOO FAR.
CRACK
株式会社 関東ビジネス マシン
Coca-Cola
OH SHIT!
CRIC CRAC
HERE, TAKE THIS SUITCASE. IT'S A BIT RATTY, SO YOU CAN JUST THROW IT OUT ONCE YOU GET THERE.
AND IT'S ONE LESS THING IN THE HOUSE!
AND MISTER MADE IN CHINA...
...GETS TO END HIS DAYS WHERE THEY STARTED, ASIA!

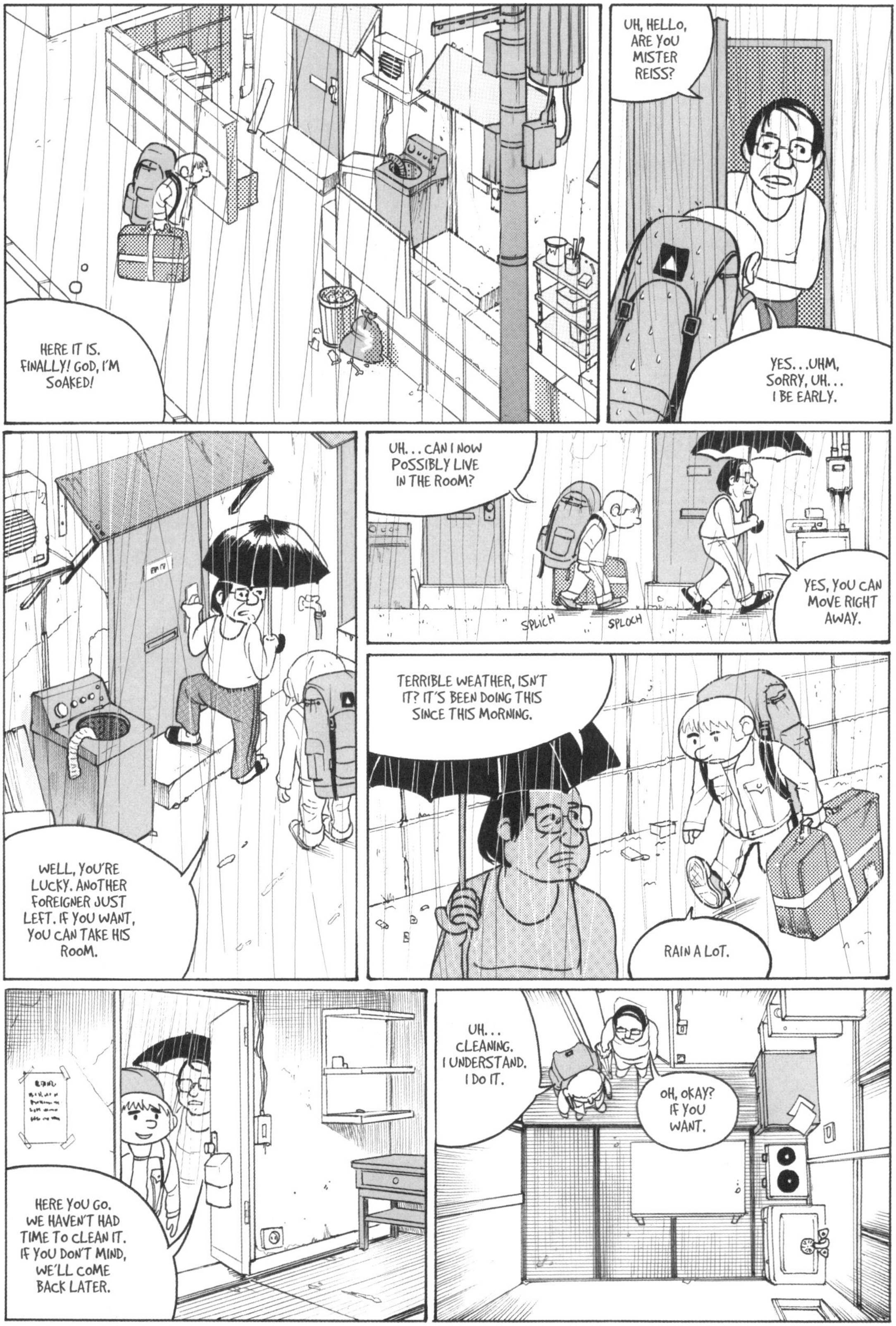
HERE IT IS. FINALLY! GOD, I'M SOAKED!
UH, HELLO, ARE YOU MISTER REISS?
YES...UHM, SORRY, UH... I BE EARLY.
WELL, YOU'RE LUCKY. ANOTHER FOREIGNER JUST LEFT. IF YOU WANT, YOU CAN TAKE HIS ROOM.
UH... CAN I NOW POSSIBLY LIVE IN THE ROOM?
YES, YOU CAN MOVE RIGHT AWAY.
SPLICH
SPLOCH
TERRIBLE WEATHER, ISN'T IT? IT'S BEEN DOING THIS SINCE THIS MORNING.
RAIN A LOT.
HERE YOU GO. WE HAVEN'T HAD TIME TO CLEAN IT. IF YOU DON'T MIND, WE'LL COME BACK LATER.
UH... CLEANING. I UNDERSTAND. I DO IT.
OH, OKAY? IF YOU WANT.

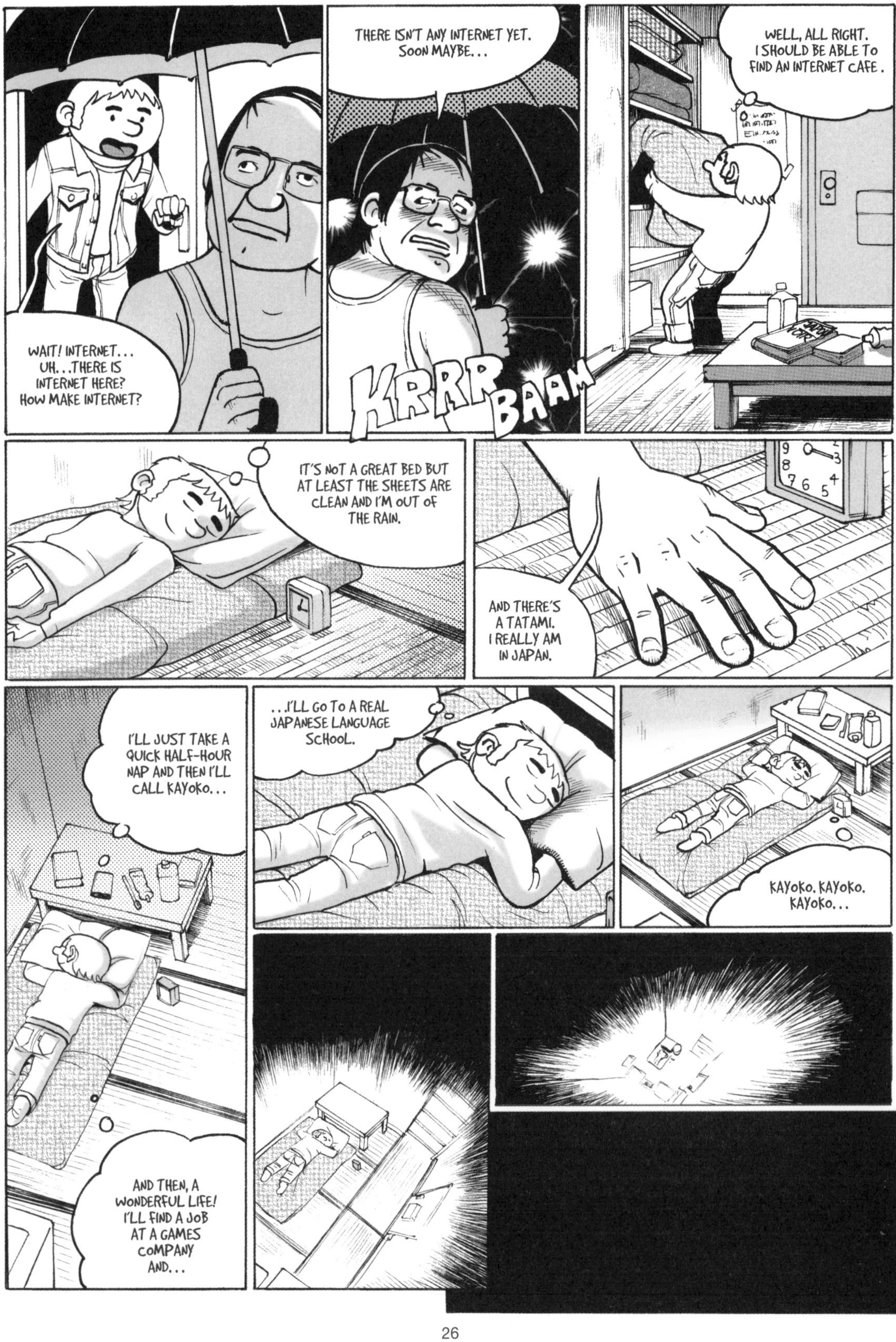
WAIT! INTERNET... UH...THERE IS INTERNET HERE? HOW MAKE INTERNET?
THERE ISN'T ANY INTERNET YET. SOON MAYBE...
KRRR BAAM
WELL, ALL RIGHT. I SHOULD BE ABLE TO FIND AN INTERNET CAFE.
IT'S NOT A GREAT BED BUT AT LEAST THE SHEETS ARE CLEAN AND I'M OUT OF THE RAIN.
AND THERE'S A TATAMI. I REALLY AM IN JAPAN.
I'LL JUST TAKE A QUICK HALF-HOUR NAP AND THEN I'LL CALL KAYOKO...
AND THEN, A WONDERFUL LIFE! I'LL FIND A JOB AT A GAMES COMPANY AND...
...I'LL GO TO A REAL JAPANESE LANGUAGE SCHOOL.
KAYOKO. KAYOKO. KAYOKO...

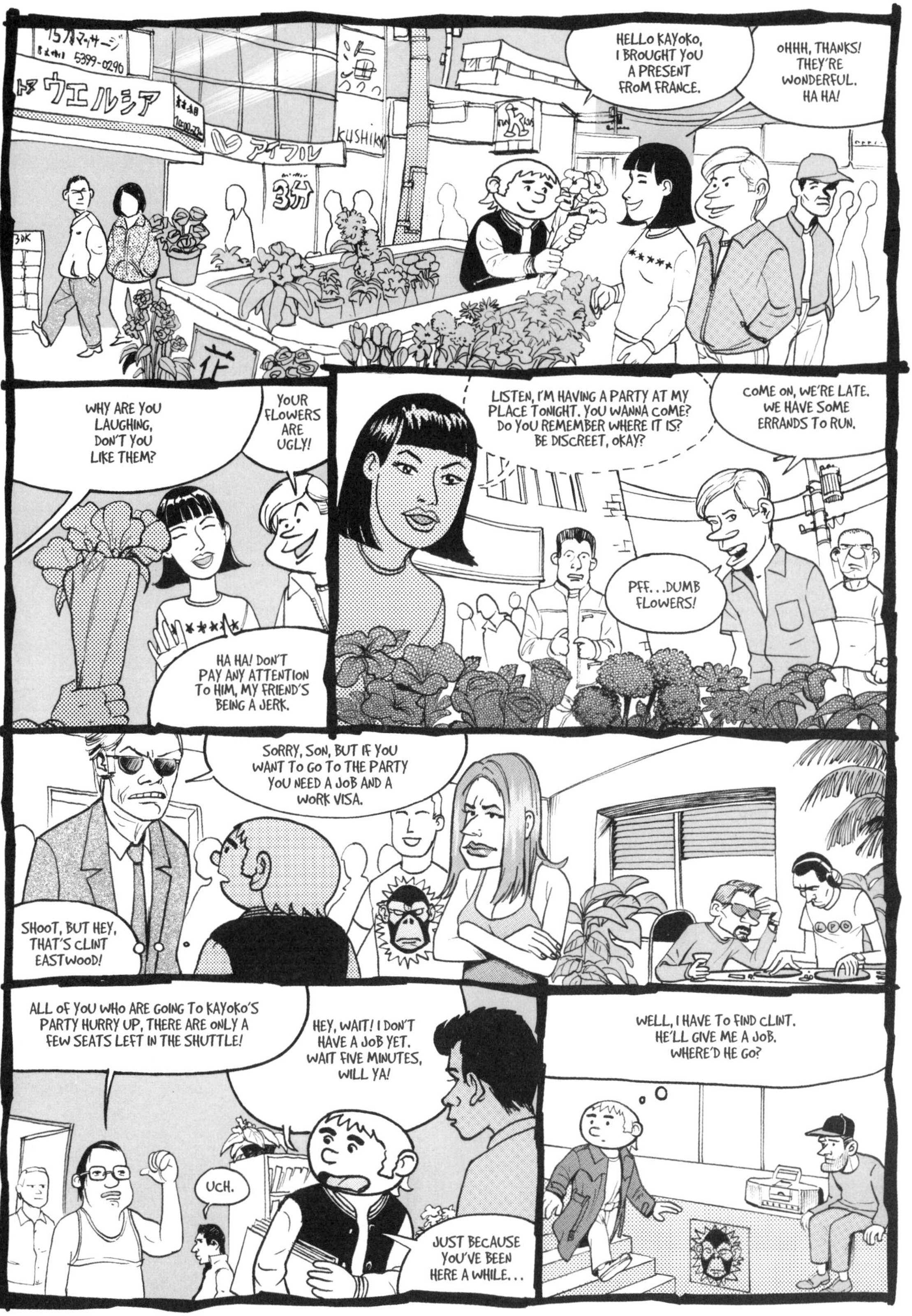
HELLO KAYOKO, I BROUGHT YOU A PRESENT FROM FRANCE.
OHHH, THANKS! THEY'RE WONDERFUL. HA HA!
WHY ARE YOU LAUGHING, DON'T YOU LIKE THEM?
YOUR FLOWERS ARE UGLY!
HA HA! DON'T PAY ANY ATTENTION TO HIM, MY FRIEND'S BEING A JERK.
LISTEN, I'M HAVING A PARTY AT MY PLACE TONIGHT. YOU WANNA COME? DO YOU REMEMBER WHERE IT IS? BE DISCREET, OKAY?
COME ON, WE'RE LATE. WE HAVE SOME ERRANDS TO RUN.
PFF...DUMB FLOWERS!
SORRY, SON, BUT IF YOU WANT TO GO TO THE PARTY YOU NEED A JOB AND A WORK VISA.
SHOOT, BUT HEY, THAT'S CLINT EASTWOOD!
ALL OF YOU WHO ARE GOING TO KAYOKO'S PARTY HURRY UP, THERE ARE ONLY A FEW SEATS LEFT IN THE SHUTTLE!
HEY, WAIT! I DON'T HAVE A JOB YET. WAIT FIVE MINUTES, WILL YA!
UCH.
JUST BECAUSE YOU'VE BEEN HERE A WHILE...
WELL, I HAVE TO FIND CLINT. HE'LL GIVE ME A JOB. WHERE'D HE GO?

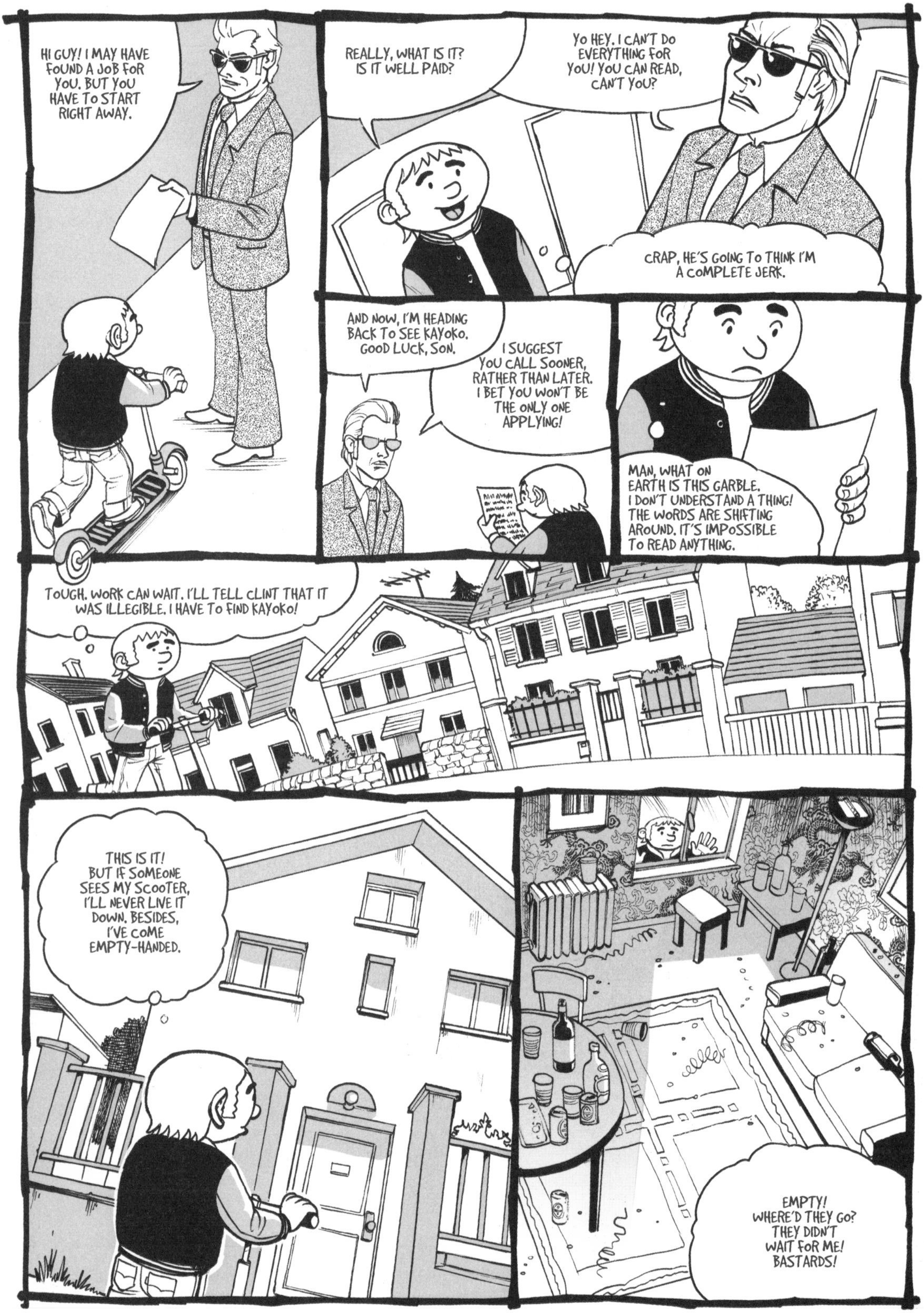
HI GUY! I MAY HAVE FOUND A JOB FOR YOU. BUT YOU HAVE TO START RIGHT AWAY.
REALLY, WHAT IS IT? IS IT WELL PAID?
YO HEY. I CAN'T DO EVERYTHING FOR YOU! YOU CAN READ, CAN'T YOU?
CRAP, HE'S GOING TO THINK I'M A COMPLETE JERK.
AND NOW, I'M HEADING BACK TO SEE KAYOKO. GOOD LUCK, SON.
I SUGGEST YOU CALL SOONER, RATHER THAN LATER. I BET YOU WON'T BE THE ONLY ONE APPLYING!
MAN, WHAT ON EARTH IS THIS GARBLE. I DON'T UNDERSTAND A THING! THE WORDS ARE SHIFTING AROUND. IT'S IMPOSSIBLE TO READ ANYTHING.
TOUGH. WORK CAN WAIT. I'LL TELL CLINT THAT IT WAS ILLEGIBLE. I HAVE TO FIND KAYOKO!
THIS IS IT! BUT IF SOMEONE SEES MY SCOOTER, I'LL NEVER LIVE IT DOWN. BESIDES, I'VE COME EMPTY-HANDED.
EMPTY! WHERE'D THEY GO? THEY DIDN'T WAIT FOR ME! BASTARDS!

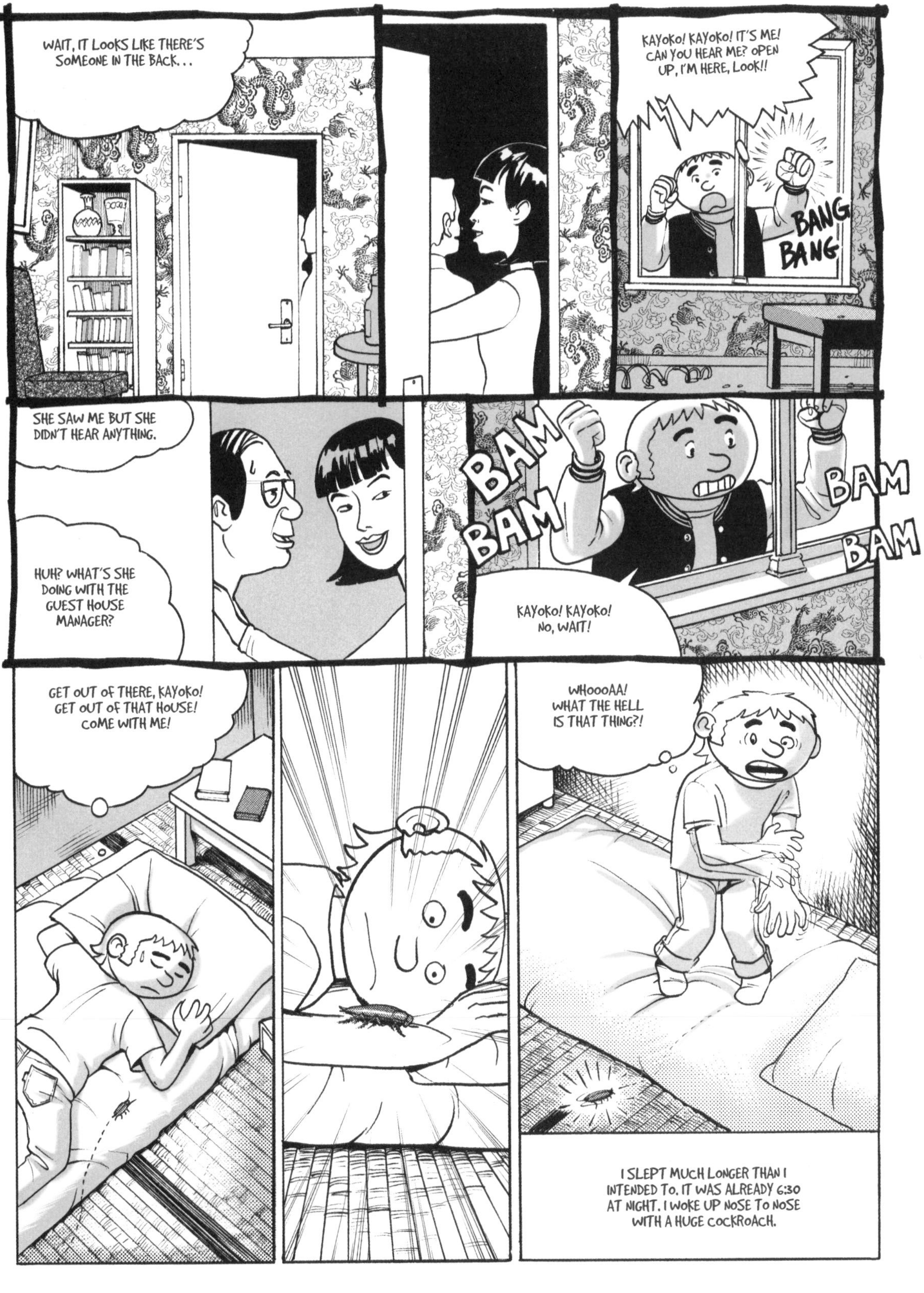
WAIT, IT LOOKS LIKE THERE'S SOMEONE IN THE BACK. . .
KAYOKO! KAYOKO! IT'S ME! CAN YOU HEAR ME? OPEN UP, I'M HERE, LOOK!!
BANG BANG
SHE SAW ME BUT SHE DIDN'T HEAR ANYTHING.
HUH? WHAT'S SHE DOING WITH THE GUEST HOUSE MANAGER?
BAM BAM
BAM BAM
KAYOKO! KAYOKO! NO, WAIT!
GET OUT OF THERE, KAYOKO! GET OUT OF THAT HOUSE! COME WITH ME!
WHOOOAA! WHAT THE HELL IS THAT THING?!
I SLEPT MUCH LONGER THAN I INTENDED TO. IT WAS ALREADY 6:30 AT NIGHT. I WOKE UP NOSE TO NOSE WITH A HUGE COCKROACH.

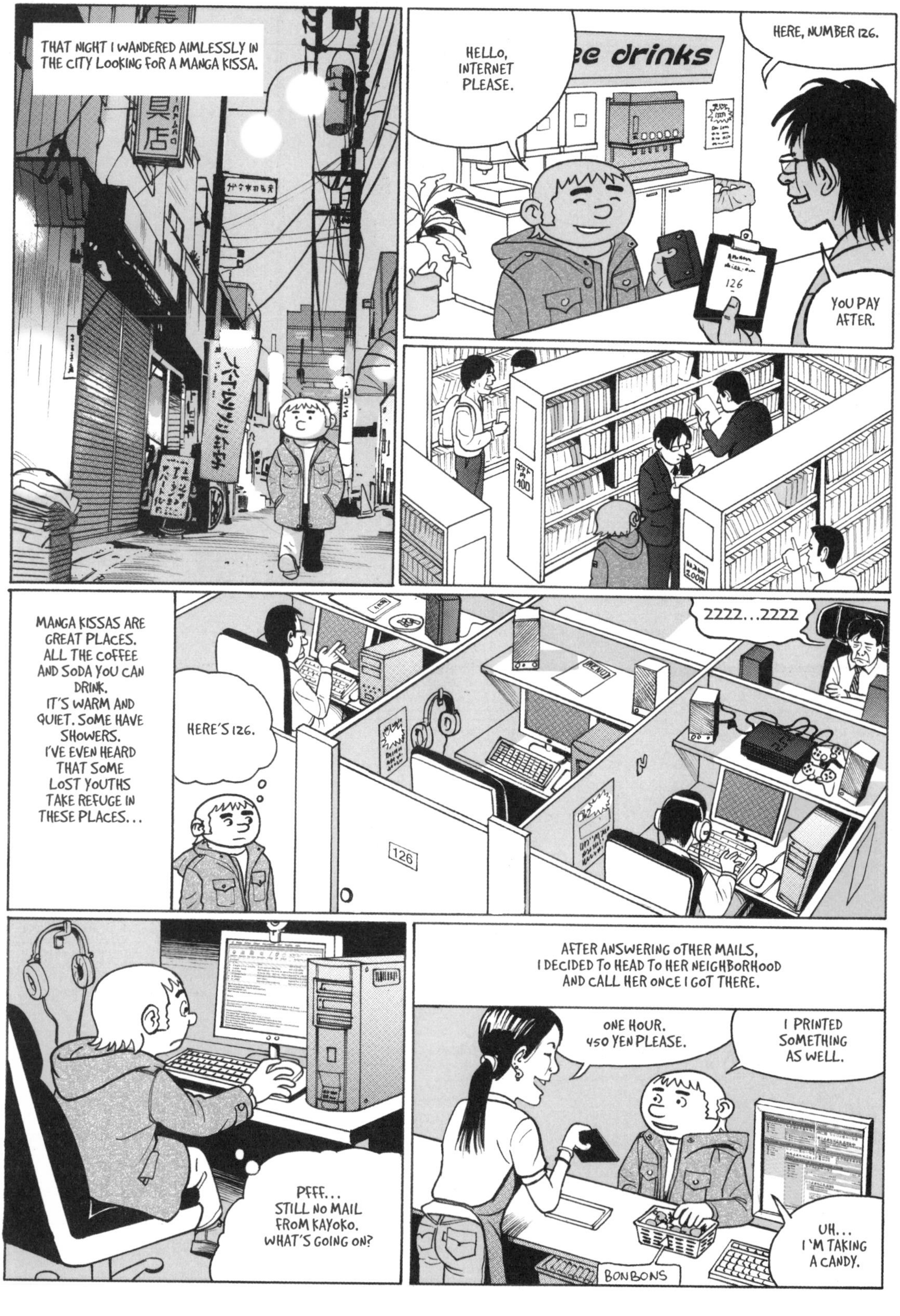

THAT NIGHT I WANDERED AIMLESSLY IN THE CITY LOOKING FOR A MANGA KISSA.
HELLO, INTERNET PLEASE.
HERE, NUMBER 126.
YOU PAY AFTER.
MANGA KISSAS ARE GREAT PLACES. ALL THE COFFEE AND SODA YOU CAN DRINK. IT'S WARM AND QUIET. SOME HAVE SHOWERS. I'VE EVEN HEARD THAT SOME LOST YOUTHS TAKE REFUGE IN THESE PLACES...
HERE'S 126.
126
ZZZZ...ZZZZ
PFFF... STILL NO MAIL FROM KAYOKO. WHAT'S GOING ON?
AFTER ANSWERING OTHER MAILS, I DECIDED TO HEAD TO HER NEIGHBORHOOD AND CALL HER ONCE I GOT THERE.
ONE HOUR. 450 YEN PLEASE.
I PRINTED SOMETHING AS WELL.
UH... I'M TAKING A CANDY.
BONBONS

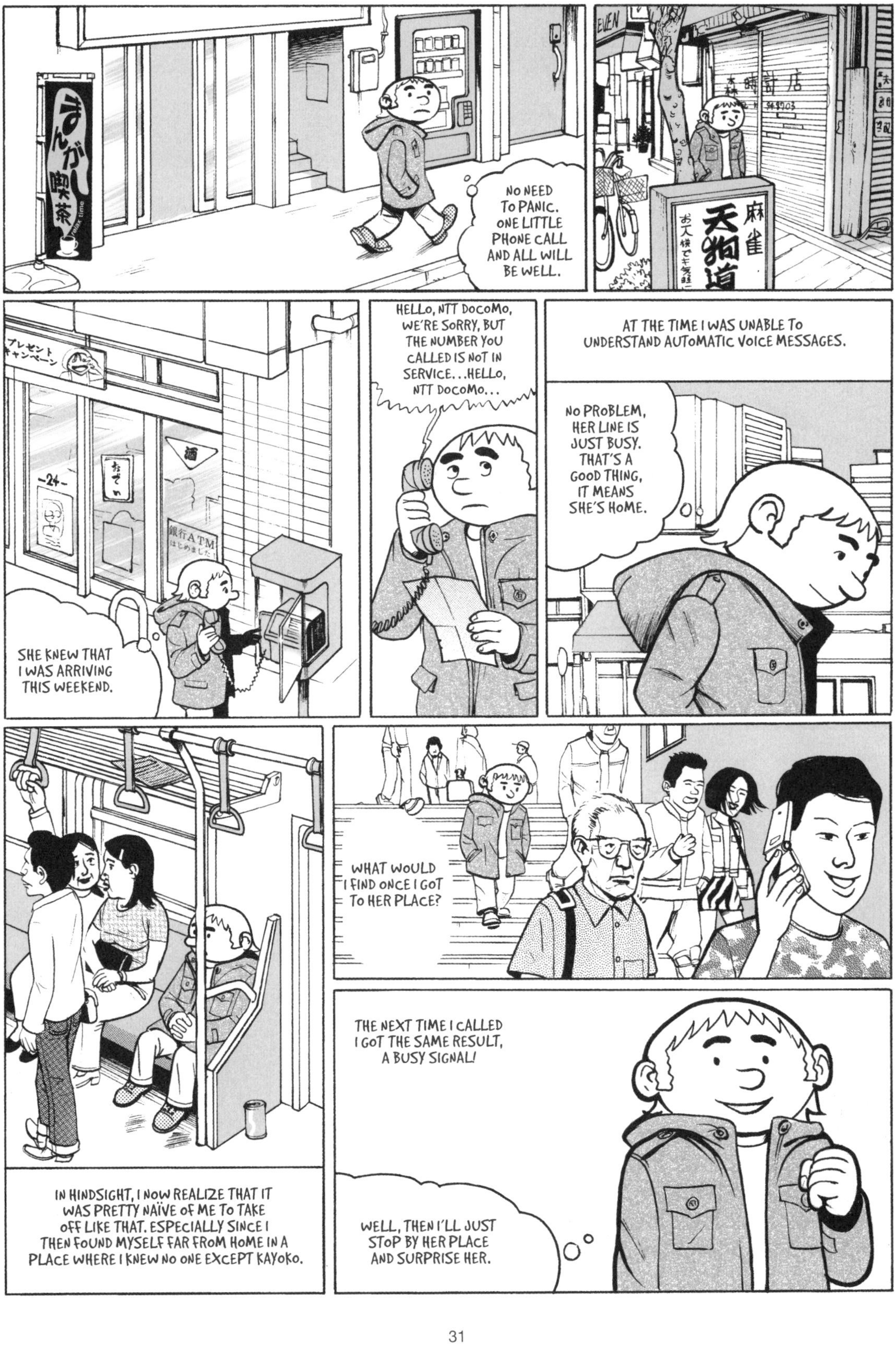

NO NEED TO PANIC. ONE LITTLE PHONE CALL AND ALL WILL BE WELL.
麻雀
天狗道
HELLO, NTT DOCOMO, WE'RE SORRY, BUT THE NUMBER YOU CALLED IS NOT IN SERVICE...HELLO, NTT DOCOMO...
SHE KNEW THAT I WAS ARRIVING THIS WEEKEND.
AT THE TIME I WAS UNABLE TO UNDERSTAND AUTOMATIC VOICE MESSAGES.
NO PROBLEM, HER LINE IS JUST BUSY. THAT'S A GOOD THING, IT MEANS SHE'S HOME.
IN HINDSIGHT, I NOW REALIZE THAT IT WAS PRETTY NAÏVE OF ME TO TAKE OFF LIKE THAT. ESPECIALLY SINCE I THEN FOUND MYSELF FAR FROM HOME IN A PLACE WHERE I KNEW NO ONE EXCEPT KAYOKO.
WHAT WOULD I FIND ONCE I GOT TO HER PLACE?
THE NEXT TIME I CALLED I GOT THE SAME RESULT, A BUSY SIGNAL!
WELL, THEN I'LL JUST STOP BY HER PLACE AND SURPRISE HER.

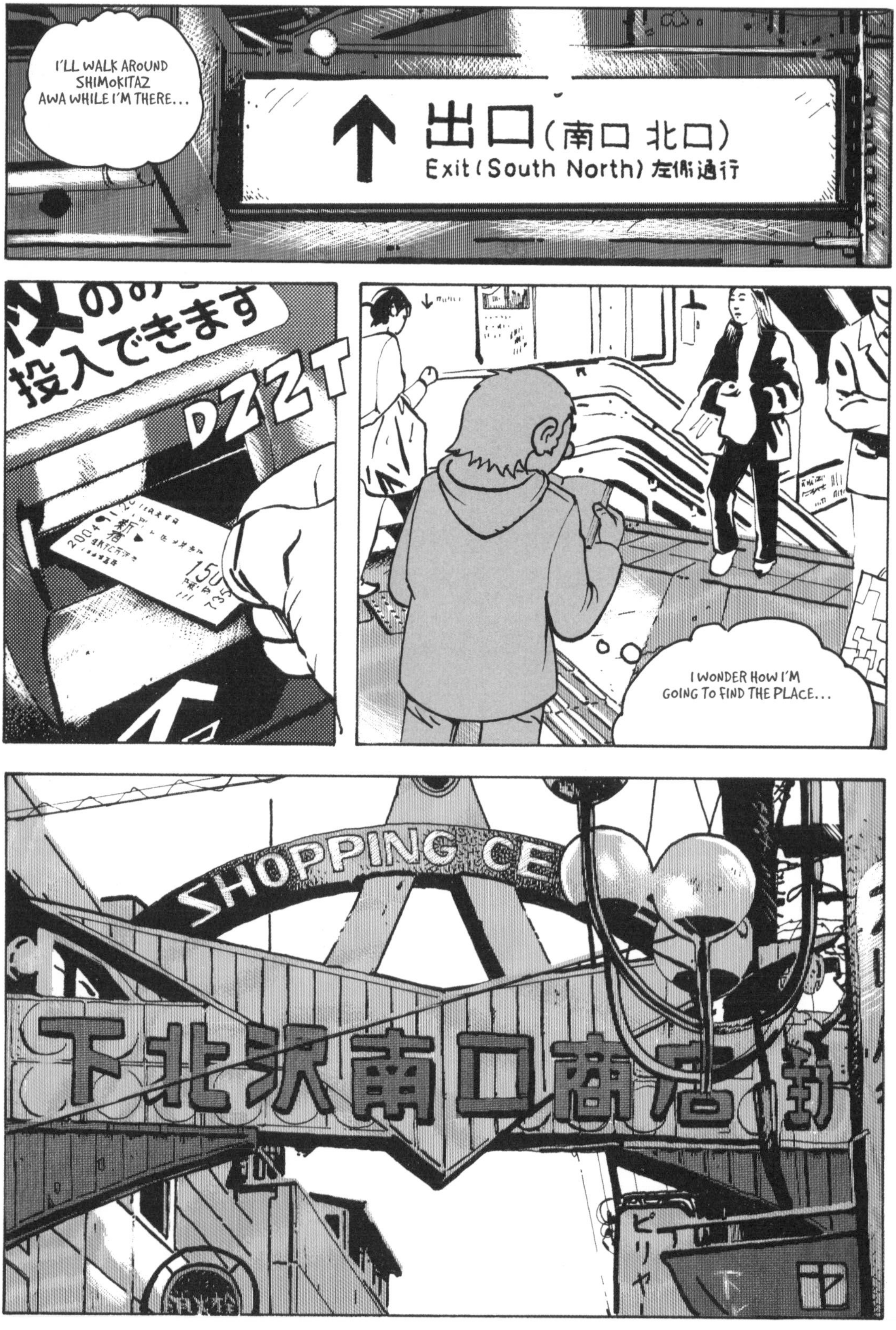
I'LL WALK AROUND SHIMOKITAZ AWA WHILE I'M THERE...
出口(南口 北口)
Exit (South North) 左側通行
投入できます
DZZT
I WONDER HOW I'M GOING TO FIND THE PLACE...
SHOPPING CE
下北沢南口商店

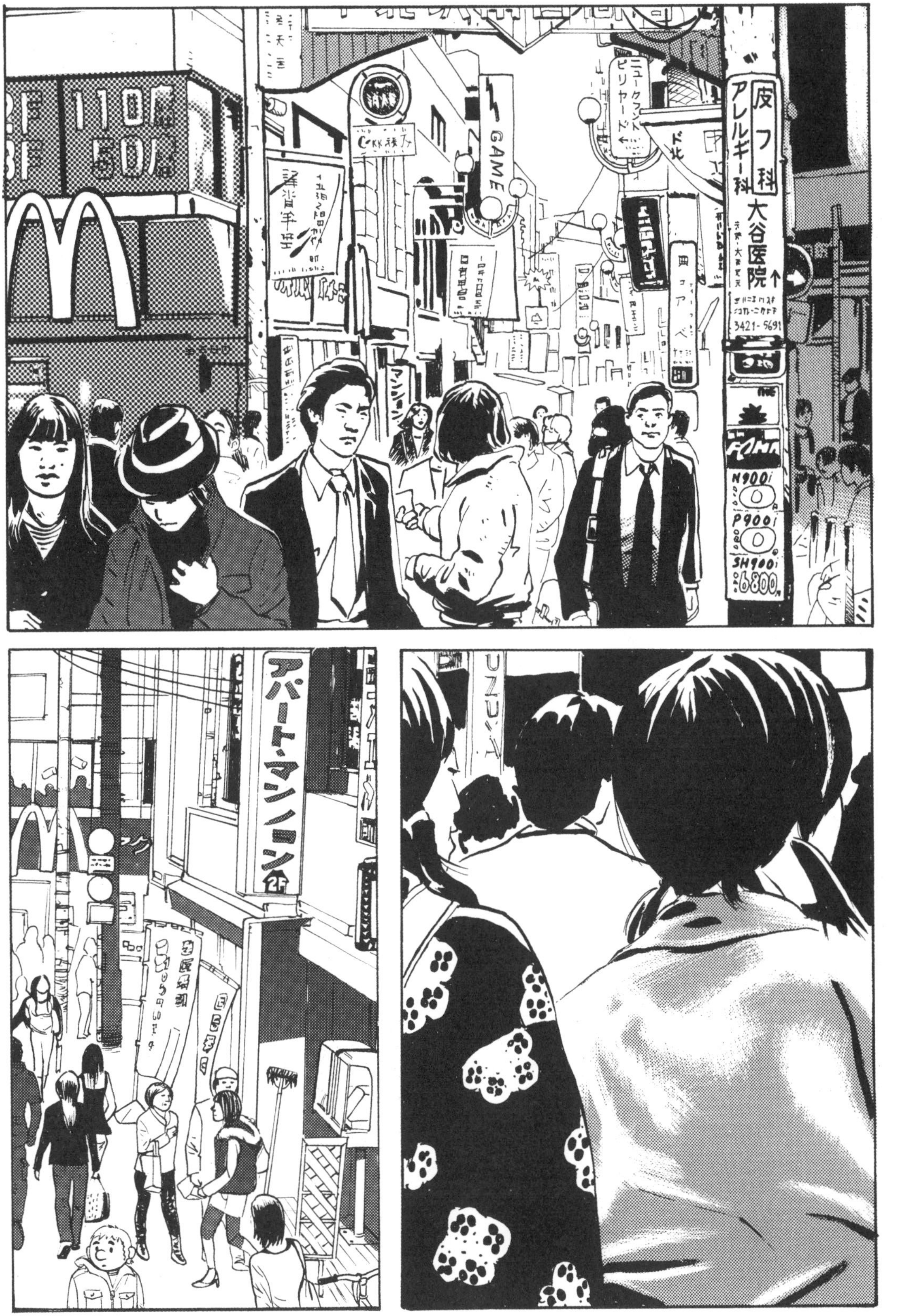
GAME
皮フ科
アレルギー科
大谷医院
3421-5691
N900i
P900i
SH900i
6800
アパート・マンション
2F

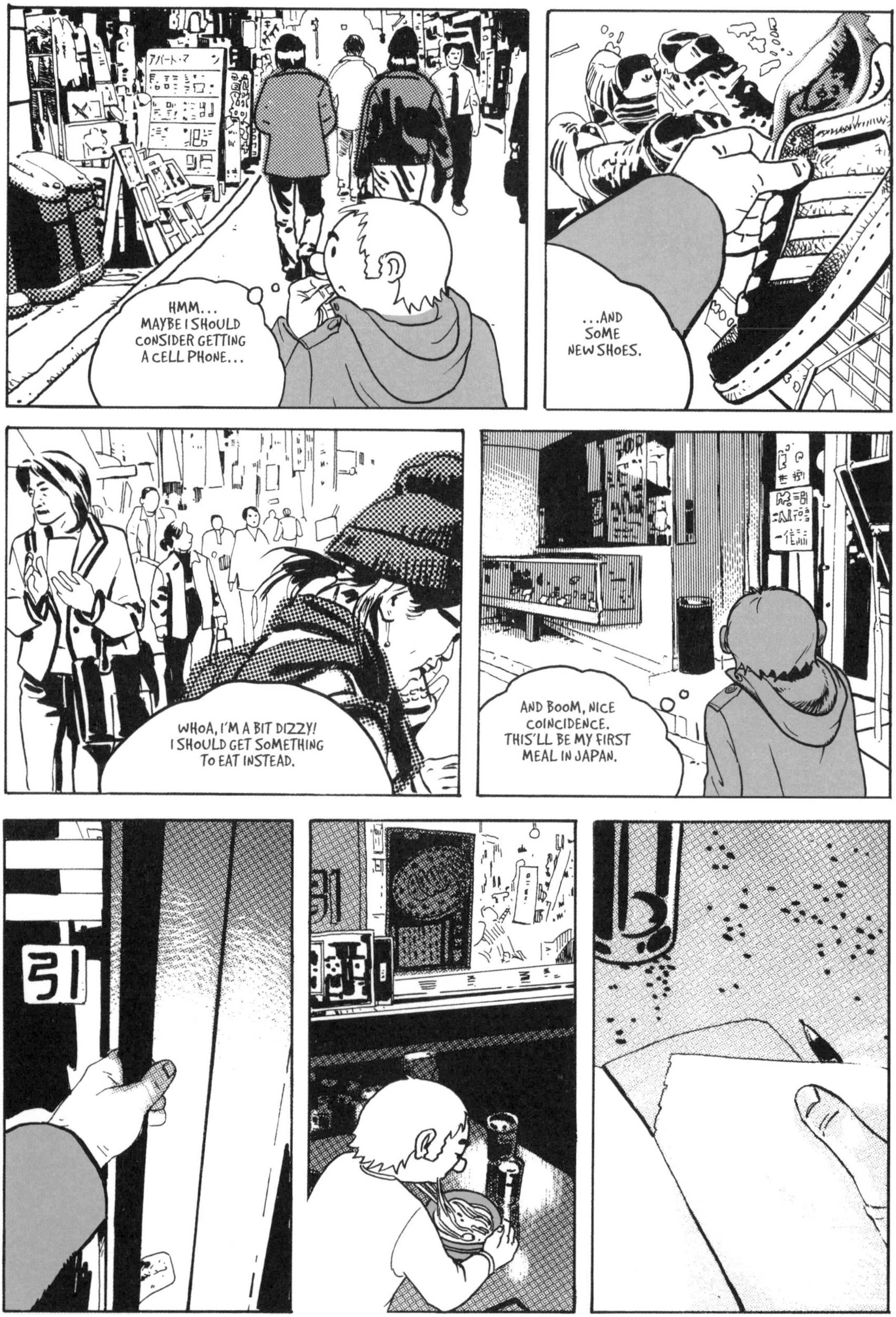
HMM... MAYBE I SHOULD CONSIDER GETTING A CELL PHONE...
...AND SOME NEW SHOES.
WHOA, I'M A BIT DIZZY! I SHOULD GET SOMETHING TO EAT INSTEAD.
AND BOOM, NICE COINCIDENCE. THIS'LL BE MY FIRST MEAL IN JAPAN.
引

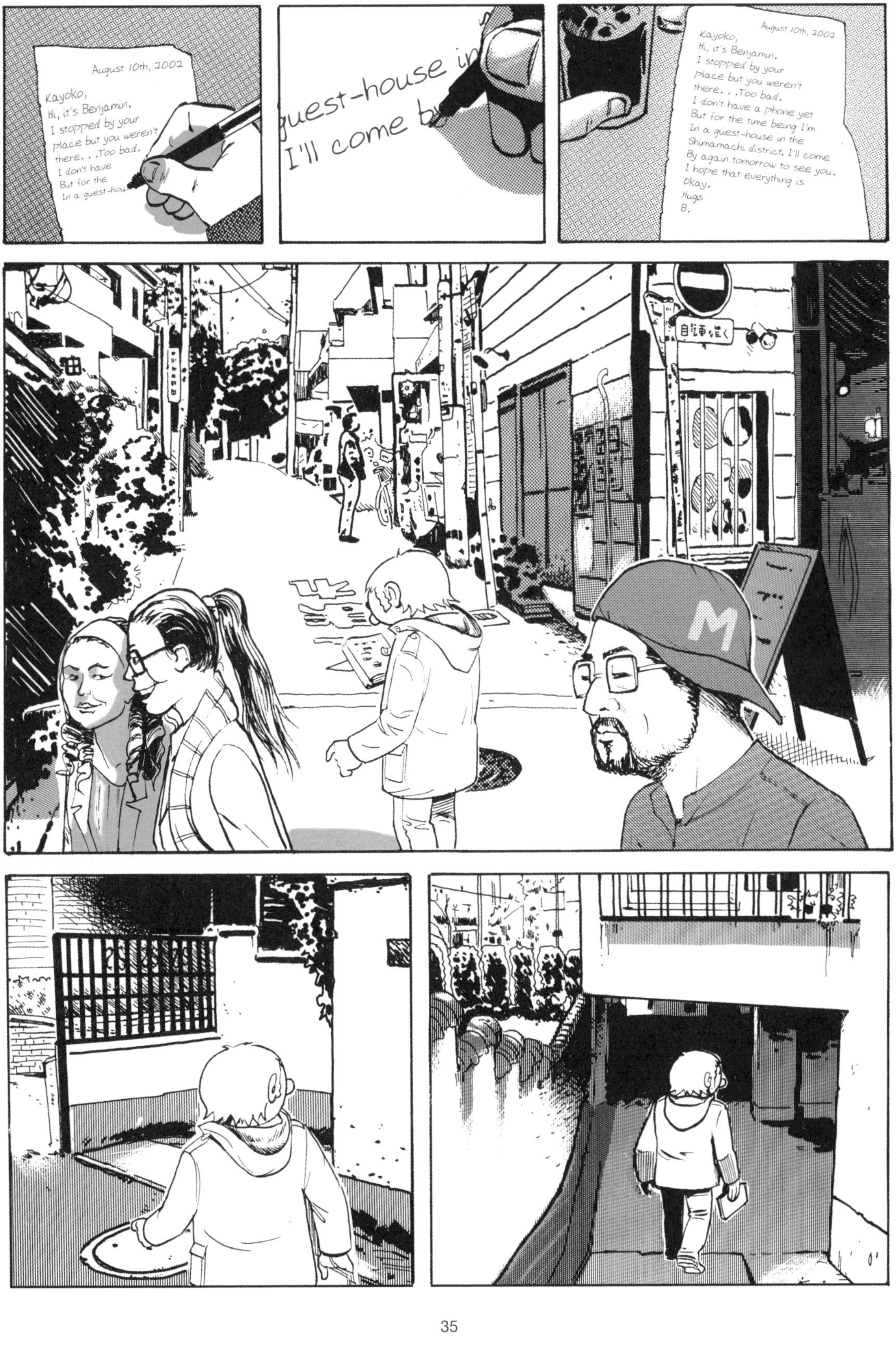
August 10th, 2002
Kayoko,
Hi, it's Benjamin.
I stopped by your
place but you weren't
there. . .Too bad.
I don't have
But for the
In a guest-hou
guest-house in
I'll come by
August 10th, 2002
Kayoko,
Hi, it's Benjamin.
I stopped by your
place but you weren't
there. . .Too bad.
I don't have a phone yet
But for the time being I'm
In a guest-house in the
Shimamachi district. I'll come
By again tomorrow to see you.
I hope that everything is
Okay.
Hugs
B.
自転車を除く

HUH? THERE'S ONLY THIS NAME ON THIS FLOOR?
東京新聞北澤
MAYBE I'VE GOT THE ADDRESS WRONG... LET'S SEE.
東京新聞北澤
TOC TOC TOC
HMMM!

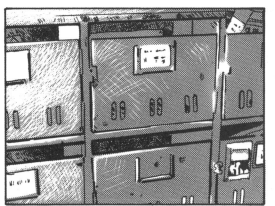

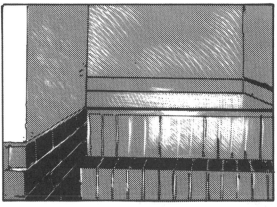

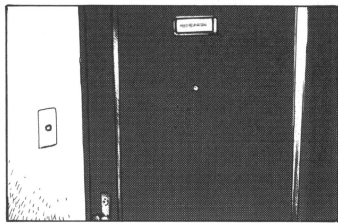

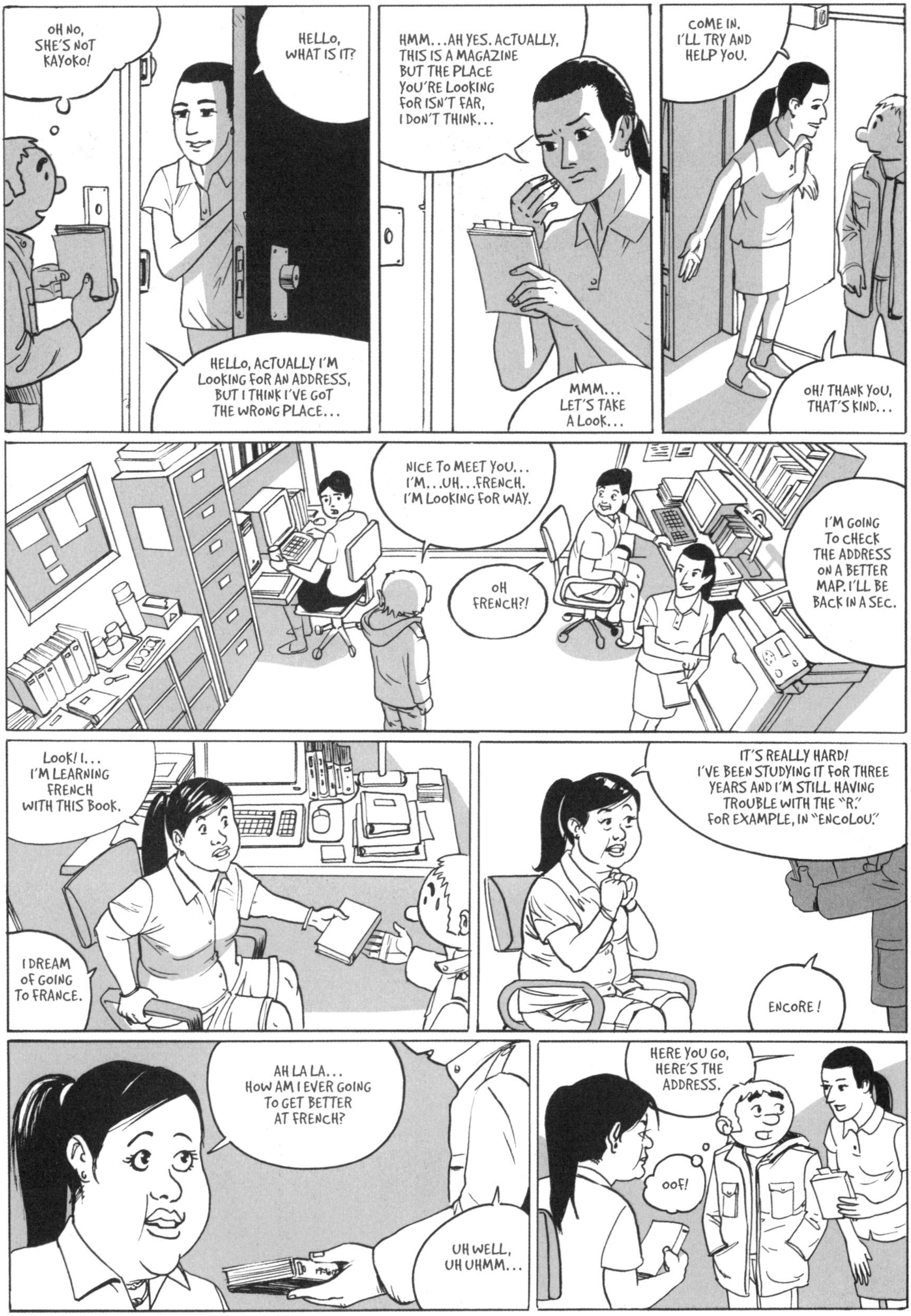
OH NO, SHE'S NOT KAYOKO!
HELLO, WHAT IS IT?
HELLO, ACTUALLY I'M LOOKING FOR AN ADDRESS, BUT I THINK I'VE GOT THE WRONG PLACE...
HMM...AH YES. ACTUALLY, THIS IS A MAGAZINE BUT THE PLACE YOU'RE LOOKING FOR ISN'T FAR, I DON'T THINK...
MMM... LET'S TAKE A LOOK...
COME IN. I'LL TRY AND HELP YOU.
OH! THANK YOU, THAT'S KIND...
NICE TO MEET YOU... I'M...UH...FRENCH. I'M LOOKING FOR WAY.
OH FRENCH?!
I'M GOING TO CHECK THE ADDRESS ON A BETTER MAP. I'LL BE BACK IN A SEC.
LOOK! I... I'M LEARNING FRENCH WITH THIS BOOK.
I DREAM OF GOING TO FRANCE.
IT'S REALLY HARD! I'VE BEEN STUDYING IT FOR THREE YEARS AND I'M STILL HAVING TROUBLE WITH THE "R." FOR EXAMPLE, IN "ENCOLOU."
ENCORE!
AH LA LA... HOW AM I EVER GOING TO GET BETTER AT FRENCH?
UH WELL, UH UHMM...
HERE YOU GO, HERE'S THE ADDRESS.
OOF!

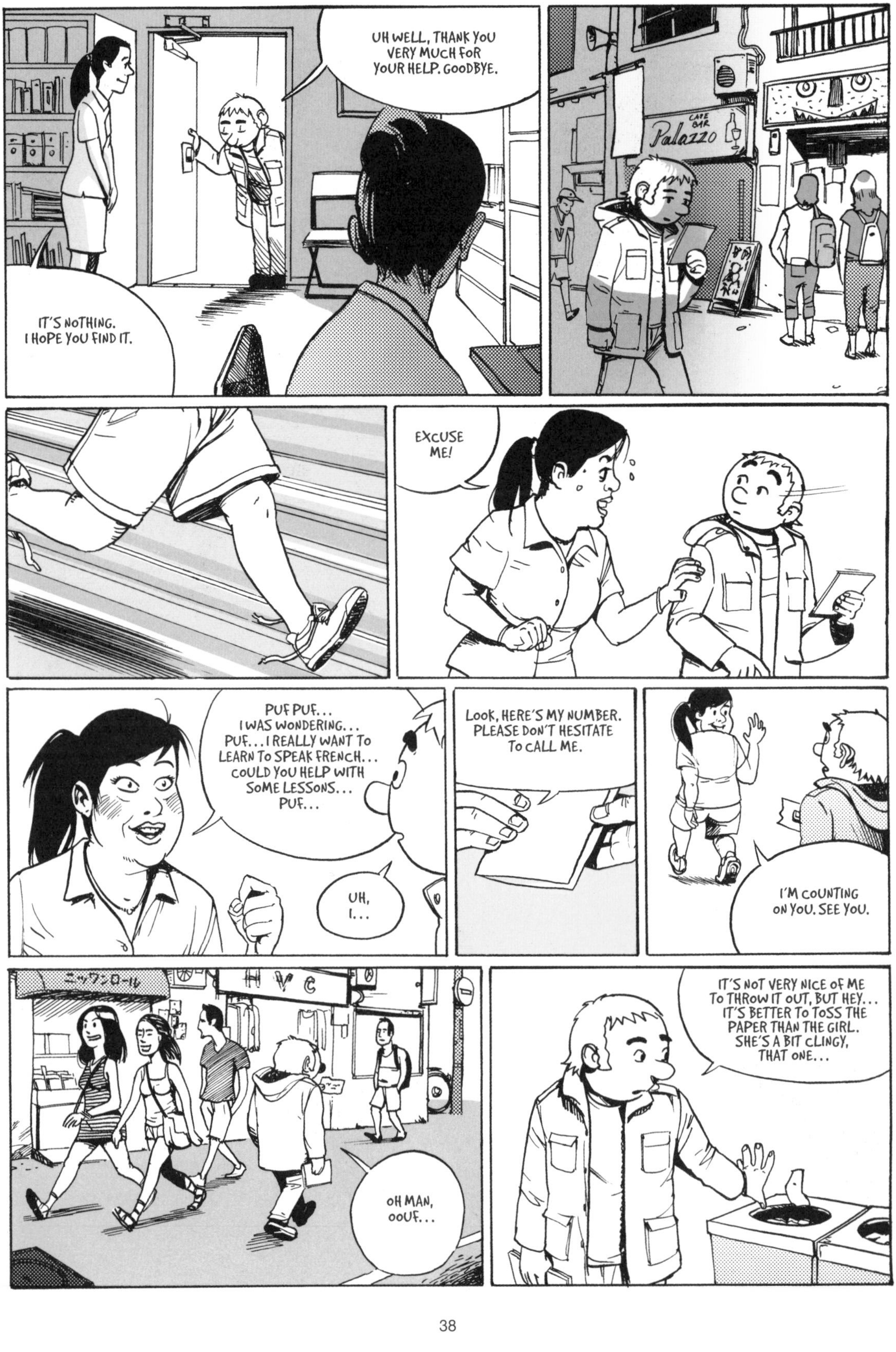
UH WELL, THANK YOU VERY MUCH FOR YOUR HELP. GOODBYE.
IT'S NOTHING. I HOPE YOU FIND IT.
CAFE BAR Palazzo
EXCUSE ME!
PUF PUF... I WAS WONDERING... PUF... I REALLY WANT TO LEARN TO SPEAK FRENCH... COULD YOU HELP WITH SOME LESSONS... PUF...
UH, I...
Look, HERE'S MY NUMBER. PLEASE DON'T HESITATE TO CALL ME.
I'M COUNTING ON YOU. SEE YOU.
OH MAN, OOUF...
IT'S NOT VERY NICE OF ME TO THROW IT OUT, BUT HEY... IT'S BETTER TO TOSS THE PAPER THAN THE GIRL. SHE'S A BIT CLINGY, THAT ONE...

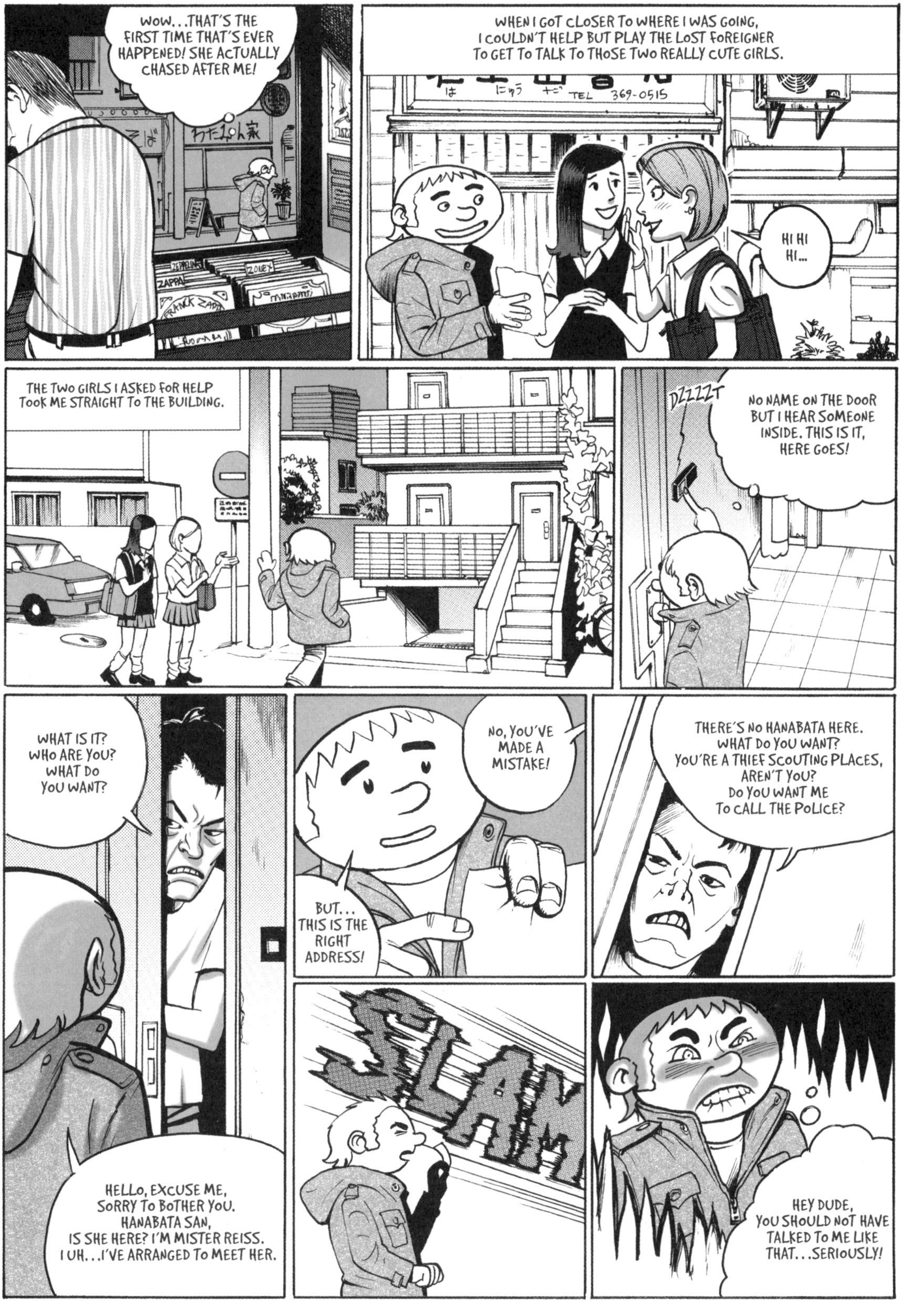
WOW... THAT'S THE FIRST TIME THAT'S EVER HAPPENED! SHE ACTUALLY CHASED AFTER ME!
ZAPPA
FRANCK ZAPPA
WHEN I GOT CLOSER TO WHERE I WAS GOING, I COULDN'T HELP BUT PLAY THE LOST FOREIGNER TO GET TO TALK TO THOSE TWO REALLY CUTE GIRLS.
TEL 369-0515
HI HI HI...
THE TWO GIRLS I ASKED FOR HELP TOOK ME STRAIGHT TO THE BUILDING.
DZZZZT
NO NAME ON THE DOOR BUT I HEAR SOMEONE INSIDE. THIS IS IT, HERE GOES!
WHAT IS IT? WHO ARE YOU? WHAT DO YOU WANT?
HELLO, EXCUSE ME, SORRY TO BOTHER YOU. HANABATA SAN, IS SHE HERE? I'M MISTER REISS. I UH... I'VE ARRANGED TO MEET HER.
NO, YOU'VE MADE A MISTAKE!
BUT... THIS IS THE RIGHT ADDRESS!
THERE'S NO HANABATA HERE. WHAT DO YOU WANT? YOU'RE A THIEF SCOUTING PLACES, AREN'T YOU? DO YOU WANT ME TO CALL THE POLICE?
SLAM
HEY DUDE, YOU SHOULD NOT HAVE TALKED TO ME LIKE THAT... SERIOUSLY!

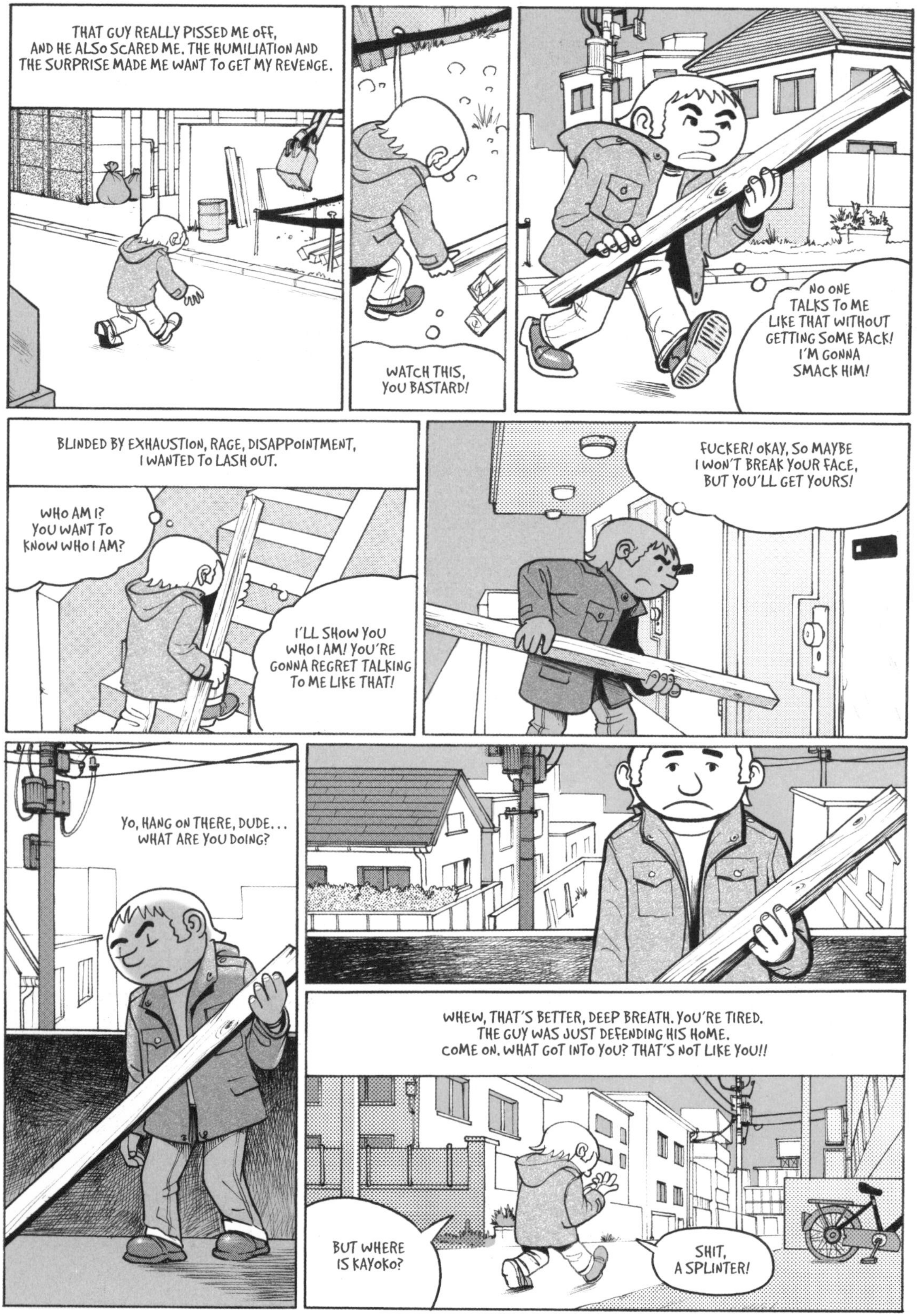
THAT GUY REALLY PISSED ME OFF, AND HE ALSO SCARED ME. THE HUMILIATION AND THE SURPRISE MADE ME WANT TO GET MY REVENGE.
WATCH THIS, YOU BASTARD!
NO ONE TALKS TO ME LIKE THAT WITHOUT GETTING SOME BACK! I'M GONNA SMACK HIM!
BLINDED BY EXHAUSTION, RAGE, DISAPPOINTMENT, I WANTED TO LASH OUT.
WHO AM I? YOU WANT TO KNOW WHO I AM?
I'LL SHOW YOU WHO I AM! YOU'RE GONNA REGRET TALKING TO ME LIKE THAT!
FUCKER! OKAY, SO MAYBE I WON'T BREAK YOUR FACE, BUT YOU'LL GET YOURS!
YO, HANG ON THERE, DUDE... WHAT ARE YOU DOING?
WHEW, THAT'S BETTER, DEEP BREATH. YOU'RE TIRED. THE GUY WAS JUST DEFENDING HIS HOME. COME ON. WHAT GOT INTO YOU? THAT'S NOT LIKE YOU!!
BUT WHERE IS KAYOKO?
SHIT, A SPLINTER!

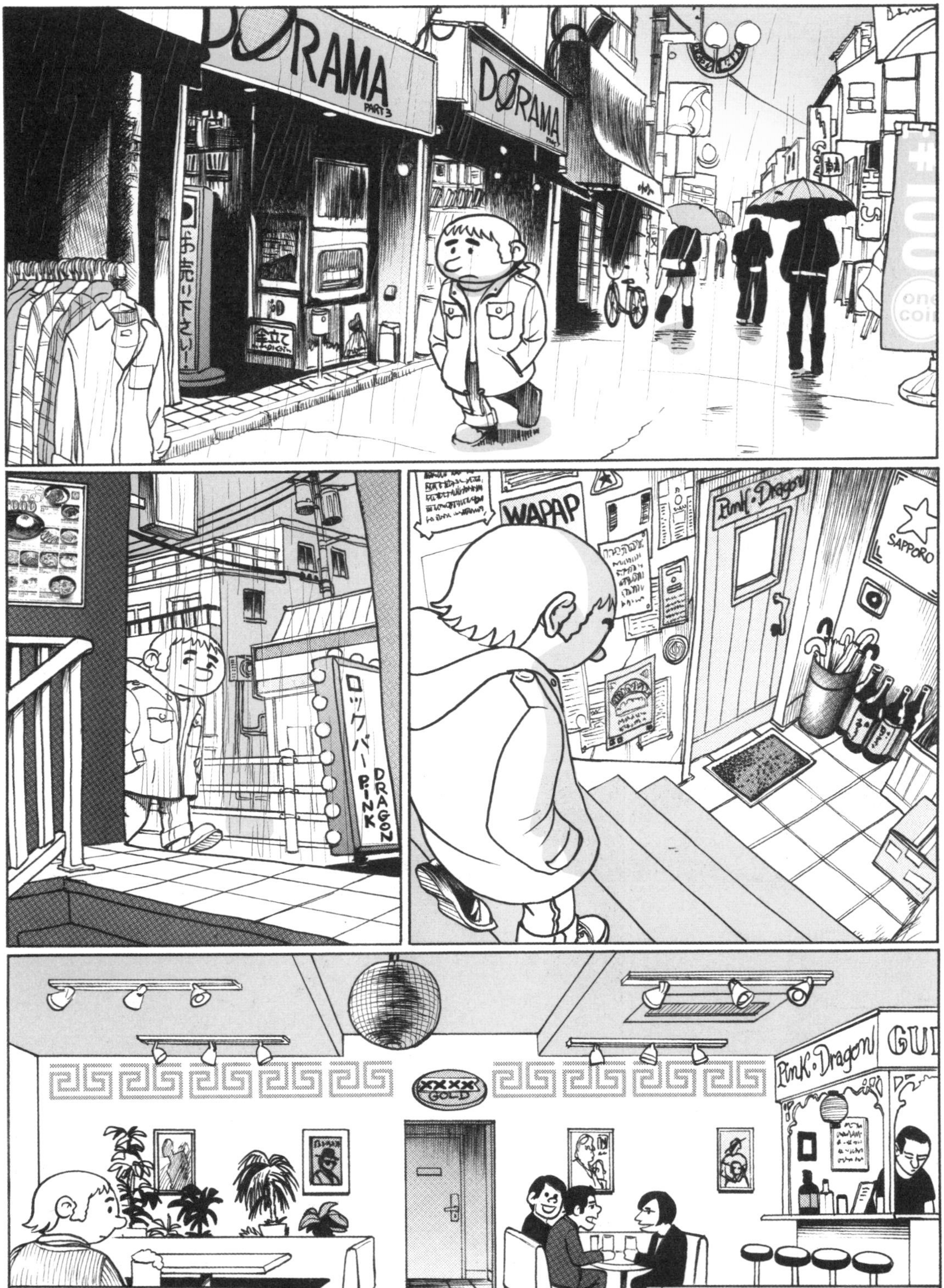
DORAMA
PART 3
DORAMA
お売り下さい
ロックバー
PINK DRAGON
WAPAP
Pink・Dragon
SAPPORO
XXXX GOLD
Pink・Dragon

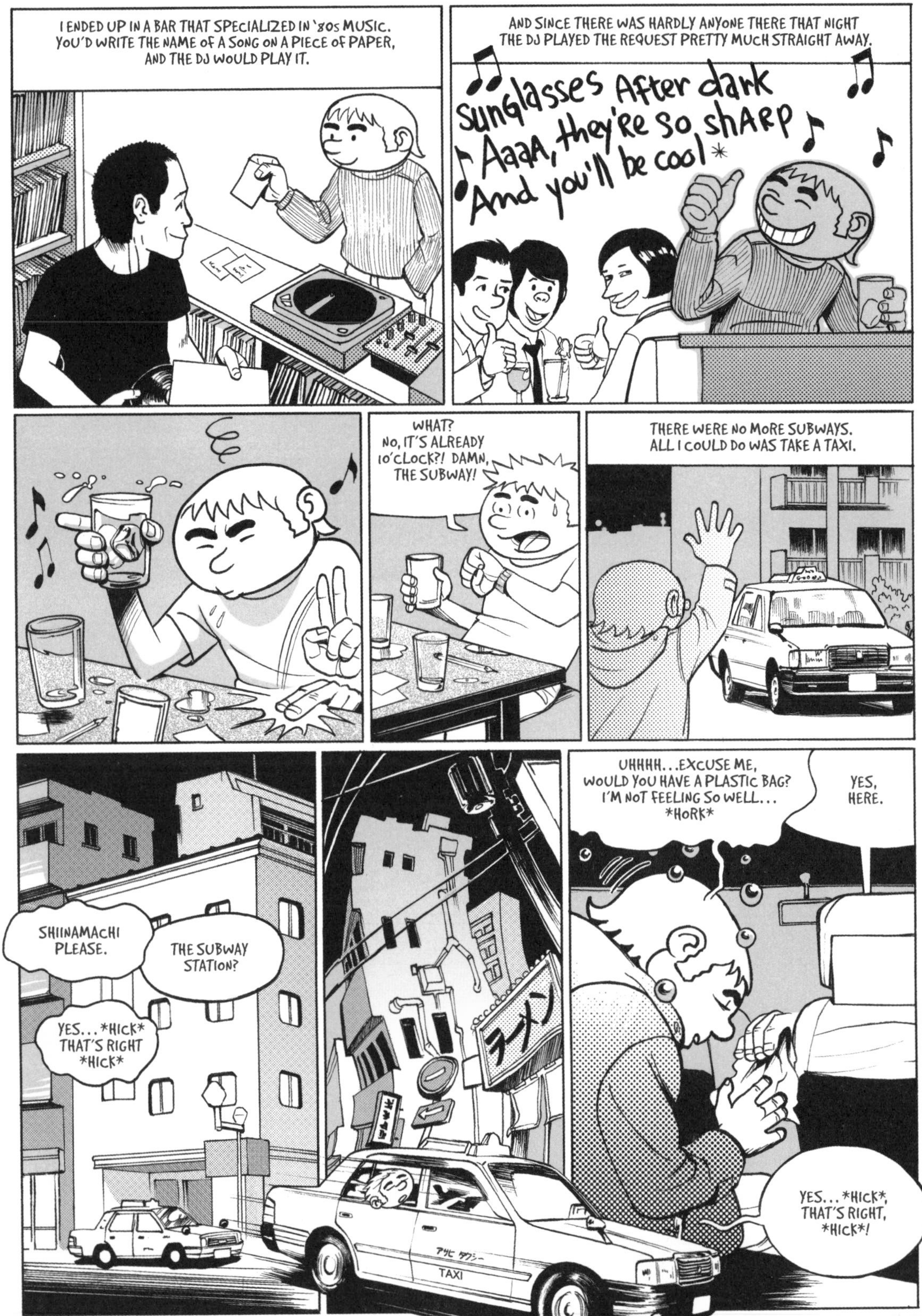
I ENDED UP IN A BAR THAT SPECIALIZED IN '80s MUSIC. YOU'D WRITE THE NAME OF A SONG ON A PIECE OF PAPER, AND THE DJ WOULD PLAY IT.
AND SINCE THERE WAS HARDLY ANYONE THERE THAT NIGHT THE DJ PLAYED THE REQUEST PRETTY MUCH STRAIGHT AWAY.
Sunglasses After dark
Aaaa, they're so sharp
And you'll be cool*
WHAT? NO, IT'S ALREADY 10'CLOCK?! DAMN, THE SUBWAY!
THERE WERE NO MORE SUBWAYS. ALL I COULD DO WAS TAKE A TAXI.
SHIINAMACHI PLEASE.
THE SUBWAY STATION?
YES... *HICK* THAT'S RIGHT *HICK*
ラーメン
TAXI
UHHHH...EXCUSE ME, WOULD YOU HAVE A PLASTIC BAG? I'M NOT FEELING SO WELL... *HORK*
YES, HERE.
YES... *HICK*, THAT'S RIGHT, *HICK*!

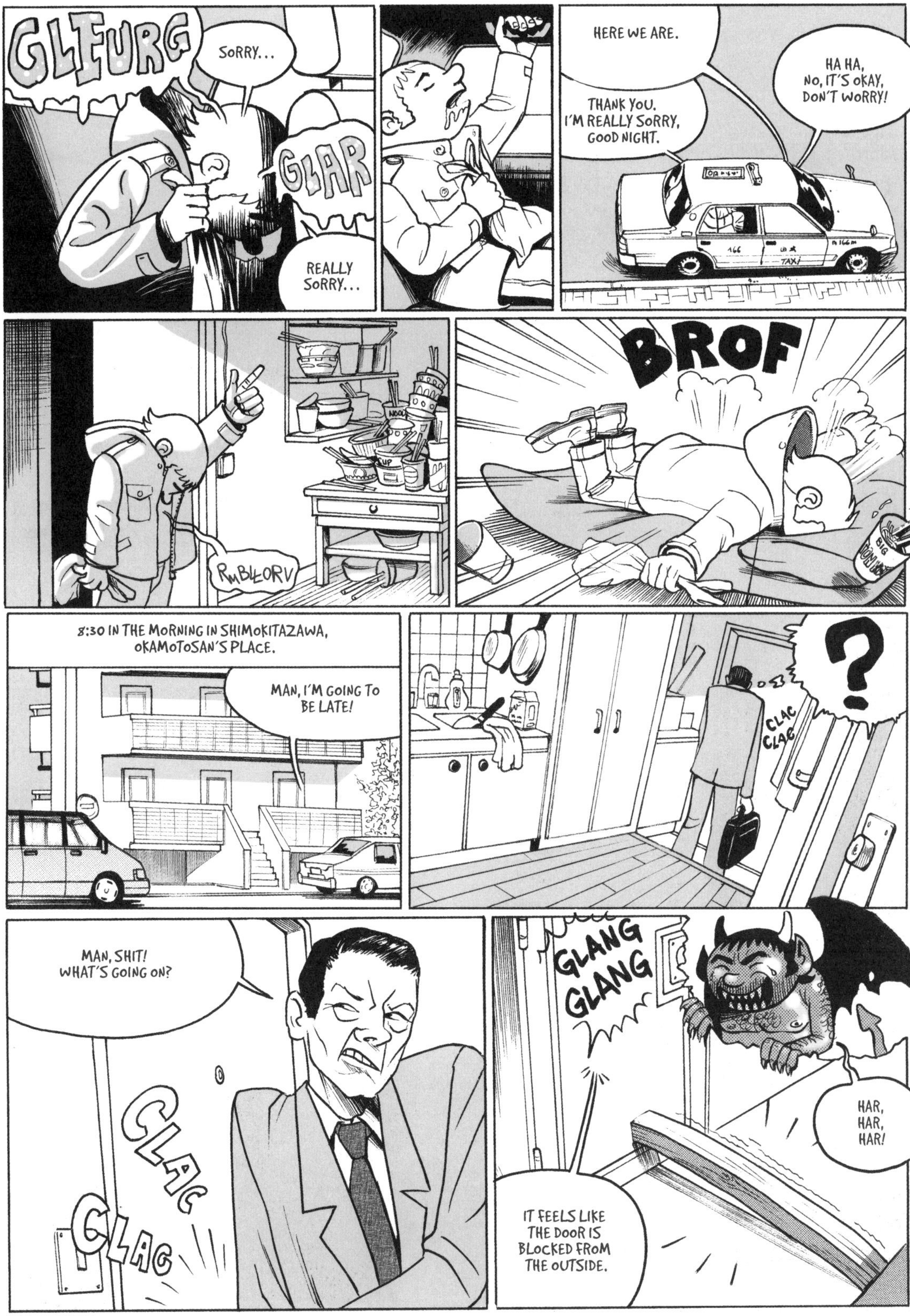
GLEURG
SORRY...
GLAR
REALLY SORRY...
HERE WE ARE.
THANK YOU. I'M REALLY SORRY, GOOD NIGHT.
HA HA, NO, IT'S OKAY, DON'T WORRY!
TAXI
RMBLLORV
BROF
8:30 IN THE MORNING IN SHIMOKITAZAWA, OKAMOTOSAN'S PLACE.
MAN, I'M GOING TO BE LATE!
CLAC CLAC
?
MAN, SHIT! WHAT'S GOING ON?
CLAC
CLAG
GLANG GLANG
HAR, HAR, HAR!
IT FEELS LIKE THE DOOR IS BLOCKED FROM THE OUTSIDE.

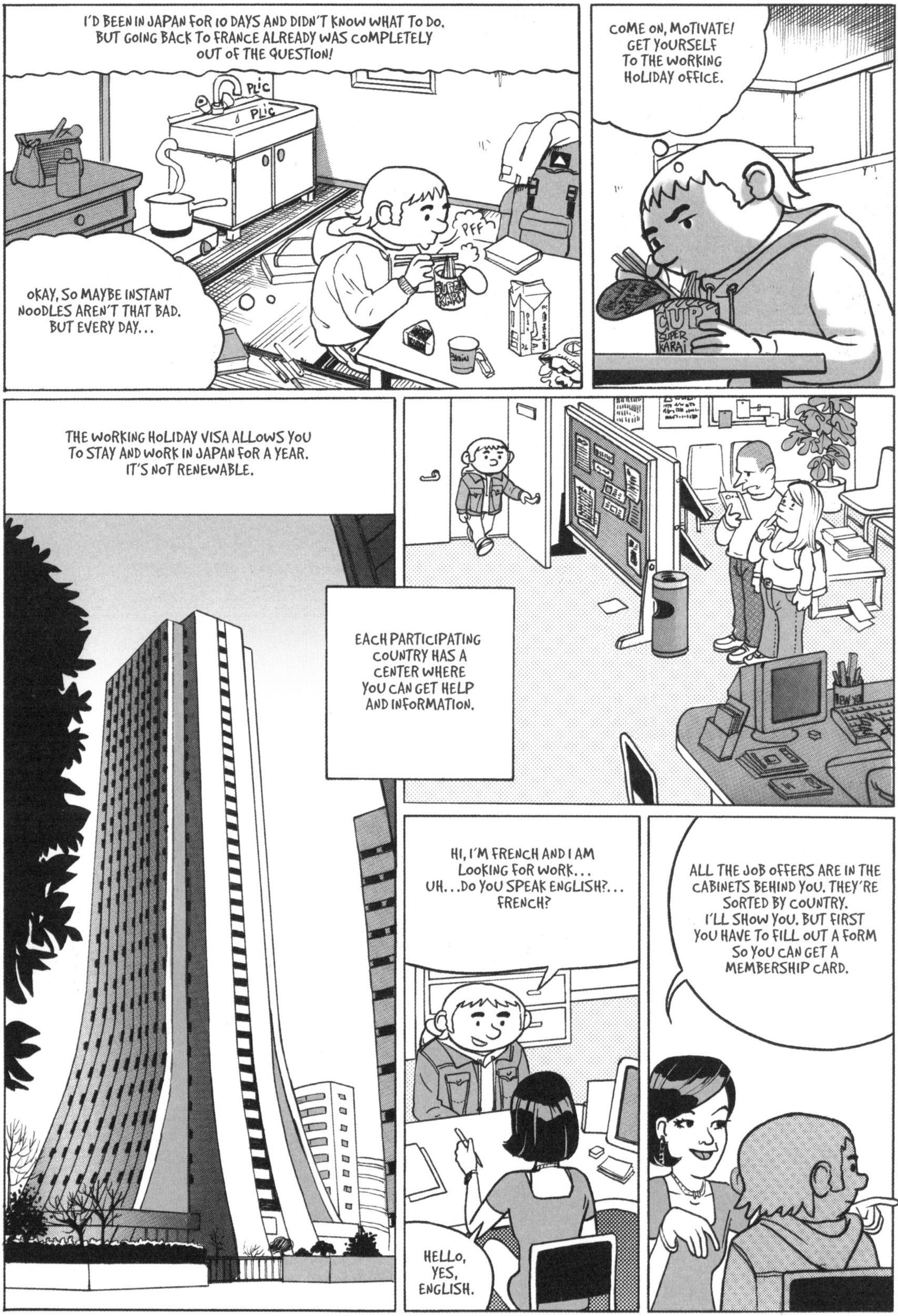

I'D BEEN IN JAPAN FOR 10 DAYS AND DIDN'T KNOW WHAT TO DO. BUT GOING BACK TO FRANCE ALREADY WAS COMPLETELY OUT OF THE QUESTION!
PLIC
PLIC
PFF
OKAY, SO MAYBE INSTANT NOODLES AREN'T THAT BAD. BUT EVERY DAY...
COME ON, MOTIVATE! GET YOURSELF TO THE WORKING HOLIDAY OFFICE.
CUP SUPER KARAI
THE WORKING HOLIDAY VISA ALLOWS YOU TO STAY AND WORK IN JAPAN FOR A YEAR. IT'S NOT RENEWABLE.
EACH PARTICIPATING COUNTRY HAS A CENTER WHERE YOU CAN GET HELP AND INFORMATION.
HI, I'M FRENCH AND I AM LOOKING FOR WORK... UH...DO YOU SPEAK ENGLISH?... FRENCH?
HELLO, YES, ENGLISH.
ALL THE JOB OFFERS ARE IN THE CABINETS BEHIND YOU. THEY'RE SORTED BY COUNTRY. I'LL SHOW YOU. BUT FIRST YOU HAVE TO FILL OUT A FORM SO YOU CAN GET A MEMBERSHIP CARD.

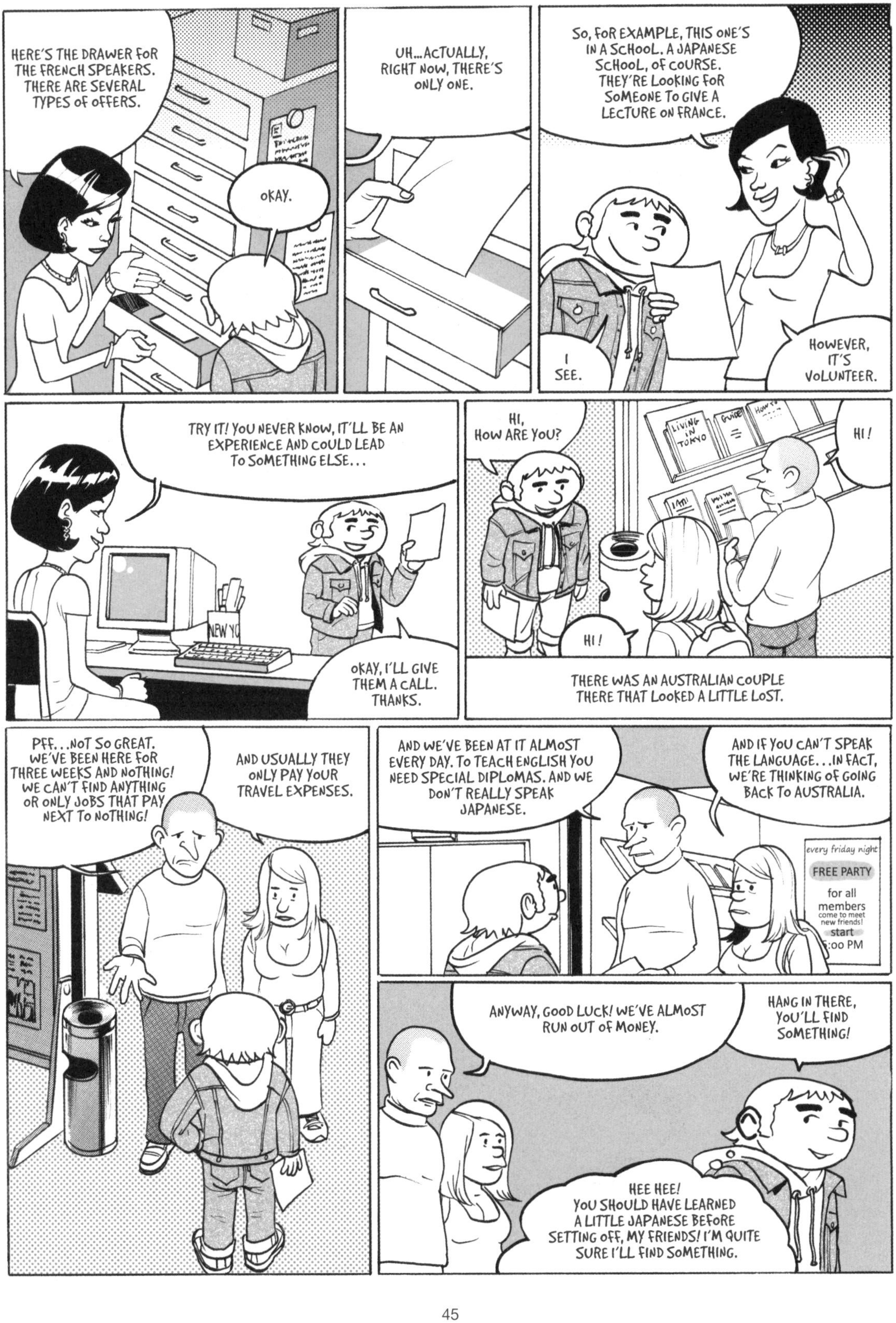
HERE'S THE DRAWER FOR THE FRENCH SPEAKERS. THERE ARE SEVERAL TYPES OF OFFERS.
OKAY.
UH...ACTUALLY, RIGHT NOW, THERE'S ONLY ONE.
SO, FOR EXAMPLE, THIS ONE'S IN A SCHOOL. A JAPANESE SCHOOL, OF COURSE. THEY'RE LOOKING FOR SOMEONE TO GIVE A LECTURE ON FRANCE.
I SEE.
HOWEVER, IT'S VOLUNTEER.
TRY IT! YOU NEVER KNOW, IT'LL BE AN EXPERIENCE AND COULD LEAD TO SOMETHING ELSE...
OKAY, I'LL GIVE THEM A CALL. THANKS.
HI, HOW ARE YOU?
HI!
HI!
THERE WAS AN AUSTRALIAN COUPLE THERE THAT LOOKED A LITTLE LOST.
PFF...NOT SO GREAT. WE'VE BEEN HERE FOR THREE WEEKS AND NOTHING! WE CAN'T FIND ANYTHING OR ONLY JOBS THAT PAY NEXT TO NOTHING!
AND USUALLY THEY ONLY PAY YOUR TRAVEL EXPENSES.
AND WE'VE BEEN AT IT ALMOST EVERY DAY. TO TEACH ENGLISH YOU NEED SPECIAL DIPLOMAS. AND WE DON'T REALLY SPEAK JAPANESE.
AND IF YOU CAN'T SPEAK THE LANGUAGE...IN FACT, WE'RE THINKING OF GOING BACK TO AUSTRALIA.
every friday night
FREE PARTY
for all members
come to meet new friends!
start
ANYWAY, GOOD LUCK! WE'VE ALMOST RUN OUT OF MONEY.
HANG IN THERE, YOU'LL FIND SOMETHING!
HEE HEE! YOU SHOULD HAVE LEARNED A LITTLE JAPANESE BEFORE SETTING OFF, MY FRIENDS! I'M QUITE SURE I'LL FIND SOMETHING.

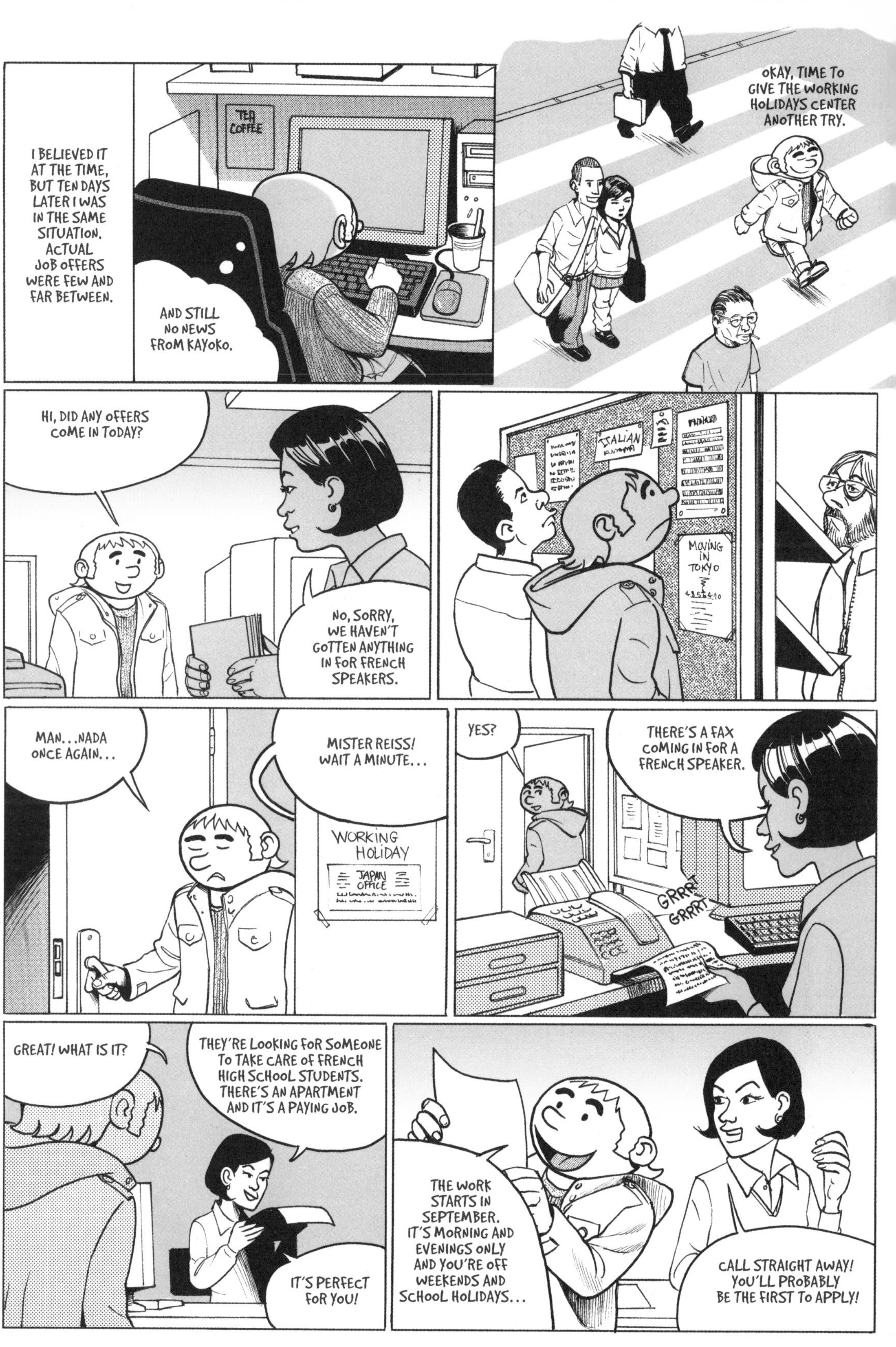
I BELIEVED IT AT THE TIME, BUT TEN DAYS LATER I WAS IN THE SAME SITUATION. ACTUAL JOB OFFERS WERE FEW AND FAR BETWEEN.
TEA COFFEE
AND STILL NO NEWS FROM KAYOKO.
OKAY, TIME TO GIVE THE WORKING HOLIDAYS CENTER ANOTHER TRY.
HI, DID ANY OFFERS COME IN TODAY?
NO, SORRY, WE HAVEN'T GOTTEN ANYTHING IN FOR FRENCH SPEAKERS.
ITALIAN
MOVING IN TOKYO
MAN...NADA ONCE AGAIN...
MISTER REISS! WAIT A MINUTE...
WORKING HOLIDAY
JAPAN OFFICE
YES?
THERE'S A FAX COMING IN FOR A FRENCH SPEAKER.
GRRRT GRRRT
GREAT! WHAT IS IT?
THEY'RE LOOKING FOR SOMEONE TO TAKE CARE OF FRENCH HIGH SCHOOL STUDENTS. THERE'S AN APARTMENT AND IT'S A PAYING JOB.
IT'S PERFECT FOR YOU!
THE WORK STARTS IN SEPTEMBER. IT'S MORNING AND EVENINGS ONLY AND YOU'RE OFF WEEKENDS AND SCHOOL HOLIDAYS...
CALL STRAIGHT AWAY! YOU'LL PROBABLY BE THE FIRST TO APPLY!

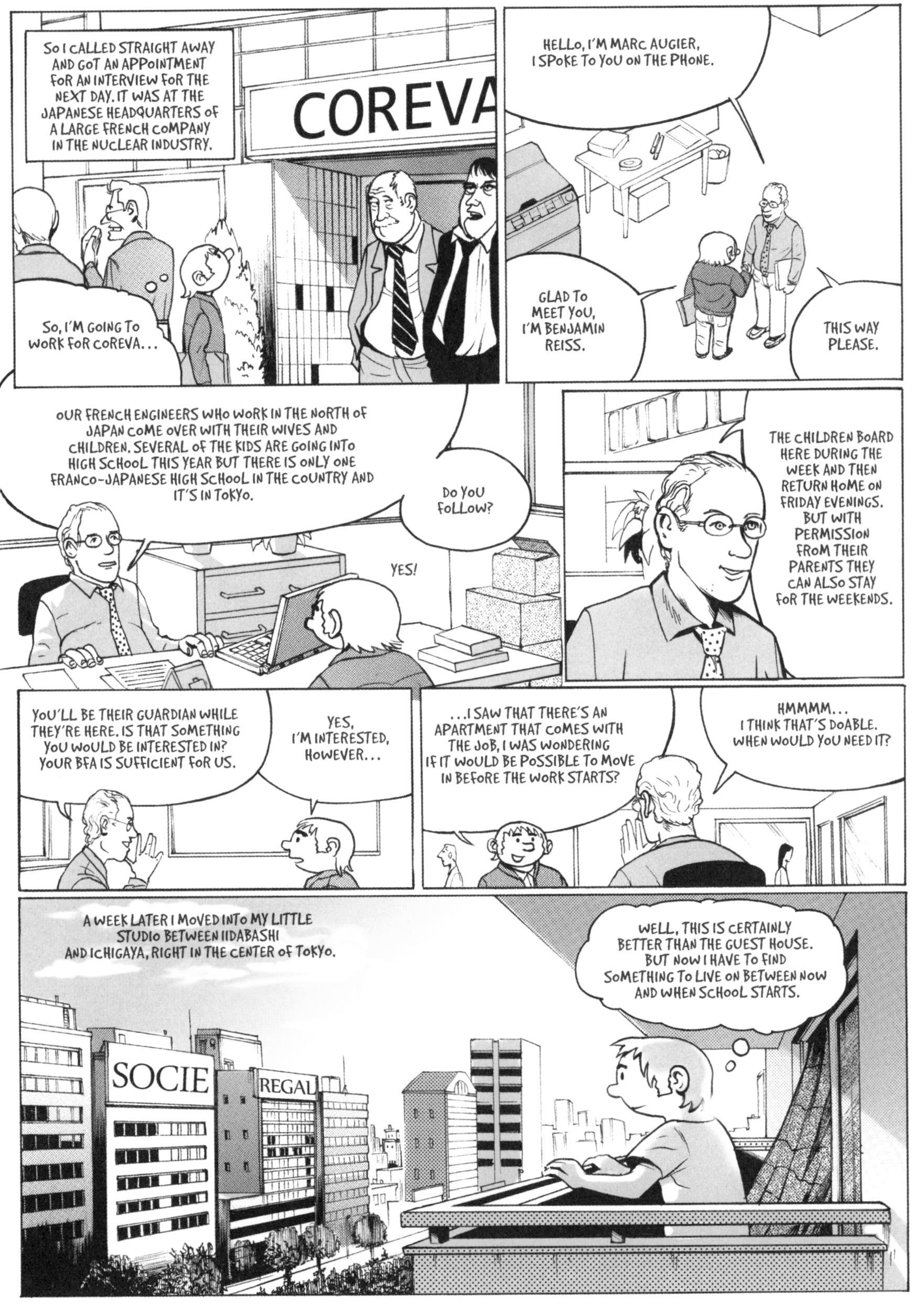
So I CALLED STRAIGHT AWAY AND GOT AN APPOINTMENT FOR AN INTERVIEW FOR THE NEXT DAY. IT WAS AT THE JAPANESE HEADQUARTERS OF A LARGE FRENCH COMPANY IN THE NUCLEAR INDUSTRY.
COREVA
So, I'M GOING TO WORK FOR COREVA...
HELLO, I'M MARC AUGIER, I SPOKE TO YOU ON THE PHONE.
GLAD TO MEET YOU, I'M BENJAMIN REISS.
THIS WAY PLEASE.
OUR FRENCH ENGINEERS WHO WORK IN THE NORTH OF JAPAN COME OVER WITH THEIR WIVES AND CHILDREN. SEVERAL OF THE KIDS ARE GOING INTO HIGH SCHOOL THIS YEAR BUT THERE IS ONLY ONE FRANCO-JAPANESE HIGH SCHOOL IN THE COUNTRY AND IT'S IN TOKYO.
DO YOU FOLLOW?
YES!
THE CHILDREN BOARD HERE DURING THE WEEK AND THEN RETURN HOME ON FRIDAY EVENINGS. BUT WITH PERMISSION FROM THEIR PARENTS THEY CAN ALSO STAY FOR THE WEEKENDS.
YOU'LL BE THEIR GUARDIAN WHILE THEY'RE HERE. IS THAT SOMETHING YOU WOULD BE INTERESTED IN? YOUR BFA IS SUFFICIENT FOR US.
YES, I'M INTERESTED, HOWEVER...
...I SAW THAT THERE'S AN APARTMENT THAT COMES WITH THE JOB, I WAS WONDERING IF IT WOULD BE POSSIBLE TO MOVE IN BEFORE THE WORK STARTS?
HMMMM... I THINK THAT'S DOABLE. WHEN WOULD YOU NEED IT?
A WEEK LATER I MOVED INTO MY LITTLE STUDIO BETWEEN IIDABASHI AND ICHIGAYA, RIGHT IN THE CENTER OF TOKYO.
WELL, THIS IS CERTAINLY BETTER THAN THE GUEST HOUSE. BUT NOW I HAVE TO FIND SOMETHING TO LIVE ON BETWEEN NOW AND WHEN SCHOOL STARTS.
SOCIE
REGAL

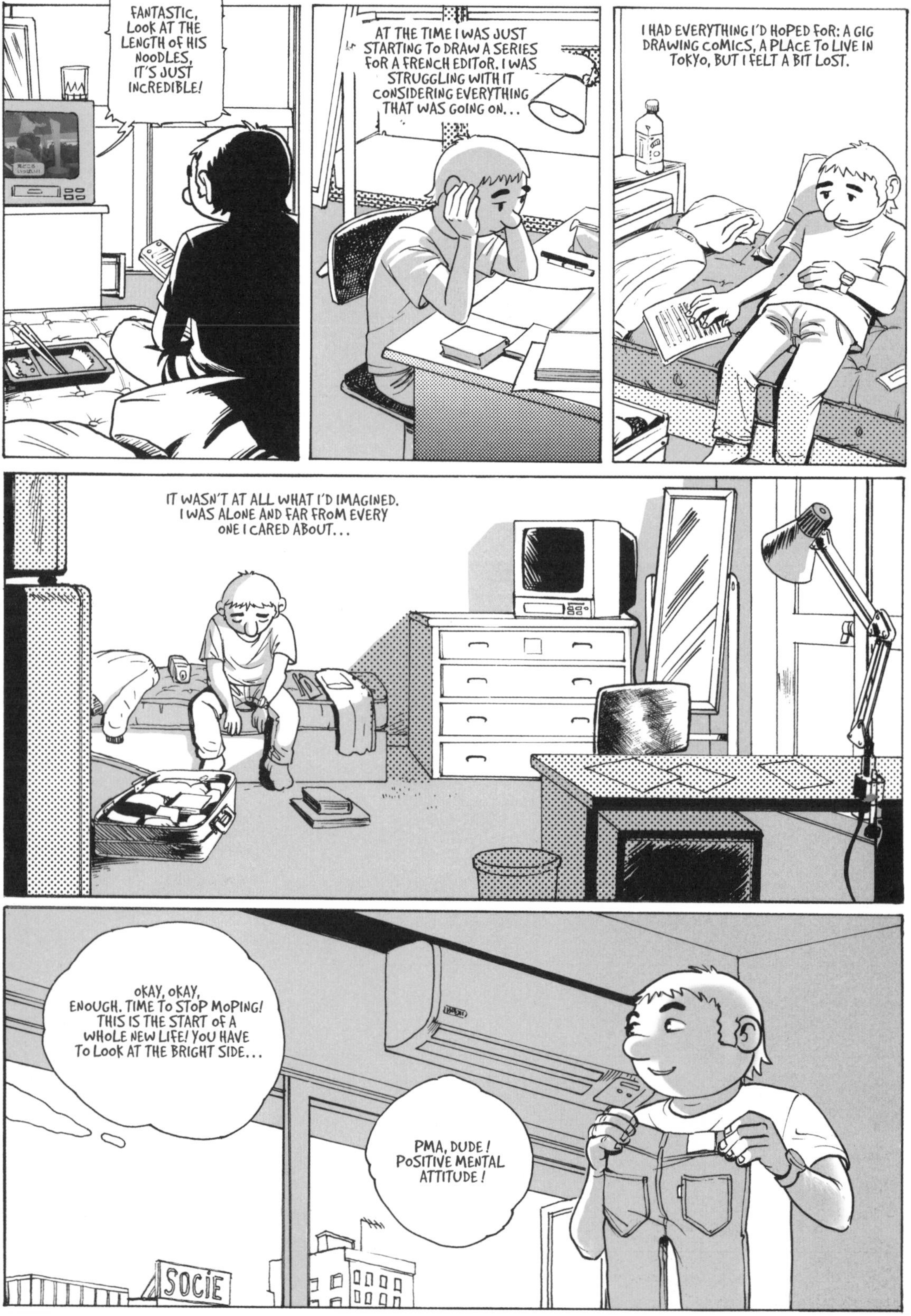
FANTASTIC, LOOK AT THE LENGTH OF HIS NOODLES, IT'S JUST INCREDIBLE!
AT THE TIME I WAS JUST STARTING TO DRAW A SERIES FOR A FRENCH EDITOR. I WAS STRUGGLING WITH IT CONSIDERING EVERYTHING THAT WAS GOING ON...
I HAD EVERYTHING I'D HOPED FOR: A GIG DRAWING COMICS, A PLACE TO LIVE IN TOKYO, BUT I FELT A BIT LOST.
IT WASN'T AT ALL WHAT I'D IMAGINED. I WAS ALONE AND FAR FROM EVERY ONE I CARED ABOUT...
OKAY, OKAY, ENOUGH. TIME TO STOP MOPING! THIS IS THE START OF A WHOLE NEW LIFE! YOU HAVE TO LOOK AT THE BRIGHT SIDE...
PMA, DUDE! POSITIVE MENTAL ATTITUDE!
SOCIE

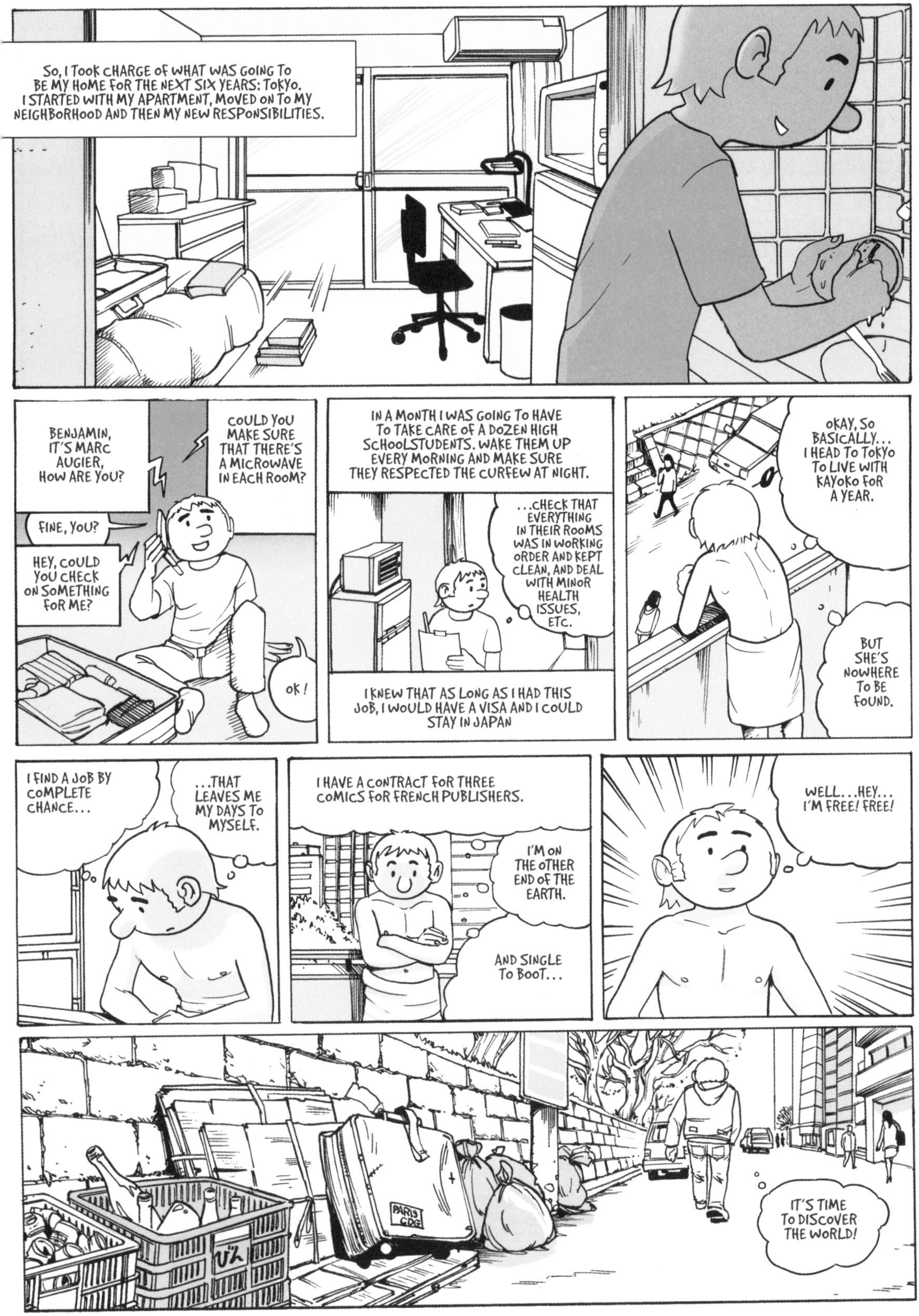
So, I took charge of what was going to be my home for the next six years: Tokyo. I started with my apartment, moved on to my neighborhood and then my new responsibilities.
Benjamin, it's Marc Augier, how are you?
Could you make sure that there's a microwave in each room?
Fine, you?
Hey, could you check on something for me?
Ok!
In a month I was going to have to take care of a dozen high schoolstudents. Wake them up every morning and make sure they respected the curfew at night.
...check that everything in their rooms was in working order and kept clean, and deal with minor health issues, etc.
I knew that as long as I had this job, I would have a visa and I could stay in Japan
Okay, so basically... I head to Tokyo to live with Kayoko for a year.
But she's nowhere to be found.
I find a job by complete chance...
...that leaves me my days to myself.
I have a contract for three comics for French publishers.
I'm on the other end of the earth.
And single to boot...
Well... hey... I'm free! Free!
Paris CDG
It's time to discover the world!

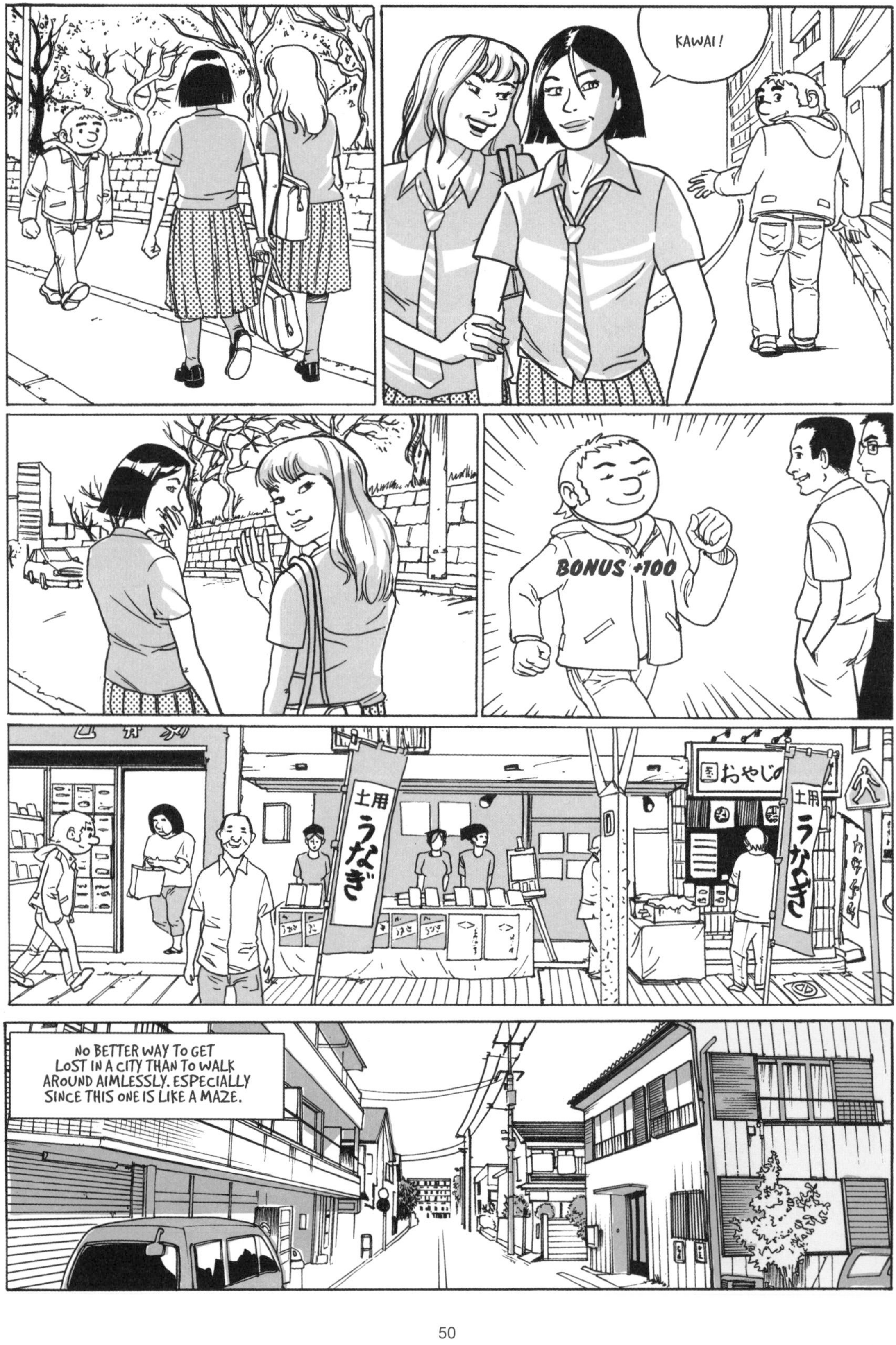
KAWAI!
BONUS +100
土用
うなぎ
おやじの
土用
うなぎ
NO BETTER WAY TO GET LOST IN A CITY THAN TO WALK AROUND AIMLESSLY. ESPECIALLY SINCE THIS ONE IS LIKE A MAZE.

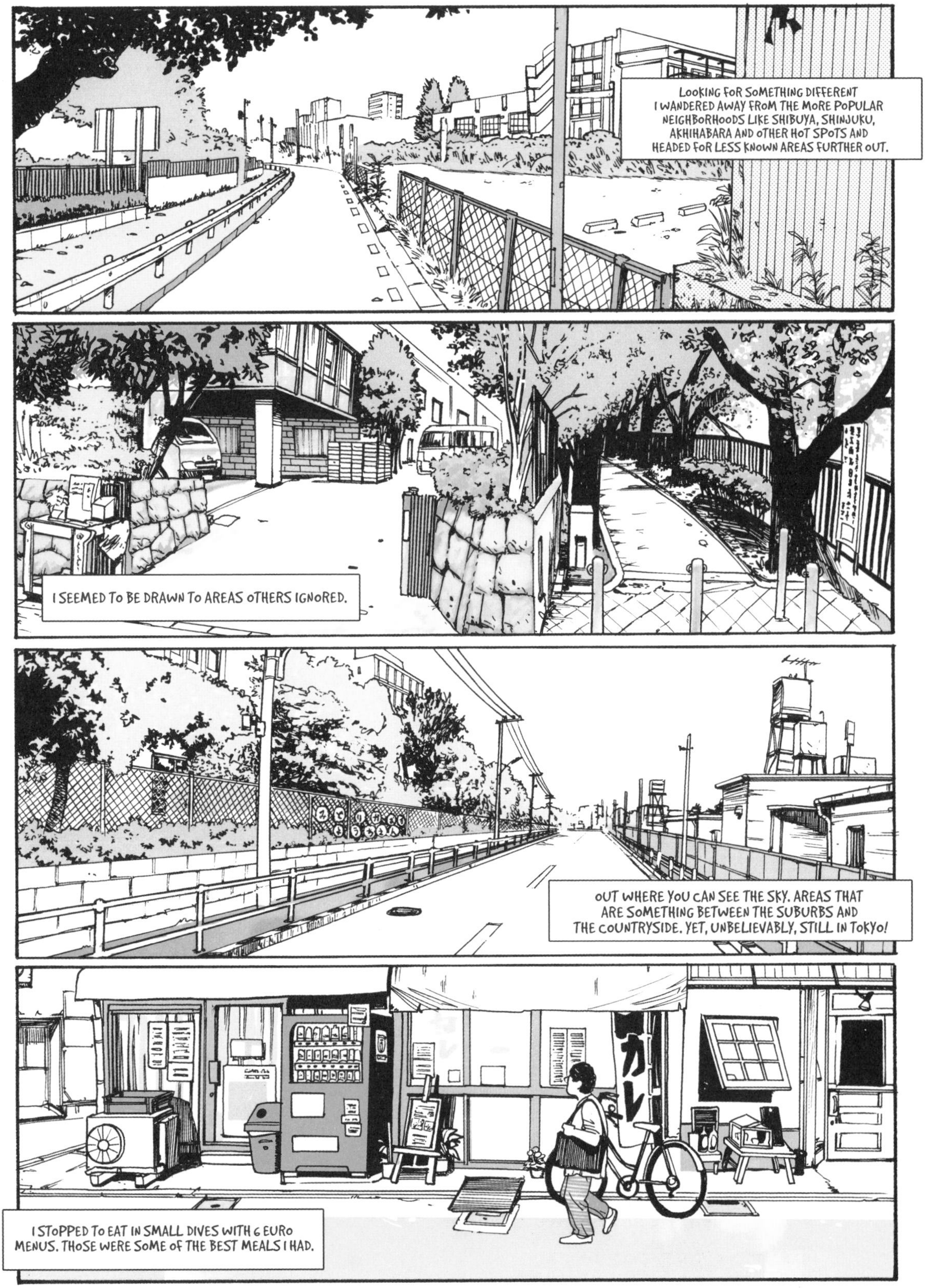
LOOKING FOR SOMETHING DIFFERENT
I WANDERED AWAY FROM THE MORE POPULAR
NEIGHBORHOODS LIKE SHIBUYA, SHINJUKU,
AKHIHABARA AND OTHER HOT SPOTS AND
HEADED FOR LESS KNOWN AREAS FURTHER OUT.
I SEEMED TO BE DRAWN TO AREAS OTHERS IGNORED.
OUT WHERE YOU CAN SEE THE SKY. AREAS THAT
ARE SOMETHING BETWEEN THE SUBURBS AND
THE COUNTRYSIDE. YET, UNBELIEVABLY, STILL IN TOKYO!
カレ
I STOPPED TO EAT IN SMALL DIVES WITH 6 EURO
MENUS. THOSE WERE SOME OF THE BEST MEALS I HAD.

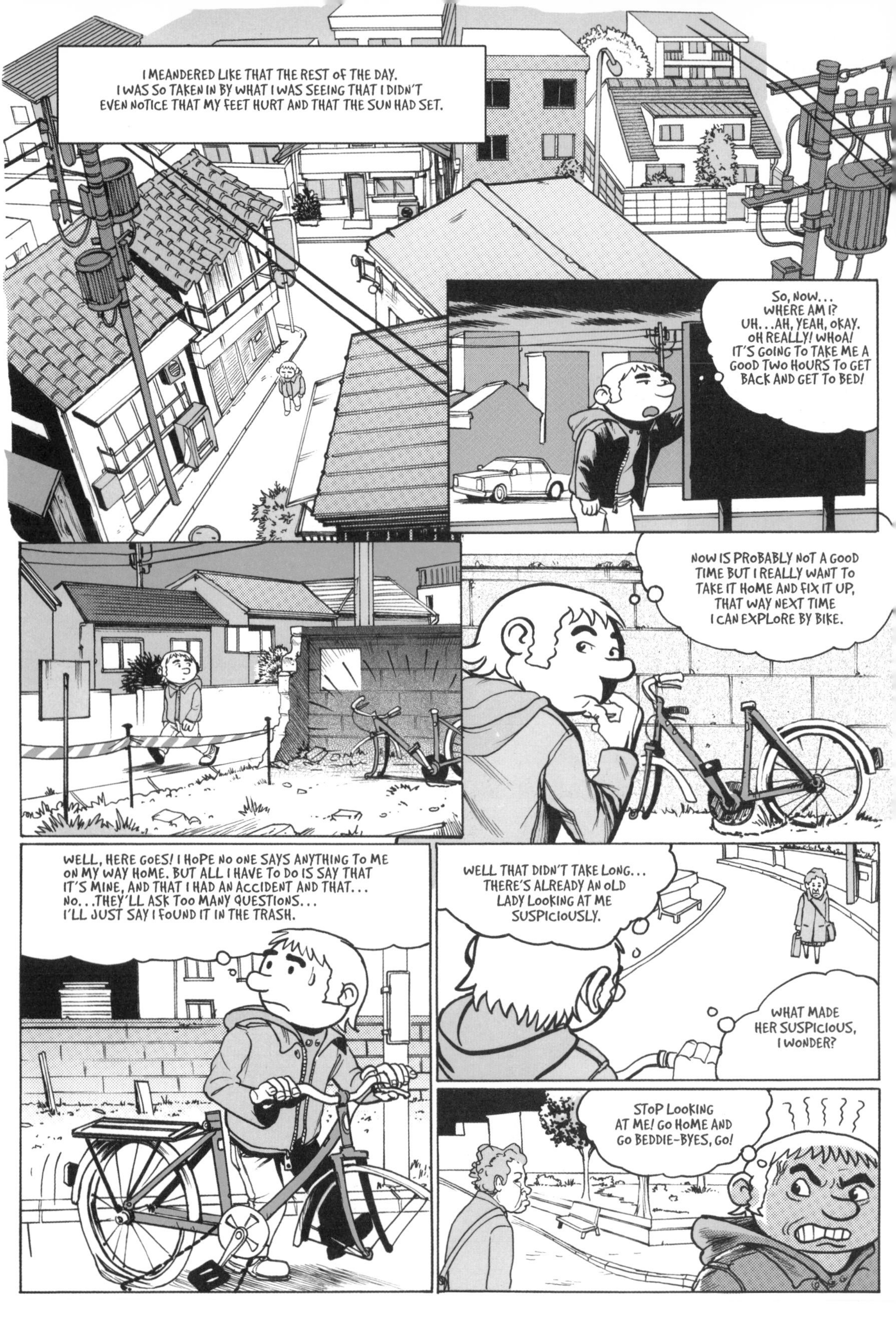

I MEANDERED LIKE THAT THE REST OF THE DAY. I WAS SO TAKEN IN BY WHAT I WAS SEEING THAT I DIDN'T EVEN NOTICE THAT MY FEET HURT AND THAT THE SUN HAD SET.
SO, NOW... WHERE AM I? UH...AH, YEAH, OKAY. OH REALLY! WHOA! IT'S GOING TO TAKE ME A GOOD TWO HOURS TO GET BACK AND GET TO BED!
NOW IS PROBABLY NOT A GOOD TIME BUT I REALLY WANT TO TAKE IT HOME AND FIX IT UP, THAT WAY NEXT TIME I CAN EXPLORE BY BIKE.
WELL, HERE GOES! I HOPE NO ONE SAYS ANYTHING TO ME ON MY WAY HOME. BUT ALL I HAVE TO DO IS SAY THAT IT'S MINE, AND THAT I HAD AN ACCIDENT AND THAT... NO...THEY'LL ASK TOO MANY QUESTIONS... I'LL JUST SAY I FOUND IT IN THE TRASH.
WELL THAT DIDN'T TAKE LONG... THERE'S ALREADY AN OLD LADY LOOKING AT ME SUSPICIOUSLY.
WHAT MADE HER SUSPICIOUS, I WONDER?
STOP LOOKING AT ME! GO HOME AND GO BEDDIE-BYES, GO!

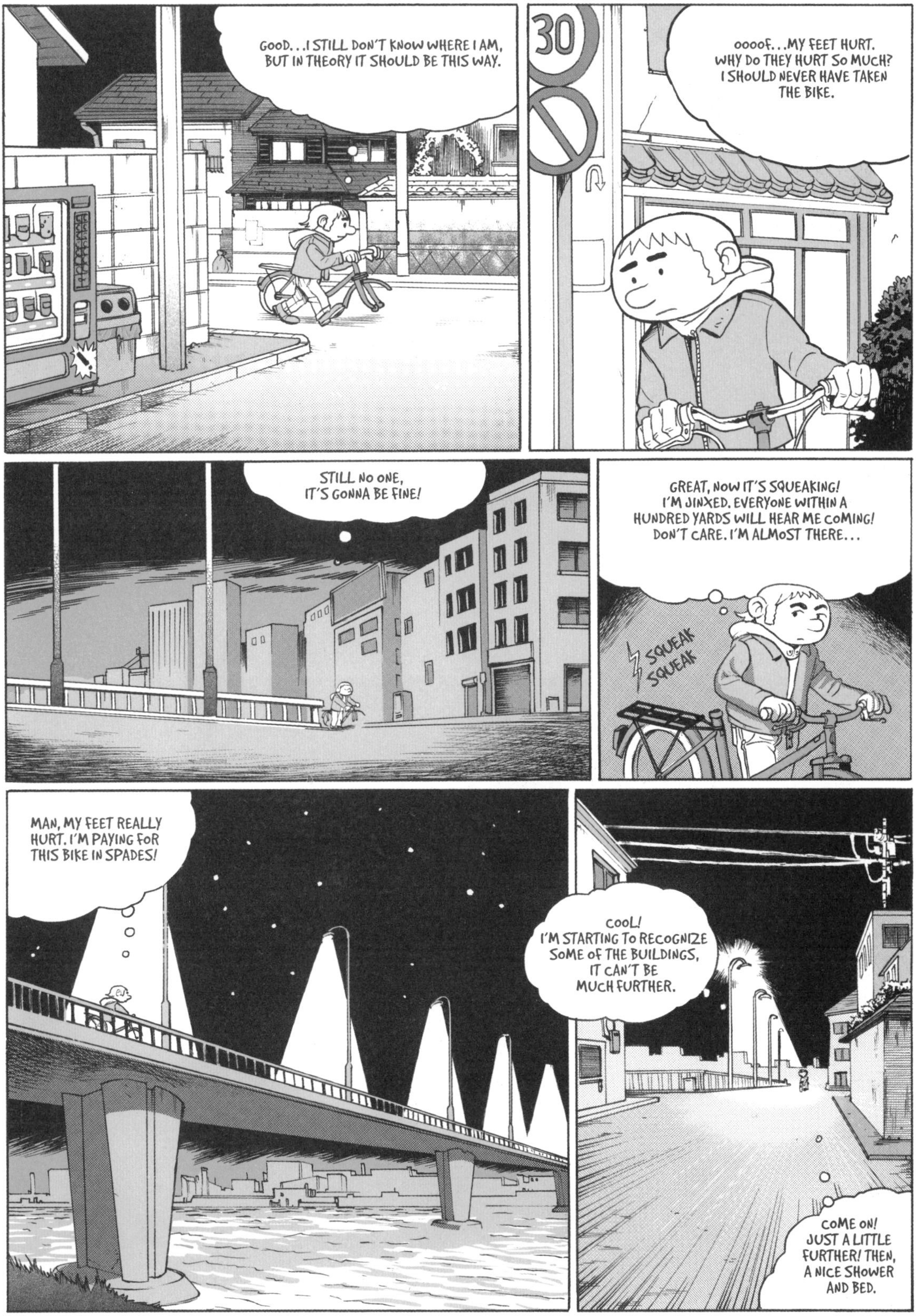
GOOD...I STILL DON'T KNOW WHERE I AM, BUT IN THEORY IT SHOULD BE THIS WAY.
30
OOOOF...MY FEET HURT. WHY DO THEY HURT SO MUCH? I SHOULD NEVER HAVE TAKEN THE BIKE.
STILL NO ONE, IT'S GONNA BE FINE!
GREAT, NOW IT'S SQUEAKING! I'M JINXED. EVERYONE WITHIN A HUNDRED YARDS WILL HEAR ME COMING! DON'T CARE. I'M ALMOST THERE...
SQUEAK SQUEAK
MAN, MY FEET REALLY HURT. I'M PAYING FOR THIS BIKE IN SPADES!
COOL! I'M STARTING TO RECOGNIZE SOME OF THE BUILDINGS, IT CAN'T BE MUCH FURTHER.
COME ON! JUST A LITTLE FURTHER! THEN, A NICE SHOWER AND BED.

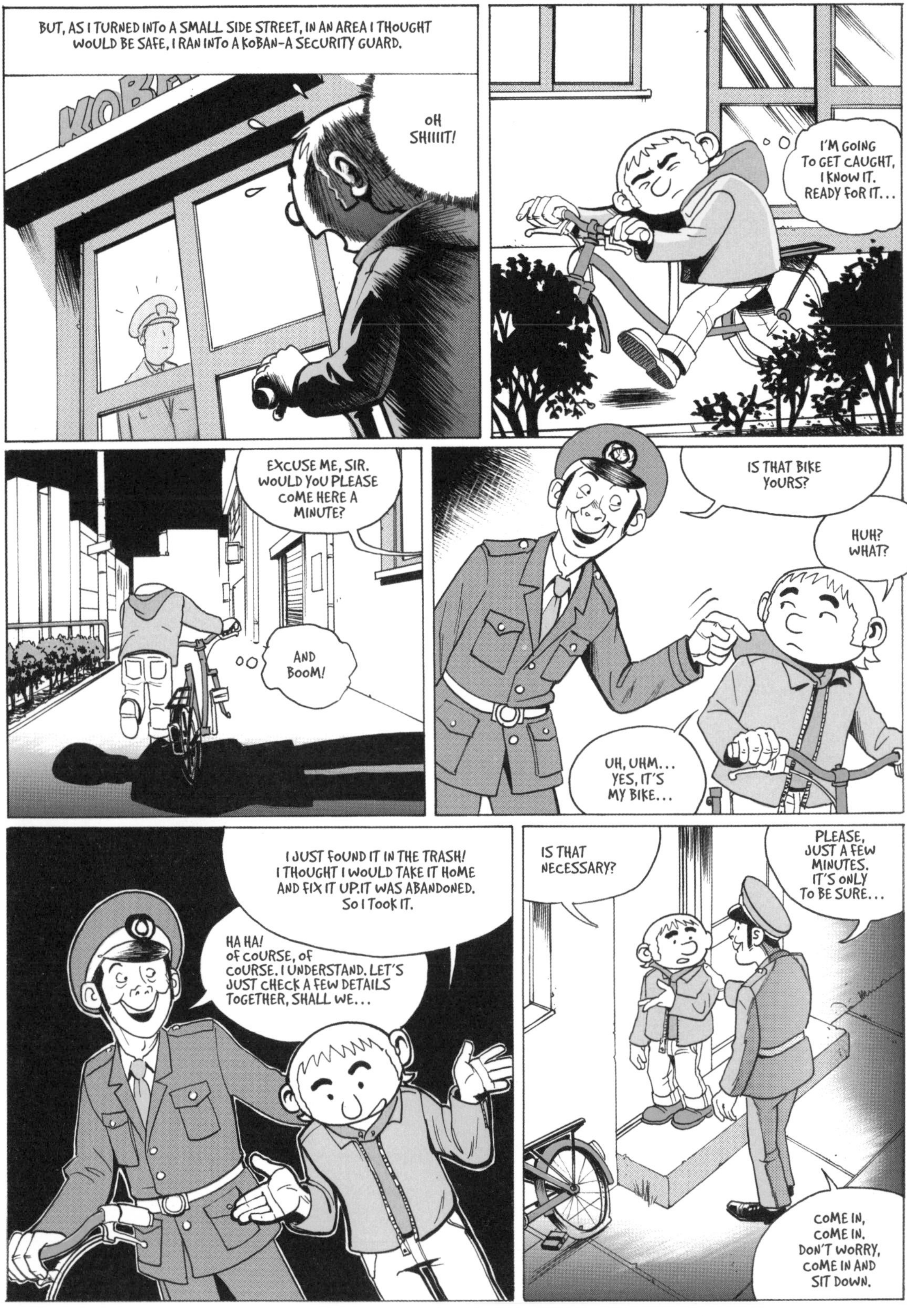
BUT, AS I TURNED INTO A SMALL SIDE STREET, IN AN AREA I THOUGHT WOULD BE SAFE, I RAN INTO A KOBAN–A SECURITY GUARD.
OH SHIIIT!
I'M GOING TO GET CAUGHT, I KNOW IT. READY FOR IT...
EXCUSE ME, SIR. WOULD YOU PLEASE COME HERE A MINUTE?
AND BOOM!
IS THAT BIKE YOURS?
HUH? WHAT?
UH, UHM... YES, IT'S MY BIKE...
I JUST FOUND IT IN THE TRASH! I THOUGHT I WOULD TAKE IT HOME AND FIX IT UP.IT WAS ABANDONED. SO I TOOK IT.
HA HA! OF COURSE, OF COURSE. I UNDERSTAND. LET'S JUST CHECK A FEW DETAILS TOGETHER, SHALL WE...
IS THAT NECESSARY?
PLEASE, JUST A FEW MINUTES. IT'S ONLY TO BE SURE...
COME IN, COME IN. DON'T WORRY, COME IN AND SIT DOWN.

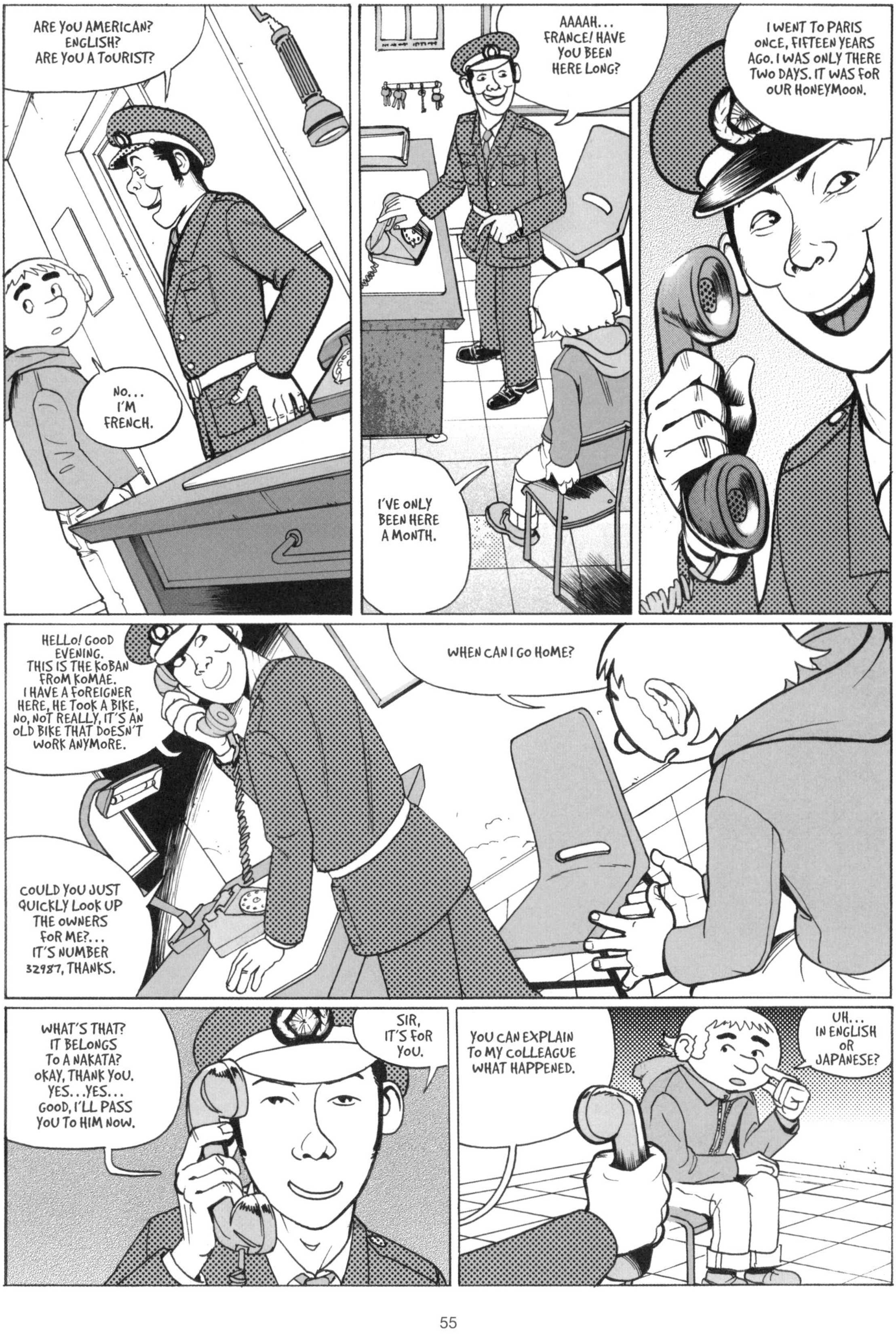
ARE YOU AMERICAN? ENGLISH? ARE YOU A TOURIST?
NO... I'M FRENCH.
AAAAH... FRANCE! HAVE YOU BEEN HERE LONG?
I'VE ONLY BEEN HERE A MONTH.
I WENT TO PARIS ONCE, FIFTEEN YEARS AGO. I WAS ONLY THERE TWO DAYS. IT WAS FOR OUR HONEYMOON.
HELLO! GOOD EVENING. THIS IS THE KOBAN FROM KOMAE. I HAVE A FOREIGNER HERE, HE TOOK A BIKE, NO, NOT REALLY, IT'S AN OLD BIKE THAT DOESN'T WORK ANYMORE.
COULD YOU JUST QUICKLY LOOK UP THE OWNERS FOR ME?... IT'S NUMBER 32987, THANKS.
WHEN CAN I GO HOME?
WHAT'S THAT? IT BELONGS TO A NAKATA? OKAY, THANK YOU. YES... YES... GOOD, I'LL PASS YOU TO HIM NOW.
SIR, IT'S FOR YOU.
YOU CAN EXPLAIN TO MY COLLEAGUE WHAT HAPPENED.
UH... IN ENGLISH OR JAPANESE?

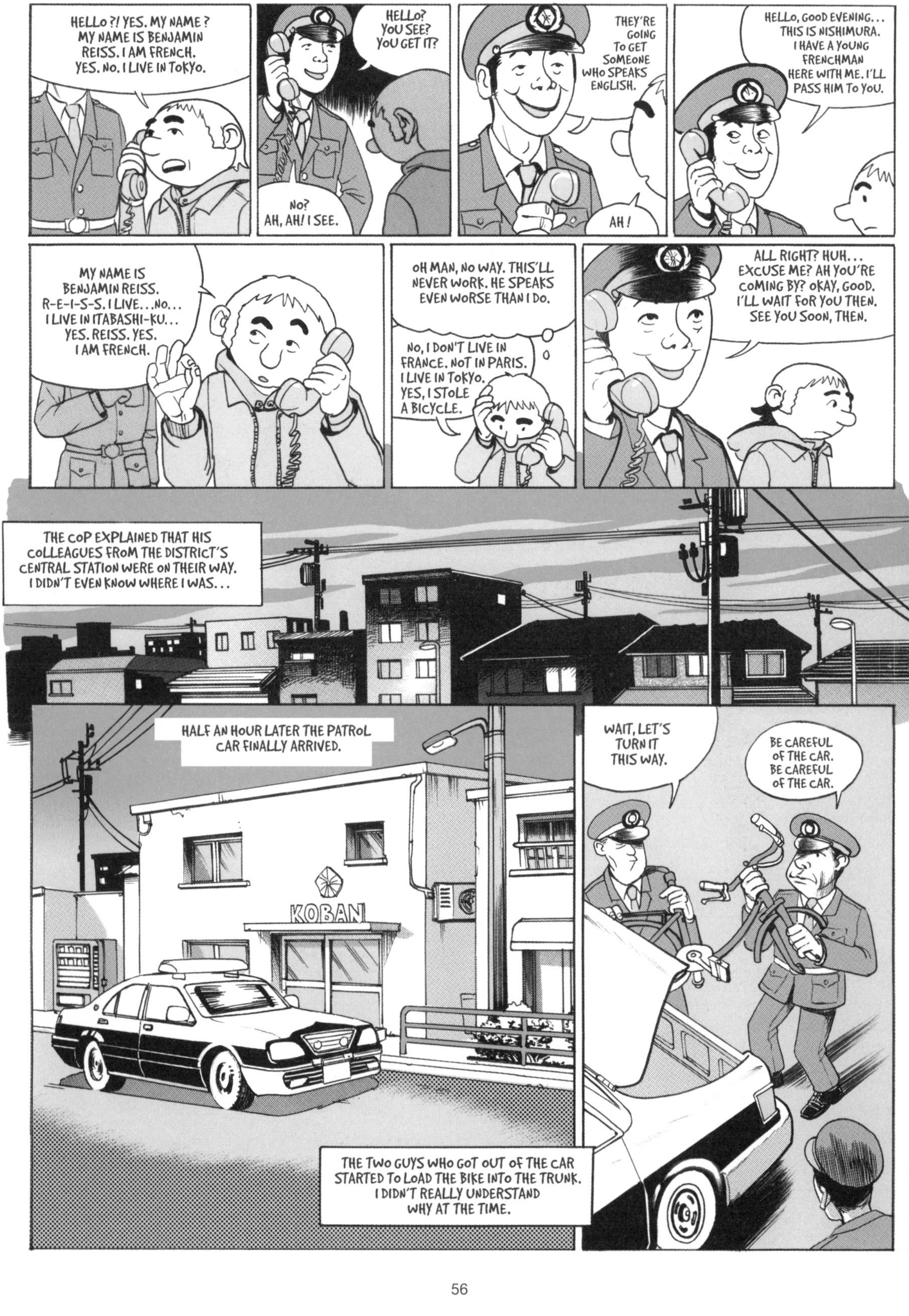
HELLO?! YES. MY NAME? MY NAME IS BENJAMIN REISS. I AM FRENCH. YES. NO. I LIVE IN TOKYO.
HELLO? YOU SEE? YOU GET IT?
NO? AH, AH! I SEE.
THEY'RE GOING TO GET SOMEONE WHO SPEAKS ENGLISH.
AH!
HELLO, GOOD EVENING... THIS IS NISHIMURA. I HAVE A YOUNG FRENCHMAN HERE WITH ME. I'LL PASS HIM TO YOU.
MY NAME IS BENJAMIN REISS. R-E-I-S-S. I LIVE... NO... I LIVE IN ITABASHI-KU... YES. REISS. YES. I AM FRENCH.
OH MAN, NO WAY. THIS'LL NEVER WORK. HE SPEAKS EVEN WORSE THAN I DO.
NO, I DON'T LIVE IN FRANCE. NOT IN PARIS. I LIVE IN TOKYO. YES, I STOLE A BICYCLE.
ALL RIGHT? HUH... EXCUSE ME? AH YOU'RE COMING BY? OKAY, GOOD. I'LL WAIT FOR YOU THEN. SEE YOU SOON, THEN.
THE COP EXPLAINED THAT HIS COLLEAGUES FROM THE DISTRICT'S CENTRAL STATION WERE ON THEIR WAY. I DIDN'T EVEN KNOW WHERE I WAS...
HALF AN HOUR LATER THE PATROL CAR FINALLY ARRIVED.
KOBAN
THE TWO GUYS WHO GOT OUT OF THE CAR STARTED TO LOAD THE BIKE INTO THE TRUNK. I DIDN'T REALLY UNDERSTAND WHY AT THE TIME.
WAIT, LET'S TURN IT THIS WAY.
BE CAREFUL OF THE CAR. BE CAREFUL OF THE CAR.

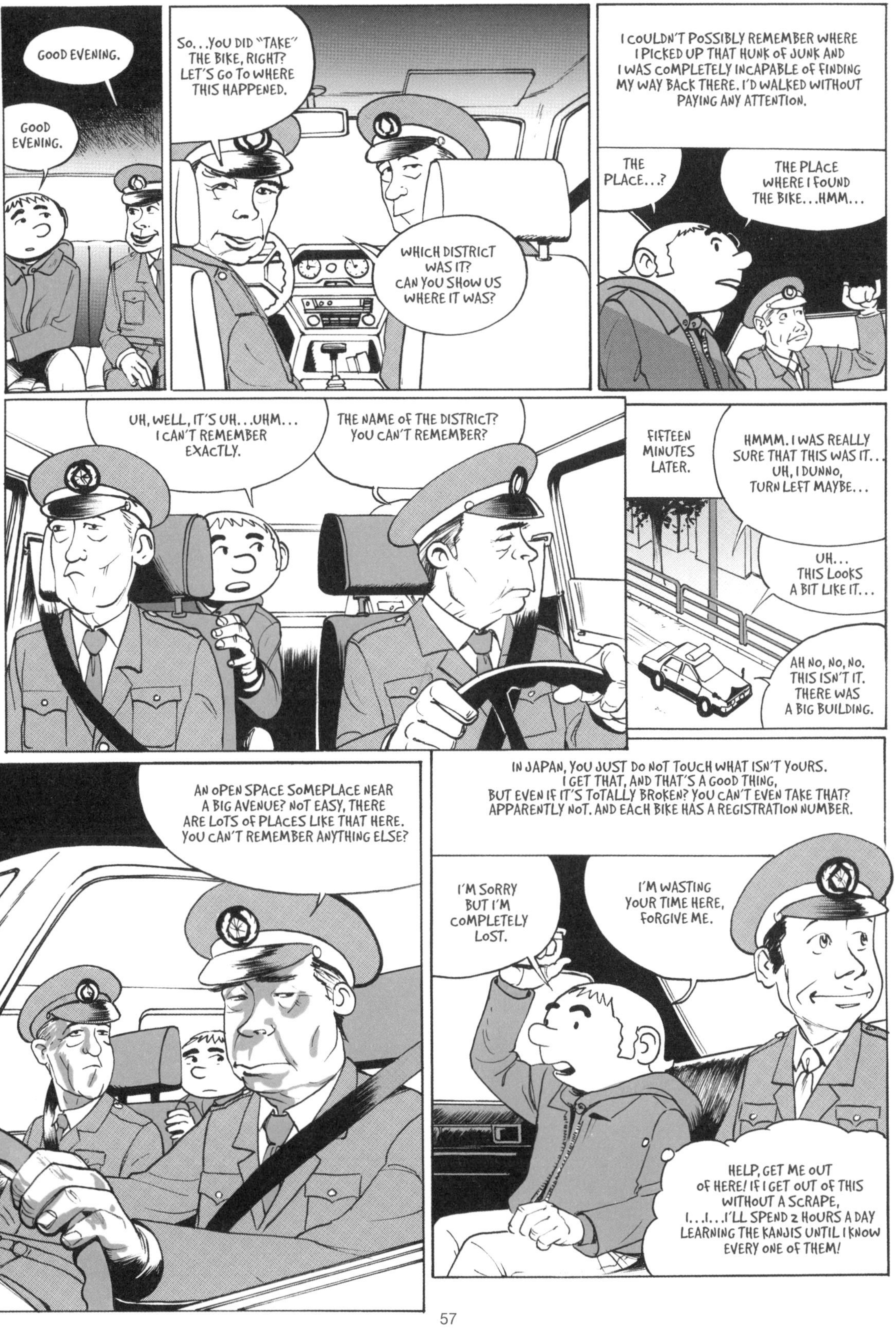

GOOD EVENING.
GOOD EVENING.
SO...YOU DID "TAKE" THE BIKE, RIGHT? LET'S GO TO WHERE THIS HAPPENED.
WHICH DISTRICT WAS IT? CAN YOU SHOW US WHERE IT WAS?
I COULDN'T POSSIBLY REMEMBER WHERE I PICKED UP THAT HUNK OF JUNK AND I WAS COMPLETELY INCAPABLE OF FINDING MY WAY BACK THERE. I'D WALKED WITHOUT PAYING ANY ATTENTION.
THE PLACE...?
THE PLACE WHERE I FOUND THE BIKE...HMM...
UH, WELL, IT'S UH...UHM... I CAN'T REMEMBER EXACTLY.
THE NAME OF THE DISTRICT? YOU CAN'T REMEMBER?
FIFTEEN MINUTES LATER.
HMMM. I WAS REALLY SURE THAT THIS WAS IT... UH, I DUNNO, TURN LEFT MAYBE...
UH... THIS LOOKS A BIT LIKE IT...
AH NO, NO, NO. THIS ISN'T IT. THERE WAS A BIG BUILDING.
AN OPEN SPACE SOMEPLACE NEAR A BIG AVENUE? NOT EASY, THERE ARE LOTS OF PLACES LIKE THAT HERE. YOU CAN'T REMEMBER ANYTHING ELSE?
IN JAPAN, YOU JUST DO NOT TOUCH WHAT ISN'T YOURS. I GET THAT, AND THAT'S A GOOD THING, BUT EVEN IF IT'S TOTALLY BROKEN? YOU CAN'T EVEN TAKE THAT? APPARENTLY NOT. AND EACH BIKE HAS A REGISTRATION NUMBER.
I'M SORRY BUT I'M COMPLETELY LOST.
I'M WASTING YOUR TIME HERE, FORGIVE ME.
HELP, GET ME OUT OF HERE! IF I GET OUT OF THIS WITHOUT A SCRAPE, I...I...I'LL SPEND 2 HOURS A DAY LEARNING THE KANJIS UNTIL I KNOW EVERY ONE OF THEM!

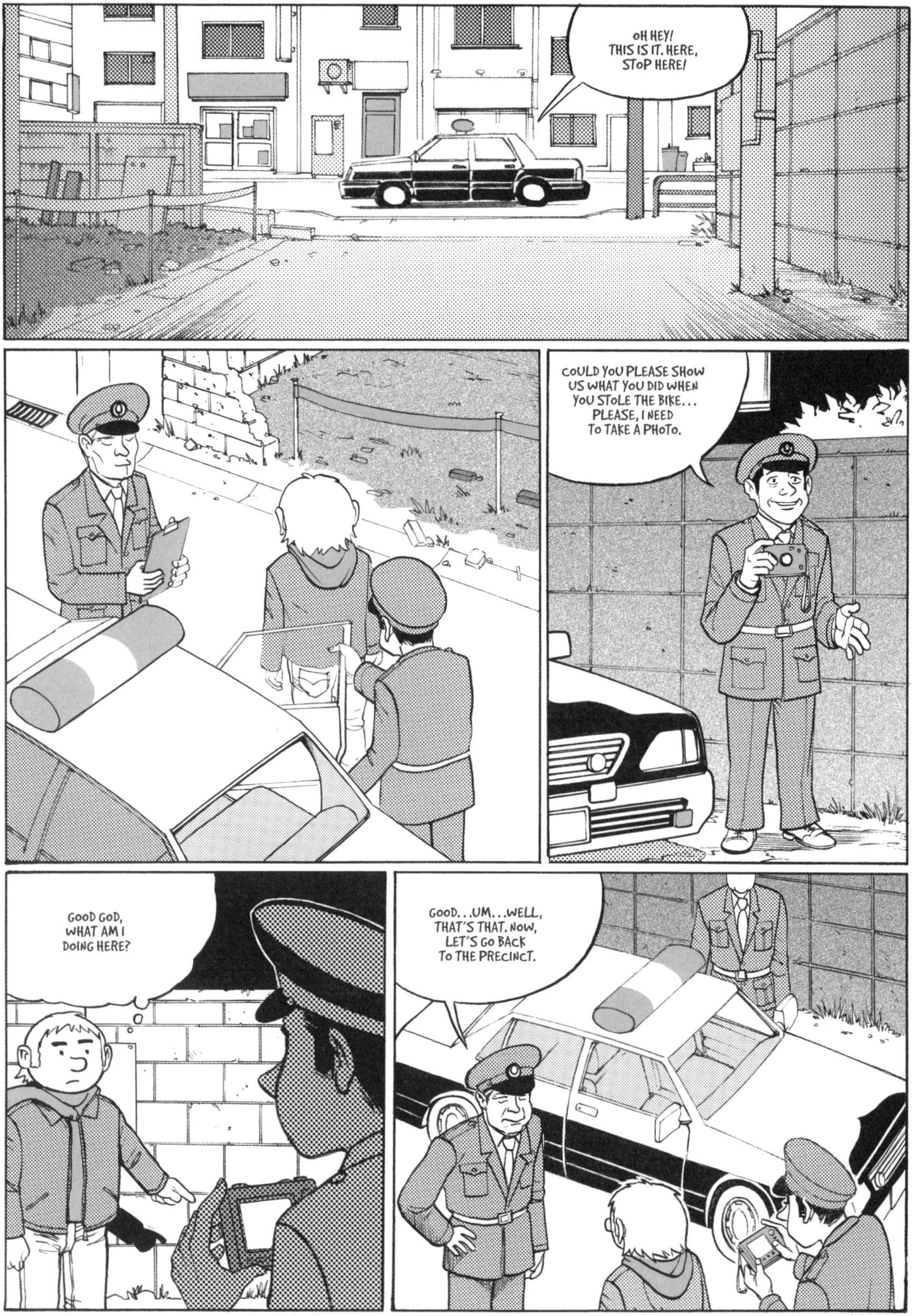
OH HEY! THIS IS IT. HERE, STOP HERE!
COULD YOU PLEASE SHOW US WHAT YOU DID WHEN YOU STOLE THE BIKE... PLEASE, I NEED TO TAKE A PHOTO.
GOOD GOD, WHAT AM I DOING HERE?
GOOD...UM...WELL, THAT'S THAT. NOW, LET'S GO BACK TO THE PRECINCT.

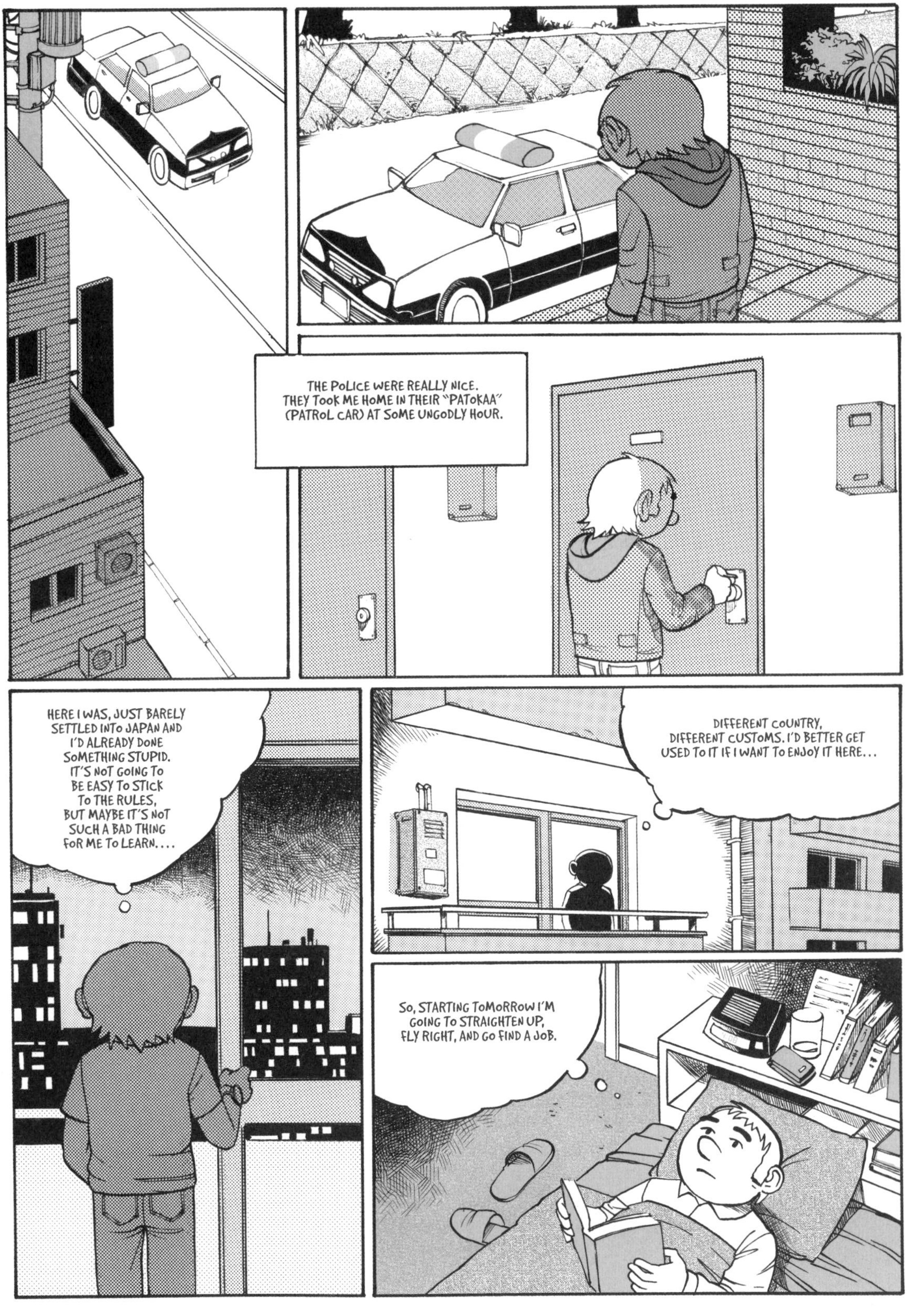
THE POLICE WERE REALLY NICE. THEY TOOK ME HOME IN THEIR "PATOKAA" (PATROL CAR) AT SOME UNGODLY HOUR.
HERE I WAS, JUST BARELY SETTLED INTO JAPAN AND I'D ALREADY DONE SOMETHING STUPID. IT'S NOT GOING TO BE EASY TO STICK TO THE RULES, BUT MAYBE IT'S NOT SUCH A BAD THING FOR ME TO LEARN....
DIFFERENT COUNTRY, DIFFERENT CUSTOMS. I'D BETTER GET USED TO IT IF I WANT TO ENJOY IT HERE...
SO, STARTING TOMORROW I'M GOING TO STRAIGHTEN UP, FLY RIGHT, AND GO FIND A JOB.

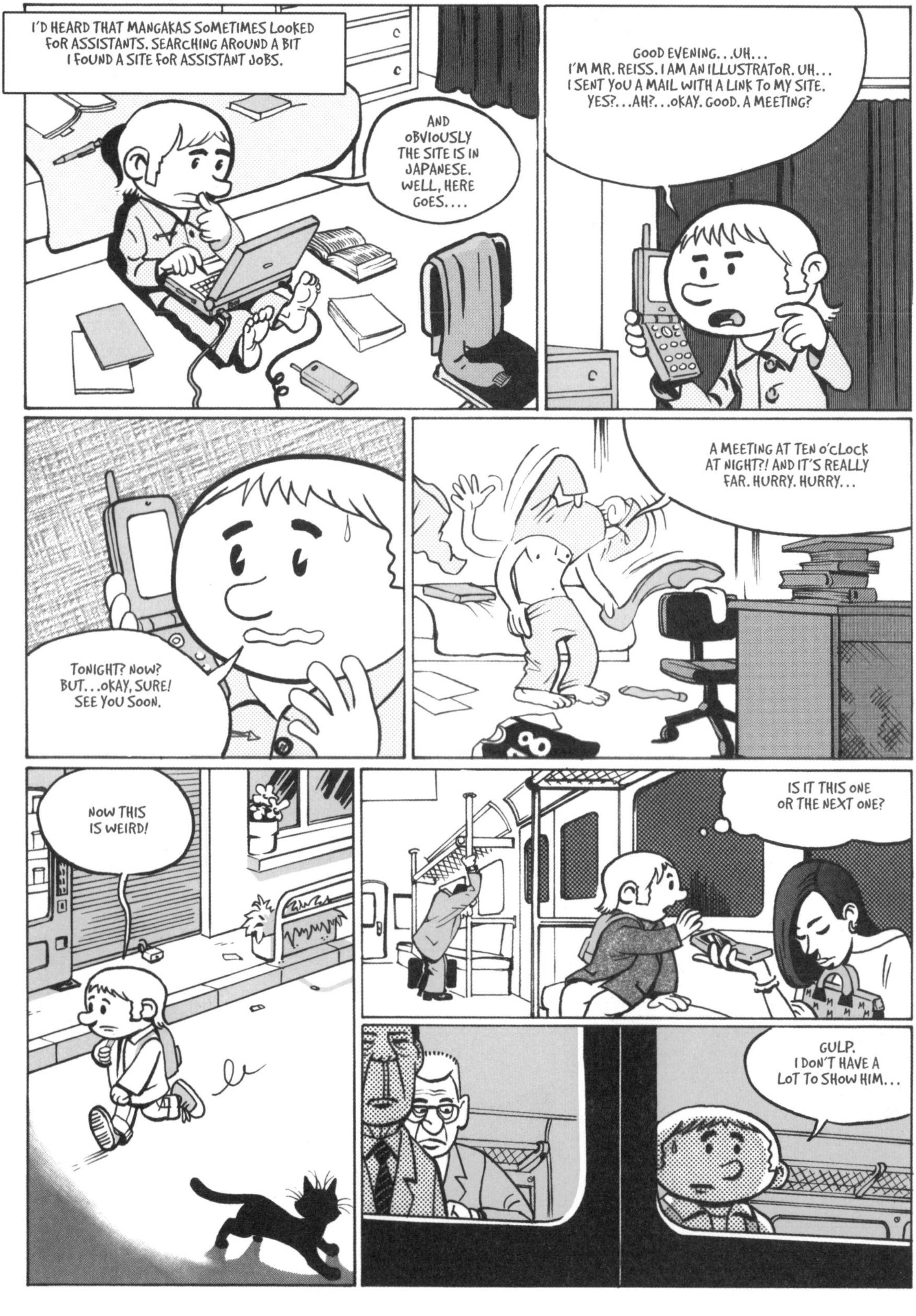
I'D HEARD THAT MANGAKAS SOMETIMES LOOKED FOR ASSISTANTS. SEARCHING AROUND A BIT I FOUND A SITE FOR ASSISTANT JOBS.
AND OBVIOUSLY THE SITE IS IN JAPANESE. WELL, HERE GOES....
GOOD EVENING...UH... I'M MR. REISS. I AM AN ILLUSTRATOR. UH... I SENT YOU A MAIL WITH A LINK TO MY SITE. YES?...AH?...OKAY. GOOD. A MEETING?
TONIGHT? NOW? BUT...OKAY, SURE! SEE YOU SOON.
A MEETING AT TEN O'CLOCK AT NIGHT?! AND IT'S REALLY FAR. HURRY. HURRY...
NOW THIS IS WEIRD!
IS IT THIS ONE OR THE NEXT ONE?
GULP. I DON'T HAVE A LOT TO SHOW HIM...

I ARRIVED A LITTLE EARLY AT THE MEETING POINT AND IT WAS POURING. I WAS WONDERING IF I WOULD BE ABLE TO CATCH THE LAST SUBWAY BACK.

YOU'RE MISTER REISS, RIGHT? HERE'S AN UMBRELLA...

I THOUGHT HE WAS THE SERIES CREATOR, BUT HE WAS THE HEAD ASSISTANT.

UH... I SAW YOUR WEB SITE. I LOVE YOUR WORK!

WHAT WAS A BIT STRANGE WAS THAT HE DIDN'T CORRECT ME.

MMM... NO, NOT REALLY.

YOU DRAW REALLY FAST, DON'T YOU?

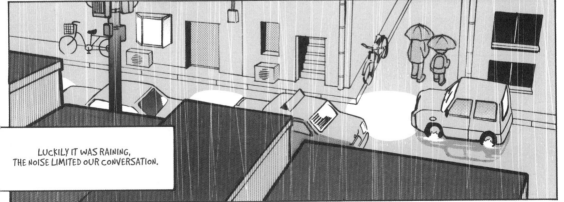

LUCKILY IT WAS RAINING, THE NOISE LIMITED OUR CONVERSATION.

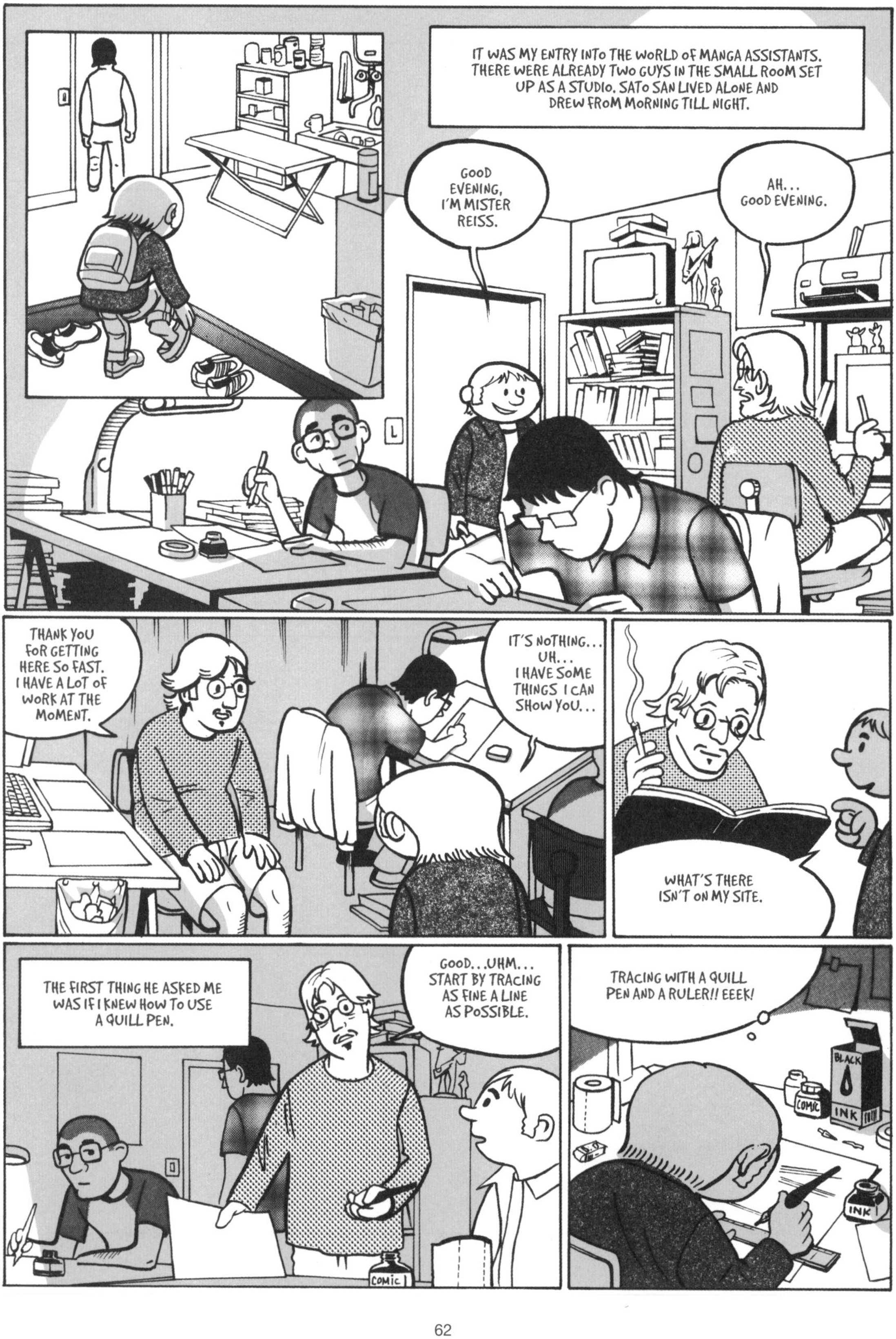
IT WAS MY ENTRY INTO THE WORLD OF MANGA ASSISTANTS. THERE WERE ALREADY TWO GUYS IN THE SMALL ROOM SET UP AS A STUDIO. SATO SAN LIVED ALONE AND DREW FROM MORNING TILL NIGHT.
GOOD EVENING, I'M MISTER REISS.
AH... GOOD EVENING.
THANK YOU FOR GETTING HERE SO FAST. I HAVE A LOT OF WORK AT THE MOMENT.
IT'S NOTHING... UH... I HAVE SOME THINGS I CAN SHOW YOU...
WHAT'S THERE ISN'T ON MY SITE.
THE FIRST THING HE ASKED ME WAS IF I KNEW HOW TO USE A QUILL PEN.
GOOD...UHM... START BY TRACING AS FINE A LINE AS POSSIBLE.
COMIC
TRACING WITH A QUILL PEN AND A RULER!! EEEK!
BLACK
INK
COMIC
INK

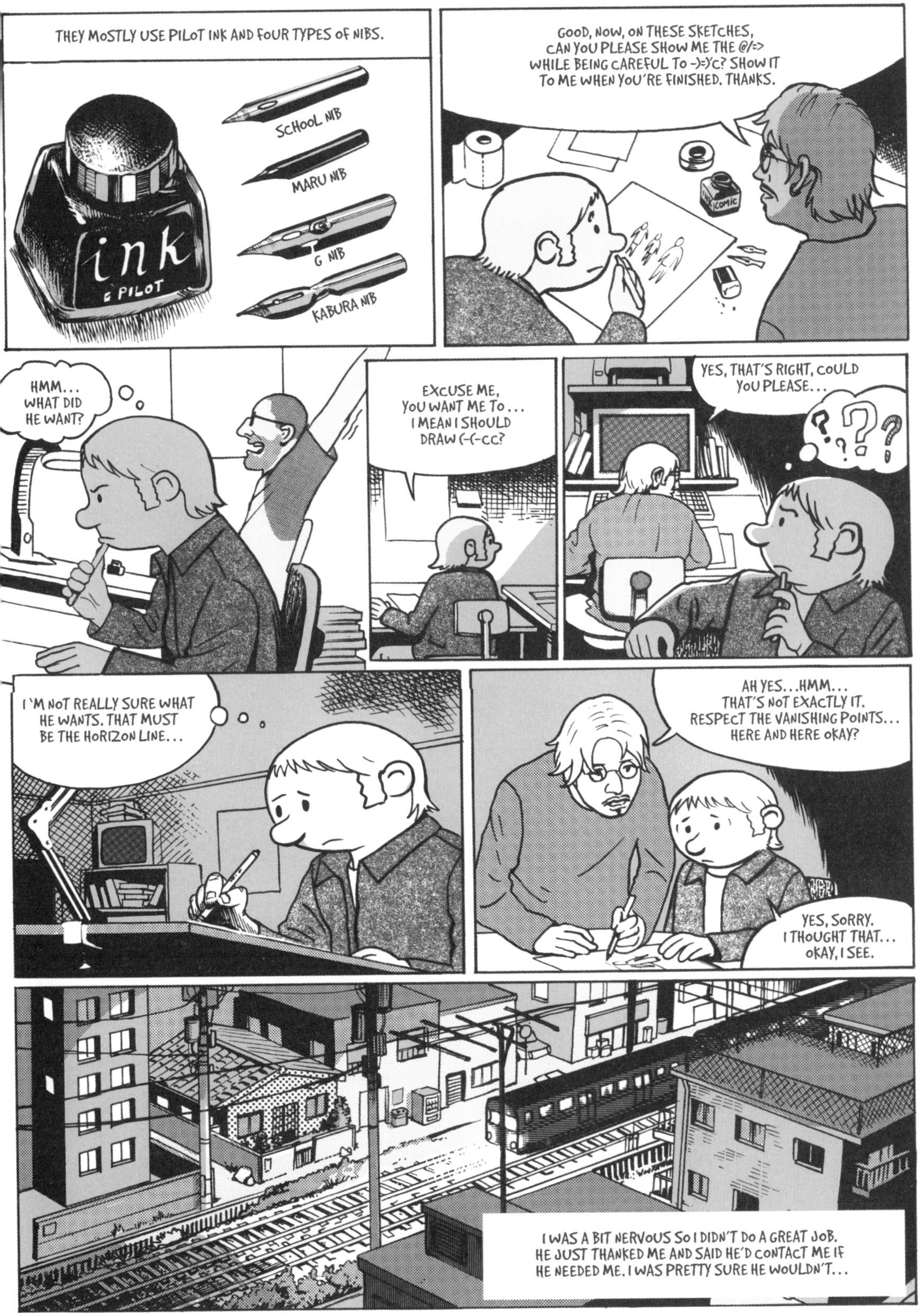
THEY MOSTLY USE PILOT INK AND FOUR TYPES OF NIBS.
ink
PILOT
SCHOOL NIB
MARU NIB
G NIB
KABURA NIB
GOOD, NOW, ON THESE SKETCHES, CAN YOU PLEASE SHOW ME THE @/=> WHILE BEING CAREFUL TO -)=)'c? SHOW IT TO ME WHEN YOU'RE FINISHED. THANKS.
INK COMIC
HMM... WHAT DID HE WANT?
EXCUSE ME, YOU WANT ME TO... I MEAN I SHOULD DRAW (-(-cc?
YES, THAT'S RIGHT, COULD YOU PLEASE...
? ? ? ?
I'M NOT REALLY SURE WHAT HE WANTS. THAT MUST BE THE HORIZON LINE...
AH YES... HMM... THAT'S NOT EXACTLY IT. RESPECT THE VANISHING POINTS... HERE AND HERE OKAY?
YES, SORRY. I THOUGHT THAT... OKAY, I SEE.
I WAS A BIT NERVOUS SO I DIDN'T DO A GREAT JOB. HE JUST THANKED ME AND SAID HE'D CONTACT ME IF HE NEEDED ME. I WAS PRETTY SURE HE WOULDN'T...

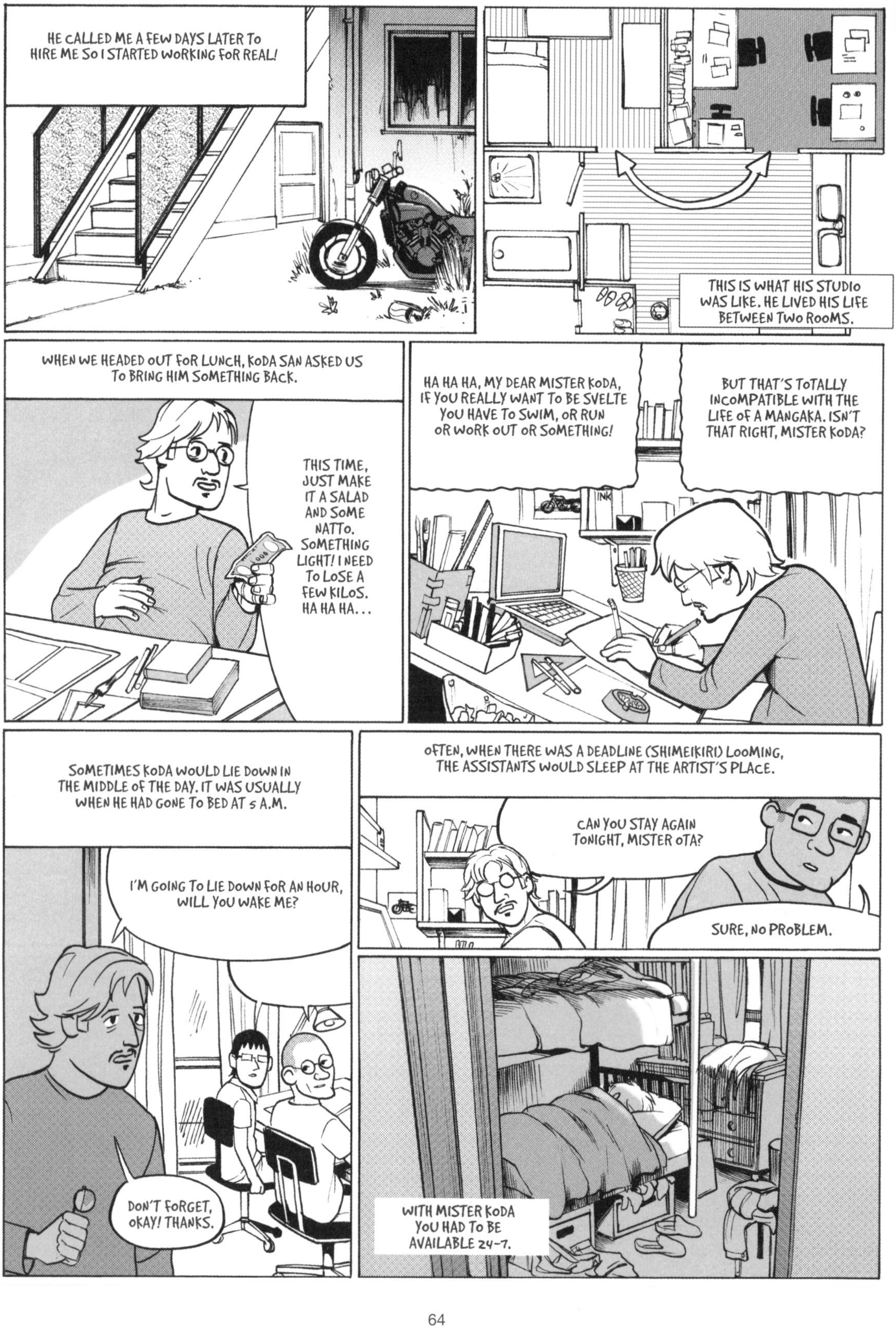

HE CALLED ME A FEW DAYS LATER TO HIRE ME SO I STARTED WORKING FOR REAL!
THIS IS WHAT HIS STUDIO WAS LIKE. HE LIVED HIS LIFE BETWEEN TWO ROOMS.
WHEN WE HEADED OUT FOR LUNCH, KODA SAN ASKED US TO BRING HIM SOMETHING BACK.
THIS TIME, JUST MAKE IT A SALAD AND SOME NATTO. SOMETHING LIGHT! I NEED TO LOSE A FEW KILOS. HA HA HA...
HA HA HA, MY DEAR MISTER KODA, IF YOU REALLY WANT TO BE SVELTE YOU HAVE TO SWIM, OR RUN OR WORK OUT OR SOMETHING!
BUT THAT'S TOTALLY INCOMPATIBLE WITH THE LIFE OF A MANGAKA. ISN'T THAT RIGHT, MISTER KODA?
INK
SOMETIMES KODA WOULD LIE DOWN IN THE MIDDLE OF THE DAY. IT WAS USUALLY WHEN HE HAD GONE TO BED AT 5 A.M.
I'M GOING TO LIE DOWN FOR AN HOUR, WILL YOU WAKE ME?
DON'T FORGET, OKAY! THANKS.
OFTEN, WHEN THERE WAS A DEADLINE (SHIMEIKIRI) LOOMING, THE ASSISTANTS WOULD SLEEP AT THE ARTIST'S PLACE.
CAN YOU STAY AGAIN TONIGHT, MISTER OTA?
SURE, NO PROBLEM.
WITH MISTER KODA YOU HAD TO BE AVAILABLE 24-7.

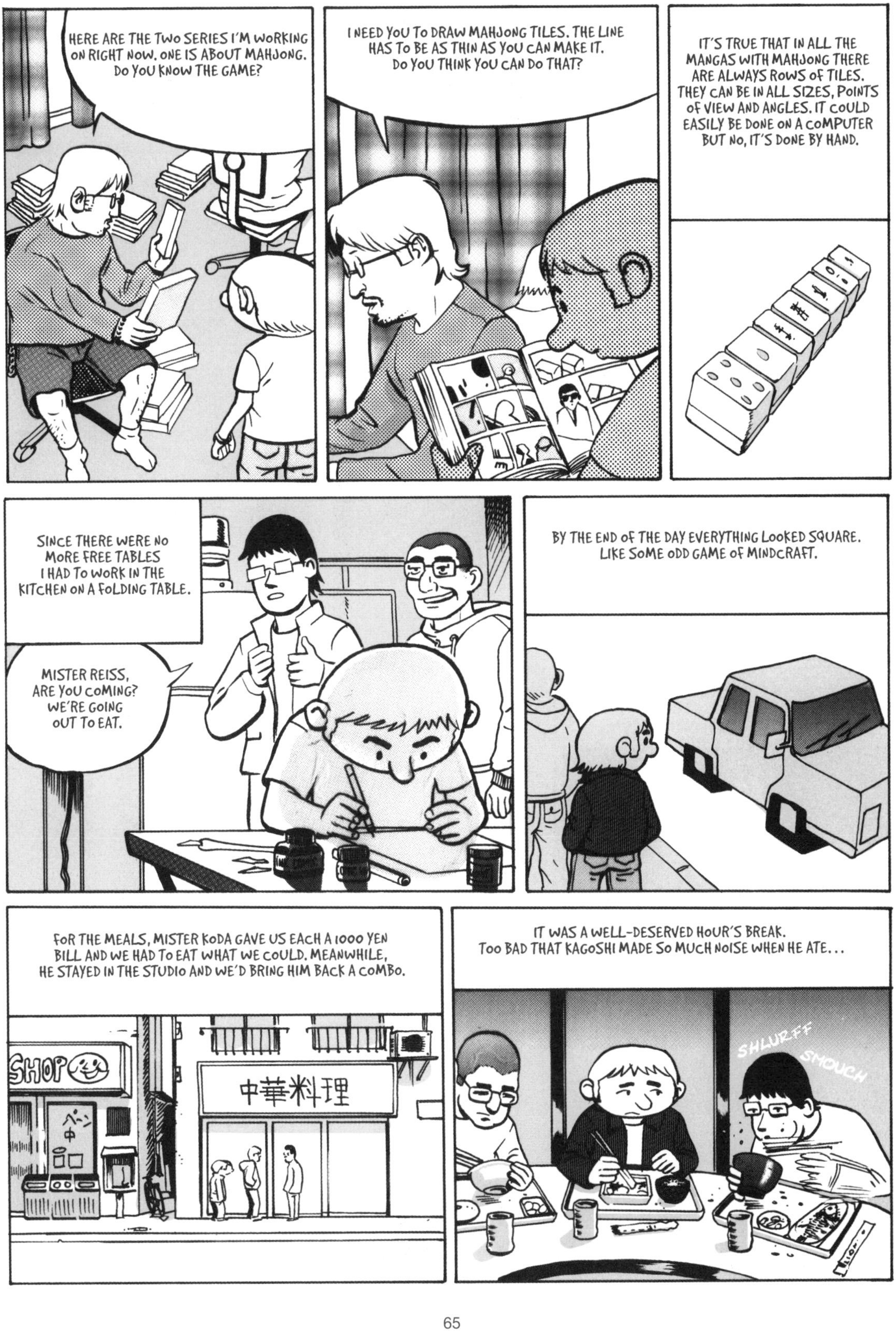
HERE ARE THE TWO SERIES I'M WORKING ON RIGHT NOW. ONE IS ABOUT MAHJONG. DO YOU KNOW THE GAME?
I NEED YOU TO DRAW MAHJONG TILES. THE LINE HAS TO BE AS THIN AS YOU CAN MAKE IT. DO YOU THINK YOU CAN DO THAT?
IT'S TRUE THAT IN ALL THE MANGAS WITH MAHJONG THERE ARE ALWAYS ROWS OF TILES. THEY CAN BE IN ALL SIZES, POINTS OF VIEW AND ANGLES. IT COULD EASILY BE DONE ON A COMPUTER BUT NO, IT'S DONE BY HAND.
SINCE THERE WERE NO MORE FREE TABLES I HAD TO WORK IN THE KITCHEN ON A FOLDING TABLE.
MISTER REISS, ARE YOU COMING? WE'RE GOING OUT TO EAT.
BY THE END OF THE DAY EVERYTHING LOOKED SQUARE. LIKE SOME ODD GAME OF MINDCRAFT.
FOR THE MEALS, MISTER KODA GAVE US EACH A 1000 YEN BILL AND WE HAD TO EAT WHAT WE COULD. MEANWHILE, HE STAYED IN THE STUDIO AND WE'D BRING HIM BACK A COMBO.
SHOP
中華料理
IT WAS A WELL-DESERVED HOUR'S BREAK. TOO BAD THAT KAGOSHI MADE SO MUCH NOISE WHEN HE ATE...
SHLURFF
SMOUCH

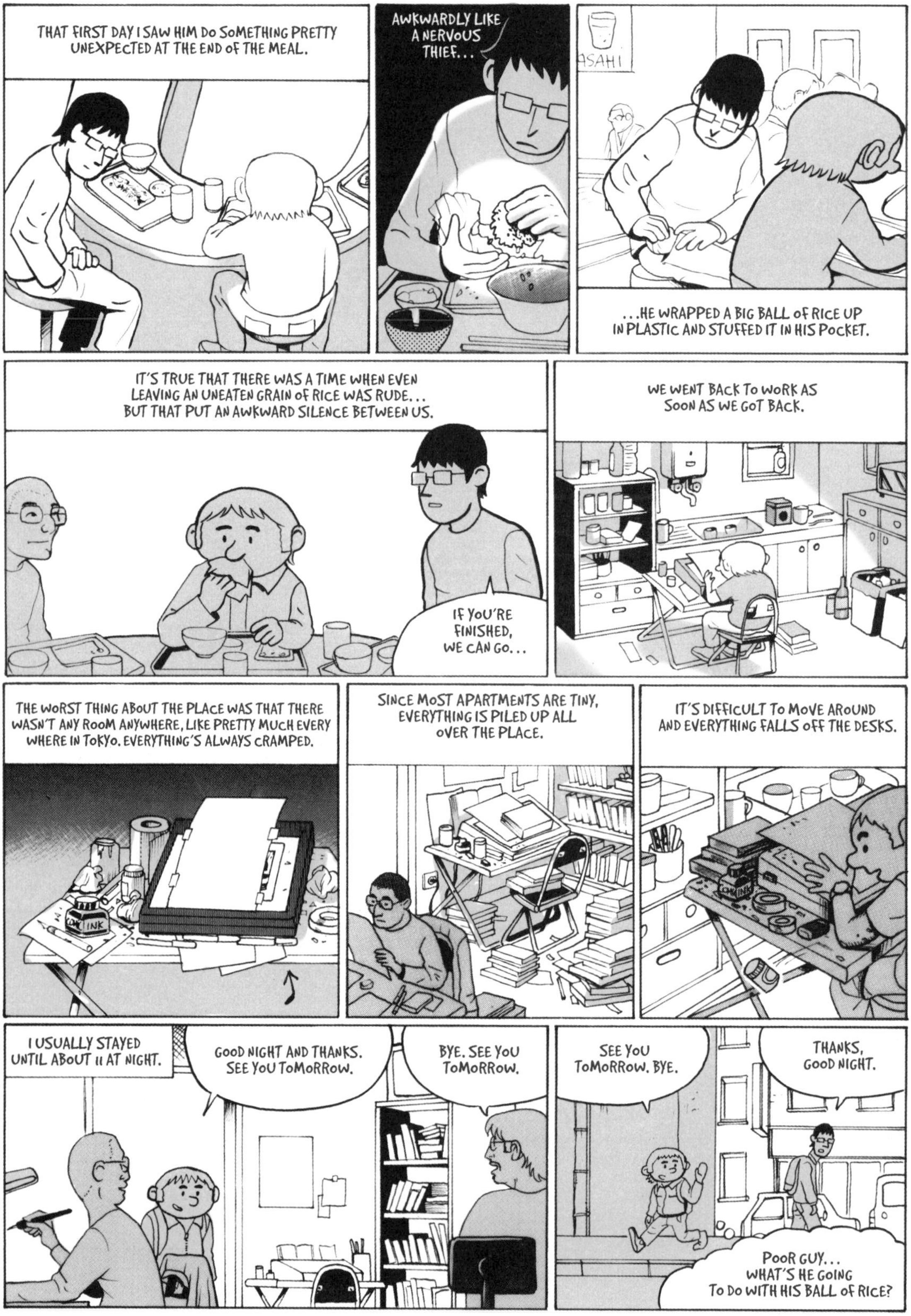
THAT FIRST DAY I SAW HIM DO SOMETHING PRETTY UNEXPECTED AT THE END OF THE MEAL.
AWKWARDLY LIKE A NERVOUS THIEF...
ASAHI
...HE WRAPPED A BIG BALL OF RICE UP IN PLASTIC AND STUFFED IT IN HIS POCKET.
IT'S TRUE THAT THERE WAS A TIME WHEN EVEN LEAVING AN UNEATEN GRAIN OF RICE WAS RUDE... BUT THAT PUT AN AWKWARD SILENCE BETWEEN US.
IF YOU'RE FINISHED, WE CAN GO...
WE WENT BACK TO WORK AS SOON AS WE GOT BACK.
THE WORST THING ABOUT THE PLACE WAS THAT THERE WASN'T ANY ROOM ANYWHERE, LIKE PRETTY MUCH EVERY WHERE IN TOKYO. EVERYTHING'S ALWAYS CRAMPED.
INK
SINCE MOST APARTMENTS ARE TINY, EVERYTHING IS PILED UP ALL OVER THE PLACE.
IT'S DIFFICULT TO MOVE AROUND AND EVERYTHING FALLS OFF THE DESKS.
INK
I USUALLY STAYED UNTIL ABOUT 11 AT NIGHT.
GOOD NIGHT AND THANKS. SEE YOU TOMORROW.
BYE. SEE YOU TOMORROW.
SEE YOU TOMORROW. BYE.
THANKS, GOOD NIGHT.
POOR GUY... WHAT'S HE GOING TO DO WITH HIS BALL OF RICE?

ALL FOR A HANDFUL OF RICE

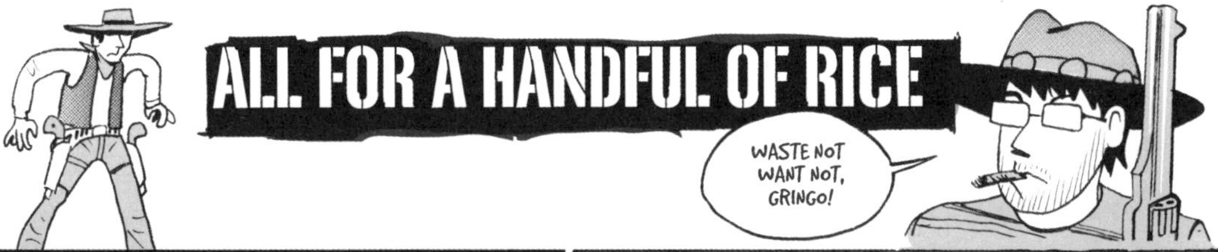
WASTE NOT WANT NOT, GRINGO!

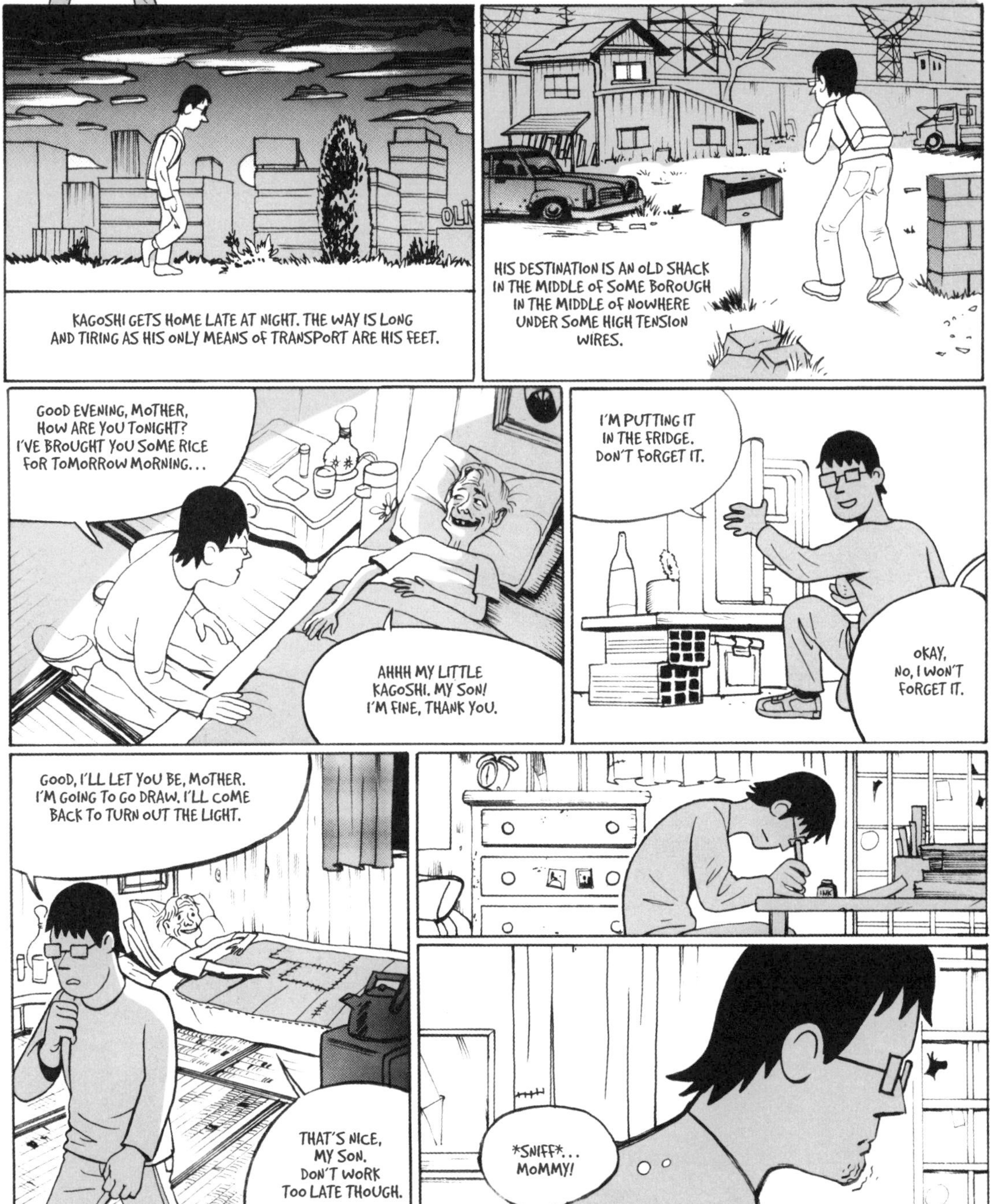
KAGOSHI GETS HOME LATE AT NIGHT. THE WAY IS LONG AND TIRING AS HIS ONLY MEANS OF TRANSPORT ARE HIS FEET.
HIS DESTINATION IS AN OLD SHACK IN THE MIDDLE OF SOME BOROUGH IN THE MIDDLE OF NOWHERE UNDER SOME HIGH TENSION WIRES.
GOOD EVENING, MOTHER, HOW ARE YOU TONIGHT? I'VE BROUGHT YOU SOME RICE FOR TOMORROW MORNING...
AHHH MY LITTLE KAGOSHI. MY SON! I'M FINE, THANK YOU.
I'M PUTTING IT IN THE FRIDGE. DON'T FORGET IT.
OKAY, NO, I WON'T FORGET IT.
GOOD, I'LL LET YOU BE, MOTHER. I'M GOING TO GO DRAW. I'LL COME BACK TO TURN OUT THE LIGHT.
THAT'S NICE, MY SON. DON'T WORK TOO LATE THOUGH.
SNIFF... MOMMY!

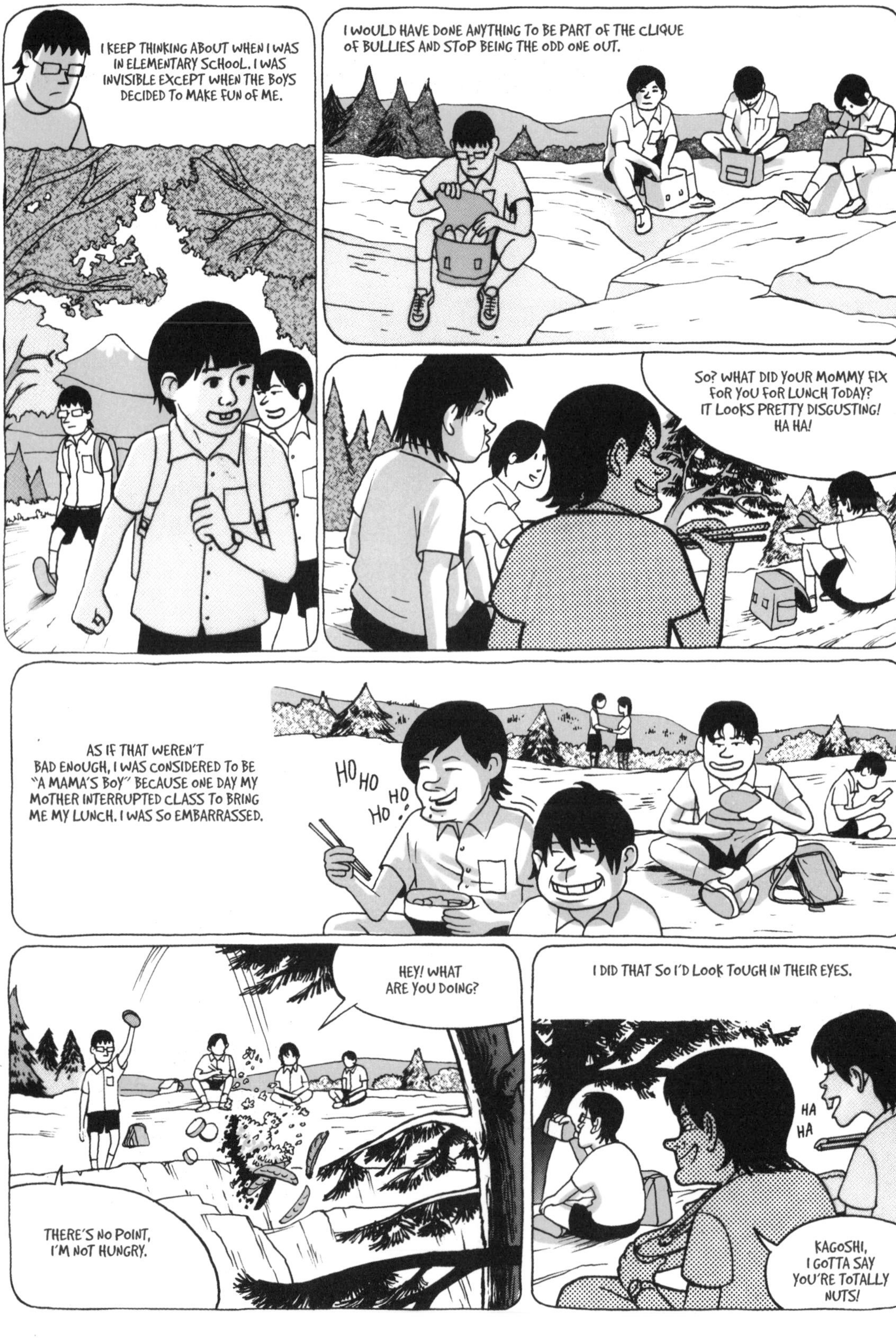

I KEEP THINKING ABOUT WHEN I WAS IN ELEMENTARY SCHOOL. I WAS INVISIBLE EXCEPT WHEN THE BOYS DECIDED TO MAKE FUN OF ME.
I WOULD HAVE DONE ANYTHING TO BE PART OF THE CLIQUE OF BULLIES AND STOP BEING THE ODD ONE OUT.
SO? WHAT DID YOUR MOMMY FIX FOR YOU FOR LUNCH TODAY? IT LOOKS PRETTY DISGUSTING! HA HA!
AS IF THAT WEREN'T BAD ENOUGH, I WAS CONSIDERED TO BE "A MAMA'S BOY" BECAUSE ONE DAY MY MOTHER INTERRUPTED CLASS TO BRING ME MY LUNCH. I WAS SO EMBARRASSED.
HO HO HO HO
HEY! WHAT ARE YOU DOING?
THERE'S NO POINT, I'M NOT HUNGRY.
I DID THAT SO I'D LOOK TOUGH IN THEIR EYES.
HA HA
KAGOSHI, I GOTTA SAY YOU'RE TOTALLY NUTS!

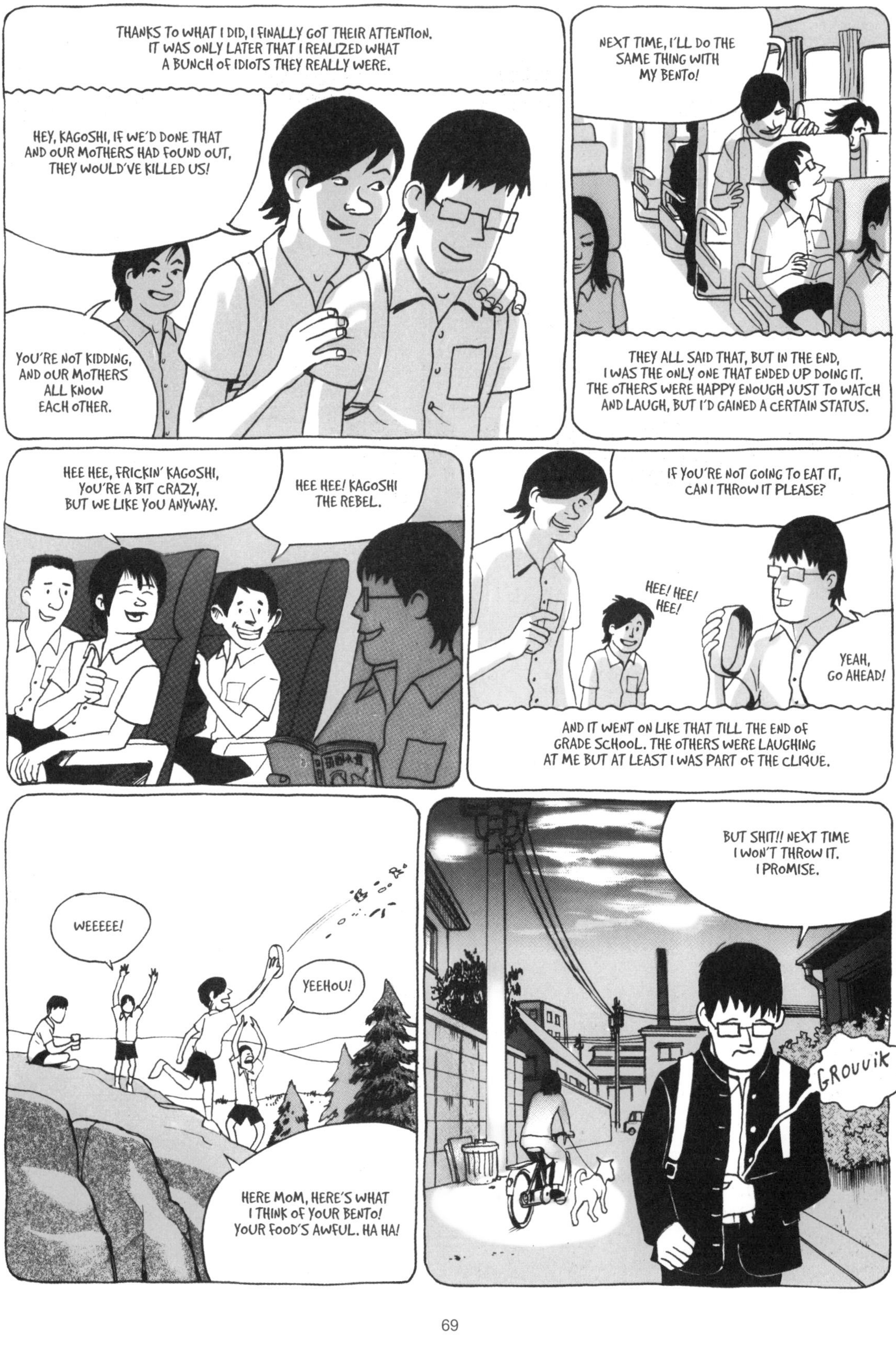
THANKS TO WHAT I DID, I FINALLY GOT THEIR ATTENTION. IT WAS ONLY LATER THAT I REALIZED WHAT A BUNCH OF IDIOTS THEY REALLY WERE.
HEY, KAGOSHI, IF WE'D DONE THAT AND OUR MOTHERS HAD FOUND OUT, THEY WOULD'VE KILLED US!
YOU'RE NOT KIDDING, AND OUR MOTHERS ALL KNOW EACH OTHER.
NEXT TIME, I'LL DO THE SAME THING WITH MY BENTO!
THEY ALL SAID THAT, BUT IN THE END, I WAS THE ONLY ONE THAT ENDED UP DOING IT. THE OTHERS WERE HAPPY ENOUGH JUST TO WATCH AND LAUGH, BUT I'D GAINED A CERTAIN STATUS.
HEE HEE, FRICKIN' KAGOSHI, YOU'RE A BIT CRAZY, BUT WE LIKE YOU ANYWAY.
HEE HEE! KAGOSHI THE REBEL.
IF YOU'RE NOT GOING TO EAT IT, CAN I THROW IT PLEASE?
HEE! HEE! HEE!
YEAH, GO AHEAD!
AND IT WENT ON LIKE THAT TILL THE END OF GRADE SCHOOL. THE OTHERS WERE LAUGHING AT ME BUT AT LEAST I WAS PART OF THE CLIQUE.
WEEEEE!
YEEHOU!
HERE MOM, HERE'S WHAT I THINK OF YOUR BENTO! YOUR FOOD'S AWFUL. HA HA!
BUT SHIT!! NEXT TIME I WON'T THROW IT. I PROMISE.
GROUUIK

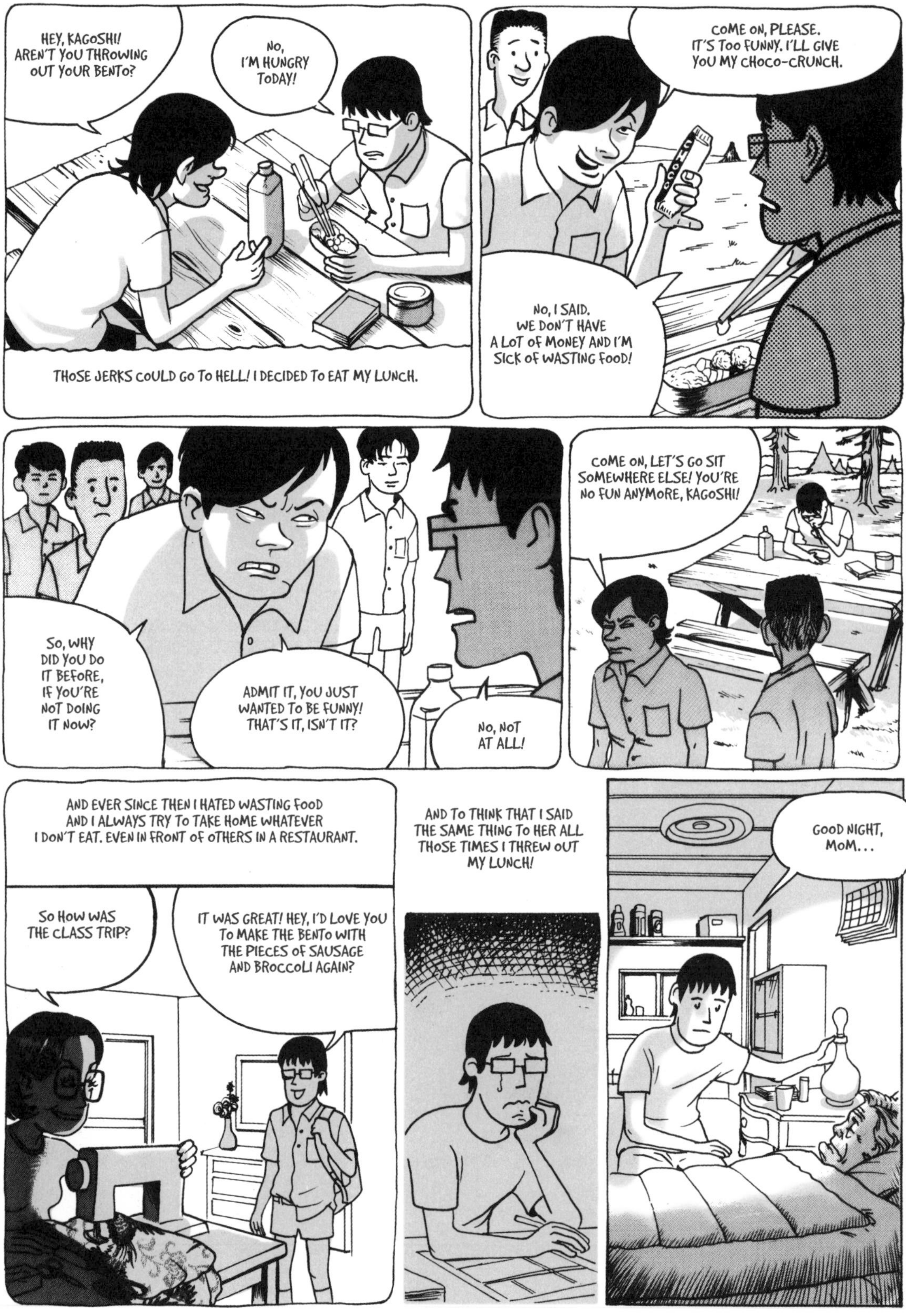
HEY, KAGOSHI! AREN'T YOU THROWING OUT YOUR BENTO?
NO, I'M HUNGRY TODAY!
THOSE JERKS COULD GO TO HELL! I DECIDED TO EAT MY LUNCH.
COME ON, PLEASE. IT'S TOO FUNNY. I'LL GIVE YOU MY CHOCO-CRUNCH.
NO, I SAID. WE DON'T HAVE A LOT OF MONEY AND I'M SICK OF WASTING FOOD!
SO, WHY DID YOU DO IT BEFORE, IF YOU'RE NOT DOING IT NOW?
ADMIT IT, YOU JUST WANTED TO BE FUNNY! THAT'S IT, ISN'T IT?
NO, NOT AT ALL!
COME ON, LET'S GO SIT SOMEWHERE ELSE! YOU'RE NO FUN ANYMORE, KAGOSHI!
AND EVER SINCE THEN I HATED WASTING FOOD AND I ALWAYS TRY TO TAKE HOME WHATEVER I DON'T EAT. EVEN IN FRONT OF OTHERS IN A RESTAURANT.
SO HOW WAS THE CLASS TRIP?
IT WAS GREAT! HEY, I'D LOVE YOU TO MAKE THE BENTO WITH THE PIECES OF SAUSAGE AND BROCCOLI AGAIN?
AND TO THINK THAT I SAID THE SAME THING TO HER ALL THOSE TIMES I THREW OUT MY LUNCH!
GOOD NIGHT, MOM...

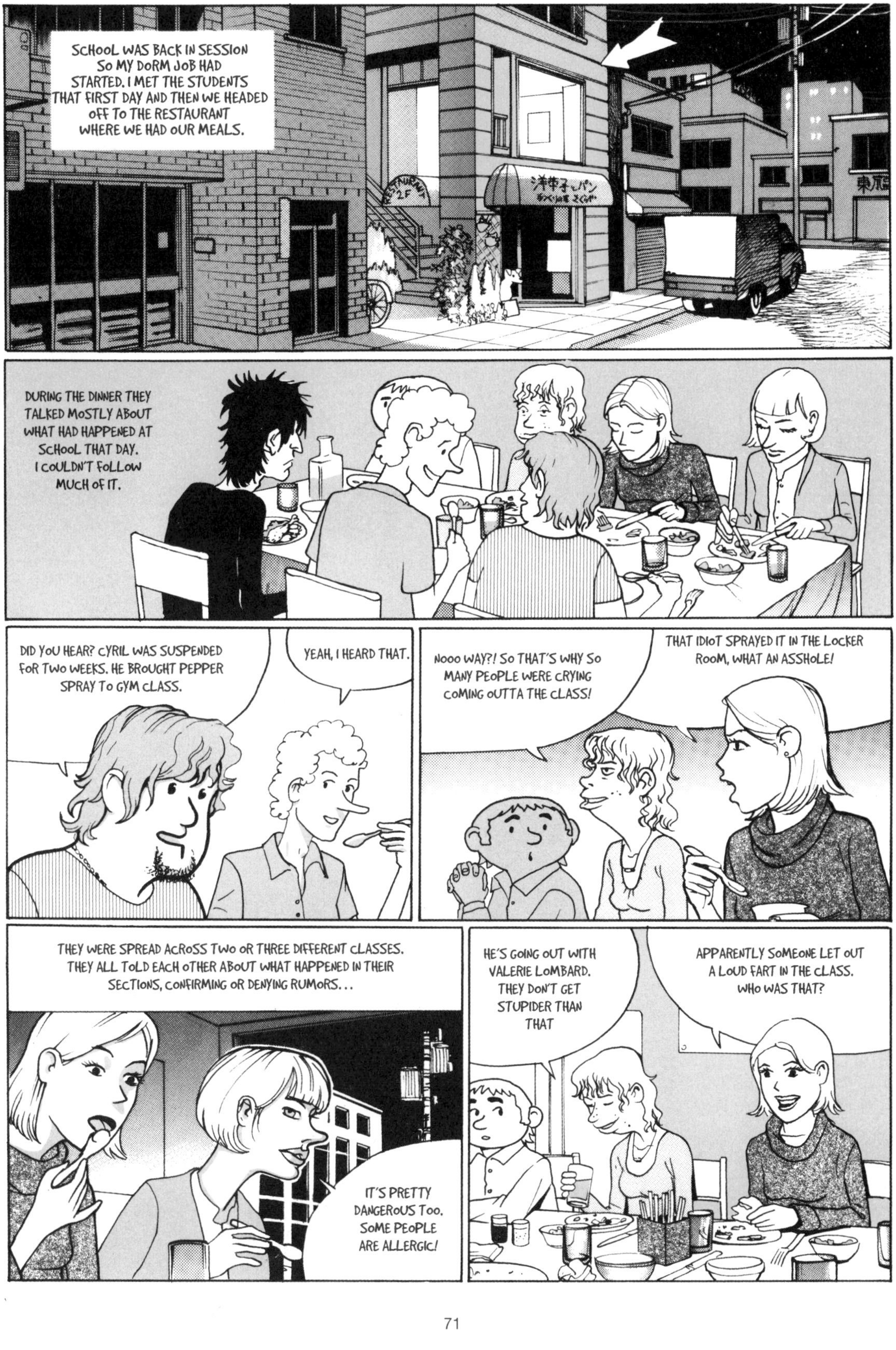
SCHOOL WAS BACK IN SESSION SO MY DORM JOB HAD STARTED. I MET THE STUDENTS THAT FIRST DAY AND THEN WE HEADED OFF TO THE RESTAURANT WHERE WE HAD OUR MEALS.
DURING THE DINNER THEY TALKED MOSTLY ABOUT WHAT HAD HAPPENED AT SCHOOL THAT DAY. I COULDN'T FOLLOW MUCH OF IT.
DID YOU HEAR? CYRIL WAS SUSPENDED FOR TWO WEEKS. HE BROUGHT PEPPER SPRAY TO GYM CLASS.
YEAH, I HEARD THAT.
NOOO WAY?! SO THAT'S WHY SO MANY PEOPLE WERE CRYING COMING OUTTA THE CLASS!
THAT IDIOT SPRAYED IT IN THE LOCKER ROOM, WHAT AN ASSHOLE!
THEY WERE SPREAD ACROSS TWO OR THREE DIFFERENT CLASSES. THEY ALL TOLD EACH OTHER ABOUT WHAT HAPPENED IN THEIR SECTIONS, CONFIRMING OR DENYING RUMORS...
IT'S PRETTY DANGEROUS TOO. SOME PEOPLE ARE ALLERGIC!
HE'S GOING OUT WITH VALERIE LOMBARD. THEY DON'T GET STUPIDER THAN THAT
APPARENTLY SOMEONE LET OUT A LOUD FART IN THE CLASS. WHO WAS THAT?

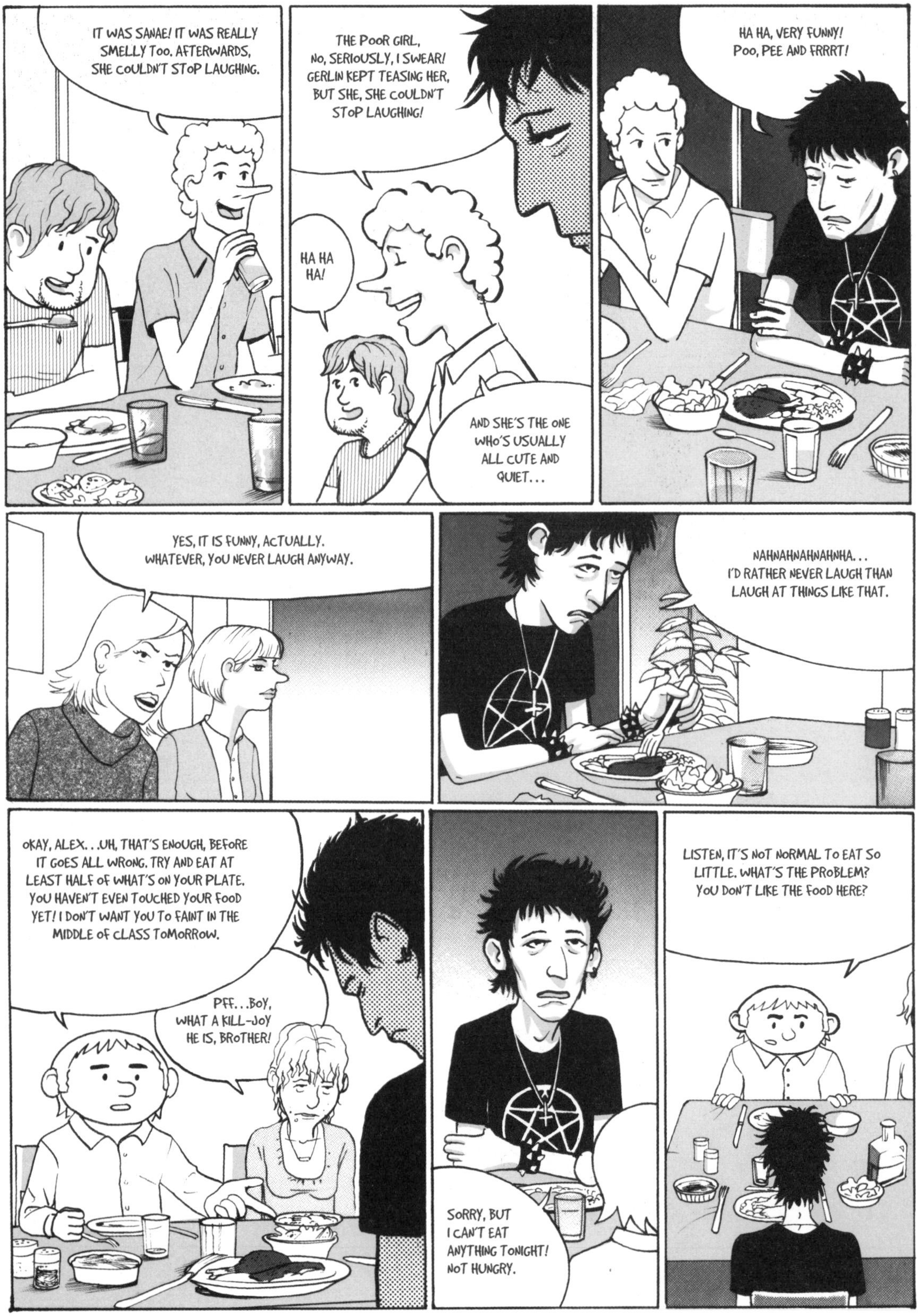

IT WAS SANAE! IT WAS REALLY SMELLY TOO. AFTERWARDS, SHE COULDN'T STOP LAUGHING.
THE POOR GIRL, NO, SERIOUSLY, I SWEAR! GERLIN KEPT TEASING HER, BUT SHE, SHE COULDN'T STOP LAUGHING!
HA HA HA!
AND SHE'S THE ONE WHO'S USUALLY ALL CUTE AND QUIET...
HA HA, VERY FUNNY! POO, PEE AND FRRRT!
YES, IT IS FUNNY, ACTUALLY. WHATEVER, YOU NEVER LAUGH ANYWAY.
NAHNAHNAHNAHNHA... I'D RATHER NEVER LAUGH THAN LAUGH AT THINGS LIKE THAT.
OKAY, ALEX...UH, THAT'S ENOUGH, BEFORE IT GOES ALL WRONG. TRY AND EAT AT LEAST HALF OF WHAT'S ON YOUR PLATE. YOU HAVEN'T EVEN TOUCHED YOUR FOOD YET! I DON'T WANT YOU TO FAINT IN THE MIDDLE OF CLASS TOMORROW.
PFF...BOY, WHAT A KILL-JOY HE IS, BROTHER!
SORRY, BUT I CAN'T EAT ANYTHING TONIGHT! NOT HUNGRY.
LISTEN, IT'S NOT NORMAL TO EAT SO LITTLE. WHAT'S THE PROBLEM? YOU DON'T LIKE THE FOOD HERE?

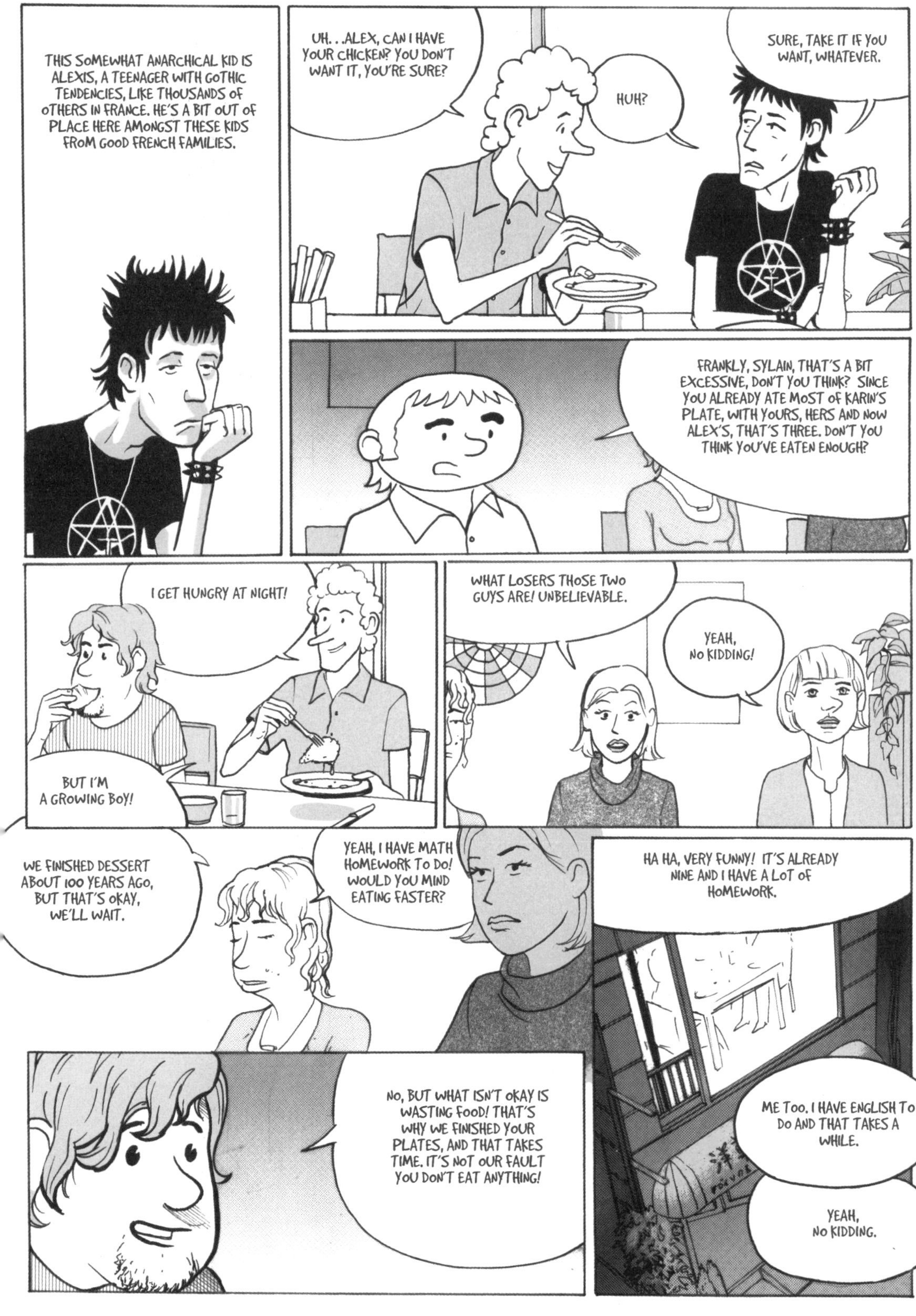
THIS SOMEWHAT ANARCHICAL KID IS ALEXIS, A TEENAGER WITH GOTHIC TENDENCIES, LIKE THOUSANDS OF OTHERS IN FRANCE. HE'S A BIT OUT OF PLACE HERE AMONGST THESE KIDS FROM GOOD FRENCH FAMILIES.
UH. . .ALEX, CAN I HAVE YOUR CHICKEN? YOU DON'T WANT IT, YOU'RE SURE?
HUH?
SURE, TAKE IT IF YOU WANT, WHATEVER.
FRANKLY, SYLAIN, THAT'S A BIT EXCESSIVE, DON'T YOU THINK? SINCE YOU ALREADY ATE MOST OF KARIN'S PLATE, WITH YOURS, HERS AND NOW ALEX'S, THAT'S THREE. DON'T YOU THINK YOU'VE EATEN ENOUGH?
I GET HUNGRY AT NIGHT!
BUT I'M A GROWING BOY!
WHAT LOSERS THOSE TWO GUYS ARE! UNBELIEVABLE.
YEAH, NO KIDDING!
WE FINISHED DESSERT ABOUT 100 YEARS AGO, BUT THAT'S OKAY, WE'LL WAIT.
YEAH, I HAVE MATH HOMEWORK TO DO! WOULD YOU MIND EATING FASTER?
NO, BUT WHAT ISN'T OKAY IS WASTING FOOD! THAT'S WHY WE FINISHED YOUR PLATES, AND THAT TAKES TIME. IT'S NOT OUR FAULT YOU DON'T EAT ANYTHING!
HA HA, VERY FUNNY! IT'S ALREADY NINE AND I HAVE A LOT OF HOMEWORK.
ME TOO. I HAVE ENGLISH TO DO AND THAT TAKES A WHILE.
YEAH, NO KIDDING.

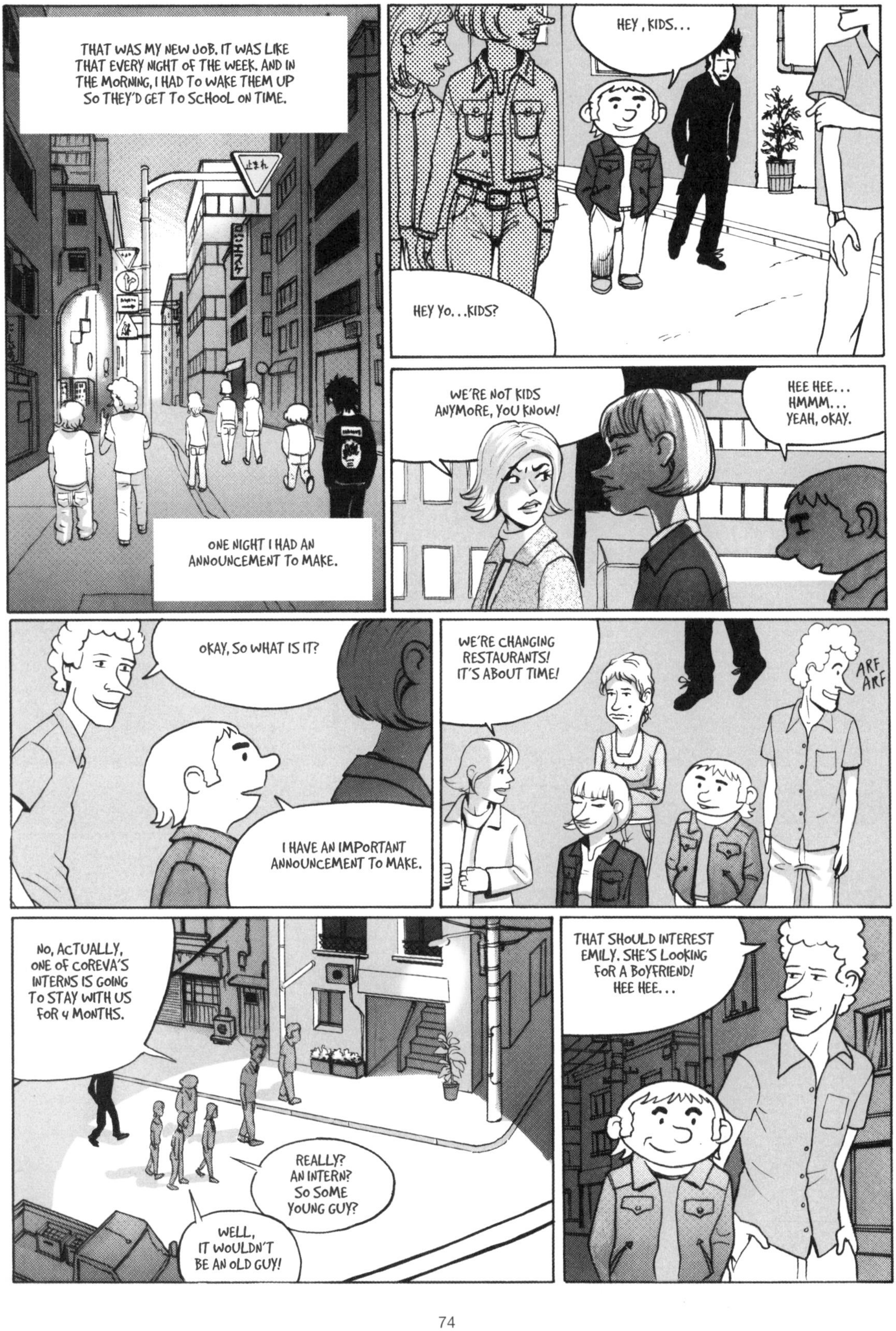
THAT WAS MY NEW JOB. IT WAS LIKE THAT EVERY NIGHT OF THE WEEK. AND IN THE MORNING, I HAD TO WAKE THEM UP SO THEY'D GET TO SCHOOL ON TIME.
ONE NIGHT I HAD AN ANNOUNCEMENT TO MAKE.
HEY, KIDS...
HEY YO...KIDS?
WE'RE NOT KIDS ANYMORE, YOU KNOW!
HEE HEE... HMMM... YEAH, OKAY.
OKAY, SO WHAT IS IT?
I HAVE AN IMPORTANT ANNOUNCEMENT TO MAKE.
WE'RE CHANGING RESTAURANTS! IT'S ABOUT TIME!
ARF ARF
NO, ACTUALLY, ONE OF COREVA'S INTERNS IS GOING TO STAY WITH US FOR 4 MONTHS.
REALLY? AN INTERN? SO SOME YOUNG GUY?
WELL, IT WOULDN'T BE AN OLD GUY!
THAT SHOULD INTEREST EMILY. SHE'S LOOKING FOR A BOYFRIEND! HEE HEE...

THE RULES ARE THE RULES

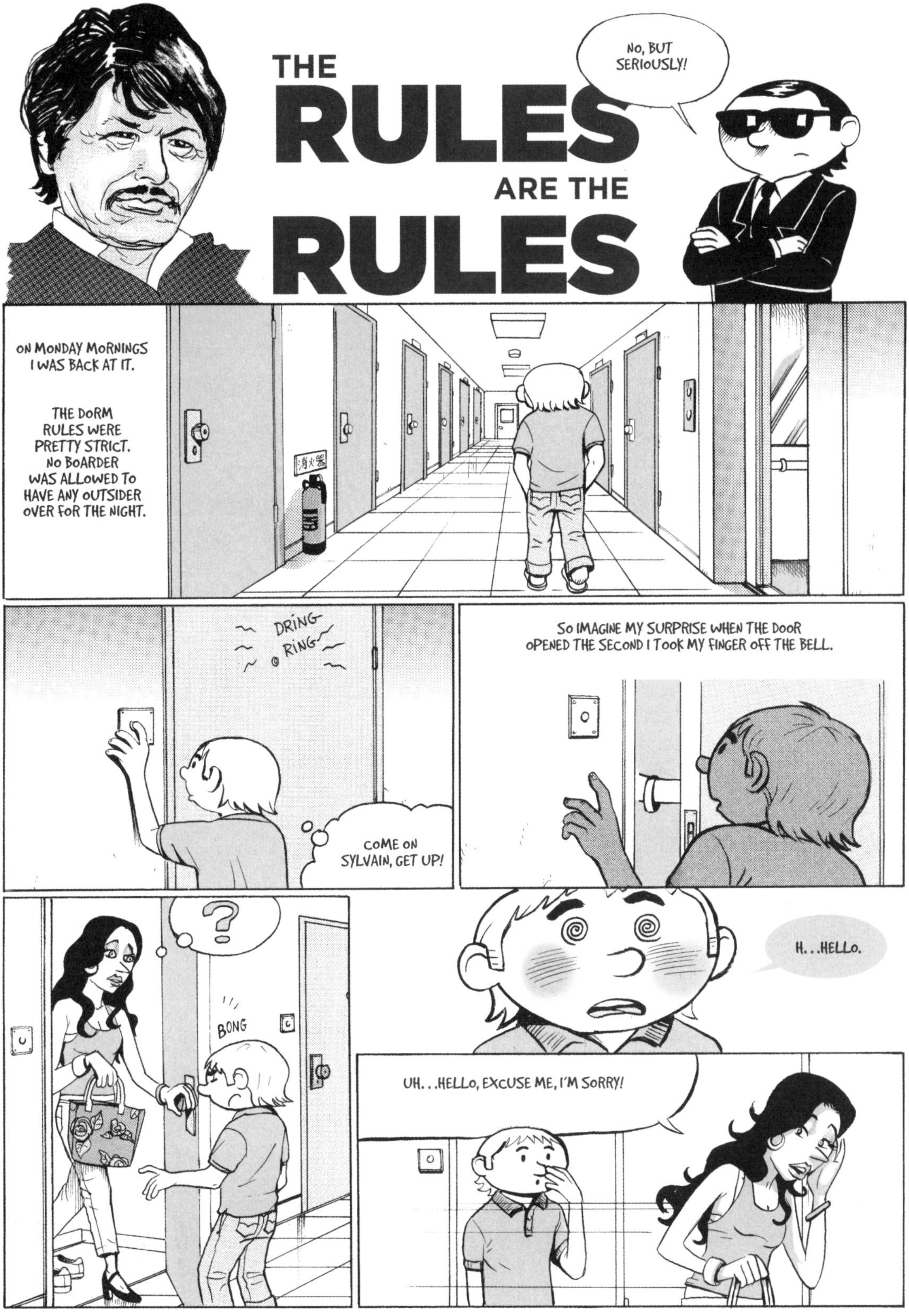
NO, BUT SERIOUSLY!
ON MONDAY MORNINGS I WAS BACK AT IT.
THE DORM RULES WERE PRETTY STRICT. NO BOARDER WAS ALLOWED TO HAVE ANY OUTSIDER OVER FOR THE NIGHT.
消火器
DRING RING
COME ON SYLVAIN, GET UP!
SO IMAGINE MY SURPRISE WHEN THE DOOR OPENED THE SECOND I TOOK MY FINGER OFF THE BELL.
?
BONG
H...HELLO.
UH...HELLO, EXCUSE ME, I'M SORRY!

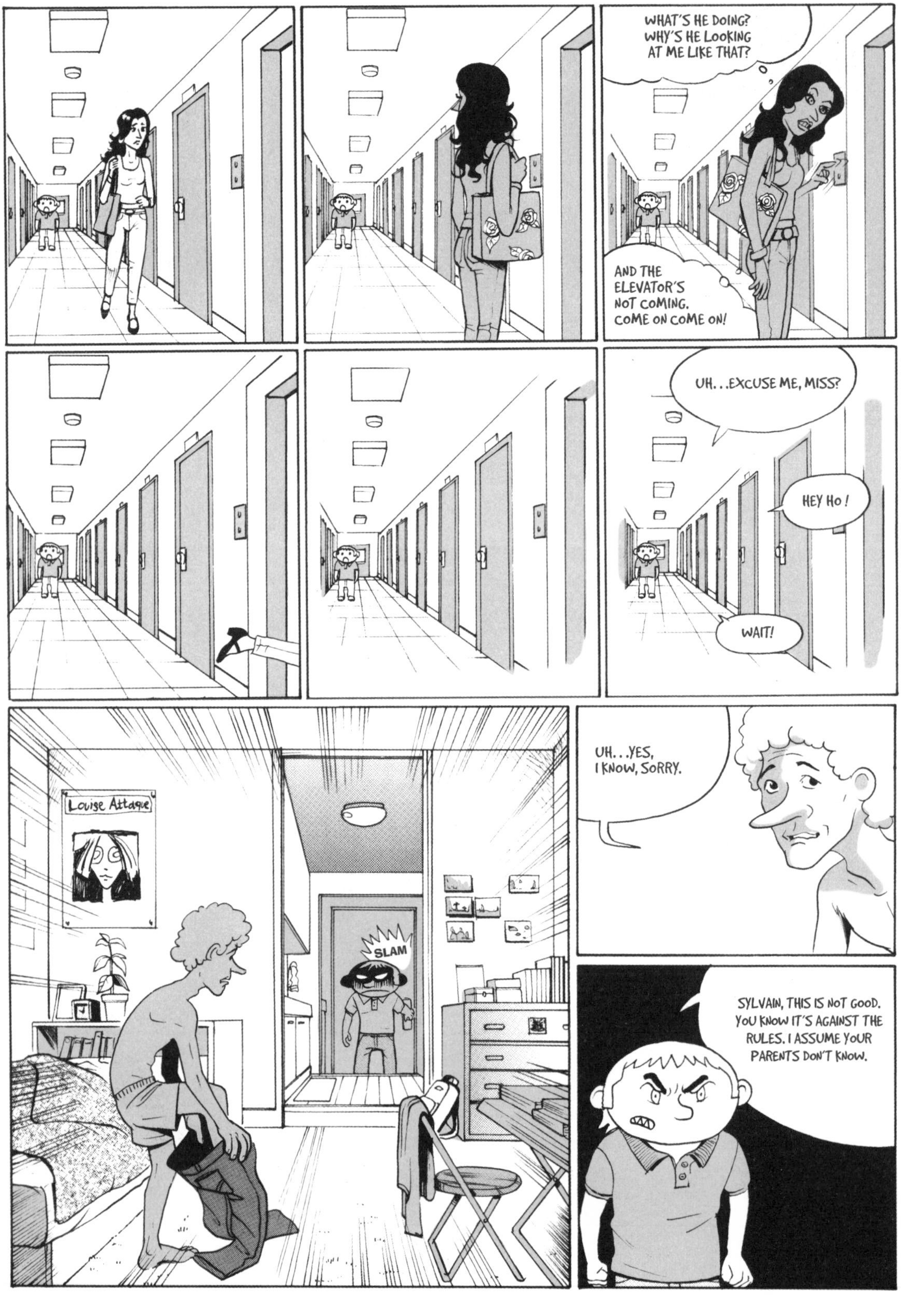
WHAT'S HE DOING? WHY'S HE LOOKING AT ME LIKE THAT?
AND THE ELEVATOR'S NOT COMING. COME ON COME ON!
UH...EXCUSE ME, MISS?
HEY HO!
WAIT!
Louise Attaque
SLAM
UH...YES, I KNOW, SORRY.
SYLVAIN, THIS IS NOT GOOD. YOU KNOW IT'S AGAINST THE RULES. I ASSUME YOUR PARENTS DON'T KNOW.

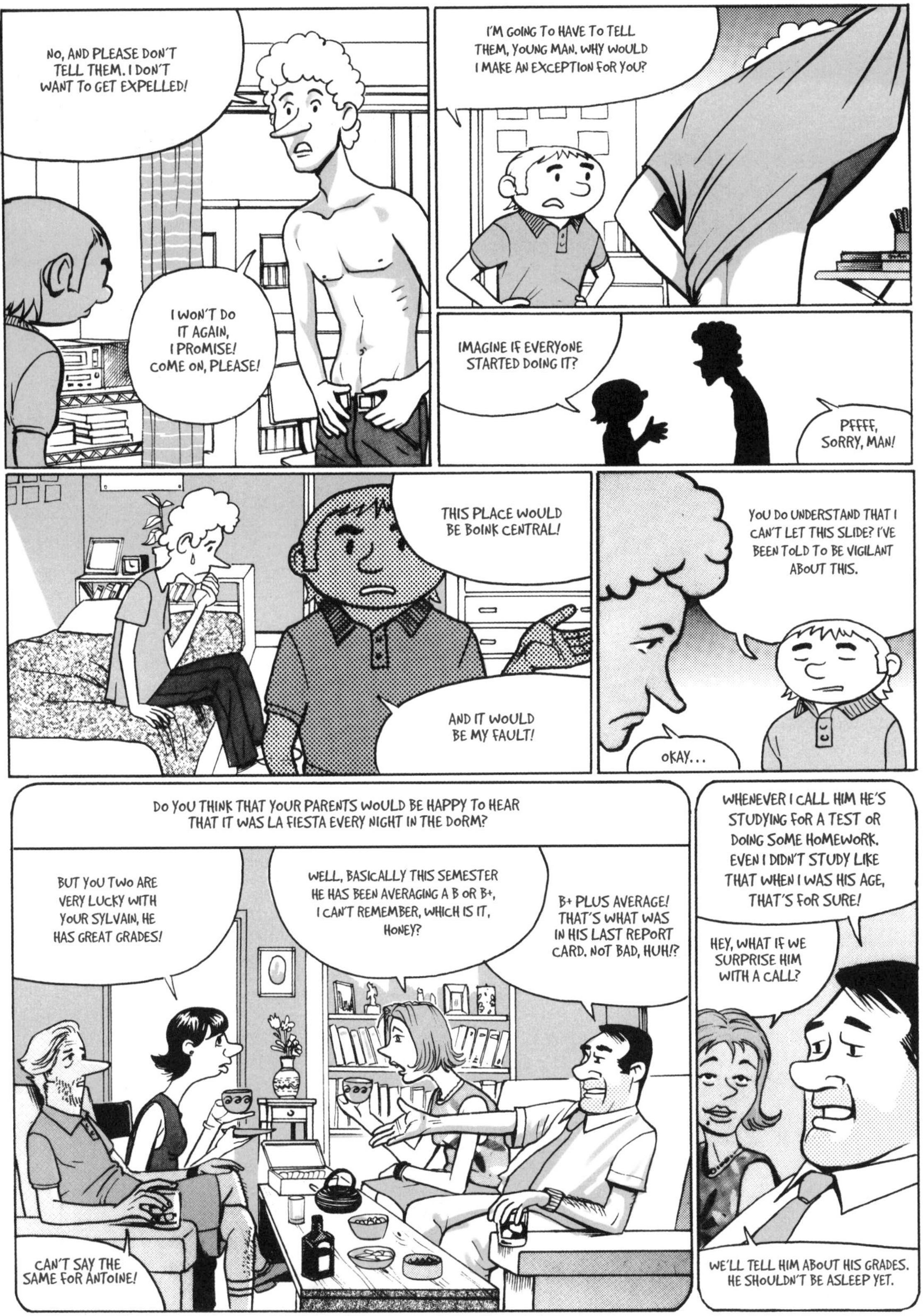
NO, AND PLEASE DON'T TELL THEM. I DON'T WANT TO GET EXPELLED!
I WON'T DO IT AGAIN, I PROMISE! COME ON, PLEASE!
I'M GOING TO HAVE TO TELL THEM, YOUNG MAN. WHY WOULD I MAKE AN EXCEPTION FOR YOU?
IMAGINE IF EVERYONE STARTED DOING IT?
PFFFF, SORRY, MAN!
THIS PLACE WOULD BE BOINK CENTRAL!
AND IT WOULD BE MY FAULT!
YOU DO UNDERSTAND THAT I CAN'T LET THIS SLIDE? I'VE BEEN TOLD TO BE VIGILANT ABOUT THIS.
OKAY...
DO YOU THINK THAT YOUR PARENTS WOULD BE HAPPY TO HEAR THAT IT WAS LA FIESTA EVERY NIGHT IN THE DORM?
BUT YOU TWO ARE VERY LUCKY WITH YOUR SYLVAIN, HE HAS GREAT GRADES!
WELL, BASICALLY THIS SEMESTER HE HAS BEEN AVERAGING A B OR B+, I CAN'T REMEMBER, WHICH IS IT, HONEY?
B+ PLUS AVERAGE! THAT'S WHAT WAS IN HIS LAST REPORT CARD. NOT BAD, HUH!?
CAN'T SAY THE SAME FOR ANTOINE!
WHENEVER I CALL HIM HE'S STUDYING FOR A TEST OR DOING SOME HOMEWORK. EVEN I DIDN'T STUDY LIKE THAT WHEN I WAS HIS AGE, THAT'S FOR SURE!
HEY, WHAT IF WE SURPRISE HIM WITH A CALL?
WE'LL TELL HIM ABOUT HIS GRADES. HE SHOULDN'T BE ASLEEP YET.

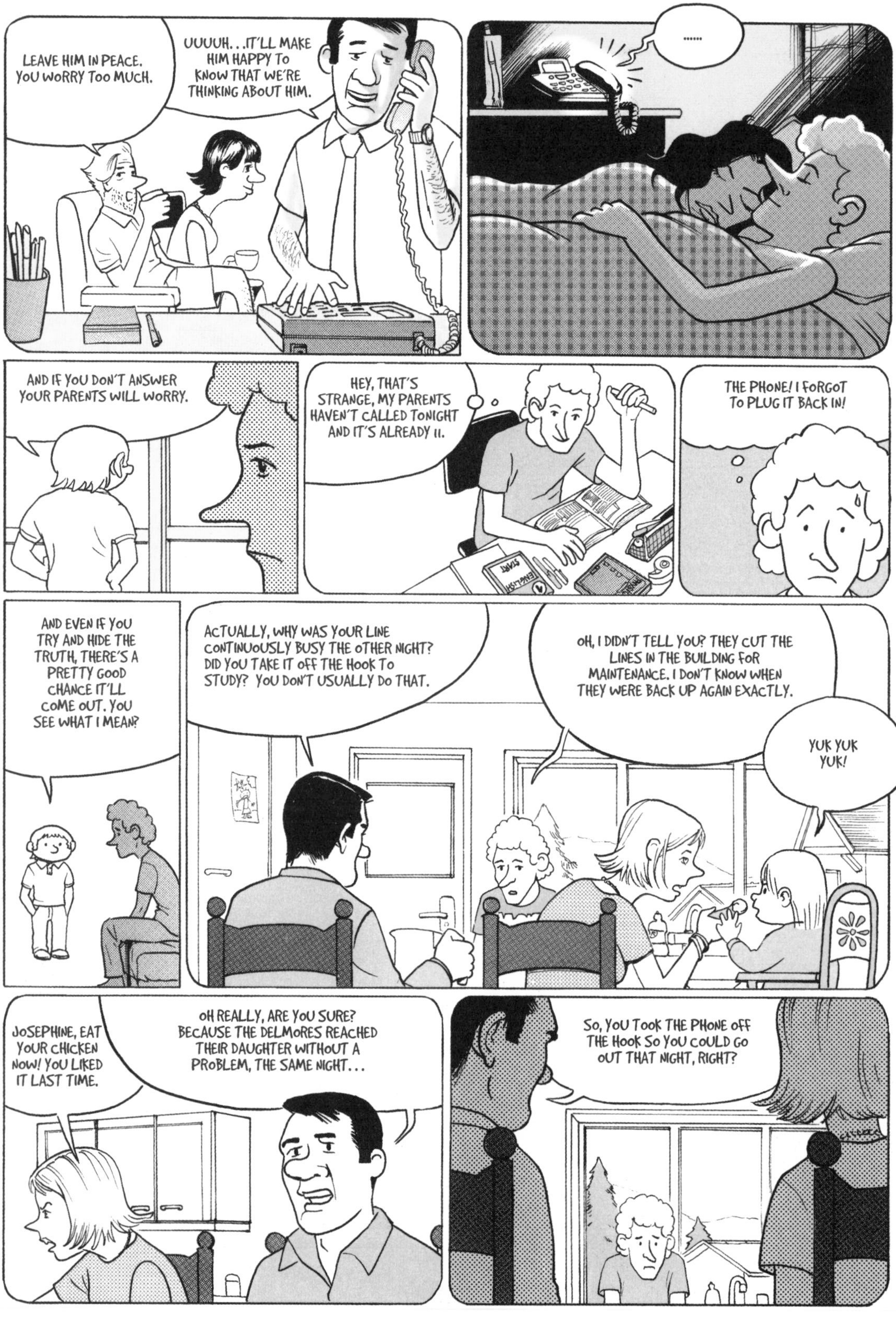
LEAVE HIM IN PEACE. YOU WORRY TOO MUCH.
UUUUH...IT'LL MAKE HIM HAPPY TO KNOW THAT WE'RE THINKING ABOUT HIM.
......
AND IF YOU DON'T ANSWER YOUR PARENTS WILL WORRY.
HEY, THAT'S STRANGE, MY PARENTS HAVEN'T CALLED TONIGHT AND IT'S ALREADY 11.
THE PHONE! I FORGOT TO PLUG IT BACK IN!
AND EVEN IF YOU TRY AND HIDE THE TRUTH, THERE'S A PRETTY GOOD CHANCE IT'LL COME OUT. YOU SEE WHAT I MEAN?
ACTUALLY, WHY WAS YOUR LINE CONTINUOUSLY BUSY THE OTHER NIGHT? DID YOU TAKE IT OFF THE HOOK TO STUDY? YOU DON'T USUALLY DO THAT.
OH, I DIDN'T TELL YOU? THEY CUT THE LINES IN THE BUILDING FOR MAINTENANCE. I DON'T KNOW WHEN THEY WERE BACK UP AGAIN EXACTLY.
YUK YUK YUK!
JOSEPHINE, EAT YOUR CHICKEN NOW! YOU LIKED IT LAST TIME.
OH REALLY, ARE YOU SURE? BECAUSE THE DELMORES REACHED THEIR DAUGHTER WITHOUT A PROBLEM, THE SAME NIGHT...
SO, YOU TOOK THE PHONE OFF THE HOOK SO YOU COULD GO OUT THAT NIGHT, RIGHT?

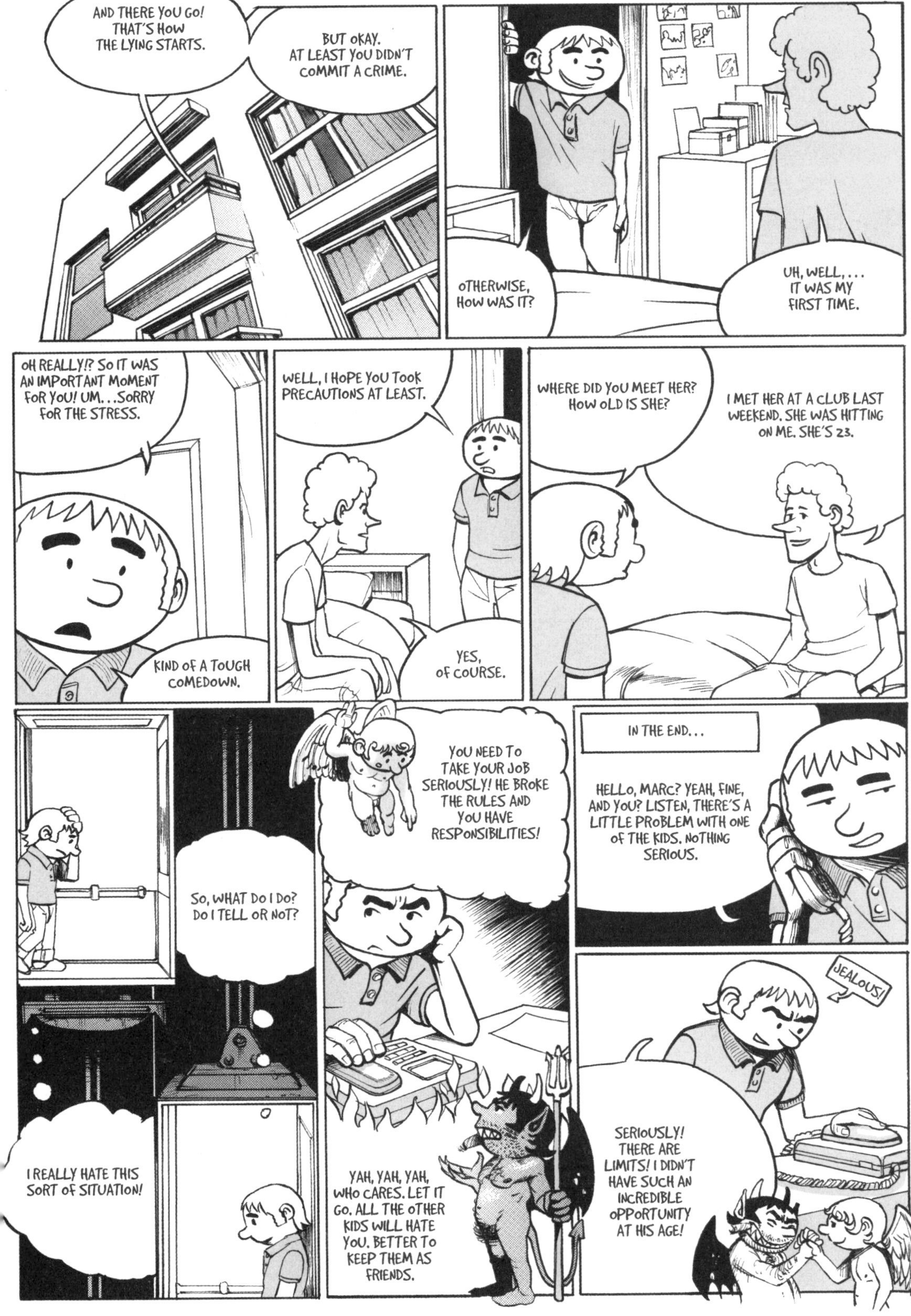
AND THERE YOU GO! THAT'S HOW THE LYING STARTS.
BUT OKAY. AT LEAST YOU DIDN'T COMMIT A CRIME.
OTHERWISE, HOW WAS IT?
UH, WELL, . . . IT WAS MY FIRST TIME.
OH REALLY!? SO IT WAS AN IMPORTANT MOMENT FOR YOU! UM. . . SORRY FOR THE STRESS.
KIND OF A TOUGH COMEDOWN.
WELL, I HOPE YOU TOOK PRECAUTIONS AT LEAST.
YES, OF COURSE.
WHERE DID YOU MEET HER? HOW OLD IS SHE?
I MET HER AT A CLUB LAST WEEKEND. SHE WAS HITTING ON ME. SHE'S 23.
SO, WHAT DO I DO? DO I TELL OR NOT?
I REALLY HATE THIS SORT OF SITUATION!
YOU NEED TO TAKE YOUR JOB SERIOUSLY! HE BROKE THE RULES AND YOU HAVE RESPONSIBILITIES!
YAH, YAH, YAH, WHO CARES. LET IT GO. ALL THE OTHER KIDS WILL HATE YOU. BETTER TO KEEP THEM AS FRIENDS.
IN THE END. . .
HELLO, MARC? YEAH, FINE, AND YOU? LISTEN, THERE'S A LITTLE PROBLEM WITH ONE OF THE KIDS. NOTHING SERIOUS.
JEALOUS!
SERIOUSLY! THERE ARE LIMITS! I DIDN'T HAVE SUCH AN INCREDIBLE OPPORTUNITY AT HIS AGE!

MY BOSS ASKED ME TO PICK UP JEROME THE INTERN. I NEEDED TO GET HIM UP TO SPEED ON DORM LIFE.

HE'S PROBABLY GOING TO BE A KNIGHTS OF THE ZODIAC OR A NARUTO FAN.

WELL, WHERE IS THE GUY? DID HE GET STOPPED AT CUSTOMS OR WHAT?

HELLO! ARE YOU BENJAMIN?

YEAH... HELLO, HOW ARE YOU?

ZEN MAN! SO WHERE IS IT? I'M ALL YOURS.

UH... LET'S GO, COME ON.

EASY BOY, NOW, TAKE IT EASY!

I WASN'T EXPECTING THIS KIND OF GUY. INSTEAD OF A STRAIGHT-LACED ENGINEER, BENJAMIN WAS A WALKING/TALKING MANNEQUIN FOR HUGO BOSS.

SHIT, MAN, IT'S GREAT TO BE BACK IN TOKYO! IT'S BEEN A WHILE.

OH, YOU KNOW IT?

TOTALLY! I WAS COMING HERE REGULARLY FOR NINE YEARS. I ALSO WENT TO THE FRANCO-JAPANESE HIGH SCHOOL.

HIS OLD MAN WAS A BIGWIG AT COREVA. HE'D PULLED STRINGS TO GET THE GIG.

IT'S HERE.

THIS IS YOUR ROOM. IF THERE AREN'T ANY SHEETS ON THE BED, I'LL BRING YOU SOME. OTHERWISE WE MEET DOWNSTAIRS AT 7 TO HEAD TO DINNER.

GREAT! I THINK IN THE MEANTIME I'M GOING TO TAKE A FUCKIN' NAP.

OKAY FINE, DON'T HESITATE TO COME SEE ME IF YOU NEED ANYTHING. I'M IN APARTMENT 201.

OKAY.

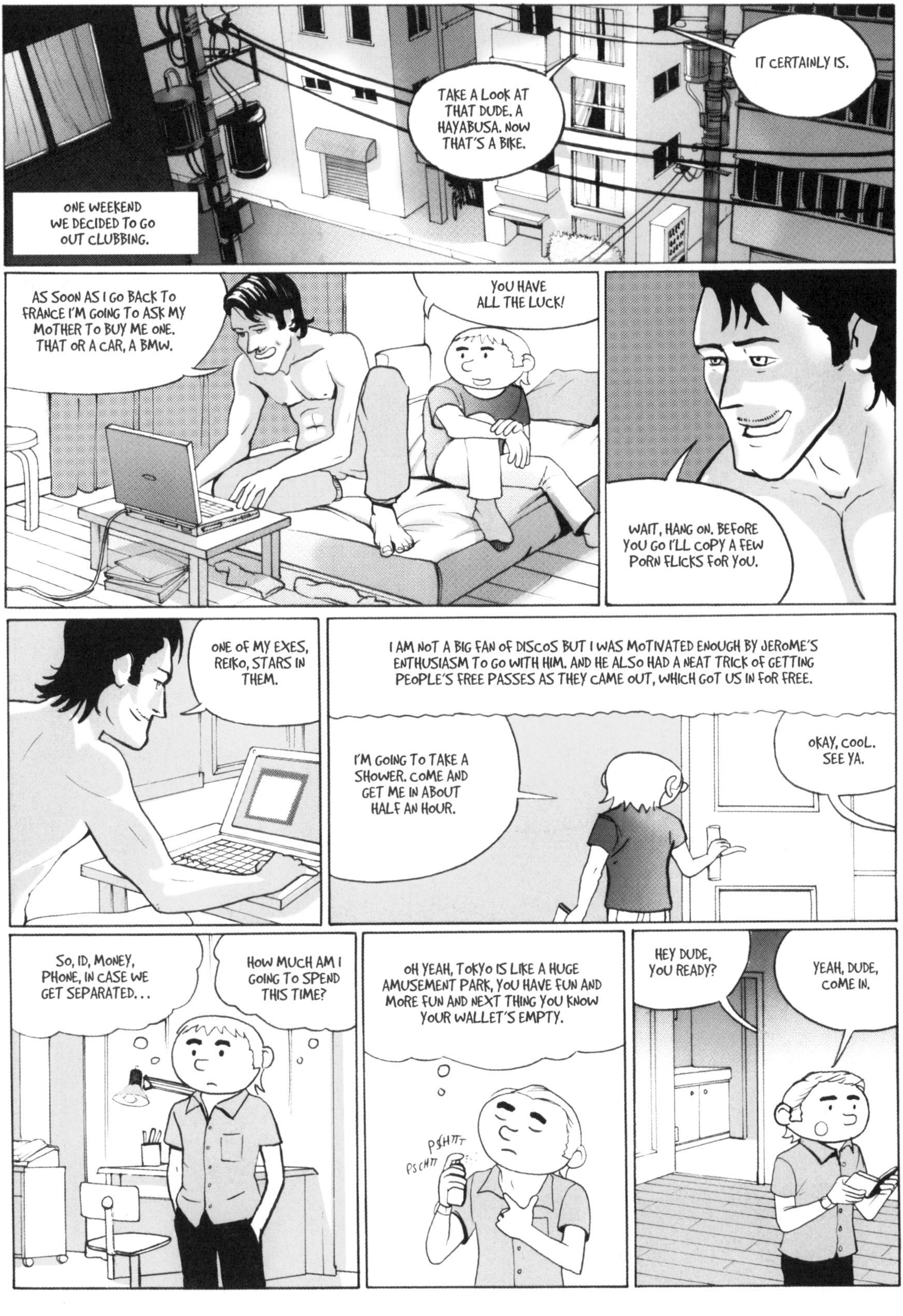
ONE WEEKEND WE DECIDED TO GO OUT CLUBBING.
TAKE A LOOK AT THAT DUDE. A HAYABUSA. NOW THAT'S A BIKE.
IT CERTAINLY IS.
AS SOON AS I GO BACK TO FRANCE I'M GOING TO ASK MY MOTHER TO BUY ME ONE. THAT OR A CAR, A BMW.
YOU HAVE ALL THE LUCK!
WAIT, HANG ON. BEFORE YOU GO I'LL COPY A FEW PORN FLICKS FOR YOU.
ONE OF MY EXES, REIKO, STARS IN THEM.
I AM NOT A BIG FAN OF DISCOS BUT I WAS MOTIVATED ENOUGH BY JEROME'S ENTHUSIASM TO GO WITH HIM. AND HE ALSO HAD A NEAT TRICK OF GETTING PEOPLE'S FREE PASSES AS THEY CAME OUT, WHICH GOT US IN FOR FREE.
I'M GOING TO TAKE A SHOWER. COME AND GET ME IN ABOUT HALF AN HOUR.
OKAY, COOL. SEE YA.
SO, ID, MONEY, PHONE, IN CASE WE GET SEPARATED...
HOW MUCH AM I GOING TO SPEND THIS TIME?
OH YEAH, TOKYO IS LIKE A HUGE AMUSEMENT PARK, YOU HAVE FUN AND MORE FUN AND NEXT THING YOU KNOW YOUR WALLET'S EMPTY.
PSHTT
PSCHTT
HEY DUDE, YOU READY?
YEAH, DUDE, COME IN.

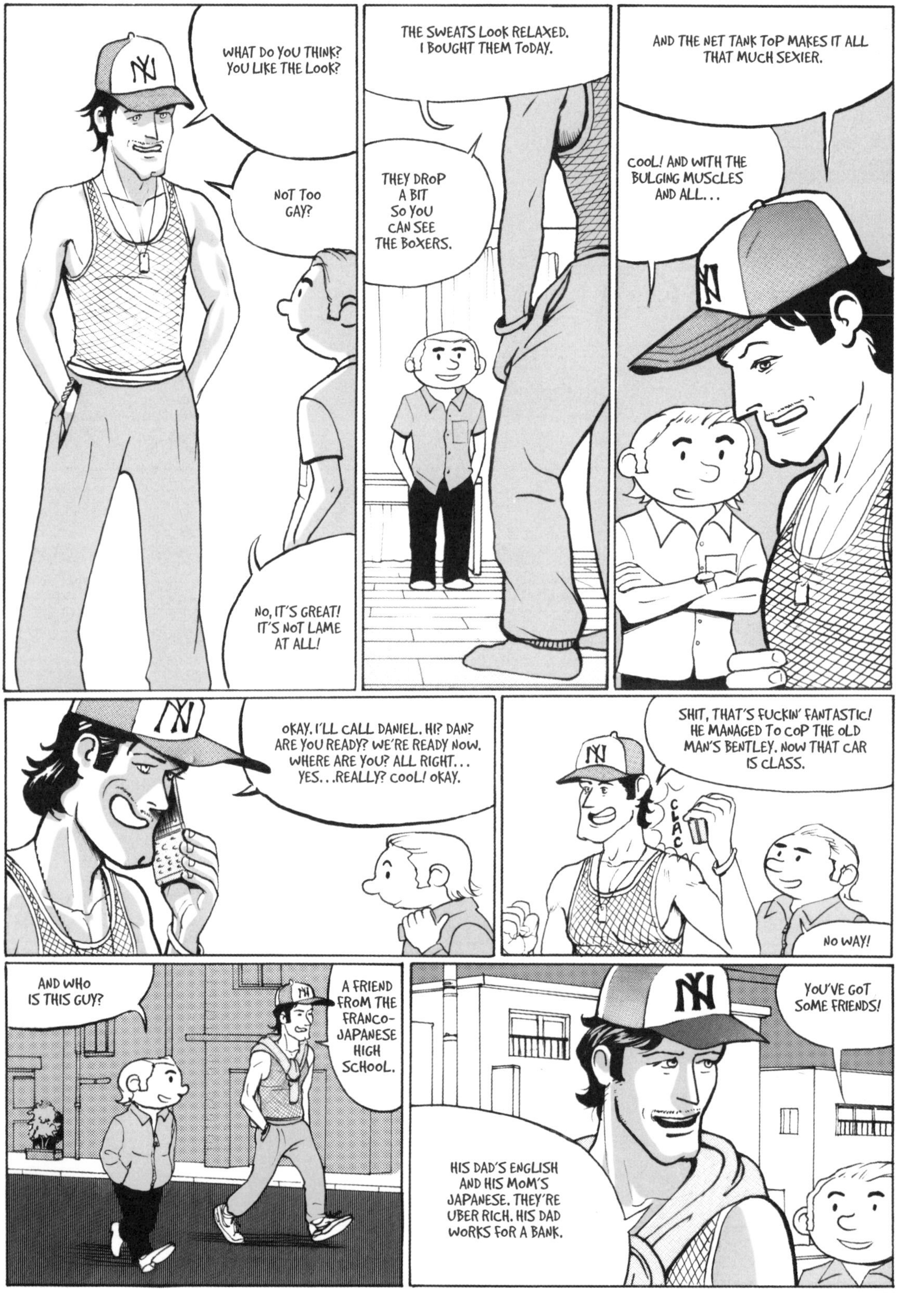
WHAT DO YOU THINK? YOU LIKE THE LOOK?
NOT TOO GAY?
NO, IT'S GREAT! IT'S NOT LAME AT ALL!
THE SWEATS LOOK RELAXED. I BOUGHT THEM TODAY.
THEY DROP A BIT SO YOU CAN SEE THE BOXERS.
AND THE NET TANK TOP MAKES IT ALL THAT MUCH SEXIER.
COOL! AND WITH THE BULGING MUSCLES AND ALL...
OKAY. I'LL CALL DANIEL. HI? DAN? ARE YOU READY? WE'RE READY NOW. WHERE ARE YOU? ALL RIGHT... YES...REALLY? COOL! OKAY.
SHIT, THAT'S FUCKIN' FANTASTIC! HE MANAGED TO COP THE OLD MAN'S BENTLEY. NOW THAT CAR IS CLASS.
CLAC
NO WAY!
AND WHO IS THIS GUY?
A FRIEND FROM THE FRANCO-JAPANESE HIGH SCHOOL.
YOU'VE GOT SOME FRIENDS!
HIS DAD'S ENGLISH AND HIS MOM'S JAPANESE. THEY'RE UBER RICH. HIS DAD WORKS FOR A BANK.

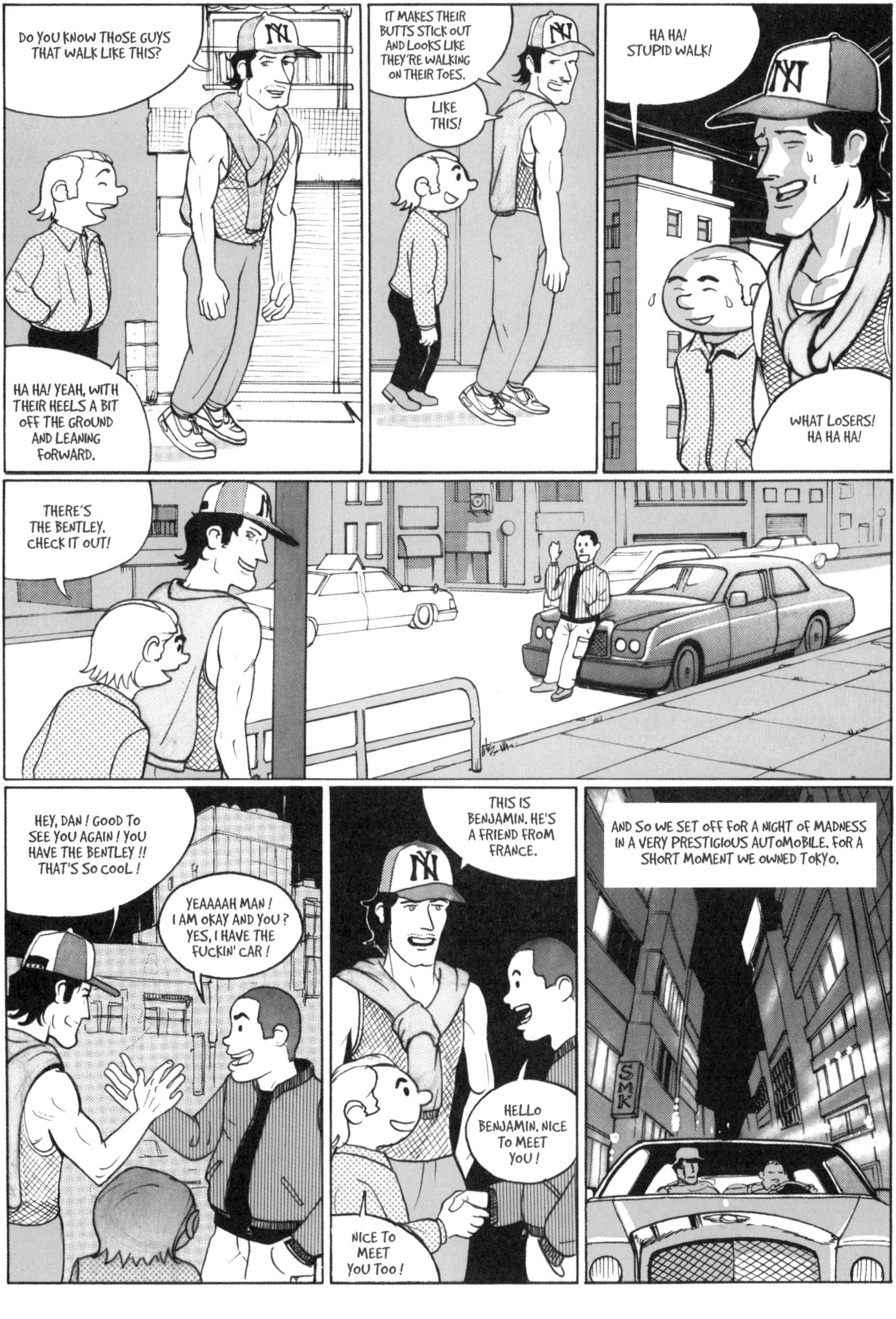
DO YOU KNOW THOSE GUYS THAT WALK LIKE THIS?
HA HA! YEAH, WITH THEIR HEELS A BIT OFF THE GROUND AND LEANING FORWARD.
IT MAKES THEIR BUTTS STICK OUT AND LOOKS LIKE THEY'RE WALKING ON THEIR TOES.
LIKE THIS!
HA HA! STUPID WALK!
WHAT LOSERS! HA HA HA!
THERE'S THE BENTLEY. CHECK IT OUT!
HEY, DAN! GOOD TO SEE YOU AGAIN! YOU HAVE THE BENTLEY!! THAT'S SO COOL!
YEAAAAH MAN! I AM OKAY AND YOU? YES, I HAVE THE FUCKIN' CAR!
THIS IS BENJAMIN. HE'S A FRIEND FROM FRANCE.
HELLO BENJAMIN. NICE TO MEET YOU!
NICE TO MEET YOU TOO!
AND SO WE SET OFF FOR A NIGHT OF MADNESS IN A VERY PRESTIGIOUS AUTOMOBILE. FOR A SHORT MOMENT WE OWNED TOKYO.
SMK

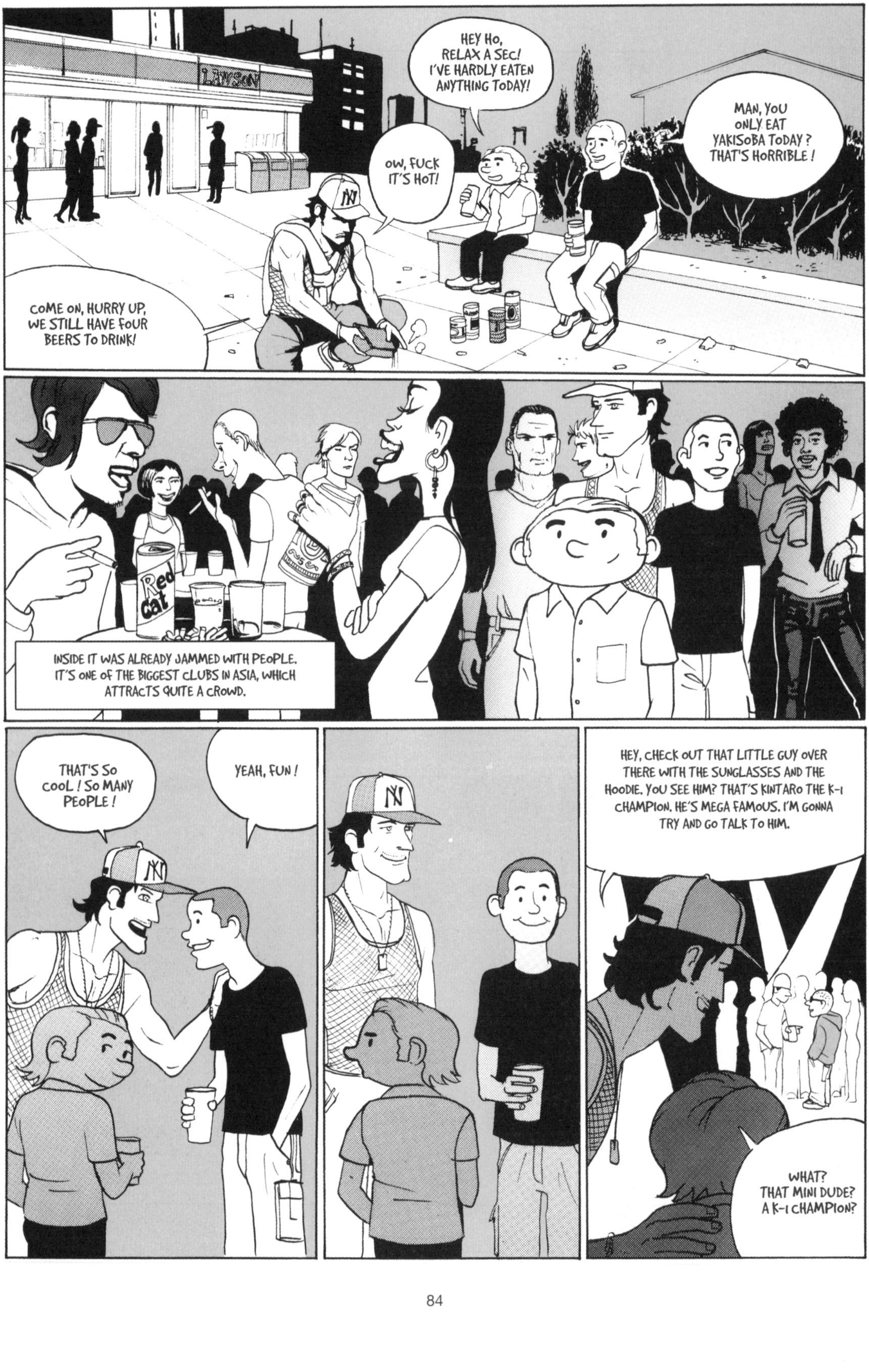
LAWSON
HEY HO, RELAX A SEC! I'VE HARDLY EATEN ANYTHING TODAY!
OW, FUCK IT'S HOT!
MAN, YOU ONLY EAT YAKISOBA TODAY ? THAT'S HORRIBLE !
COME ON, HURRY UP, WE STILL HAVE FOUR BEERS TO DRINK!
Red Cat
INSIDE IT WAS ALREADY JAMMED WITH PEOPLE. IT'S ONE OF THE BIGGEST CLUBS IN ASIA, WHICH ATTRACTS QUITE A CROWD.
THAT'S SO COOL ! SO MANY PEOPLE !
YEAH, FUN !
HEY, CHECK OUT THAT LITTLE GUY OVER THERE WITH THE SUNGLASSES AND THE HOODIE. YOU SEE HIM? THAT'S KINTARO THE K-1 CHAMPION. HE'S MEGA FAMOUS. I'M GONNA TRY AND GO TALK TO HIM.
WHAT? THAT MINI DUDE? A K-1 CHAMPION?

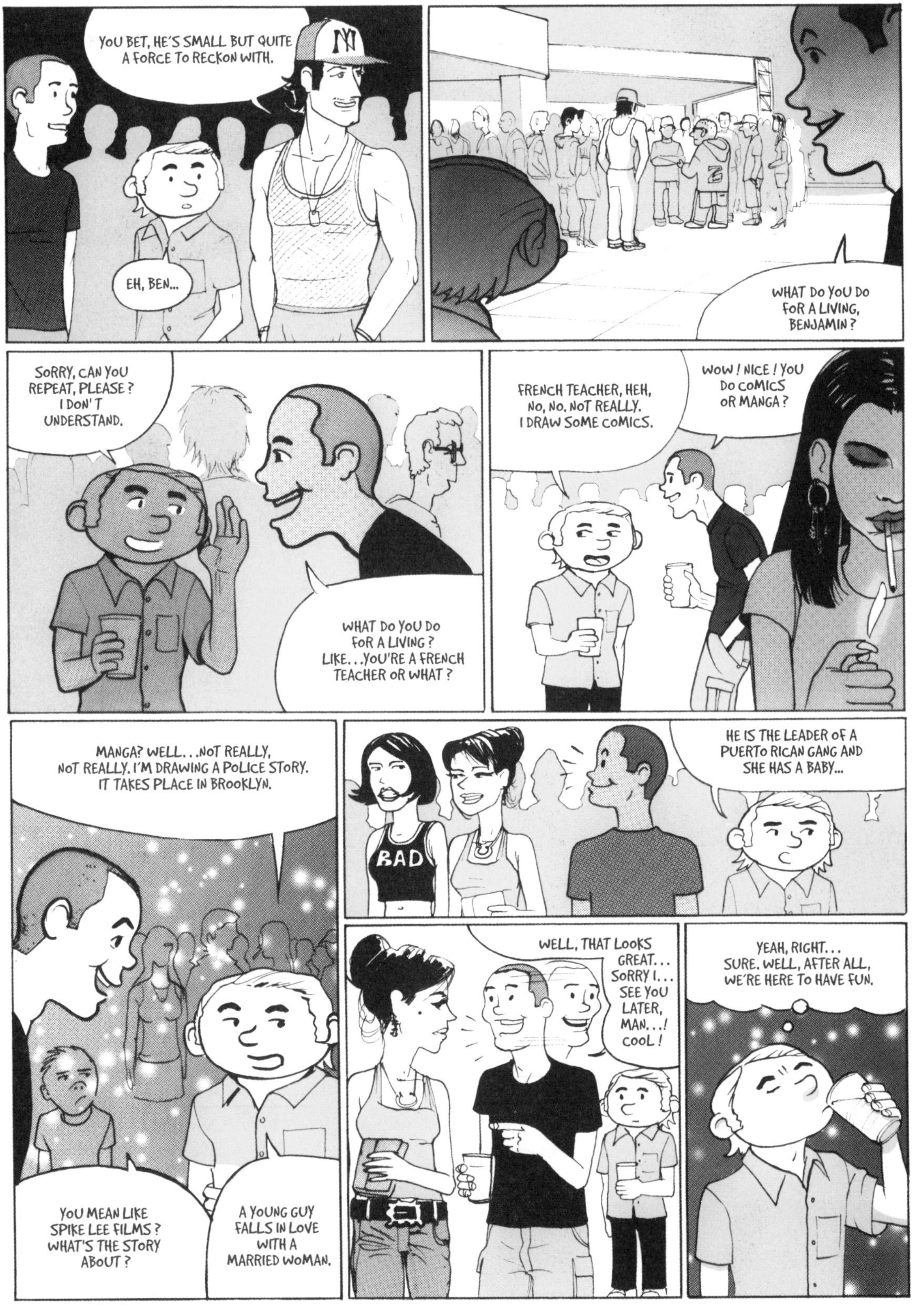
YOU BET, HE'S SMALL BUT QUITE A FORCE TO RECKON WITH.
NY
EH, BEN...
WHAT DO YOU DO FOR A LIVING, BENJAMIN?
SORRY, CAN YOU REPEAT, PLEASE? I DON'T UNDERSTAND.
WHAT DO YOU DO FOR A LIVING? LIKE...YOU'RE A FRENCH TEACHER OR WHAT?
FRENCH TEACHER, HEH, NO, NO. NOT REALLY. I DRAW SOME COMICS.
WOW! NICE! YOU DO COMICS OR MANGA?
MANGA? WELL...NOT REALLY, NOT REALLY. I'M DRAWING A POLICE STORY. IT TAKES PLACE IN BROOKLYN.
YOU MEAN LIKE SPIKE LEE FILMS? WHAT'S THE STORY ABOUT?
A YOUNG GUY FALLS IN LOVE WITH A MARRIED WOMAN.
BAD
HE IS THE LEADER OF A PUERTO RICAN GANG AND SHE HAS A BABY...
WELL, THAT LOOKS GREAT... SORRY I... SEE YOU LATER, MAN...! COOL!
YEAH, RIGHT... SURE. WELL, AFTER ALL, WE'RE HERE TO HAVE FUN.

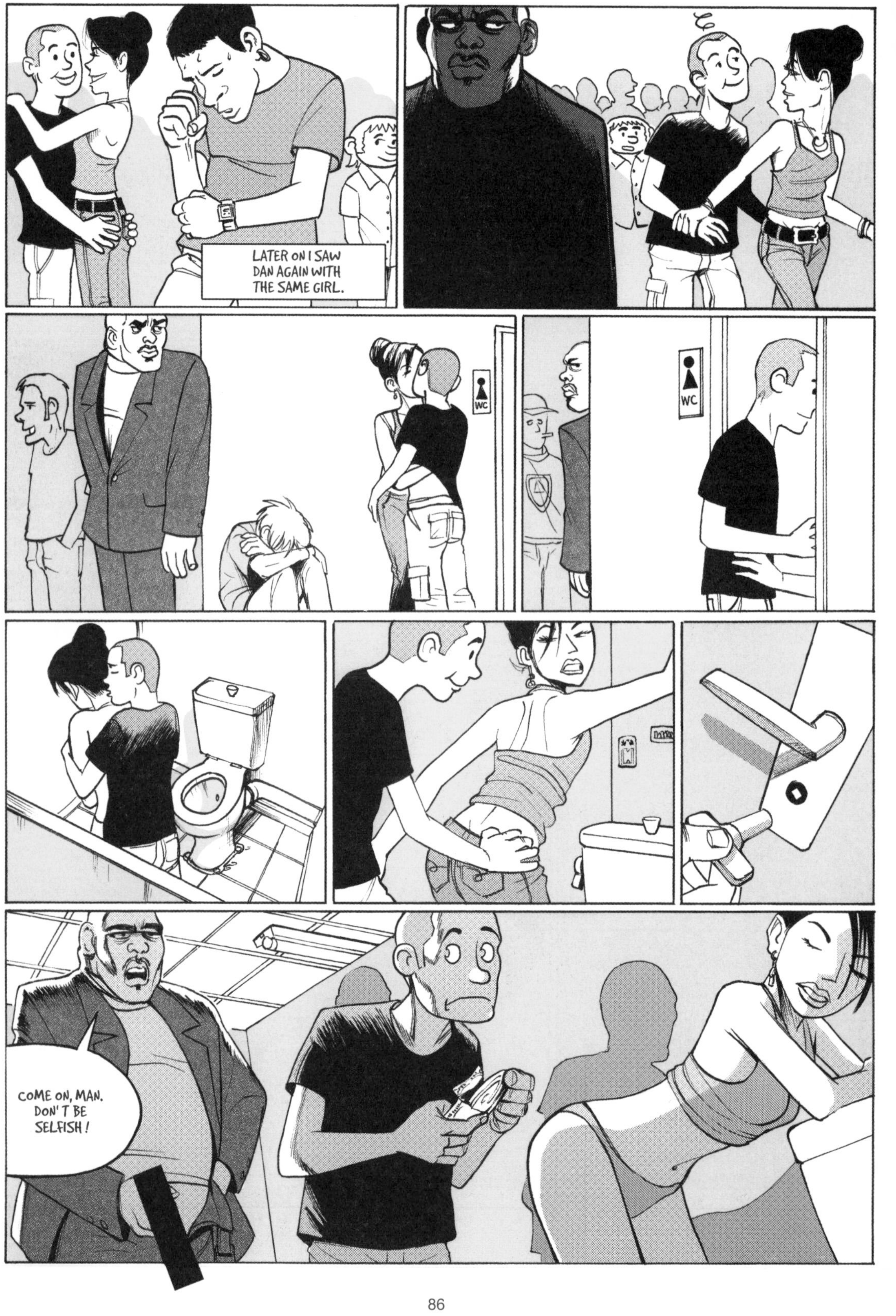
LATER ON I SAW DAN AGAIN WITH THE SAME GIRL.
WC
WC
COME ON, MAN. DON'T BE SELFISH!

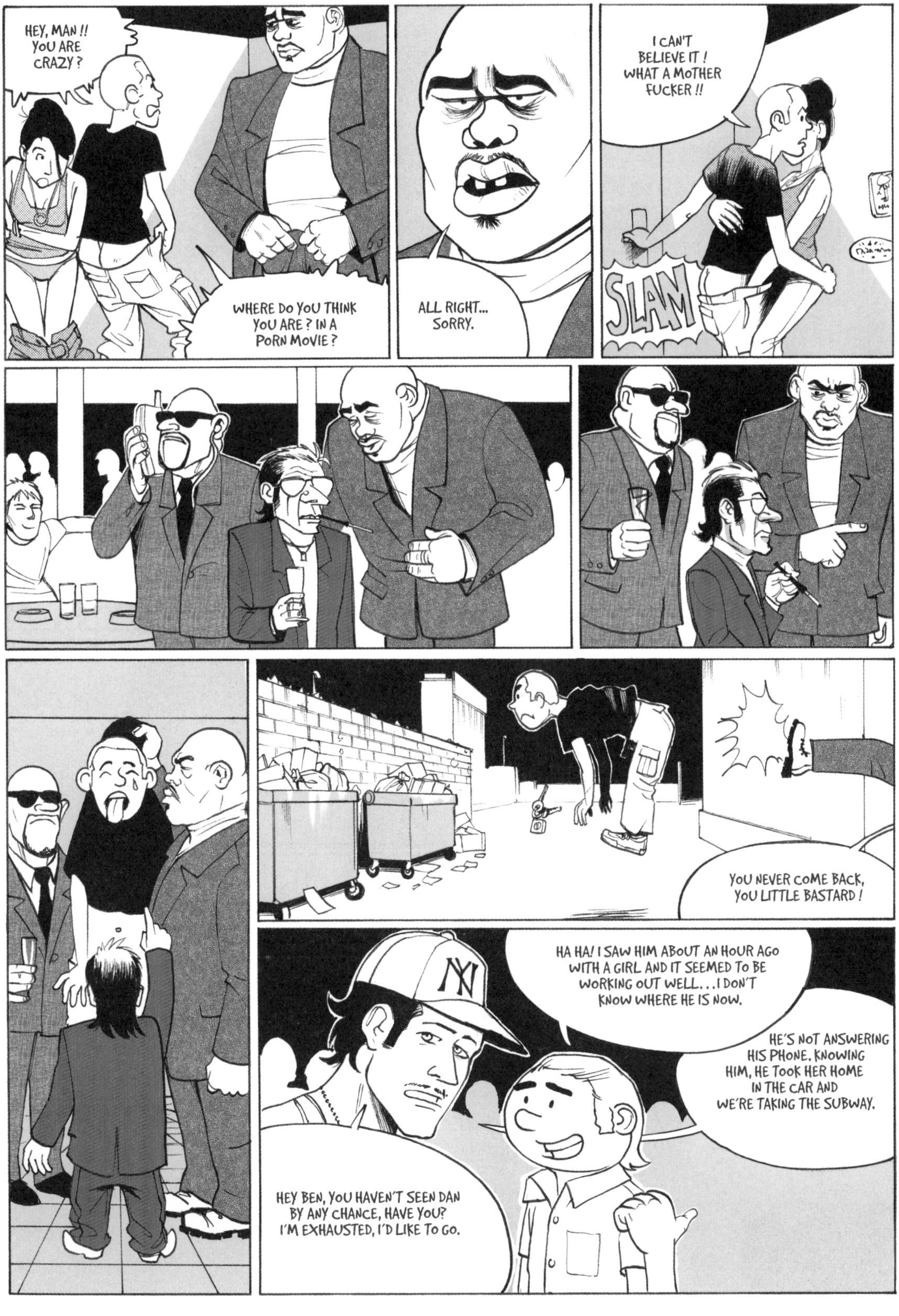
HEY, MAN !! YOU ARE CRAZY ?
WHERE DO YOU THINK YOU ARE ? IN A PORN MOVIE ?
ALL RIGHT... SORRY.
I CAN'T BELIEVE IT ! WHAT A MOTHER FUCKER !!
SLAM
YOU NEVER COME BACK, YOU LITTLE BASTARD !
HEY BEN, YOU HAVEN'T SEEN DAN BY ANY CHANCE, HAVE YOU? I'M EXHAUSTED, I'D LIKE TO GO.
HA HA! I SAW HIM ABOUT AN HOUR AGO WITH A GIRL AND IT SEEMED TO BE WORKING OUT WELL. . . I DON'T KNOW WHERE HE IS NOW.
HE'S NOT ANSWERING HIS PHONE. KNOWING HIM, HE TOOK HER HOME IN THE CAR AND WE'RE TAKING THE SUBWAY.

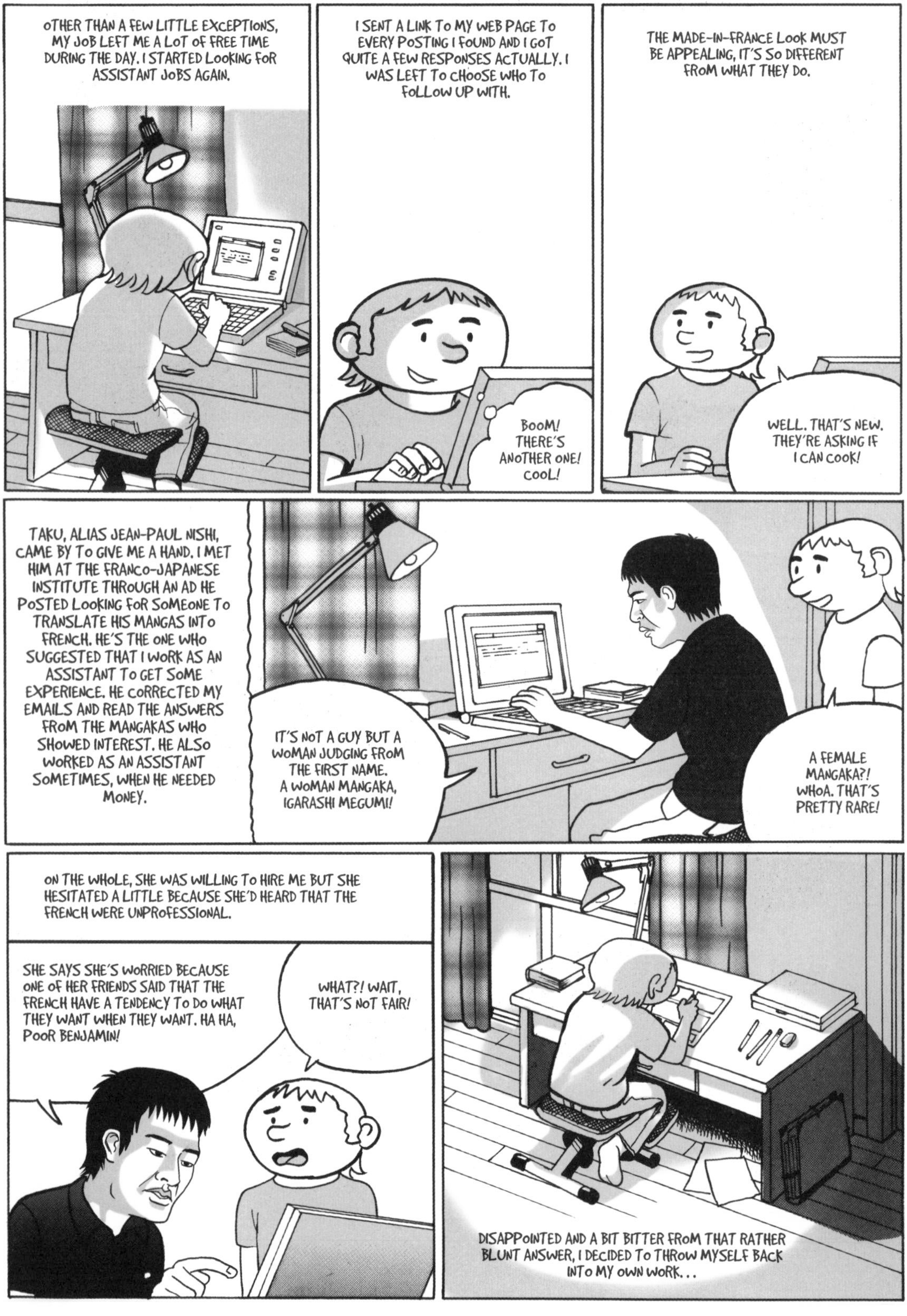
OTHER THAN A FEW LITTLE EXCEPTIONS, MY JOB LEFT ME A LOT OF FREE TIME DURING THE DAY. I STARTED LOOKING FOR ASSISTANT JOBS AGAIN.
I SENT A LINK TO MY WEB PAGE TO EVERY POSTING I FOUND AND I GOT QUITE A FEW RESPONSES ACTUALLY. I WAS LEFT TO CHOOSE WHO TO FOLLOW UP WITH.
BOOM! THERE'S ANOTHER ONE! COOL!
THE MADE-IN-FRANCE LOOK MUST BE APPEALING, IT'S SO DIFFERENT FROM WHAT THEY DO.
WELL. THAT'S NEW. THEY'RE ASKING IF I CAN COOK!
TAKU, ALIAS JEAN-PAUL NISHI, CAME BY TO GIVE ME A HAND. I MET HIM AT THE FRANCO-JAPANESE INSTITUTE THROUGH AN AD HE POSTED LOOKING FOR SOMEONE TO TRANSLATE HIS MANGAS INTO FRENCH. HE'S THE ONE WHO SUGGESTED THAT I WORK AS AN ASSISTANT TO GET SOME EXPERIENCE. HE CORRECTED MY EMAILS AND READ THE ANSWERS FROM THE MANGAKAS WHO SHOWED INTEREST. HE ALSO WORKED AS AN ASSISTANT SOMETIMES, WHEN HE NEEDED MONEY.
IT'S NOT A GUY BUT A WOMAN JUDGING FROM THE FIRST NAME. A WOMAN MANGAKA, IGARASHI MEGUMI!
A FEMALE MANGAKA?! WHOA. THAT'S PRETTY RARE!
ON THE WHOLE, SHE WAS WILLING TO HIRE ME BUT SHE HESITATED A LITTLE BECAUSE SHE'D HEARD THAT THE FRENCH WERE UNPROFESSIONAL.
SHE SAYS SHE'S WORRIED BECAUSE ONE OF HER FRIENDS SAID THAT THE FRENCH HAVE A TENDENCY TO DO WHAT THEY WANT WHEN THEY WANT. HA HA, POOR BENJAMIN!
WHAT?! WAIT, THAT'S NOT FAIR!
DISAPPOINTED AND A BIT BITTER FROM THAT RATHER BLUNT ANSWER, I DECIDED TO THROW MYSELF BACK INTO MY OWN WORK. . .

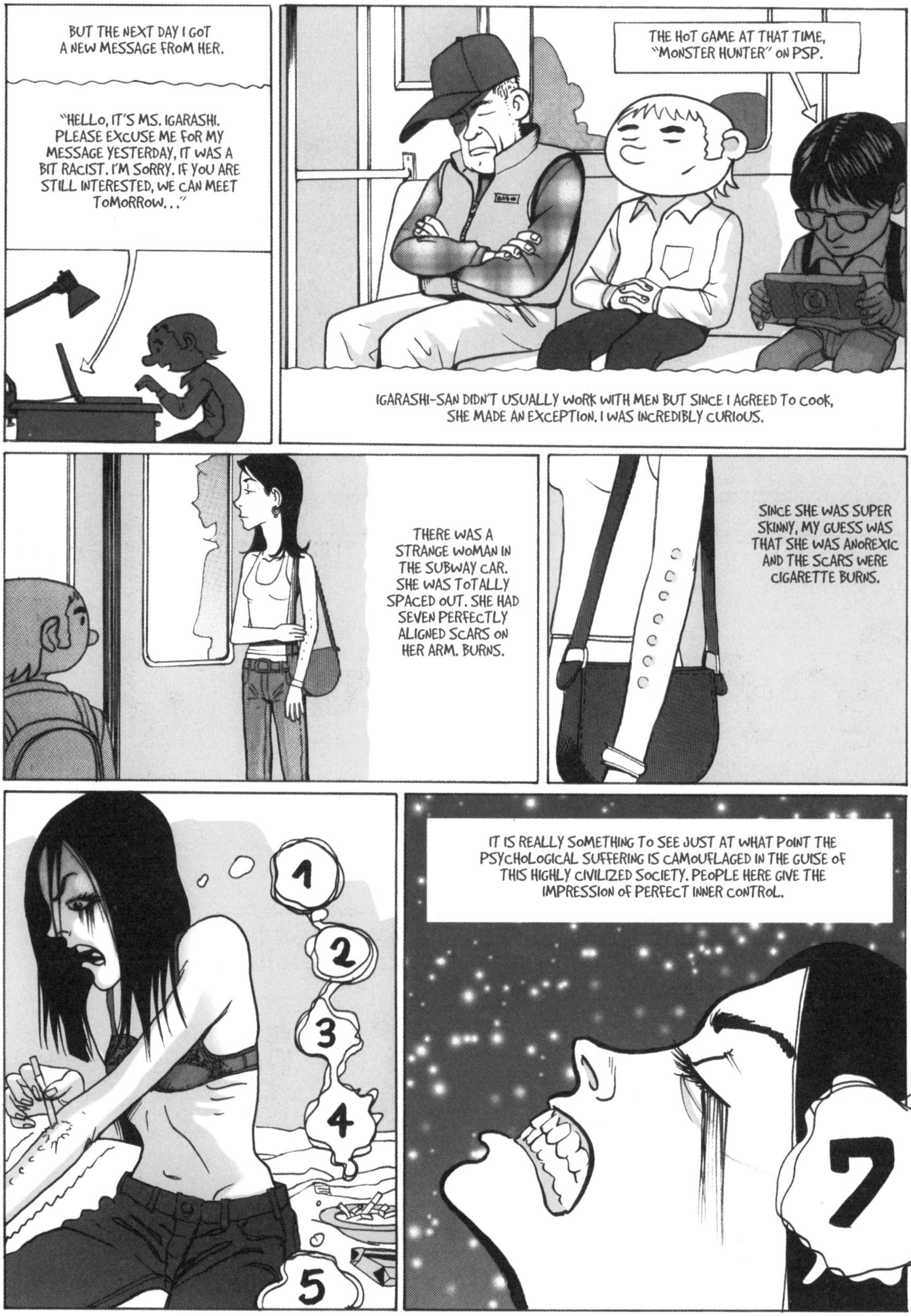

BUT THE NEXT DAY I GOT A NEW MESSAGE FROM HER.
"HELLO, IT'S MS. IGARASHI. PLEASE EXCUSE ME FOR MY MESSAGE YESTERDAY, IT WAS A BIT RACIST. I'M SORRY. IF YOU ARE STILL INTERESTED, WE CAN MEET TOMORROW..."
THE HOT GAME AT THAT TIME, "MONSTER HUNTER" ON PSP.
IGARASHI-SAN DIDN'T USUALLY WORK WITH MEN BUT SINCE I AGREED TO COOK, SHE MADE AN EXCEPTION. I WAS INCREDIBLY CURIOUS.
THERE WAS A STRANGE WOMAN IN THE SUBWAY CAR. SHE WAS TOTALLY SPACED OUT. SHE HAD SEVEN PERFECTLY ALIGNED SCARS ON HER ARM. BURNS.
SINCE SHE WAS SUPER SKINNY, MY GUESS WAS THAT SHE WAS ANOREXIC AND THE SCARS WERE CIGARETTE BURNS.
1
2
3
4
5
IT IS REALLY SOMETHING TO SEE JUST AT WHAT POINT THE PSYCHOLOGICAL SUFFERING IS CAMOUFLAGED IN THE GUISE OF THIS HIGHLY CIVILIZED SOCIETY. PEOPLE HERE GIVE THE IMPRESSION OF PERFECT INNER CONTROL.
7

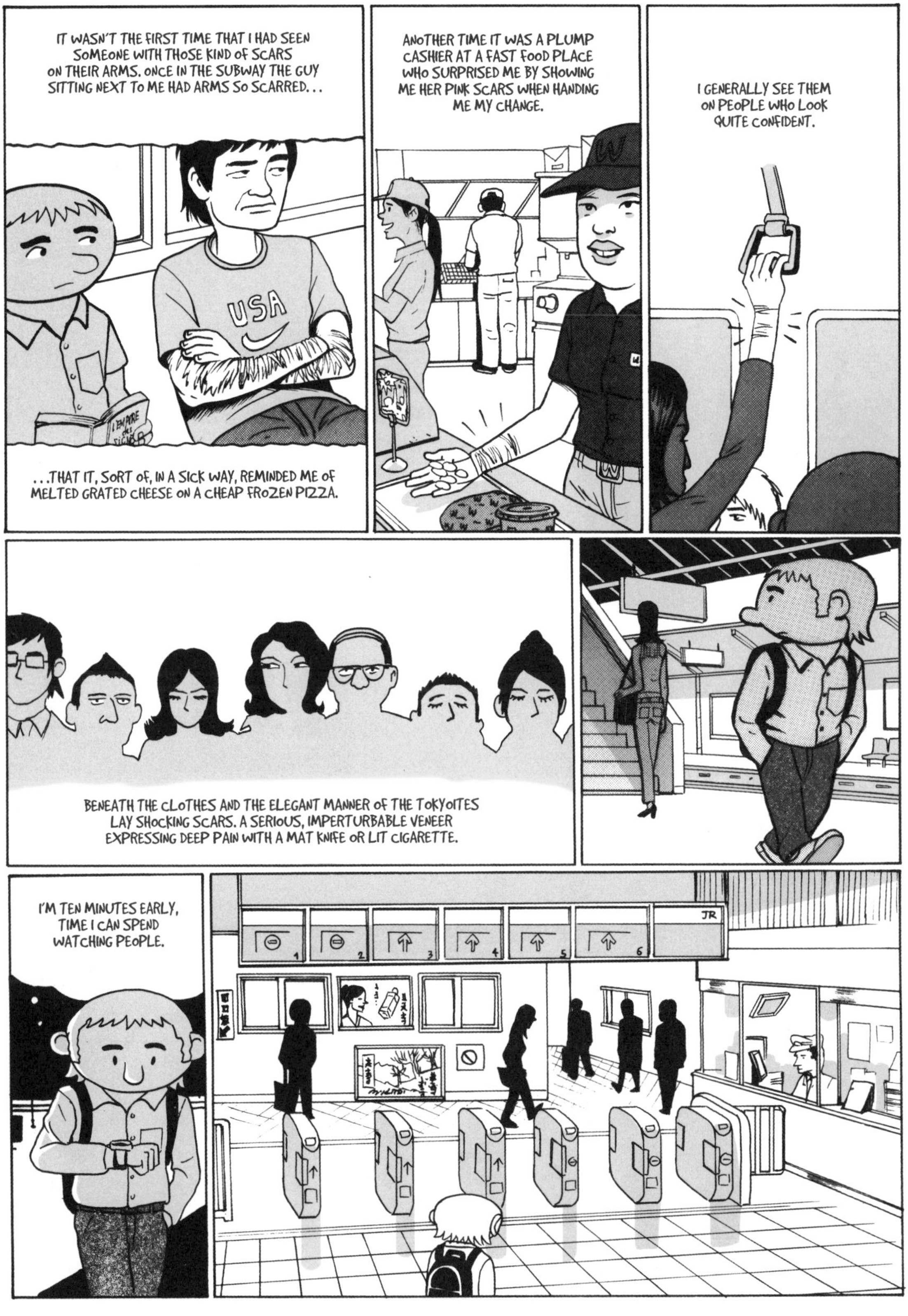
IT WASN'T THE FIRST TIME THAT I HAD SEEN SOMEONE WITH THOSE KIND OF SCARS ON THEIR ARMS. ONCE IN THE SUBWAY THE GUY SITTING NEXT TO ME HAD ARMS SO SCARRED...
USA
...THAT IT, SORT OF, IN A SICK WAY, REMINDED ME OF MELTED GRATED CHEESE ON A CHEAP FROZEN PIZZA.
ANOTHER TIME IT WAS A PLUMP CASHIER AT A FAST FOOD PLACE WHO SURPRISED ME BY SHOWING ME HER PINK SCARS WHEN HANDING ME MY CHANGE.
I GENERALLY SEE THEM ON PEOPLE WHO LOOK QUITE CONFIDENT.
BENEATH THE CLOTHES AND THE ELEGANT MANNER OF THE TOKYOITES LAY SHOCKING SCARS. A SERIOUS, IMPERTURBABLE VENEER EXPRESSING DEEP PAIN WITH A MAT KNIFE OR LIT CIGARETTE.
I'M TEN MINUTES EARLY, TIME I CAN SPEND WATCHING PEOPLE.
JR

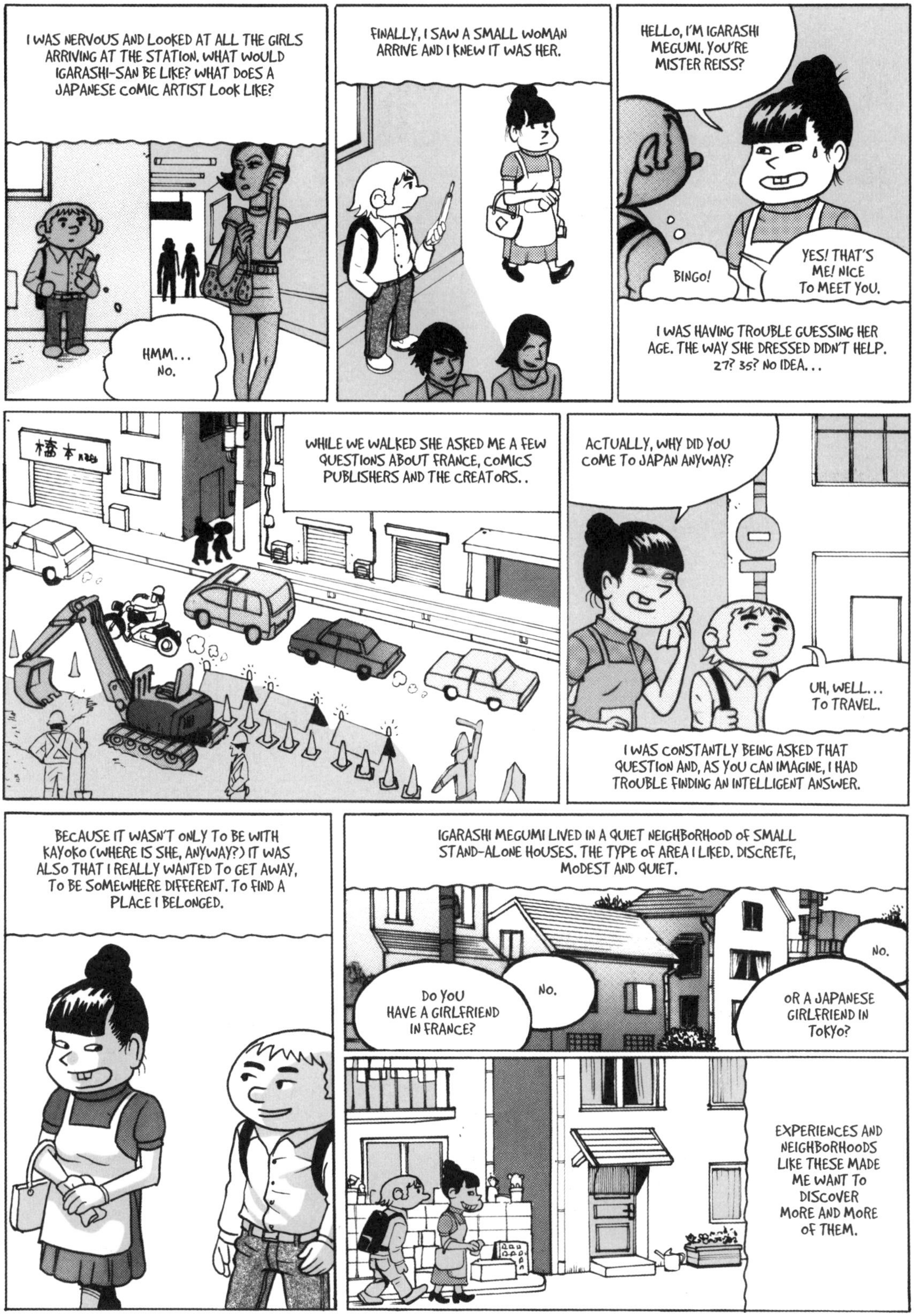
I WAS NERVOUS AND LOOKED AT ALL THE GIRLS ARRIVING AT THE STATION. WHAT WOULD IGARASHI-SAN BE LIKE? WHAT DOES A JAPANESE COMIC ARTIST LOOK LIKE?
HMM... NO.
FINALLY, I SAW A SMALL WOMAN ARRIVE AND I KNEW IT WAS HER.
HELLO, I'M IGARASHI MEGUMI. YOU'RE MISTER REISS?
BINGO!
YES! THAT'S ME! NICE TO MEET YOU.
I WAS HAVING TROUBLE GUESSING HER AGE. THE WAY SHE DRESSED DIDN'T HELP. 27? 35? NO IDEA...
橋本
WHILE WE WALKED SHE ASKED ME A FEW QUESTIONS ABOUT FRANCE, COMICS PUBLISHERS AND THE CREATORS..
ACTUALLY, WHY DID YOU COME TO JAPAN ANYWAY?
UH, WELL... TO TRAVEL.
I WAS CONSTANTLY BEING ASKED THAT QUESTION AND, AS YOU CAN IMAGINE, I HAD TROUBLE FINDING AN INTELLIGENT ANSWER.
BECAUSE IT WASN'T ONLY TO BE WITH KAYOKO (WHERE IS SHE, ANYWAY?) IT WAS ALSO THAT I REALLY WANTED TO GET AWAY, TO BE SOMEWHERE DIFFERENT. TO FIND A PLACE I BELONGED.
IGARASHI MEGUMI LIVED IN A QUIET NEIGHBORHOOD OF SMALL STAND-ALONE HOUSES. THE TYPE OF AREA I LIKED. DISCRETE, MODEST AND QUIET.
DO YOU HAVE A GIRLFRIEND IN FRANCE?
NO.
OR A JAPANESE GIRLFRIEND IN TOKYO?
NO.
EXPERIENCES AND NEIGHBORHOODS LIKE THESE MADE ME WANT TO DISCOVER MORE AND MORE OF THEM.

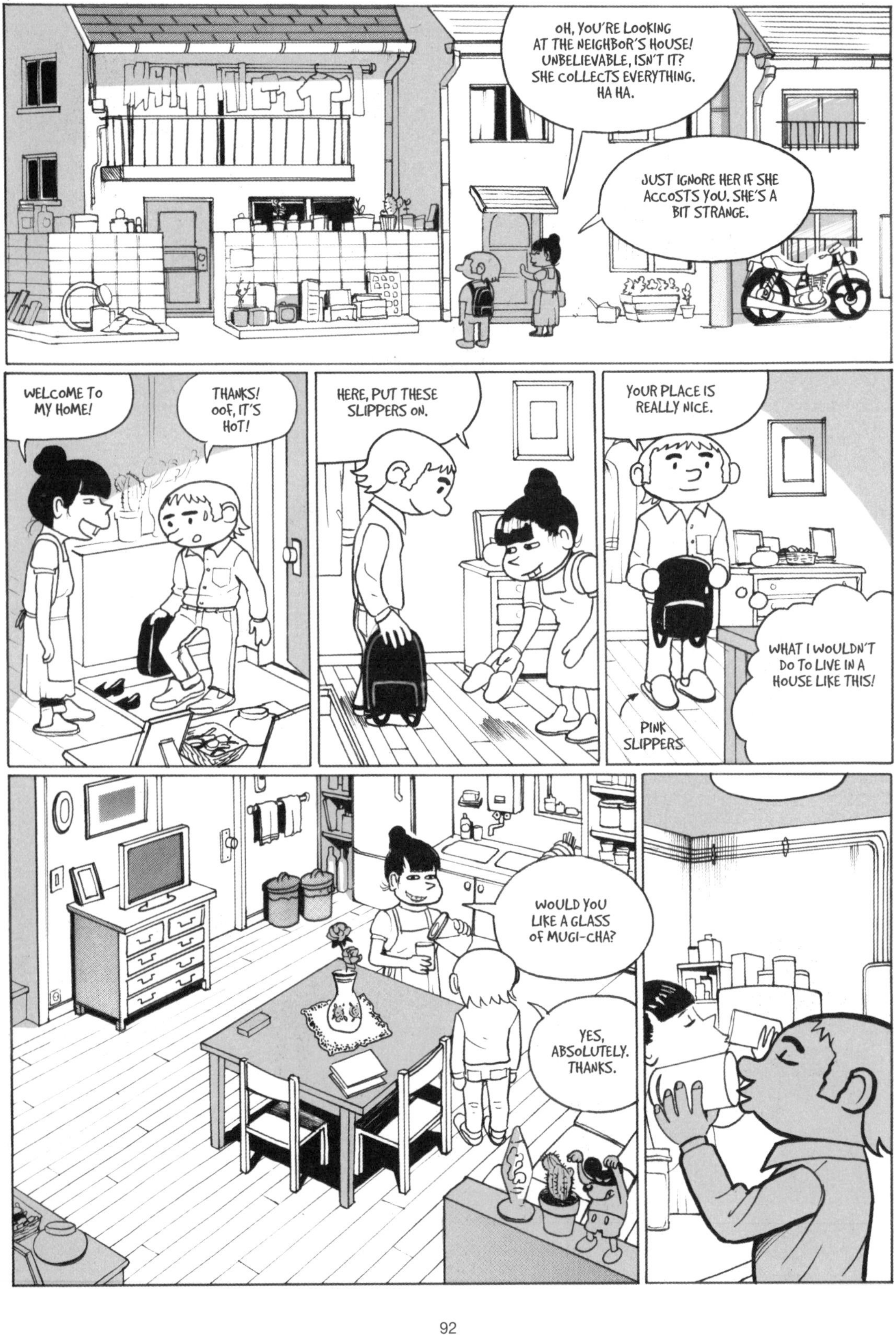
OH, YOU'RE LOOKING AT THE NEIGHBOR'S HOUSE! UNBELIEVABLE, ISN'T IT? SHE COLLECTS EVERYTHING. HA HA.
JUST IGNORE HER IF SHE ACCOSTS YOU. SHE'S A BIT STRANGE.
WELCOME TO MY HOME!
THANKS! OOF, IT'S HOT!
HERE, PUT THESE SLIPPERS ON.
YOUR PLACE IS REALLY NICE.
PINK SLIPPERS
WHAT I WOULDN'T DO TO LIVE IN A HOUSE LIKE THIS!
WOULD YOU LIKE A GLASS OF MUGI-CHA?
YES, ABSOLUTELY. THANKS.

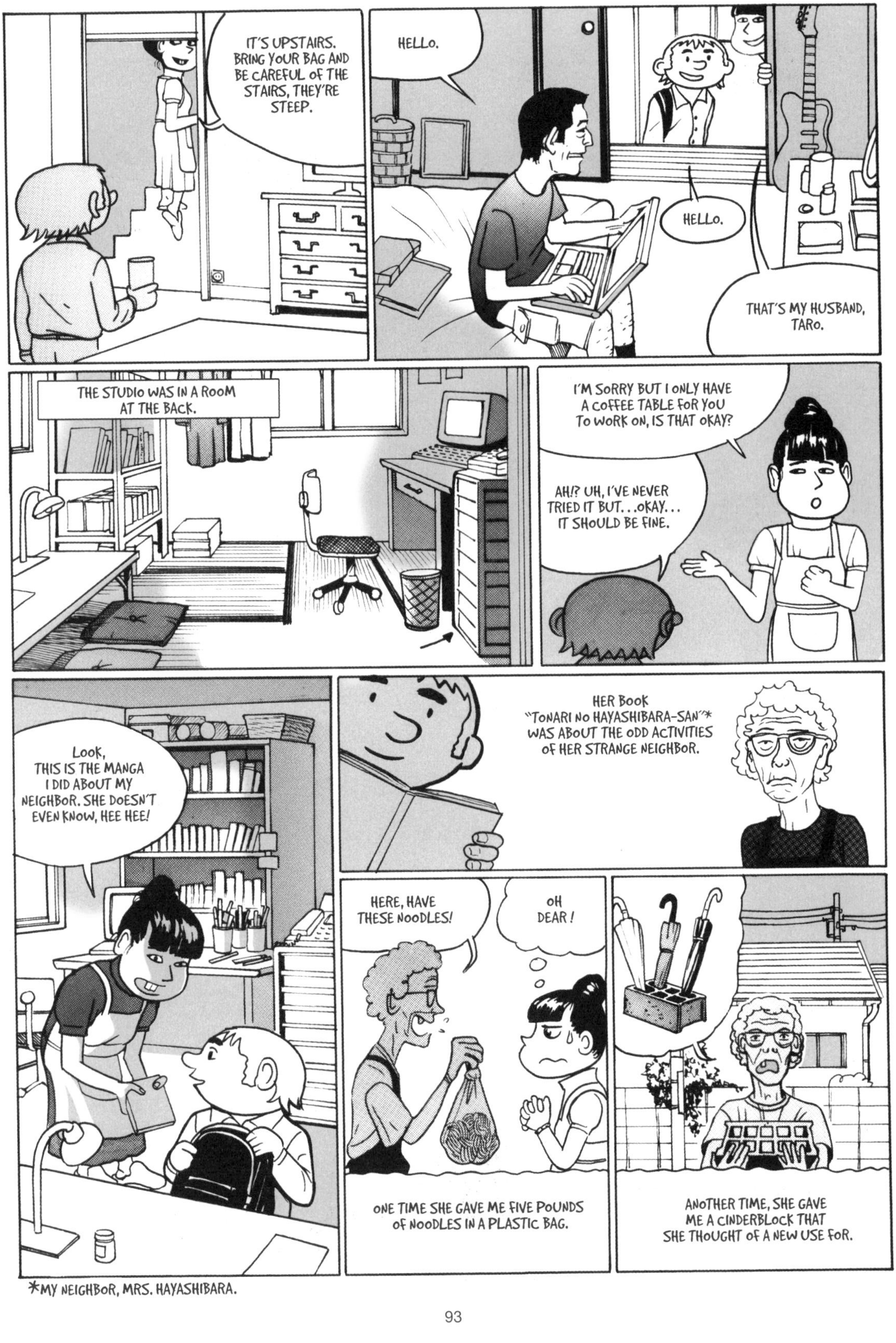
IT'S UPSTAIRS. BRING YOUR BAG AND BE CAREFUL OF THE STAIRS, THEY'RE STEEP.
HELLo.
HELLo.
THAT'S MY HUSBAND, TARo.
THE STUDIO WAS IN A RooM AT THE BACK.
I'M SORRY BUT I ONLY HAVE A COFFEE TABLE FOR YOU TO WORK ON, IS THAT OKAY?
AH!? UH, I'VE NEVER TRIED IT BUT. . .OKAY. . . IT SHOULD BE FINE.
Look, THIS IS THE MANGA I DID ABOUT MY NEIGHBOR. SHE DOESN'T EVEN KNOW, HEE HEE!
HER Book "TONARI NO HAYASHIBARA-SAN"* WAS ABOUT THE ODD ACTIVITIES OF HER STRANGE NEIGHBOR.
HERE, HAVE THESE NOODLES!
OH DEAR!
ONE TIME SHE GAVE ME FIVE POUNDS OF NOODLES IN A PLASTIC BAG.
ANOTHER TIME, SHE GAVE ME A CINDERBLOCK THAT SHE THOUGHT OF A NEW USE FOR.

*MY NEIGHBOR, MRS. HAYASHIBARA.

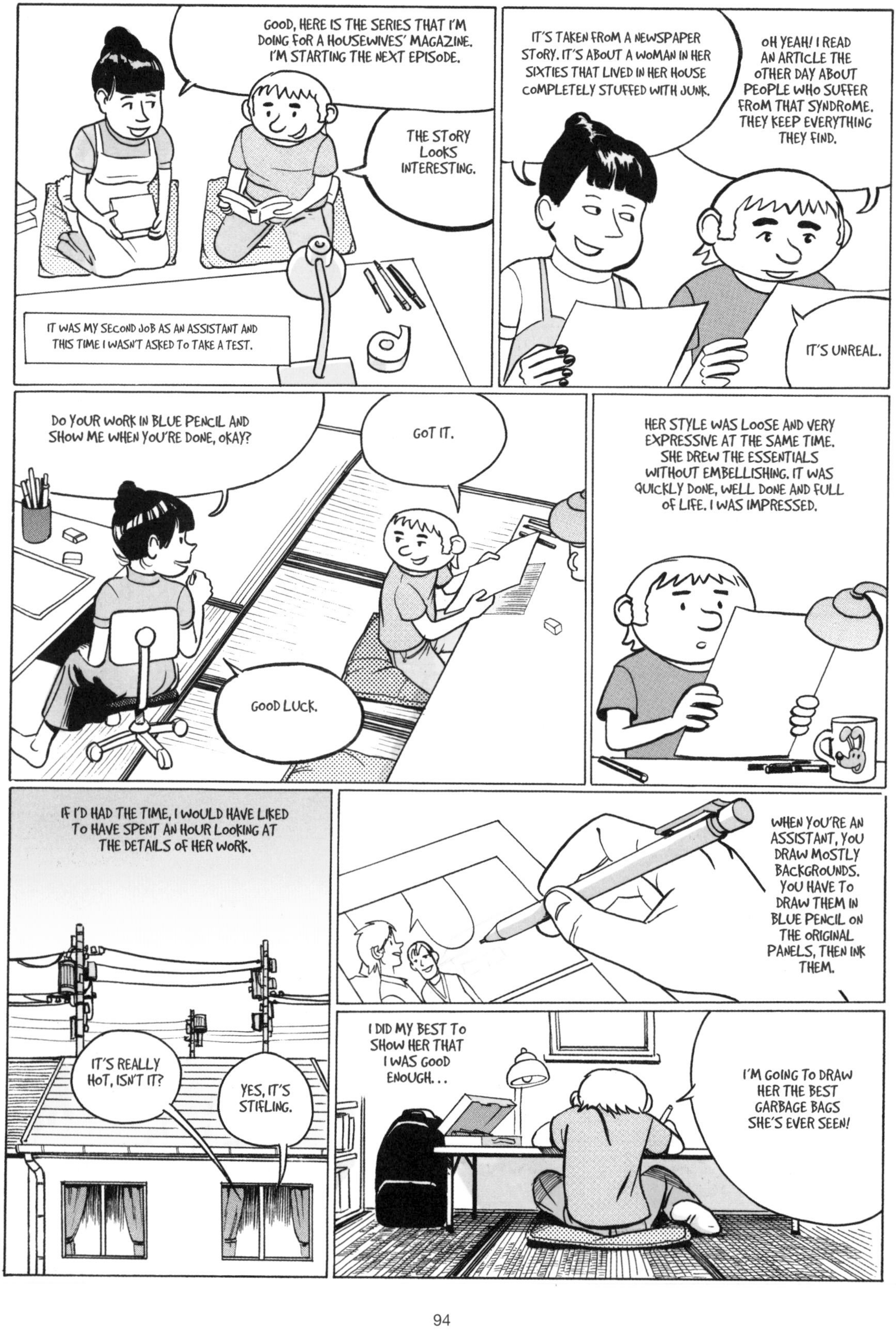
GOOD, HERE IS THE SERIES THAT I'M DOING FOR A HOUSEWIVES' MAGAZINE. I'M STARTING THE NEXT EPISODE.
THE STORY LOOKS INTERESTING.
IT WAS MY SECOND JOB AS AN ASSISTANT AND THIS TIME I WASN'T ASKED TO TAKE A TEST.
IT'S TAKEN FROM A NEWSPAPER STORY. IT'S ABOUT A WOMAN IN HER SIXTIES THAT LIVED IN HER HOUSE COMPLETELY STUFFED WITH JUNK.
OH YEAH! I READ AN ARTICLE THE OTHER DAY ABOUT PEOPLE WHO SUFFER FROM THAT SYNDROME. THEY KEEP EVERYTHING THEY FIND.
IT'S UNREAL.
DO YOUR WORK IN BLUE PENCIL AND SHOW ME WHEN YOU'RE DONE, OKAY?
GOT IT.
GOOD LUCK.
HER STYLE WAS LOOSE AND VERY EXPRESSIVE AT THE SAME TIME. SHE DREW THE ESSENTIALS WITHOUT EMBELLISHING. IT WAS QUICKLY DONE, WELL DONE AND FULL OF LIFE. I WAS IMPRESSED.
IF I'D HAD THE TIME, I WOULD HAVE LIKED TO HAVE SPENT AN HOUR LOOKING AT THE DETAILS OF HER WORK.
IT'S REALLY HOT, ISN'T IT?
YES, IT'S STIFLING.
WHEN YOU'RE AN ASSISTANT, YOU DRAW MOSTLY BACKGROUNDS. YOU HAVE TO DRAW THEM IN BLUE PENCIL ON THE ORIGINAL PANELS, THEN INK THEM.
I DID MY BEST TO SHOW HER THAT I WAS GOOD ENOUGH. . .
I'M GOING TO DRAW HER THE BEST GARBAGE BAGS SHE'S EVER SEEN!

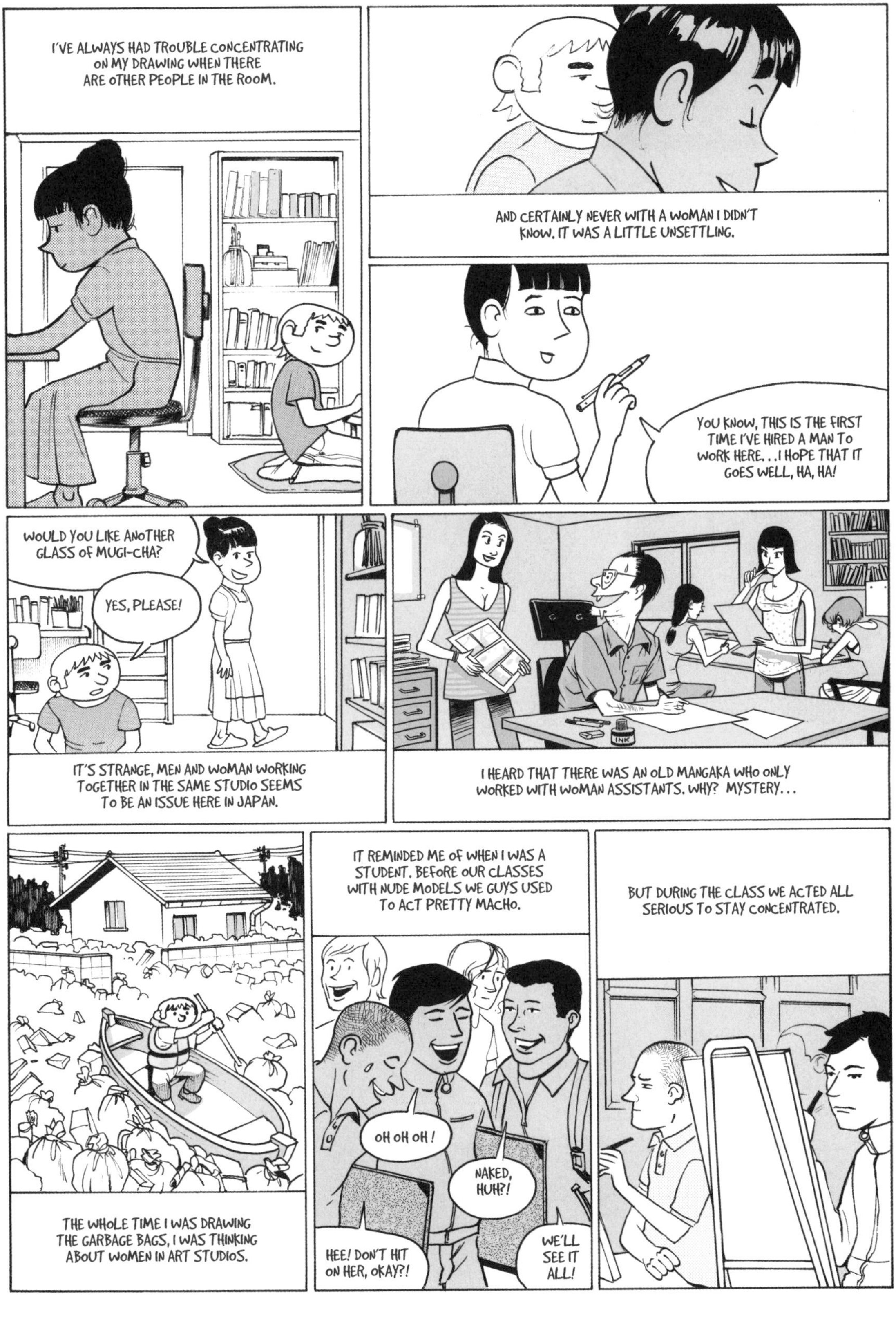
I'VE ALWAYS HAD TROUBLE CONCENTRATING ON MY DRAWING WHEN THERE ARE OTHER PEOPLE IN THE ROOM.
AND CERTAINLY NEVER WITH A WOMAN I DIDN'T KNOW. IT WAS A LITTLE UNSETTLING.
YOU KNOW, THIS IS THE FIRST TIME I'VE HIRED A MAN TO WORK HERE...I HOPE THAT IT GOES WELL, HA, HA!
WOULD YOU LIKE ANOTHER GLASS OF MUGI-CHA?
YES, PLEASE!
IT'S STRANGE, MEN AND WOMAN WORKING TOGETHER IN THE SAME STUDIO SEEMS TO BE AN ISSUE HERE IN JAPAN.
INK
I HEARD THAT THERE WAS AN OLD MANGAKA WHO ONLY WORKED WITH WOMAN ASSISTANTS. WHY? MYSTERY...
THE WHOLE TIME I WAS DRAWING THE GARBAGE BAGS, I WAS THINKING ABOUT WOMEN IN ART STUDIOS.
IT REMINDED ME OF WHEN I WAS A STUDENT. BEFORE OUR CLASSES WITH NUDE MODELS WE GUYS USED TO ACT PRETTY MACHO.
OH OH OH!
NAKED, HUH?!
HEE! DON'T HIT ON HER, OKAY?!
WE'LL SEE IT ALL!
BUT DURING THE CLASS WE ACTED ALL SERIOUS TO STAY CONCENTRATED.

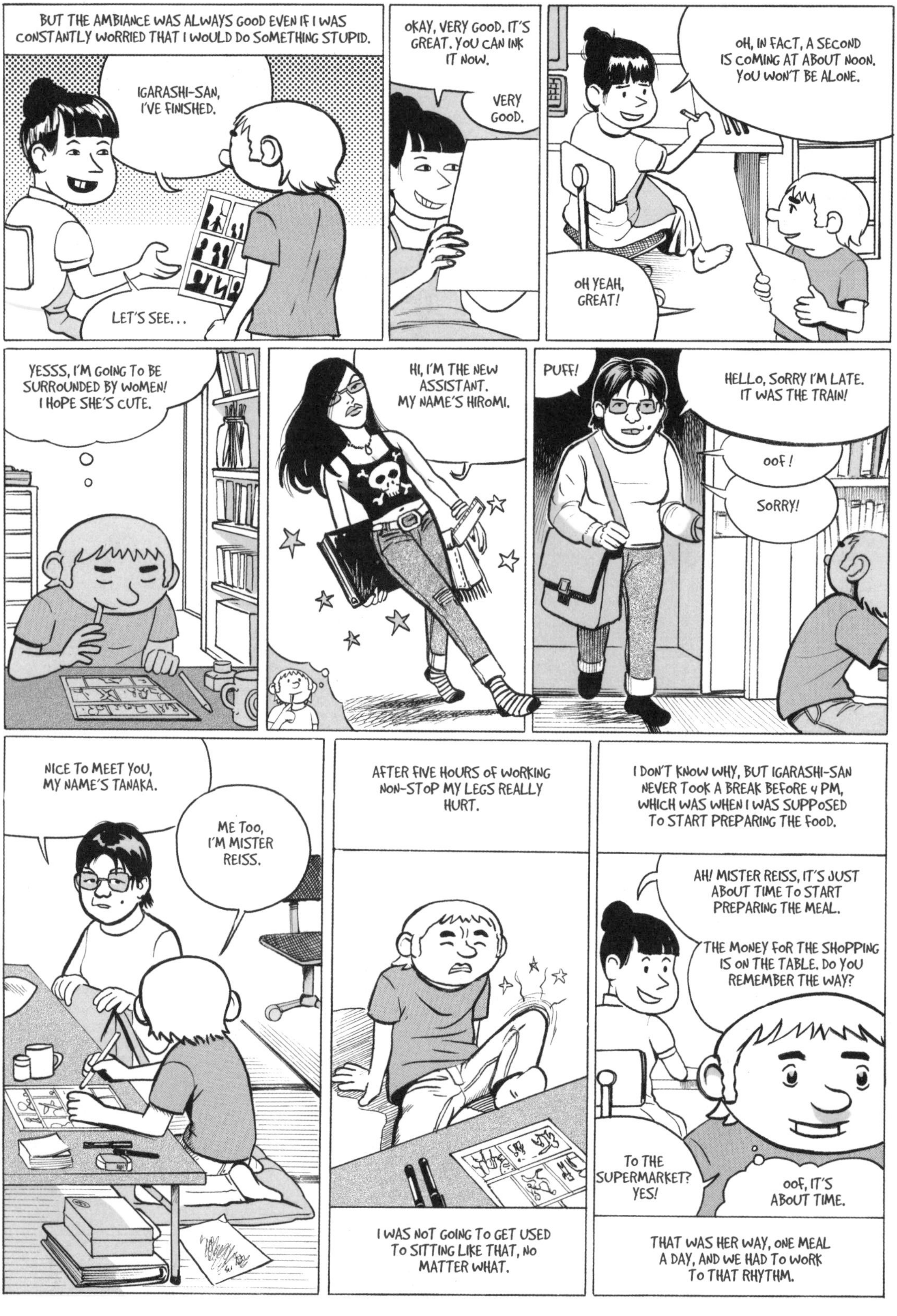

BUT THE AMBIANCE WAS ALWAYS GOOD EVEN IF I WAS CONSTANTLY WORRIED THAT I WOULD DO SOMETHING STUPID.
IGARASHI-SAN, I'VE FINISHED.
LET'S SEE...
OKAY, VERY GOOD. IT'S GREAT. YOU CAN INK IT NOW.
VERY GOOD.
OH, IN FACT, A SECOND IS COMING AT ABOUT NOON. YOU WON'T BE ALONE.
OH YEAH, GREAT!
YESSS, I'M GOING TO BE SURROUNDED BY WOMEN! I HOPE SHE'S CUTE.
HI, I'M THE NEW ASSISTANT. MY NAME'S HIROMI.
PUFF!
HELLO, SORRY I'M LATE. IT WAS THE TRAIN!
OOF!
SORRY!
NICE TO MEET YOU, MY NAME'S TANAKA.
ME TOO, I'M MISTER REISS.
AFTER FIVE HOURS OF WORKING NON-STOP MY LEGS REALLY HURT.
I WAS NOT GOING TO GET USED TO SITTING LIKE THAT, NO MATTER WHAT.
I DON'T KNOW WHY, BUT IGARASHI-SAN NEVER TOOK A BREAK BEFORE 4 PM, WHICH WAS WHEN I WAS SUPPOSED TO START PREPARING THE FOOD.
AH! MISTER REISS, IT'S JUST ABOUT TIME TO START PREPARING THE MEAL.
THE MONEY FOR THE SHOPPING IS ON THE TABLE. DO YOU REMEMBER THE WAY?
TO THE SUPERMARKET? YES!
OOF, IT'S ABOUT TIME.
THAT WAS HER WAY, ONE MEAL A DAY, AND WE HAD TO WORK TO THAT RHYTHM.

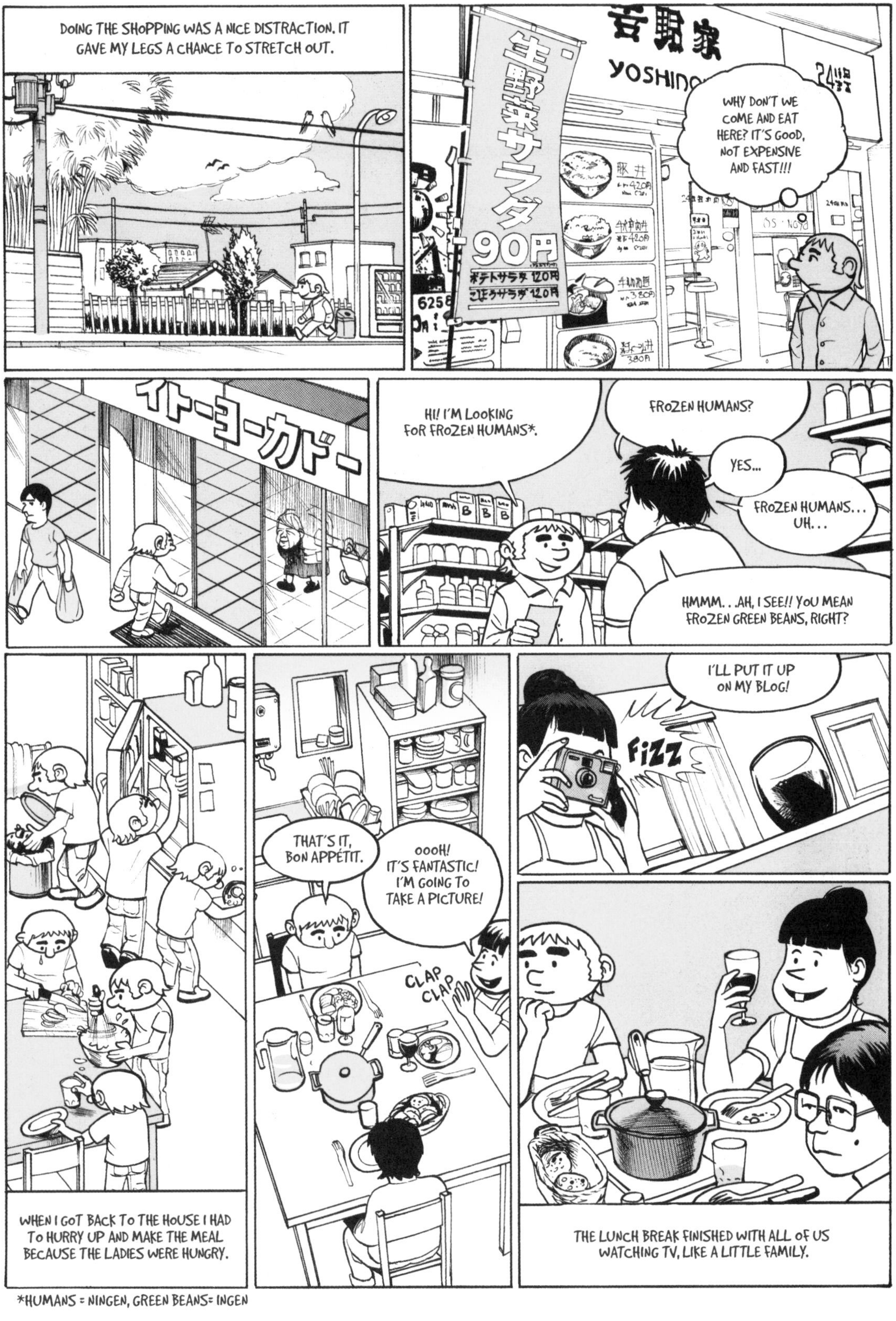
DOING THE SHOPPING WAS A NICE DISTRACTION. IT GAVE MY LEGS A CHANCE TO STRETCH OUT.
生野菜サラダ
90円
ポテトサラダ 120円
ごぼうサラダ 120円
WHY DON'T WE COME AND EAT HERE? IT'S GOOD, NOT EXPENSIVE AND FAST!!!
イトーヨーカドー
HI! I'M LOOKING FOR FROZEN HUMANS*.
FROZEN HUMANS?
YES...
FROZEN HUMANS... UH...
HMMM.. .AH, I SEE!! YOU MEAN FROZEN GREEN BEANS, RIGHT?
WHEN I GOT BACK TO THE HOUSE I HAD TO HURRY UP AND MAKE THE MEAL BECAUSE THE LADIES WERE HUNGRY.
THAT'S IT, BON APPÉTIT.
OOOH! IT'S FANTASTIC! I'M GOING TO TAKE A PICTURE!
CLAP CLAP
I'LL PUT IT UP ON MY BLOG!
FIZZ
THE LUNCH BREAK FINISHED WITH ALL OF US WATCHING TV, LIKE A LITTLE FAMILY.

*HUMANS = NINGEN, GREEN BEANS= INGEN

AFTER HAVING WORKED TOGETHER FOR 6 MONTHS, MEGUMI ANNOUNCED THAT THE SERIES HAD BEEN CANCELLED SO SHE WOULDN'T NEED ME ANYMORE. THE MAGAZINE THAT PUBLISHED IT HAD GONE BANKRUPT.

" Dear Mister Reiss,
I am very sorry but I no longer need your services for an indefinite period of time. My manga has been cancelled. . ."

TO CELEBRATE SHE TOOK ME OUT TO A OKONOMI-YAKI RESTAURANT WITH HER HUSBAND.

IGARASHI-SAN HAD QUITE AN EXPLOSIVE PERSONALITY FOR SOMEONE JAPANESE. SHE LAUGHED OUT LOUD IN THE SUBWAY.

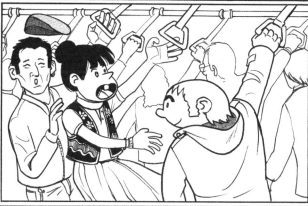

OOPS! MEGUMI WAS A BIT TIPSY!

WHEN WE SAID GOODBYE IN THE SUBWAY WE PROMISED TO GET TOGETHER AGAIN. THAT NEVER HAPPENED. PITY.

BECAUSE THAT TINY LADY HAD AN INTERESTING VIEW OF HER COUNTRY. IT CAME ACROSS THROUGH THE SUBJECTS SHE SELECTED IN HER WORK. SHE CREATED COMICAL DIORAMAS OF HER NEIGHBOR. HER MANGAS WEREN'T HER ONLY WAY OF COMMENTING ON SOCIETY'S FOIBLES.

IN JULY 2014 I READ ON THE INTERNET THAT IGARASHI SENSEI HAD GOTTEN ARRESTED FOR OBSCENITY.

HER SPECIALTY, VAGINAL REPRESENTATIVE ART. HER "CRIME", CREATING PRODUCTS IN THE FORM OF HER VULVA-LIKE VINYL FIGURINES...

...AND PHONE COVERS.

IT ALL STARTED WITH AN INTERNET CROWDFUNDING PROJECT TO RAISE MONEY FOR A KAYAK WHERE THE COCKPIT WAS MADE FROM A MOLD OF THE ARTIST. THE CAMPAIGN RAISED 1 MILLION YEN (ABOUT $8,800) AND THE BOAT WAS BUILT.

IN FACT, WHAT THE AUTHORITIES OBJECTED TO WAS THAT SHE SHARED HER 3-D IMAGES OF HER GENITALS.

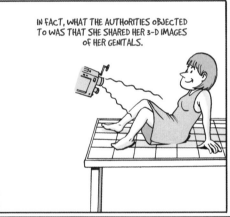

WHEN I WAS HER ASSISTANT SHE BUILT FUNNY DIORAMAS.

NOW SHE'S GOT A DIFFERENT STYLE...

IT SET OFF A CONTROVERSY IN JAPAN AROUND THE QUESTION OF FREEDOM OF EXPRESSION.

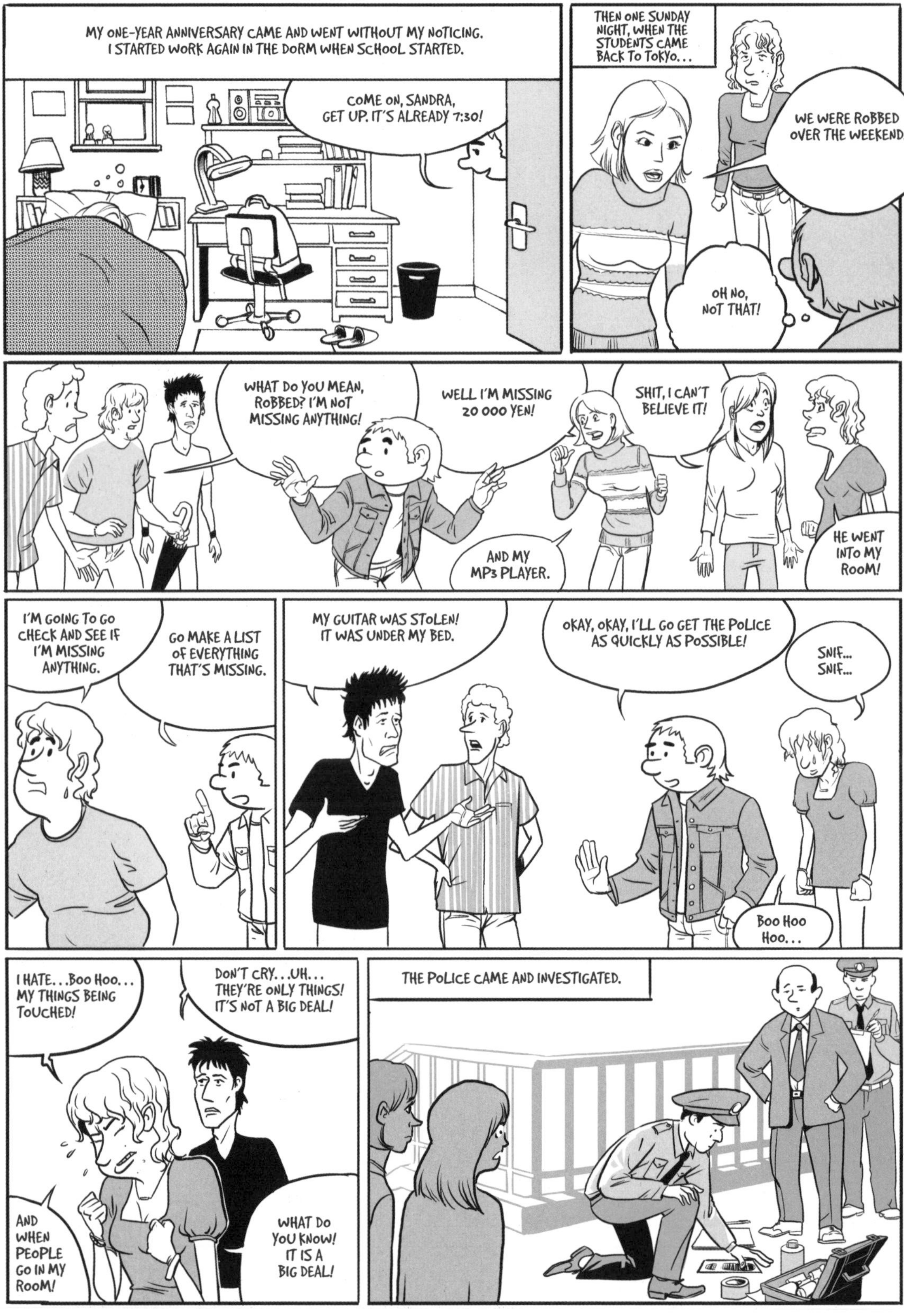
MY ONE-YEAR ANNIVERSARY CAME AND WENT WITHOUT MY NOTICING. I STARTED WORK AGAIN IN THE DORM WHEN SCHOOL STARTED.
COME ON, SANDRA, GET UP. IT'S ALREADY 7:30!
THEN ONE SUNDAY NIGHT, WHEN THE STUDENTS CAME BACK TO TOKYO...
WE WERE ROBBED OVER THE WEEKEND!
OH NO, NOT THAT!
WHAT DO YOU MEAN, ROBBED? I'M NOT MISSING ANYTHING!
WELL I'M MISSING 20 000 YEN!
AND MY MP3 PLAYER.
SHIT, I CAN'T BELIEVE IT!
HE WENT INTO MY ROOM!
I'M GOING TO GO CHECK AND SEE IF I'M MISSING ANYTHING.
GO MAKE A LIST OF EVERYTHING THAT'S MISSING.
MY GUITAR WAS STOLEN! IT WAS UNDER MY BED.
OKAY, OKAY, I'LL GO GET THE POLICE AS QUICKLY AS POSSIBLE!
SNIF... SNIF...
BOO HOO HOO...
I HATE...BOO HOO... MY THINGS BEING TOUCHED!
DON'T CRY...UH... THEY'RE ONLY THINGS! IT'S NOT A BIG DEAL!
AND WHEN PEOPLE GO IN MY ROOM!
WHAT DO YOU KNOW! IT IS A BIG DEAL!
THE POLICE CAME AND INVESTIGATED.

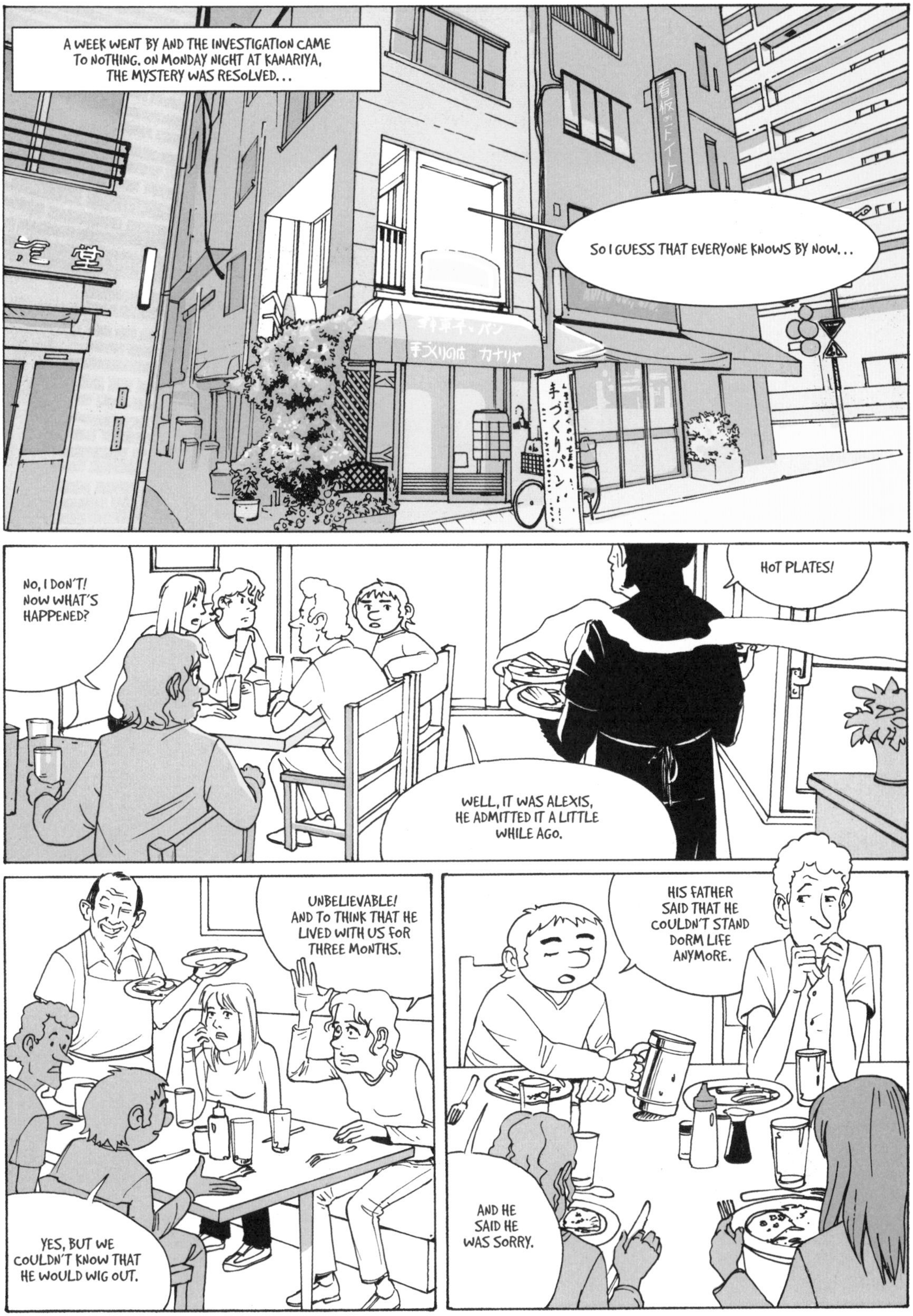
A WEEK WENT BY AND THE INVESTIGATION CAME TO NOTHING. ON MONDAY NIGHT AT KANARIYA, THE MYSTERY WAS RESOLVED...
手づくりの店 カナリヤ
SO I GUESS THAT EVERYONE KNOWS BY NOW...
NO, I DON'T! NOW WHAT'S HAPPENED?
HOT PLATES!
WELL, IT WAS ALEXIS, HE ADMITTED IT A LITTLE WHILE AGO.
UNBELIEVABLE! AND TO THINK THAT HE LIVED WITH US FOR THREE MONTHS.
YES, BUT WE COULDN'T KNOW THAT HE WOULD WIG OUT.
HIS FATHER SAID THAT HE COULDN'T STAND DORM LIFE ANYMORE.
AND HE SAID HE WAS SORRY.

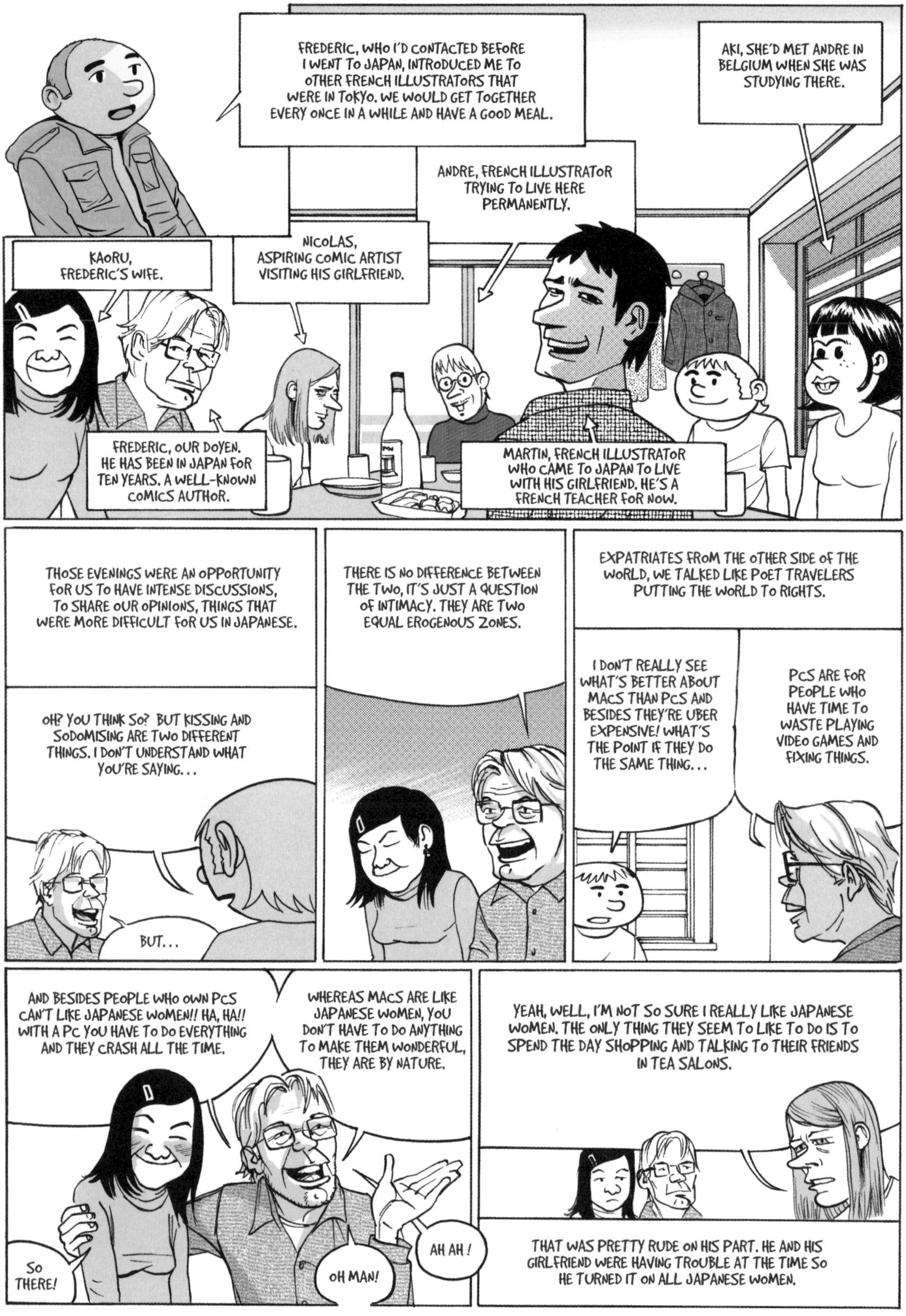
FREDERIC, WHO I'D CONTACTED BEFORE I WENT TO JAPAN, INTRODUCED ME TO OTHER FRENCH ILLUSTRATORS THAT WERE IN TOKYO. WE WOULD GET TOGETHER EVERY ONCE IN A WHILE AND HAVE A GOOD MEAL.
ANDRE, FRENCH ILLUSTRATOR TRYING TO LIVE HERE PERMANENTLY.
AKI, SHE'D MET ANDRE IN BELGIUM WHEN SHE WAS STUDYING THERE.
KAORU, FREDERIC'S WIFE.
NICOLAS, ASPIRING COMIC ARTIST VISITING HIS GIRLFRIEND.
FREDERIC, OUR DOYEN. HE HAS BEEN IN JAPAN FOR TEN YEARS. A WELL-KNOWN COMICS AUTHOR.
MARTIN, FRENCH ILLUSTRATOR WHO CAME TO JAPAN TO LIVE WITH HIS GIRLFRIEND. HE'S A FRENCH TEACHER FOR NOW.
THOSE EVENINGS WERE AN OPPORTUNITY FOR US TO HAVE INTENSE DISCUSSIONS, TO SHARE OUR OPINIONS, THINGS THAT WERE MORE DIFFICULT FOR US IN JAPANESE.
OH? YOU THINK SO? BUT KISSING AND SODOMISING ARE TWO DIFFERENT THINGS. I DON'T UNDERSTAND WHAT YOU'RE SAYING...
BUT...
THERE IS NO DIFFERENCE BETWEEN THE TWO, IT'S JUST A QUESTION OF INTIMACY. THEY ARE TWO EQUAL EROGENOUS ZONES.
EXPATRIATES FROM THE OTHER SIDE OF THE WORLD, WE TALKED LIKE POET TRAVELERS PUTTING THE WORLD TO RIGHTS.
I DON'T REALLY SEE WHAT'S BETTER ABOUT MACS THAN PCS AND BESIDES THEY'RE UBER EXPENSIVE! WHAT'S THE POINT IF THEY DO THE SAME THING...
PCS ARE FOR PEOPLE WHO HAVE TIME TO WASTE PLAYING VIDEO GAMES AND FIXING THINGS.
AND BESIDES PEOPLE WHO OWN PCS CAN'T LIKE JAPANESE WOMEN!! HA, HA!! WITH A PC YOU HAVE TO DO EVERYTHING AND THEY CRASH ALL THE TIME.
WHEREAS MACS ARE LIKE JAPANESE WOMEN, YOU DON'T HAVE TO DO ANYTHING TO MAKE THEM WONDERFUL, THEY ARE BY NATURE.
SO THERE!
OH MAN!
AH AH !
YEAH, WELL, I'M NOT SO SURE I REALLY LIKE JAPANESE WOMEN. THE ONLY THING THEY SEEM TO LIKE TO DO IS TO SPEND THE DAY SHOPPING AND TALKING TO THEIR FRIENDS IN TEA SALONS.
THAT WAS PRETTY RUDE ON HIS PART. HE AND HIS GIRLFRIEND WERE HAVING TROUBLE AT THE TIME SO HE TURNED IT ON ALL JAPANESE WOMEN.

HMM.

HEEEY, EASY, MAN, WE'RE KIDDING AROUND HERE! IT'LL WORK OUT BETWEEN THE TWO OF YOU! HAVE SOME MORE TEA.

UH, LOOK, AKIA FOUND A MANGA CONTEST IN THIS MAGAZINE CALLED IKKI.

WE HAVE TO ENTER!

THE WINNER WILL BE PUBLISHED WEEKLY IN THE MAGAZINE FOR A YEAR. I'LL MAKE COPIES OF THE REGISTRATION FORM.

OH YEAH, I'D LIKE TO. WE HAVE TO TRY, GUYS!

HOWEVER, THE DEADLINE'S IN A MONTH.

HEY, BENJAMIN, WITH YOUR ASSISTANT WORK, DO YOU HAVE ANY CONTACTS AT PUBLISHING COMPANIES?

NO, NOT ESPECIALLY...

I COULD EVENTUALLY SUBMIT SOME PAGES TO ONE PUBLISHER BUT I DON'T REALLY HAVE ANYTHING SERIOUS TO SHOW THEM RIGHT NOW. WELL, NOTHING IN BLACK AND WHITE...

WELL, WHEN YOU HAVE SOMETHING A BIT MORE DEVELOPED, I'D LIKE TO SEE IT!

UH...ME TOO...I DON'T HAVE A LOT TO SHOW ANYONE EITHER.

WITH MY TEACHING JOB, I DON'T HAVE A LOT OF TIME LEFT TO DRAW.

IN FACT, I'D LIKE TO GET OUT SLOWLY. FIRST GO PART-TIME, THEN RESIGN AND THEN SPEND ALL MY TIME DRAWING.

WE COULD START BY CREATING SOME T-SHIRTS AND POSTCARDS.

CD COVERS AND FLYERS.

YEAH, OKAY, BUT I'M MORE INTERESTED IN THE CONTEST!

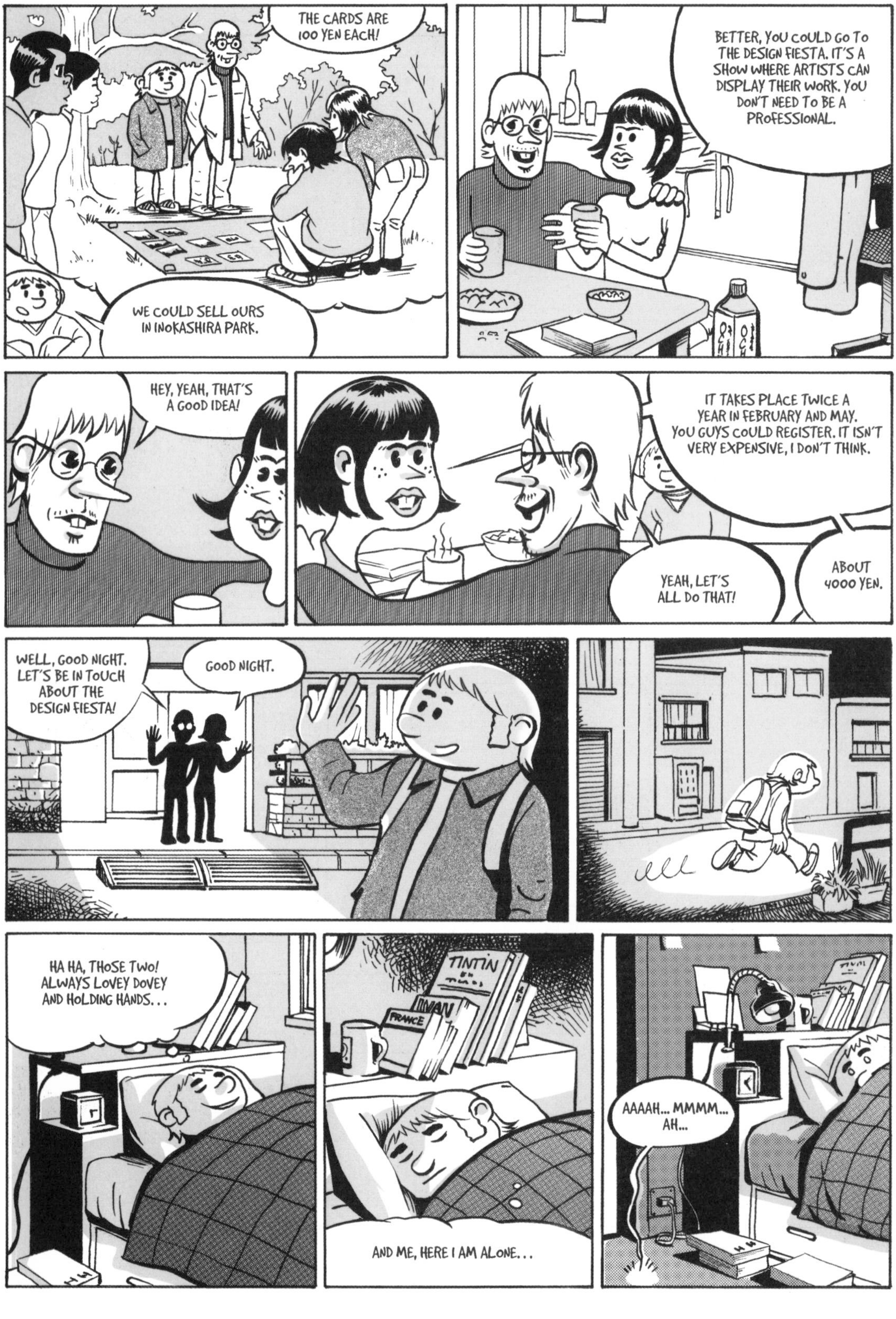
THE CARDS ARE 100 YEN EACH!
WE COULD SELL OURS IN INOKASHIRA PARK.
BETTER, YOU COULD GO TO THE DESIGN FIESTA. IT'S A SHOW WHERE ARTISTS CAN DISPLAY THEIR WORK. YOU DON'T NEED TO BE A PROFESSIONAL.
HEY, YEAH, THAT'S A GOOD IDEA!
IT TAKES PLACE TWICE A YEAR IN FEBRUARY AND MAY. YOU GUYS COULD REGISTER. IT ISN'T VERY EXPENSIVE, I DON'T THINK.
YEAH, LET'S ALL DO THAT!
ABOUT 4000 YEN.
WELL, GOOD NIGHT. LET'S BE IN TOUCH ABOUT THE DESIGN FIESTA!
GOOD NIGHT.
HA HA, THOSE TWO! ALWAYS LOVEY DOVEY AND HOLDING HANDS...
TINTIN
FRANCE
AND ME, HERE I AM ALONE...
AAAAH... MMMM... AH...

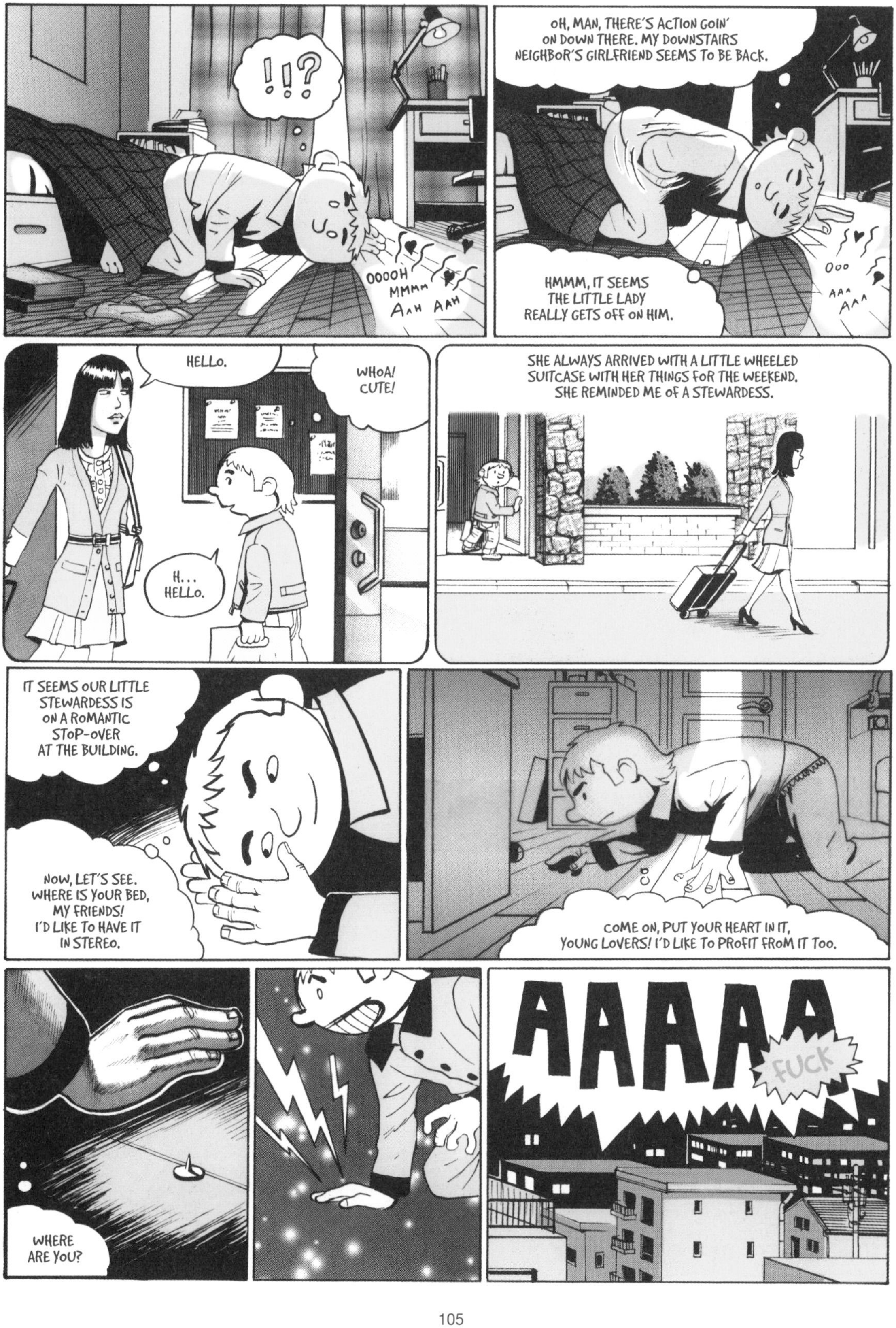
!!?
OOOOH
MMMM
AAH AAH
OH, MAN, THERE'S ACTION GOIN' ON DOWN THERE. MY DOWNSTAIRS NEIGHBOR'S GIRLFRIEND SEEMS TO BE BACK.
HMMM, IT SEEMS THE LITTLE LADY REALLY GETS OFF ON HIM.
OOO
AAA
AAA
HELLO.
WHOA! CUTE!
H... HELLO.
SHE ALWAYS ARRIVED WITH A LITTLE WHEELED SUITCASE WITH HER THINGS FOR THE WEEKEND. SHE REMINDED ME OF A STEWARDESS.
IT SEEMS OUR LITTLE STEWARDESS IS ON A ROMANTIC STOP-OVER AT THE BUILDING.
NOW, LET'S SEE. WHERE IS YOUR BED, MY FRIENDS! I'D LIKE TO HAVE IT IN STEREO.
COME ON, PUT YOUR HEART IN IT, YOUNG LOVERS! I'D LIKE TO PROFIT FROM IT TOO.
WHERE ARE YOU?
AAAAA
FUCK

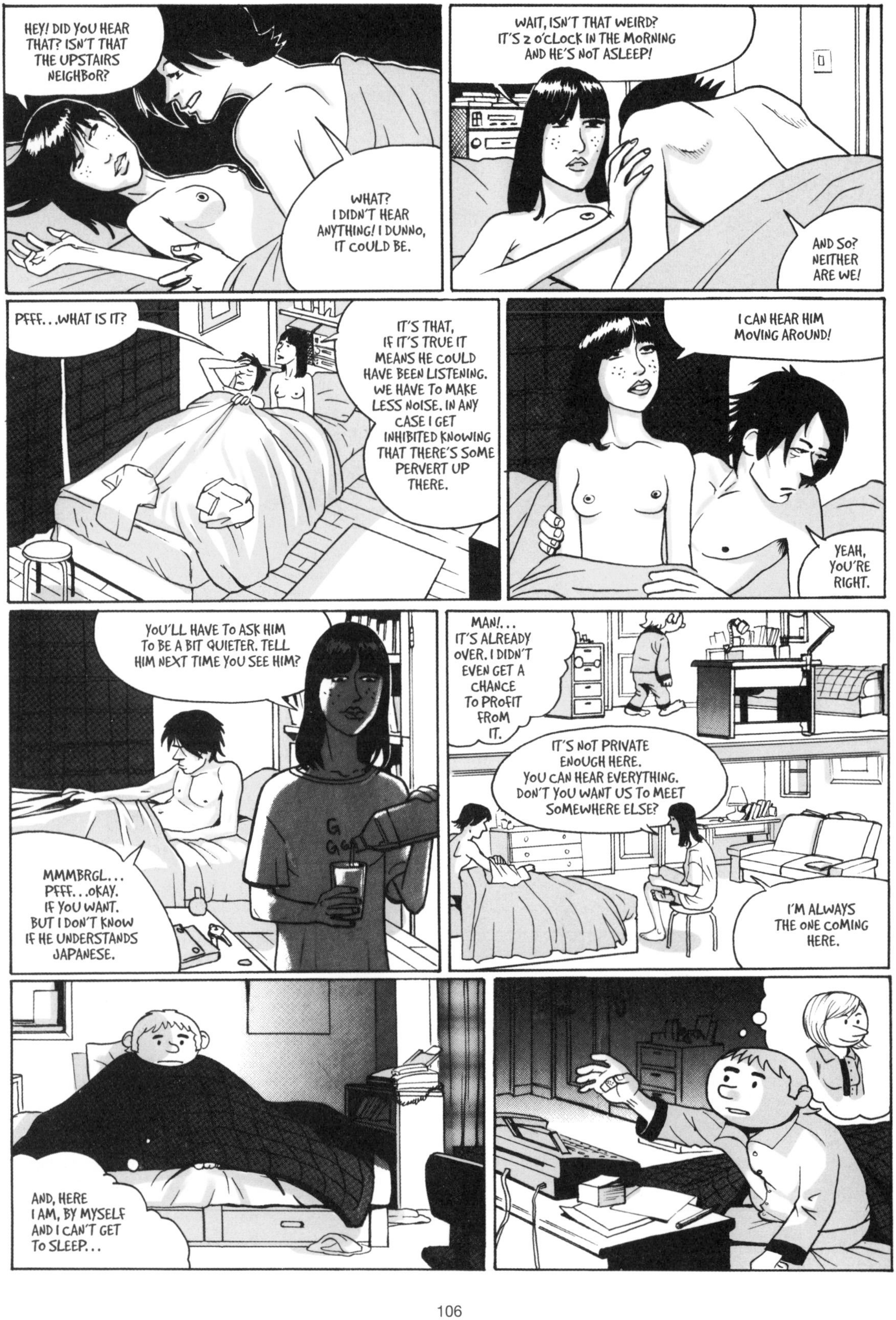

HEY! DID YOU HEAR THAT? ISN'T THAT THE UPSTAIRS NEIGHBOR?
WHAT? I DIDN'T HEAR ANYTHING! I DUNNO, IT COULD BE.
WAIT, ISN'T THAT WEIRD? IT'S 2 O'CLOCK IN THE MORNING AND HE'S NOT ASLEEP!
AND SO? NEITHER ARE WE!
PFFF... WHAT IS IT?
IT'S THAT, IF IT'S TRUE IT MEANS HE COULD HAVE BEEN LISTENING. WE HAVE TO MAKE LESS NOISE. IN ANY CASE I GET INHIBITED KNOWING THAT THERE'S SOME PERVERT UP THERE.
I CAN HEAR HIM MOVING AROUND!
YEAH, YOU'RE RIGHT.
YOU'LL HAVE TO ASK HIM TO BE A BIT QUIETER. TELL HIM NEXT TIME YOU SEE HIM?
MMMBRGL... PFFF... OKAY. IF YOU WANT. BUT I DON'T KNOW IF HE UNDERSTANDS JAPANESE.
MAN!... IT'S ALREADY OVER. I DIDN'T EVEN GET A CHANCE TO PROFIT FROM IT.
IT'S NOT PRIVATE ENOUGH HERE. YOU CAN HEAR EVERYTHING. DON'T YOU WANT US TO MEET SOMEWHERE ELSE?
I'M ALWAYS THE ONE COMING HERE.
AND, HERE I AM, BY MYSELF AND I CAN'T GET TO SLEEP...

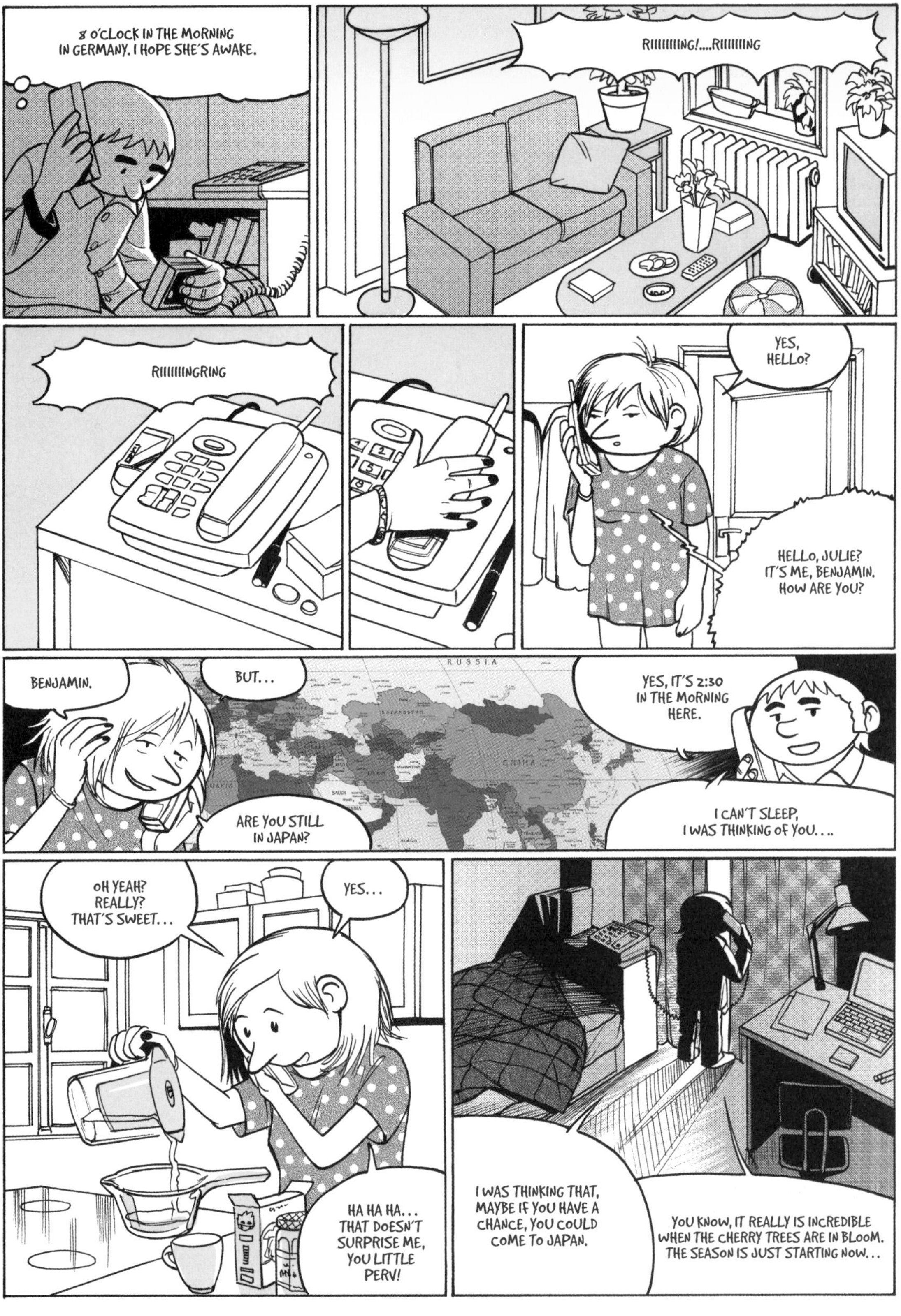
8 O'CLOCK IN THE MORNING IN GERMANY. I HOPE SHE'S AWAKE.
RIIIIIIING!....RIIIIIING
RIIIIIIINGRING
YES, HELLO?
HELLO, JULIE? IT'S ME, BENJAMIN. HOW ARE YOU?
BENJAMIN.
BUT...
ARE YOU STILL IN JAPAN?
YES, IT'S 2:30 IN THE MORNING HERE.
I CAN'T SLEEP, I WAS THINKING OF YOU....
OH YEAH? REALLY? THAT'S SWEET...
YES...
HA HA HA... THAT DOESN'T SURPRISE ME, YOU LITTLE PERV!
I WAS THINKING THAT, MAYBE IF YOU HAVE A CHANCE, YOU COULD COME TO JAPAN.
YOU KNOW, IT REALLY IS INCREDIBLE WHEN THE CHERRY TREES ARE IN BLOOM. THE SEASON IS JUST STARTING NOW...

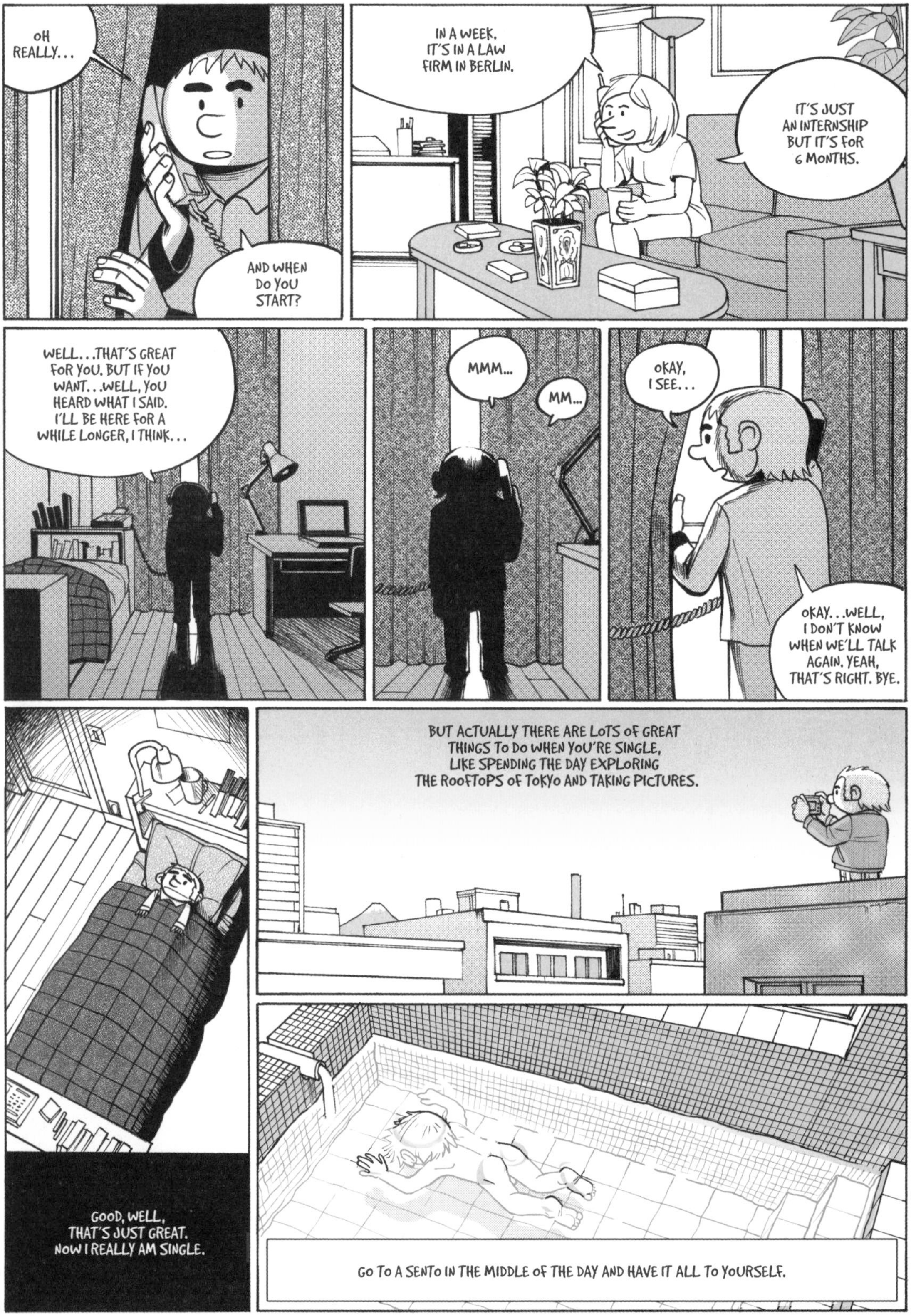
OH REALLY...
AND WHEN DO YOU START?
IN A WEEK. IT'S IN A LAW FIRM IN BERLIN.
IT'S JUST AN INTERNSHIP BUT IT'S FOR 6 MONTHS.
WELL...THAT'S GREAT FOR YOU. BUT IF YOU WANT...WELL, YOU HEARD WHAT I SAID. I'LL BE HERE FOR A WHILE LONGER, I THINK...
MMM...
MM...
OKAY, I SEE...
OKAY...WELL, I DON'T KNOW WHEN WE'LL TALK AGAIN. YEAH, THAT'S RIGHT. BYE.
GOOD, WELL, THAT'S JUST GREAT. NOW I REALLY AM SINGLE.
BUT ACTUALLY THERE ARE LOTS OF GREAT THINGS TO DO WHEN YOU'RE SINGLE, LIKE SPENDING THE DAY EXPLORING THE ROOFTOPS OF TOKYO AND TAKING PICTURES.
GO TO A SENTO IN THE MIDDLE OF THE DAY AND HAVE IT ALL TO YOURSELF.

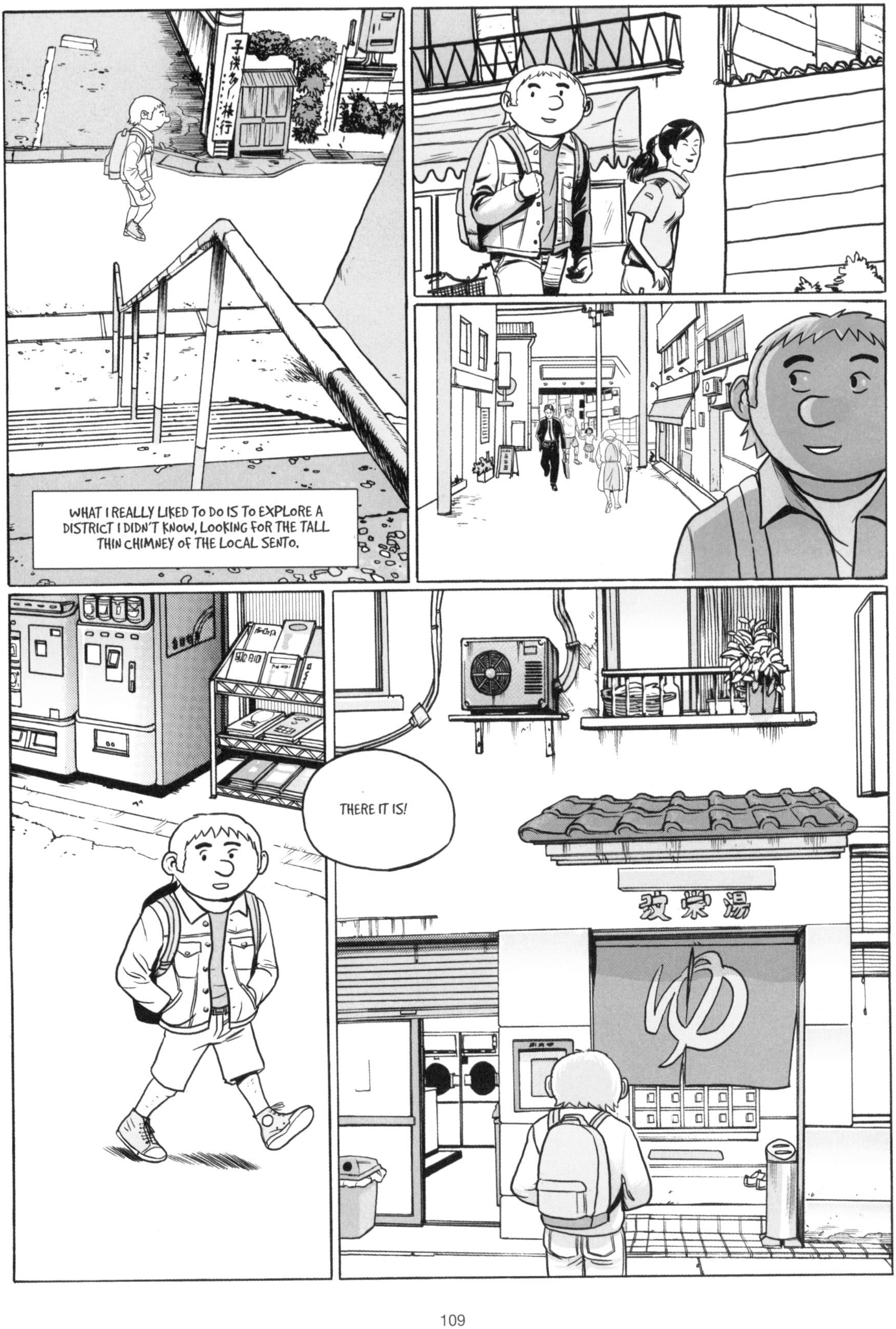
WHAT I REALLY LIKED TO DO IS TO EXPLORE A DISTRICT I DIDN'T KNOW, LOOKING FOR THE TALL THIN CHIMNEY OF THE LOCAL SENTO.
THERE IT IS!
ゆ

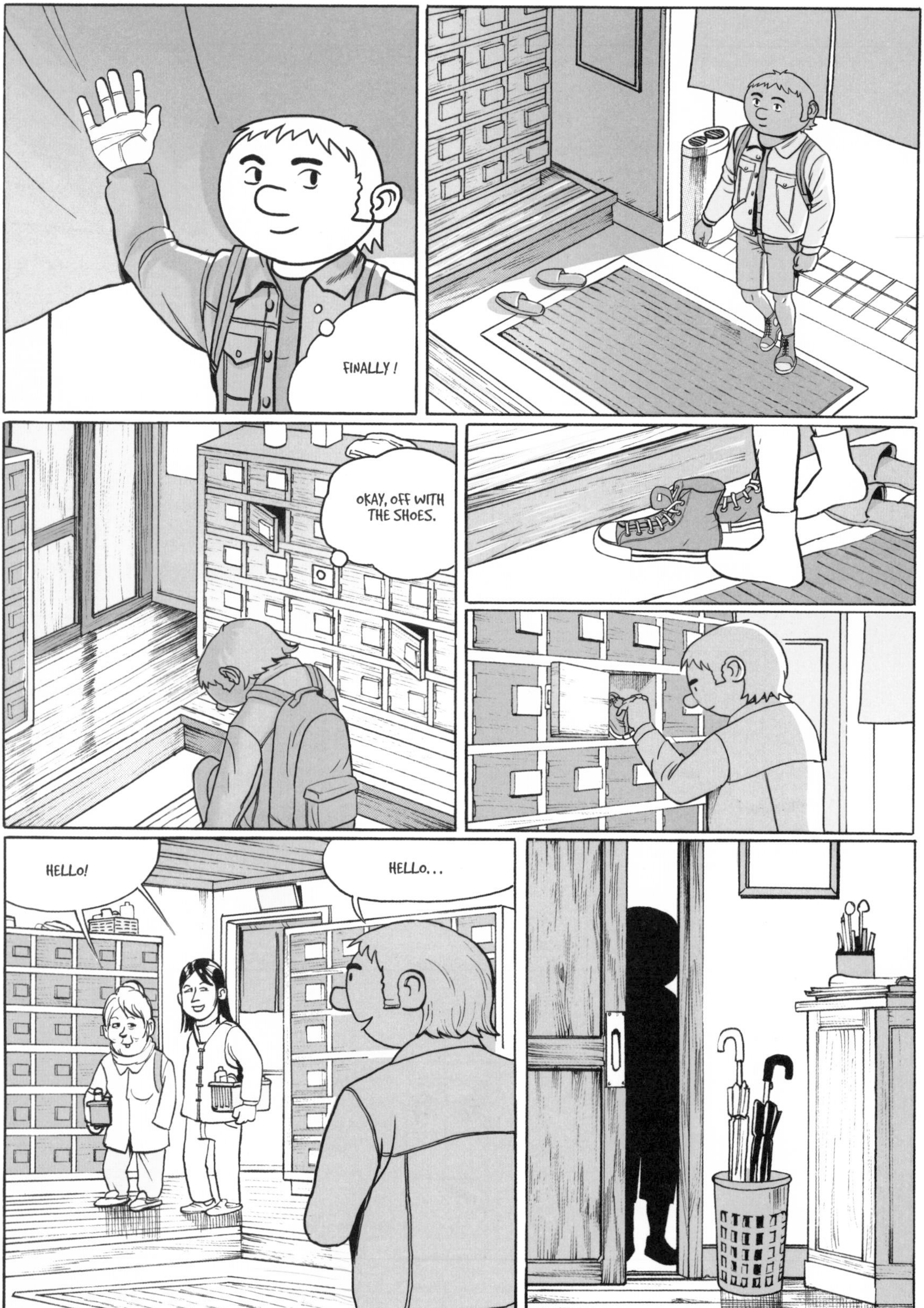
FINALLY !
OKAY, OFF WITH THE SHOES.
HELLO!
HELLO...

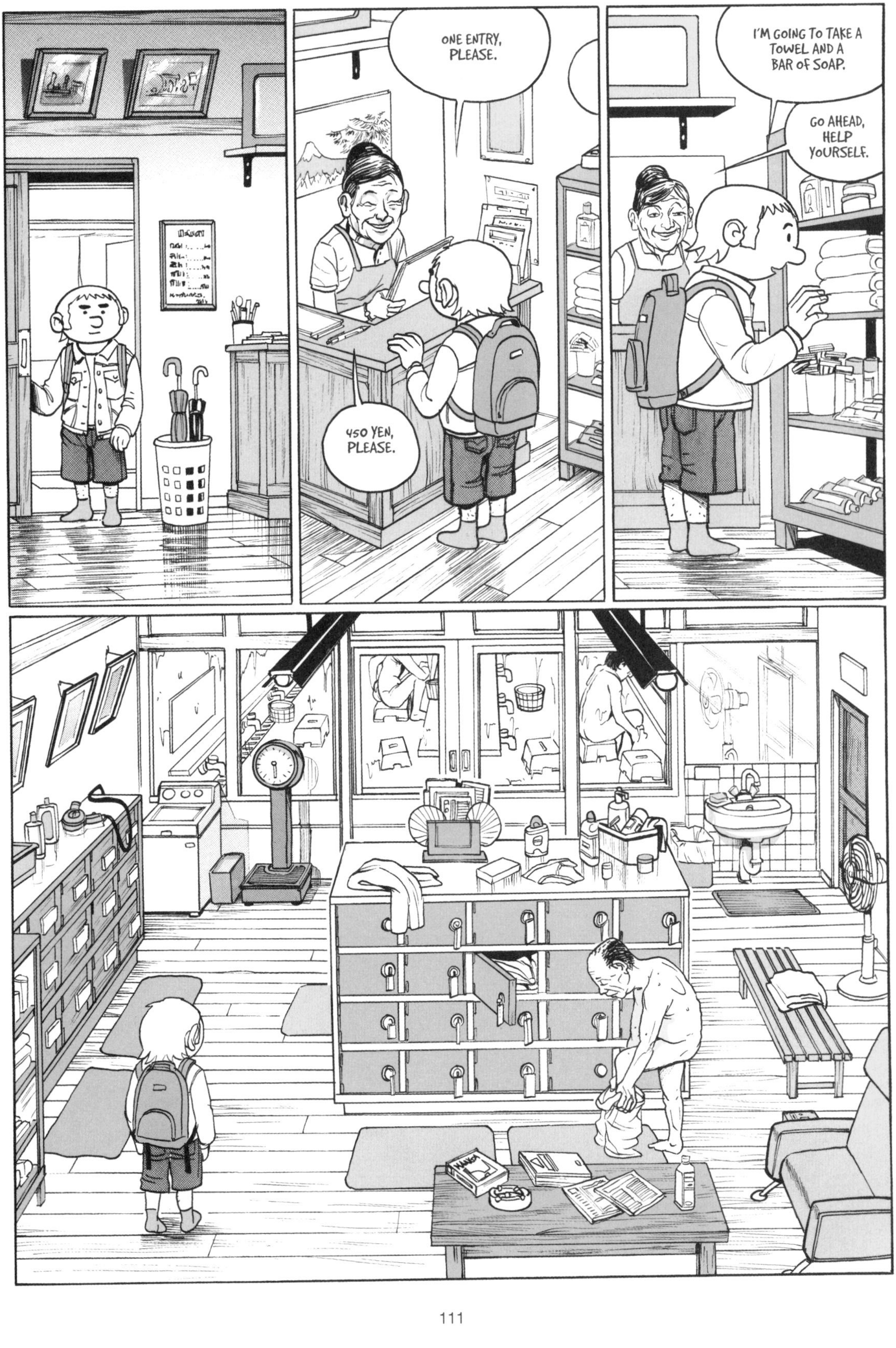
ONE ENTRY, PLEASE.
450 YEN, PLEASE.
I'M GOING TO TAKE A TOWEL AND A BAR OF SOAP.
GO AHEAD, HELP YOURSELF.

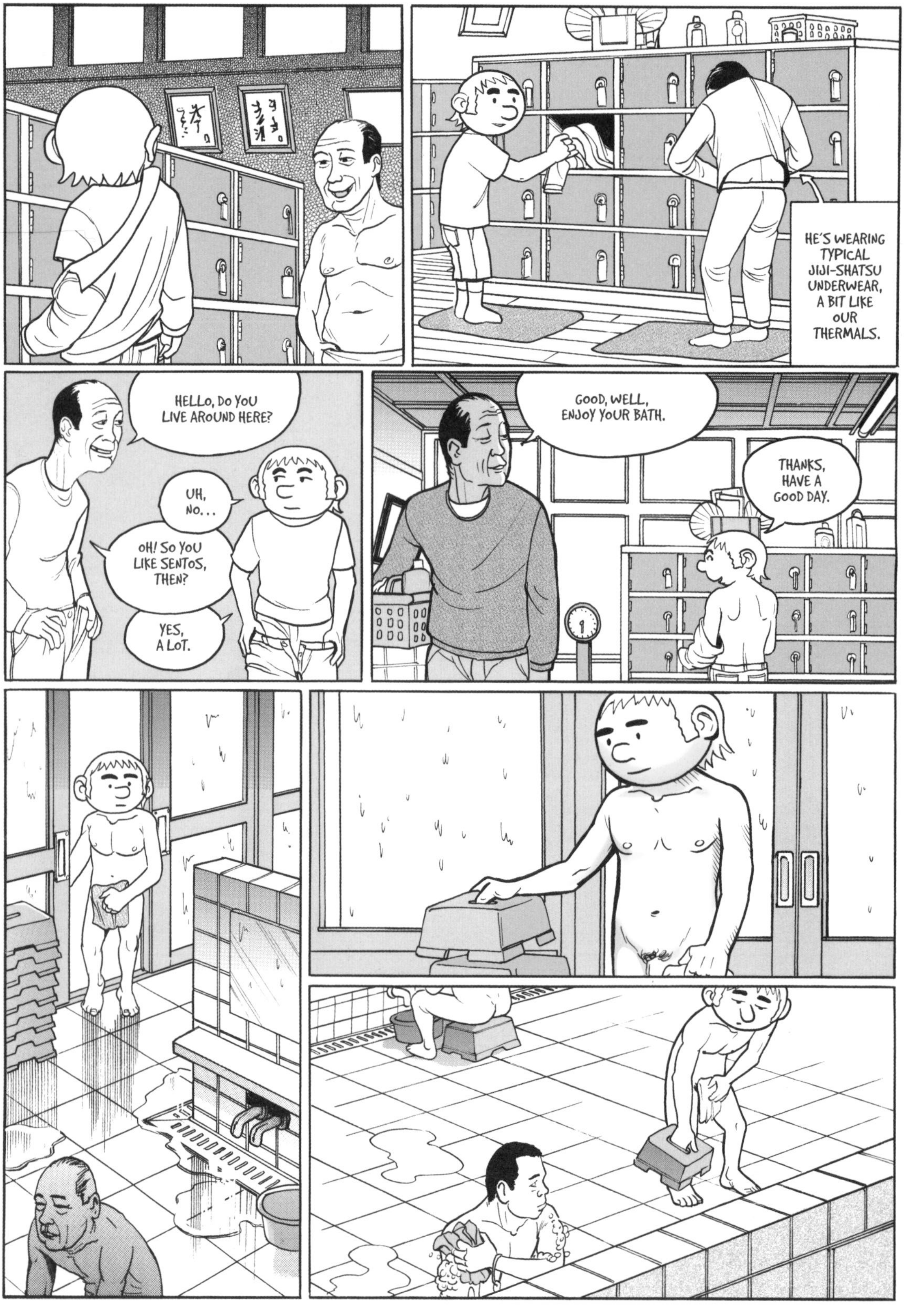
HE'S WEARING TYPICAL JIJI-SHATSU UNDERWEAR, A BIT LIKE OUR THERMALS.
HELLO, DO YOU LIVE AROUND HERE?
UH, NO...
OH! SO YOU LIKE SENTOS, THEN?
YES, A LOT.
GOOD, WELL, ENJOY YOUR BATH.
THANKS, HAVE A GOOD DAY.

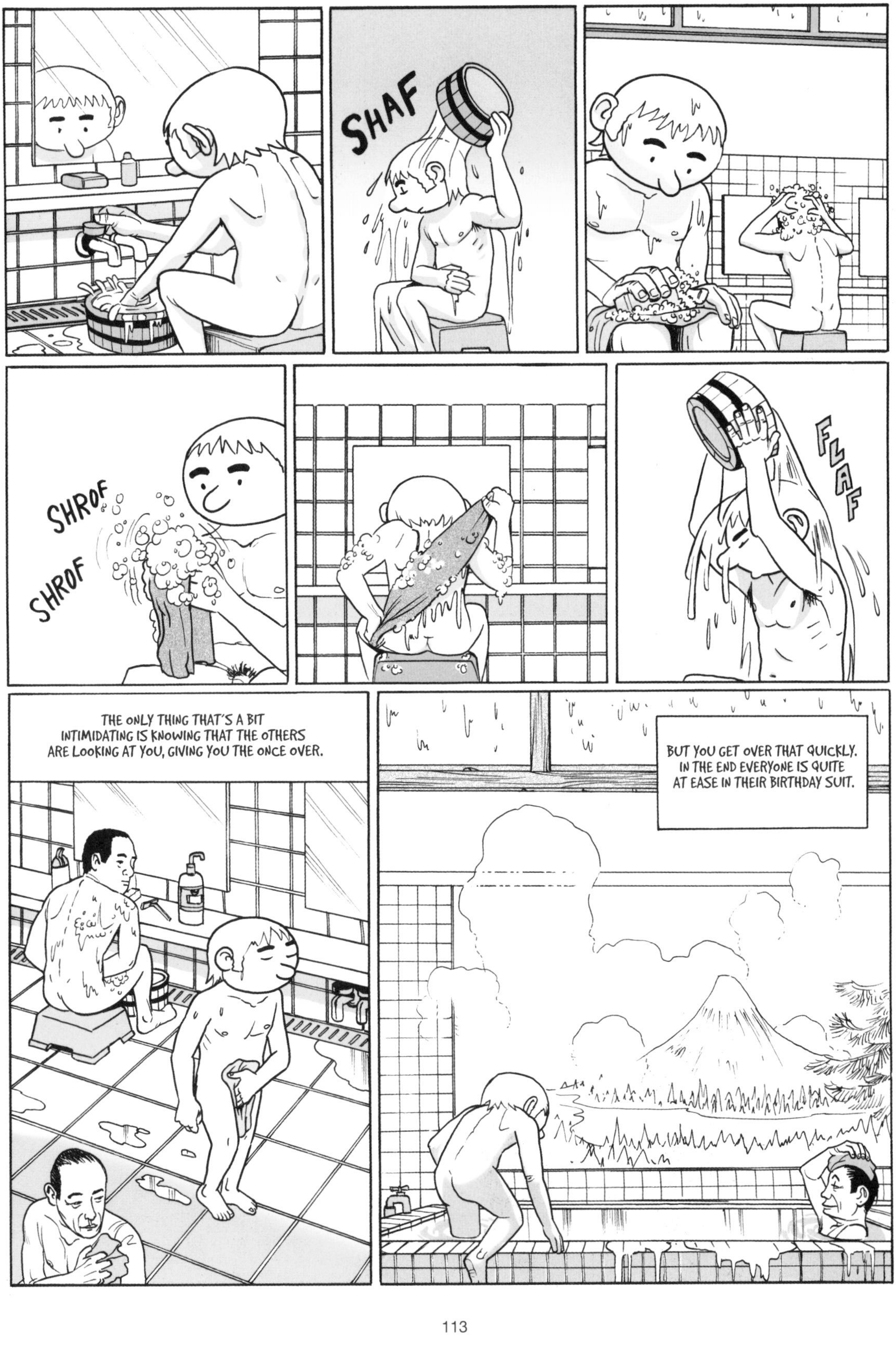
SHAF
SHROF
SHROF
FLAF
THE ONLY THING THAT'S A BIT INTIMIDATING IS KNOWING THAT THE OTHERS ARE LOOKING AT YOU, GIVING YOU THE ONCE OVER.
BUT YOU GET OVER THAT QUICKLY. IN THE END EVERYONE IS QUITE AT EASE IN THEIR BIRTHDAY SUIT.

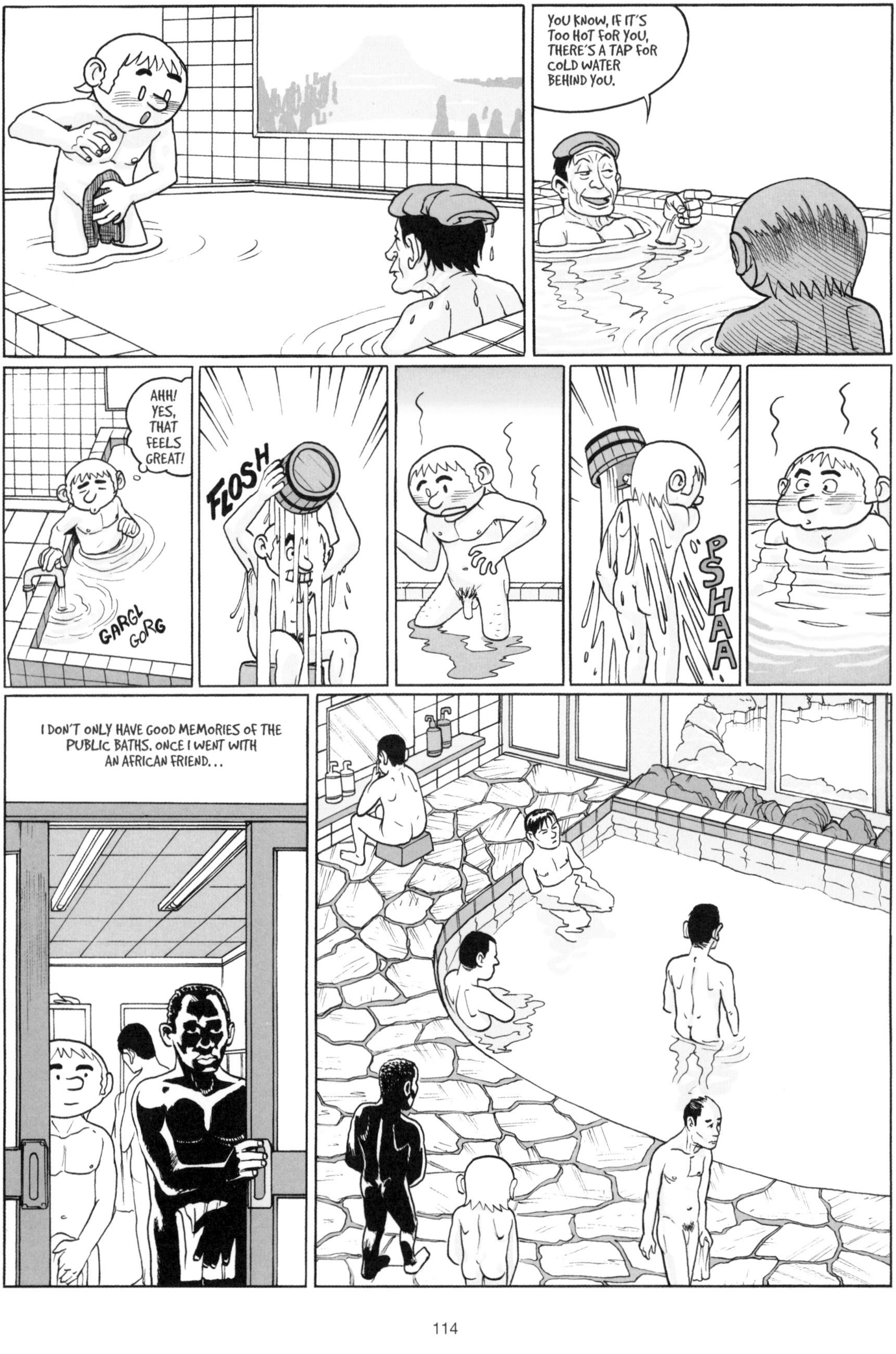
YOU KNOW, IF IT'S TOO HOT FOR YOU, THERE'S A TAP FOR COLD WATER BEHIND YOU.
AHH! YES, THAT FEELS GREAT!
GARGL GORG
FLOSH
PSHAA
I DON'T ONLY HAVE GOOD MEMORIES OF THE PUBLIC BATHS. ONCE I WENT WITH AN AFRICAN FRIEND...

HMMM! IT LOOKS LIKE THEY'RE AFRAID OF US... HA HA.

PFF... DON'T WORRY, I'M USED TO IT!

FLAF

THAT'S HOW THE XENOPHOBIA MANIFESTS ITSELF IN JAPAN. QUIETLY BUT EXPLICITLY.

THE SAME THING HAPPENED WHEN A BIG HAIRY GUY (A FOREIGNER) CAME AND SAT DOWN AMONGST THE HAIRLESS JAPANESE. HE CERTAINLY STUCK OUT.

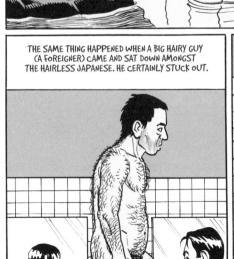

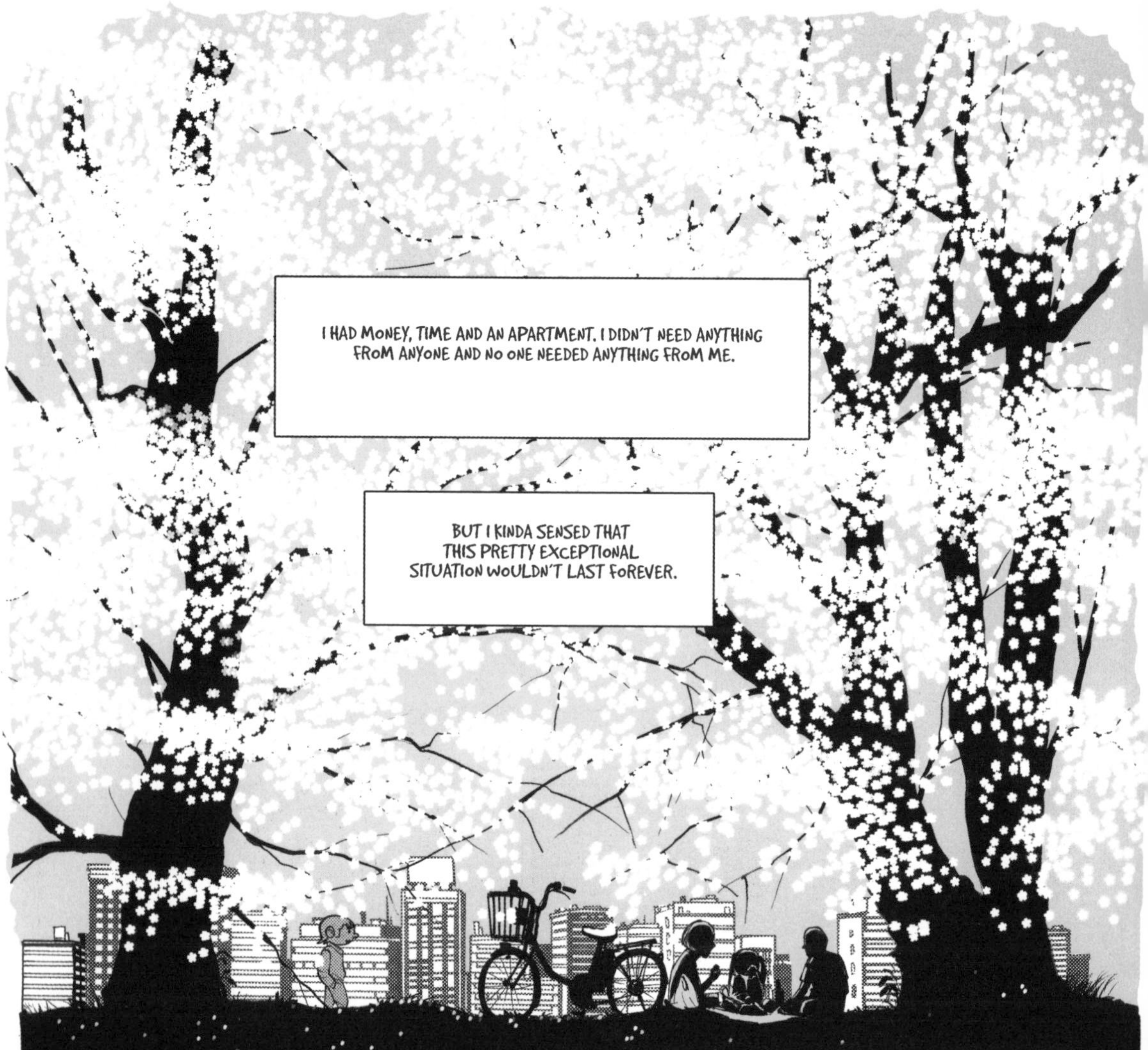
I HAD MONEY, TIME AND AN APARTMENT. I DIDN'T NEED ANYTHING FROM ANYONE AND NO ONE NEEDED ANYTHING FROM ME.
BUT I KINDA SENSED THAT THIS PRETTY EXCEPTIONAL SITUATION WOULDN'T LAST FOREVER.

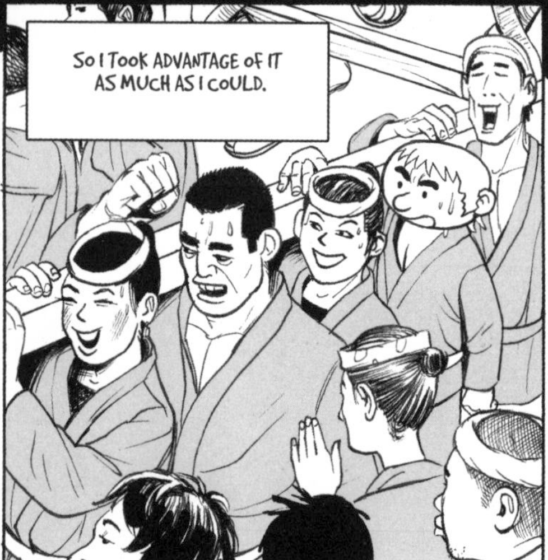
SO I TOOK ADVANTAGE OF IT AS MUCH AS I COULD.

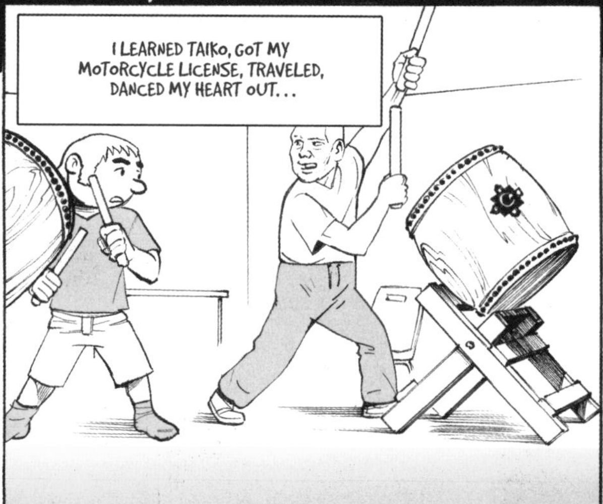
I LEARNED TAIKO, GOT MY MOTORCYCLE LICENSE, TRAVELED, DANCED MY HEART OUT...

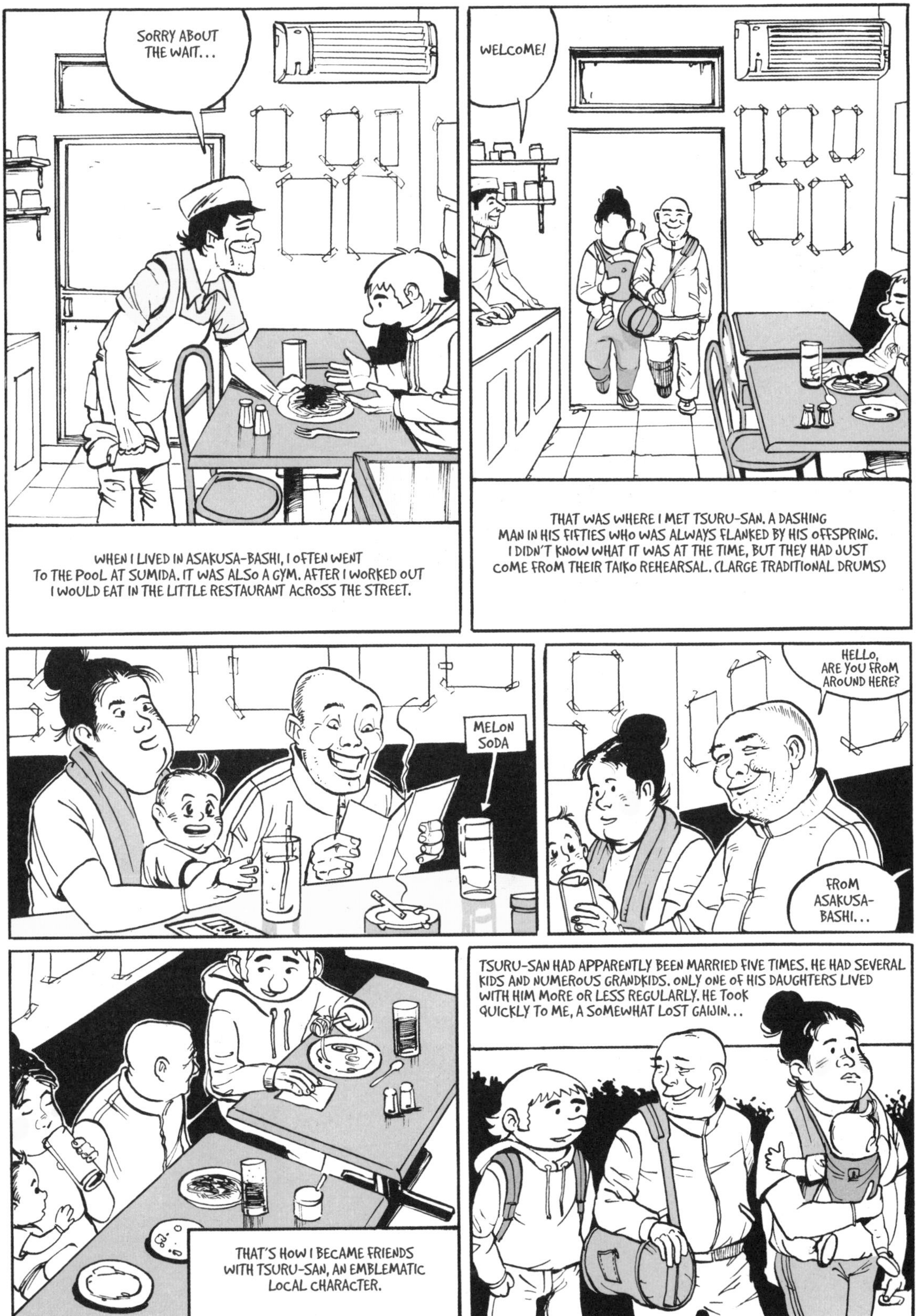
SORRY ABOUT THE WAIT...
WHEN I LIVED IN ASAKUSA-BASHI, I OFTEN WENT TO THE POOL AT SUMIDA. IT WAS ALSO A GYM. AFTER I WORKED OUT I WOULD EAT IN THE LITTLE RESTAURANT ACROSS THE STREET.
WELCOME!
THAT WAS WHERE I MET TSURU-SAN. A DASHING MAN IN HIS FIFTIES WHO WAS ALWAYS FLANKED BY HIS OFFSPRING. I DIDN'T KNOW WHAT IT WAS AT THE TIME, BUT THEY HAD JUST COME FROM THEIR TAIKO REHEARSAL. (LARGE TRADITIONAL DRUMS)
MELON SODA
HELLO, ARE YOU FROM AROUND HERE?
FROM ASAKUSA-BASHI...
THAT'S HOW I BECAME FRIENDS WITH TSURU-SAN, AN EMBLEMATIC LOCAL CHARACTER.
TSURU-SAN HAD APPARENTLY BEEN MARRIED FIVE TIMES. HE HAD SEVERAL KIDS AND NUMEROUS GRANDKIDS. ONLY ONE OF HIS DAUGHTERS LIVED WITH HIM MORE OR LESS REGULARLY. HE TOOK QUICKLY TO ME, A SOMEWHAT LOST GAIJIN...

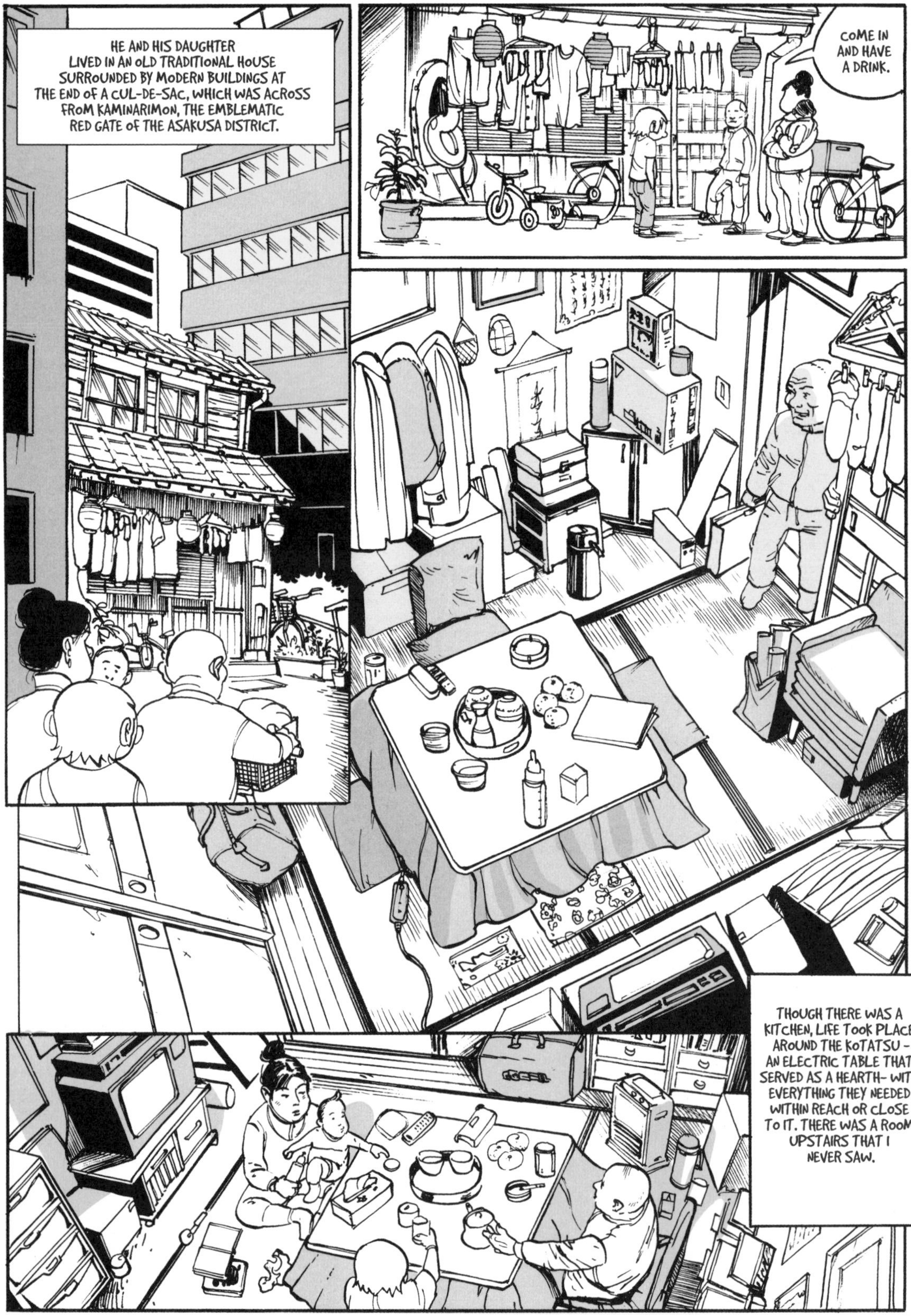
HE AND HIS DAUGHTER LIVED IN AN OLD TRADITIONAL HOUSE SURROUNDED BY MODERN BUILDINGS AT THE END OF A CUL-DE-SAC, WHICH WAS ACROSS FROM KAMINARIMON, THE EMBLEMATIC RED GATE OF THE ASAKUSA DISTRICT.
COME IN AND HAVE A DRINK.
THOUGH THERE WAS A KITCHEN, LIFE TOOK PLACE AROUND THE KOTATSU - AN ELECTRIC TABLE THAT SERVED AS A HEARTH- WITH EVERYTHING THEY NEEDED WITHIN REACH OR CLOSE TO IT. THERE WAS A ROOM UPSTAIRS THAT I NEVER SAW.

TSURU-SAN OFFERED TO TEACH ME TO PLAY THE TAIKO. HE HAD TWO OF THEM.

THEY HAD TO BE TRANSPORTED FROM HIS PLACE TO THE REHEARSAL HALL. THE MAD PENSIONER HAD THE WILD IDEA TO START A SMALL TAIKO SCHOOL.

HUMPF!

HANG IN. . .

THE TAIKO WAS AS MUCH DANCE AS DRUMMING. A FEW YEARS EARLIER I STUDIED RHYTHM MUSIC THEORY BECAUSE I WAS PLAYING THE DRUMS.

SO I PICKED UP THE RHYTHM EASILY.

GOUM DOUM

DOM DOM

DOM DOM

TA TA TA TA TA

SOMETIMES WE PRACTICED OUTDOORS ON THE BANKS OF THE SUMIDA.

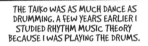

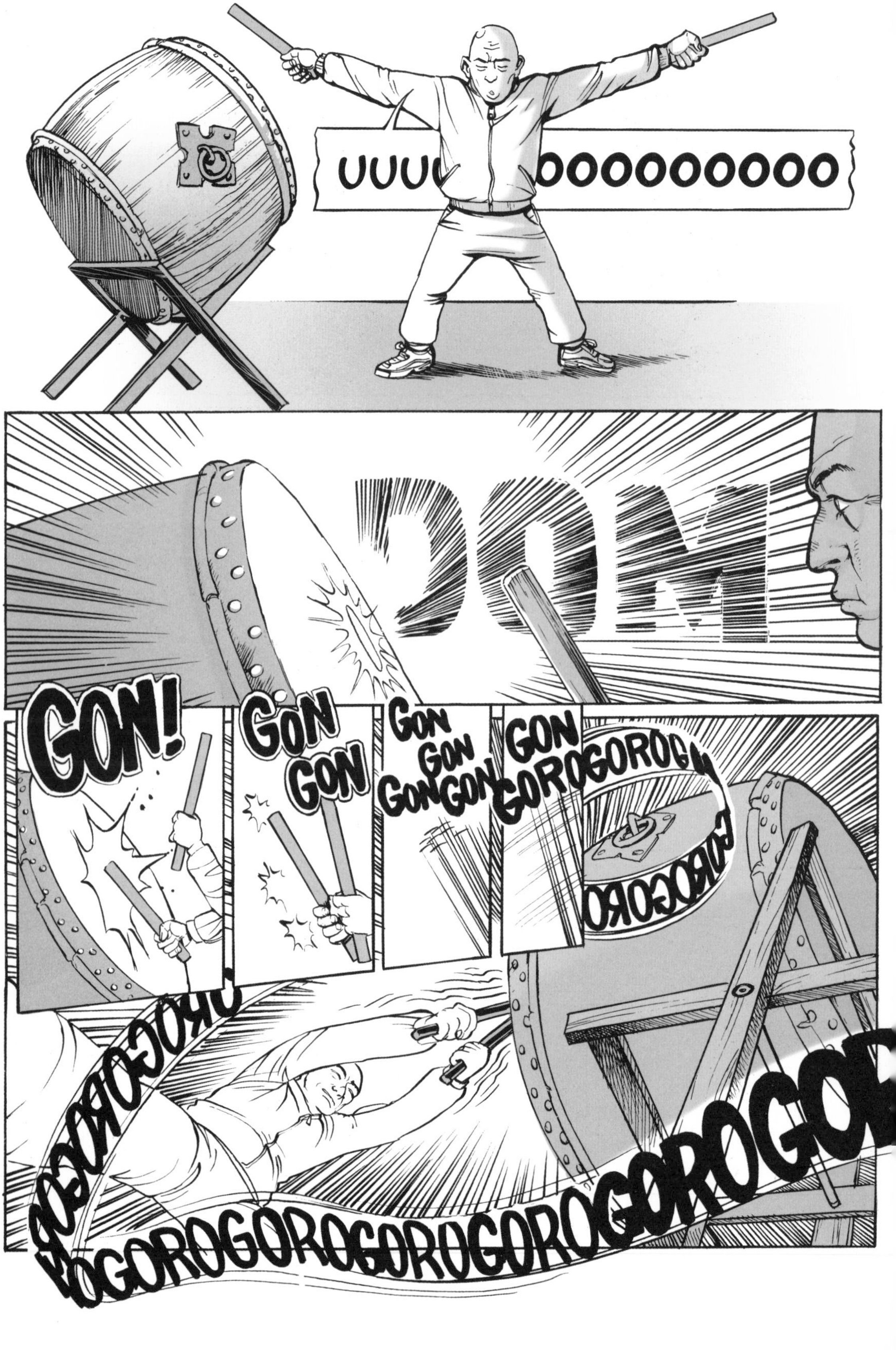
UUUOOOOOOOOOO
DOM
GON!
GON GON
GON GON GONGON
GON GOROGOROG
GOROGORO
GOROGOROGORO
GOROGOROGOROGOROGOROGOROGOROGO

I EVEN SPENT A NEW YEAR'S EVE WITH THEM AS PART OF THE FAMILY, IN FRONT OF A POT (NABE) AND WATCHING TELEVISION, AS IS THE CUSTOM.

DURING MY VISITS TSURU-SAN WOULD TELL ME STORIES ABOUT ASAKUSA, HIS NEIGHBORS AND THE LOCAL SHOPS. SUCH AND SUCH IS IN PRISON, SUCH AND SUCH GOT IN A FIGHT WITH SUCH AND SUCH, SO AND SO WAS A DRUG ADDICT.

TSURU-SAN PLAYED NANNY WILLINGLY, HELPING OUT HIS DAUGHTER. HE WAS A VERY SCRUPULOUS GRANDFATHER, WHO HAD MORE THAN ENOUGH ENERGY TO TAKE CARE OF ALL THE DETAILS THAT MAKE UP FAMILY LIFE.

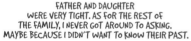

FATHER AND DAUGHTER WERE VERY TIGHT. AS FOR THE REST OF THE FAMILY, I NEVER GOT AROUND TO ASKING. MAYBE BECAUSE I DIDN'T WANT TO KNOW THEIR PAST.

TSURU-SAN SHOWED ME SOME OF HIS FAVORITE MANGAS. HE EXPLAINED TO ME WHAT, ACCORDING TO HIM, MAKES A GOOD MANGA. HE SHOWED ME THE MOMENTS THE EMOTION WAS HIGH, THE PASSAGES THAT MAKE YOU LAUGH, OR CRY...

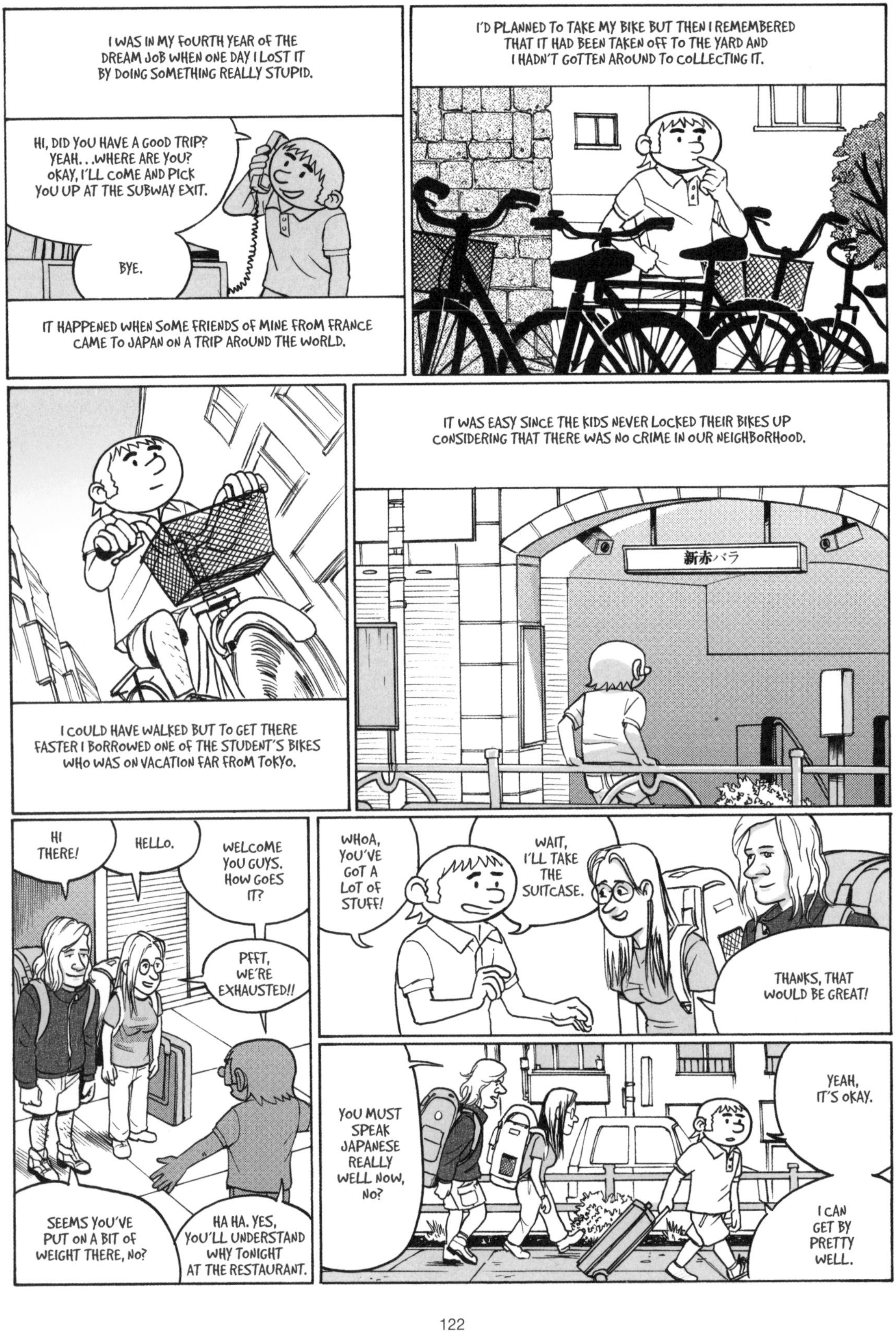
I WAS IN MY FOURTH YEAR OF THE DREAM JOB WHEN ONE DAY I LOST IT BY DOING SOMETHING REALLY STUPID.
HI, DID YOU HAVE A GOOD TRIP? YEAH. . .WHERE ARE YOU? OKAY, I'LL COME AND PICK YOU UP AT THE SUBWAY EXIT.
BYE.
IT HAPPENED WHEN SOME FRIENDS OF MINE FROM FRANCE CAME TO JAPAN ON A TRIP AROUND THE WORLD.
I'D PLANNED TO TAKE MY BIKE BUT THEN I REMEMBERED THAT IT HAD BEEN TAKEN OFF TO THE YARD AND I HADN'T GOTTEN AROUND TO COLLECTING IT.
I COULD HAVE WALKED BUT TO GET THERE FASTER I BORROWED ONE OF THE STUDENT'S BIKES WHO WAS ON VACATION FAR FROM TOKYO.
IT WAS EASY SINCE THE KIDS NEVER LOCKED THEIR BIKES UP CONSIDERING THAT THERE WAS NO CRIME IN OUR NEIGHBORHOOD.
新赤バラ
HI THERE!
HELLO.
WELCOME YOU GUYS. HOW GOES IT?
PFFT, WE'RE EXHAUSTED!!
SEEMS YOU'VE PUT ON A BIT OF WEIGHT THERE, NO?
HA HA. YES, YOU'LL UNDERSTAND WHY TONIGHT AT THE RESTAURANT.
WHOA, YOU'VE GOT A LOT OF STUFF!
WAIT, I'LL TAKE THE SUITCASE.
THANKS, THAT WOULD BE GREAT!
YOU MUST SPEAK JAPANESE REALLY WELL NOW, NO?
YEAH, IT'S OKAY.
I CAN GET BY PRETTY WELL.

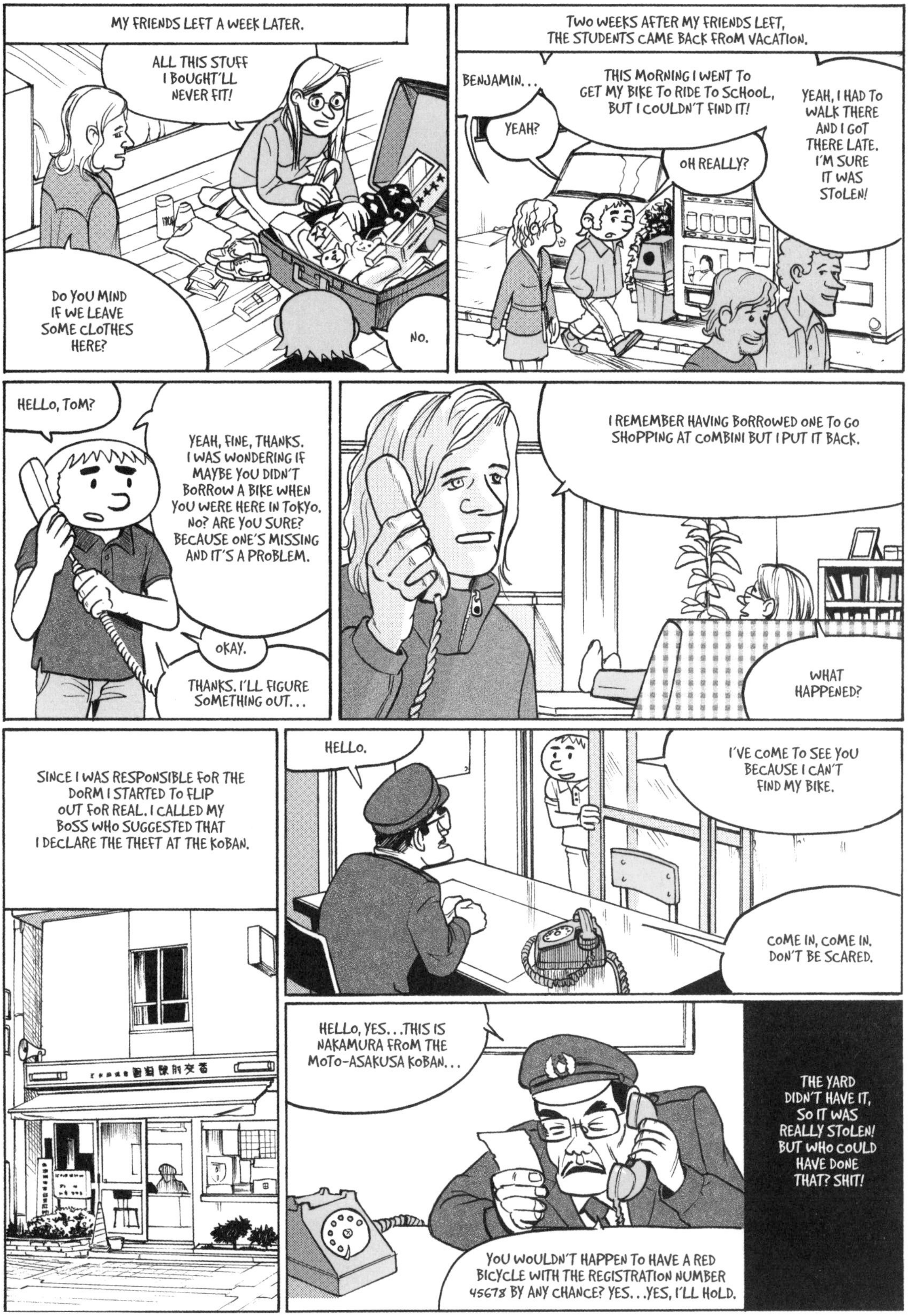
MY FRIENDS LEFT A WEEK LATER.
ALL THIS STUFF I BOUGHT'LL NEVER FIT!
DO YOU MIND IF WE LEAVE SOME CLOTHES HERE?
NO.
TWO WEEKS AFTER MY FRIENDS LEFT, THE STUDENTS CAME BACK FROM VACATION.
BENJAMIN. . .
THIS MORNING I WENT TO GET MY BIKE TO RIDE TO SCHOOL, BUT I COULDN'T FIND IT!
YEAH?
OH REALLY?
YEAH, I HAD TO WALK THERE AND I GOT THERE LATE. I'M SURE IT WAS STOLEN!
HELLO, TOM?
YEAH, FINE, THANKS. I WAS WONDERING IF MAYBE YOU DIDN'T BORROW A BIKE WHEN YOU WERE HERE IN TOKYO. NO? ARE YOU SURE? BECAUSE ONE'S MISSING AND IT'S A PROBLEM.
OKAY.
THANKS. I'LL FIGURE SOMETHING OUT. . .
I REMEMBER HAVING BORROWED ONE TO GO SHOPPING AT COMBINI BUT I PUT IT BACK.
WHAT HAPPENED?
SINCE I WAS RESPONSIBLE FOR THE DORM I STARTED TO FLIP OUT FOR REAL. I CALLED MY BOSS WHO SUGGESTED THAT I DECLARE THE THEFT AT THE KOBAN.
HELLO.
I'VE COME TO SEE YOU BECAUSE I CAN'T FIND MY BIKE.
COME IN, COME IN. DON'T BE SCARED.
HELLO, YES. . .THIS IS NAKAMURA FROM THE MOTO-ASAKUSA KOBAN. . .
YOU WOULDN'T HAPPEN TO HAVE A RED BICYCLE WITH THE REGISTRATION NUMBER 45678 BY ANY CHANCE? YES. . .YES, I'LL HOLD.
THE YARD DIDN'T HAVE IT, SO IT WAS REALLY STOLEN! BUT WHO COULD HAVE DONE THAT? SHIT!

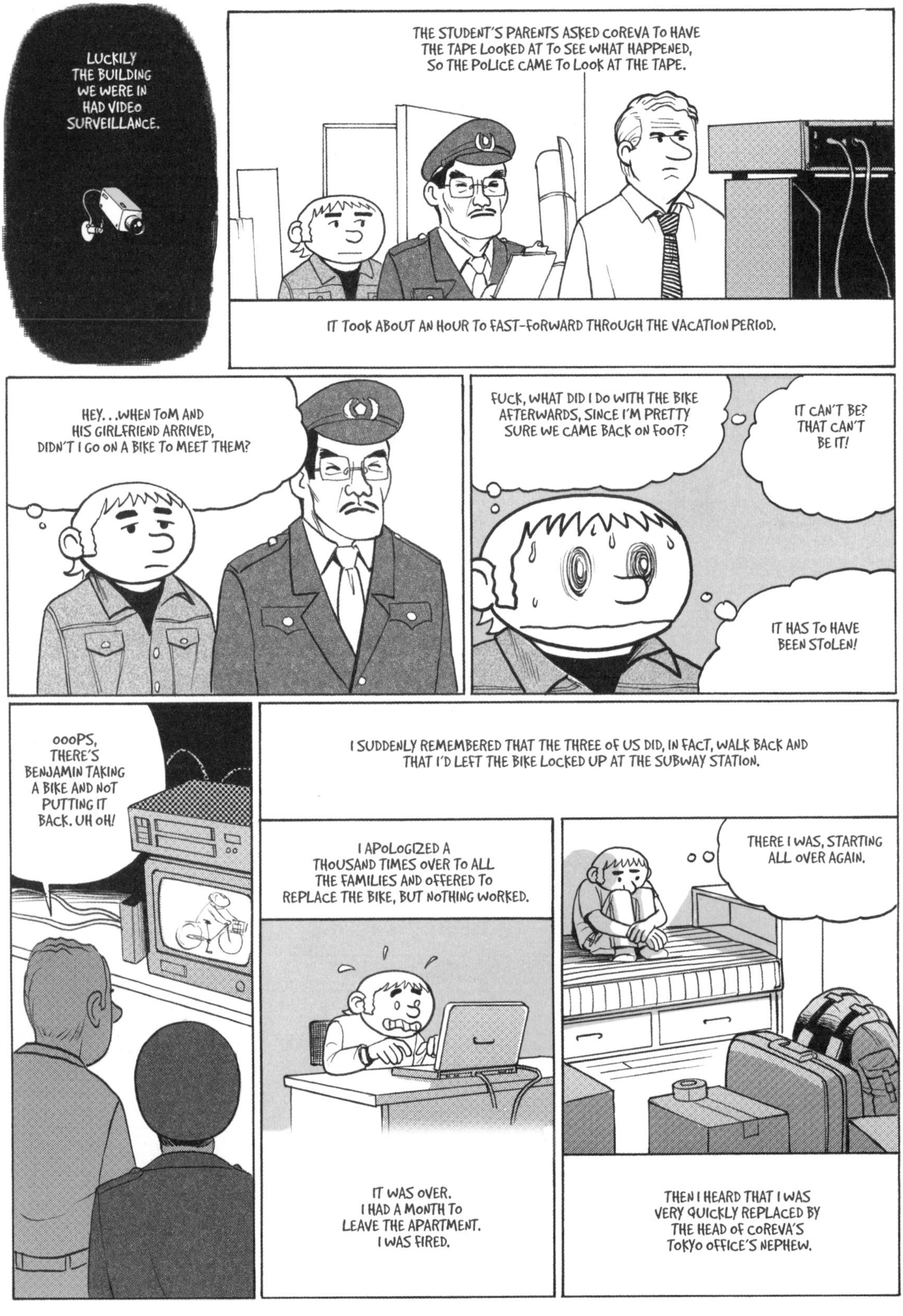
LUCKILY THE BUILDING WE WERE IN HAD VIDEO SURVEILLANCE.
THE STUDENT'S PARENTS ASKED COREVA TO HAVE THE TAPE LOOKED AT TO SEE WHAT HAPPENED, SO THE POLICE CAME TO LOOK AT THE TAPE.
IT TOOK ABOUT AN HOUR TO FAST-FORWARD THROUGH THE VACATION PERIOD.
HEY. . .WHEN TOM AND HIS GIRLFRIEND ARRIVED, DIDN'T I GO ON A BIKE TO MEET THEM?
FUCK, WHAT DID I DO WITH THE BIKE AFTERWARDS, SINCE I'M PRETTY SURE WE CAME BACK ON FOOT?
IT CAN'T BE? THAT CAN'T BE IT!
IT HAS TO HAVE BEEN STOLEN!
OOOPS, THERE'S BENJAMIN TAKING A BIKE AND NOT PUTTING IT BACK. UH OH!
I SUDDENLY REMEMBERED THAT THE THREE OF US DID, IN FACT, WALK BACK AND THAT I'D LEFT THE BIKE LOCKED UP AT THE SUBWAY STATION.
I APOLOGIZED A THOUSAND TIMES OVER TO ALL THE FAMILIES AND OFFERED TO REPLACE THE BIKE, BUT NOTHING WORKED.
IT WAS OVER. I HAD A MONTH TO LEAVE THE APARTMENT. I WAS FIRED.
THERE I WAS, STARTING ALL OVER AGAIN.
THEN I HEARD THAT I WAS VERY QUICKLY REPLACED BY THE HEAD OF COREVA'S TOKYO OFFICE'S NEPHEW.

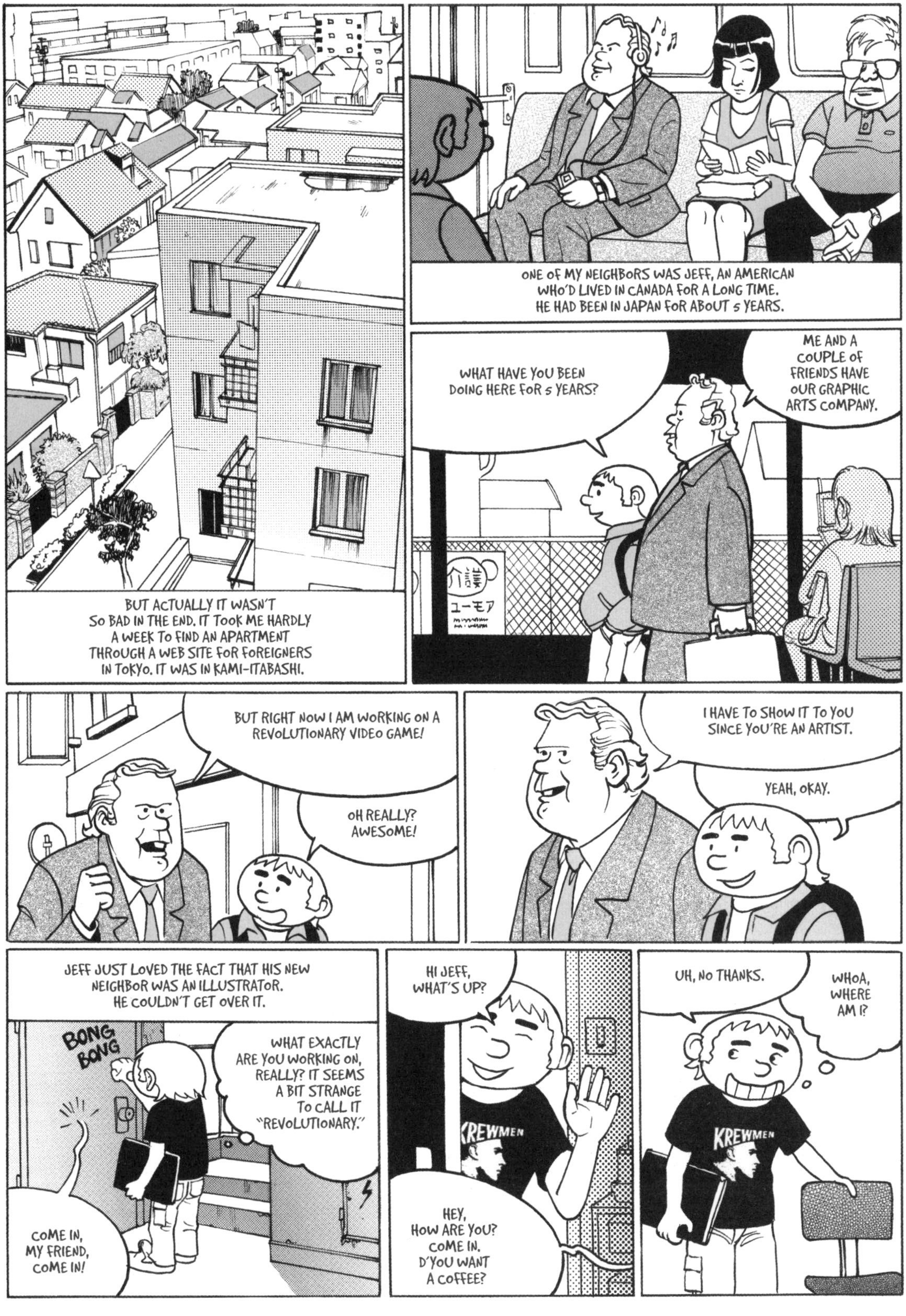
BUT ACTUALLY IT WASN'T SO BAD IN THE END. IT TOOK ME HARDLY A WEEK TO FIND AN APARTMENT THROUGH A WEB SITE FOR FOREIGNERS IN TOKYO. IT WAS IN KAMI-ITABASHI.
ONE OF MY NEIGHBORS WAS JEFF, AN AMERICAN WHO'D LIVED IN CANADA FOR A LONG TIME. HE HAD BEEN IN JAPAN FOR ABOUT 5 YEARS.
WHAT HAVE YOU BEEN DOING HERE FOR 5 YEARS?
ME AND A COUPLE OF FRIENDS HAVE OUR GRAPHIC ARTS COMPANY.
介護
ユーモア
BUT RIGHT NOW I AM WORKING ON A REVOLUTIONARY VIDEO GAME!
OH REALLY? AWESOME!
I HAVE TO SHOW IT TO YOU SINCE YOU'RE AN ARTIST.
YEAH, OKAY.
JEFF JUST LOVED THE FACT THAT HIS NEW NEIGHBOR WAS AN ILLUSTRATOR. HE COULDN'T GET OVER IT.
BONG BONG
WHAT EXACTLY ARE YOU WORKING ON, REALLY? IT SEEMS A BIT STRANGE TO CALL IT "REVOLUTIONARY."
COME IN, MY FRIEND, COME IN!
HI JEFF, WHAT'S UP?
KREWMEN
HEY, HOW ARE YOU? COME IN. D'YOU WANT A COFFEE?
UH, NO THANKS.
WHOA, WHERE AM I?
KREWMEN

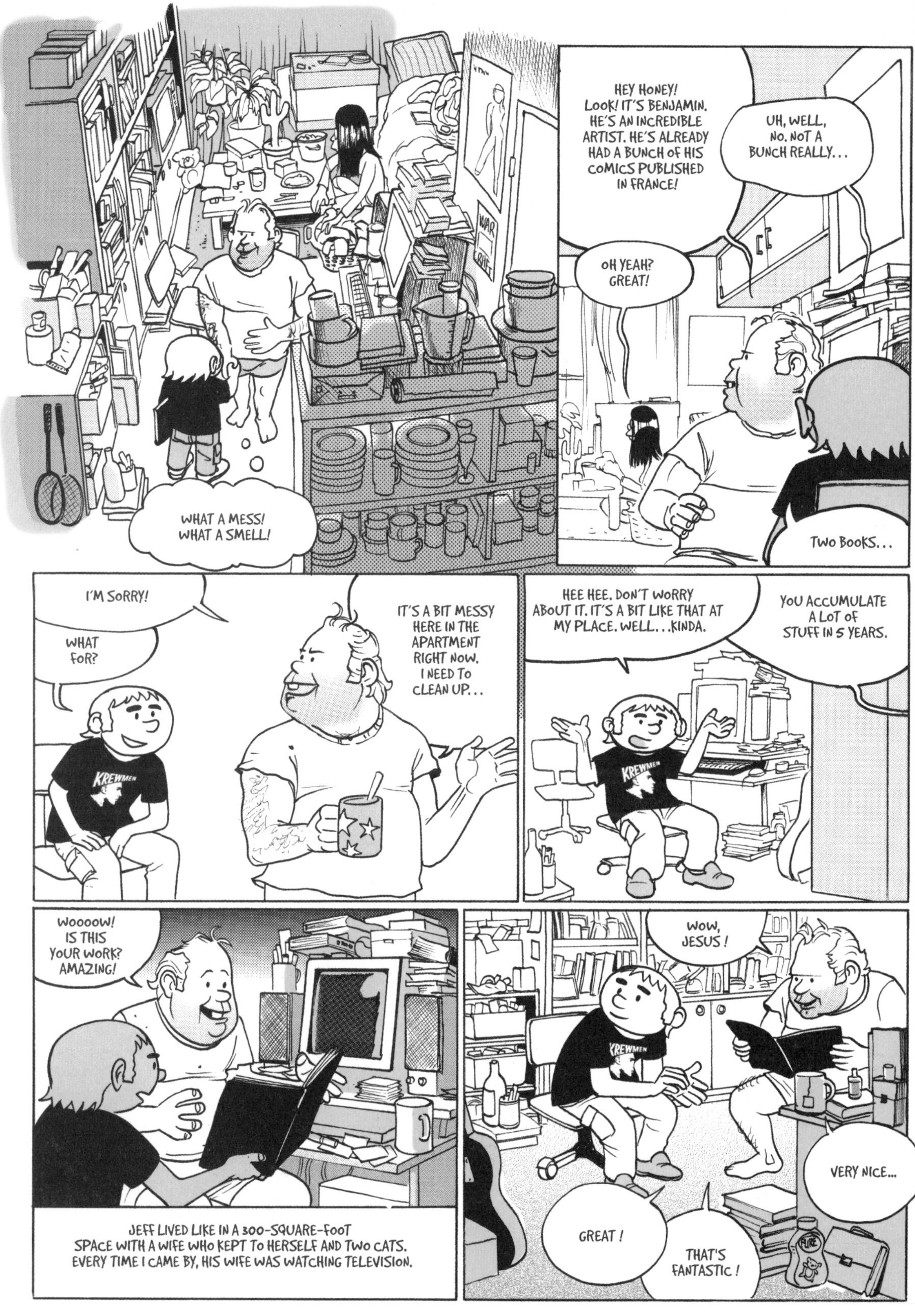
WHAT A MESS! WHAT A SMELL!
HEY HONEY! LOOK! IT'S BENJAMIN. HE'S AN INCREDIBLE ARTIST. HE'S ALREADY HAD A BUNCH OF HIS COMICS PUBLISHED IN FRANCE!
UH, WELL, NO. NOT A BUNCH REALLY...
OH YEAH? GREAT!
TWO BOOKS...
I'M SORRY!
WHAT FOR?
IT'S A BIT MESSY HERE IN THE APARTMENT RIGHT NOW. I NEED TO CLEAN UP...
HEE HEE. DON'T WORRY ABOUT IT. IT'S A BIT LIKE THAT AT MY PLACE. WELL...KINDA.
YOU ACCUMULATE A LOT OF STUFF IN 5 YEARS.
WOOOOW! IS THIS YOUR WORK? AMAZING!
JEFF LIVED LIKE IN A 300-SQUARE-FOOT SPACE WITH A WIFE WHO KEPT TO HERSELF AND TWO CATS. EVERY TIME I CAME BY, HIS WIFE WAS WATCHING TELEVISION.
WOW, JESUS!
VERY NICE...
GREAT!
THAT'S FANTASTIC!

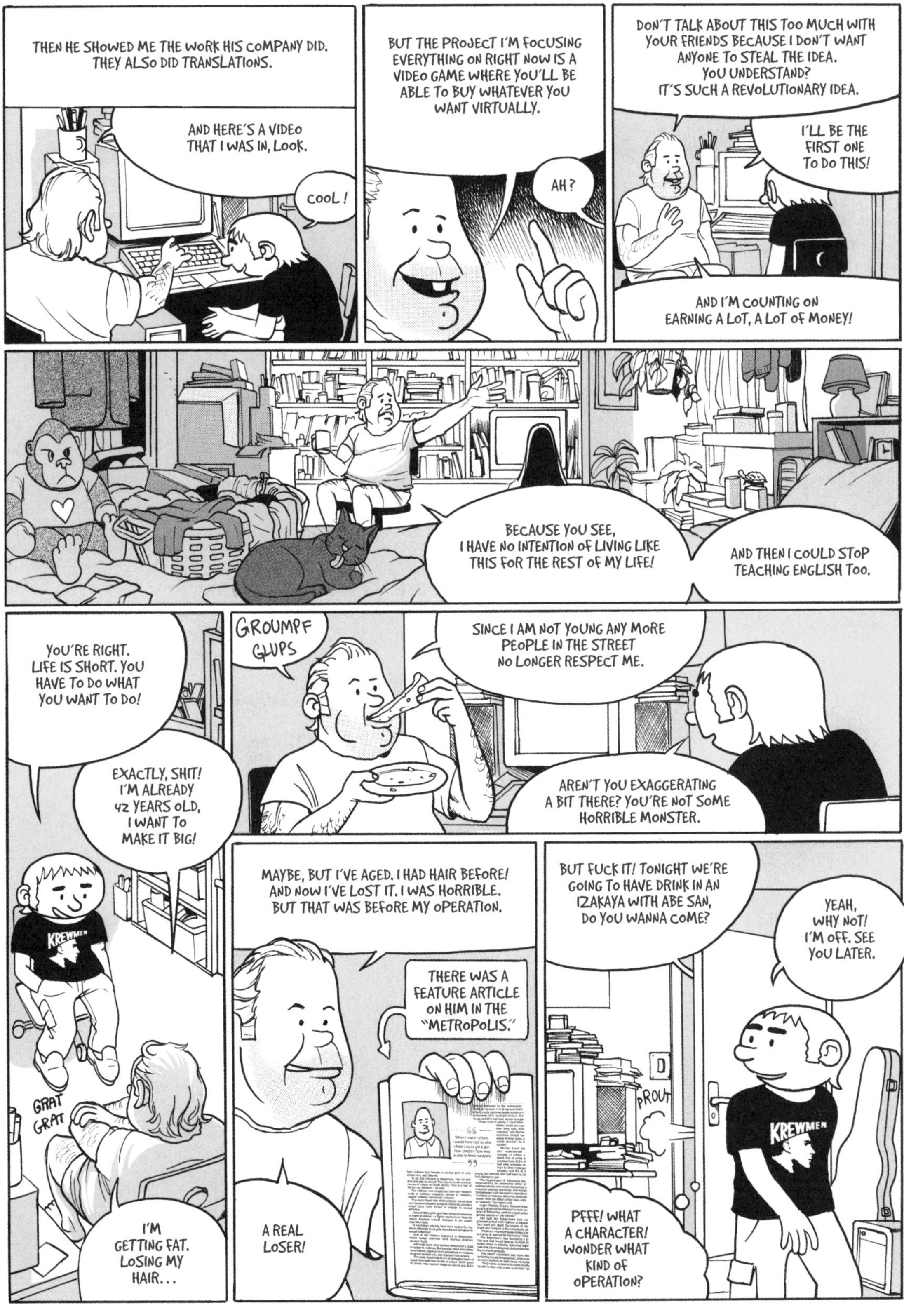
THEN HE SHOWED ME THE WORK HIS COMPANY DID. THEY ALSO DID TRANSLATIONS.
AND HERE'S A VIDEO THAT I WAS IN, LOOK.
COOL!
BUT THE PROJECT I'M FOCUSING EVERYTHING ON RIGHT NOW IS A VIDEO GAME WHERE YOU'LL BE ABLE TO BUY WHATEVER YOU WANT VIRTUALLY.
AH?
DON'T TALK ABOUT THIS TOO MUCH WITH YOUR FRIENDS BECAUSE I DON'T WANT ANYONE TO STEAL THE IDEA. YOU UNDERSTAND? IT'S SUCH A REVOLUTIONARY IDEA.
I'LL BE THE FIRST ONE TO DO THIS!
AND I'M COUNTING ON EARNING A LOT, A LOT OF MONEY!
BECAUSE YOU SEE, I HAVE NO INTENTION OF LIVING LIKE THIS FOR THE REST OF MY LIFE!
AND THEN I COULD STOP TEACHING ENGLISH TOO.
YOU'RE RIGHT. LIFE IS SHORT. YOU HAVE TO DO WHAT YOU WANT TO DO!
EXACTLY, SHIT! I'M ALREADY 42 YEARS OLD, I WANT TO MAKE IT BIG!
GROUMPF GLUPS
SINCE I AM NOT YOUNG ANY MORE PEOPLE IN THE STREET NO LONGER RESPECT ME.
AREN'T YOU EXAGGERATING A BIT THERE? YOU'RE NOT SOME HORRIBLE MONSTER.
KREWMEN
GRAT GRAT
I'M GETTING FAT. LOSING MY HAIR...
MAYBE, BUT I'VE AGED. I HAD HAIR BEFORE! AND NOW I'VE LOST IT. I WAS HORRIBLE. BUT THAT WAS BEFORE MY OPERATION.
THERE WAS A FEATURE ARTICLE ON HIM IN THE "METROPOLIS."
A REAL LOSER!
BUT FUCK IT! TONIGHT WE'RE GOING TO HAVE DRINK IN AN IZAKAYA WITH ABE SAN, DO YOU WANNA COME?
YEAH, WHY NOT! I'M OFF. SEE YOU LATER.
PROUT
KREWMEN
PFFF! WHAT A CHARACTER! WONDER WHAT KIND OF OPERATION?

JEFF EXPLAINED IT TO ME. IT CONSISTED OF TAKING HAIR FROM BEHIND HIS HEAD AND TRANSPLANTING WHERE HE HAD LOST IT.

UNDER A GENERAL AESTHETIC THE SURGEON TAKES A NICE BIG PIECE OF HEAD FROM THE NAPE OF THE NECK, WHERE THE HAIR GROWS THE THICKEST.

THERE'S SOME LEFT OVER. SHOULD I SAVE IT FOR YOU?

THE GAP IS THEN STAPLED SHUT.

SHLAK SHLAK

DANGER

DEFECTIVE HAIR HOLE

AND THE CUTTINGS THEY TAKE FROM THE FAT ARE TRANSPLANTED, ONE BY ONE, INTO THE HOLES WHERE THE HAIR'S FALLEN OUT ON THE FRONT OF THE HEAD.

FOR SEVERAL MONTHS YOU HAVE TO LIVE WITH YOUR HEAD HELD BACK.

HEY, JEFF, IT'S BEEN A WHILE SINCE WE'VE SEEN YOU!

HA HA, TERRY, GLAD TO SEE YOU. IT'S ONLY A STIFF NECK, NOTHING SERIOUS.

BUT ALL THAT SUFFERING WAS WORTH IT. JEFF GOT BACK THE LOOK HE HAD WHEN HE WAS IN HIS TWENTIES.

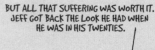

128

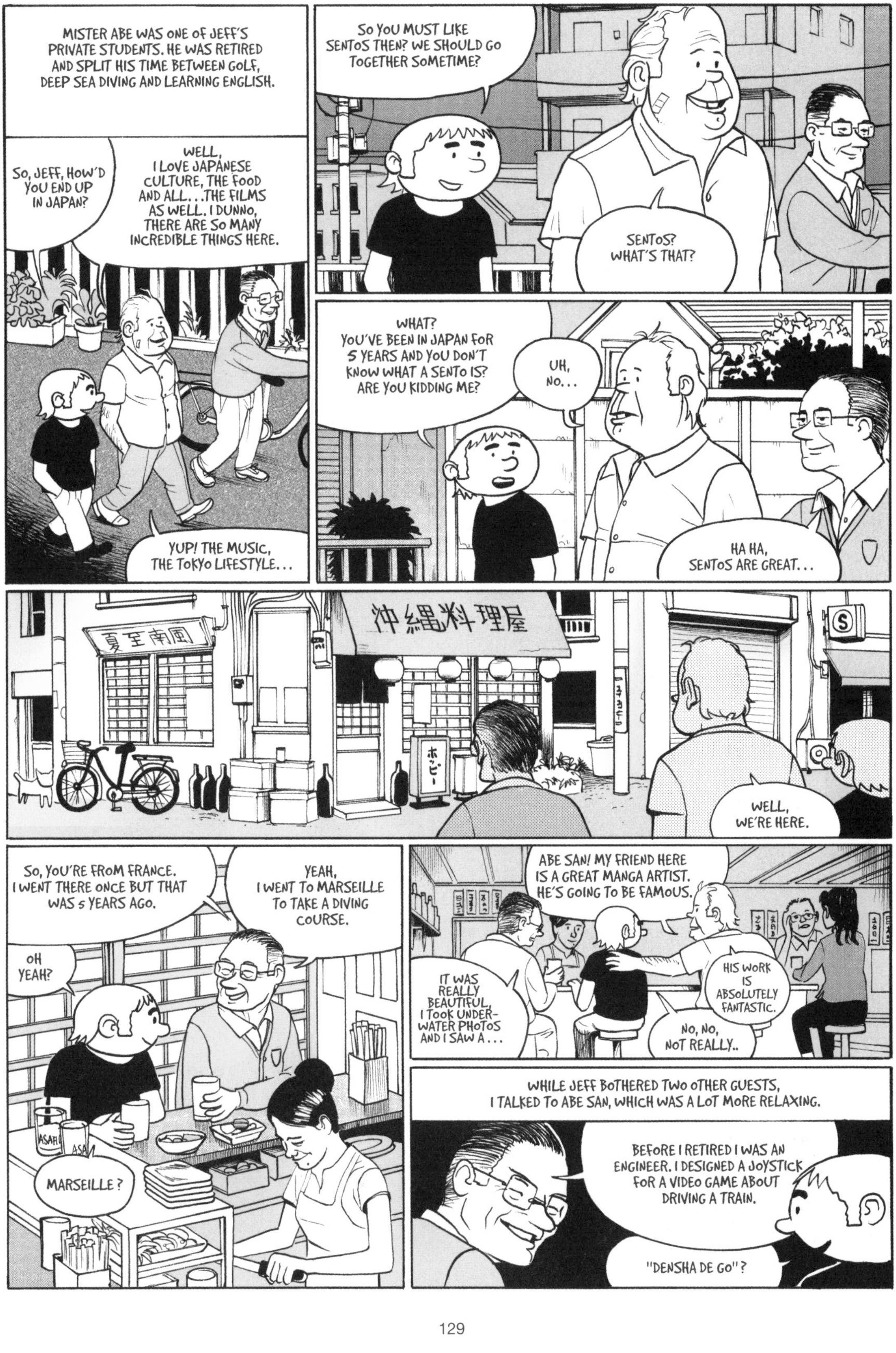

MISTER ABE WAS ONE OF JEFF'S PRIVATE STUDENTS. HE WAS RETIRED AND SPLIT HIS TIME BETWEEN GOLF, DEEP SEA DIVING AND LEARNING ENGLISH.
SO, JEFF, HOW'D YOU END UP IN JAPAN?
WELL, I LOVE JAPANESE CULTURE, THE FOOD AND ALL...THE FILMS AS WELL. I DUNNO, THERE ARE SO MANY INCREDIBLE THINGS HERE.
YUP! THE MUSIC, THE TOKYO LIFESTYLE...
SO YOU MUST LIKE SENTOS THEN? WE SHOULD GO TOGETHER SOMETIME?
SENTOS? WHAT'S THAT?
WHAT? YOU'VE BEEN IN JAPAN FOR 5 YEARS AND YOU DON'T KNOW WHAT A SENTO IS? ARE YOU KIDDING ME?
UH, NO...
HA HA, SENTOS ARE GREAT...
夏至南風
沖縄料理屋
ホッピー
WELL, WE'RE HERE.
SO, YOU'RE FROM FRANCE. I WENT THERE ONCE BUT THAT WAS 5 YEARS AGO.
YEAH, I WENT TO MARSEILLE TO TAKE A DIVING COURSE.
OH YEAH?
MARSEILLE?
ABE SAN! MY FRIEND HERE IS A GREAT MANGA ARTIST. HE'S GOING TO BE FAMOUS.
IT WAS REALLY BEAUTIFUL, I TOOK UNDER-WATER PHOTOS AND I SAW A...
HIS WORK IS ABSOLUTELY FANTASTIC.
NO, NO, NOT REALLY..
WHILE JEFF BOTHERED TWO OTHER GUESTS, I TALKED TO ABE SAN, WHICH WAS A LOT MORE RELAXING.
BEFORE I RETIRED I WAS AN ENGINEER. I DESIGNED A JOYSTICK FOR A VIDEO GAME ABOUT DRIVING A TRAIN.
"DENSHA DE GO"?

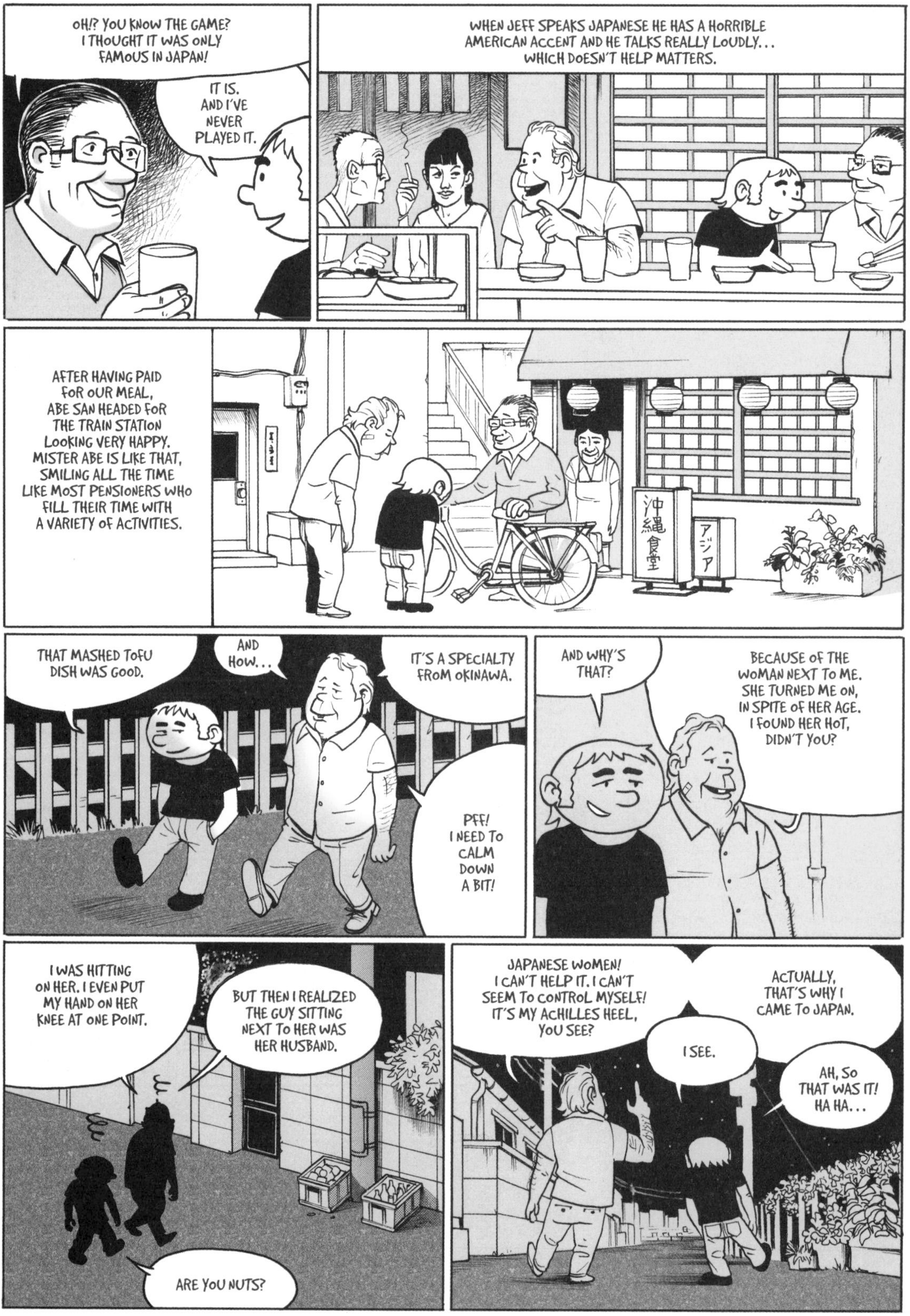
OH!? YOU KNOW THE GAME? I THOUGHT IT WAS ONLY FAMOUS IN JAPAN!
IT IS. AND I'VE NEVER PLAYED IT.
WHEN JEFF SPEAKS JAPANESE HE HAS A HORRIBLE AMERICAN ACCENT AND HE TALKS REALLY LOUDLY... WHICH DOESN'T HELP MATTERS.
AFTER HAVING PAID FOR OUR MEAL, ABE SAN HEADED FOR THE TRAIN STATION LOOKING VERY HAPPY. MISTER ABE IS LIKE THAT, SMILING ALL THE TIME LIKE MOST PENSIONERS WHO FILL THEIR TIME WITH A VARIETY OF ACTIVITIES.
沖縄食堂
アジア
THAT MASHED TOFU DISH WAS GOOD.
AND HOW...
IT'S A SPECIALTY FROM OKINAWA.
PFF! I NEED TO CALM DOWN A BIT!
AND WHY'S THAT?
BECAUSE OF THE WOMAN NEXT TO ME. SHE TURNED ME ON, IN SPITE OF HER AGE. I FOUND HER HOT, DIDN'T YOU?
I WAS HITTING ON HER. I EVEN PUT MY HAND ON HER KNEE AT ONE POINT.
BUT THEN I REALIZED THE GUY SITTING NEXT TO HER WAS HER HUSBAND.
ARE YOU NUTS?
JAPANESE WOMEN! I CAN'T HELP IT. I CAN'T SEEM TO CONTROL MYSELF! IT'S MY ACHILLES HEEL, YOU SEE?
ACTUALLY, THAT'S WHY I CAME TO JAPAN.
I SEE.
AH, SO THAT WAS IT! HA HA...

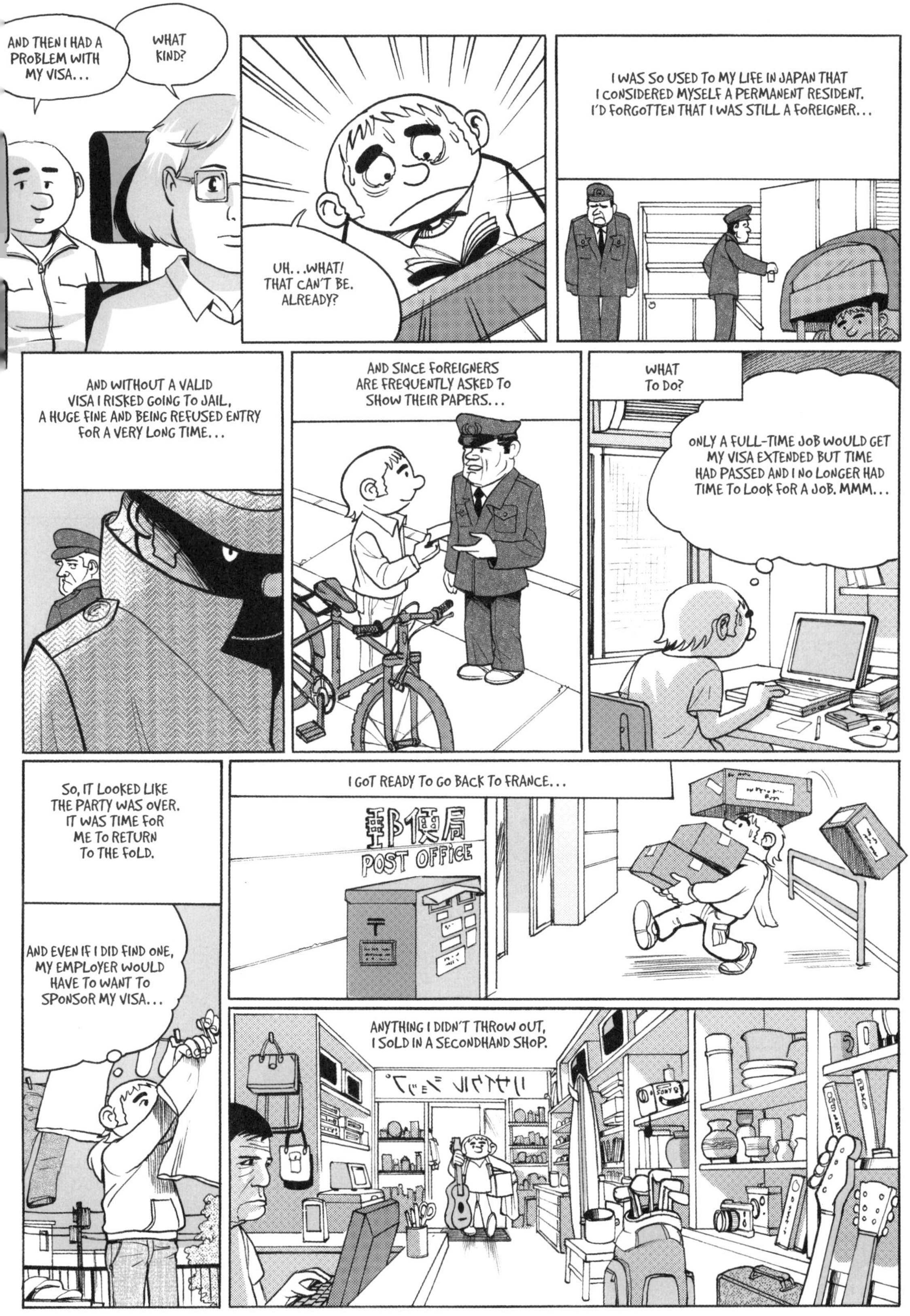
AND THEN I HAD A PROBLEM WITH MY VISA...
WHAT KIND?
UH...WHAT! THAT CAN'T BE. ALREADY?
I WAS SO USED TO MY LIFE IN JAPAN THAT I CONSIDERED MYSELF A PERMANENT RESIDENT. I'D FORGOTTEN THAT I WAS STILL A FOREIGNER...
AND WITHOUT A VALID VISA I RISKED GOING TO JAIL, A HUGE FINE AND BEING REFUSED ENTRY FOR A VERY LONG TIME...
AND SINCE FOREIGNERS ARE FREQUENTLY ASKED TO SHOW THEIR PAPERS...
WHAT TO DO?
ONLY A FULL-TIME JOB WOULD GET MY VISA EXTENDED BUT TIME HAD PASSED AND I NO LONGER HAD TIME TO LOOK FOR A JOB. MMM...
SO, IT LOOKED LIKE THE PARTY WAS OVER. IT WAS TIME FOR ME TO RETURN TO THE FOLD.
AND EVEN IF I DID FIND ONE, MY EMPLOYER WOULD HAVE TO WANT TO SPONSOR MY VISA...
I GOT READY TO GO BACK TO FRANCE...
郵便局
POST OFFICE
ANYTHING I DIDN'T THROW OUT, I SOLD IN A SECONDHAND SHOP.

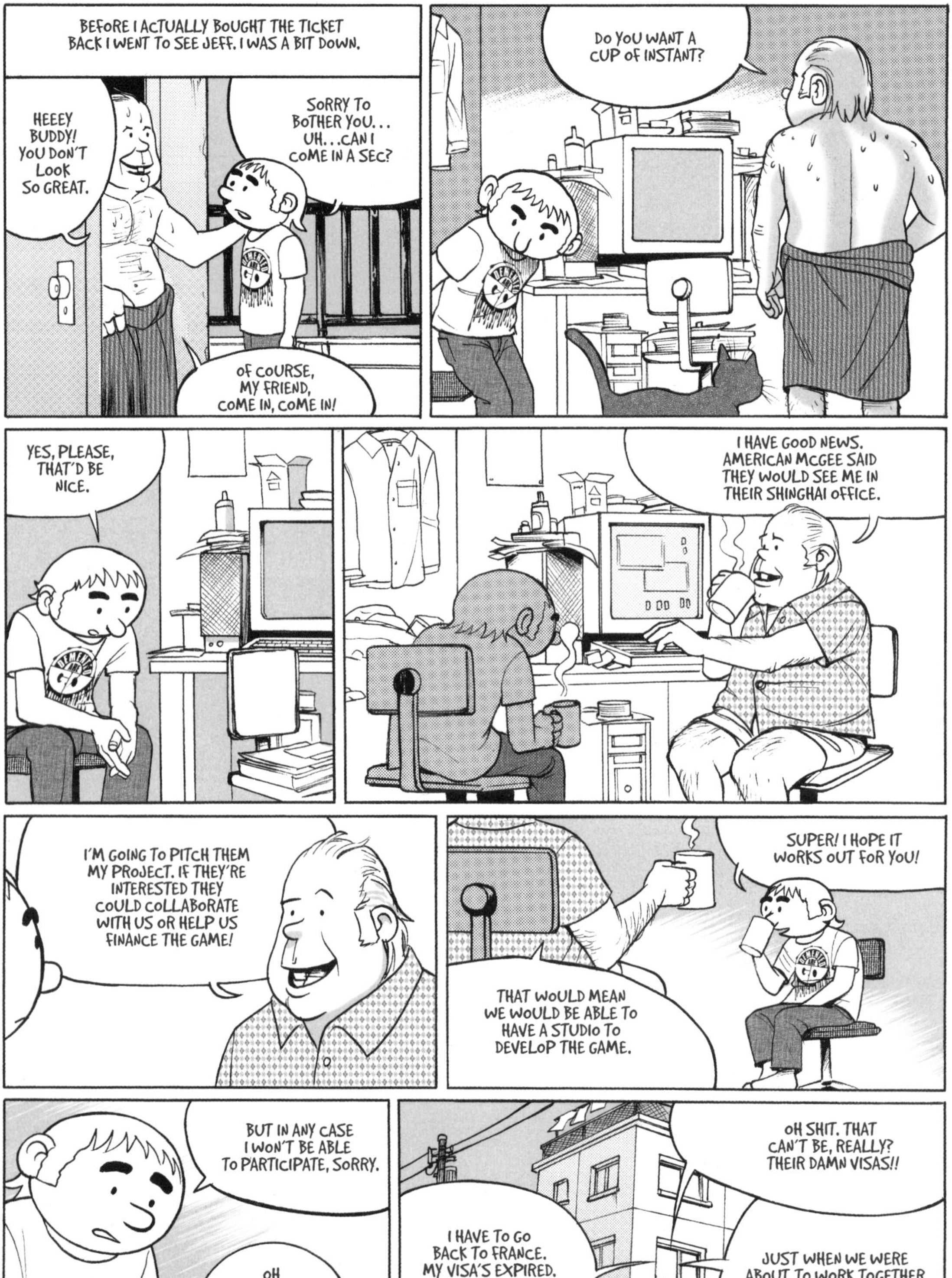
BEFORE I ACTUALLY BOUGHT THE TICKET BACK I WENT TO SEE JEFF. I WAS A BIT DOWN.
HEEEY BUDDY! YOU DON'T LOOK SO GREAT.
SORRY TO BOTHER YOU... UH...CAN I COME IN A SEC?
OF COURSE, MY FRIEND, COME IN, COME IN!
DO YOU WANT A CUP OF INSTANT?
YES, PLEASE, THAT'D BE NICE.
I HAVE GOOD NEWS. AMERICAN MCGEE SAID THEY WOULD SEE ME IN THEIR SHINGHAI OFFICE.
I'M GOING TO PITCH THEM MY PROJECT. IF THEY'RE INTERESTED THEY COULD COLLABORATE WITH US OR HELP US FINANCE THE GAME!
SUPER! I HOPE IT WORKS OUT FOR YOU!
THAT WOULD MEAN WE WOULD BE ABLE TO HAVE A STUDIO TO DEVELOP THE GAME.
BUT IN ANY CASE I WON'T BE ABLE TO PARTICIPATE, SORRY.
OH REALLY? WHY?
I HAVE TO GO BACK TO FRANCE. MY VISA'S EXPIRED. I WASN'T PAYING ATTENTION.
OH SHIT. THAT CAN'T BE, REALLY? THEIR DAMN VISAS!!
JUST WHEN WE WERE ABOUT TO WORK TOGETHER ON A GREAT PROJECT! WHEN ARE YOU COMING BACK?

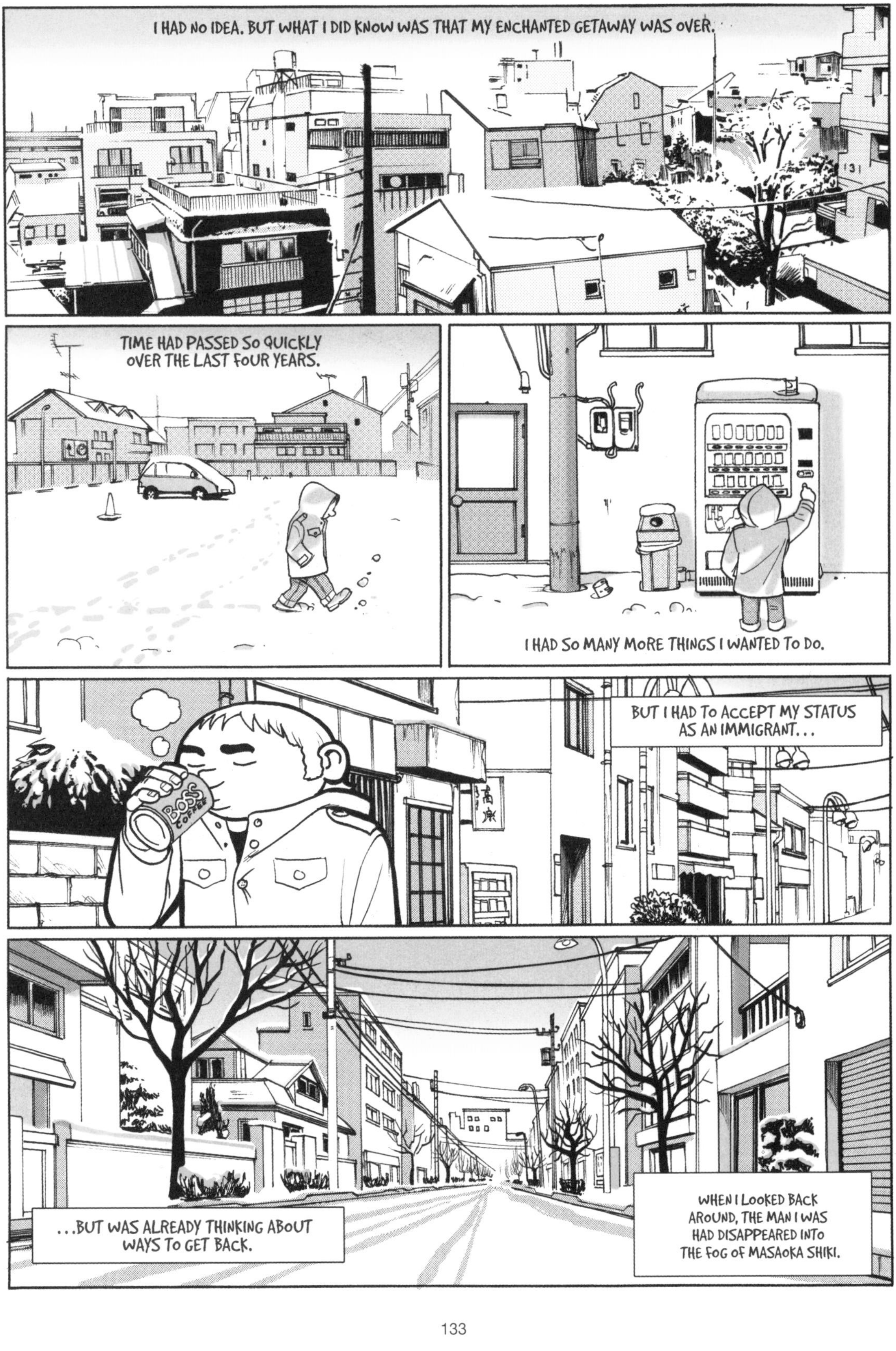
I HAD NO IDEA. BUT WHAT I DID KNOW WAS THAT MY ENCHANTED GETAWAY WAS OVER.
TIME HAD PASSED SO QUICKLY OVER THE LAST FOUR YEARS.
I HAD SO MANY MORE THINGS I WANTED TO DO.
BOSS COFFEE
BUT I HAD TO ACCEPT MY STATUS AS AN IMMIGRANT...
...BUT WAS ALREADY THINKING ABOUT WAYS TO GET BACK.
WHEN I LOOKED BACK AROUND, THE MAN I WAS HAD DISAPPEARED INTO THE FOG OF MASAOKA SHIKI.

LEAVE SO AS TO COME BACK BETTER PREPARED.

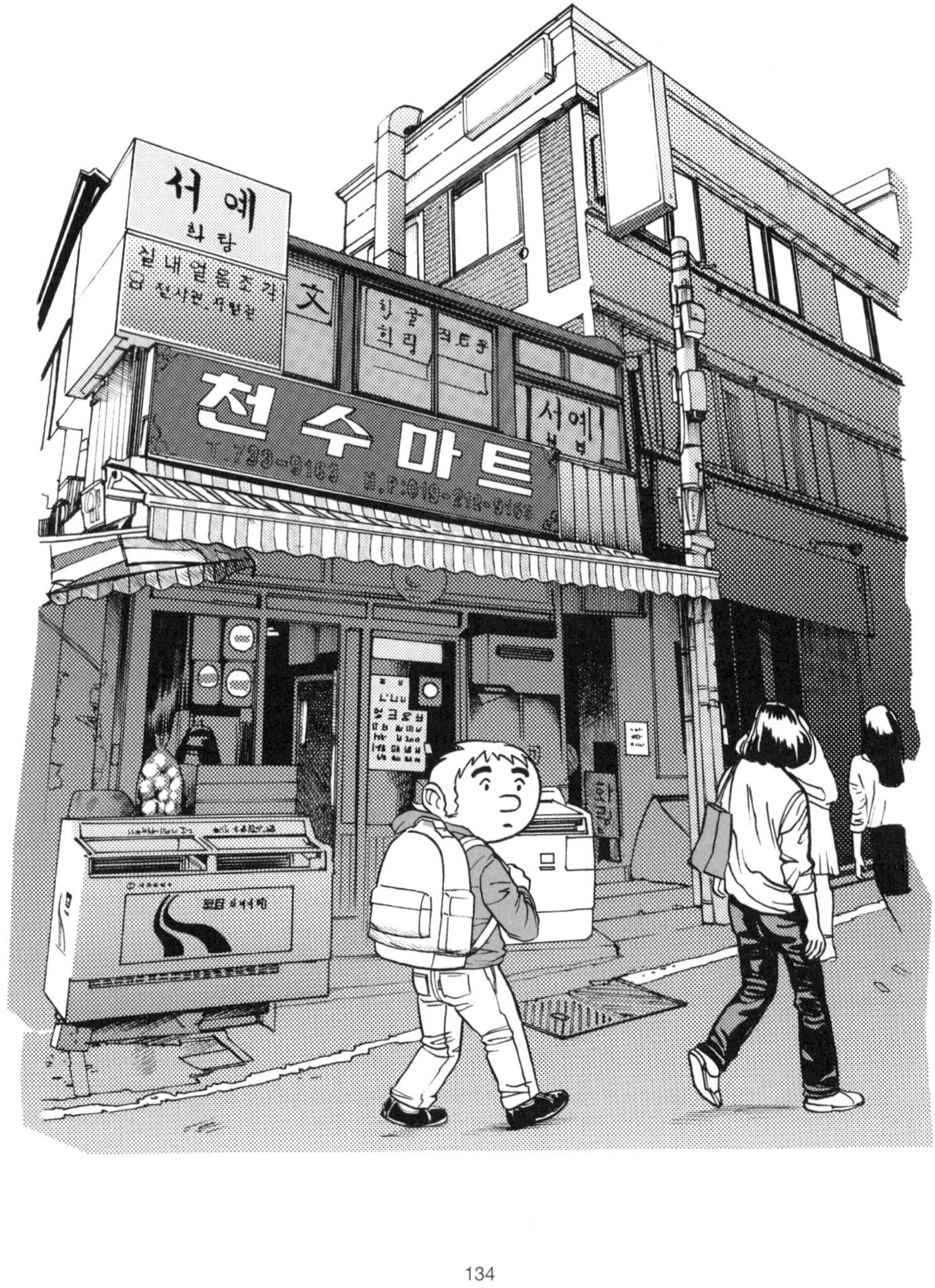
서예
文
천수마트

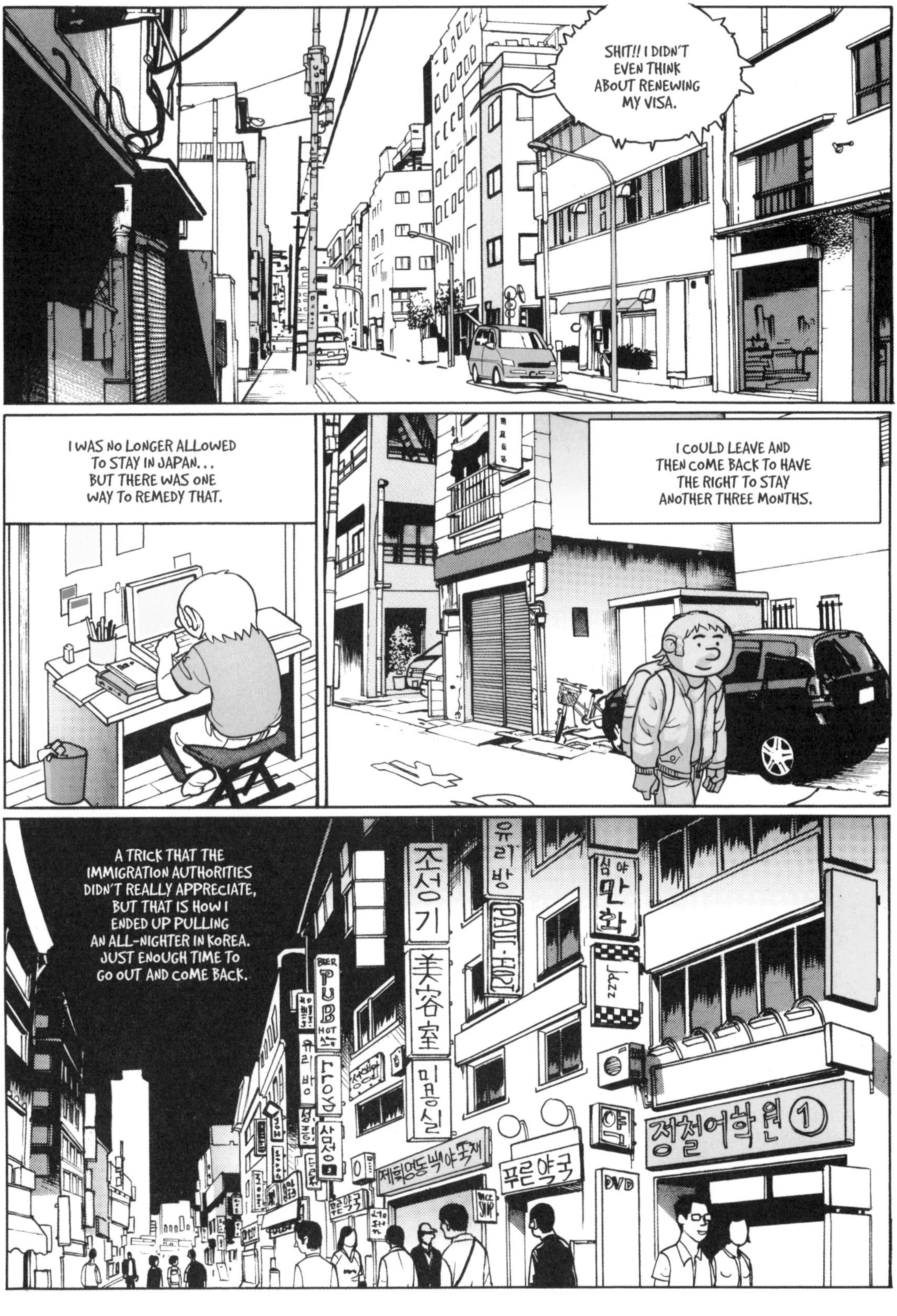
SHIT!! I DIDN'T EVEN THINK ABOUT RENEWING MY VISA.
I WAS NO LONGER ALLOWED TO STAY IN JAPAN. . . BUT THERE WAS ONE WAY TO REMEDY THAT.
I COULD LEAVE AND THEN COME BACK TO HAVE THE RIGHT TO STAY ANOTHER THREE MONTHS.
A TRICK THAT THE IMMIGRATION AUTHORITIES DIDN'T REALLY APPRECIATE, BUT THAT IS HOW I ENDED UP PULLING AN ALL-NIGHTER IN KOREA. JUST ENOUGH TIME TO GO OUT AND COME BACK.
유리방
조성기
美容室
미용실
만화
PUB
정철어학원 ①
푸른약국
DVD

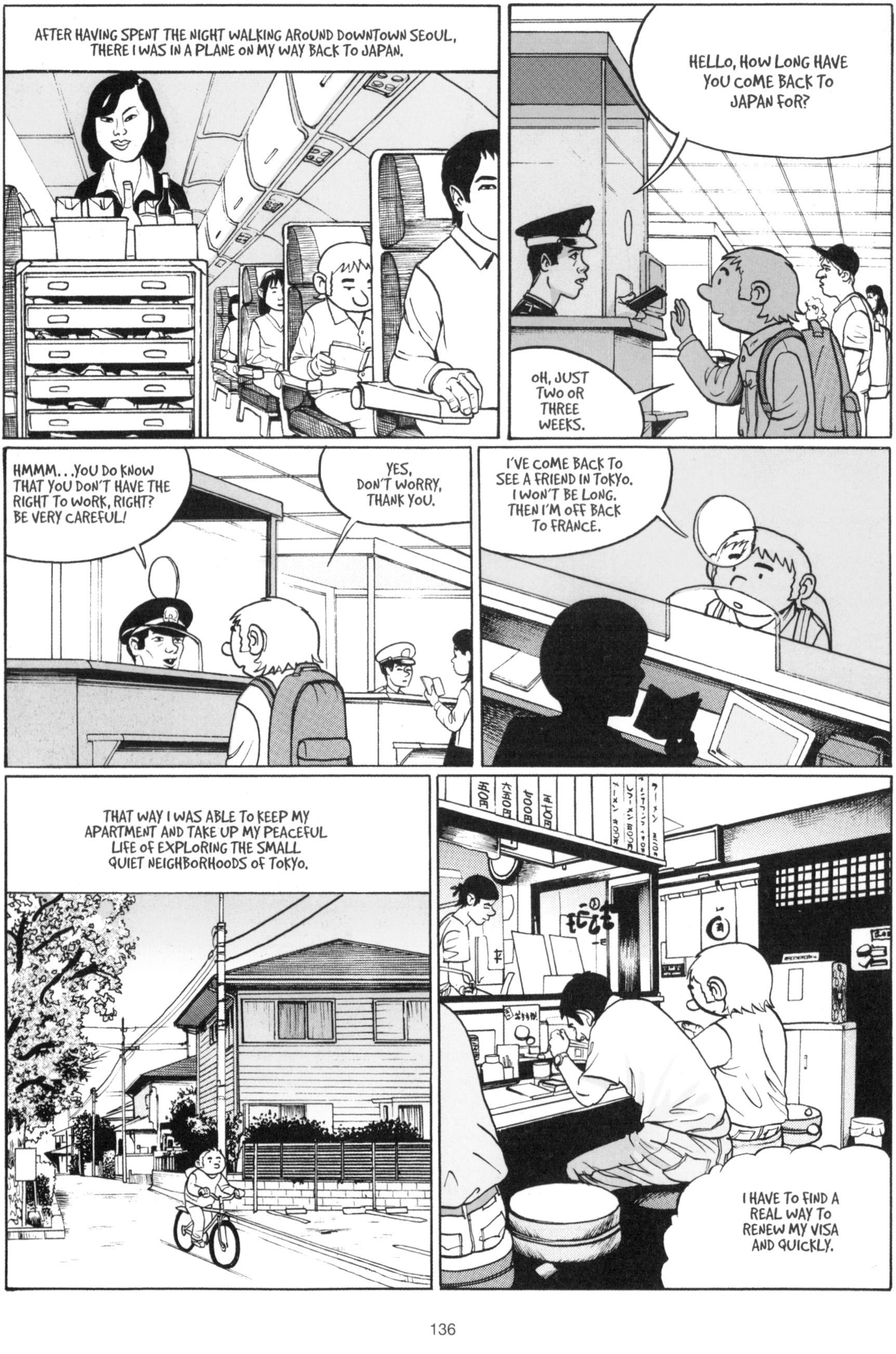
AFTER HAVING SPENT THE NIGHT WALKING AROUND DOWNTOWN SEOUL, THERE I WAS IN A PLANE ON MY WAY BACK TO JAPAN.
HELLO, HOW LONG HAVE YOU COME BACK TO JAPAN FOR?
OH, JUST TWO OR THREE WEEKS.
HMMM. . .YOU DO KNOW THAT YOU DON'T HAVE THE RIGHT TO WORK, RIGHT? BE VERY CAREFUL!
YES, DON'T WORRY, THANK YOU.
I'VE COME BACK TO SEE A FRIEND IN TOKYO. I WON'T BE LONG. THEN I'M OFF BACK TO FRANCE.
THAT WAY I WAS ABLE TO KEEP MY APARTMENT AND TAKE UP MY PEACEFUL LIFE OF EXPLORING THE SMALL QUIET NEIGHBORHOODS OF TOKYO.
I HAVE TO FIND A REAL WAY TO RENEW MY VISA AND QUICKLY.

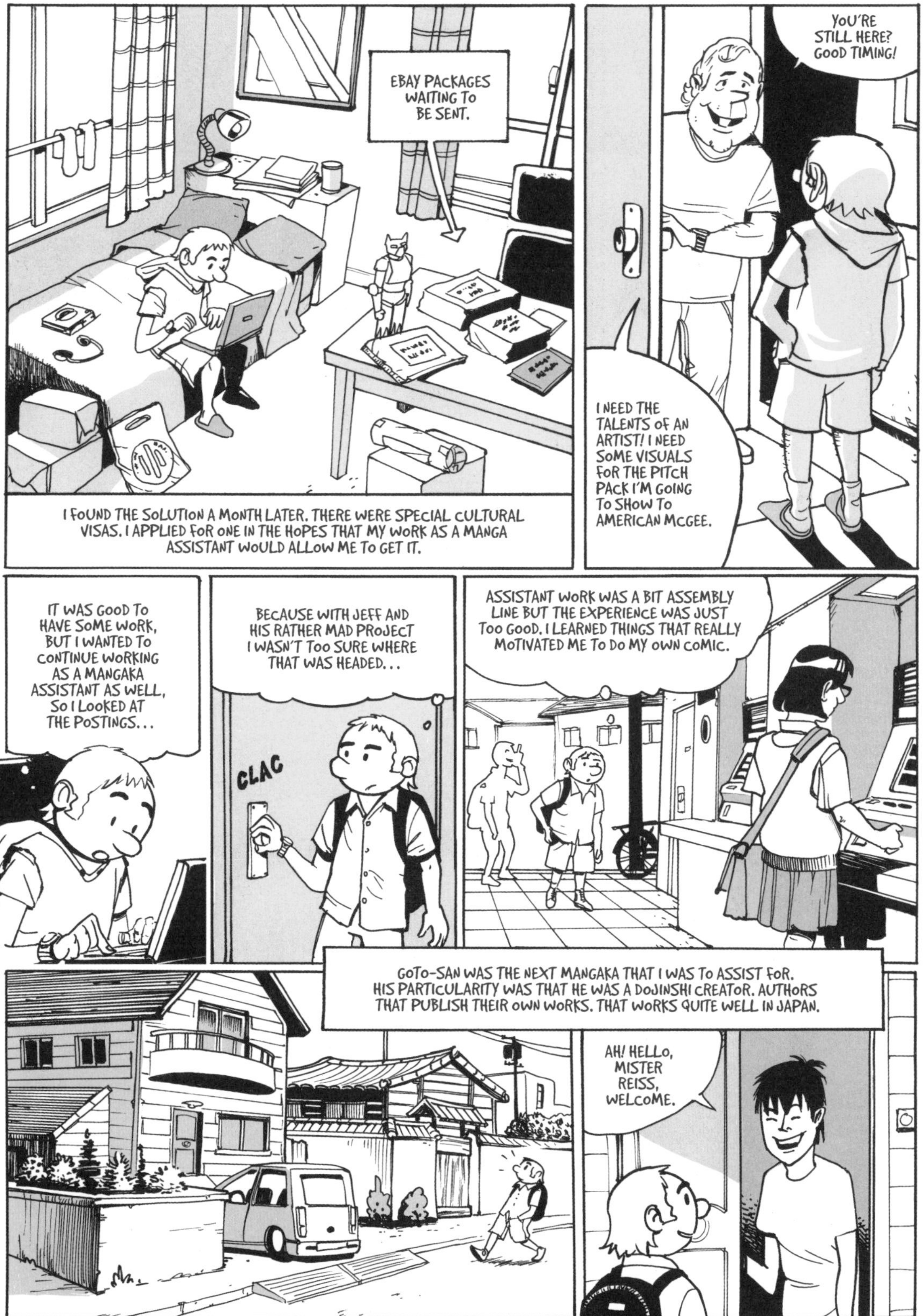
EBAY PACKAGES WAITING TO BE SENT.
I FOUND THE SOLUTION A MONTH LATER. THERE WERE SPECIAL CULTURAL VISAS. I APPLIED FOR ONE IN THE HOPES THAT MY WORK AS A MANGA ASSISTANT WOULD ALLOW ME TO GET IT.
YOU'RE STILL HERE? GOOD TIMING!
I NEED THE TALENTS OF AN ARTIST! I NEED SOME VISUALS FOR THE PITCH PACK I'M GOING TO SHOW TO AMERICAN McGEE.
IT WAS GOOD TO HAVE SOME WORK, BUT I WANTED TO CONTINUE WORKING AS A MANGAKA ASSISTANT AS WELL, SO I LOOKED AT THE POSTINGS...
BECAUSE WITH JEFF AND HIS RATHER MAD PROJECT I WASN'T TOO SURE WHERE THAT WAS HEADED...
CLAC
ASSISTANT WORK WAS A BIT ASSEMBLY LINE BUT THE EXPERIENCE WAS JUST TOO GOOD. I LEARNED THINGS THAT REALLY MOTIVATED ME TO DO MY OWN COMIC.
GOTO-SAN WAS THE NEXT MANGAKA THAT I WAS TO ASSIST FOR. HIS PARTICULARITY WAS THAT HE WAS A DOJINSHI CREATOR. AUTHORS THAT PUBLISH THEIR OWN WORKS. THAT WORKS QUITE WELL IN JAPAN.
AH! HELLO, MISTER REISS, WELCOME.

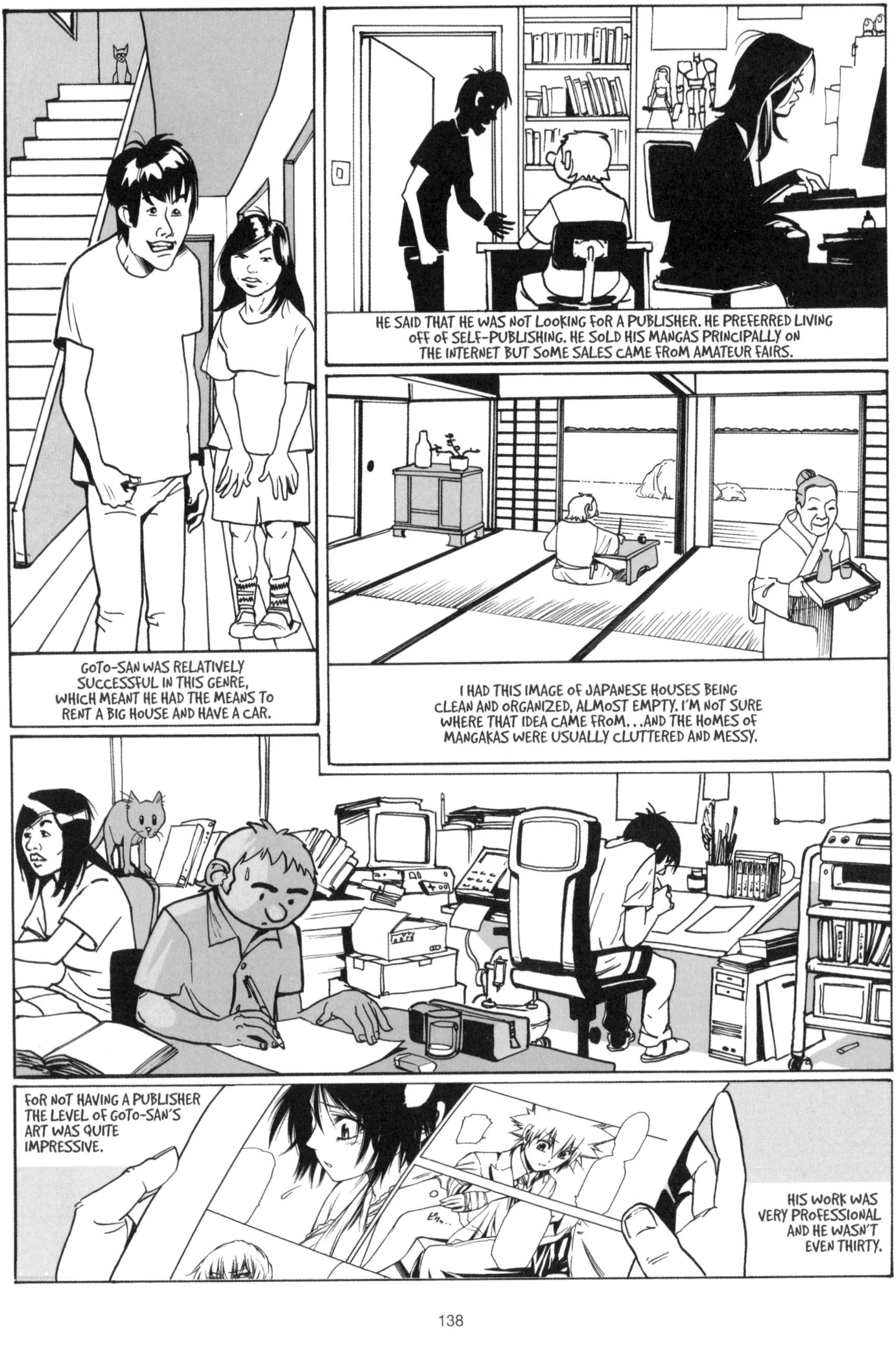
GOTO-SAN WAS RELATIVELY SUCCESSFUL IN THIS GENRE, WHICH MEANT HE HAD THE MEANS TO RENT A BIG HOUSE AND HAVE A CAR.
HE SAID THAT HE WAS NOT LOOKING FOR A PUBLISHER. HE PREFERRED LIVING OFF OF SELF-PUBLISHING. HE SOLD HIS MANGAS PRINCIPALLY ON THE INTERNET BUT SOME SALES CAME FROM AMATEUR FAIRS.
I HAD THIS IMAGE OF JAPANESE HOUSES BEING CLEAN AND ORGANIZED, ALMOST EMPTY. I'M NOT SURE WHERE THAT IDEA CAME FROM. . . AND THE HOMES OF MANGAKAS WERE USUALLY CLUTTERED AND MESSY.
FOR NOT HAVING A PUBLISHER THE LEVEL OF GOTO-SAN'S ART WAS QUITE IMPRESSIVE.
HIS WORK WAS VERY PROFESSIONAL AND HE WASN'T EVEN THIRTY.

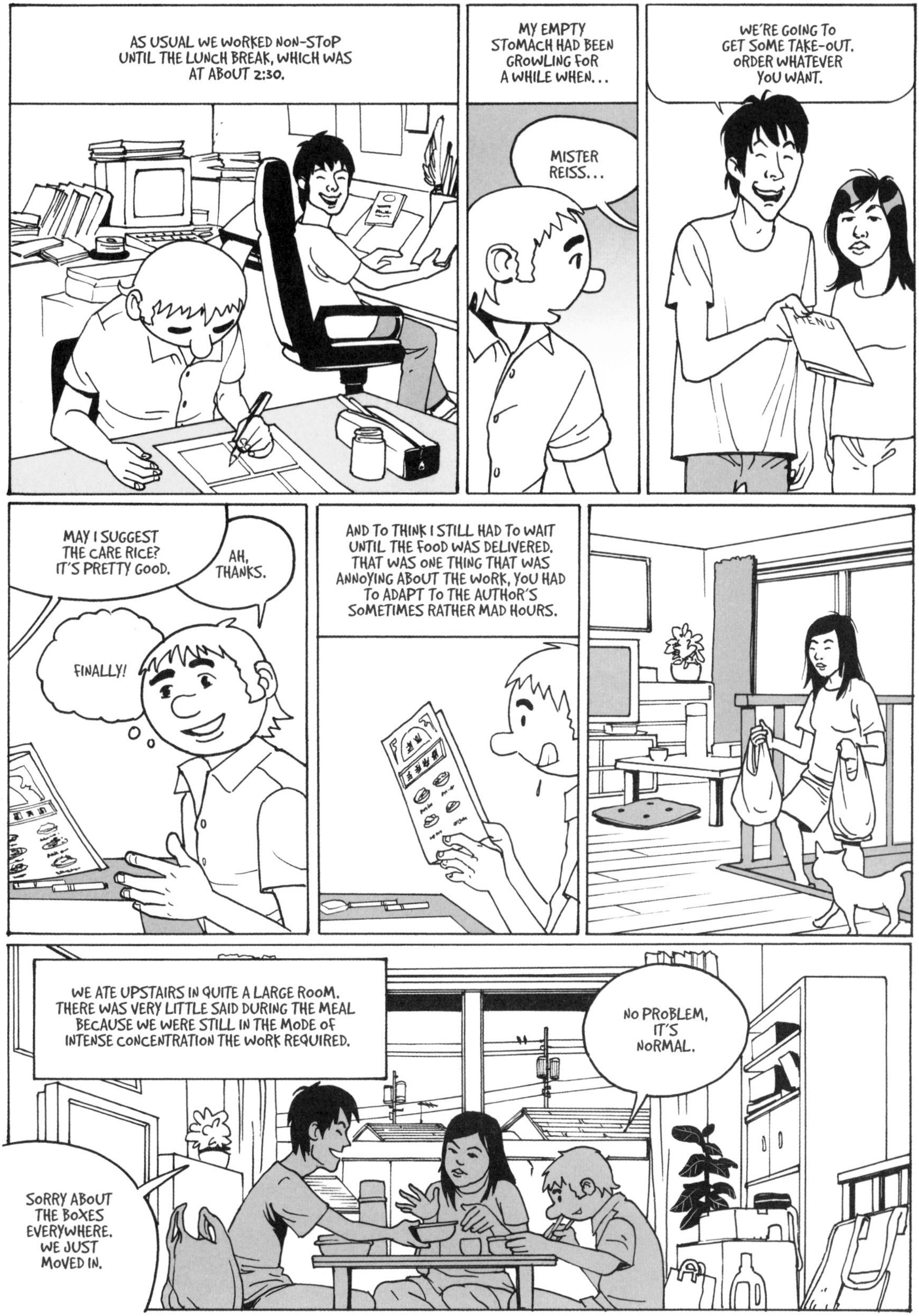
AS USUAL WE WORKED NON-STOP UNTIL THE LUNCH BREAK, WHICH WAS AT ABOUT 2:30.
MY EMPTY STOMACH HAD BEEN GROWLING FOR A WHILE WHEN...
MISTER REISS...
WE'RE GOING TO GET SOME TAKE-OUT. ORDER WHATEVER YOU WANT.
MENU
MAY I SUGGEST THE CARE RICE? IT'S PRETTY GOOD.
AH, THANKS.
FINALLY!
AND TO THINK I STILL HAD TO WAIT UNTIL THE FOOD WAS DELIVERED. THAT WAS ONE THING THAT WAS ANNOYING ABOUT THE WORK, YOU HAD TO ADAPT TO THE AUTHOR'S SOMETIMES RATHER MAD HOURS.
WE ATE UPSTAIRS IN QUITE A LARGE ROOM. THERE WAS VERY LITTLE SAID DURING THE MEAL BECAUSE WE WERE STILL IN THE MODE OF INTENSE CONCENTRATION THE WORK REQUIRED.
SORRY ABOUT THE BOXES EVERYWHERE. WE JUST MOVED IN.
NO PROBLEM, IT'S NORMAL.

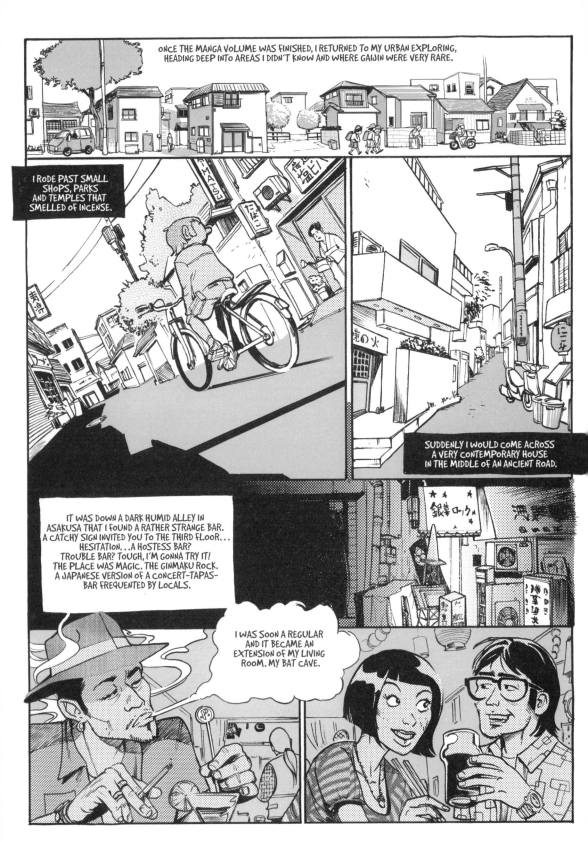

ONCE THE MANGA VOLUME WAS FINISHED, I RETURNED TO MY URBAN EXPLORING, HEADING DEEP INTO AREAS I DIDN'T KNOW AND WHERE GAIJIN WERE VERY RARE.

I RODE PAST SMALL SHOPS, PARKS AND TEMPLES THAT SMELLED OF INCENSE.

SUDDENLY I WOULD COME ACROSS A VERY CONTEMPORARY HOUSE IN THE MIDDLE OF AN ANCIENT ROAD.

IT WAS DOWN A DARK HUMID ALLEY IN ASAKUSA THAT I FOUND A RATHER STRANGE BAR. A CATCHY SIGN INVITED YOU TO THE THIRD FLOOR... HESITATION...A HOSTESS BAR? TROUBLE BAR? TOUGH, I'M GONNA TRY IT! THE PLACE WAS MAGIC. THE GINMAKU ROCK. A JAPANESE VERSION OF A CONCERT-TAPAS-BAR FREQUENTED BY LOCALS.

I WAS SOON A REGULAR AND IT BECAME AN EXTENSION OF MY LIVING ROOM. MY BAT CAVE.

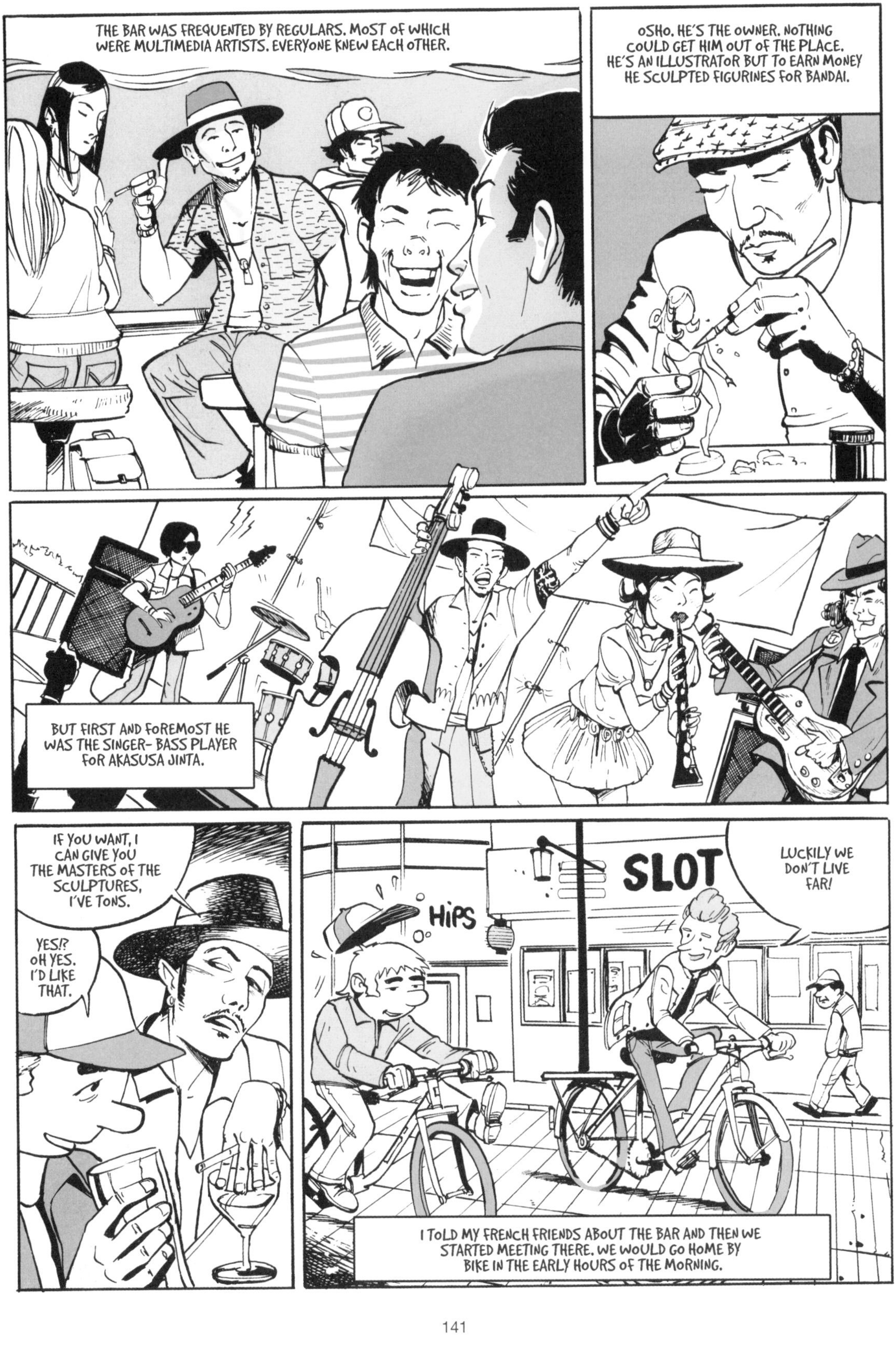
THE BAR WAS FREQUENTED BY REGULARS. MOST OF WHICH WERE MULTIMEDIA ARTISTS. EVERYONE KNEW EACH OTHER.
OSHO. HE'S THE OWNER. NOTHING COULD GET HIM OUT OF THE PLACE. HE'S AN ILLUSTRATOR BUT TO EARN MONEY HE SCULPTED FIGURINES FOR BANDAI.
BUT FIRST AND FOREMOST HE WAS THE SINGER- BASS PLAYER FOR AKASUSA JINTA.
IF YOU WANT, I CAN GIVE YOU THE MASTERS OF THE SCULPTURES, I'VE TONS.
YES!? OH YES. I'D LIKE THAT.
SLOT
LUCKILY WE DON'T LIVE FAR!
HIPS
I TOLD MY FRENCH FRIENDS ABOUT THE BAR AND THEN WE STARTED MEETING THERE. WE WOULD GO HOME BY BIKE IN THE EARLY HOURS OF THE MORNING.

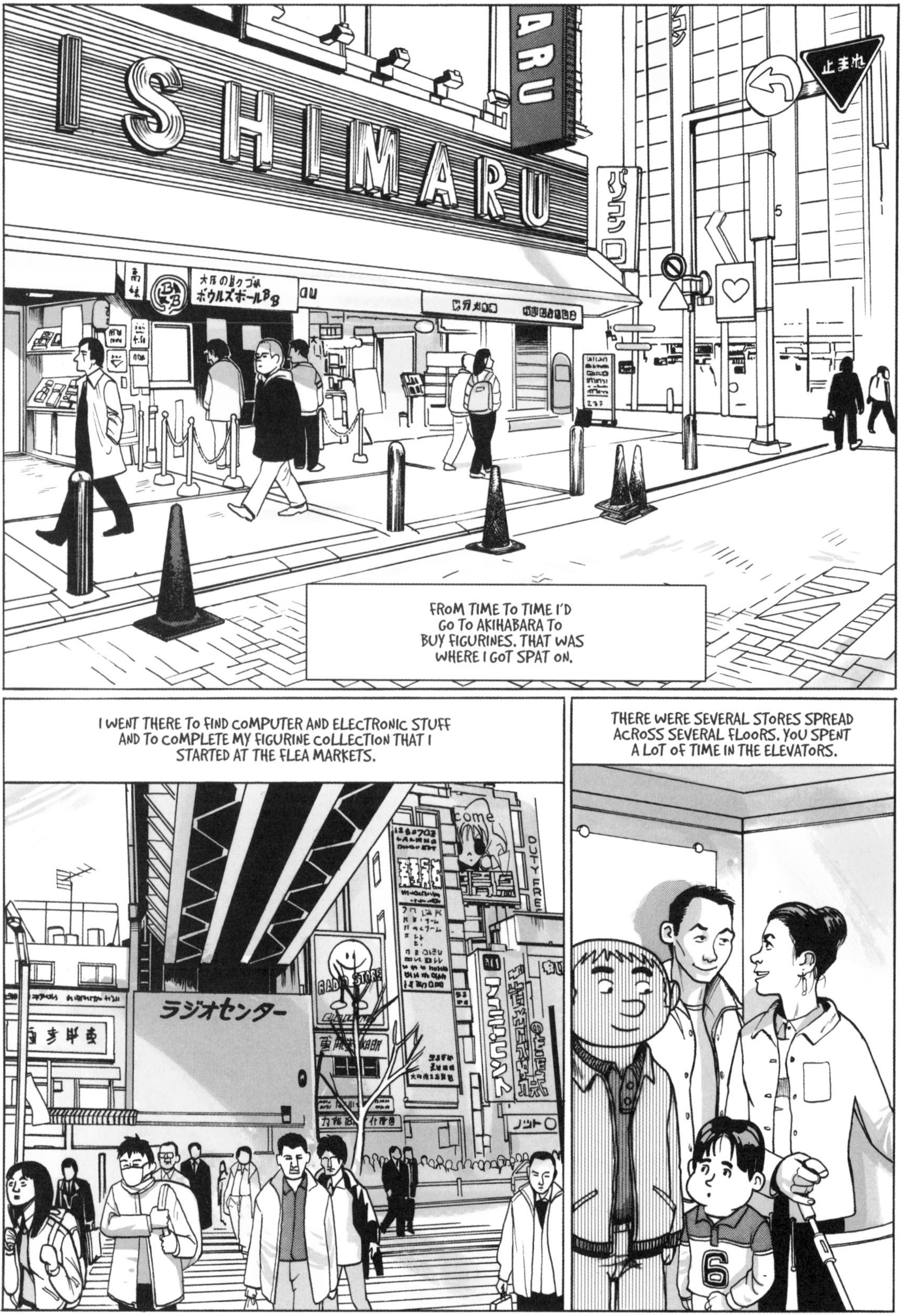
FROM TIME TO TIME I'D GO TO AKIHABARA TO BUY FIGURINES. THAT WAS WHERE I GOT SPAT ON.
I WENT THERE TO FIND COMPUTER AND ELECTRONIC STUFF AND TO COMPLETE MY FIGURINE COLLECTION THAT I STARTED AT THE FLEA MARKETS.
THERE WERE SEVERAL STORES SPREAD ACROSS SEVERAL FLOORS. YOU SPENT A LOT OF TIME IN THE ELEVATORS.

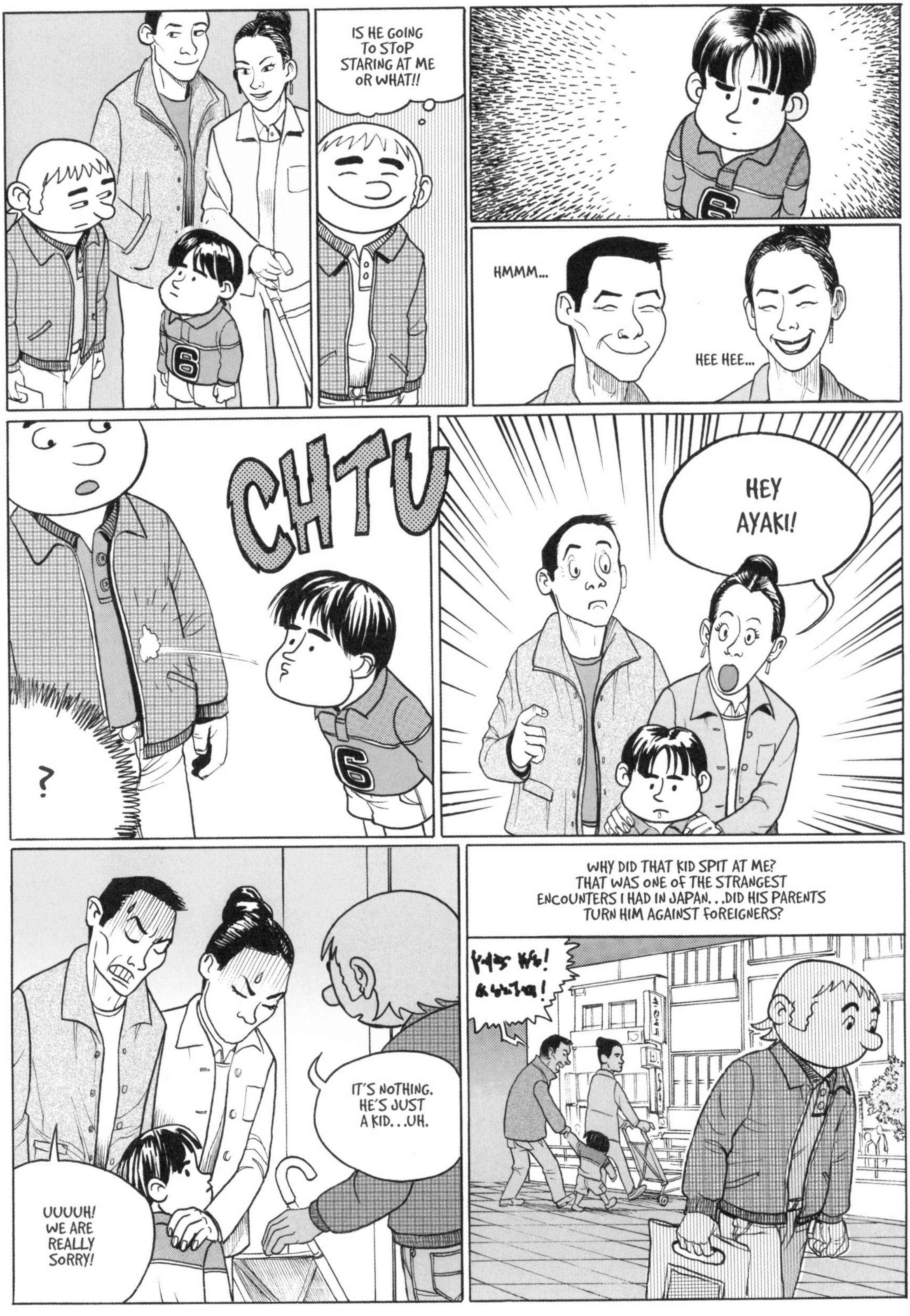
IS HE GOING TO STOP STARING AT ME OR WHAT!!
HMMM...
HEE HEE...
CHTU
?
HEY AYAKI!
UUUUH! WE ARE REALLY SORRY!
IT'S NOTHING. HE'S JUST A KID. . .UH.
WHY DID THAT KID SPIT AT ME? THAT WAS ONE OF THE STRANGEST ENCOUNTERS I HAD IN JAPAN. . .DID HIS PARENTS TURN HIM AGAINST FOREIGNERS?

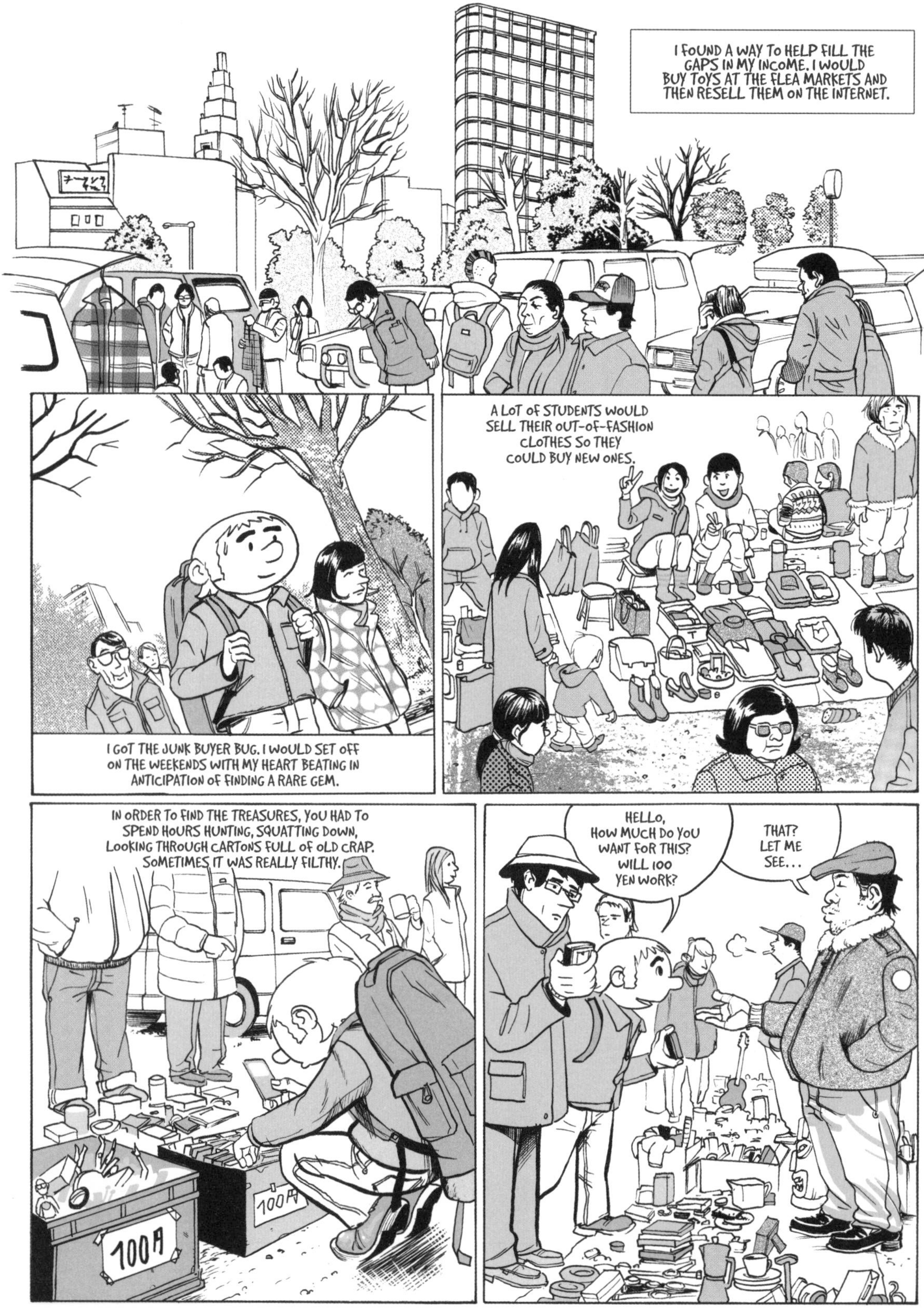
I FOUND A WAY TO HELP FILL THE GAPS IN MY INCOME. I WOULD BUY TOYS AT THE FLEA MARKETS AND THEN RESELL THEM ON THE INTERNET.
I GOT THE JUNK BUYER BUG. I WOULD SET OFF ON THE WEEKENDS WITH MY HEART BEATING IN ANTICIPATION OF FINDING A RARE GEM.
A LOT OF STUDENTS WOULD SELL THEIR OUT-OF-FASHION CLOTHES SO THEY COULD BUY NEW ONES.
IN ORDER TO FIND THE TREASURES, YOU HAD TO SPEND HOURS HUNTING, SQUATTING DOWN, LOOKING THROUGH CARTONS FULL OF OLD CRAP. SOMETIMES IT WAS REALLY FILTHY.
100円
100円
HELLO, HOW MUCH DO YOU WANT FOR THIS? WILL 100 YEN WORK?
THAT? LET ME SEE...

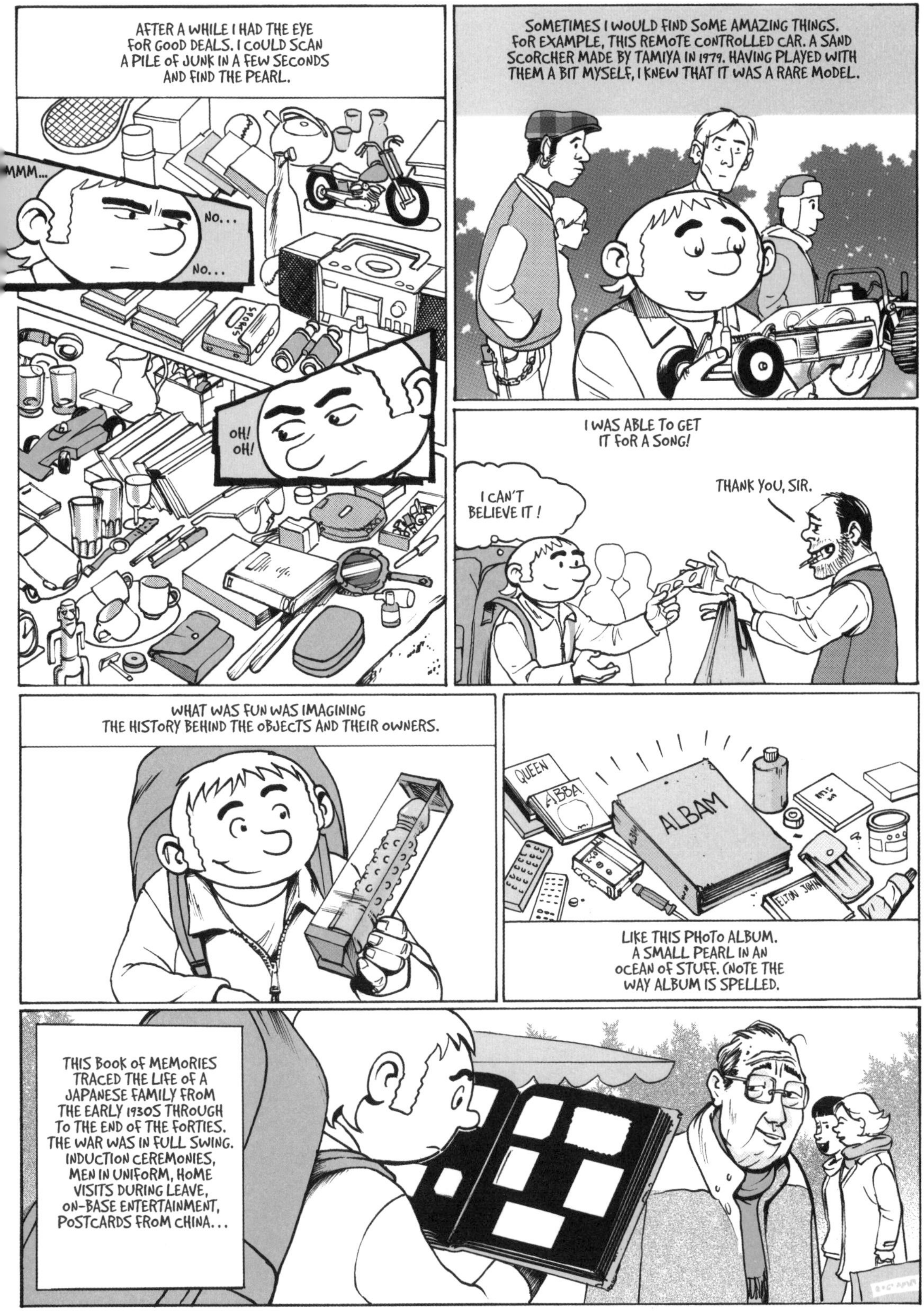
AFTER A WHILE I HAD THE EYE FOR GOOD DEALS. I COULD SCAN A PILE OF JUNK IN A FEW SECONDS AND FIND THE PEARL.
MMM...
NO...
NO...
OH! OH!
SOMETIMES I WOULD FIND SOME AMAZING THINGS. FOR EXAMPLE, THIS REMOTE CONTROLLED CAR. A SAND SCORCHER MADE BY TAMIYA IN 1979. HAVING PLAYED WITH THEM A BIT MYSELF, I KNEW THAT IT WAS A RARE MODEL.
I WAS ABLE TO GET IT FOR A SONG!
I CAN'T BELIEVE IT !
THANK YOU, SIR.
WHAT WAS FUN WAS IMAGINING THE HISTORY BEHIND THE OBJECTS AND THEIR OWNERS.
QUEEN
ABBA
ALBAM
ELTON JOHN
LIKE THIS PHOTO ALBUM. A SMALL PEARL IN AN OCEAN OF STUFF. (NOTE THE WAY ALBUM IS SPELLED.
THIS BOOK OF MEMORIES TRACED THE LIFE OF A JAPANESE FAMILY FROM THE EARLY 1930S THROUGH TO THE END OF THE FORTIES. THE WAR WAS IN FULL SWING. INDUCTION CEREMONIES, MEN IN UNIFORM, HOME VISITS DURING LEAVE, ON-BASE ENTERTAINMENT, POSTCARDS FROM CHINA...

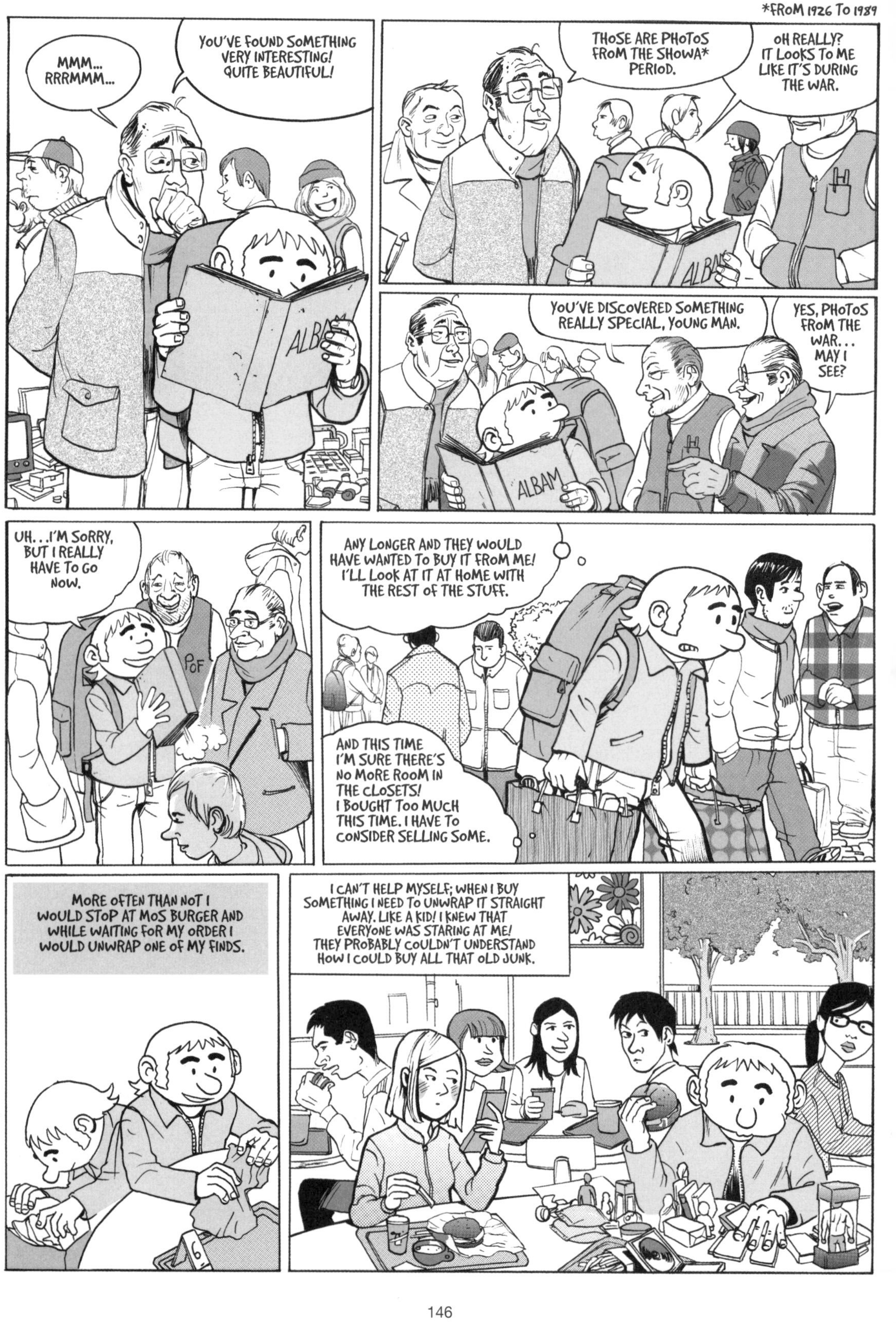
*FROM 1926 TO 1989
MMM... RRRMMM...
YOU'VE FOUND SOMETHING VERY INTERESTING! QUITE BEAUTIFUL!
ALBAM
THOSE ARE PHOTOS FROM THE SHOWA* PERIOD.
OH REALLY? IT LOOKS TO ME LIKE IT'S DURING THE WAR.
ALBAM
YOU'VE DISCOVERED SOMETHING REALLY SPECIAL, YOUNG MAN.
YES, PHOTOS FROM THE WAR... MAY I SEE?
ALBAM
UH...I'M SORRY, BUT I REALLY HAVE TO GO NOW.
POF
ANY LONGER AND THEY WOULD HAVE WANTED TO BUY IT FROM ME! I'LL LOOK AT IT AT HOME WITH THE REST OF THE STUFF.
AND THIS TIME I'M SURE THERE'S NO MORE ROOM IN THE CLOSETS! I BOUGHT TOO MUCH THIS TIME. I HAVE TO CONSIDER SELLING SOME.
MORE OFTEN THAN NOT I WOULD STOP AT MOS BURGER AND WHILE WAITING FOR MY ORDER I WOULD UNWRAP ONE OF MY FINDS.
I CAN'T HELP MYSELF; WHEN I BUY SOMETHING I NEED TO UNWRAP IT STRAIGHT AWAY. LIKE A KID! I KNEW THAT EVERYONE WAS STARING AT ME! THEY PROBABLY COULDN'T UNDERSTAND HOW I COULD BUY ALL THAT OLD JUNK.

GAMES

HELP JEREMY THE GEEK GET HIS MEMORY BACK BY TRYING TO REMEMBER THE NAMES OF ALL OF THE CONSOLES BELOW. YOU HAVE ONE MINUTE!

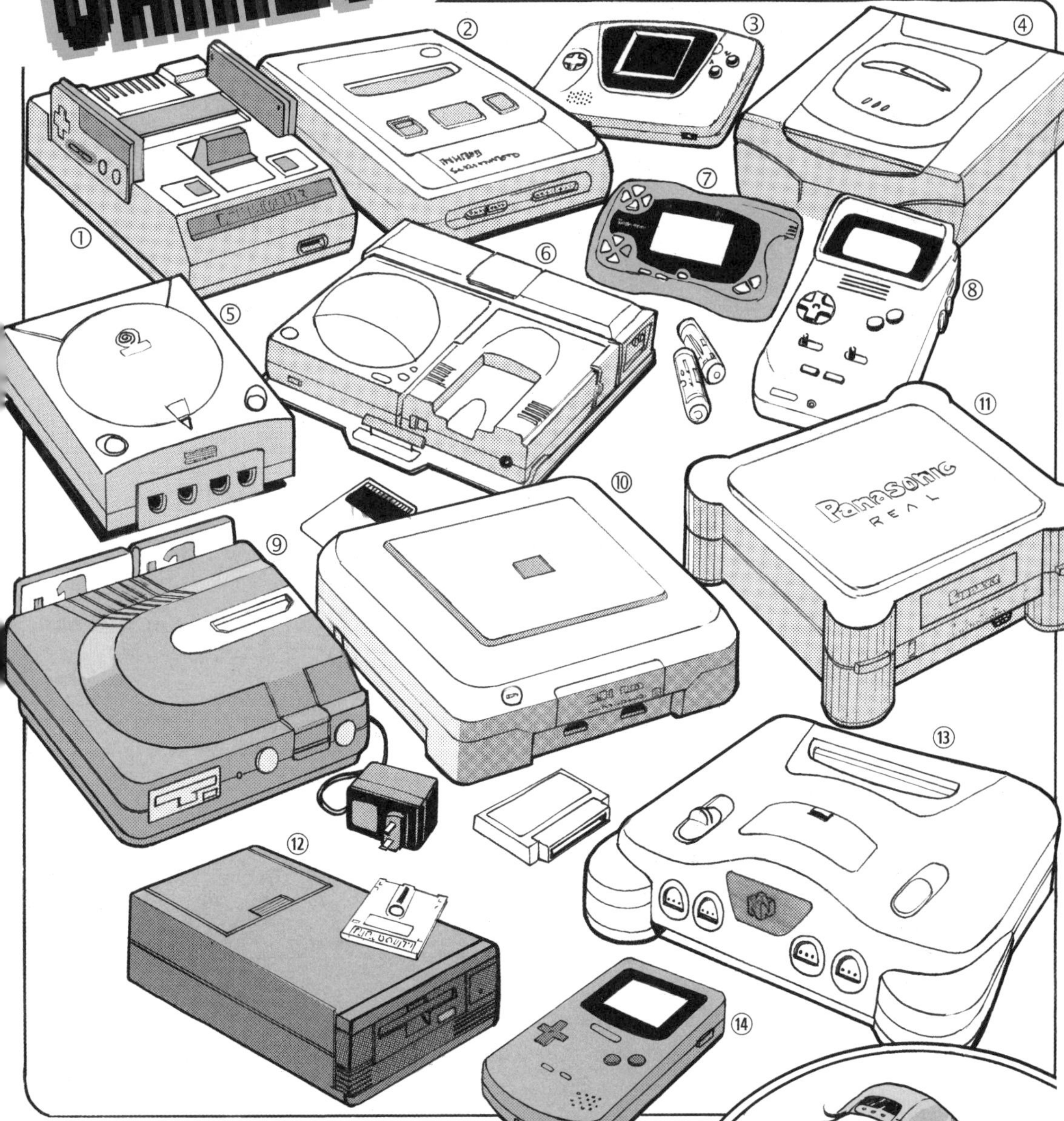

①
②
③
④
⑤
⑥
⑦
⑧
⑨
⑩
⑪
Panasonic
REAL
⑫
⑬
⑭

SOLUTION

① Famicom ② Super Famicom ③ Sega Game Gear ④ Sega Saturn
⑤ Sega Dreamcast ⑥ Nec PC Engine CD-ROM ⑦ Bandai WonderSwan color
⑧ Nec PC Engine GT ⑨ Sharp TwinFamicom ⑩ Neo-Geo CD(front loading)
⑪ Panasonic 3DO ⑫ Nintendo Disk system ⑬ Nintendo N64
⑭ Nintendo Game Boy color

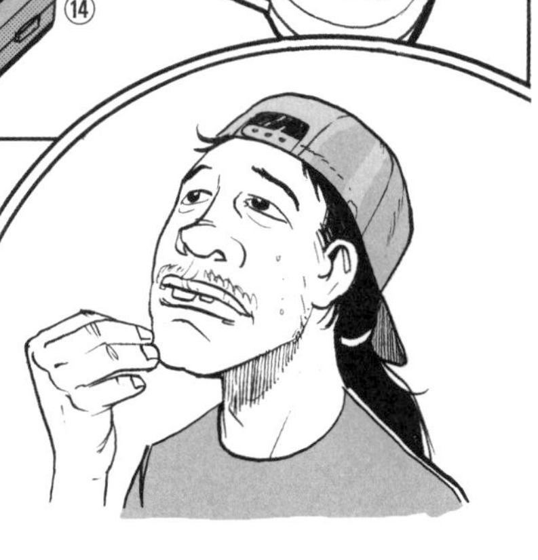

JEREMY WAS CONFRONTED BY A GROUP OF JAPANESE PEOPLE.
HE WANTED TO APPEAR IN THE KNOW, SAYING HE LOVED MANGA. AS A RESULT,
THE JAPANESE SAID: OH, REALLY? COOL! WHAT MANGAS DO YOU LIKE?
HELP JEREMY REMEMBER THE TITLES OF THE MANGAS THAT HE HAS READ RECENTLY.

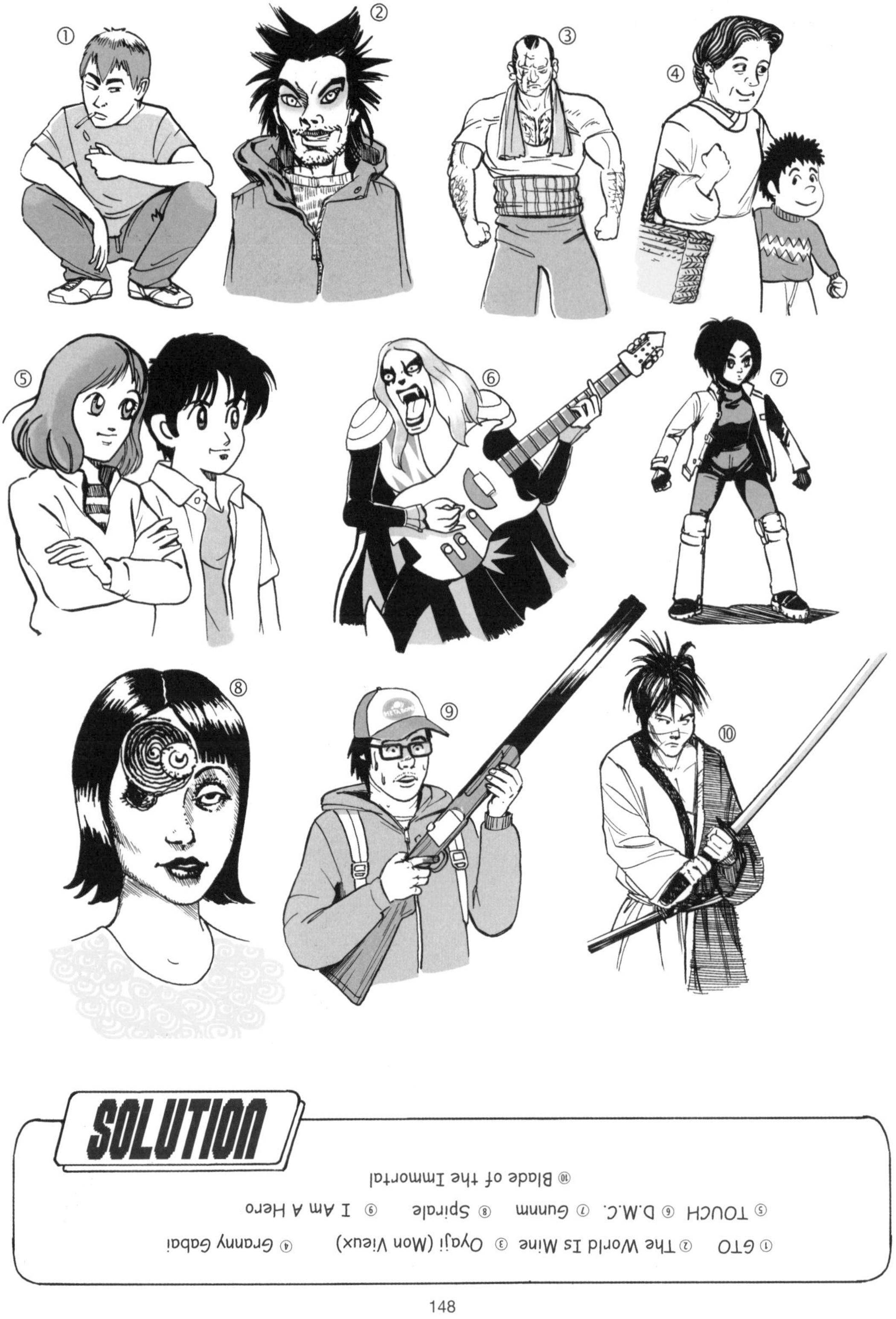
①
②
③
④
⑤
⑥
⑦
⑧
⑨
⑩

SOLUTION

① GTO ② The World Is Mine ③ Oyaji (Mon Vieux) ④ Granny Gabai

⑤ TOUCH ⑥ D.M.C. ⑦ Gunnm ⑧ Spirale ⑨ I Am A Hero

⑩ Blade of the Immortal

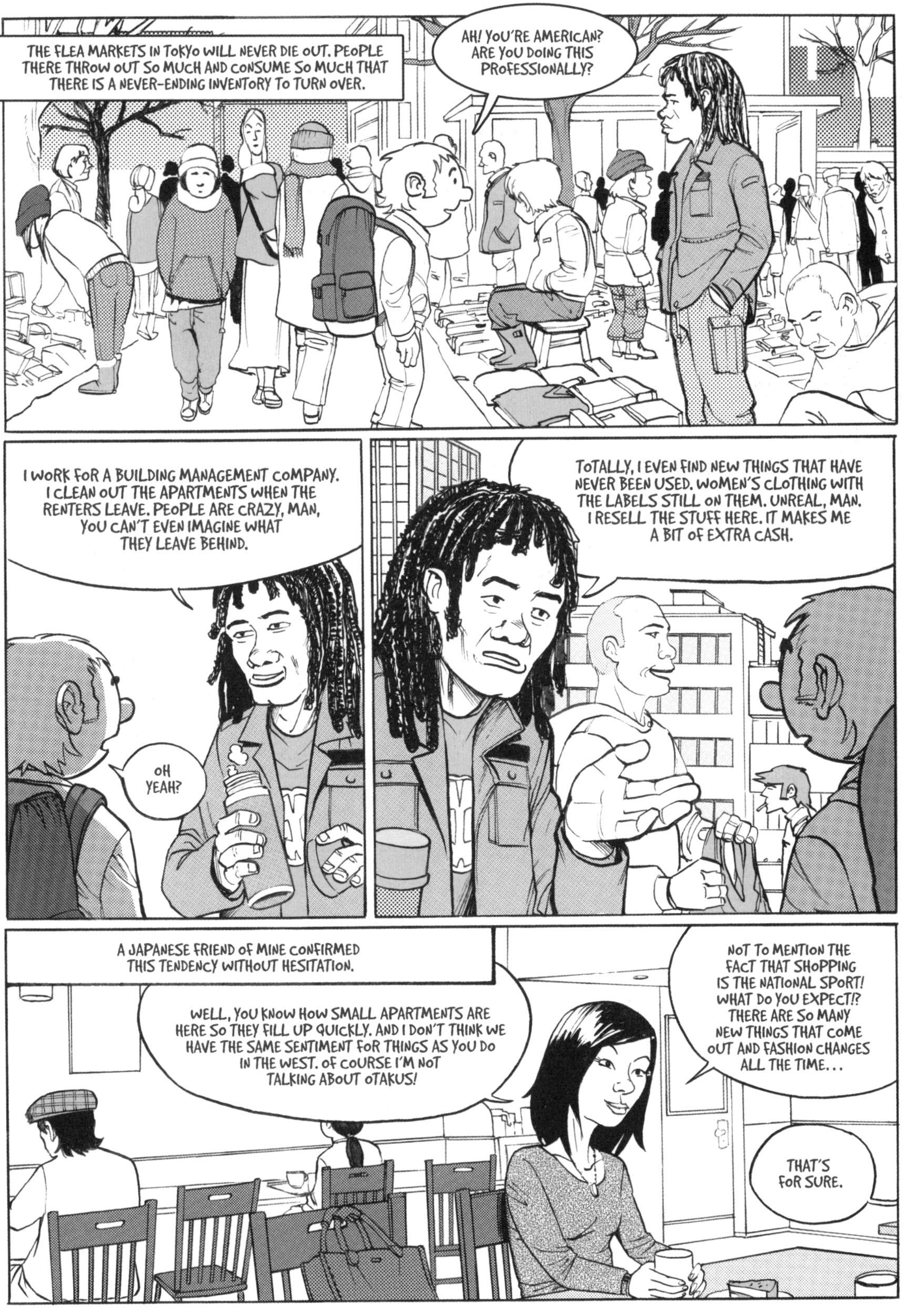
THE FLEA MARKETS IN TOKYO WILL NEVER DIE OUT. PEOPLE THERE THROW OUT SO MUCH AND CONSUME SO MUCH THAT THERE IS A NEVER-ENDING INVENTORY TO TURN OVER.
AH! YOU'RE AMERICAN? ARE YOU DOING THIS PROFESSIONALLY?
I WORK FOR A BUILDING MANAGEMENT COMPANY. I CLEAN OUT THE APARTMENTS WHEN THE RENTERS LEAVE. PEOPLE ARE CRAZY, MAN, YOU CAN'T EVEN IMAGINE WHAT THEY LEAVE BEHIND.
OH YEAH?
TOTALLY, I EVEN FIND NEW THINGS THAT HAVE NEVER BEEN USED. WOMEN'S CLOTHING WITH THE LABELS STILL ON THEM. UNREAL, MAN. I RESELL THE STUFF HERE. IT MAKES ME A BIT OF EXTRA CASH.
A JAPANESE FRIEND OF MINE CONFIRMED THIS TENDENCY WITHOUT HESITATION.
WELL, YOU KNOW HOW SMALL APARTMENTS ARE HERE SO THEY FILL UP QUICKLY. AND I DON'T THINK WE HAVE THE SAME SENTIMENT FOR THINGS AS YOU DO IN THE WEST. OF COURSE I'M NOT TALKING ABOUT OTAKUS!
NOT TO MENTION THE FACT THAT SHOPPING IS THE NATIONAL SPORT! WHAT DO YOU EXPECT!? THERE ARE SO MANY NEW THINGS THAT COME OUT AND FASHION CHANGES ALL THE TIME...
THAT'S FOR SURE.

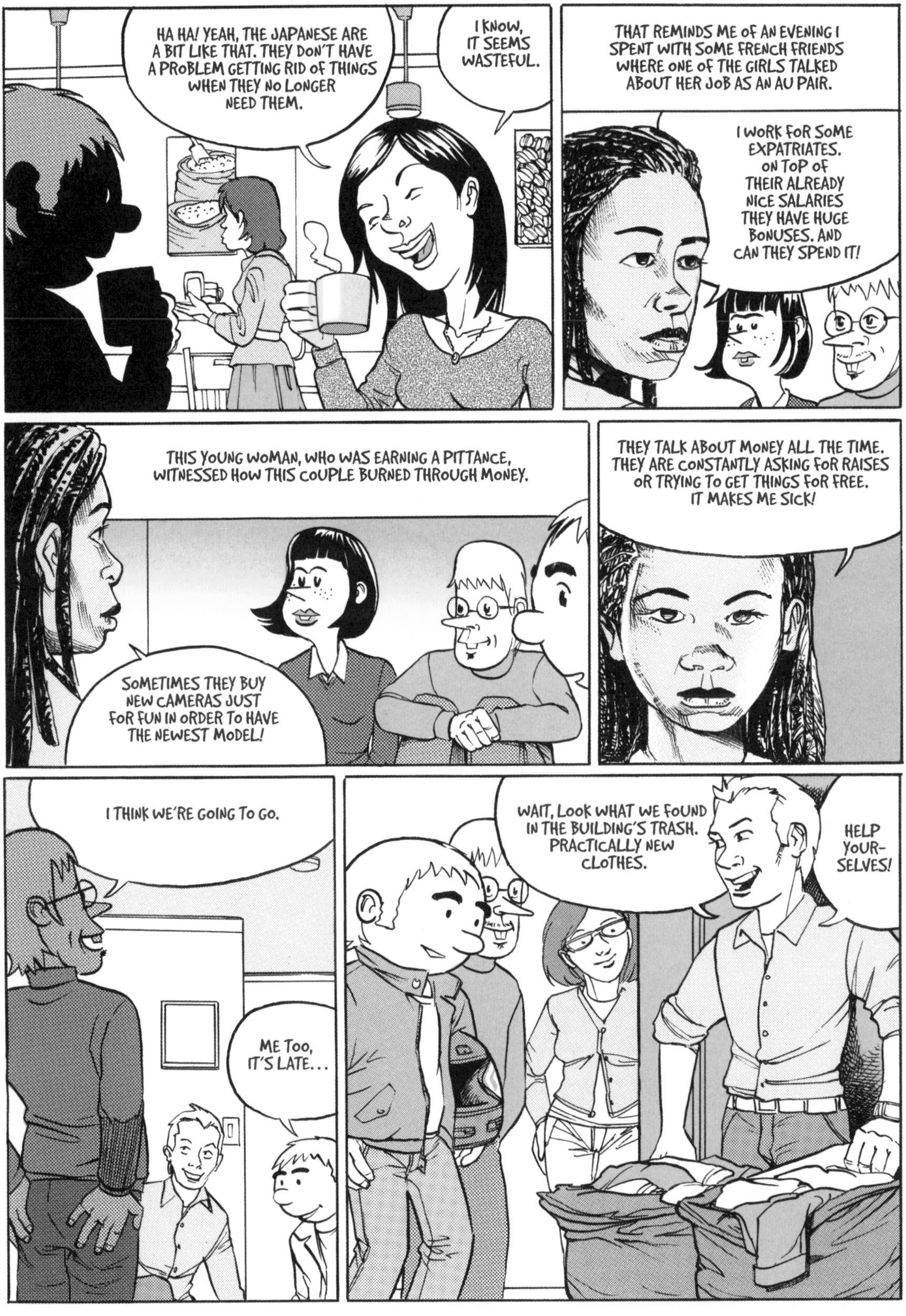
HA HA! YEAH, THE JAPANESE ARE A BIT LIKE THAT. THEY DON'T HAVE A PROBLEM GETTING RID OF THINGS WHEN THEY NO LONGER NEED THEM.
I KNOW, IT SEEMS WASTEFUL.
THAT REMINDS ME OF AN EVENING I SPENT WITH SOME FRENCH FRIENDS WHERE ONE OF THE GIRLS TALKED ABOUT HER JOB AS AN AU PAIR.
I WORK FOR SOME EXPATRIATES. ON TOP OF THEIR ALREADY NICE SALARIES THEY HAVE HUGE BONUSES. AND CAN THEY SPEND IT!
THIS YOUNG WOMAN, WHO WAS EARNING A PITTANCE, WITNESSED HOW THIS COUPLE BURNED THROUGH MONEY.
SOMETIMES THEY BUY NEW CAMERAS JUST FOR FUN IN ORDER TO HAVE THE NEWEST MODEL!
THEY TALK ABOUT MONEY ALL THE TIME. THEY ARE CONSTANTLY ASKING FOR RAISES OR TRYING TO GET THINGS FOR FREE. IT MAKES ME SICK!
I THINK WE'RE GOING TO GO.
ME TOO, IT'S LATE...
WAIT, LOOK WHAT WE FOUND IN THE BUILDING'S TRASH. PRACTICALLY NEW CLOTHES.
HELP YOURSELVES!

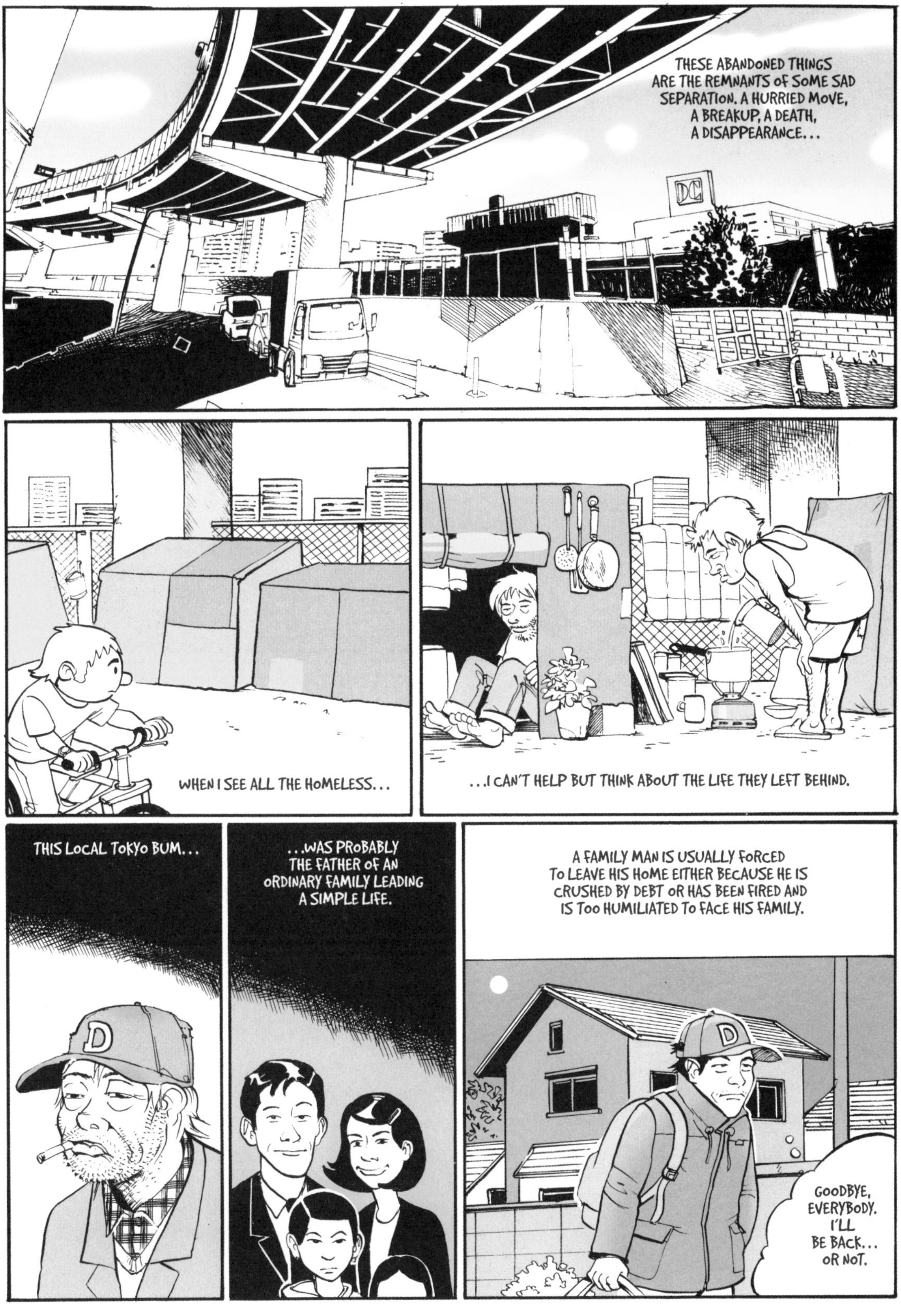
THESE ABANDONED THINGS ARE THE REMNANTS OF SOME SAD SEPARATION. A HURRIED MOVE, A BREAKUP, A DEATH, A DISAPPEARANCE...
WHEN I SEE ALL THE HOMELESS...
...I CAN'T HELP BUT THINK ABOUT THE LIFE THEY LEFT BEHIND.
THIS LOCAL TOKYO BUM...
...WAS PROBABLY THE FATHER OF AN ORDINARY FAMILY LEADING A SIMPLE LIFE.
A FAMILY MAN IS USUALLY FORCED TO LEAVE HIS HOME EITHER BECAUSE HE IS CRUSHED BY DEBT OR HAS BEEN FIRED AND IS TOO HUMILIATED TO FACE HIS FAMILY.
GOODBYE, EVERYBODY. I'LL BE BACK... OR NOT.

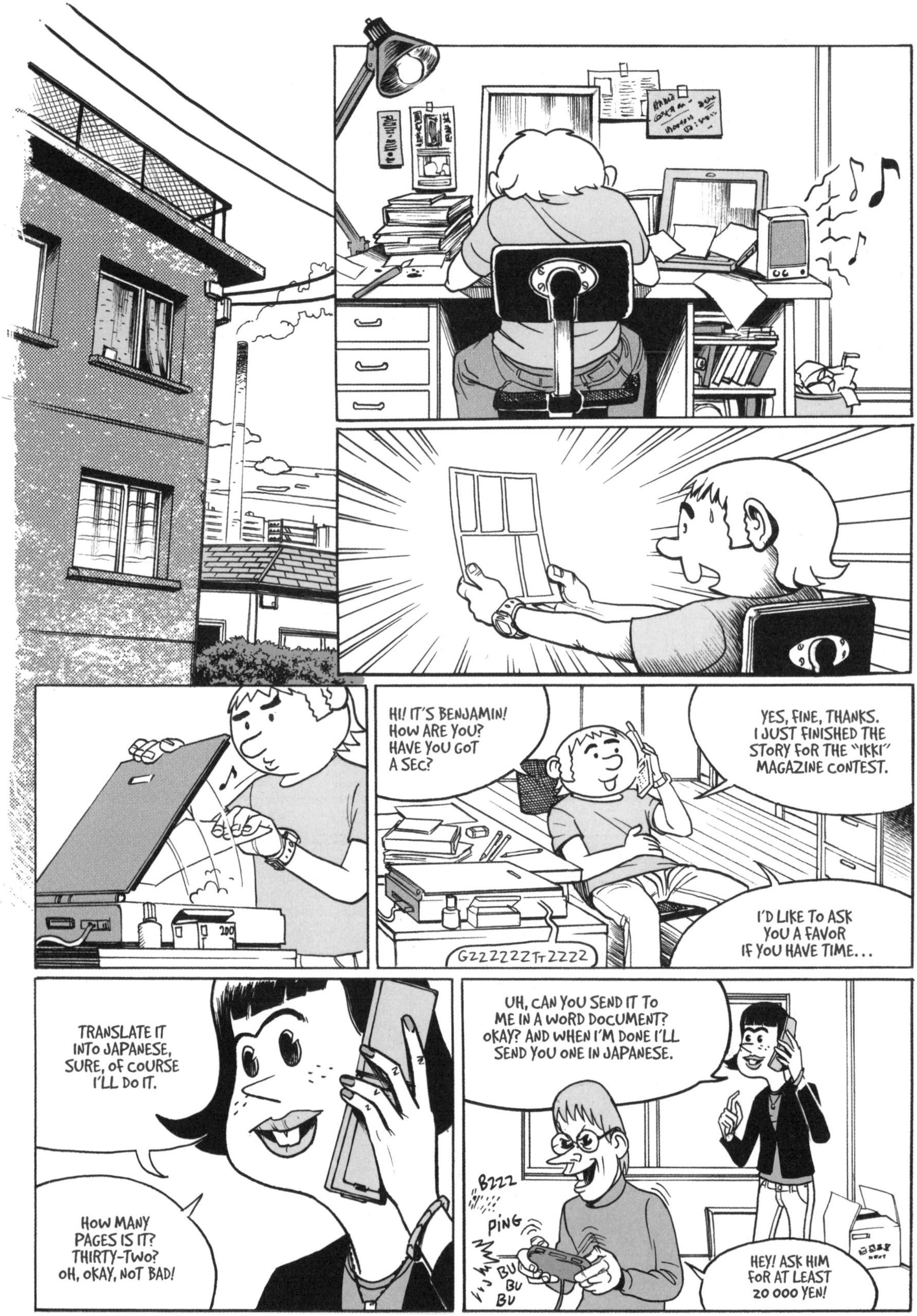
HI! IT'S BENJAMIN! HOW ARE YOU? HAVE YOU GOT A SEC?
YES, FINE, THANKS. I JUST FINISHED THE STORY FOR THE "IKKI" MAGAZINE CONTEST.
I'D LIKE TO ASK YOU A FAVOR IF YOU HAVE TIME...
GZZZZZZTTZZZZ
TRANSLATE IT INTO JAPANESE, SURE, OF COURSE I'LL DO IT.
HOW MANY PAGES IS IT? THIRTY-TWO? OH, OKAY, NOT BAD!
UH, CAN YOU SEND IT TO ME IN A WORD DOCUMENT? OKAY? AND WHEN I'M DONE I'LL SEND YOU ONE IN JAPANESE.
BZZZ
PING
BU BU BU
HEY! ASK HIM FOR AT LEAST 20 000 YEN!

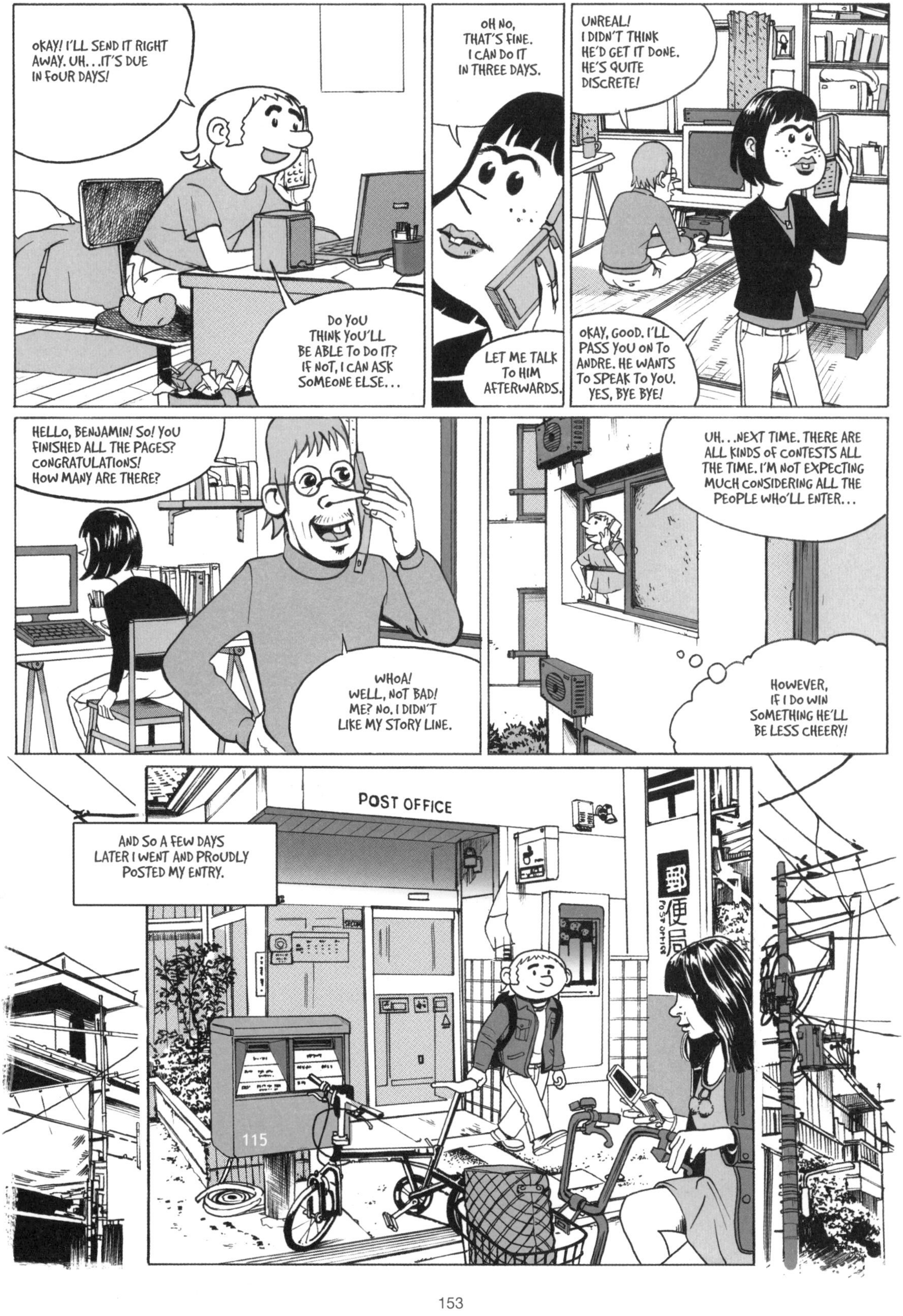

OKAY! I'LL SEND IT RIGHT AWAY. UH...IT'S DUE IN FOUR DAYS!
DO YOU THINK YOU'LL BE ABLE TO DO IT? IF NOT, I CAN ASK SOMEONE ELSE...
OH NO, THAT'S FINE. I CAN DO IT IN THREE DAYS.
LET ME TALK TO HIM AFTERWARDS.
UNREAL! I DIDN'T THINK HE'D GET IT DONE. HE'S QUITE DISCRETE!
OKAY, GOOD. I'LL PASS YOU ON TO ANDRE. HE WANTS TO SPEAK TO YOU. YES, BYE BYE!
HELLO, BENJAMIN! SO! YOU FINISHED ALL THE PAGES? CONGRATULATIONS! HOW MANY ARE THERE?
WHOA! WELL, NOT BAD! ME? NO. I DIDN'T LIKE MY STORY LINE.
UH...NEXT TIME. THERE ARE ALL KINDS OF CONTESTS ALL THE TIME. I'M NOT EXPECTING MUCH CONSIDERING ALL THE PEOPLE WHO'LL ENTER...
HOWEVER, IF I DO WIN SOMETHING HE'LL BE LESS CHEERY!
AND SO A FEW DAYS LATER I WENT AND PROUDLY POSTED MY ENTRY.
POST OFFICE
郵便局
POST OFFICE
115

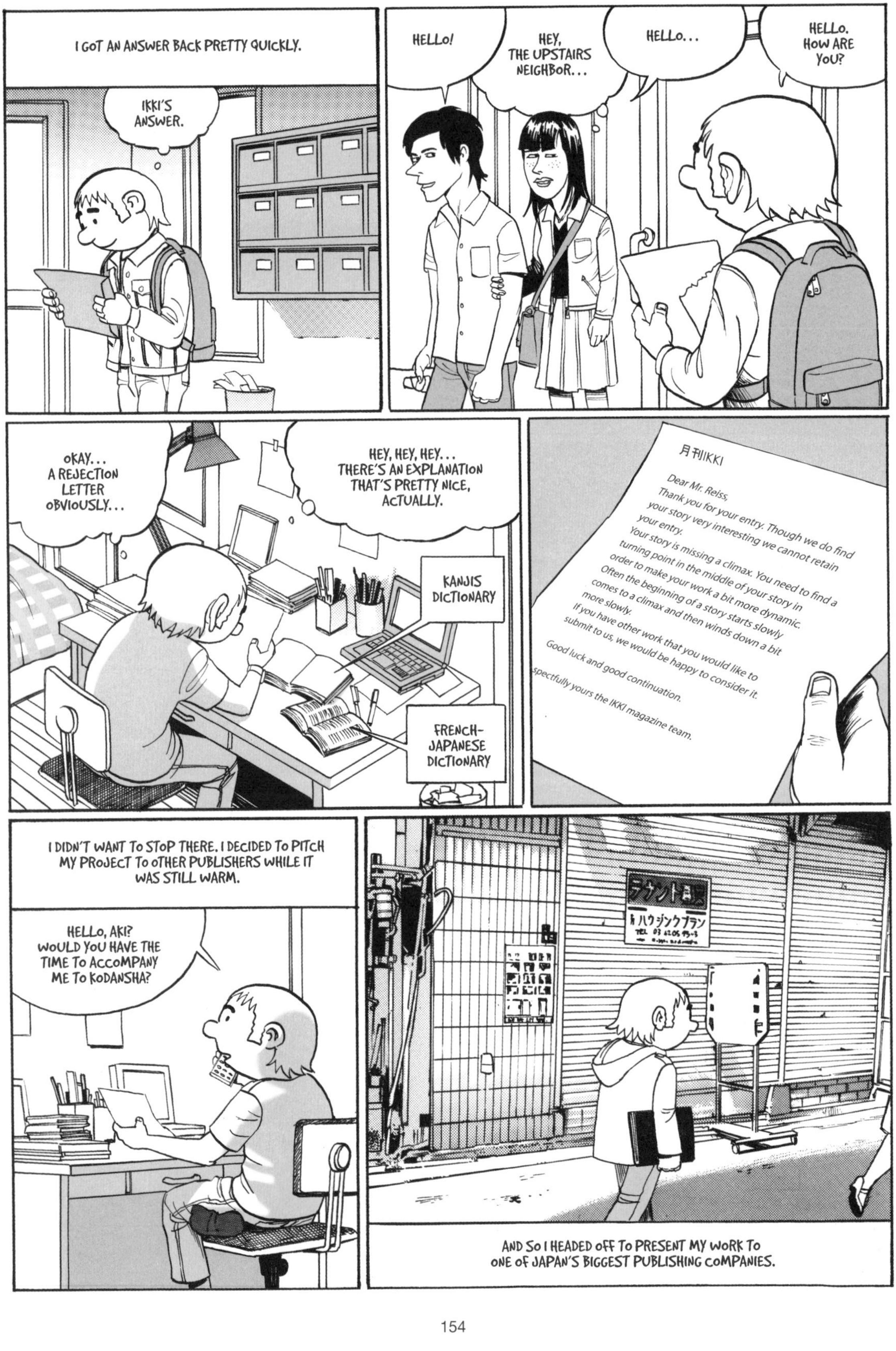
I GOT AN ANSWER BACK PRETTY QUICKLY.
IKKI'S ANSWER.
HELLO!
HEY, THE UPSTAIRS NEIGHBOR...
HELLO...
HELLO. HOW ARE YOU?
OKAY... A REJECTION LETTER OBVIOUSLY...
HEY, HEY, HEY... THERE'S AN EXPLANATION THAT'S PRETTY NICE, ACTUALLY.
KANJIS DICTIONARY
FRENCH-JAPANESE DICTIONARY
月刊IKKI
Dear Mr. Reiss,
Thank you for your entry. Though we do find your story very interesting we cannot retain your entry.
Your story is missing a climax. You need to find a turning point in the middle of your story in order to make your work a bit more dynamic.
Often the beginning of a story starts slowly comes to a climax and then winds down a bit more slowly.
If you have other work that you would like to submit to us, we would be happy to consider it.
Good luck and good continuation.
spectfully yours the IKKI magazine team.
I DIDN'T WANT TO STOP THERE. I DECIDED TO PITCH MY PROJECT TO OTHER PUBLISHERS WHILE IT WAS STILL WARM.
HELLO, AKI? WOULD YOU HAVE THE TIME TO ACCOMPANY ME TO KODANSHA?
AND SO I HEADED OFF TO PRESENT MY WORK TO ONE OF JAPAN'S BIGGEST PUBLISHING COMPANIES.

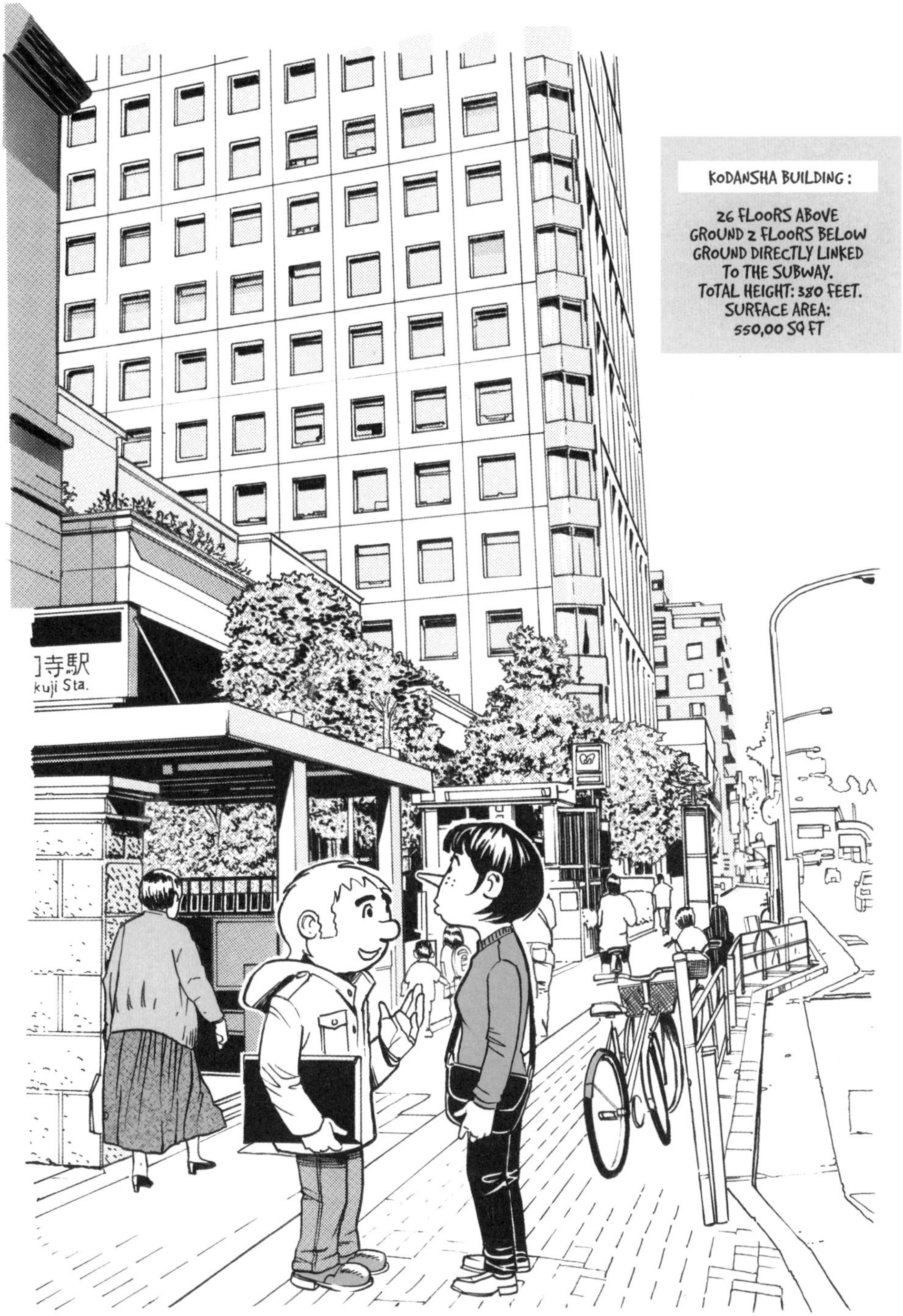
KODANSHA BUILDING:
26 FLOORS ABOVE GROUND 2 FLOORS BELOW GROUND DIRECTLY LINKED TO THE SUBWAY. TOTAL HEIGHT: 380 FEET. SURFACE AREA: 550,00 SQ FT

I WASN'T TOO NERVOUS ACTUALLY. I WAITED FOR AKI NEAR THE GOKOKUJI (BUNKYO-KU) SUBWAY EXIT. A MIDDLE-AGED WOMAN CAME AND STOOD RIGHT IN FRONT OF ME. I WASN'T TOO SURE WHAT SHE WANTED.

HMM... WHAT DOES SHE WANT?

THE WOMAN WAS REALLY STARING AT ME. IT WAS AS THOUGH SHE WANTED SOMETHING.

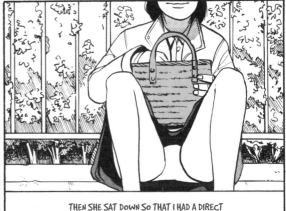

THEN SHE SAT DOWN SO THAT I HAD A DIRECT VIEW OF HER UNDERWEAR. I WAS SHOCKED.

THEN I SAW HER TEAR OFF SMALL BITS OF PAPER AND START WRITING ON ONE OF THEM.

I GOT UP, INTRIGUED BY HER ACTIONS.

I WASN'T SHY ABOUT IT...

OOF...HELLO! PFF... SORRY. I'M LATE. HAVE YOU BEEN WAITING LONG?

HOW ARE YOU?

OH UH... GOOD, YEAH. IT'S OKAY.

UH, HEY, THANKS FOR COMING!

SHALL WE GO?

GONE!!

THE ENTRANCE WAS PRETTY IMPRESSIVE. IT WAS LIKE ENTERING INTO A MANGA TEMPLE EVEN THOUGH KODANSHA PUBLISHES LOTS OF OTHER THINGS.

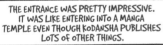

HELLO.

HELLO, WELCOME!

157

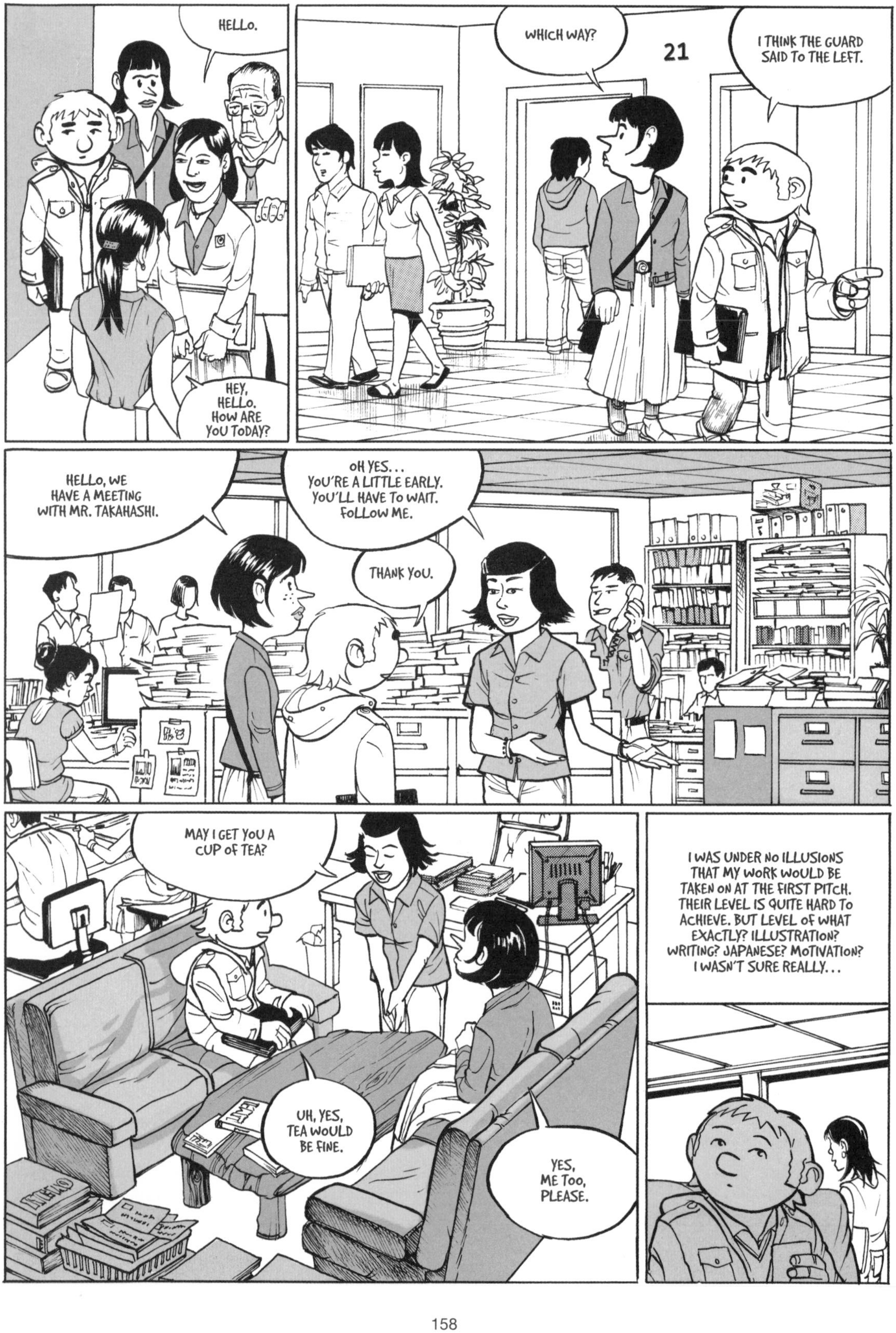
HELLO.
HEY, HELLO. HOW ARE YOU TODAY?
WHICH WAY?
21
I THINK THE GUARD SAID TO THE LEFT.
HELLO, WE HAVE A MEETING WITH MR. TAKAHASHI.
OH YES... YOU'RE A LITTLE EARLY. YOU'LL HAVE TO WAIT. FOLLOW ME.
THANK YOU.
MAY I GET YOU A CUP OF TEA?
UH, YES, TEA WOULD BE FINE.
YES, ME TOO, PLEASE.
I WAS UNDER NO ILLUSIONS THAT MY WORK WOULD BE TAKEN ON AT THE FIRST PITCH. THEIR LEVEL IS QUITE HARD TO ACHIEVE. BUT LEVEL OF WHAT EXACTLY? ILLUSTRATION? WRITING? JAPANESE? MOTIVATION? I WASN'T SURE REALLY...

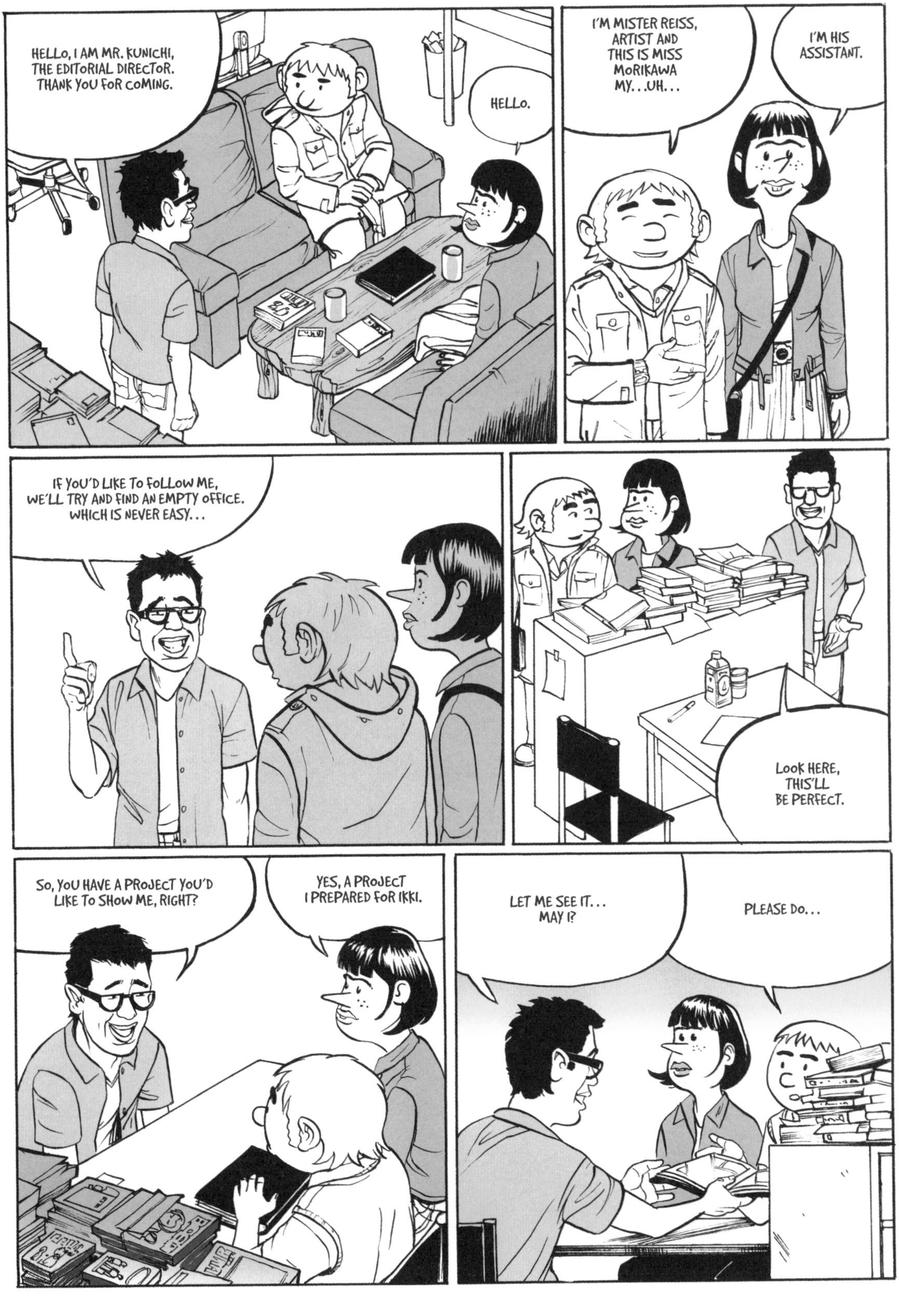
HELLO, I AM MR. KUNICHI, THE EDITORIAL DIRECTOR. THANK YOU FOR COMING.
HELLO.
I'M MISTER REISS, ARTIST AND THIS IS MISS MORIKAWA MY...UH...
I'M HIS ASSISTANT.
IF YOU'D LIKE TO FOLLOW ME, WE'LL TRY AND FIND AN EMPTY OFFICE. WHICH IS NEVER EASY...
LOOK HERE, THIS'LL BE PERFECT.
SO, YOU HAVE A PROJECT YOU'D LIKE TO SHOW ME, RIGHT?
YES, A PROJECT I PREPARED FOR IKKI.
LET ME SEE IT... MAY I?
PLEASE DO...

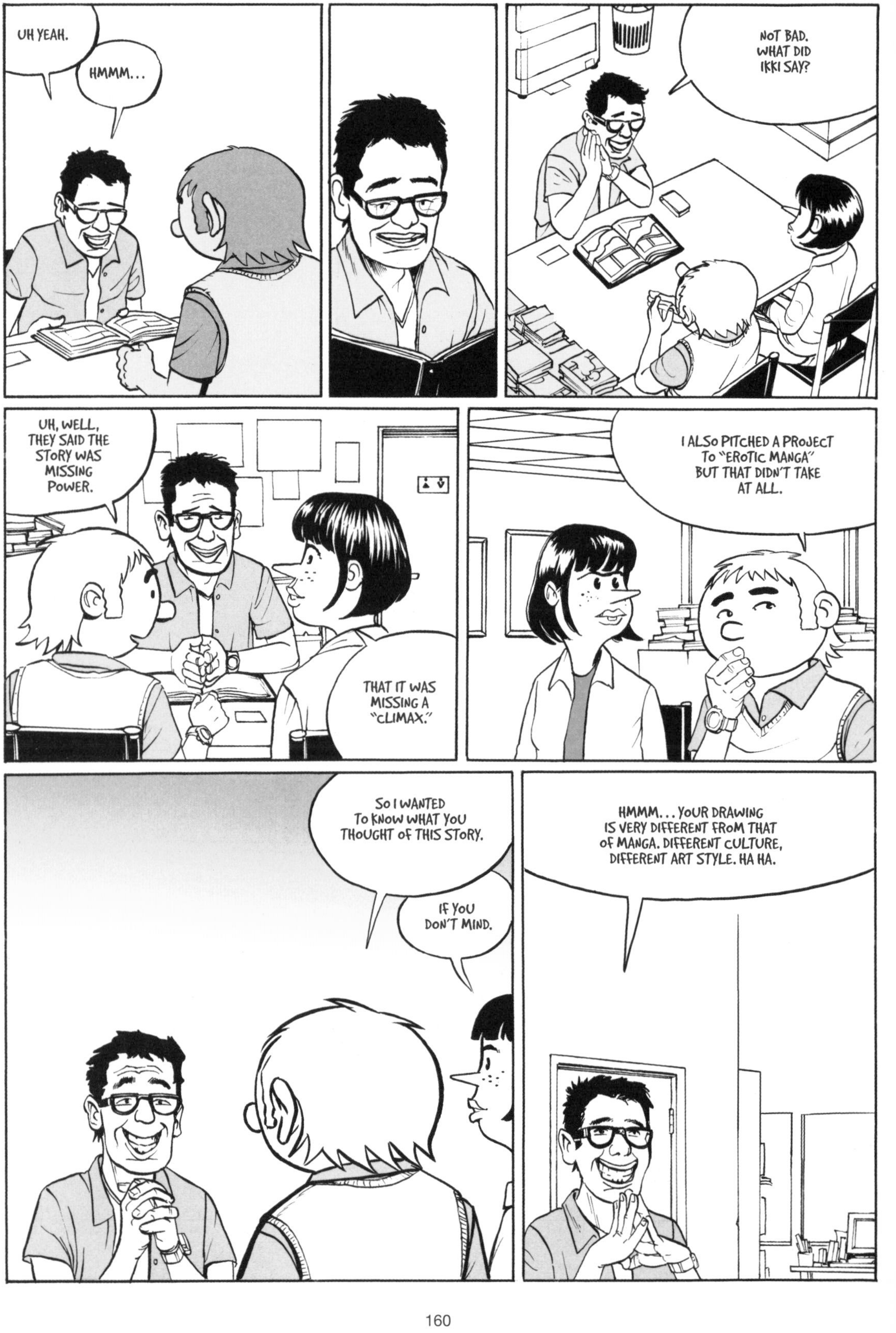
UH YEAH.
HMMM...
NOT BAD. WHAT DID IKKI SAY?
UH, WELL, THEY SAID THE STORY WAS MISSING POWER.
THAT IT WAS MISSING A "CLIMAX."
I ALSO PITCHED A PROJECT TO "EROTIC MANGA" BUT THAT DIDN'T TAKE AT ALL.
SO I WANTED TO KNOW WHAT YOU THOUGHT OF THIS STORY.
IF YOU DON'T MIND.
HMMM... YOUR DRAWING IS VERY DIFFERENT FROM THAT OF MANGA. DIFFERENT CULTURE, DIFFERENT ART STYLE. HA HA.

FOR EXAMPLE, THE WAY YOU DRAW WOMEN ISN'T RIGHT. IT'S NOT THE WAY IT SHOULD BE DONE.

OH BOY!

WAIT, I'LL SHOW YOU SOME EXAMPLES...

LOOK HERE. THE GIRLS ARE CUTE, SEXY. THAT'S WHAT THE READERS LIKE.

AH YES, I SEE.

OH NO PLEASE, NOT THE "THIS IS HOW IT'S DONE" LECTURE.

BUT WHAT YOU DO IS GOOD. YOU HAVE A GOOD NARRATIVE SENSE AND YOUR DRAWINGS ARE INTERESTING.

MMBMM, IT'S NOT LOOKING SO GOOD THOUGH.

THE PROBLEM IS...WELL, I WONDER IF YOU'RE GOING TO BE ABLE TO COMMUNICATE WITH THE EDITORIAL TEAM. YOU KNOW THAT IN THE MANGA BUSINESS WE COMMUNICATE MORE OFTEN THAN NOT BY FAX. IF YOU HAVE TO CHANGE DRAWINGS OR SCRIPTS YOU HAVE TO RESPOND IMMEDIATELY, AS IF YOU WERE JAPANESE. DO YOU SEE WHAT I MEAN?

NOT EASY, HUH?

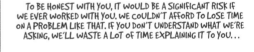

TO BE HONEST WITH YOU, IT WOULD BE A SIGNIFICANT RISK IF WE EVER WORKED WITH YOU. WE COULDN'T AFFORD TO LOSE TIME ON A PROBLEM LIKE THAT. IF YOU DON'T UNDERSTAND WHAT WE'RE ASKING, WE'LL WASTE A LOT OF TIME EXPLAINING IT TO YOU...

YES, THAT'S TRUE.

I SEE...

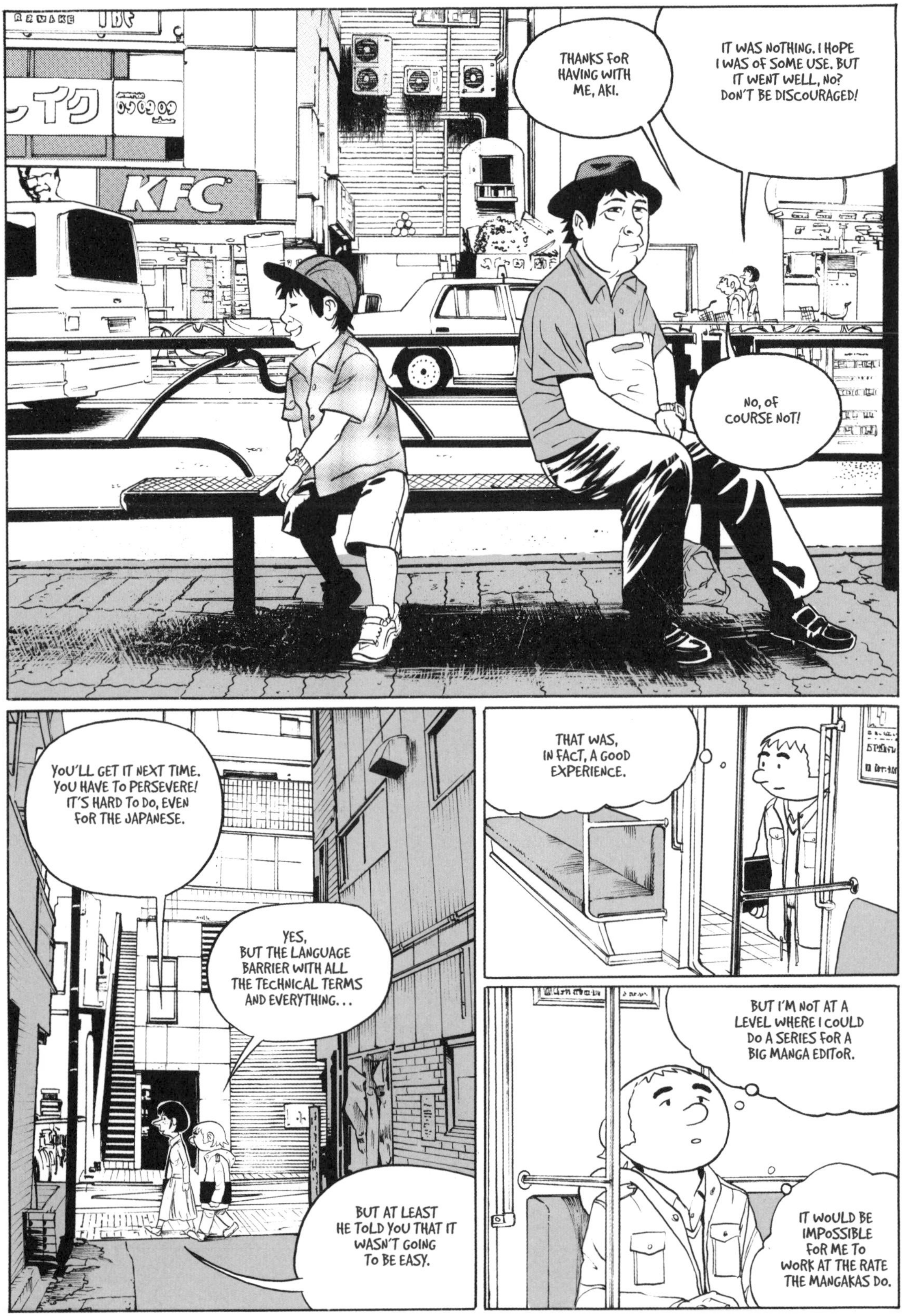
KFC
THANKS FOR HAVING WITH ME, AKI.
IT WAS NOTHING. I HOPE I WAS OF SOME USE. BUT IT WENT WELL, NO? DON'T BE DISCOURAGED!
NO, OF COURSE NOT!
YOU'LL GET IT NEXT TIME. YOU HAVE TO PERSEVERE! IT'S HARD TO DO, EVEN FOR THE JAPANESE.
YES, BUT THE LANGUAGE BARRIER WITH ALL THE TECHNICAL TERMS AND EVERYTHING...
BUT AT LEAST HE TOLD YOU THAT IT WASN'T GOING TO BE EASY.
THAT WAS, IN FACT, A GOOD EXPERIENCE.
BUT I'M NOT AT A LEVEL WHERE I COULD DO A SERIES FOR A BIG MANGA EDITOR.
IT WOULD BE IMPOSSIBLE FOR ME TO WORK AT THE RATE THE MANGAKAS DO.

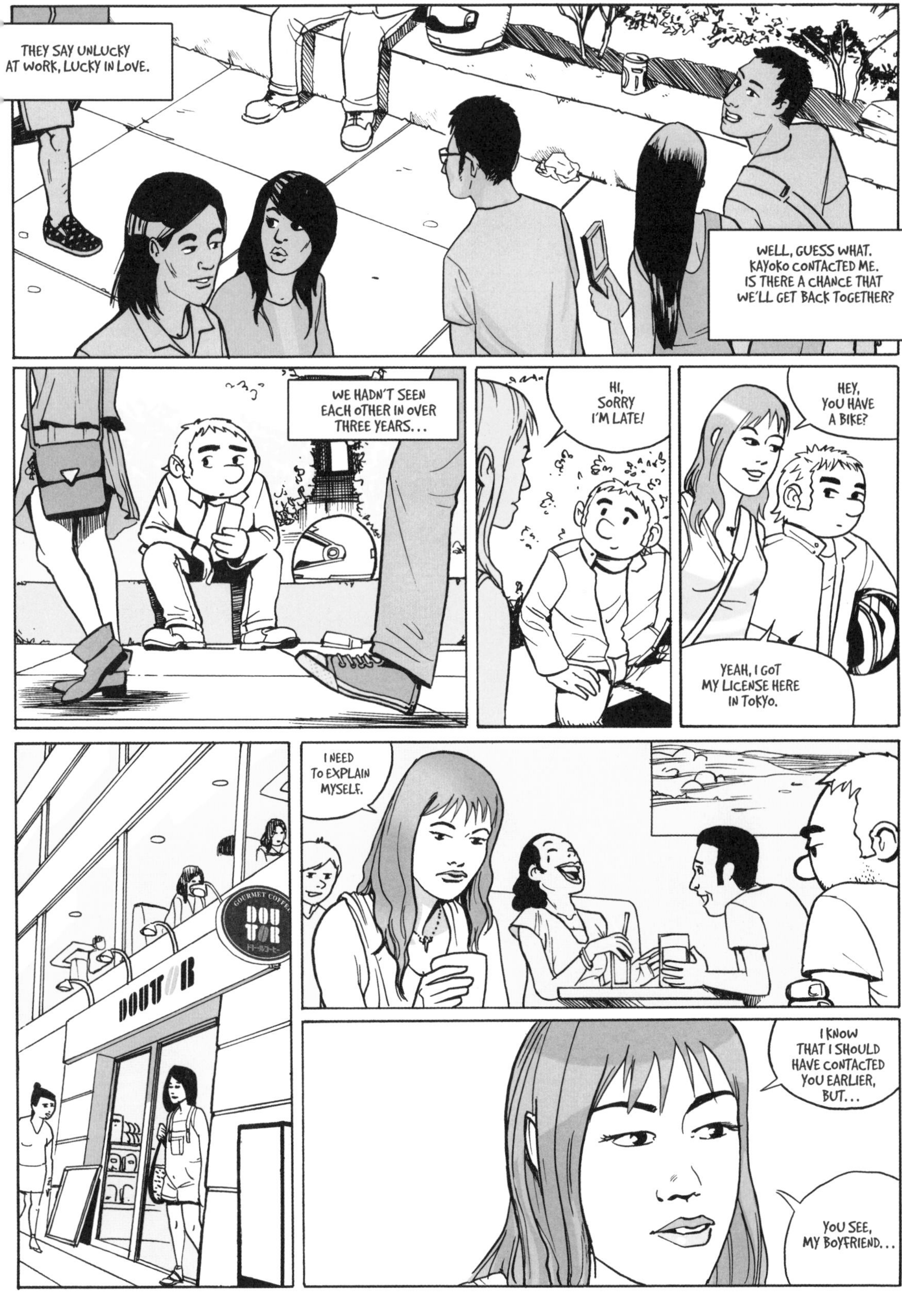
THEY SAY UNLUCKY AT WORK, LUCKY IN LOVE.
WELL, GUESS WHAT. KAYOKO CONTACTED ME. IS THERE A CHANCE THAT WE'LL GET BACK TOGETHER?
WE HADN'T SEEN EACH OTHER IN OVER THREE YEARS...
HI, SORRY I'M LATE!
HEY, YOU HAVE A BIKE?
YEAH, I GOT MY LICENSE HERE IN TOKYO.
GOURMET COFFEE
DOUTOR
DOUTOR
I NEED TO EXPLAIN MYSELF.
I KNOW THAT I SHOULD HAVE CONTACTED YOU EARLIER, BUT...
YOU SEE, MY BOYFRIEND...

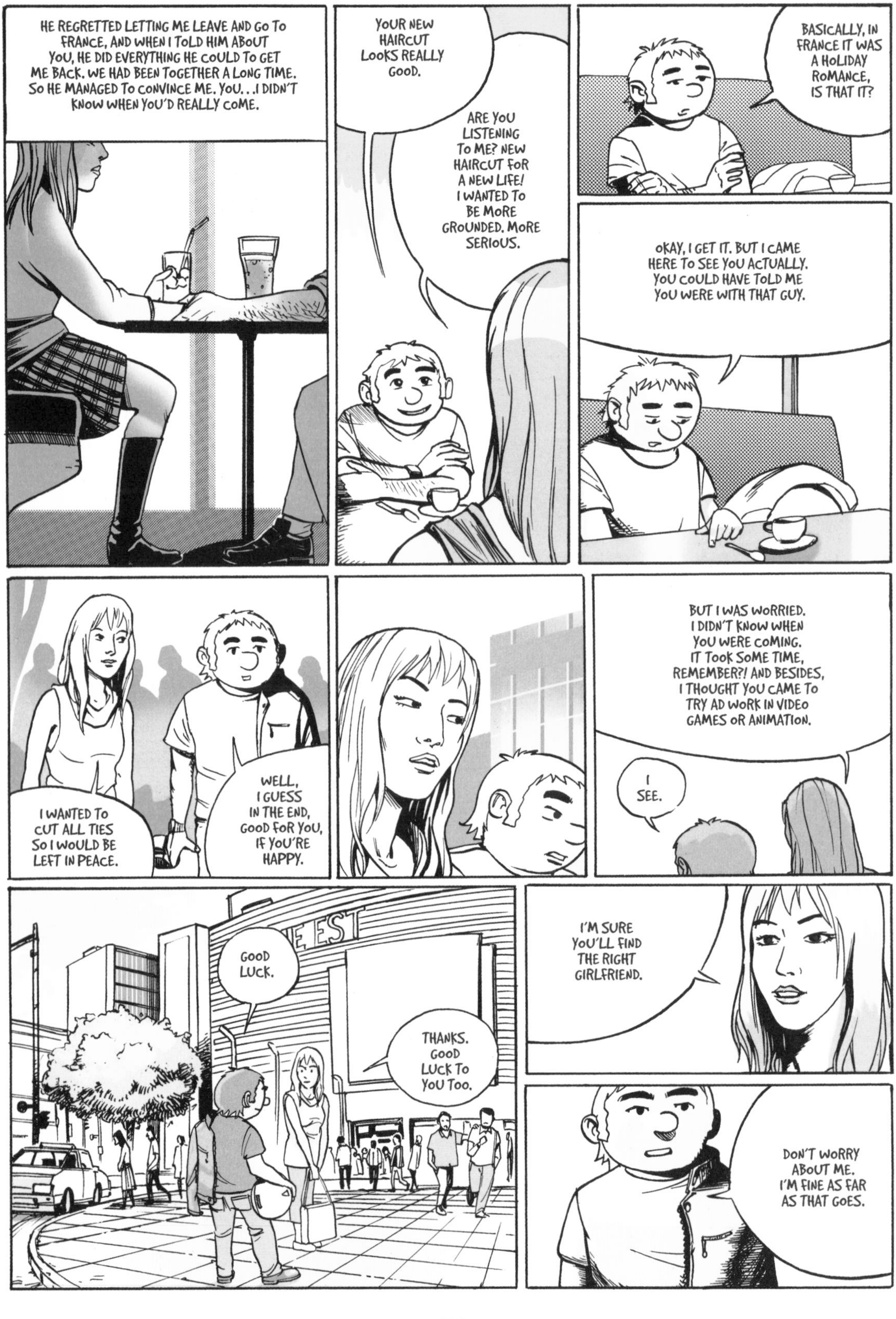
HE REGRETTED LETTING ME LEAVE AND GO TO FRANCE, AND WHEN I TOLD HIM ABOUT YOU, HE DID EVERYTHING HE COULD TO GET ME BACK. WE HAD BEEN TOGETHER A LONG TIME. SO HE MANAGED TO CONVINCE ME. YOU. . .I DIDN'T KNOW WHEN YOU'D REALLY COME.
YOUR NEW HAIRCUT LOOKS REALLY GOOD.
ARE YOU LISTENING TO ME? NEW HAIRCUT FOR A NEW LIFE! I WANTED TO BE MORE GROUNDED. MORE SERIOUS.
BASICALLY, IN FRANCE IT WAS A HOLIDAY ROMANCE, IS THAT IT?
OKAY, I GET IT. BUT I CAME HERE TO SEE YOU ACTUALLY. YOU COULD HAVE TOLD ME YOU WERE WITH THAT GUY.
I WANTED TO CUT ALL TIES SO I WOULD BE LEFT IN PEACE.
WELL, I GUESS IN THE END, GOOD FOR YOU, IF YOU'RE HAPPY.
BUT I WAS WORRIED. I DIDN'T KNOW WHEN YOU WERE COMING. IT TOOK SOME TIME, REMEMBER?! AND BESIDES, I THOUGHT YOU CAME TO TRY AD WORK IN VIDEO GAMES OR ANIMATION.
I SEE.
GOOD LUCK.
THANKS. GOOD LUCK TO YOU TOO.
I'M SURE YOU'LL FIND THE RIGHT GIRLFRIEND.
DON'T WORRY ABOUT ME. I'M FINE AS FAR AS THAT GOES.

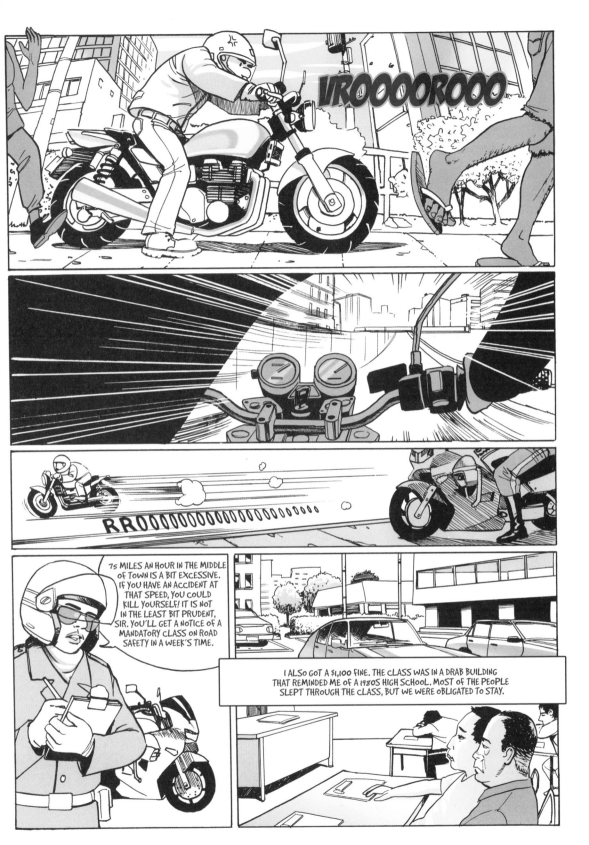

VROOOOROOO

RROOOOOOOOOOOOOOOOOOOOO

75 MILES AN HOUR IN THE MIDDLE OF TOWN IS A BIT EXCESSIVE. IF YOU HAVE AN ACCIDENT AT THAT SPEED, YOU COULD KILL YOURSELF! IT IS NOT IN THE LEAST BIT PRUDENT, SIR. YOU'LL GET A NOTICE OF A MANDATORY CLASS ON ROAD SAFETY IN A WEEK'S TIME.

I ALSO GOT A $1,100 FINE. THE CLASS WAS IN A DRAB BUILDING THAT REMINDED ME OF A 1980S HIGH SCHOOL. MOST OF THE PEOPLE SLEPT THROUGH THE CLASS, BUT WE WERE OBLIGATED TO STAY.

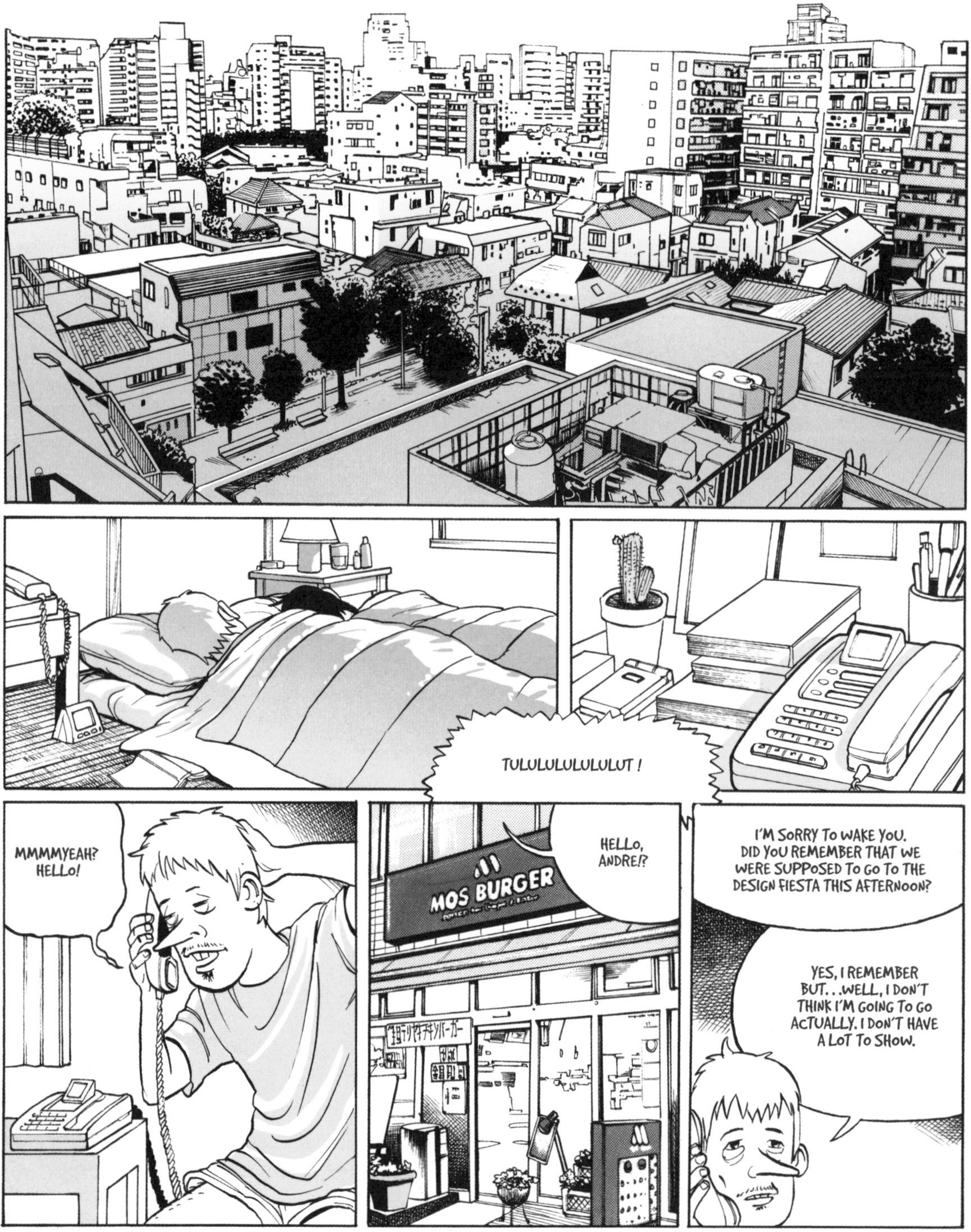
TULULULULULULUT !
MMMMYEAH? HELLo!
MOS BURGER
HELLo, ANDRE!?
I'M SORRY TO WAKE YoU. DID YOU REMEMBER THAT WE WERE SUPPOSED TO GO TO THE DESIGN FIESTA THIS AFTERNOoN?
YES, I REMEMBER BUT. . .WELL, I DON'T THINK I'M GOING TO GO ACTUALLY. I DON'T HAVE A LoT To SHOW.

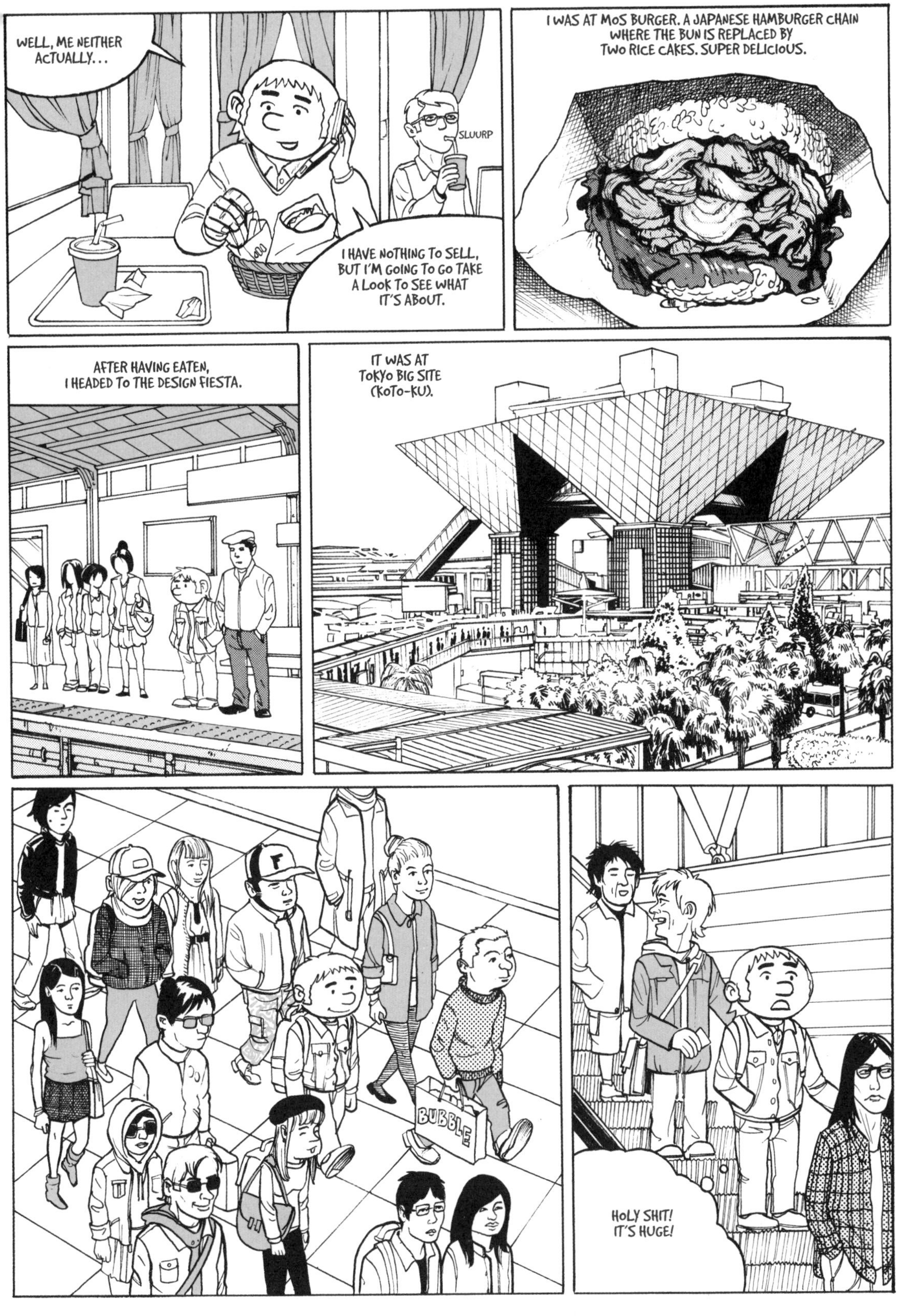
WELL, ME NEITHER ACTUALLY...
SLUURP
I HAVE NOTHING TO SELL, BUT I'M GOING TO GO TAKE A LOOK TO SEE WHAT IT'S ABOUT.
I WAS AT MOS BURGER. A JAPANESE HAMBURGER CHAIN WHERE THE BUN IS REPLACED BY TWO RICE CAKES. SUPER DELICIOUS.
AFTER HAVING EATEN, I HEADED TO THE DESIGN FIESTA.
IT WAS AT TOKYO BIG SITE (KOTO-KU).
BUBBLE
HOLY SHIT! IT'S HUGE!

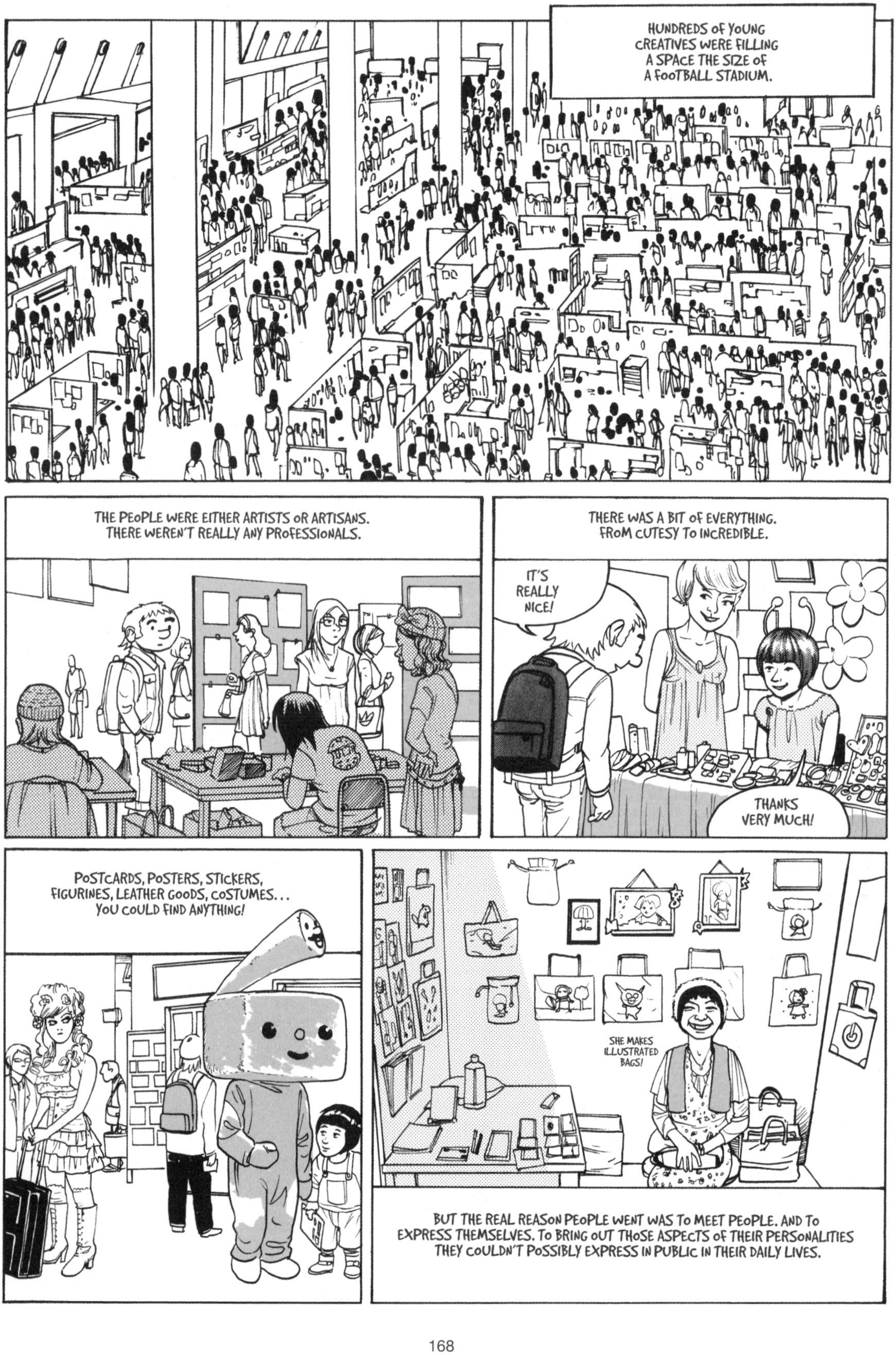
HUNDREDS OF YOUNG CREATIVES WERE FILLING A SPACE THE SIZE OF A FOOTBALL STADIUM.
THE PEOPLE WERE EITHER ARTISTS OR ARTISANS. THERE WEREN'T REALLY ANY PROFESSIONALS.
THERE WAS A BIT OF EVERYTHING. FROM CUTESY TO INCREDIBLE.
IT'S REALLY NICE!
THANKS VERY MUCH!
POSTCARDS, POSTERS, STICKERS, FIGURINES, LEATHER GOODS, COSTUMES... YOU COULD FIND ANYTHING!
SHE MAKES ILLUSTRATED BAGS!
BUT THE REAL REASON PEOPLE WENT WAS TO MEET PEOPLE. AND TO EXPRESS THEMSELVES. TO BRING OUT THOSE ASPECTS OF THEIR PERSONALITIES THEY COULDN'T POSSIBLY EXPRESS IN PUBLIC IN THEIR DAILY LIVES.

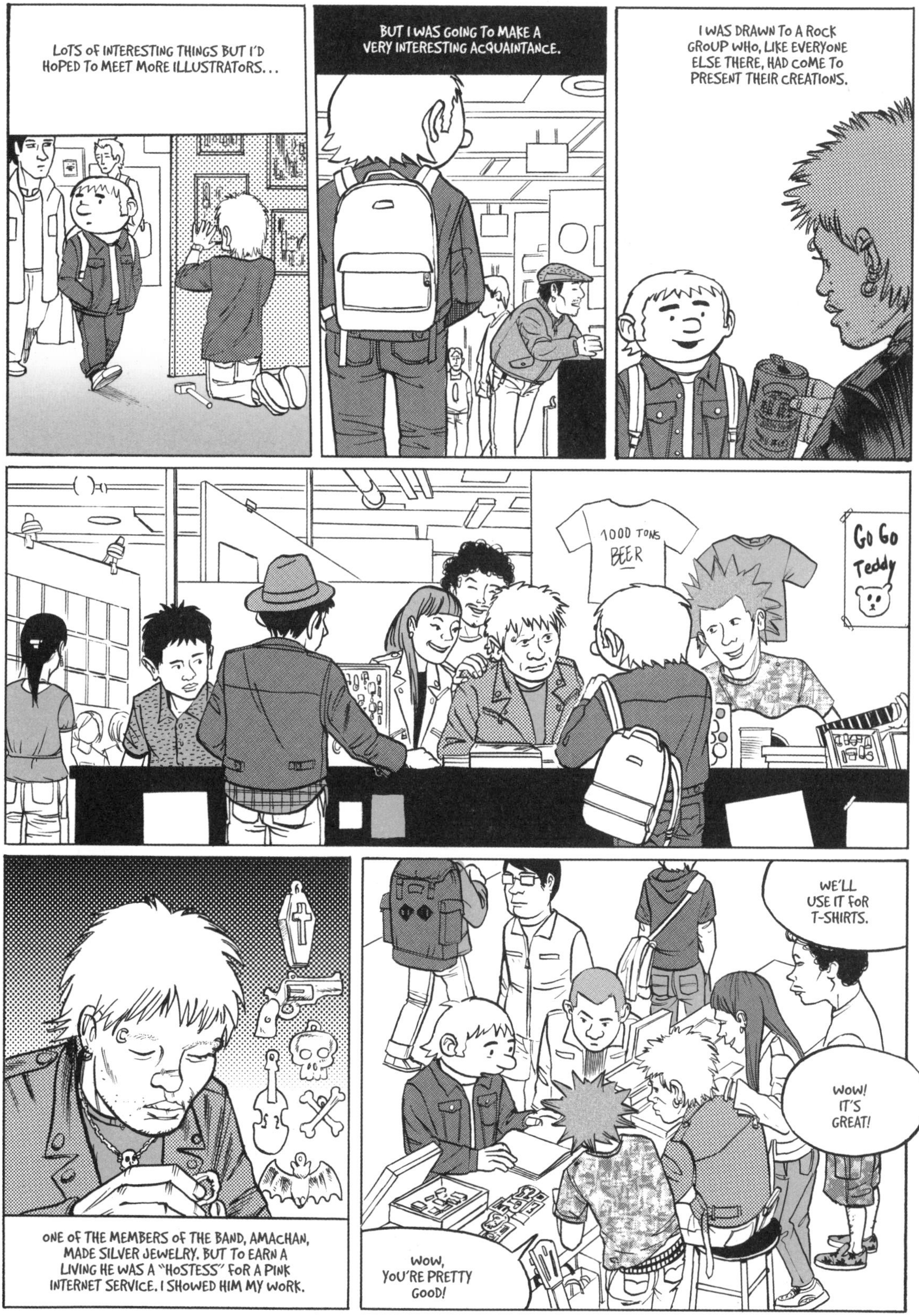
LOTS OF INTERESTING THINGS BUT I'D HOPED TO MEET MORE ILLUSTRATORS...
BUT I WAS GOING TO MAKE A VERY INTERESTING ACQUAINTANCE.
I WAS DRAWN TO A ROCK GROUP WHO, LIKE EVERYONE ELSE THERE, HAD COME TO PRESENT THEIR CREATIONS.
1000 TONS BEER
Go Go Teddy
ONE OF THE MEMBERS OF THE BAND, AMACHAN, MADE SILVER JEWELRY. BUT TO EARN A LIVING HE WAS A "HOSTESS" FOR A PINK INTERNET SERVICE. I SHOWED HIM MY WORK.
WE'LL USE IT FOR T-SHIRTS.
WOW! IT'S GREAT!
WOW, YOU'RE PRETTY GOOD!

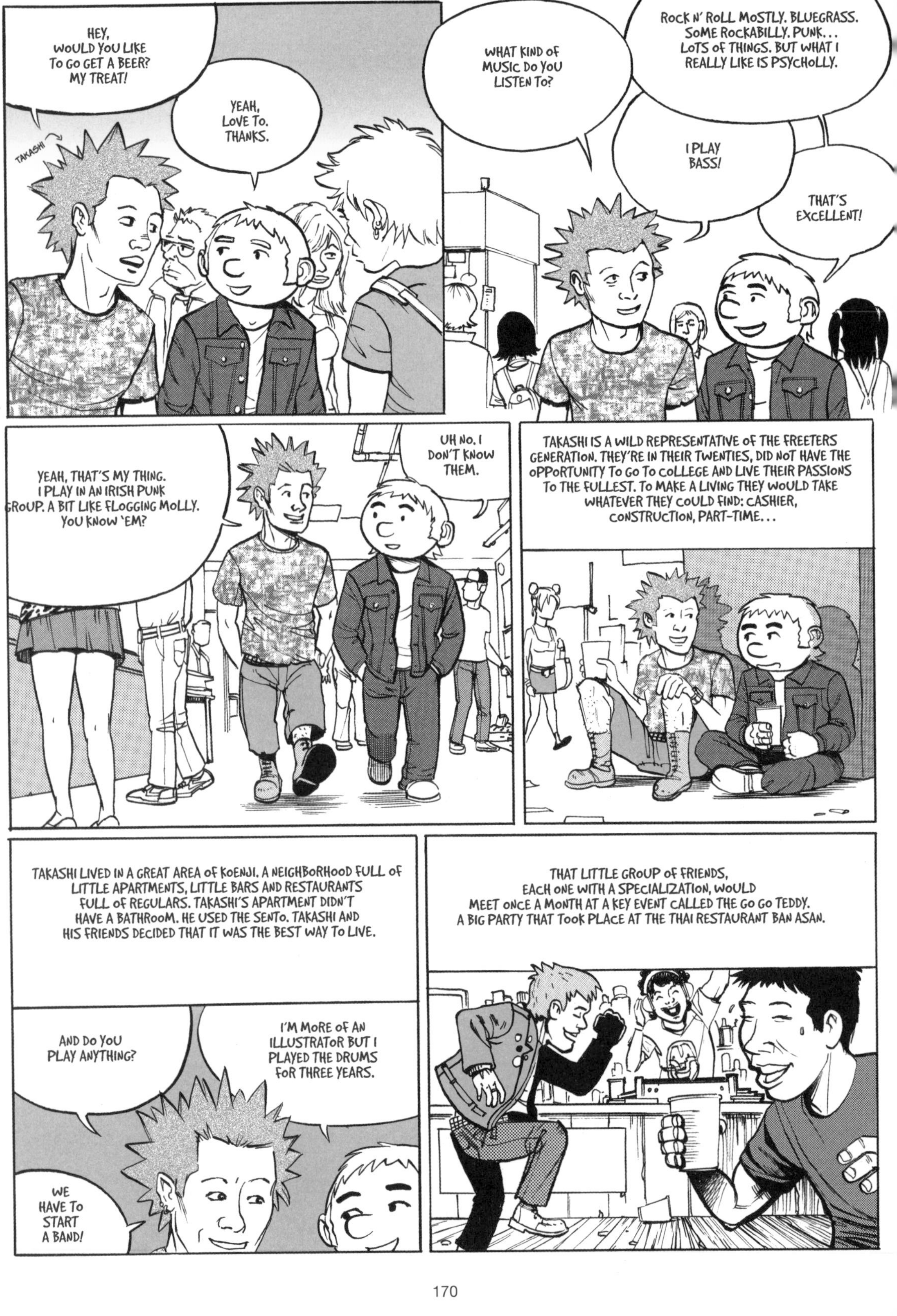
HEY, WOULD YOU LIKE TO GO GET A BEER? MY TREAT!
TAKASHI
YEAH, LOVE TO. THANKS.
WHAT KIND OF MUSIC DO YOU LISTEN TO?
ROCK N' ROLL MOSTLY. BLUEGRASS. SOME ROCKABILLY. PUNK... LOTS OF THINGS. BUT WHAT I REALLY LIKE IS PSYCHOLLY.
I PLAY BASS!
THAT'S EXCELLENT!
YEAH, THAT'S MY THING. I PLAY IN AN IRISH PUNK GROUP. A BIT LIKE FLOGGING MOLLY. YOU KNOW 'EM?
UH NO. I DON'T KNOW THEM.
TAKASHI IS A WILD REPRESENTATIVE OF THE FREETERS GENERATION. THEY'RE IN THEIR TWENTIES, DID NOT HAVE THE OPPORTUNITY TO GO TO COLLEGE AND LIVE THEIR PASSIONS TO THE FULLEST. TO MAKE A LIVING THEY WOULD TAKE WHATEVER THEY COULD FIND: CASHIER, CONSTRUCTION, PART-TIME...
TAKASHI LIVED IN A GREAT AREA OF KOENJI. A NEIGHBORHOOD FULL OF LITTLE APARTMENTS, LITTLE BARS AND RESTAURANTS FULL OF REGULARS. TAKASHI'S APARTMENT DIDN'T HAVE A BATHROOM. HE USED THE SENTO. TAKASHI AND HIS FRIENDS DECIDED THAT IT WAS THE BEST WAY TO LIVE.
AND DO YOU PLAY ANYTHING?
I'M MORE OF AN ILLUSTRATOR BUT I PLAYED THE DRUMS FOR THREE YEARS.
WE HAVE TO START A BAND!
THAT LITTLE GROUP OF FRIENDS, EACH ONE WITH A SPECIALIZATION, WOULD MEET ONCE A MONTH AT A KEY EVENT CALLED THE GO GO TEDDY. A BIG PARTY THAT TOOK PLACE AT THE THAI RESTAURANT BAN ASAN.

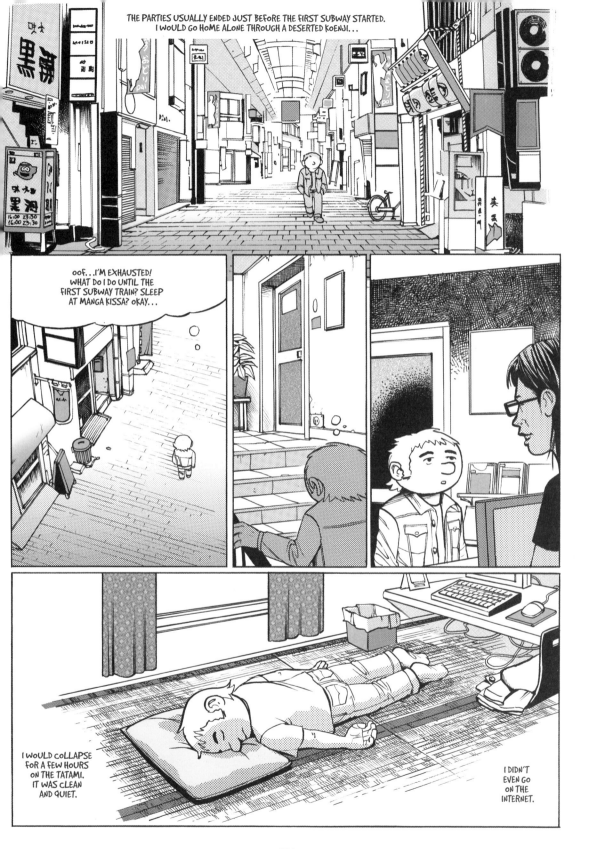

THE PARTIES USUALLY ENDED JUST BEFORE THE FIRST SUBWAY STARTED. I WOULD GO HOME ALONE THROUGH A DESERTED KOENJI...

OOF...I'M EXHAUSTED! WHAT DO I DO UNTIL THE FIRST SUBWAY TRAIN? SLEEP AT MANGA KISSA? OKAY...

I WOULD COLLAPSE FOR A FEW HOURS ON THE TATAMI. IT WAS CLEAN AND QUIET.

I DIDN'T EVEN GO ON THE INTERNET.

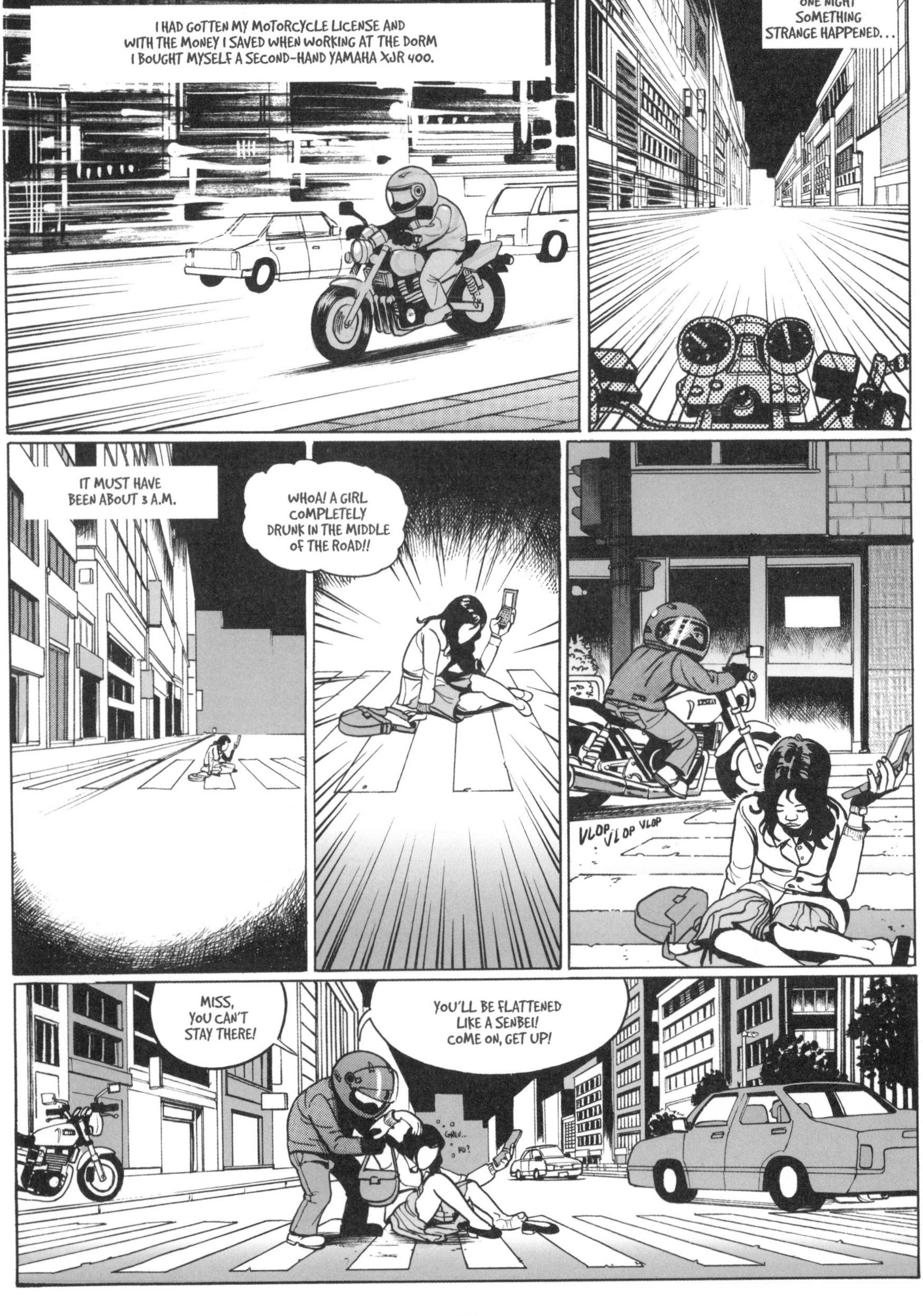
I HAD GOTTEN MY MOTORCYCLE LICENSE AND WITH THE MONEY I SAVED WHEN WORKING AT THE DORM I BOUGHT MYSELF A SECOND-HAND YAMAHA XJR 400.
ONE NIGHT SOMETHING STRANGE HAPPENED...
IT MUST HAVE BEEN ABOUT 3 A.M.
WHOA! A GIRL COMPLETELY DRUNK IN THE MIDDLE OF THE ROAD!!
VLOP VLOP VLOP
MISS, YOU CAN'T STAY THERE!
YOU'LL BE FLATTENED LIKE A SENBEI! COME ON, GET UP!
GNEU...
HU?

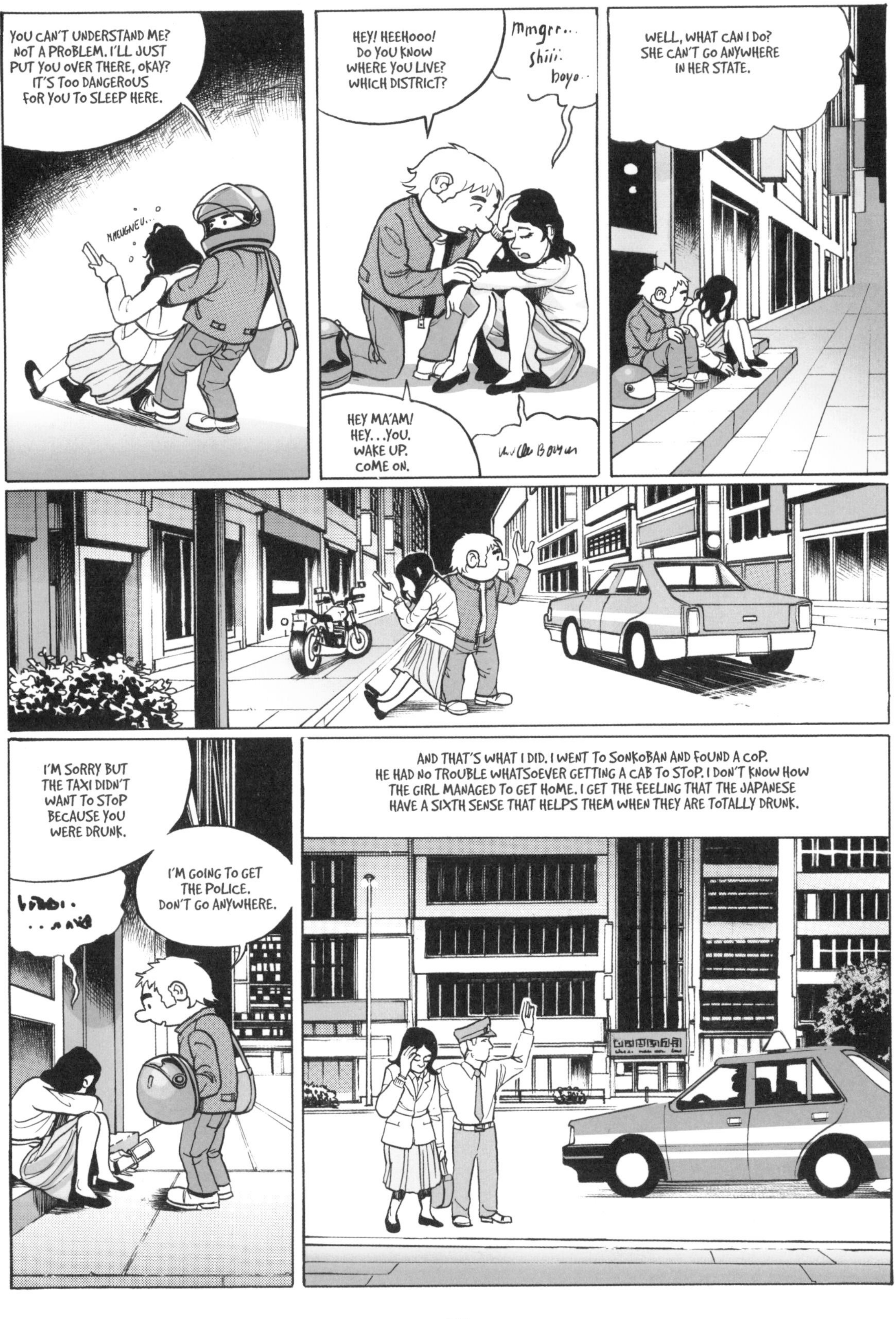
YOU CAN'T UNDERSTAND ME? NOT A PROBLEM. I'LL JUST PUT YOU OVER THERE, OKAY? IT'S TOO DANGEROUS FOR YOU TO SLEEP HERE.
MMEUGNEU...
HEY! HEEHOOO! DO YOU KNOW WHERE YOU LIVE? WHICH DISTRICT?
mmgrr... shiii boyo..
HEY MA'AM! HEY...YOU. WAKE UP. COME ON.
WELL, WHAT CAN I DO? SHE CAN'T GO ANYWHERE IN HER STATE.
I'M SORRY BUT THE TAXI DIDN'T WANT TO STOP BECAUSE YOU WERE DRUNK.
I'M GOING TO GET THE POLICE. DON'T GO ANYWHERE.
AND THAT'S WHAT I DID. I WENT TO SONKOBAN AND FOUND A COP. HE HAD NO TROUBLE WHATSOEVER GETTING A CAB TO STOP. I DON'T KNOW HOW THE GIRL MANAGED TO GET HOME. I GET THE FEELING THAT THE JAPANESE HAVE A SIXTH SENSE THAT HELPS THEM WHEN THEY ARE TOTALLY DRUNK.

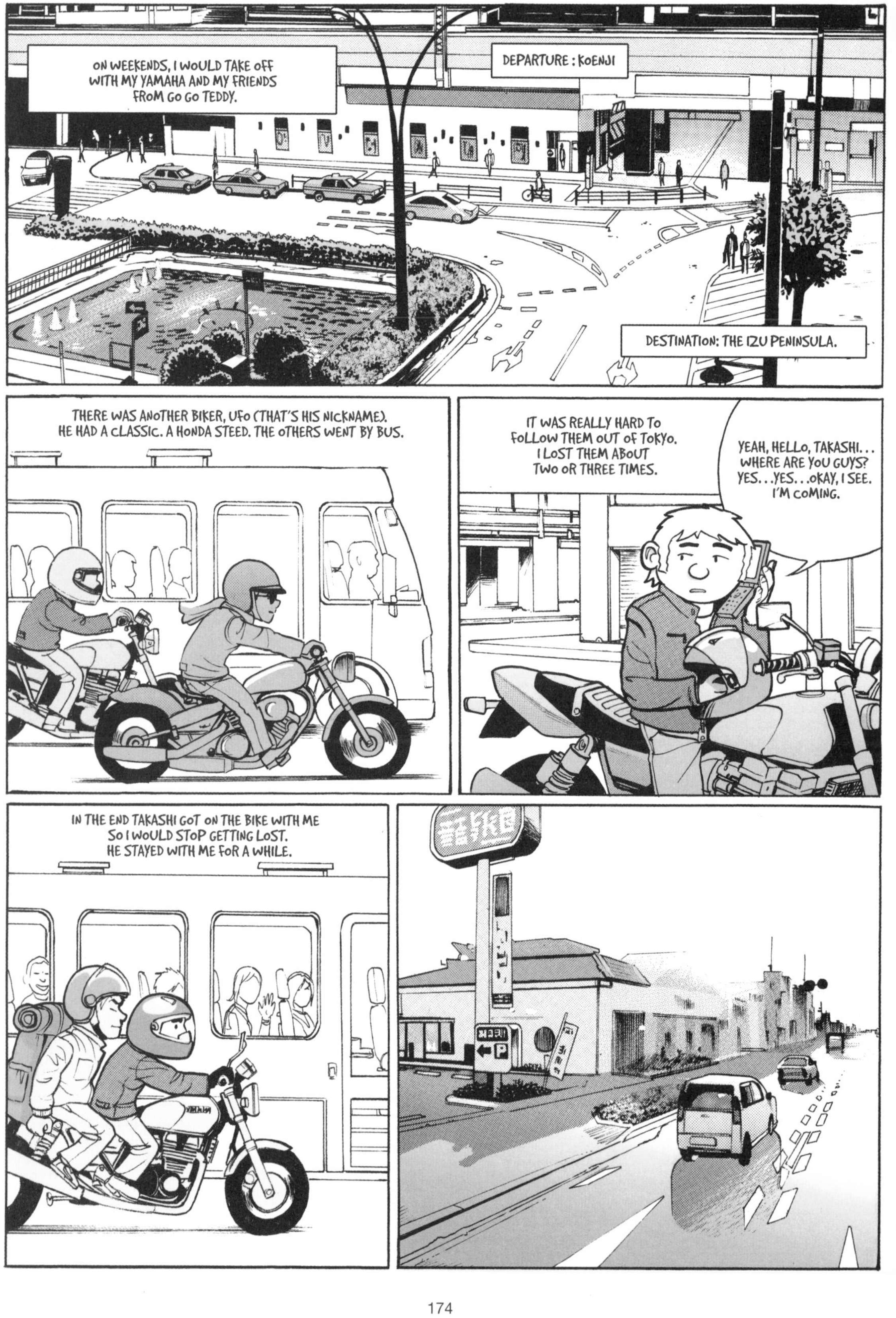
ON WEEKENDS, I WOULD TAKE OFF WITH MY YAMAHA AND MY FRIENDS FROM GO GO TEDDY.
DEPARTURE : KOENJI
DESTINATION: THE IZU PENINSULA.
THERE WAS ANOTHER BIKER, UFO (THAT'S HIS NICKNAME). HE HAD A CLASSIC. A HONDA STEED. THE OTHERS WENT BY BUS.
IT WAS REALLY HARD TO FOLLOW THEM OUT OF TOKYO. I LOST THEM ABOUT TWO OR THREE TIMES.
YEAH, HELLO, TAKASHI... WHERE ARE YOU GUYS? YES...YES...OKAY, I SEE. I'M COMING.
IN THE END TAKASHI GOT ON THE BIKE WITH ME SO I WOULD STOP GETTING LOST. HE STAYED WITH ME FOR A WHILE.

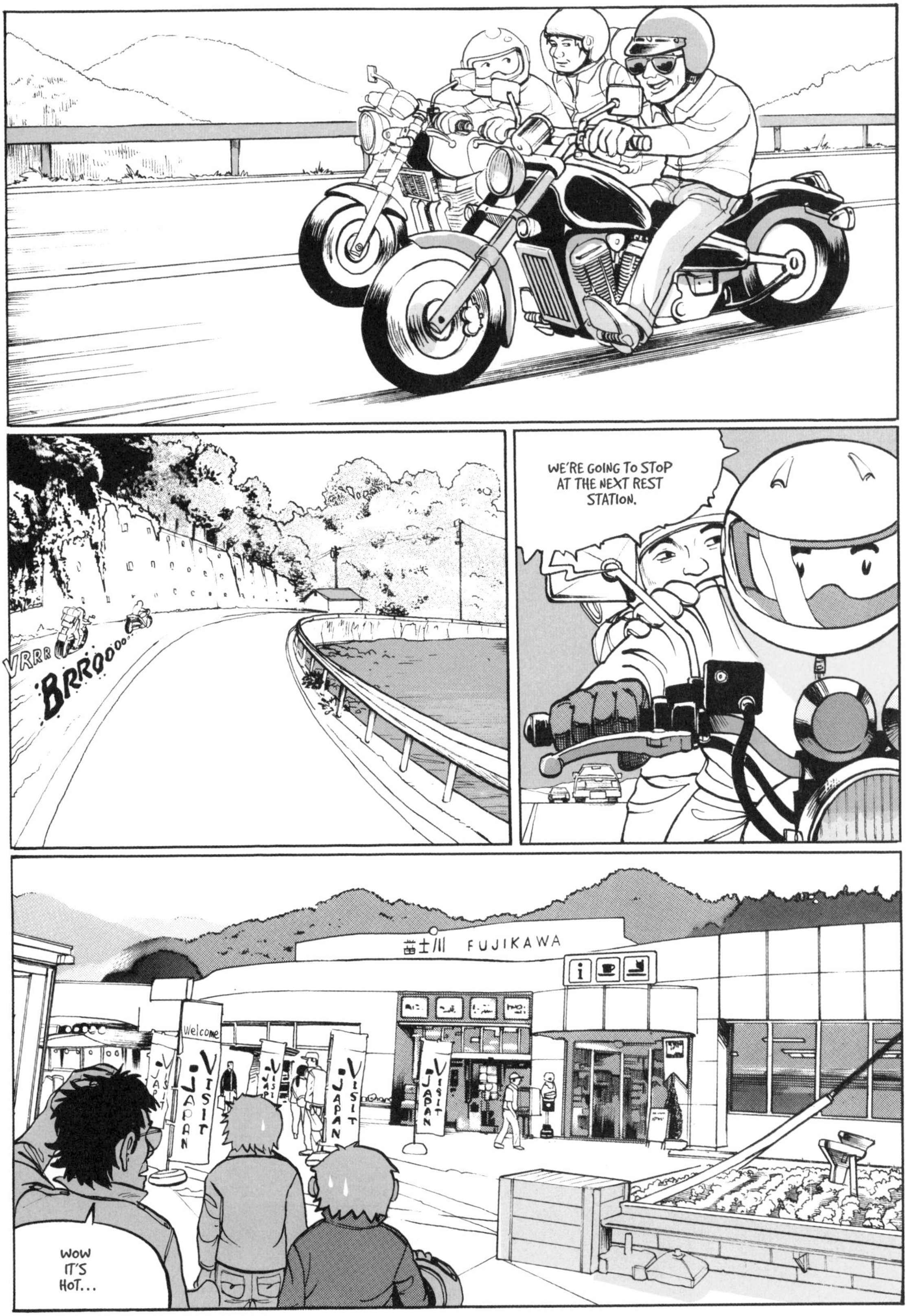
VRRR
BRROooo...
WE'RE GOING TO STOP AT THE NEXT REST STATION.
FUJIKAWA
Welcome
VISIT JAPAN
VISIT JAPAN
VISIT JAPAN
VISIT JAPAN
WOW IT'S HOT...

THE REST STOP LOOKED LIKE A MINI SHOPPING CENTER...
AND AS USUAL YOU WERE ABLE TO GET THE LOCAL
SPECIALTIES. HERE IT WAS YAKISOBAS.

A GOOD PORTION OF THE TRIP WAS DOWN THE COAST.
WE WERE HEADED FOR A SMALL PRIVATE BEACH WITH
A BIG BUNGALOW TO KEEP OUT OF THE SUN.

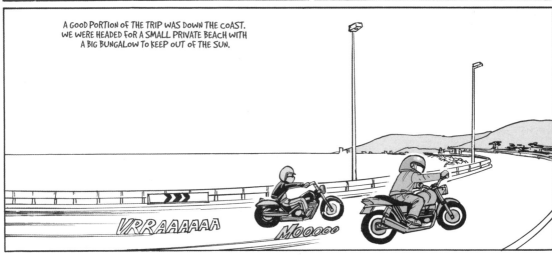

VRRAAAAAAA

MOOOOO

WE FINALLY GOT THERE...
JUST ABOUT EVERYONE WAS EXHAUSTED.

I SWAM TO THE ROCKS!

YUUKI PLAYED
THE UKULELE.

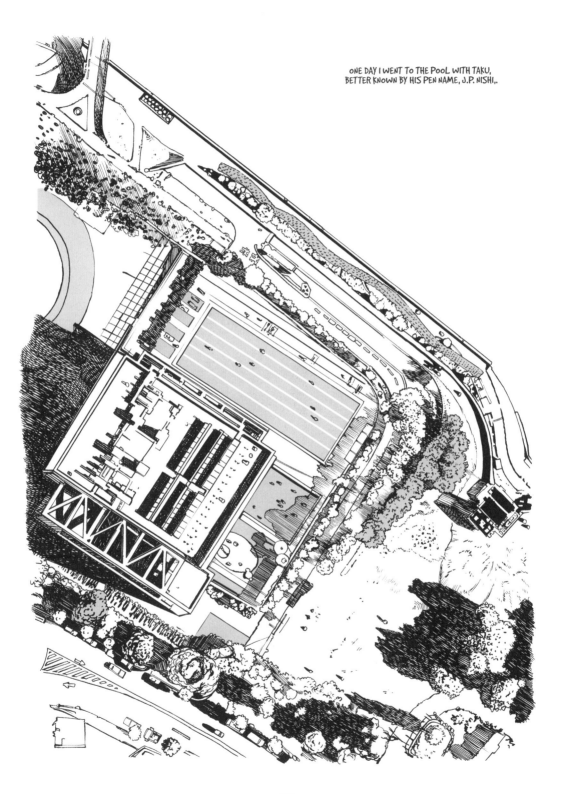

ONE DAY I WENT TO THE POOL WITH TAKU,
BETTER KNOWN BY HIS PEN NAME, J.P. NISHI,.

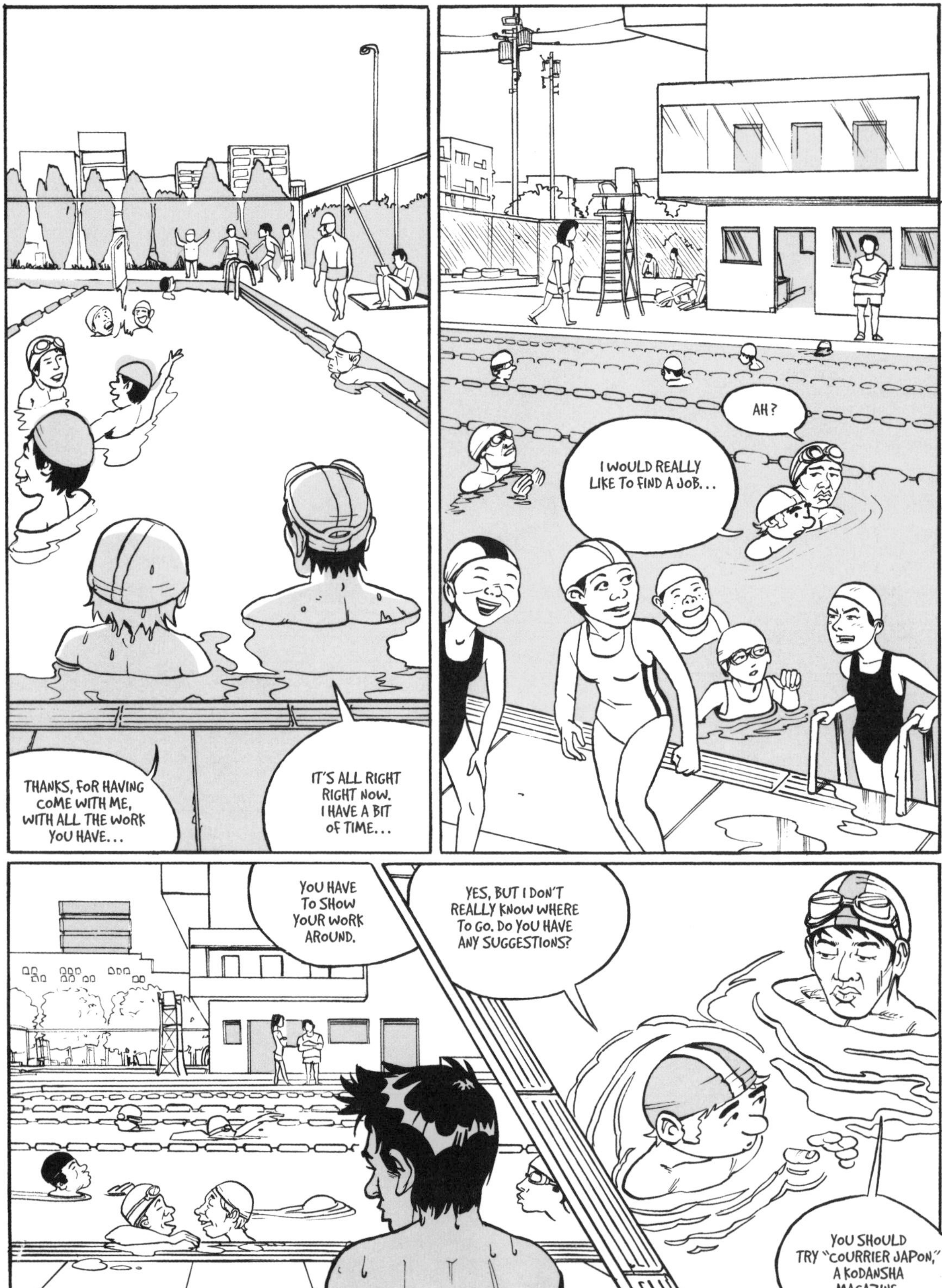
THANKS, FOR HAVING COME WITH ME, WITH ALL THE WORK YOU HAVE...
IT'S ALL RIGHT RIGHT NOW. I HAVE A BIT OF TIME...
AH?
I WOULD REALLY LIKE TO FIND A JOB...
YOU HAVE TO SHOW YOUR WORK AROUND.
YES, BUT I DON'T REALLY KNOW WHERE TO GO. DO YOU HAVE ANY SUGGESTIONS?
YOU SHOULD TRY "COURRIER JAPON," A KODANSHA MAGAZINE.

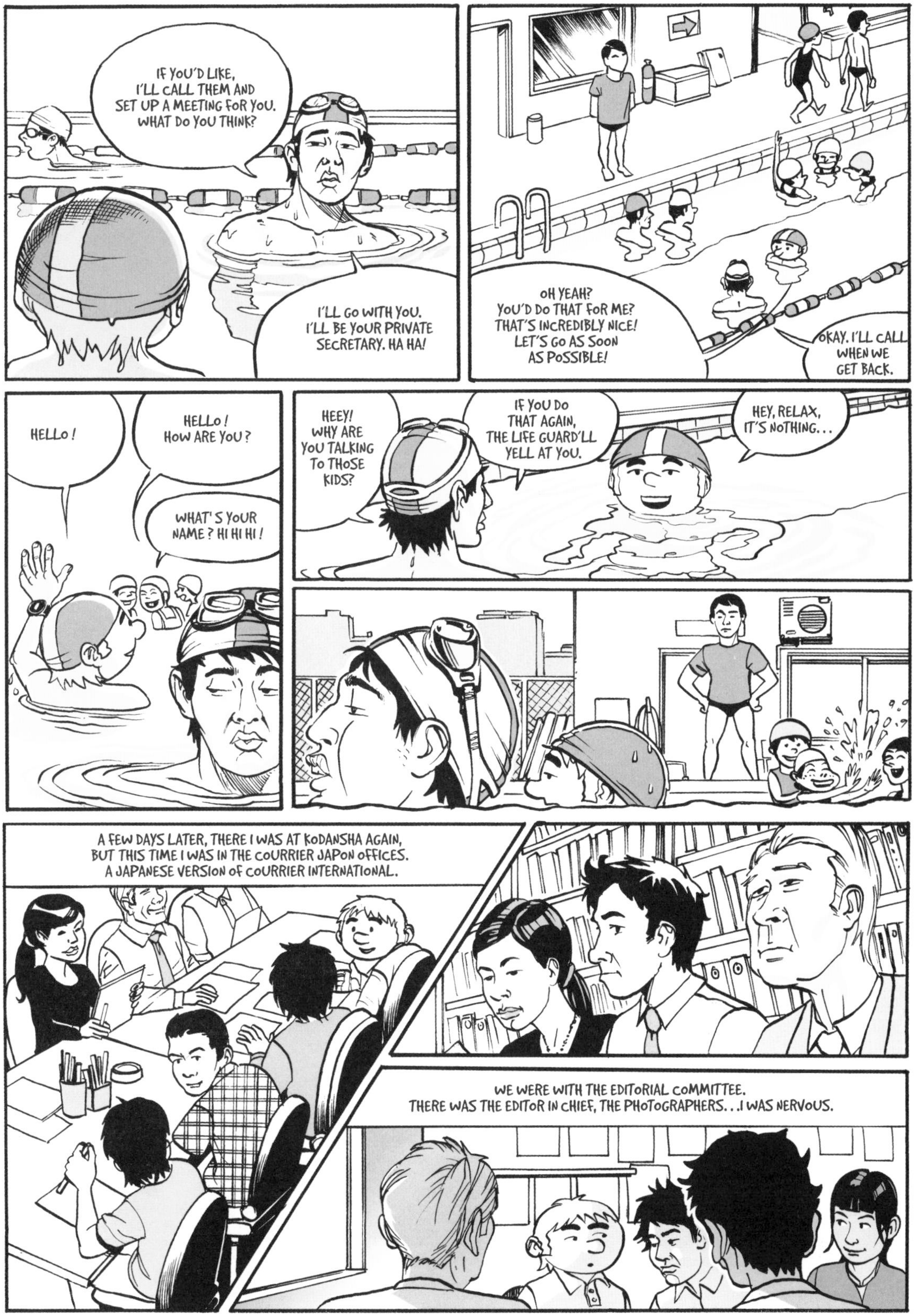
IF YOU'D LIKE, I'LL CALL THEM AND SET UP A MEETING FOR YOU. WHAT DO YOU THINK?
I'LL GO WITH YOU. I'LL BE YOUR PRIVATE SECRETARY. HA HA!
OH YEAH? YOU'D DO THAT FOR ME? THAT'S INCREDIBLY NICE! LET'S GO AS SOON AS POSSIBLE!
OKAY. I'LL CALL WHEN WE GET BACK.
HELLO!
HELLO! HOW ARE YOU?
WHAT'S YOUR NAME? HI HI HI!
HEEY! WHY ARE YOU TALKING TO THOSE KIDS?
IF YOU DO THAT AGAIN, THE LIFE GUARD'LL YELL AT YOU.
HEY, RELAX, IT'S NOTHING...
A FEW DAYS LATER, THERE I WAS AT KODANSHA AGAIN, BUT THIS TIME I WAS IN THE COURRIER JAPON OFFICES. A JAPANESE VERSION OF COURRIER INTERNATIONAL.
WE WERE WITH THE EDITORIAL COMMITTEE. THERE WAS THE EDITOR IN CHIEF, THE PHOTOGRAPHERS...I WAS NERVOUS.

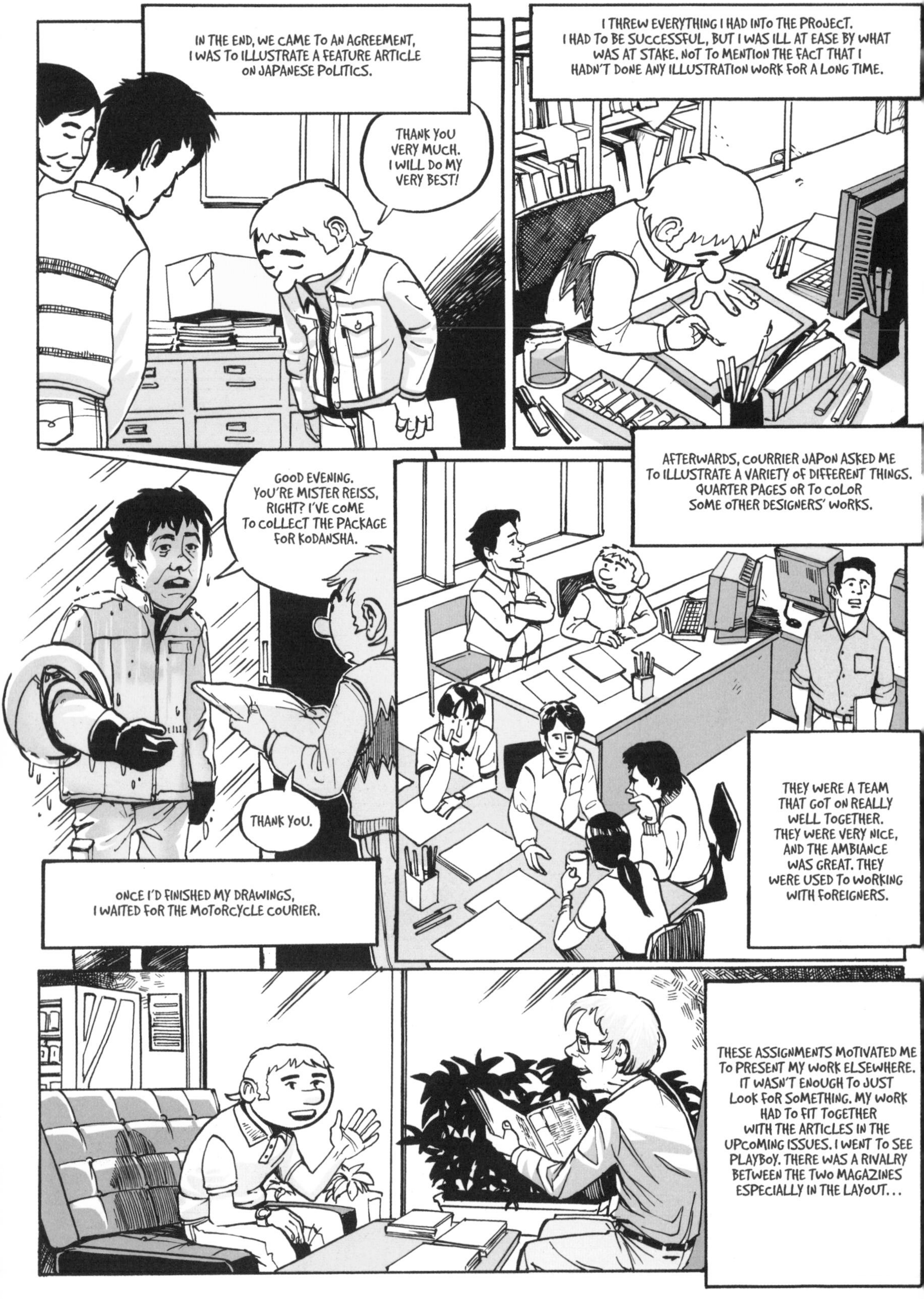
IN THE END, WE CAME TO AN AGREEMENT, I WAS TO ILLUSTRATE A FEATURE ARTICLE ON JAPANESE POLITICS.
THANK YOU VERY MUCH. I WILL DO MY VERY BEST!
I THREW EVERYTHING I HAD INTO THE PROJECT. I HAD TO BE SUCCESSFUL, BUT I WAS ILL AT EASE BY WHAT WAS AT STAKE. NOT TO MENTION THE FACT THAT I HADN'T DONE ANY ILLUSTRATION WORK FOR A LONG TIME.
GOOD EVENING. YOU'RE MISTER REISS, RIGHT? I'VE COME TO COLLECT THE PACKAGE FOR KODANSHA.
THANK YOU.
ONCE I'D FINISHED MY DRAWINGS, I WAITED FOR THE MOTORCYCLE COURIER.
AFTERWARDS, COURRIER JAPON ASKED ME TO ILLUSTRATE A VARIETY OF DIFFERENT THINGS. QUARTER PAGES OR TO COLOR SOME OTHER DESIGNERS' WORKS.
THEY WERE A TEAM THAT GOT ON REALLY WELL TOGETHER. THEY WERE VERY NICE, AND THE AMBIANCE WAS GREAT. THEY WERE USED TO WORKING WITH FOREIGNERS.
THESE ASSIGNMENTS MOTIVATED ME TO PRESENT MY WORK ELSEWHERE. IT WASN'T ENOUGH TO JUST LOOK FOR SOMETHING. MY WORK HAD TO FIT TOGETHER WITH THE ARTICLES IN THE UPCOMING ISSUES. I WENT TO SEE PLAYBOY. THERE WAS A RIVALRY BETWEEN THE TWO MAGAZINES ESPECIALLY IN THE LAYOUT...

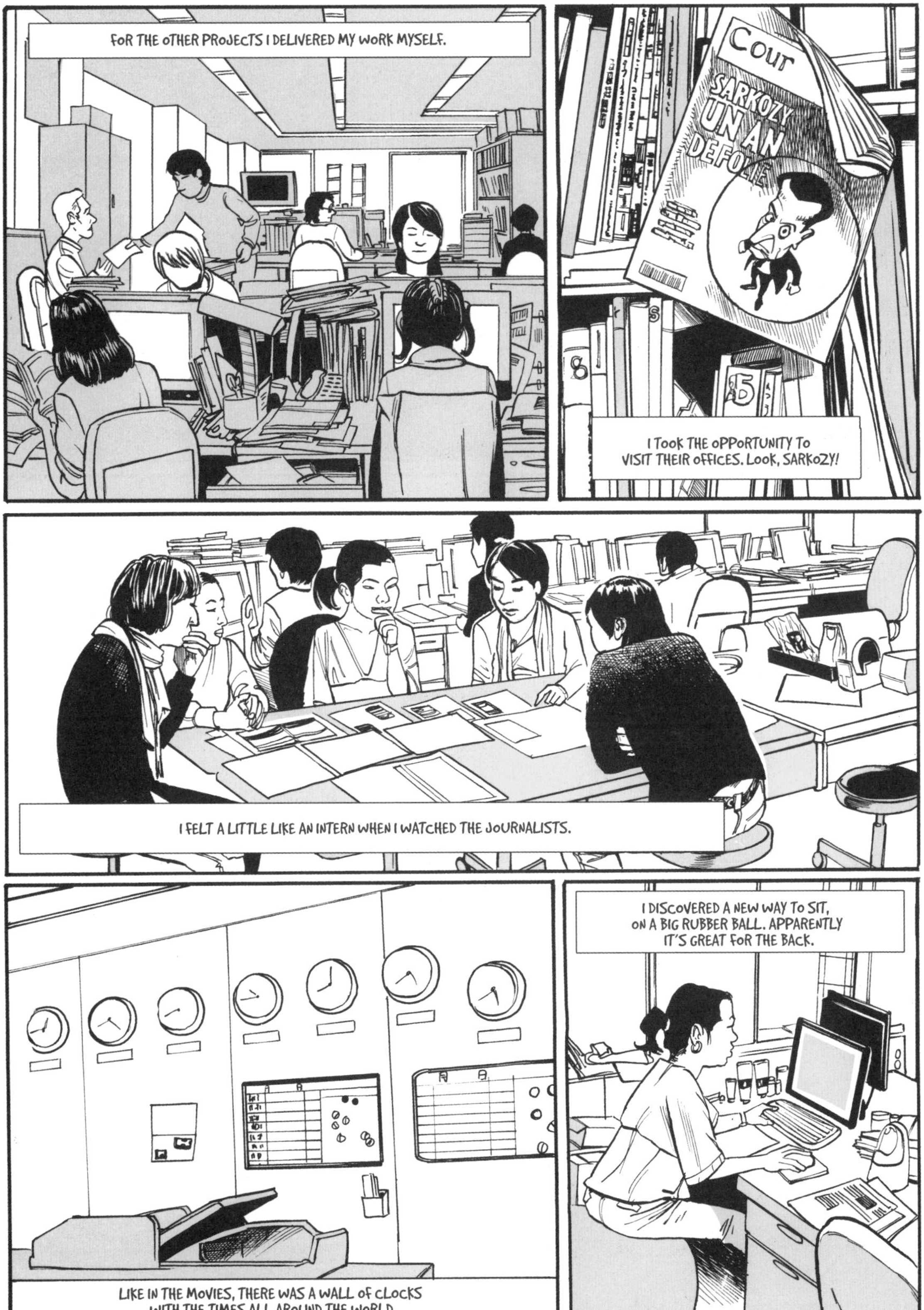
FOR THE OTHER PROJECTS I DELIVERED MY WORK MYSELF.
Cour
SARKOZY UN AN DE FOLIE
I TOOK THE OPPORTUNITY TO VISIT THEIR OFFICES. LOOK, SARKOZY!
I FELT A LITTLE LIKE AN INTERN WHEN I WATCHED THE JOURNALISTS.
LIKE IN THE MOVIES, THERE WAS A WALL OF CLOCKS WITH THE TIMES ALL AROUND THE WORLD.
I DISCOVERED A NEW WAY TO SIT, ON A BIG RUBBER BALL. APPARENTLY IT'S GREAT FOR THE BACK.

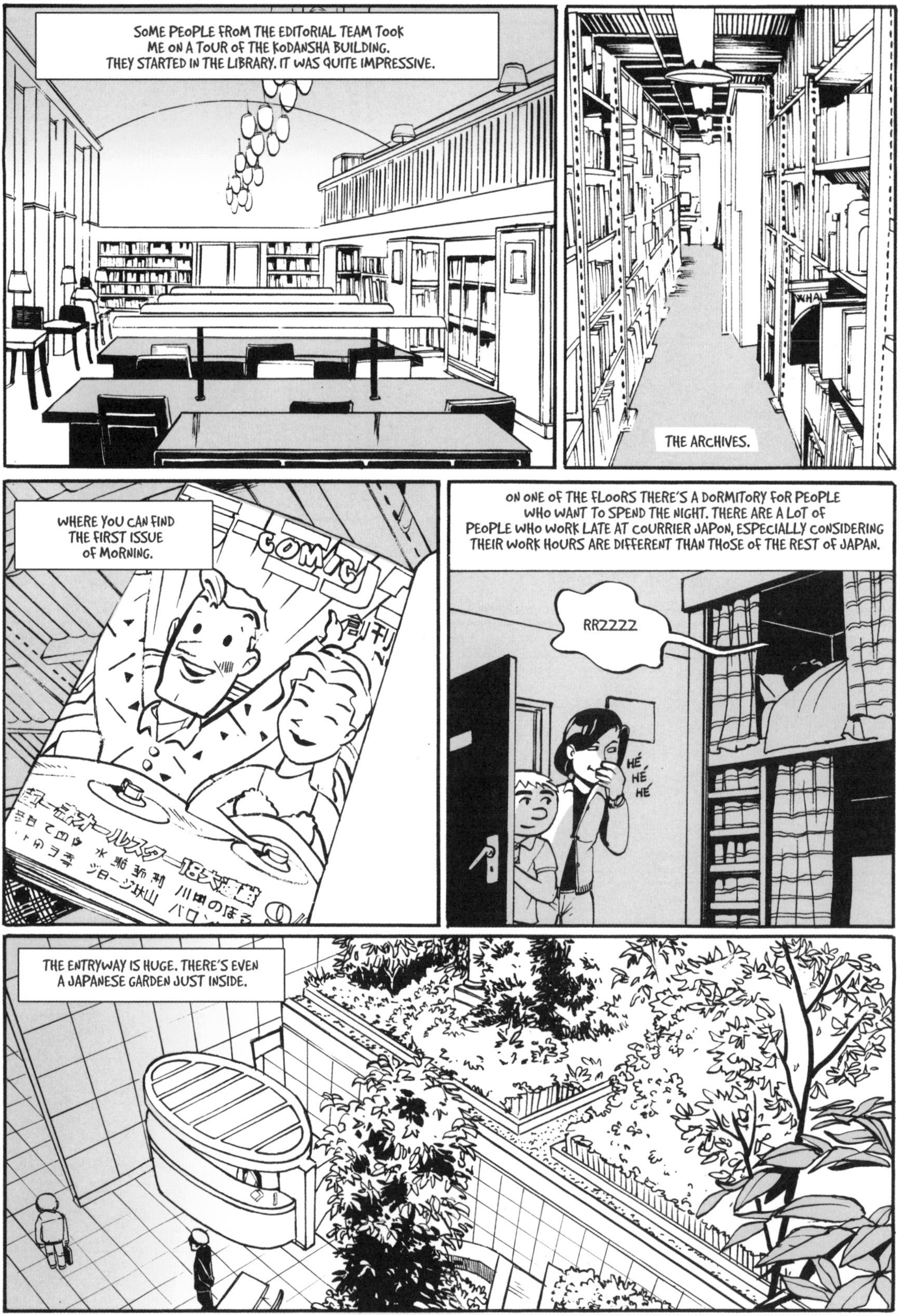
SOME PEOPLE FROM THE EDITORIAL TEAM TOOK ME ON A TOUR OF THE KODANSHA BUILDING. THEY STARTED IN THE LIBRARY. IT WAS QUITE IMPRESSIVE.
THE ARCHIVES.
WHERE YOU CAN FIND THE FIRST ISSUE OF MORNING.
COMIC
ON ONE OF THE FLOORS THERE'S A DORMITORY FOR PEOPLE WHO WANT TO SPEND THE NIGHT. THERE ARE A LOT OF PEOPLE WHO WORK LATE AT COURRIER JAPON, ESPECIALLY CONSIDERING THEIR WORK HOURS ARE DIFFERENT THAN THOSE OF THE REST OF JAPAN.
RR2222
HÉ HÉ HÉ
THE ENTRYWAY IS HUGE. THERE'S EVEN A JAPANESE GARDEN JUST INSIDE.

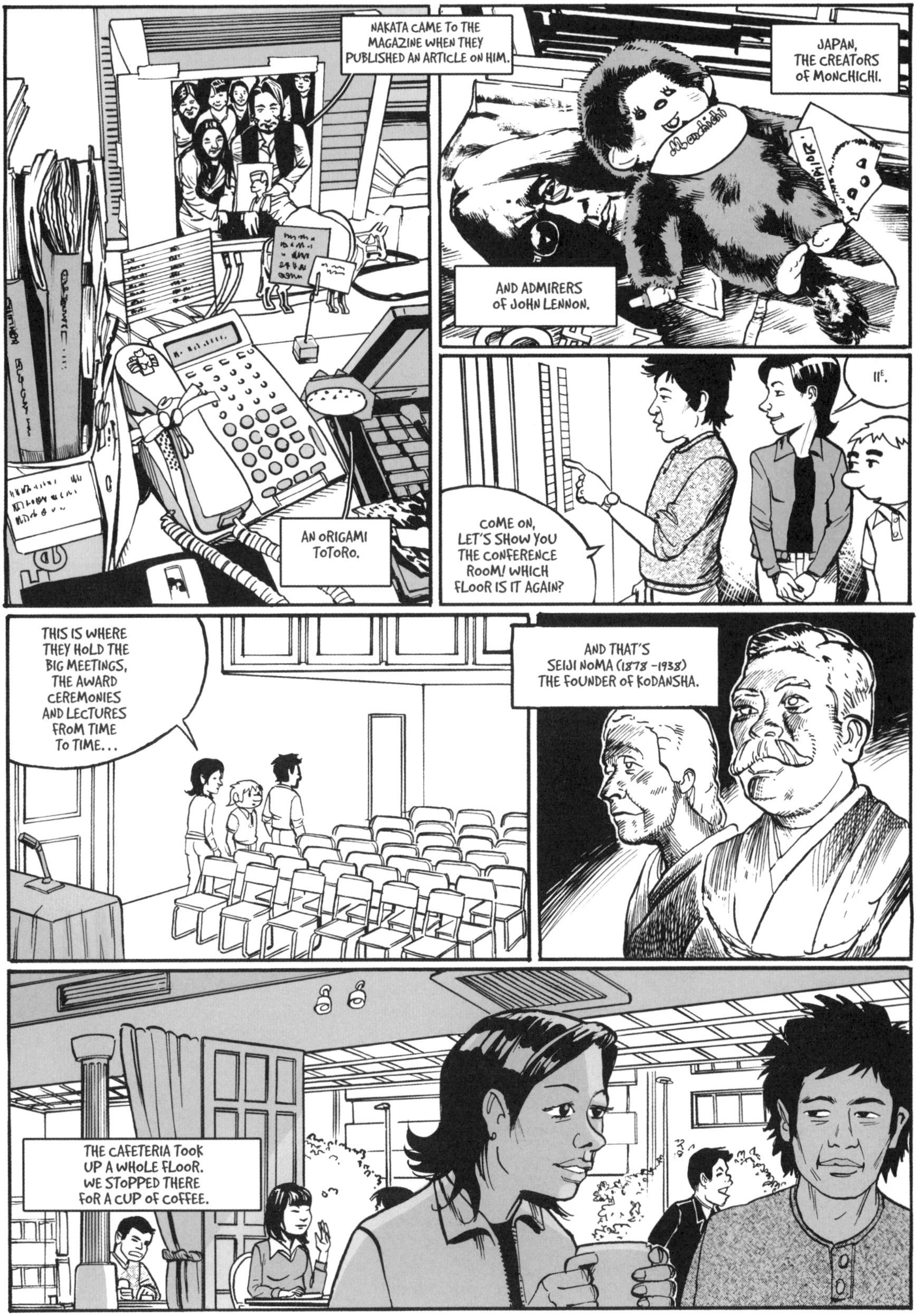
NAKATA CAME TO THE MAGAZINE WHEN THEY PUBLISHED AN ARTICLE ON HIM.
AN ORIGAMI TOTORO.
JAPAN, THE CREATORS OF MONCHICHI.
AND ADMIRERS OF JOHN LENNON.
COME ON, LET'S SHOW YOU THE CONFERENCE ROOM! WHICH FLOOR IS IT AGAIN?
IIE.
THIS IS WHERE THEY HOLD THE BIG MEETINGS, THE AWARD CEREMONIES AND LECTURES FROM TIME TO TIME...
AND THAT'S SEIJI NOMA (1878 -1938) THE FOUNDER OF KODANSHA.
THE CAFETERIA TOOK UP A WHOLE FLOOR. WE STOPPED THERE FOR A CUP OF COFFEE.

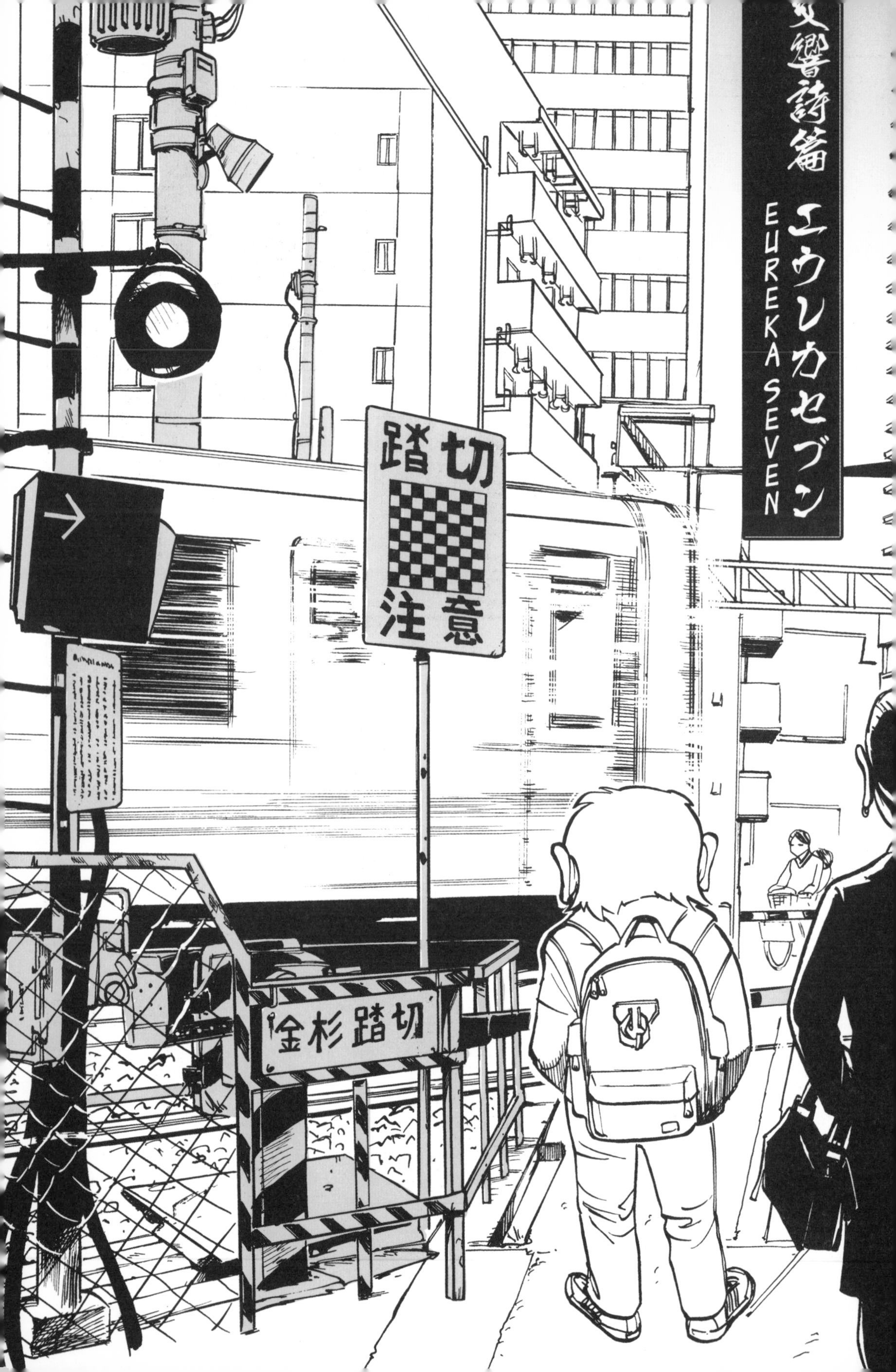
交響詩篇 エウレカセブン
EUREKA SEVEN
踏切
注意
金杉踏切

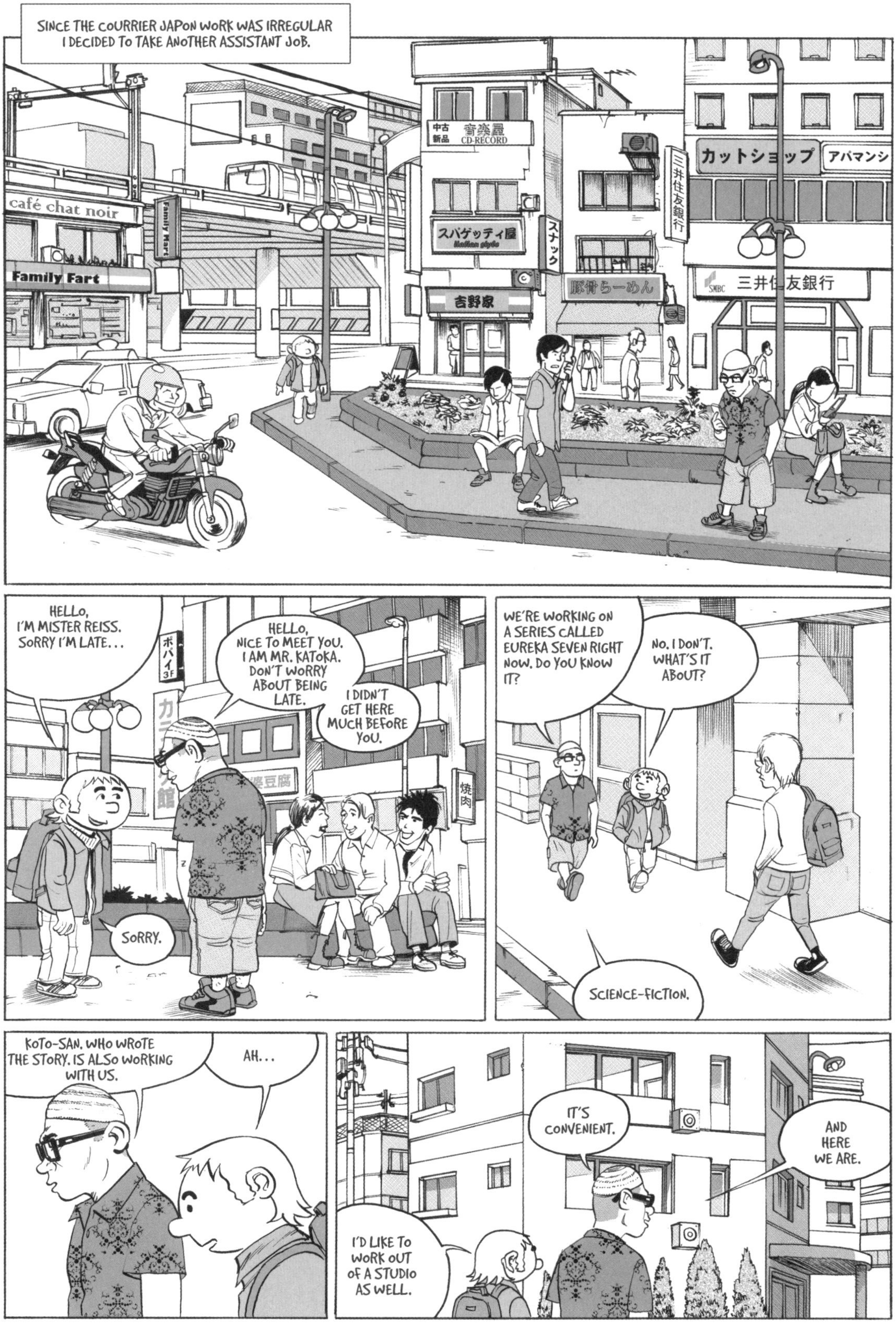
SINCE THE COURRIER JAPON WORK WAS IRREGULAR I DECIDED TO TAKE ANOTHER ASSISTANT JOB.
café chat noir
Family Fart
Family Mart
中古 新品 音楽屋 CD-RECORD
スパゲッティ屋
スナック
吉野家
豚骨らーめん
三井住友銀行
カットショップ
アパマンシ
SMBC 三井住友銀行
HELLO, I'M MISTER REISS. SORRY I'M LATE...
HELLO, NICE TO MEET YOU. I AM MR. KATOKA. DON'T WORRY ABOUT BEING LATE.
I DIDN'T GET HERE MUCH BEFORE YOU.
SORRY.
ポパイ 3F
焼肉
WE'RE WORKING ON A SERIES CALLED EUREKA SEVEN RIGHT NOW. DO YOU KNOW IT?
NO, I DON'T. WHAT'S IT ABOUT?
SCIENCE-FICTION.
KOTO-SAN, WHO WROTE THE STORY, IS ALSO WORKING WITH US.
AH...
IT'S CONVENIENT.
AND HERE WE ARE.
I'D LIKE TO WORK OUT OF A STUDIO AS WELL.

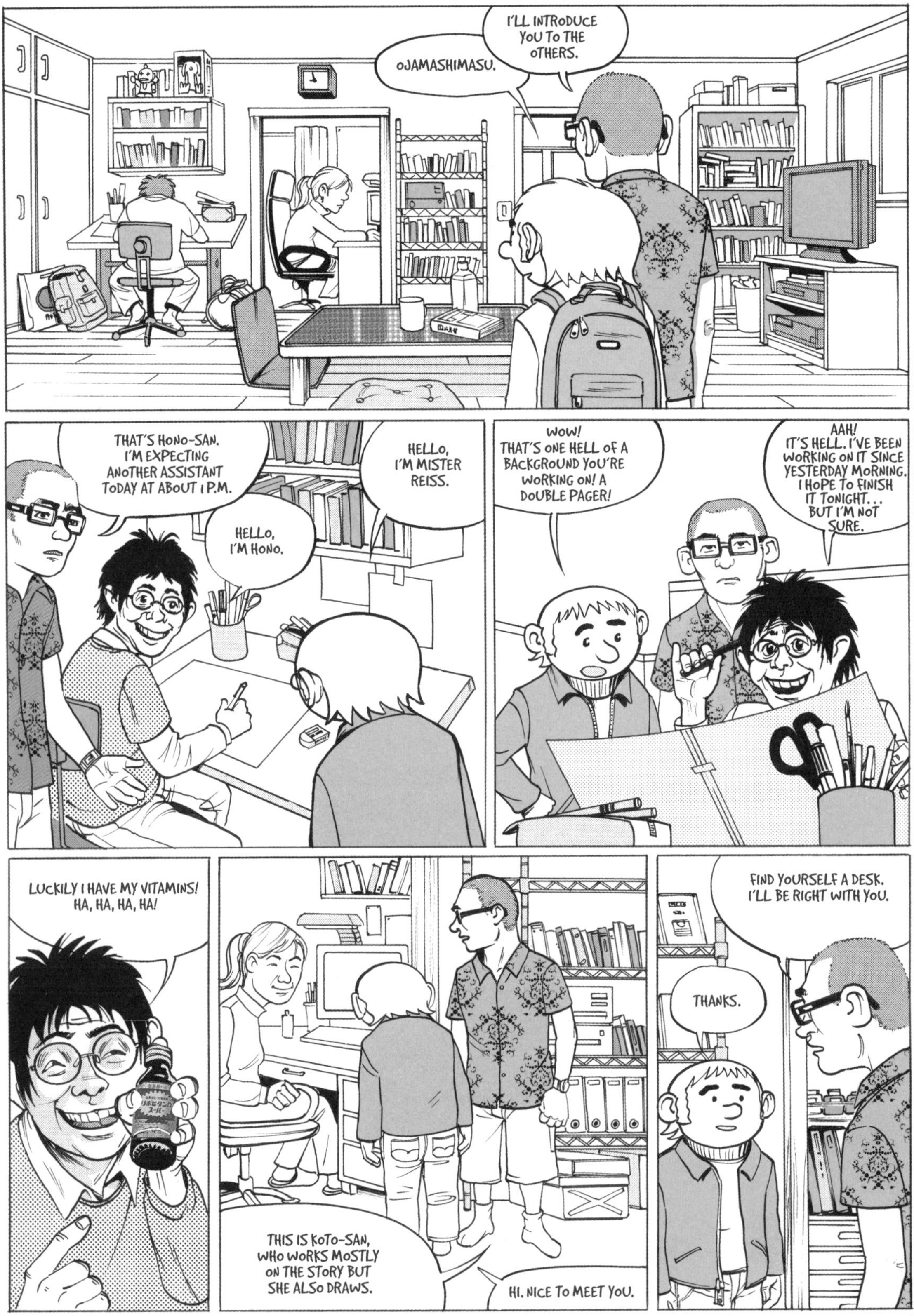
OJAMASHIMASU.
I'LL INTRODUCE YOU TO THE OTHERS.
THAT'S HONO-SAN. I'M EXPECTING ANOTHER ASSISTANT TODAY AT ABOUT 1 P.M.
HELLO, I'M HONO.
HELLO, I'M MISTER REISS.
WOW! THAT'S ONE HELL OF A BACKGROUND YOU'RE WORKING ON! A DOUBLE PAGER!
AAH! IT'S HELL. I'VE BEEN WORKING ON IT SINCE YESTERDAY MORNING. I HOPE TO FINISH IT TONIGHT... BUT I'M NOT SURE.
LUCKILY I HAVE MY VITAMINS! HA, HA, HA, HA!
THIS IS KOTO-SAN, WHO WORKS MOSTLY ON THE STORY BUT SHE ALSO DRAWS.
HI. NICE TO MEET YOU.
FIND YOURSELF A DESK. I'LL BE RIGHT WITH YOU.
THANKS.

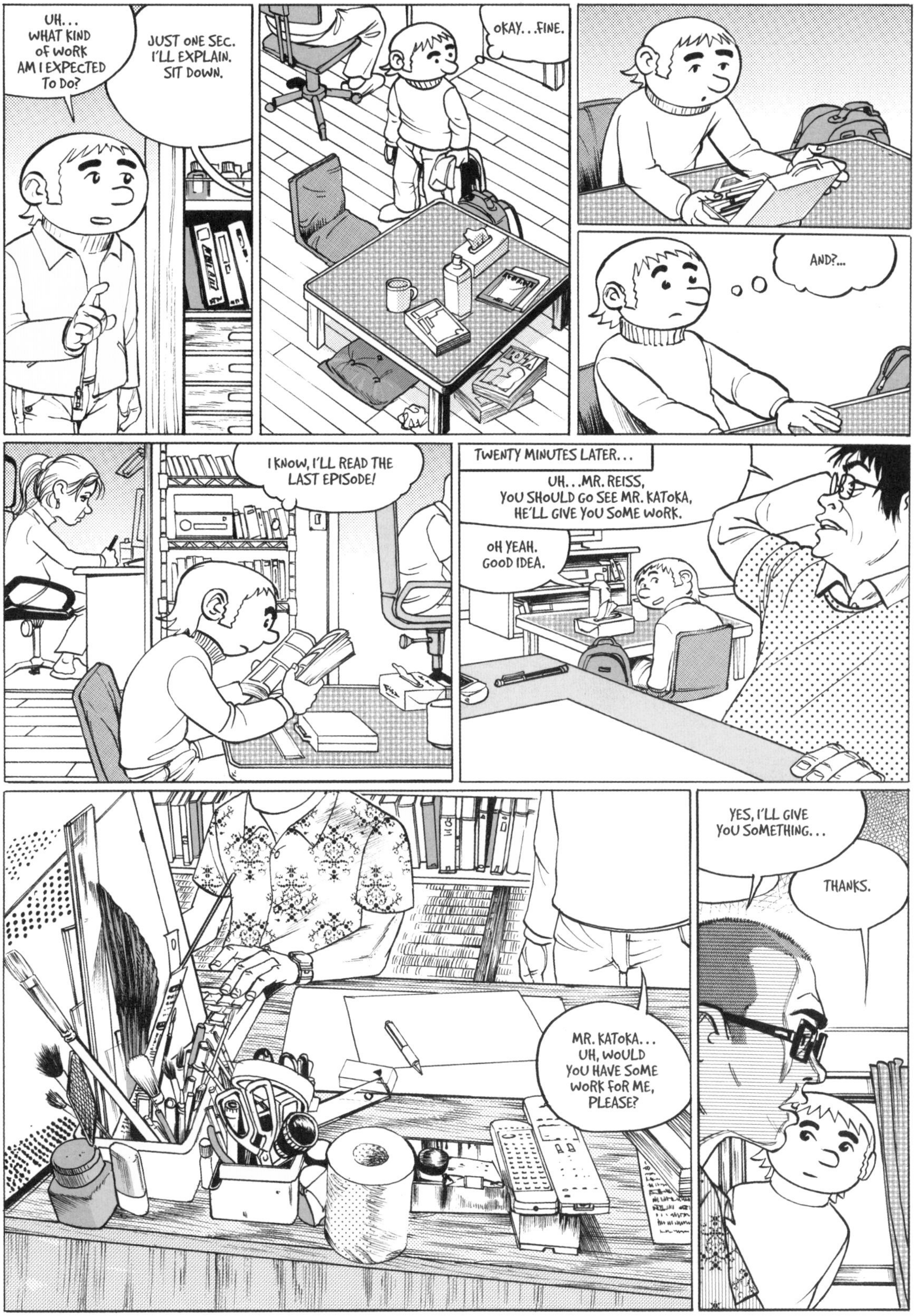
UH... WHAT KIND OF WORK AM I EXPECTED TO DO?
JUST ONE SEC. I'LL EXPLAIN. SIT DOWN.
OKAY...FINE.
AND?...
I KNOW, I'LL READ THE LAST EPISODE!
TWENTY MINUTES LATER...
UH...MR. REISS, YOU SHOULD GO SEE MR. KATOKA, HE'LL GIVE YOU SOME WORK.
OH YEAH. GOOD IDEA.
MR. KATOKA... UH, WOULD YOU HAVE SOME WORK FOR ME, PLEASE?
YES, I'LL GIVE YOU SOMETHING...
THANKS.

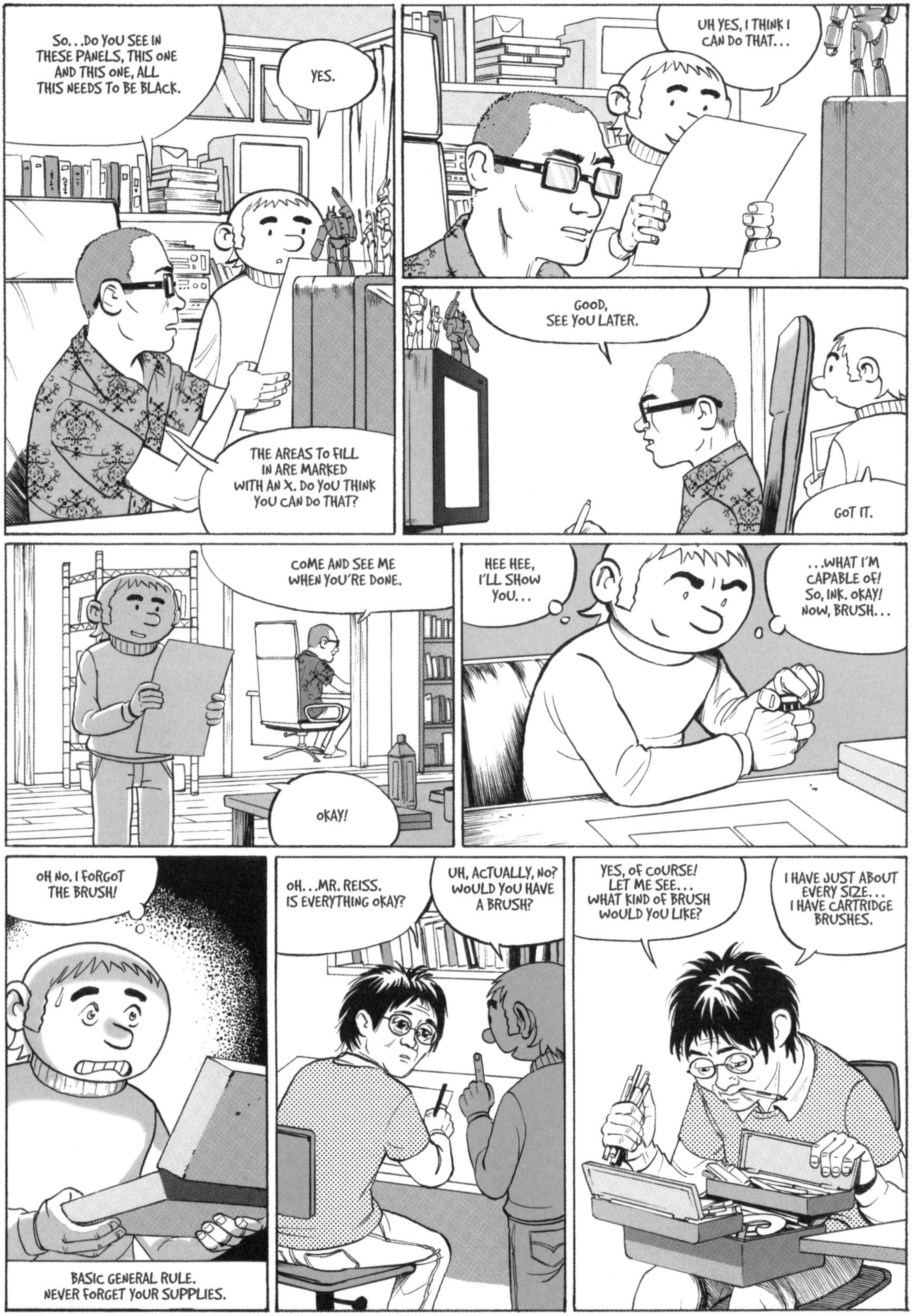
So. . .Do you see in these panels, this one and this one, all this needs to be black.
Yes.
The areas to fill in are marked with an X. Do you think you can do that?
Uh yes, I think I can do that. . .
Good, see you later.
Got it.
Come and see me when you're done.
Okay!
Hee hee, I'll show you. . .
. . .what I'm capable of! So, ink. Okay! Now, brush. . .
Oh no. I forgot the brush!
Basic general rule. Never forget your supplies.
Oh. . .Mr. Reiss. Is everything okay?
Uh, actually, no? Would you have a brush?
Yes, of course! Let me see. . . What kind of brush would you like?
I have just about every size. . . I have cartridge brushes.

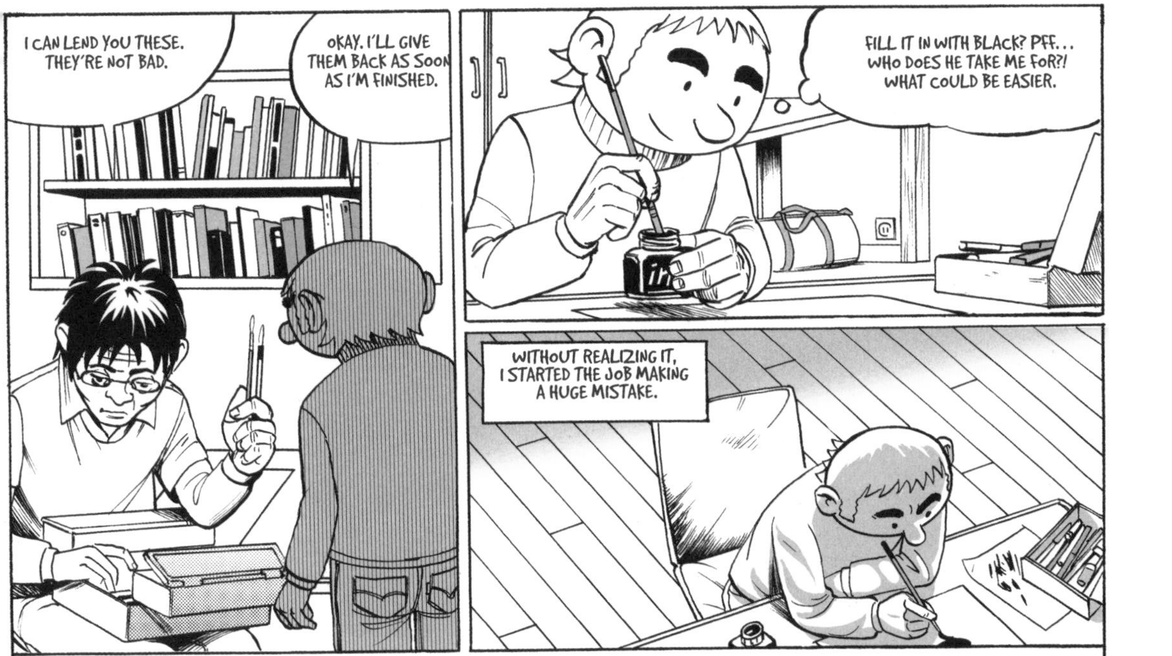
I CAN LEND YOU THESE. THEY'RE NOT BAD.
OKAY. I'LL GIVE THEM BACK AS SOON AS I'M FINISHED.
FILL IT IN WITH BLACK? PFF... WHO DOES HE TAKE ME FOR?! WHAT COULD BE EASIER.
WITHOUT REALIZING IT, I STARTED THE JOB MAKING A HUGE MISTAKE.

HOW TO DRAW MANGA
WITH MIMI AND NONO!

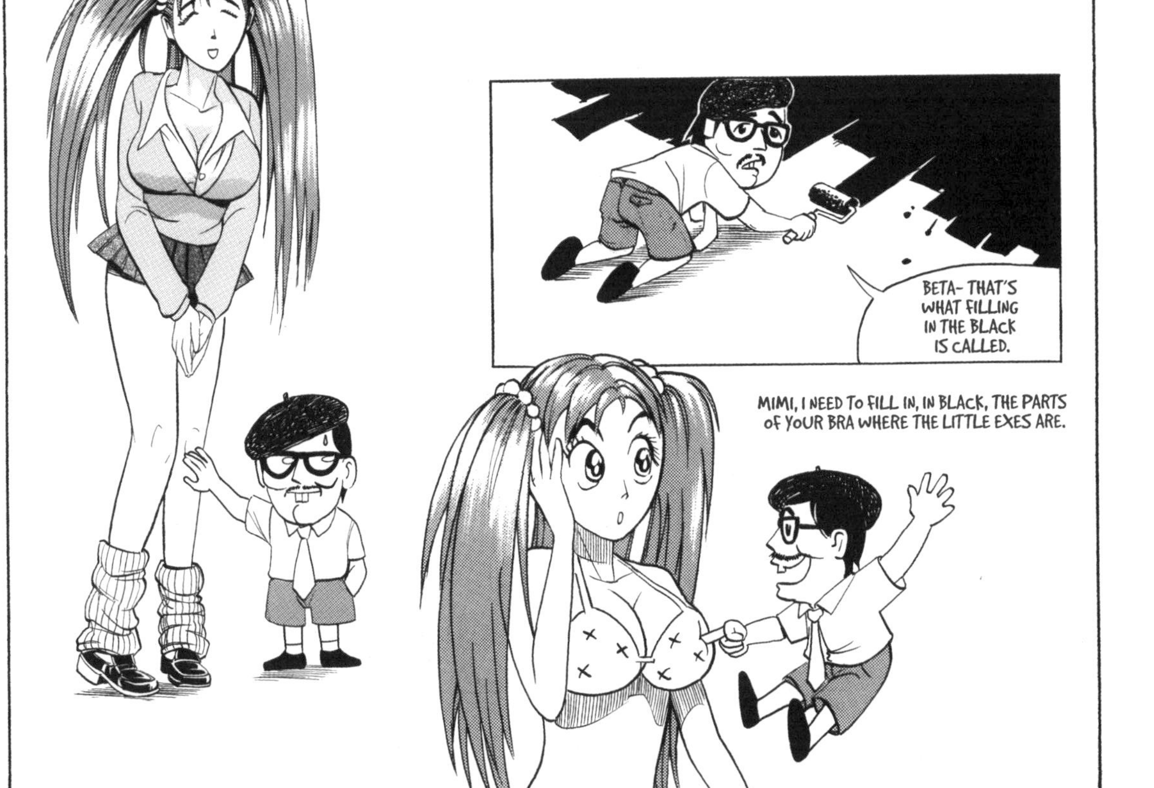
BETA- THAT'S WHAT FILLING IN THE BLACK IS CALLED.
MIMI, I NEED TO FILL IN, IN BLACK, THE PARTS OF YOUR BRA WHERE THE LITTLE EXES ARE.

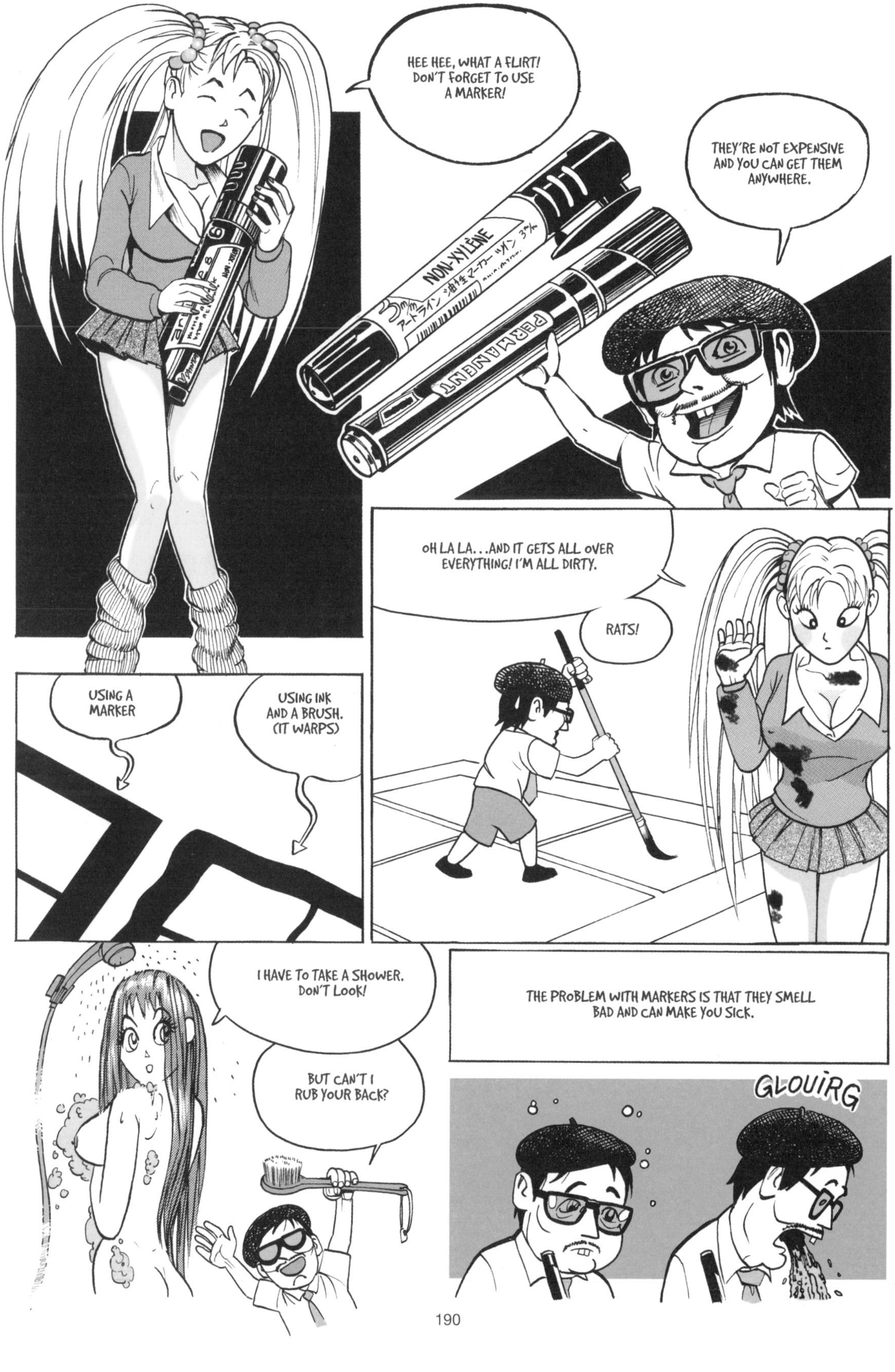
HEE HEE, WHAT A FLIRT! DON'T FORGET TO USE A MARKER!
NON-XYLÈNE
PERMANENT
THEY'RE NOT EXPENSIVE AND YOU CAN GET THEM ANYWHERE.
USING A MARKER
USING INK AND A BRUSH. (IT WARPS)
OH LA LA...AND IT GETS ALL OVER EVERYTHING! I'M ALL DIRTY.
RATS!
I HAVE TO TAKE A SHOWER. DON'T LOOK!
BUT CAN'T I RUB YOUR BACK?
THE PROBLEM WITH MARKERS IS THAT THEY SMELL BAD AND CAN MAKE YOU SICK.
GLOUIRG

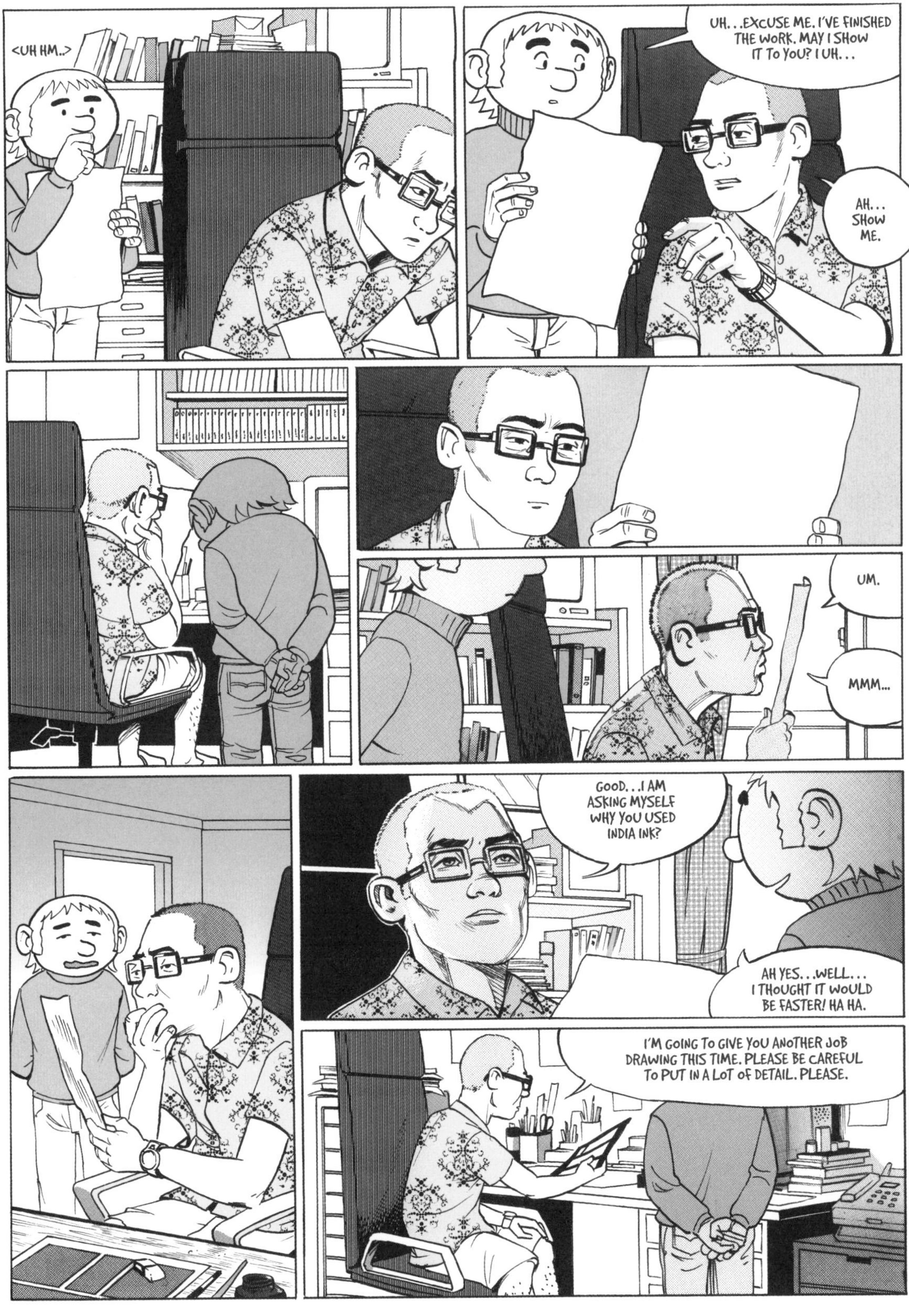
<UH HM..>
UH...EXCUSE ME. I'VE FINISHED THE WORK. MAY I SHOW IT TO YOU? I UH...
AH... SHOW ME.
UM.
MMM...
GOOD...I AM ASKING MYSELF WHY YOU USED INDIA INK?
AH YES...WELL... I THOUGHT IT WOULD BE FASTER! HA HA.
I'M GOING TO GIVE YOU ANOTHER JOB DRAWING THIS TIME. PLEASE BE CAREFUL TO PUT IN A LOT OF DETAIL. PLEASE.

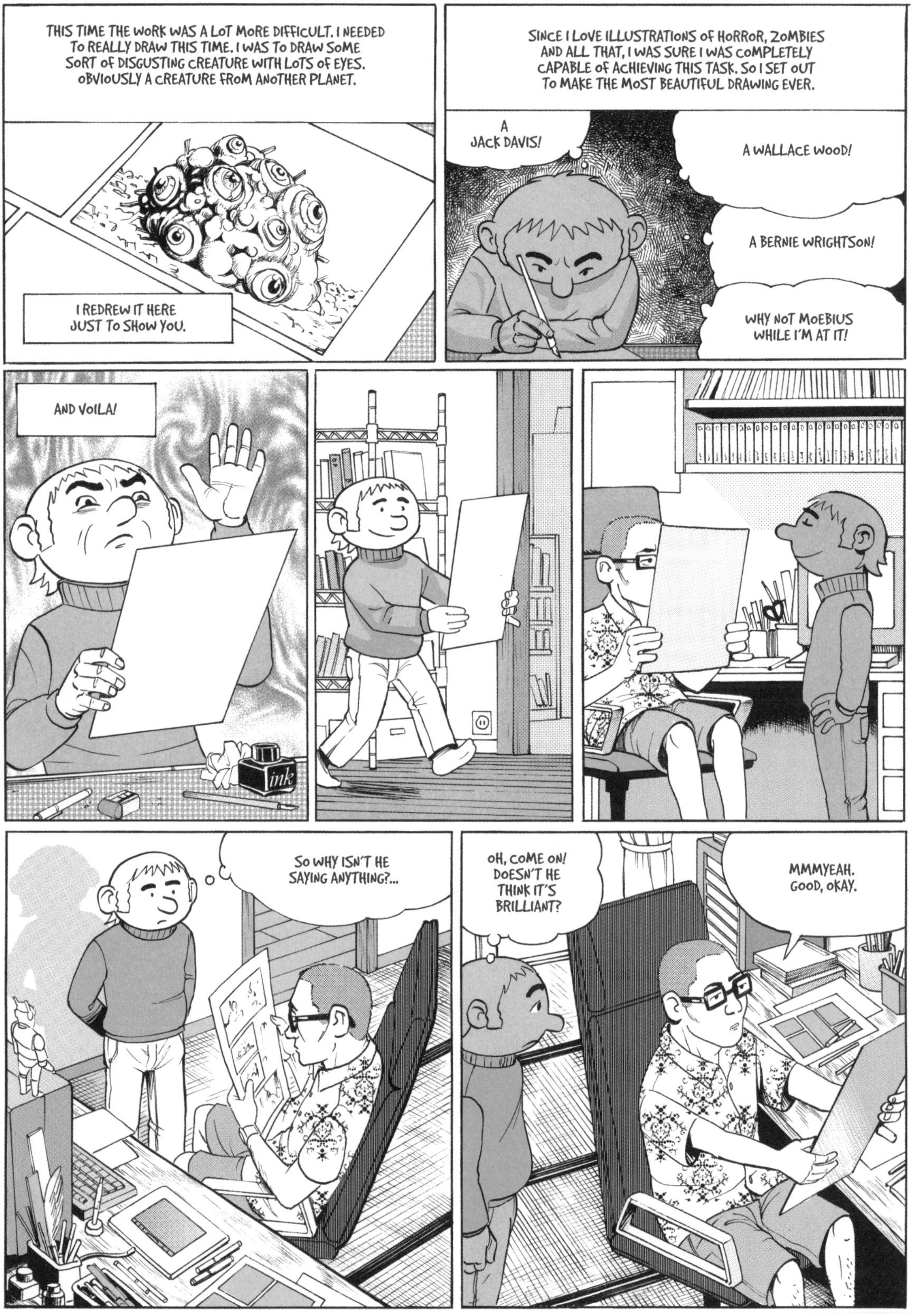
THIS TIME THE WORK WAS A LOT MORE DIFFICULT. I NEEDED TO REALLY DRAW THIS TIME. I WAS TO DRAW SOME SORT OF DISGUSTING CREATURE WITH LOTS OF EYES. OBVIOUSLY A CREATURE FROM ANOTHER PLANET.
I REDREW IT HERE JUST TO SHOW YOU.
SINCE I LOVE ILLUSTRATIONS OF HORROR, ZOMBIES AND ALL THAT, I WAS SURE I WAS COMPLETELY CAPABLE OF ACHIEVING THIS TASK. SO I SET OUT TO MAKE THE MOST BEAUTIFUL DRAWING EVER.
A JACK DAVIS!
A WALLACE WOOD!
A BERNIE WRIGHTSON!
WHY NOT MOEBIUS WHILE I'M AT IT!
AND VOILA!
ink
SO WHY ISN'T HE SAYING ANYTHING?...
OH, COME ON! DOESN'T HE THINK IT'S BRILLIANT?
MMMYEAH. GOOD, OKAY.

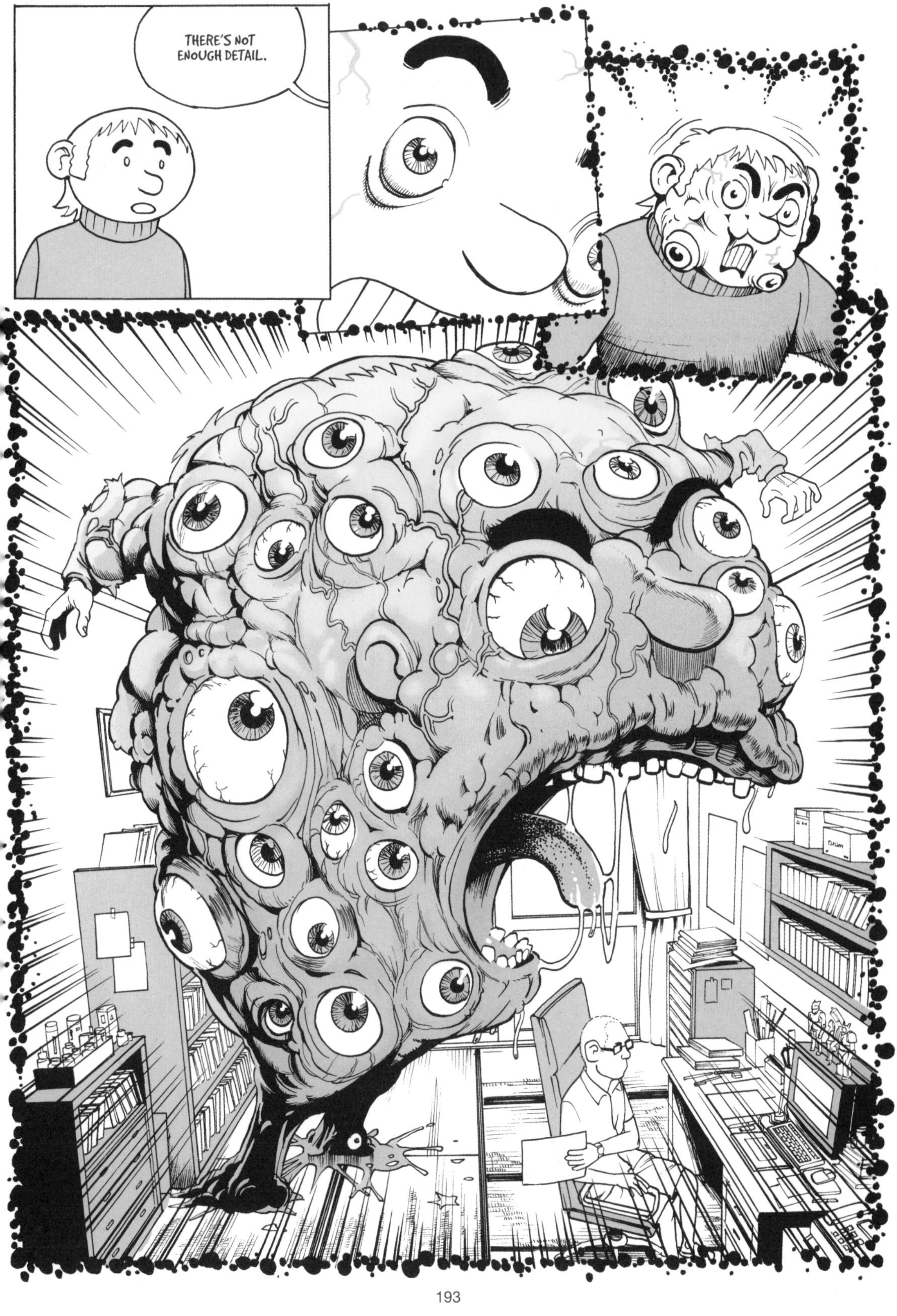
THERE'S NOT ENOUGH DETAIL.

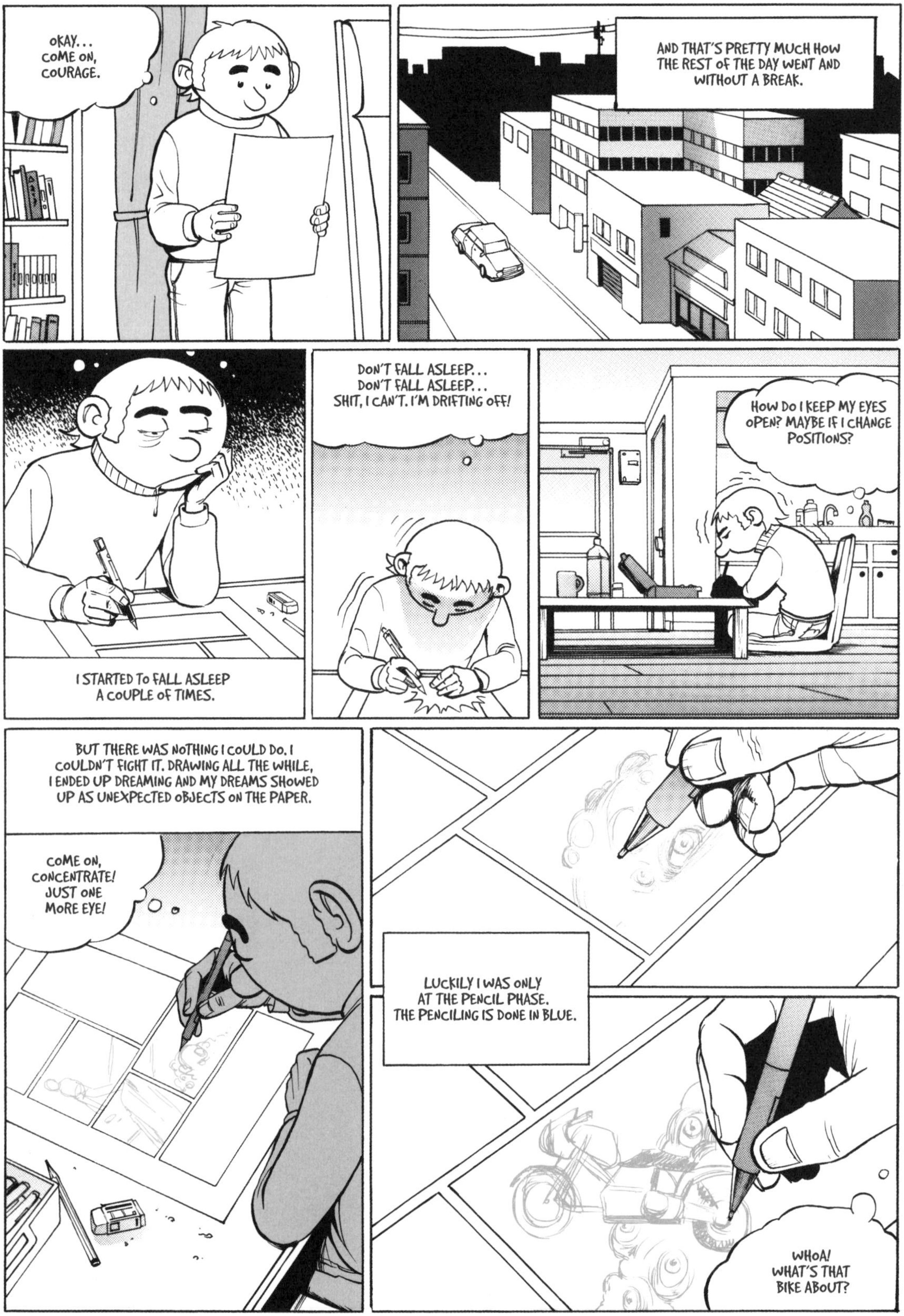
OKAY... COME ON, COURAGE.
AND THAT'S PRETTY MUCH HOW THE REST OF THE DAY WENT AND WITHOUT A BREAK.
I STARTED TO FALL ASLEEP A COUPLE OF TIMES.
DON'T FALL ASLEEP... DON'T FALL ASLEEP... SHIT, I CAN'T. I'M DRIFTING OFF!
HOW DO I KEEP MY EYES OPEN? MAYBE IF I CHANGE POSITIONS?
BUT THERE WAS NOTHING I COULD DO. I COULDN'T FIGHT IT. DRAWING ALL THE WHILE, I ENDED UP DREAMING AND MY DREAMS SHOWED UP AS UNEXPECTED OBJECTS ON THE PAPER.
COME ON, CONCENTRATE! JUST ONE MORE EYE!
LUCKILY I WAS ONLY AT THE PENCIL PHASE. THE PENCILING IS DONE IN BLUE.
WHOA! WHAT'S THAT BIKE ABOUT?

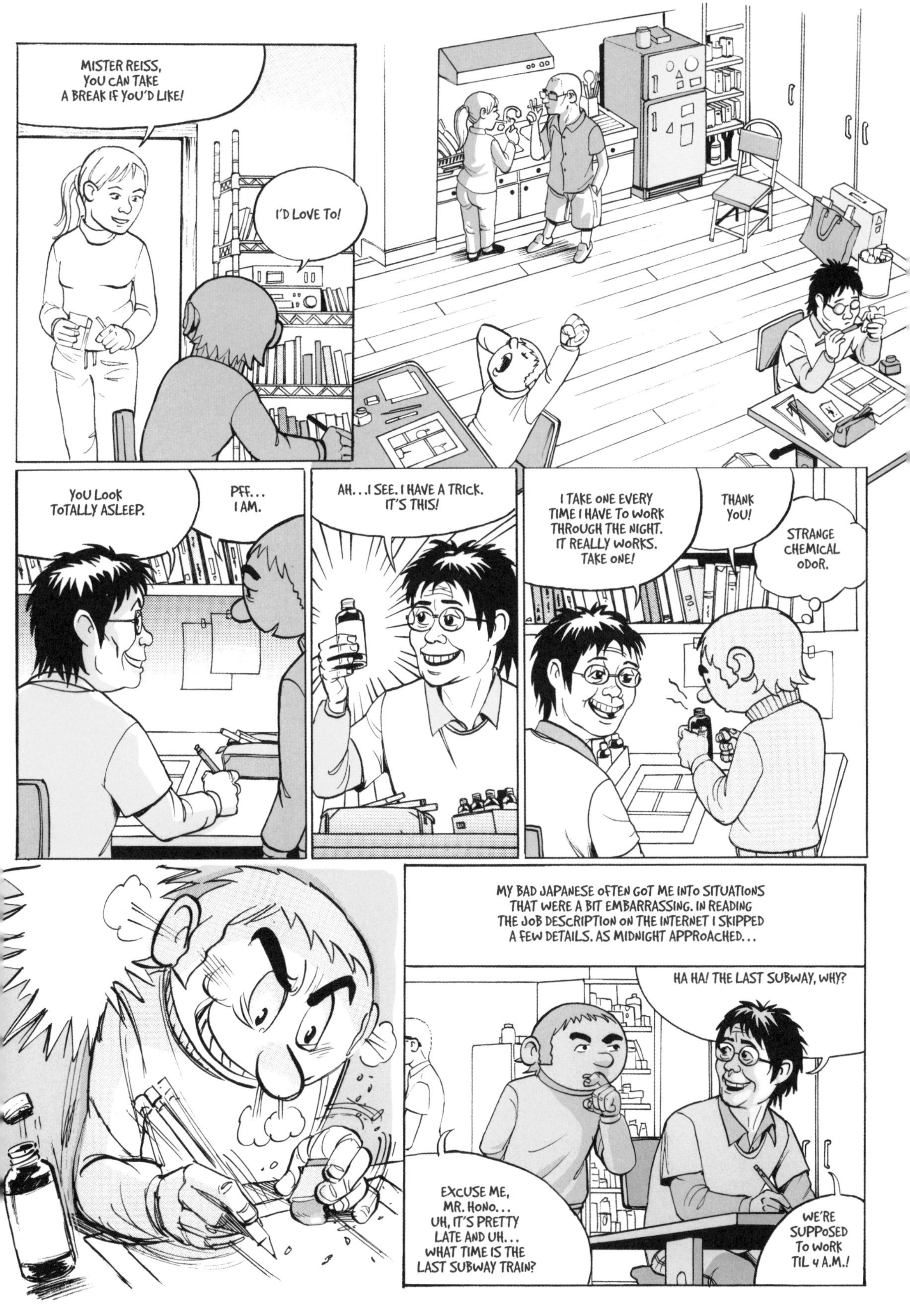
MISTER REISS, YOU CAN TAKE A BREAK IF YOU'D LIKE!
I'D LOVE TO!
YOU LOOK TOTALLY ASLEEP.
PFF... I AM.
AH...I SEE. I HAVE A TRICK. IT'S THIS!
I TAKE ONE EVERY TIME I HAVE TO WORK THROUGH THE NIGHT. IT REALLY WORKS. TAKE ONE!
THANK YOU!
STRANGE CHEMICAL ODOR.
MY BAD JAPANESE OFTEN GOT ME INTO SITUATIONS THAT WERE A BIT EMBARRASSING. IN READING THE JOB DESCRIPTION ON THE INTERNET I SKIPPED A FEW DETAILS. AS MIDNIGHT APPROACHED...
EXCUSE ME, MR. HONO... UH, IT'S PRETTY LATE AND UH... WHAT TIME IS THE LAST SUBWAY TRAIN?
HA HA! THE LAST SUBWAY, WHY?
WE'RE SUPPOSED TO WORK TIL 4 A.M.!

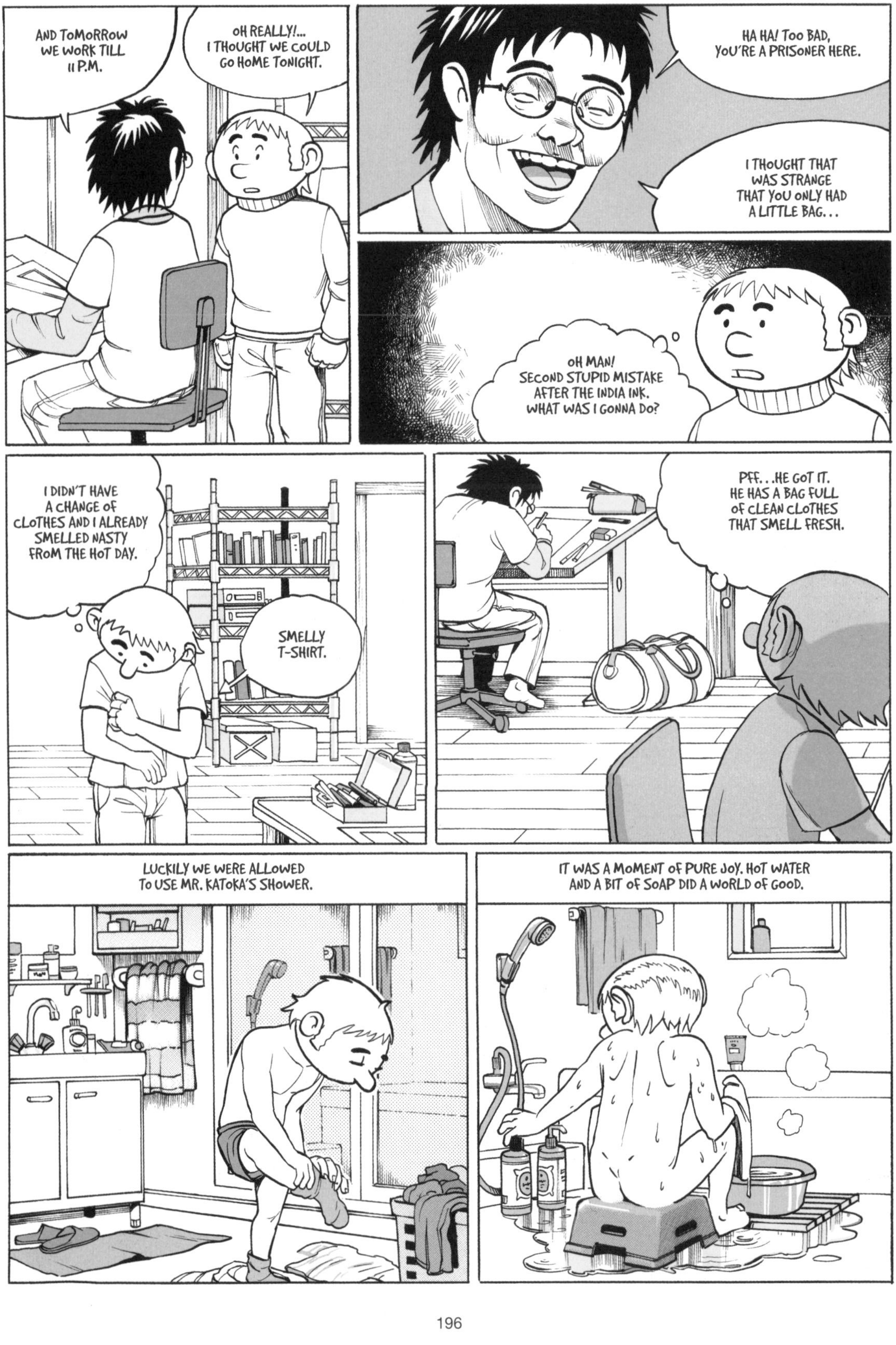
AND TOMORROW WE WORK TILL 11 P.M.
OH REALLY!... I THOUGHT WE COULD GO HOME TONIGHT.
HA HA! TOO BAD, YOU'RE A PRISONER HERE.
I THOUGHT THAT WAS STRANGE THAT YOU ONLY HAD A LITTLE BAG...
OH MAN! SECOND STUPID MISTAKE AFTER THE INDIA INK. WHAT WAS I GONNA DO?
I DIDN'T HAVE A CHANGE OF CLOTHES AND I ALREADY SMELLED NASTY FROM THE HOT DAY.
SMELLY T-SHIRT.
PFF...HE GOT IT. HE HAS A BAG FULL OF CLEAN CLOTHES THAT SMELL FRESH.
LUCKILY WE WERE ALLOWED TO USE MR. KATOKA'S SHOWER.
IT WAS A MOMENT OF PURE JOY. HOT WATER AND A BIT OF SOAP DID A WORLD OF GOOD.

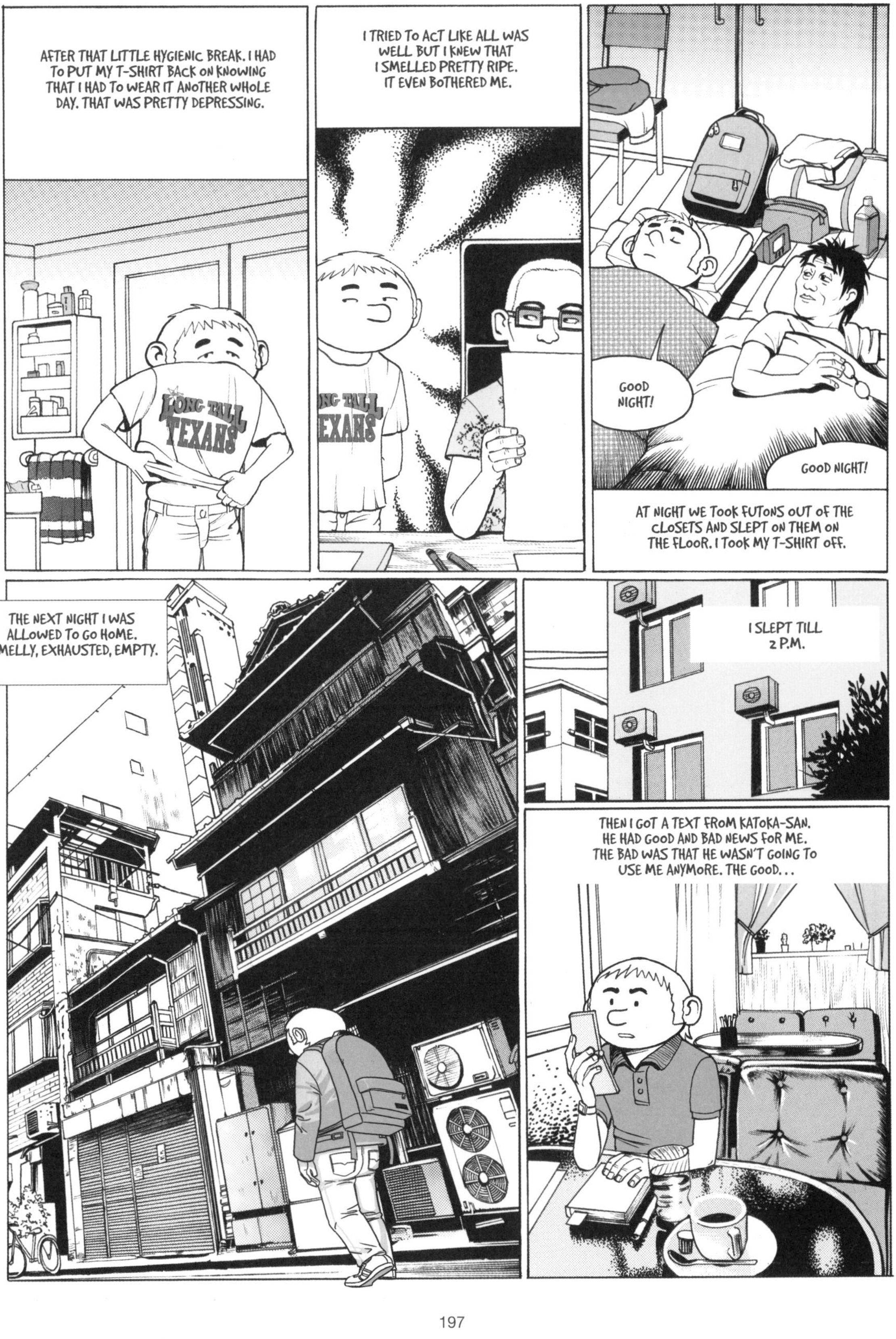
AFTER THAT LITTLE HYGIENIC BREAK. I HAD TO PUT MY T-SHIRT BACK ON KNOWING THAT I HAD TO WEAR IT ANOTHER WHOLE DAY. THAT WAS PRETTY DEPRESSING.
LONG TALL TEXANS
I TRIED TO ACT LIKE ALL WAS WELL BUT I KNEW THAT I SMELLED PRETTY RIPE. IT EVEN BOTHERED ME.
GOOD NIGHT!
GOOD NIGHT!
AT NIGHT WE TOOK FUTONS OUT OF THE CLOSETS AND SLEPT ON THEM ON THE FLOOR. I TOOK MY T-SHIRT OFF.
THE NEXT NIGHT I WAS ALLOWED TO GO HOME. SMELLY, EXHAUSTED, EMPTY.
I SLEPT TILL 2 P.M.
THEN I GOT A TEXT FROM KATOKA-SAN. HE HAD GOOD AND BAD NEWS FOR ME. THE BAD WAS THAT HE WASN'T GOING TO USE ME ANYMORE. THE GOOD...

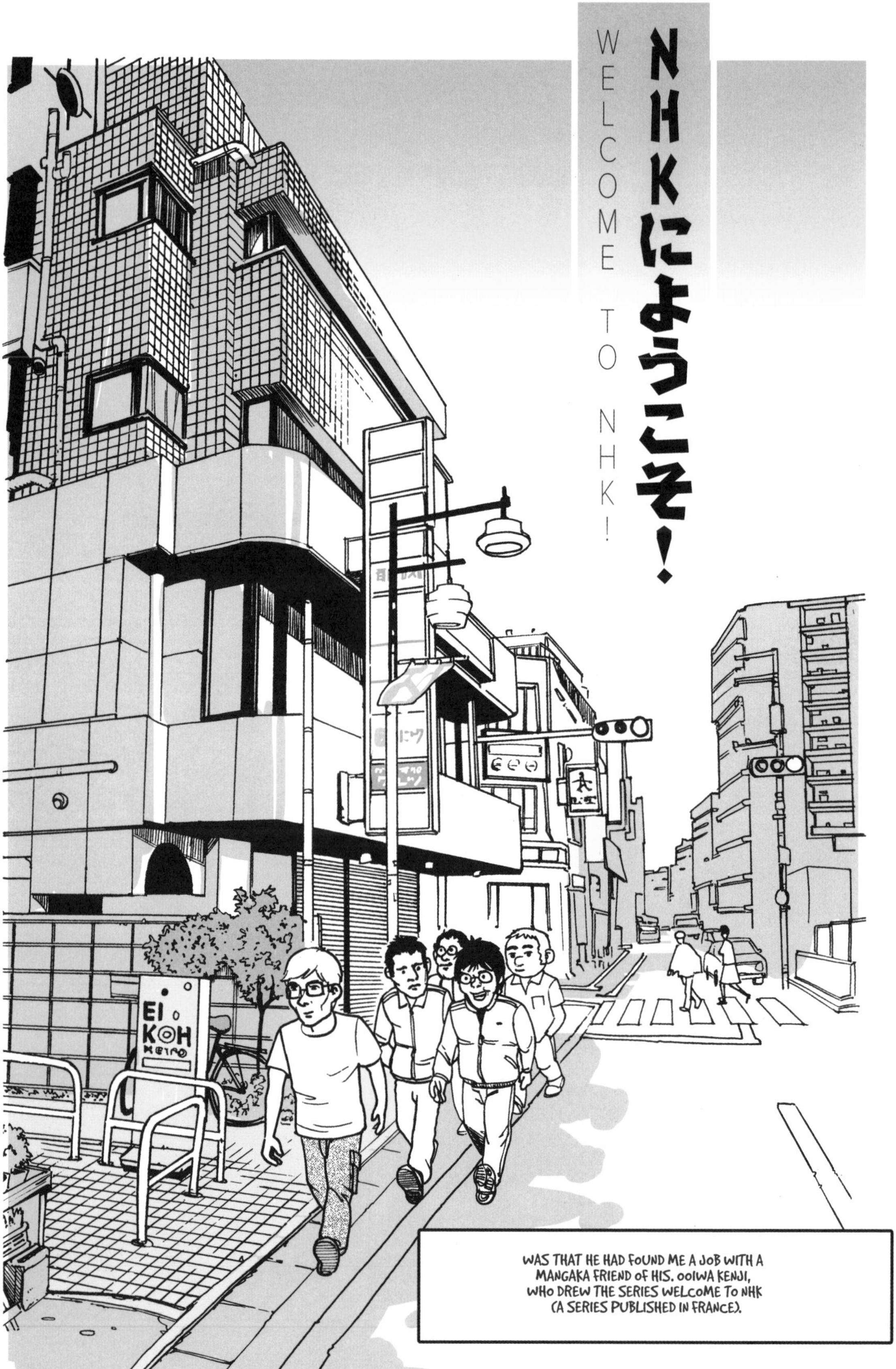
NHKにようこそ!
WELCOME TO NHK!
EI KOH METRO
WAS THAT HE HAD FOUND ME A JOB WITH A MANGAKA FRIEND OF HIS. OOIWA KENJI, WHO DREW THE SERIES WELCOME TO NHK (A SERIES PUBLISHED IN FRANCE).

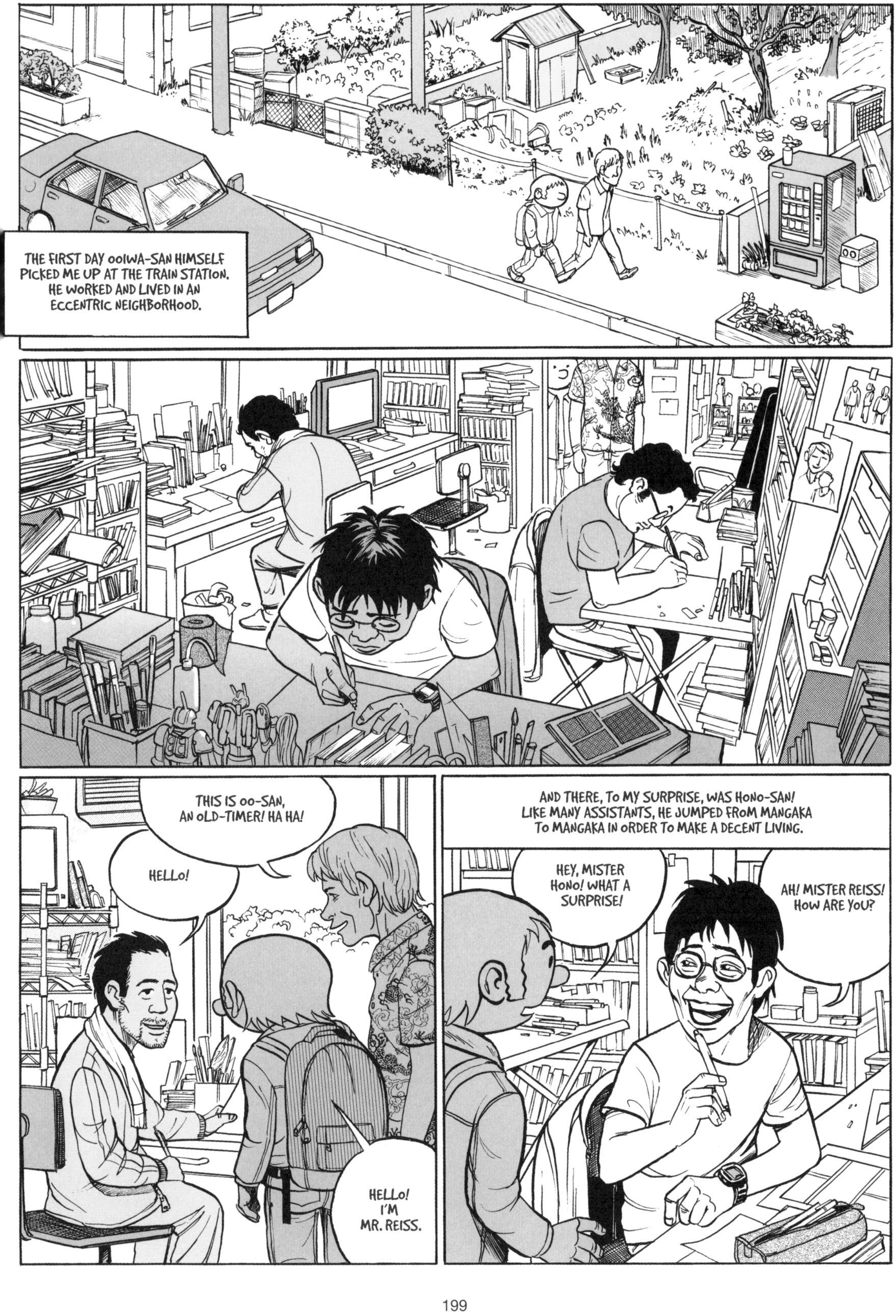
THE FIRST DAY OOIWA-SAN HIMSELF PICKED ME UP AT THE TRAIN STATION. HE WORKED AND LIVED IN AN ECCENTRIC NEIGHBORHOOD.
THIS IS OO-SAN, AN OLD-TIMER! HA HA!
HELLO!
HELLO! I'M MR. REISS.
AND THERE, TO MY SURPRISE, WAS HONO-SAN! LIKE MANY ASSISTANTS, HE JUMPED FROM MANGAKA TO MANGAKA IN ORDER TO MAKE A DECENT LIVING.
HEY, MISTER HONO! WHAT A SURPRISE!
AH! MISTER REISS! HOW ARE YOU?

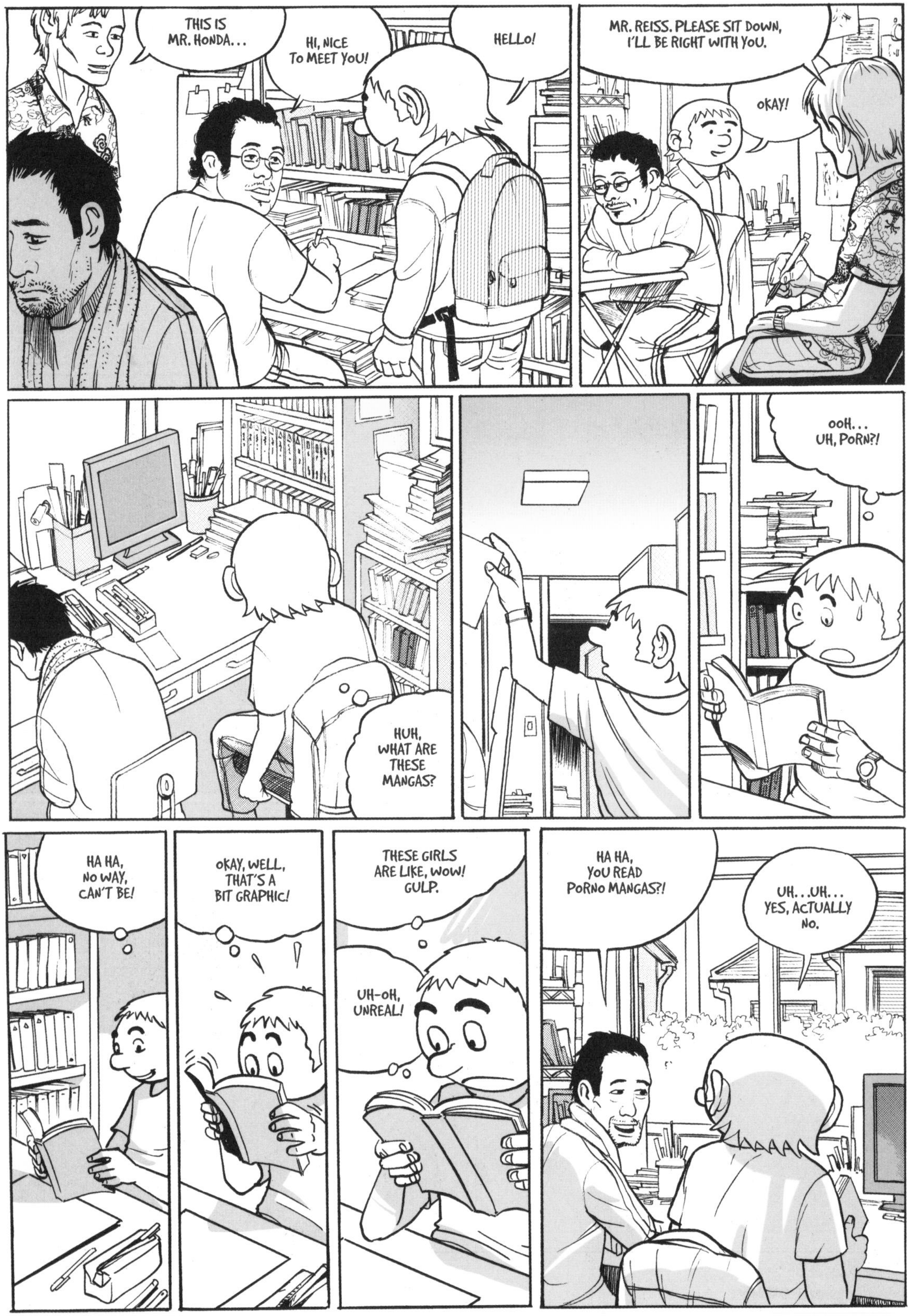
THIS IS MR. HONDA...
HI, NICE TO MEET YOU!
HELLO!
MR. REISS. PLEASE SIT DOWN, I'LL BE RIGHT WITH YOU.
OKAY!
HUH, WHAT ARE THESE MANGAS?
OOH... UH, PORN?!
HA HA, NO WAY, CAN'T BE!
OKAY, WELL, THAT'S A BIT GRAPHIC!
THESE GIRLS ARE LIKE, WOW! GULP.
UH-OH, UNREAL!
HA HA, YOU READ PORNO MANGAS?!
UH...UH... YES, ACTUALLY NO.

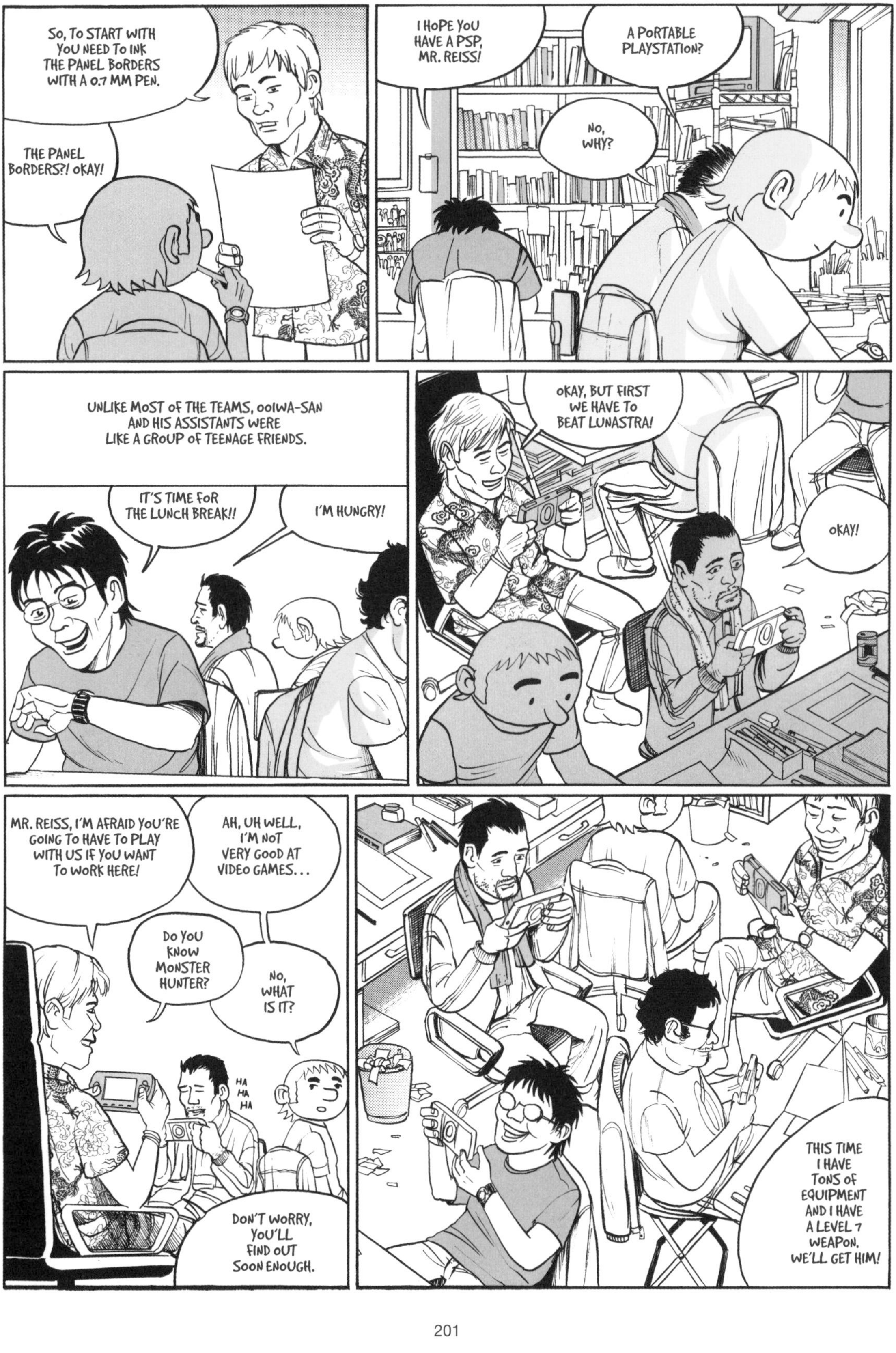
SO, TO START WITH YOU NEED TO INK THE PANEL BORDERS WITH A 0.7 MM PEN.
THE PANEL BORDERS?! OKAY!
I HOPE YOU HAVE A PSP, MR. REISS!
A PORTABLE PLAYSTATION?
NO, WHY?
UNLIKE MOST OF THE TEAMS, OOIWA-SAN AND HIS ASSISTANTS WERE LIKE A GROUP OF TEENAGE FRIENDS.
IT'S TIME FOR THE LUNCH BREAK!!
I'M HUNGRY!
OKAY, BUT FIRST WE HAVE TO BEAT LUNASTRA!
OKAY!
MR. REISS, I'M AFRAID YOU'RE GOING TO HAVE TO PLAY WITH US IF YOU WANT TO WORK HERE!
AH, UH WELL, I'M NOT VERY GOOD AT VIDEO GAMES...
DO YOU KNOW MONSTER HUNTER?
NO, WHAT IS IT?
HA HA HA
DON'T WORRY, YOU'LL FIND OUT SOON ENOUGH.
THIS TIME I HAVE TONS OF EQUIPMENT AND I HAVE A LEVEL 7 WEAPON. WE'LL GET HIM!

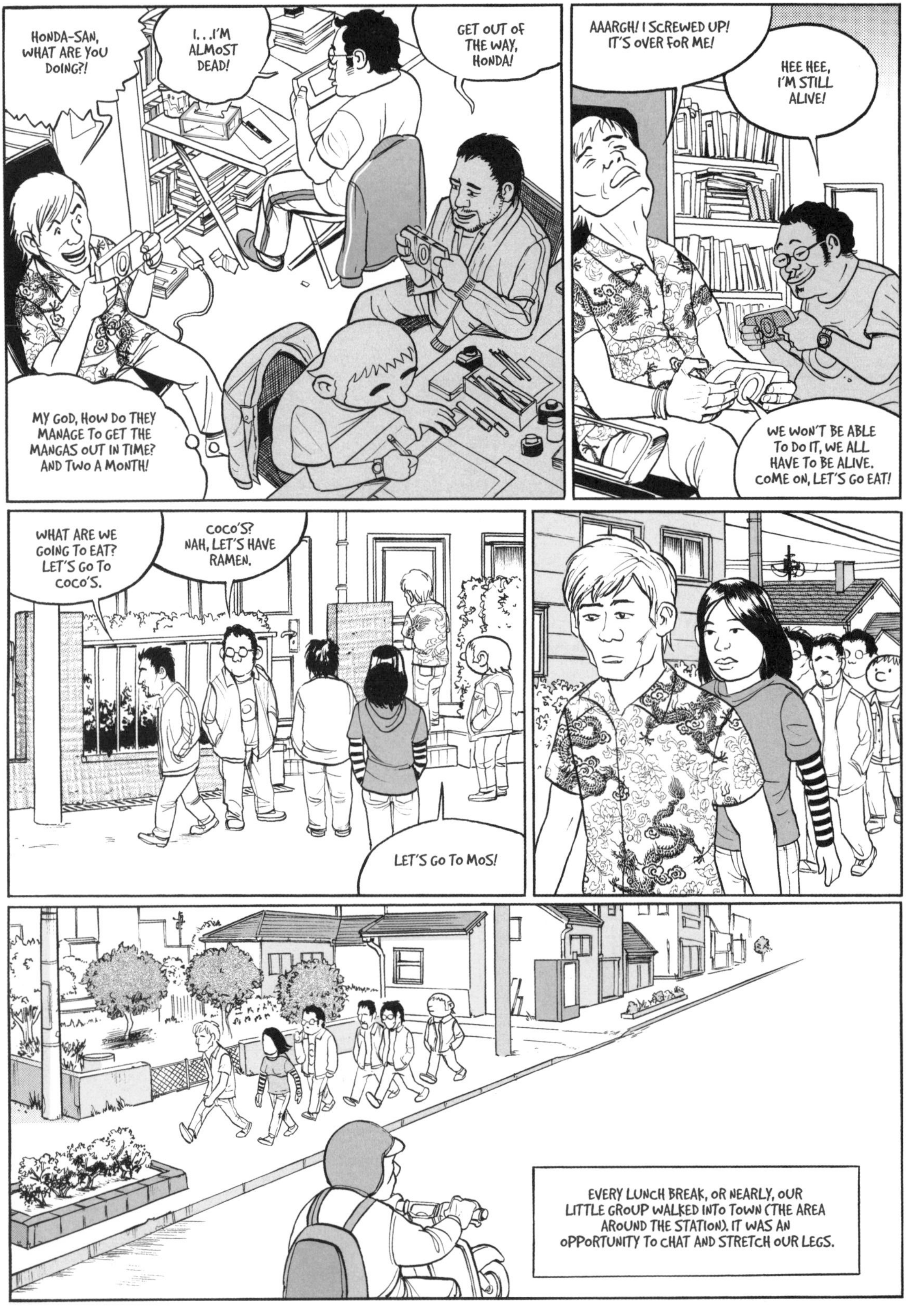
HONDA-SAN, WHAT ARE YOU DOING?!
I...I'M ALMOST DEAD!
GET OUT OF THE WAY, HONDA!
MY GOD, HOW DO THEY MANAGE TO GET THE MANGAS OUT IN TIME? AND TWO A MONTH!
AAARGH! I SCREWED UP! IT'S OVER FOR ME!
HEE HEE, I'M STILL ALIVE!
WE WON'T BE ABLE TO DO IT, WE ALL HAVE TO BE ALIVE. COME ON, LET'S GO EAT!
WHAT ARE WE GOING TO EAT? LET'S GO TO COCO'S.
COCO'S? NAH, LET'S HAVE RAMEN.
LET'S GO TO MOS!
EVERY LUNCH BREAK, OR NEARLY, OUR LITTLE GROUP WALKED INTO TOWN (THE AREA AROUND THE STATION). IT WAS AN OPPORTUNITY TO CHAT AND STRETCH OUR LEGS.

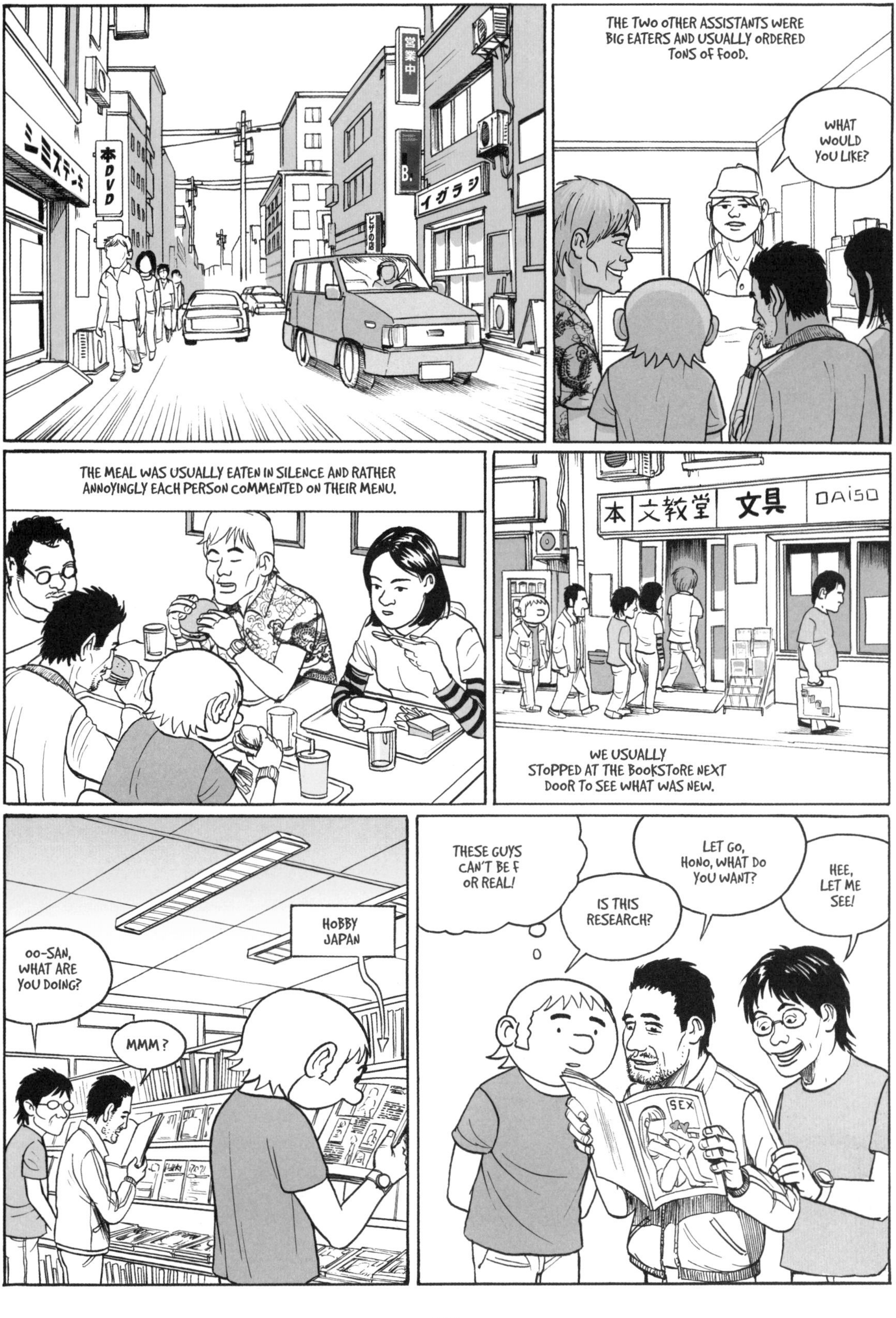
本 DVD
営業中
イガラシ
ピザの店
THE TWO OTHER ASSISTANTS WERE BIG EATERS AND USUALLY ORDERED TONS OF FOOD.
WHAT WOULD YOU LIKE?
THE MEAL WAS USUALLY EATEN IN SILENCE AND RATHER ANNOYINGLY EACH PERSON COMMENTED ON THEIR MENU.
本 文教堂 文具 DAISO
WE USUALLY STOPPED AT THE BOOKSTORE NEXT DOOR TO SEE WHAT WAS NEW.
OO-SAN, WHAT ARE YOU DOING?
HOBBY JAPAN
MMM?
THESE GUYS CAN'T BE F OR REAL!
LET GO, HONO, WHAT DO YOU WANT?
HEE, LET ME SEE!
IS THIS RESEARCH?
SEX

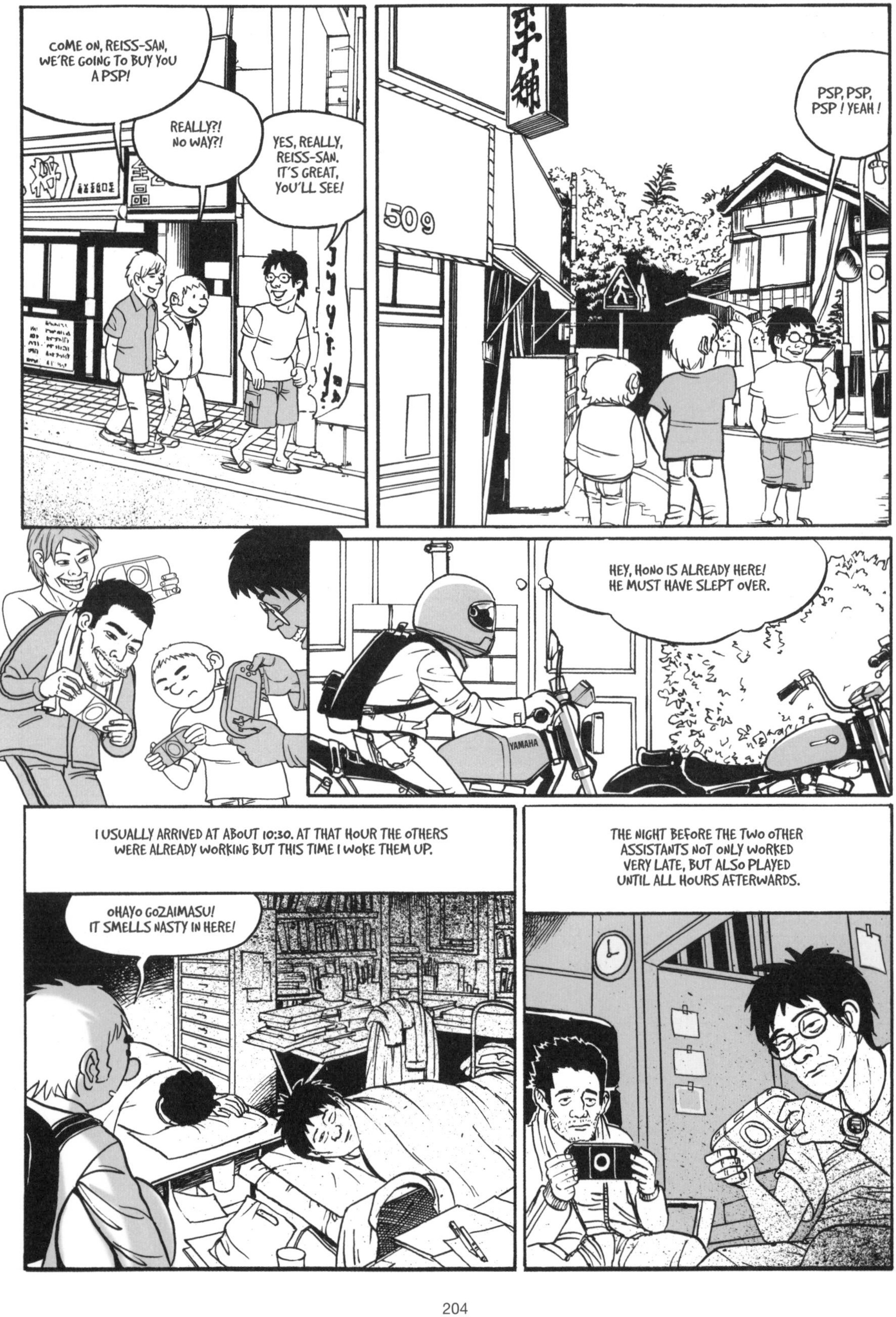

COME ON, REISS-SAN, WE'RE GOING TO BUY YOU A PSP!
REALLY?! NO WAY?!
YES, REALLY, REISS-SAN. IT'S GREAT, YOU'LL SEE!
509
PSP, PSP, PSP ! YEAH !
HEY, HONO IS ALREADY HERE! HE MUST HAVE SLEPT OVER.
YAMAHA
I USUALLY ARRIVED AT ABOUT 10:30. AT THAT HOUR THE OTHERS WERE ALREADY WORKING BUT THIS TIME I WOKE THEM UP.
OHAYO GOZAIMASU! IT SMELLS NASTY IN HERE!
THE NIGHT BEFORE THE TWO OTHER ASSISTANTS NOT ONLY WORKED VERY LATE, BUT ALSO PLAYED UNTIL ALL HOURS AFTERWARDS.

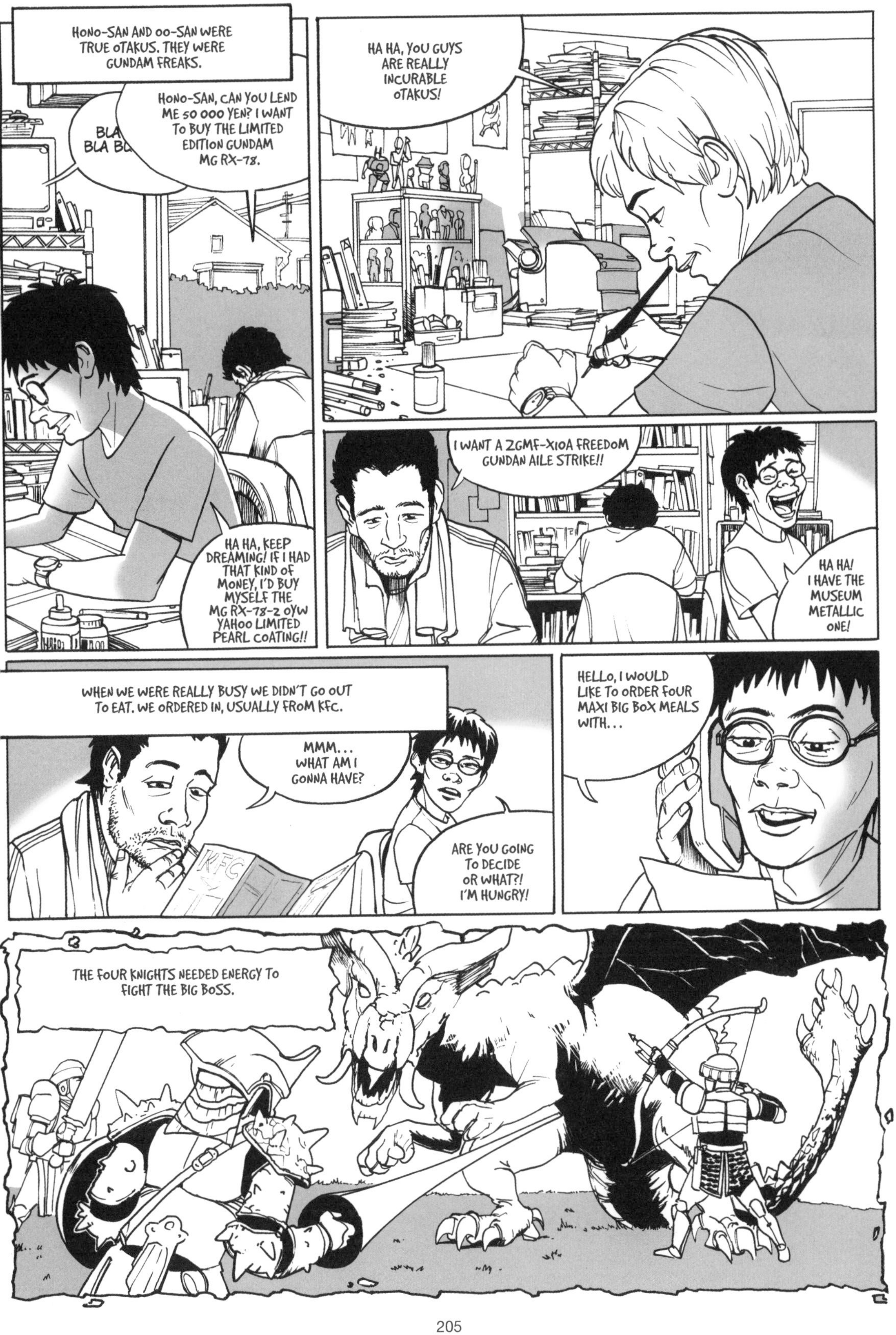
HONO-SAN AND OO-SAN WERE TRUE OTAKUS. THEY WERE GUNDAM FREAKS.
BLA BLA BL
HONO-SAN, CAN YOU LEND ME 50 000 YEN? I WANT TO BUY THE LIMITED EDITION GUNDAM MG RX-78.
HA HA, KEEP DREAMING! IF I HAD THAT KIND OF MONEY, I'D BUY MYSELF THE MG RX-78-2 OYW YAHOO LIMITED PEARL COATING!!
HA HA, YOU GUYS ARE REALLY INCURABLE OTAKUS!
I WANT A ZGMF-X10A FREEDOM GUNDAN AILE STRIKE!!
HA HA! I HAVE THE MUSEUM METALLIC ONE!
WHEN WE WERE REALLY BUSY WE DIDN'T GO OUT TO EAT. WE ORDERED IN, USUALLY FROM KFC.
MMM... WHAT AM I GONNA HAVE?
KFC
ARE YOU GOING TO DECIDE OR WHAT?! I'M HUNGRY!
HELLO, I WOULD LIKE TO ORDER FOUR MAXI BIG BOX MEALS WITH...
THE FOUR KNIGHTS NEEDED ENERGY TO FIGHT THE BIG BOSS.

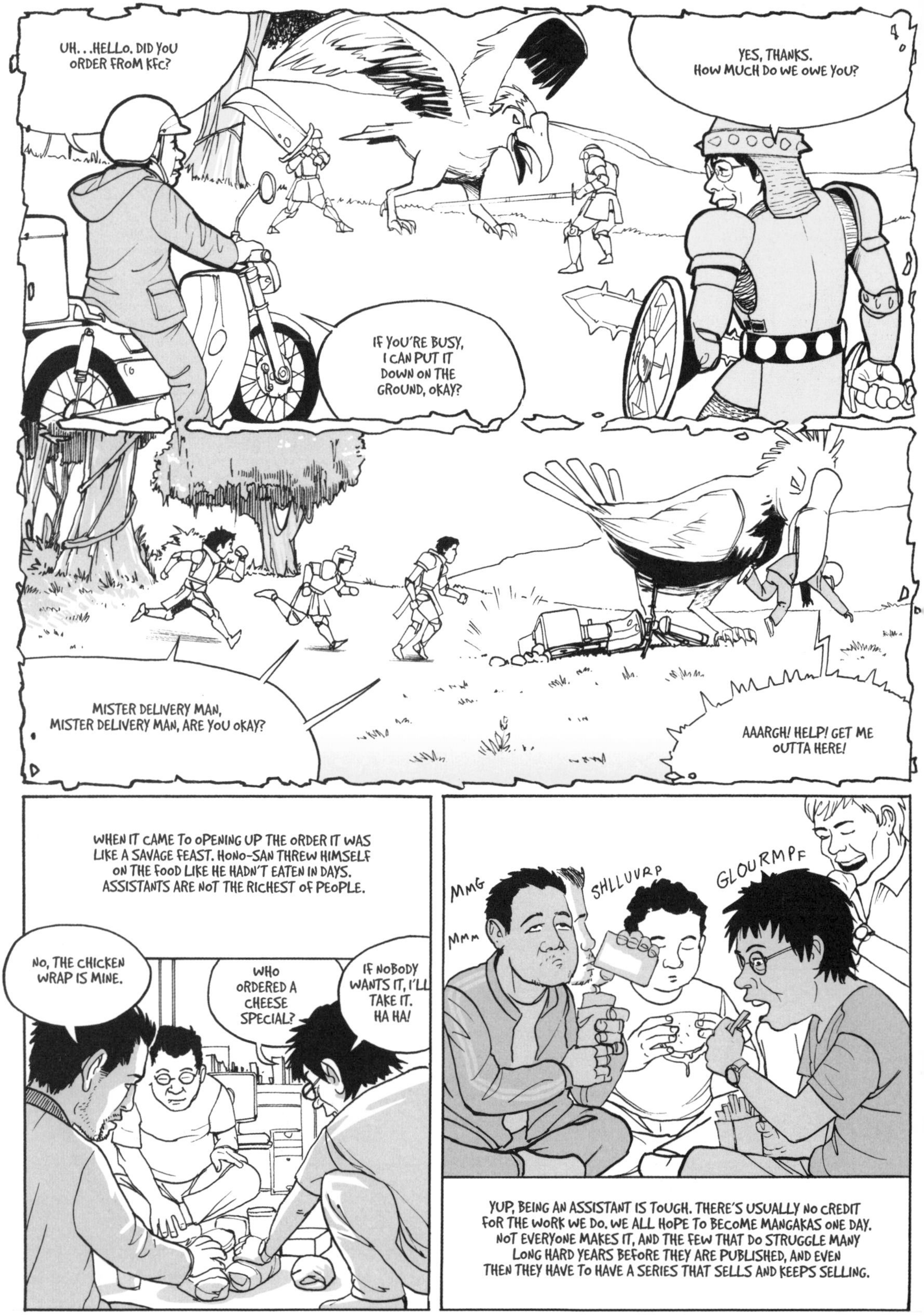

UH...HELLO. DID YOU ORDER FROM KFC?
YES, THANKS. HOW MUCH DO WE OWE YOU?
IF YOU'RE BUSY, I CAN PUT IT DOWN ON THE GROUND, OKAY?
MISTER DELIVERY MAN, MISTER DELIVERY MAN, ARE YOU OKAY?
AAARGH! HELP! GET ME OUTTA HERE!
WHEN IT CAME TO OPENING UP THE ORDER IT WAS LIKE A SAVAGE FEAST. HONO-SAN THREW HIMSELF ON THE FOOD LIKE HE HADN'T EATEN IN DAYS. ASSISTANTS ARE NOT THE RICHEST OF PEOPLE.
NO, THE CHICKEN WRAP IS MINE.
WHO ORDERED A CHEESE SPECIAL?
IF NOBODY WANTS IT, I'LL TAKE IT. HA HA!
MMG
MMM
SHLLUURP
GLOURMPF
YUP, BEING AN ASSISTANT IS TOUGH. THERE'S USUALLY NO CREDIT FOR THE WORK WE DO. WE ALL HOPE TO BECOME MANGAKAS ONE DAY. NOT EVERYONE MAKES IT, AND THE FEW THAT DO STRUGGLE MANY LONG HARD YEARS BEFORE THEY ARE PUBLISHED, AND EVEN THEN THEY HAVE TO HAVE A SERIES THAT SELLS AND KEEPS SELLING.

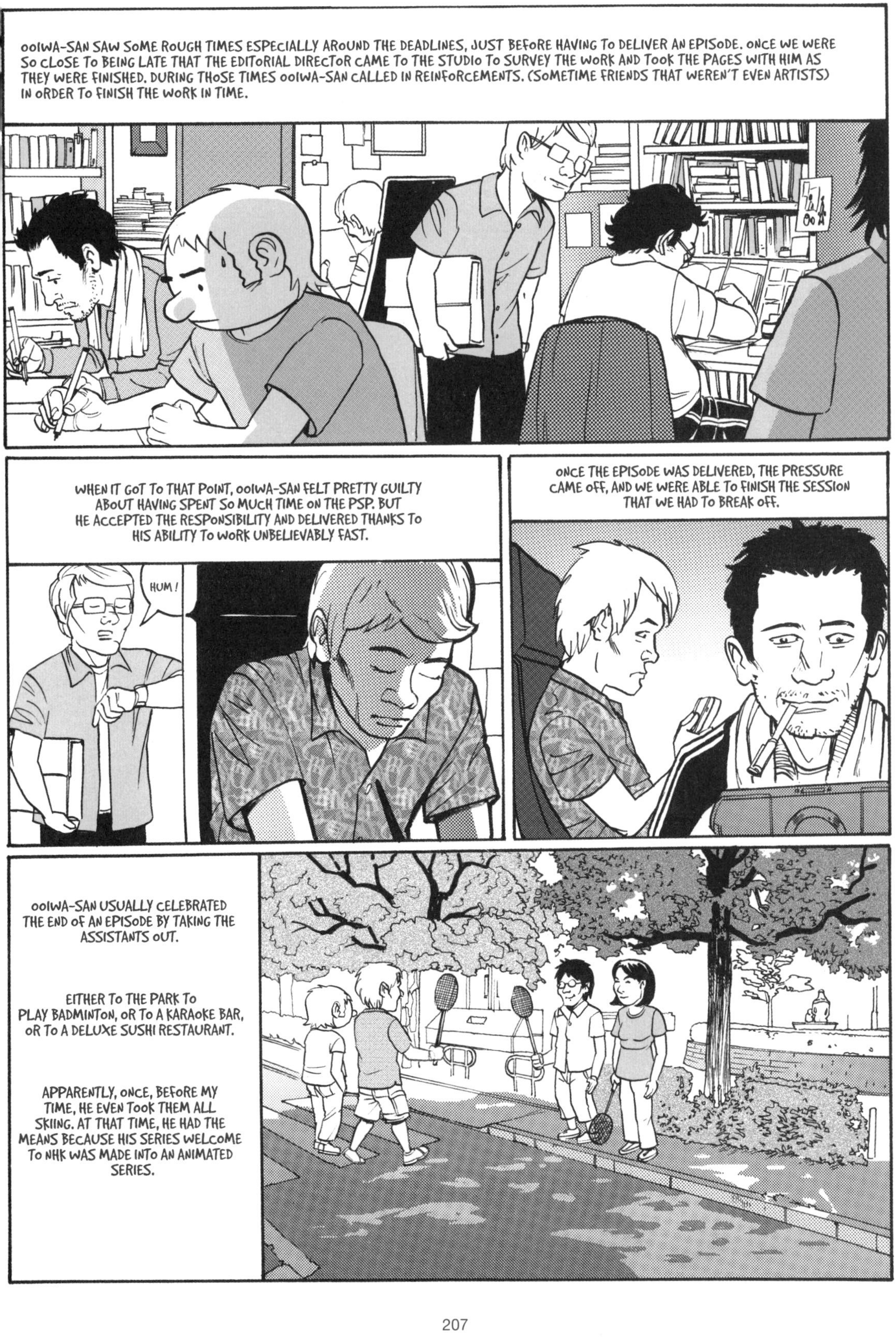

OOIWA-SAN SAW SOME ROUGH TIMES ESPECIALLY AROUND THE DEADLINES, JUST BEFORE HAVING TO DELIVER AN EPISODE. ONCE WE WERE SO CLOSE TO BEING LATE THAT THE EDITORIAL DIRECTOR CAME TO THE STUDIO TO SURVEY THE WORK AND TOOK THE PAGES WITH HIM AS THEY WERE FINISHED. DURING THOSE TIMES OOIWA-SAN CALLED IN REINFORCEMENTS. (SOMETIME FRIENDS THAT WEREN'T EVEN ARTISTS) IN ORDER TO FINISH THE WORK IN TIME.
WHEN IT GOT TO THAT POINT, OOIWA-SAN FELT PRETTY GUILTY ABOUT HAVING SPENT SO MUCH TIME ON THE PSP. BUT HE ACCEPTED THE RESPONSIBILITY AND DELIVERED THANKS TO HIS ABILITY TO WORK UNBELIEVABLY FAST.
HUM!
ONCE THE EPISODE WAS DELIVERED, THE PRESSURE CAME OFF, AND WE WERE ABLE TO FINISH THE SESSION THAT WE HAD TO BREAK OFF.
OOIWA-SAN USUALLY CELEBRATED THE END OF AN EPISODE BY TAKING THE ASSISTANTS OUT.
EITHER TO THE PARK TO PLAY BADMINTON, OR TO A KARAOKE BAR, OR TO A DELUXE SUSHI RESTAURANT.
APPARENTLY, ONCE, BEFORE MY TIME, HE EVEN TOOK THEM ALL SKIING. AT THAT TIME, HE HAD THE MEANS BECAUSE HIS SERIES WELCOME TO NHK WAS MADE INTO AN ANIMATED SERIES.

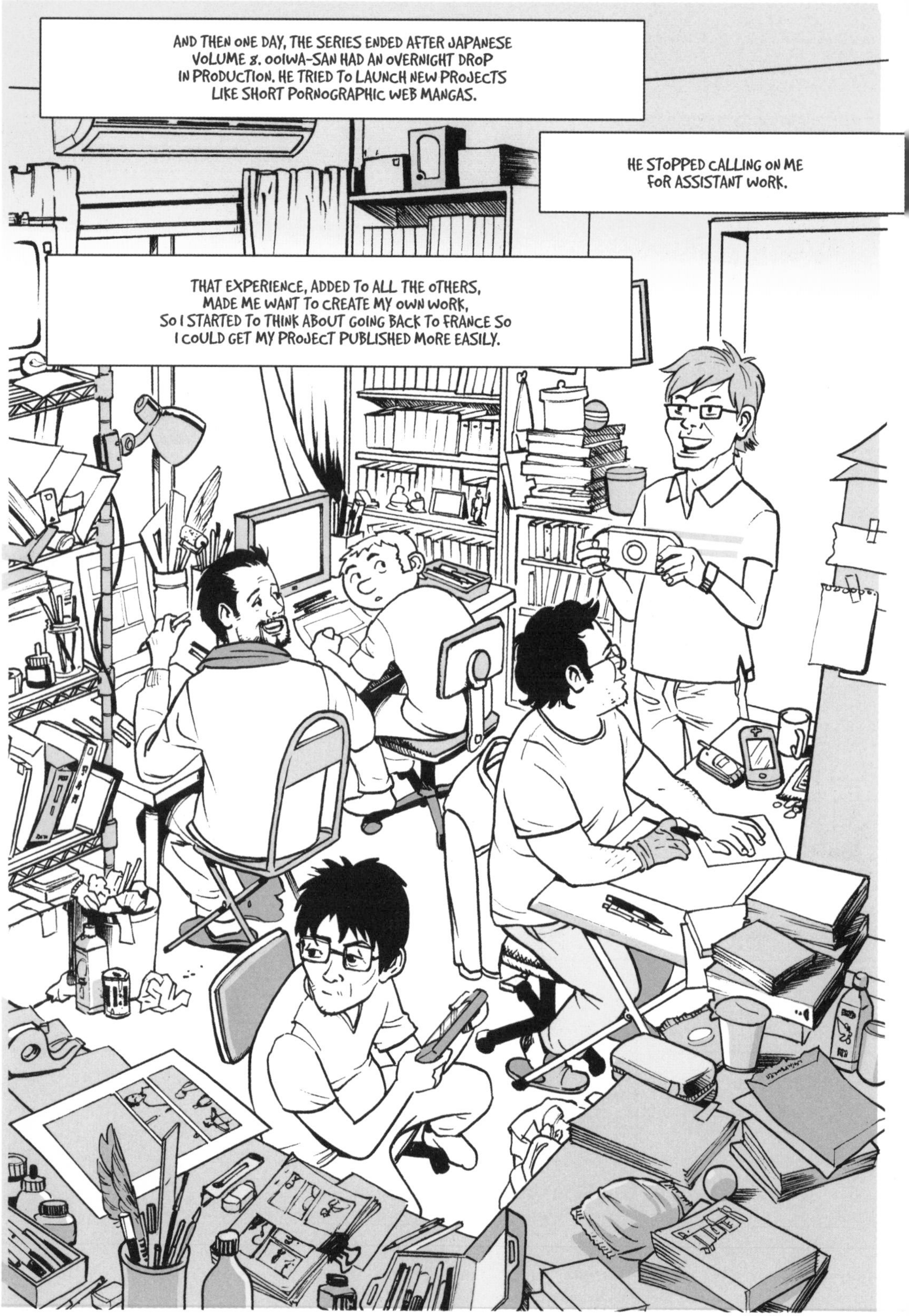
AND THEN ONE DAY, THE SERIES ENDED AFTER JAPANESE VOLUME 8. OOIWA-SAN HAD AN OVERNIGHT DROP IN PRODUCTION. HE TRIED TO LAUNCH NEW PROJECTS LIKE SHORT PORNOGRAPHIC WEB MANGAS.
HE STOPPED CALLING ON ME FOR ASSISTANT WORK.
THAT EXPERIENCE, ADDED TO ALL THE OTHERS, MADE ME WANT TO CREATE MY OWN WORK, SO I STARTED TO THINK ABOUT GOING BACK TO FRANCE SO I COULD GET MY PROJECT PUBLISHED MORE EASILY.

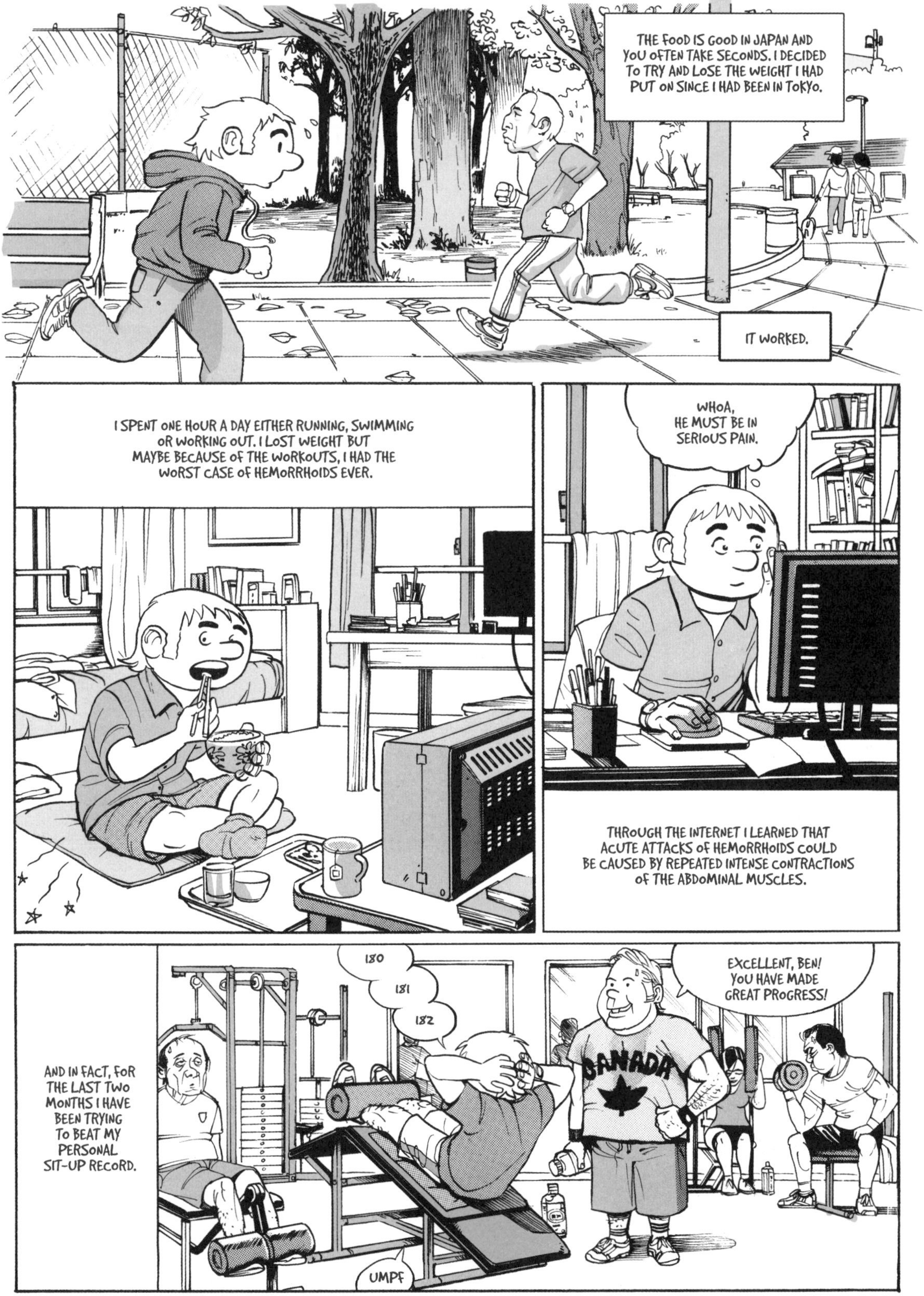
THE FOOD IS GOOD IN JAPAN AND YOU OFTEN TAKE SECONDS. I DECIDED TO TRY AND LOSE THE WEIGHT I HAD PUT ON SINCE I HAD BEEN IN TOKYO.
IT WORKED.
I SPENT ONE HOUR A DAY EITHER RUNNING, SWIMMING OR WORKING OUT. I LOST WEIGHT BUT MAYBE BECAUSE OF THE WORKOUTS, I HAD THE WORST CASE OF HEMORRHOIDS EVER.
WHOA, HE MUST BE IN SERIOUS PAIN.
THROUGH THE INTERNET I LEARNED THAT ACUTE ATTACKS OF HEMORRHOIDS COULD BE CAUSED BY REPEATED INTENSE CONTRACTIONS OF THE ABDOMINAL MUSCLES.
AND IN FACT, FOR THE LAST TWO MONTHS I HAVE BEEN TRYING TO BEAT MY PERSONAL SIT-UP RECORD.
180
181
182
CANADA
EXCELLENT, BEN! YOU HAVE MADE GREAT PROGRESS!
UMPF

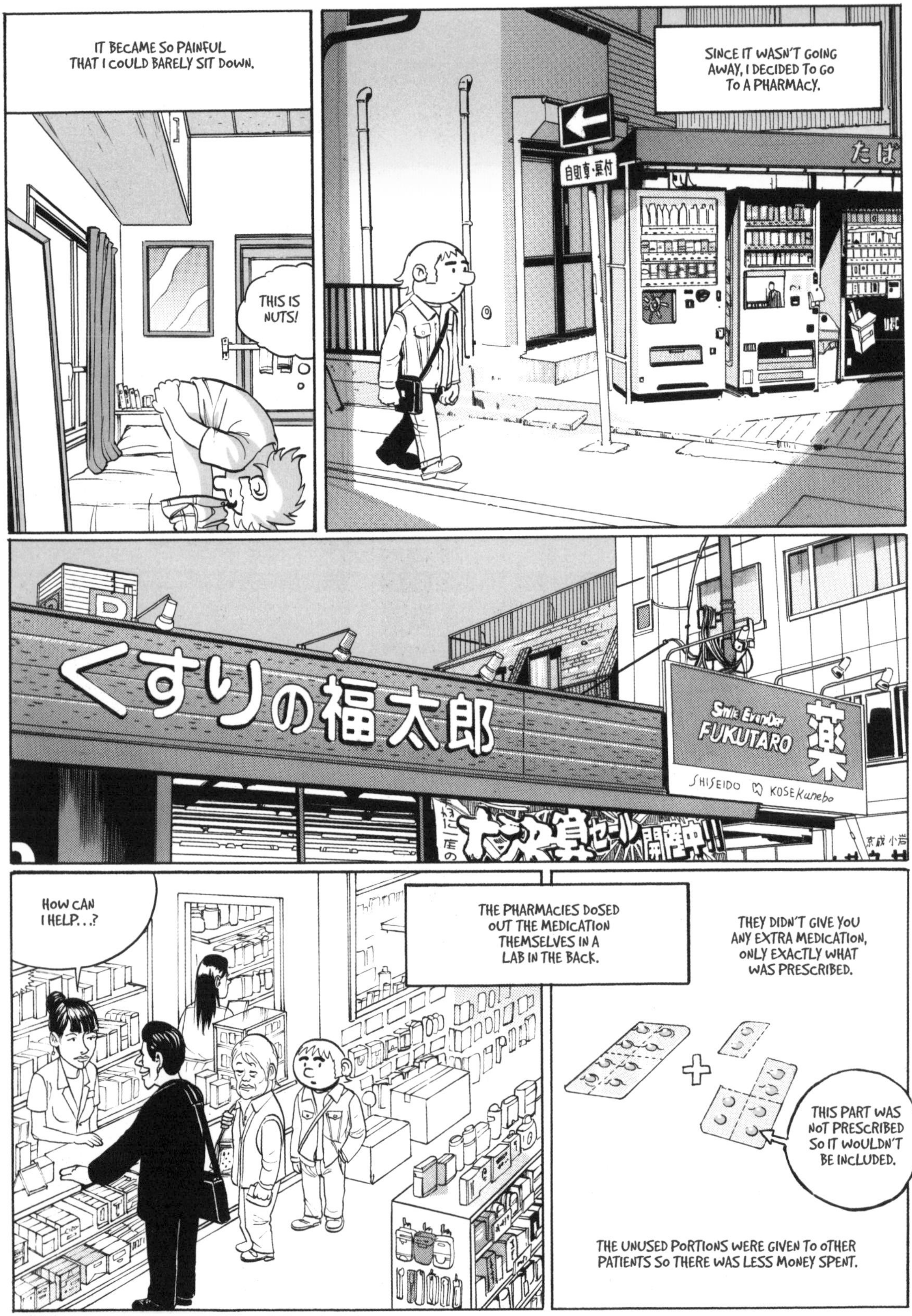
IT BECAME SO PAINFUL THAT I COULD BARELY SIT DOWN.
THIS IS NUTS!
SINCE IT WASN'T GOING AWAY, I DECIDED TO GO TO A PHARMACY.
くすりの福太郎
Smile EveryDay FUKUTARO 薬
SHISEIDO KOSE Kanebo
HOW CAN I HELP...?
THE PHARMACIES DOSED OUT THE MEDICATION THEMSELVES IN A LAB IN THE BACK.
THEY DIDN'T GIVE YOU ANY EXTRA MEDICATION, ONLY EXACTLY WHAT WAS PRESCRIBED.
THIS PART WAS NOT PRESCRIBED SO IT WOULDN'T BE INCLUDED.
THE UNUSED PORTIONS WERE GIVEN TO OTHER PATIENTS SO THERE WAS LESS MONEY SPENT.

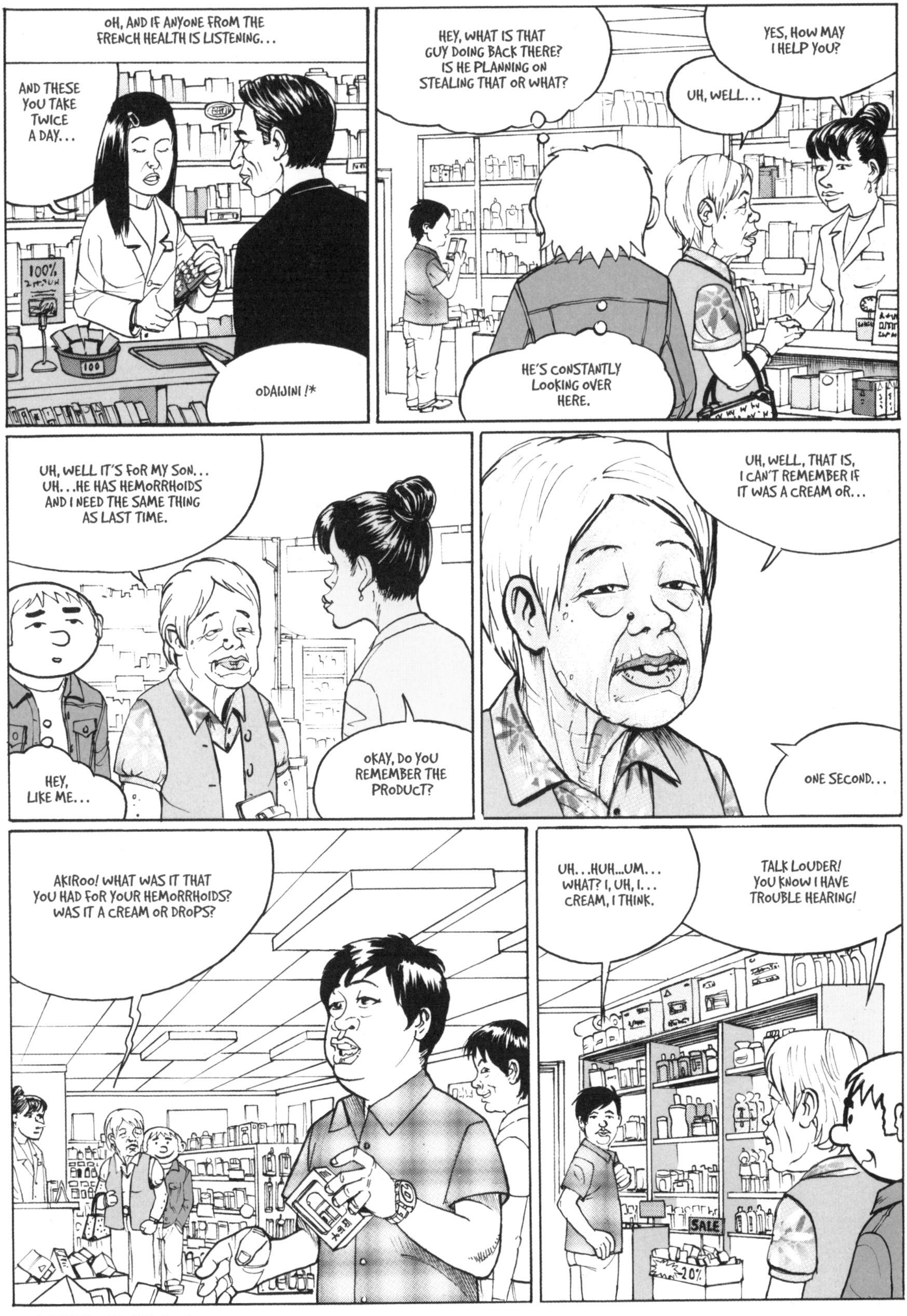
OH, AND IF ANYONE FROM THE FRENCH HEALTH IS LISTENING...
AND THESE YOU TAKE TWICE A DAY...
ODAIJINI !*
HEY, WHAT IS THAT GUY DOING BACK THERE? IS HE PLANNING ON STEALING THAT OR WHAT?
YES, HOW MAY I HELP YOU?
UH, WELL...
HE'S CONSTANTLY LOOKING OVER HERE.
UH, WELL IT'S FOR MY SON... UH...HE HAS HEMORRHOIDS AND I NEED THE SAME THING AS LAST TIME.
HEY, LIKE ME...
OKAY, DO YOU REMEMBER THE PRODUCT?
UH, WELL, THAT IS, I CAN'T REMEMBER IF IT WAS A CREAM OR...
ONE SECOND...
AKIROO! WHAT WAS IT THAT YOU HAD FOR YOUR HEMORRHOIDS? WAS IT A CREAM OR DROPS?
UH...HUH...UM... WHAT? I, UH, I... CREAM, I THINK.
TALK LOUDER! YOU KNOW I HAVE TROUBLE HEARING!

*ODAIJINI : GET WELL SOON

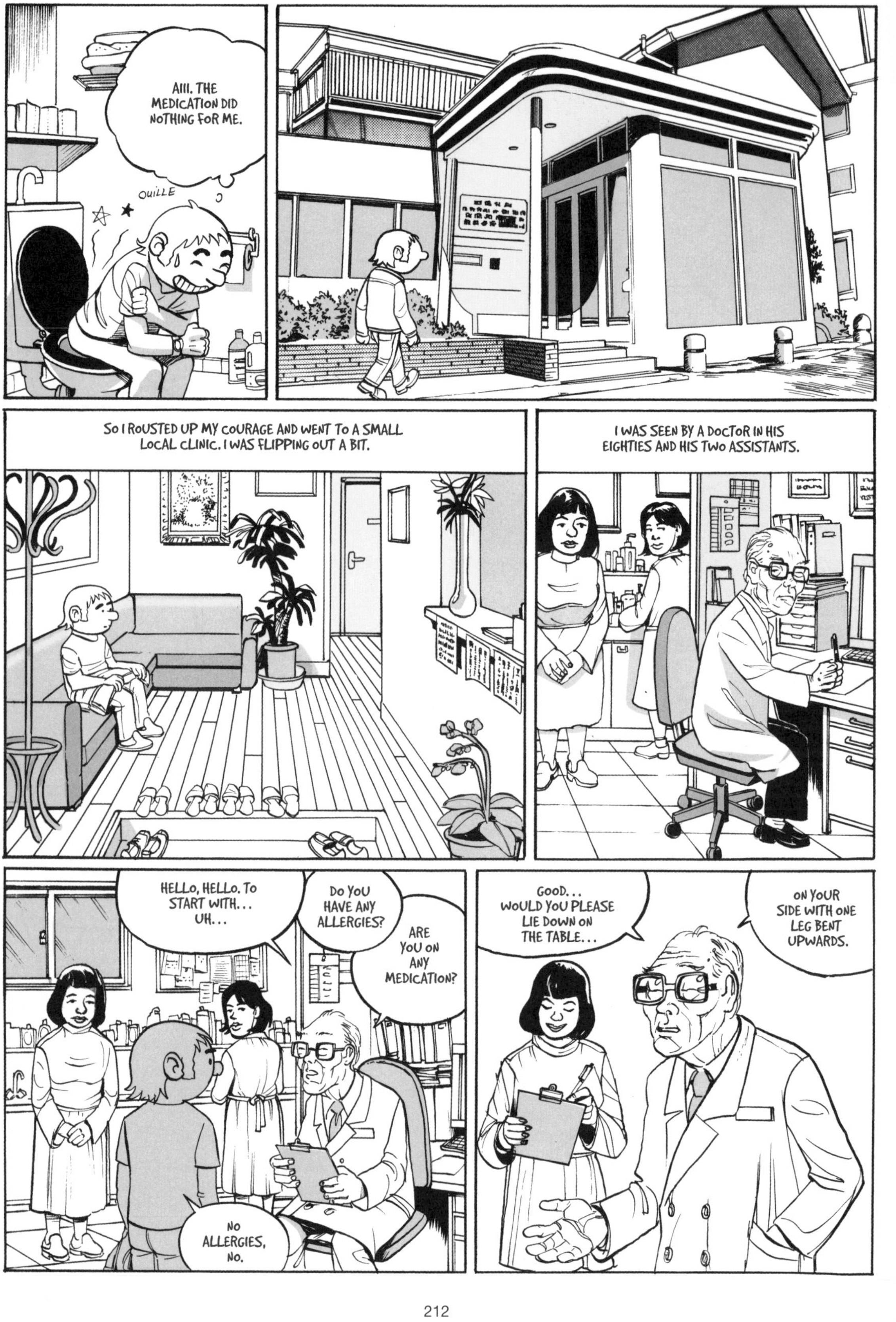
AIII. THE MEDICATION DID NOTHING FOR ME.
OUILLE
SO I ROUSTED UP MY COURAGE AND WENT TO A SMALL LOCAL CLINIC. I WAS FLIPPING OUT A BIT.
I WAS SEEN BY A DOCTOR IN HIS EIGHTIES AND HIS TWO ASSISTANTS.
HELLO, HELLO. TO START WITH... UH...
DO YOU HAVE ANY ALLERGIES?
ARE YOU ON ANY MEDICATION?
NO ALLERGIES, NO.
GOOD... WOULD YOU PLEASE LIE DOWN ON THE TABLE...
ON YOUR SIDE WITH ONE LEG BENT UPWARDS.

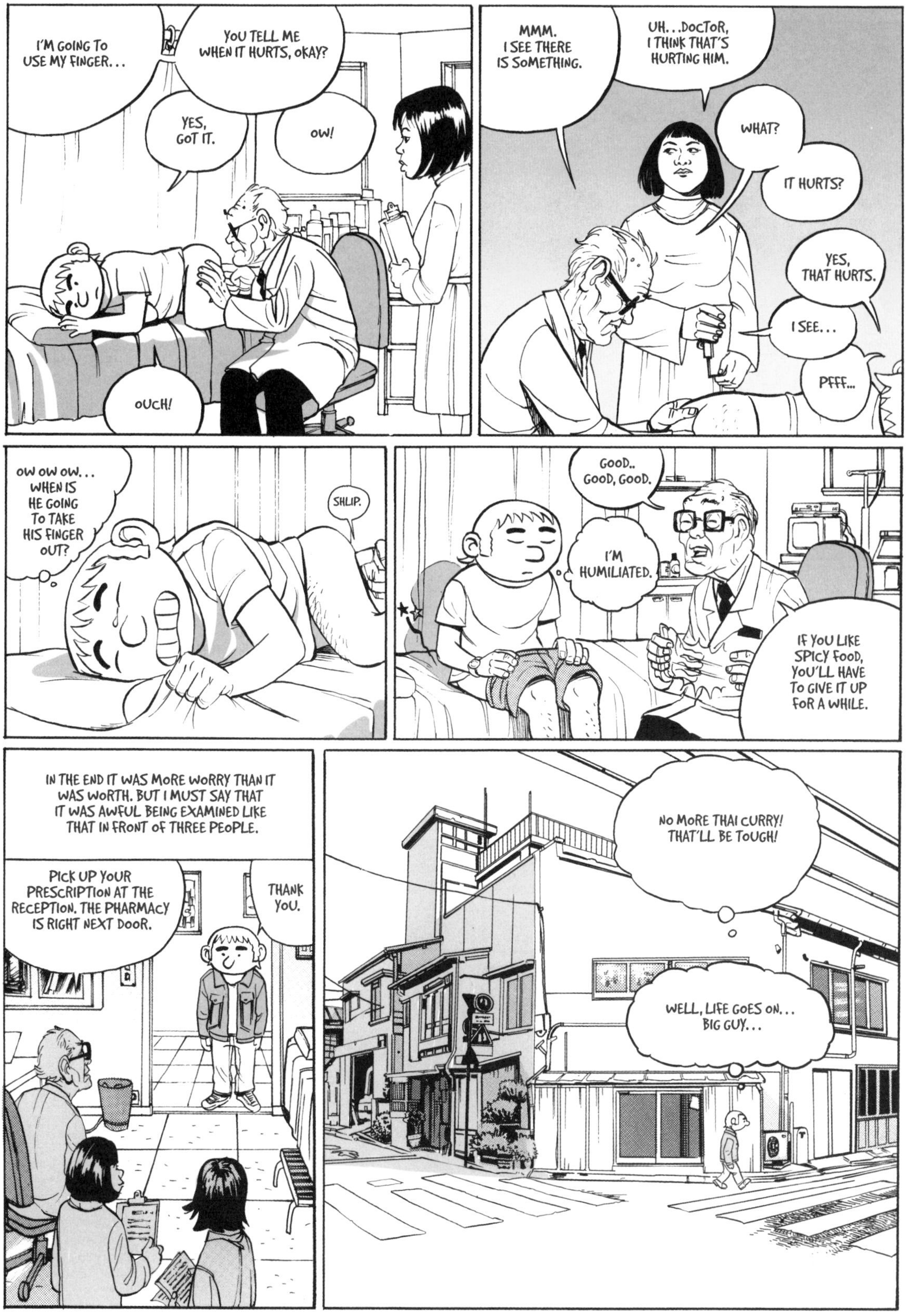
I'M GOING TO USE MY FINGER...
YOU TELL ME WHEN IT HURTS, OKAY?
YES, GOT IT.
OW!
OUCH!
MMM. I SEE THERE IS SOMETHING.
UH...DOCTOR, I THINK THAT'S HURTING HIM.
WHAT?
IT HURTS?
YES, THAT HURTS.
I SEE...
PFFF...
OW OW OW... WHEN IS HE GOING TO TAKE HIS FINGER OUT?
SHLIP.
GOOD.. GOOD, GOOD.
I'M HUMILIATED.
IF YOU LIKE SPICY FOOD, YOU'LL HAVE TO GIVE IT UP FOR A WHILE.
IN THE END IT WAS MORE WORRY THAN IT WAS WORTH. BUT I MUST SAY THAT IT WAS AWFUL BEING EXAMINED LIKE THAT IN FRONT OF THREE PEOPLE.
PICK UP YOUR PRESCRIPTION AT THE RECEPTION. THE PHARMACY IS RIGHT NEXT DOOR.
THANK YOU.
NO MORE THAI CURRY! THAT'LL BE TOUGH!
WELL, LIFE GOES ON... BIG GUY...

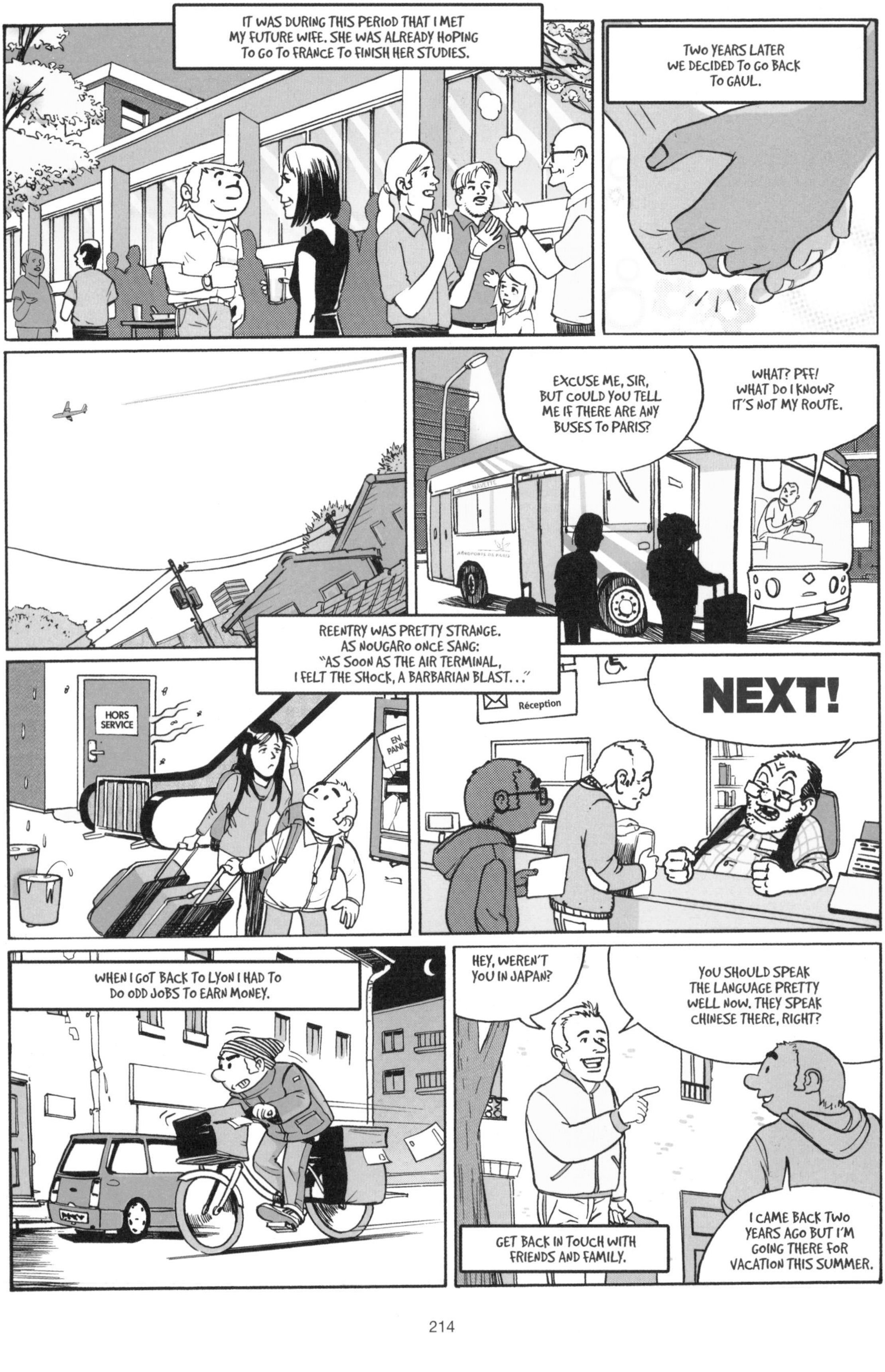
IT WAS DURING THIS PERIOD THAT I MET MY FUTURE WIFE. SHE WAS ALREADY HOPING TO GO TO FRANCE TO FINISH HER STUDIES.
TWO YEARS LATER WE DECIDED TO GO BACK TO GAUL.
EXCUSE ME, SIR, BUT COULD YOU TELL ME IF THERE ARE ANY BUSES TO PARIS?
WHAT? PFF! WHAT DO I KNOW? IT'S NOT MY ROUTE.
REENTRY WAS PRETTY STRANGE. AS NOUGARO ONCE SANG: "AS SOON AS THE AIR TERMINAL, I FELT THE SHOCK, A BARBARIAN BLAST. . ."
HORS SERVICE
EN PANN
Réception
NEXT!
WHEN I GOT BACK TO LYON I HAD TO DO ODD JOBS TO EARN MONEY.
HEY, WEREN'T YOU IN JAPAN?
YOU SHOULD SPEAK THE LANGUAGE PRETTY WELL NOW. THEY SPEAK CHINESE THERE, RIGHT?
GET BACK IN TOUCH WITH FRIENDS AND FAMILY.
I CAME BACK TWO YEARS AGO BUT I'M GOING THERE FOR VACATION THIS SUMMER.

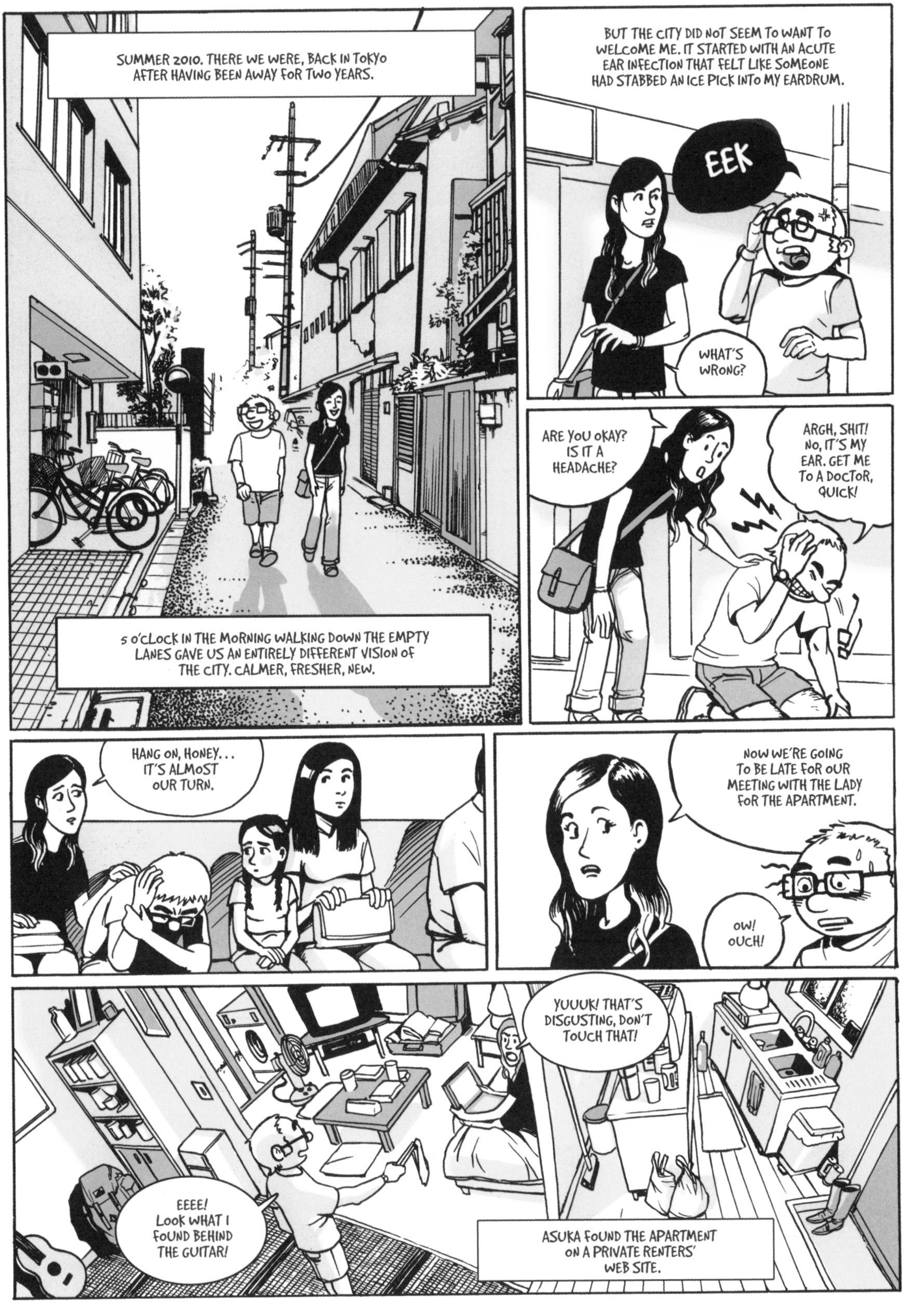
SUMMER 2010. THERE WE WERE, BACK IN TOKYO AFTER HAVING BEEN AWAY FOR TWO YEARS.
5 O'CLOCK IN THE MORNING WALKING DOWN THE EMPTY LANES GAVE US AN ENTIRELY DIFFERENT VISION OF THE CITY. CALMER, FRESHER, NEW.
BUT THE CITY DID NOT SEEM TO WANT TO WELCOME ME. IT STARTED WITH AN ACUTE EAR INFECTION THAT FELT LIKE SOMEONE HAD STABBED AN ICE PICK INTO MY EARDRUM.
EEK
WHAT'S WRONG?
ARE YOU OKAY? IS IT A HEADACHE?
ARGH, SHIT! NO, IT'S MY EAR. GET ME TO A DOCTOR, QUICK!
HANG ON, HONEY... IT'S ALMOST OUR TURN.
NOW WE'RE GOING TO BE LATE FOR OUR MEETING WITH THE LADY FOR THE APARTMENT.
OW! OUCH!
EEEE! LOOK WHAT I FOUND BEHIND THE GUITAR!
YUUUK! THAT'S DISGUSTING, DON'T TOUCH THAT!
ASUKA FOUND THE APARTMENT ON A PRIVATE RENTERS' WEB SITE.

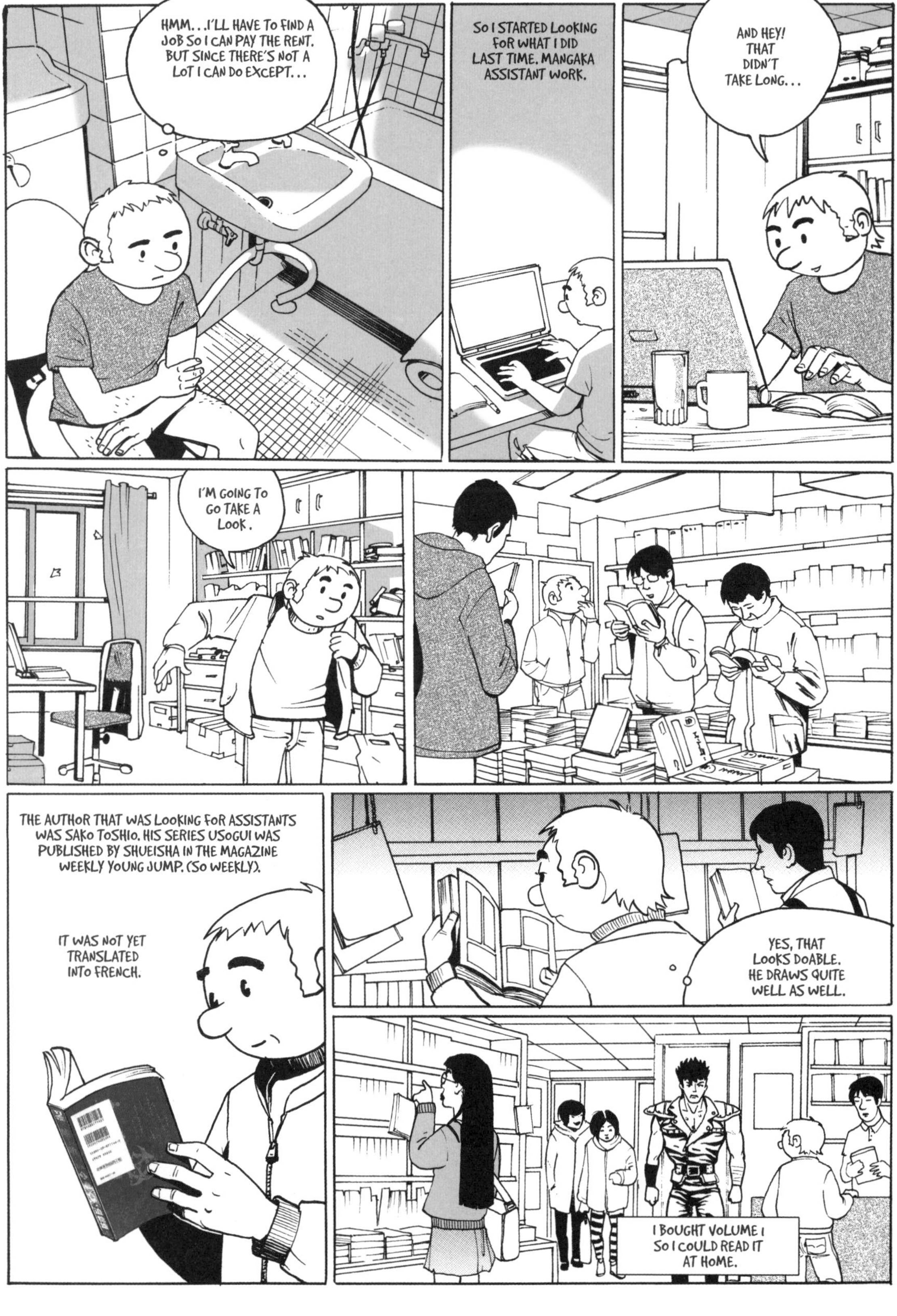
HMM... I'LL HAVE TO FIND A JOB SO I CAN PAY THE RENT. BUT SINCE THERE'S NOT A LOT I CAN DO EXCEPT...
SO I STARTED LOOKING FOR WHAT I DID LAST TIME. MANGAKA ASSISTANT WORK.
AND HEY! THAT DIDN'T TAKE LONG...
I'M GOING TO GO TAKE A LOOK.
THE AUTHOR THAT WAS LOOKING FOR ASSISTANTS WAS SAKO TOSHIO. HIS SERIES USOGUI WAS PUBLISHED BY SHUEISHA IN THE MAGAZINE WEEKLY YOUNG JUMP. (SO WEEKLY).
IT WAS NOT YET TRANSLATED INTO FRENCH.
YES, THAT LOOKS DOABLE. HE DRAWS QUITE WELL AS WELL.
I BOUGHT VOLUME 1 SO I COULD READ IT AT HOME.

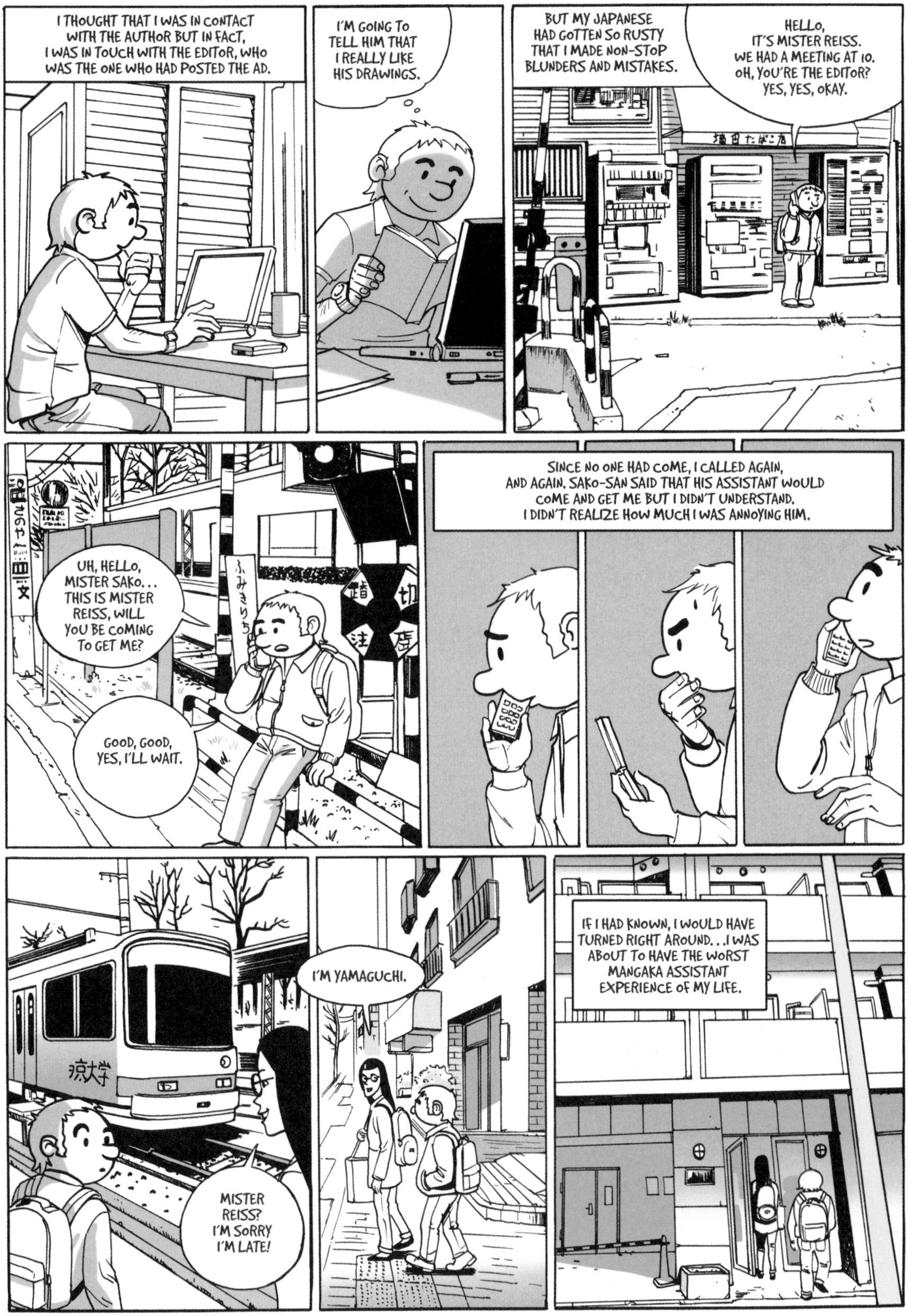
I THOUGHT THAT I WAS IN CONTACT WITH THE AUTHOR BUT IN FACT, I WAS IN TOUCH WITH THE EDITOR, WHO WAS THE ONE WHO HAD POSTED THE AD.
I'M GOING TO TELL HIM THAT I REALLY LIKE HIS DRAWINGS.
BUT MY JAPANESE HAD GOTTEN SO RUSTY THAT I MADE NON-STOP BLUNDERS AND MISTAKES.
HELLO, IT'S MISTER REISS. WE HAD A MEETING AT 10. OH, YOU'RE THE EDITOR? YES, YES, OKAY.
UH, HELLO, MISTER SAKO... THIS IS MISTER REISS, WILL YOU BE COMING TO GET ME?
GOOD, GOOD, YES, I'LL WAIT.
SINCE NO ONE HAD COME, I CALLED AGAIN, AND AGAIN. SAKO-SAN SAID THAT HIS ASSISTANT WOULD COME AND GET ME BUT I DIDN'T UNDERSTAND. I DIDN'T REALIZE HOW MUCH I WAS ANNOYING HIM.
MISTER REISS? I'M SORRY I'M LATE!
I'M YAMAGUCHI.
IF I HAD KNOWN, I WOULD HAVE TURNED RIGHT AROUND... I WAS ABOUT TO HAVE THE WORST MANGAKA ASSISTANT EXPERIENCE OF MY LIFE.

HELLO.

HELLO. NICE TO MEET YOU.

COME, FOLLOW ME, I'LL INTRODUCE YOU TO THE REST OF THE TEAM.

SAKO-SAN, SORRY FOR BEING LATE, I'VE BROUGHT THE NEW ASSISTANT.

MMMN

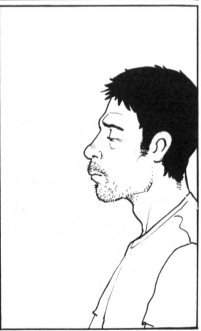

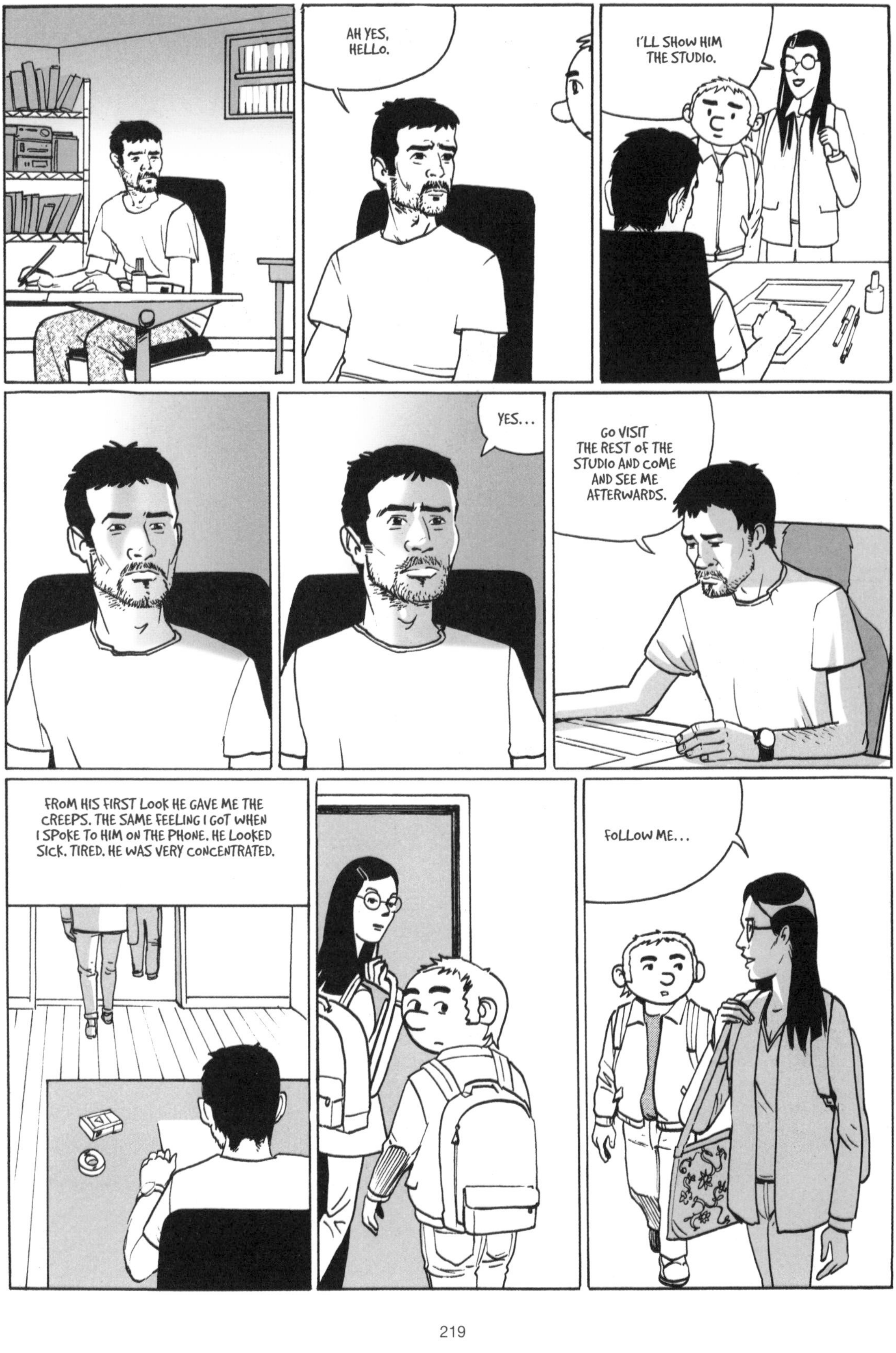
AH YES, HELLO.
I'LL SHOW HIM THE STUDIO.
YES...
GO VISIT THE REST OF THE STUDIO AND COME AND SEE ME AFTERWARDS.
FROM HIS FIRST LOOK HE GAVE ME THE CREEPS. THE SAME FEELING I GOT WHEN I SPOKE TO HIM ON THE PHONE. HE LOOKED SICK. TIRED. HE WAS VERY CONCENTRATED.
FOLLOW ME...

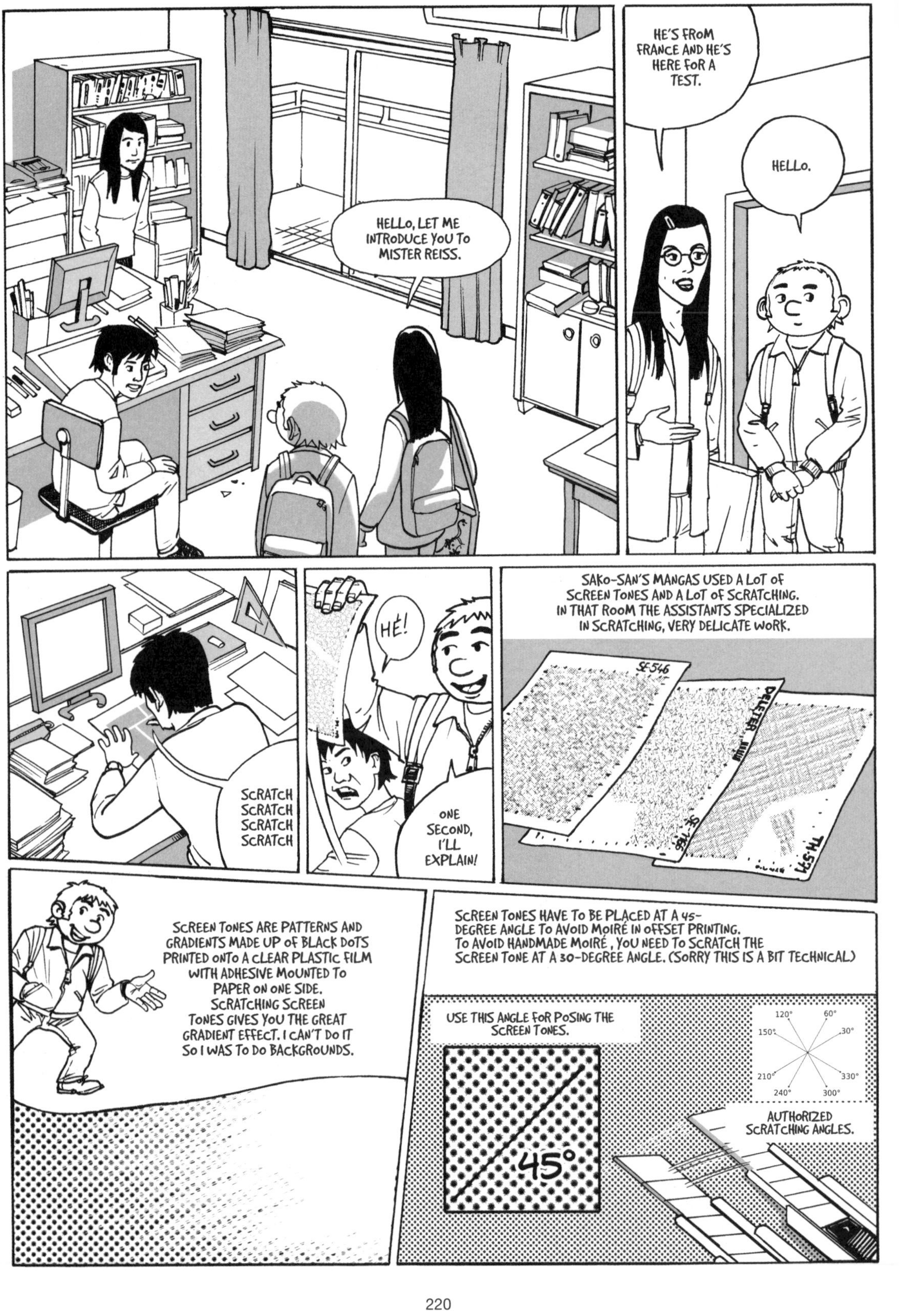
HELLO, LET ME INTRODUCE YOU TO MISTER REISS.
HE'S FROM FRANCE AND HE'S HERE FOR A TEST.
HELLO.
SCRATCH SCRATCH SCRATCH SCRATCH
HÉ!
ONE SECOND, I'LL EXPLAIN!
SAKO-SAN'S MANGAS USED A LOT OF SCREEN TONES AND A LOT OF SCRATCHING. IN THAT ROOM THE ASSISTANTS SPECIALIZED IN SCRATCHING, VERY DELICATE WORK.
SE-546
DELETER
SCREEN TONES ARE PATTERNS AND GRADIENTS MADE UP OF BLACK DOTS PRINTED ONTO A CLEAR PLASTIC FILM WITH ADHESIVE MOUNTED TO PAPER ON ONE SIDE. SCRATCHING SCREEN TONES GIVES YOU THE GREAT GRADIENT EFFECT. I CAN'T DO IT SO I WAS TO DO BACKGROUNDS.
SCREEN TONES HAVE TO BE PLACED AT A 45-DEGREE ANGLE TO AVOID MOIRÉ IN OFFSET PRINTING. TO AVOID HANDMADE MOIRÉ, YOU NEED TO SCRATCH THE SCREEN TONE AT A 30-DEGREE ANGLE. (SORRY THIS IS A BIT TECHNICAL)
USE THIS ANGLE FOR POSING THE SCREEN TONES.
45°
120° 60° 150° 30° 210° 330° 240° 300°
AUTHORIZED SCRATCHING ANGLES.

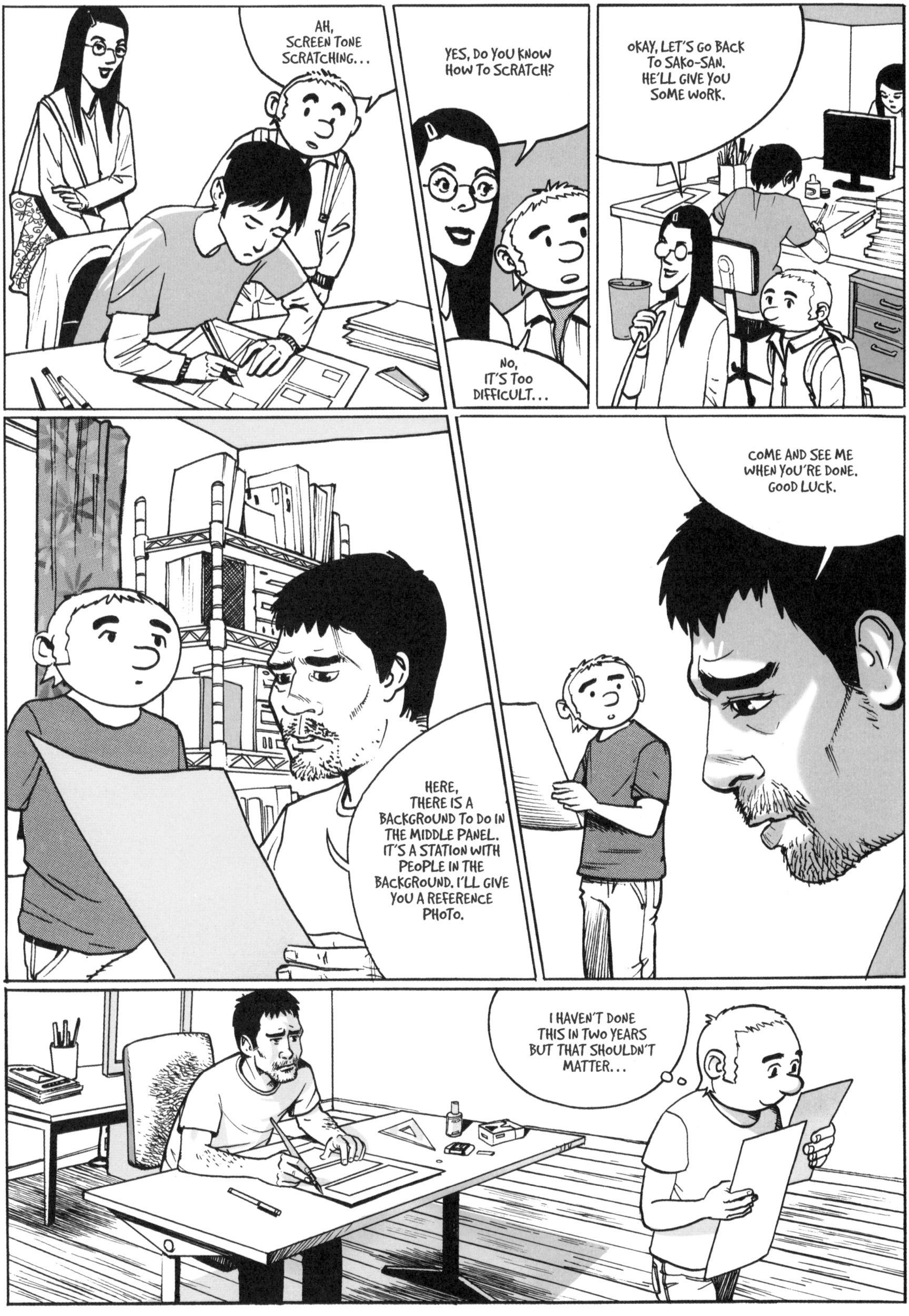
AH, SCREEN TONE SCRATCHING...
YES, DO YOU KNOW HOW TO SCRATCH?
NO, IT'S TOO DIFFICULT...
OKAY, LET'S GO BACK TO SAKO-SAN. HE'LL GIVE YOU SOME WORK.
HERE, THERE IS A BACKGROUND TO DO IN THE MIDDLE PANEL. IT'S A STATION WITH PEOPLE IN THE BACKGROUND. I'LL GIVE YOU A REFERENCE PHOTO.
COME AND SEE ME WHEN YOU'RE DONE. GOOD LUCK.
I HAVEN'T DONE THIS IN TWO YEARS BUT THAT SHOULDN'T MATTER...

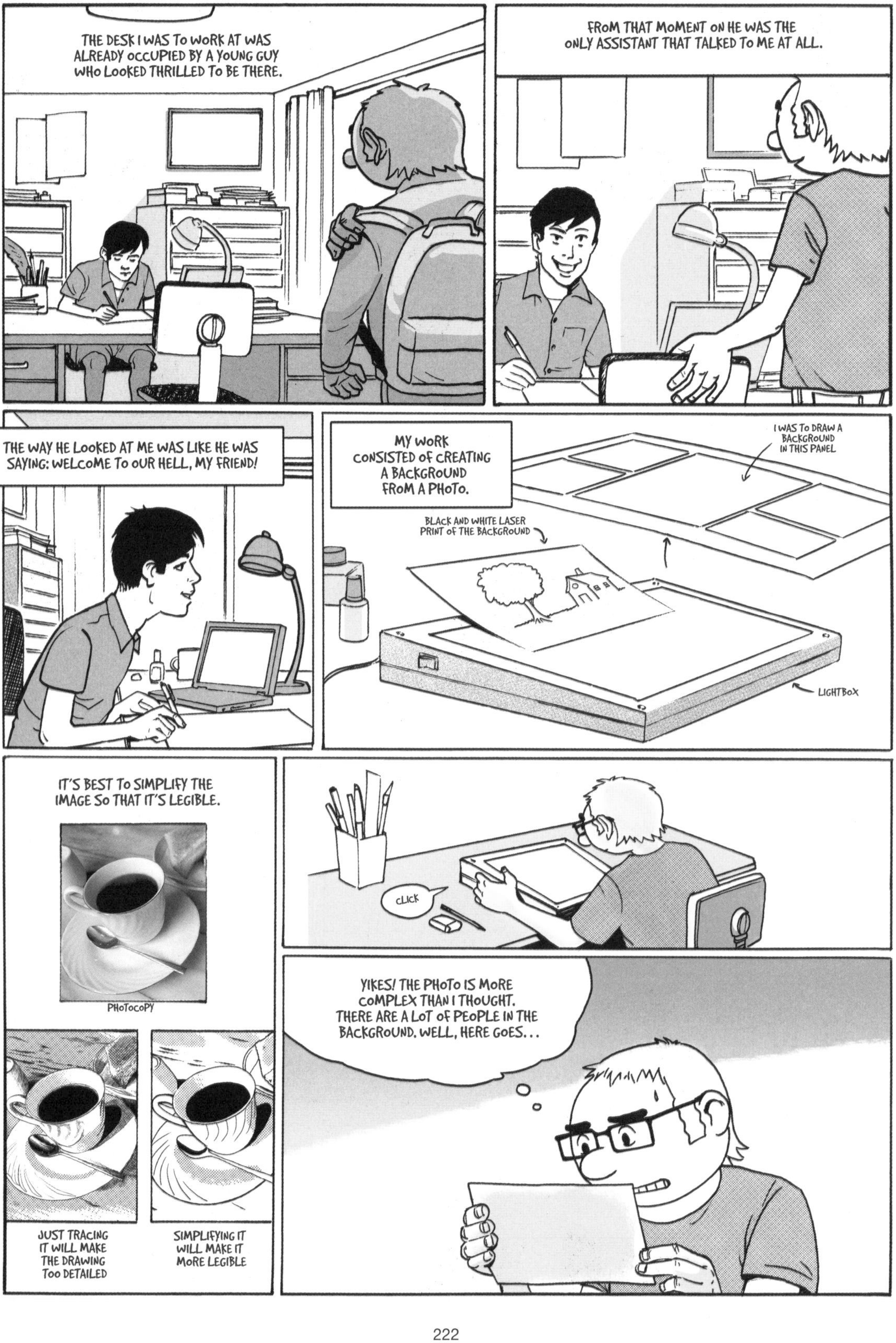
THE DESK I WAS TO WORK AT WAS ALREADY OCCUPIED BY A YOUNG GUY WHO LOOKED THRILLED TO BE THERE.
FROM THAT MOMENT ON HE WAS THE ONLY ASSISTANT THAT TALKED TO ME AT ALL.
THE WAY HE LOOKED AT ME WAS LIKE HE WAS SAYING: WELCOME TO OUR HELL, MY FRIEND!
MY WORK CONSISTED OF CREATING A BACKGROUND FROM A PHOTO.
I WAS TO DRAW A BACKGROUND IN THIS PANEL
BLACK AND WHITE LASER PRINT OF THE BACKGROUND
LIGHTBOX
IT'S BEST TO SIMPLIFY THE IMAGE SO THAT IT'S LEGIBLE.
PHOTOCOPY
JUST TRACING IT WILL MAKE THE DRAWING TOO DETAILED
SIMPLIFYING IT WILL MAKE IT MORE LEGIBLE
CLICK
YIKES! THE PHOTO IS MORE COMPLEX THAN I THOUGHT. THERE ARE A LOT OF PEOPLE IN THE BACKGROUND. WELL, HERE GOES...

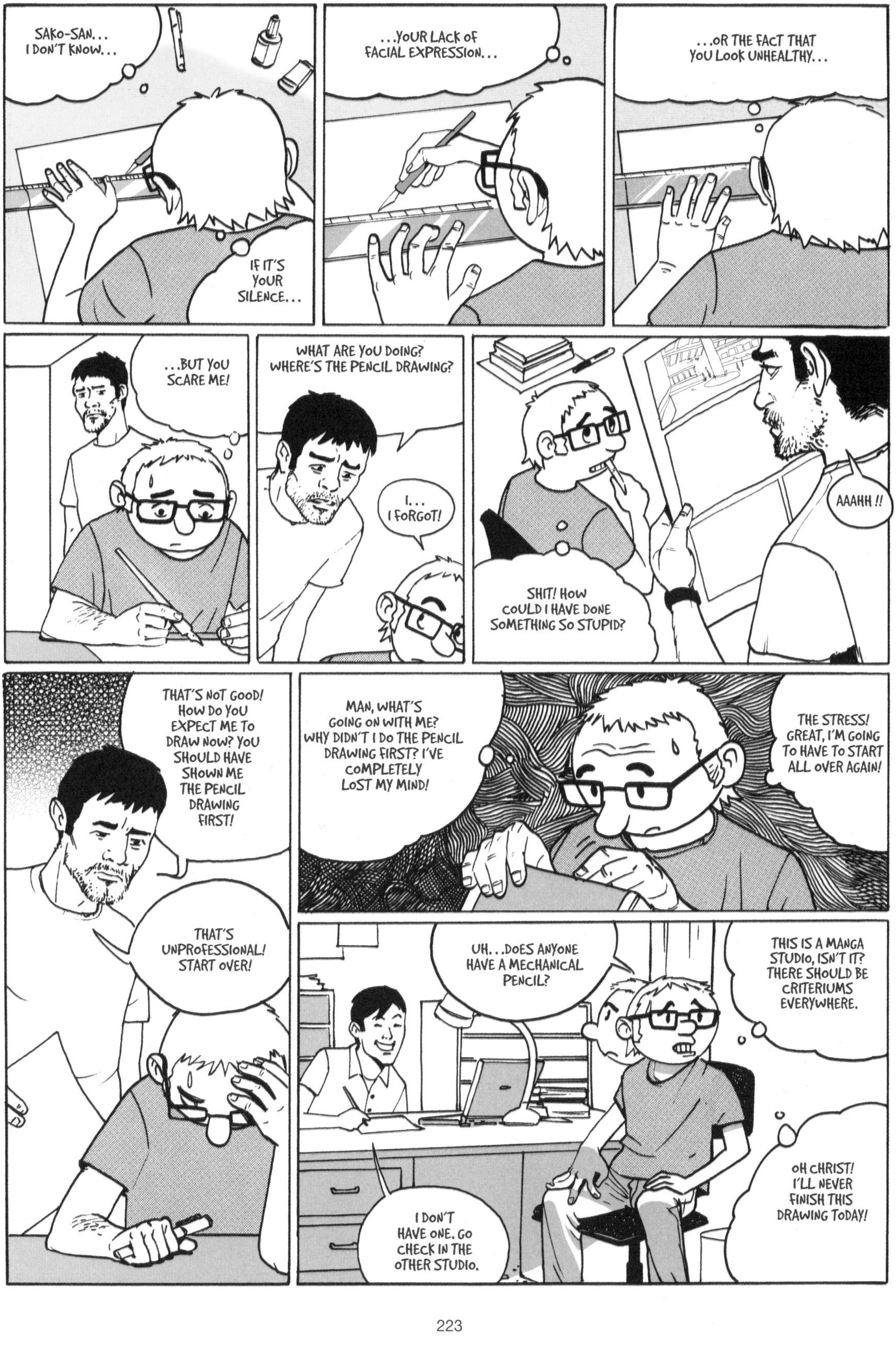
SAKO-SAN... I DON'T KNOW...
IF IT'S YOUR SILENCE...
...YOUR LACK OF FACIAL EXPRESSION...
...OR THE FACT THAT YOU LOOK UNHEALTHY...
...BUT YOU SCARE ME!
WHAT ARE YOU DOING? WHERE'S THE PENCIL DRAWING?
I... I FORGOT!
AAAHH !!
SHIT! HOW COULD I HAVE DONE SOMETHING SO STUPID?
THAT'S NOT GOOD! HOW DO YOU EXPECT ME TO DRAW NOW? YOU SHOULD HAVE SHOWN ME THE PENCIL DRAWING FIRST!
THAT'S UNPROFESSIONAL! START OVER!
MAN, WHAT'S GOING ON WITH ME? WHY DIDN'T I DO THE PENCIL DRAWING FIRST? I'VE COMPLETELY LOST MY MIND!
THE STRESS! GREAT, I'M GOING TO HAVE TO START ALL OVER AGAIN!
UH...DOES ANYONE HAVE A MECHANICAL PENCIL?
THIS IS A MANGA STUDIO, ISN'T IT? THERE SHOULD BE CRITERIUMS EVERYWHERE.
I DON'T HAVE ONE. GO CHECK IN THE OTHER STUDIO.
OH CHRIST! I'LL NEVER FINISH THIS DRAWING TODAY!

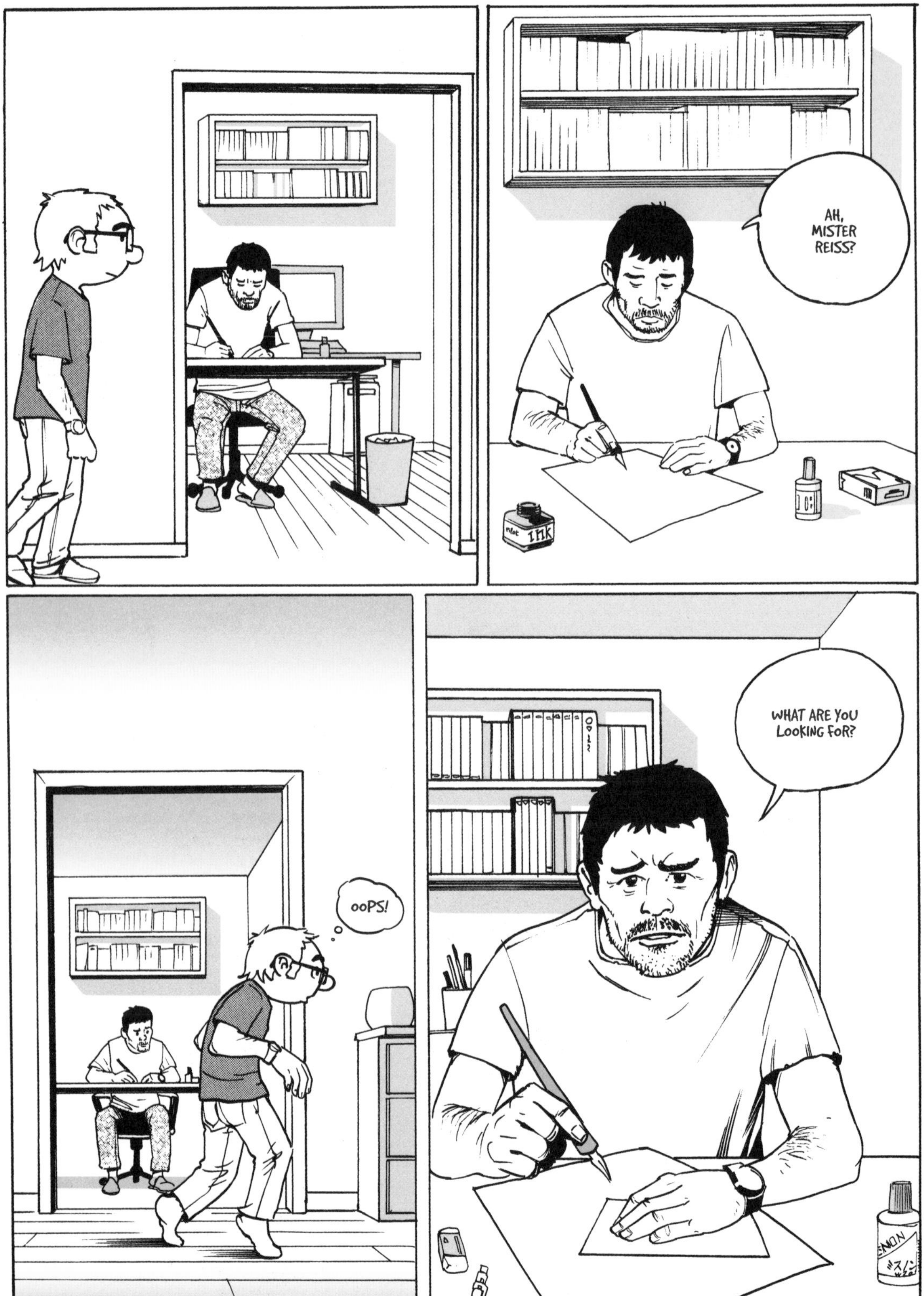
AH, MISTER REISS?
ooPS!
WHAT ARE YOU LOOKING FoR?

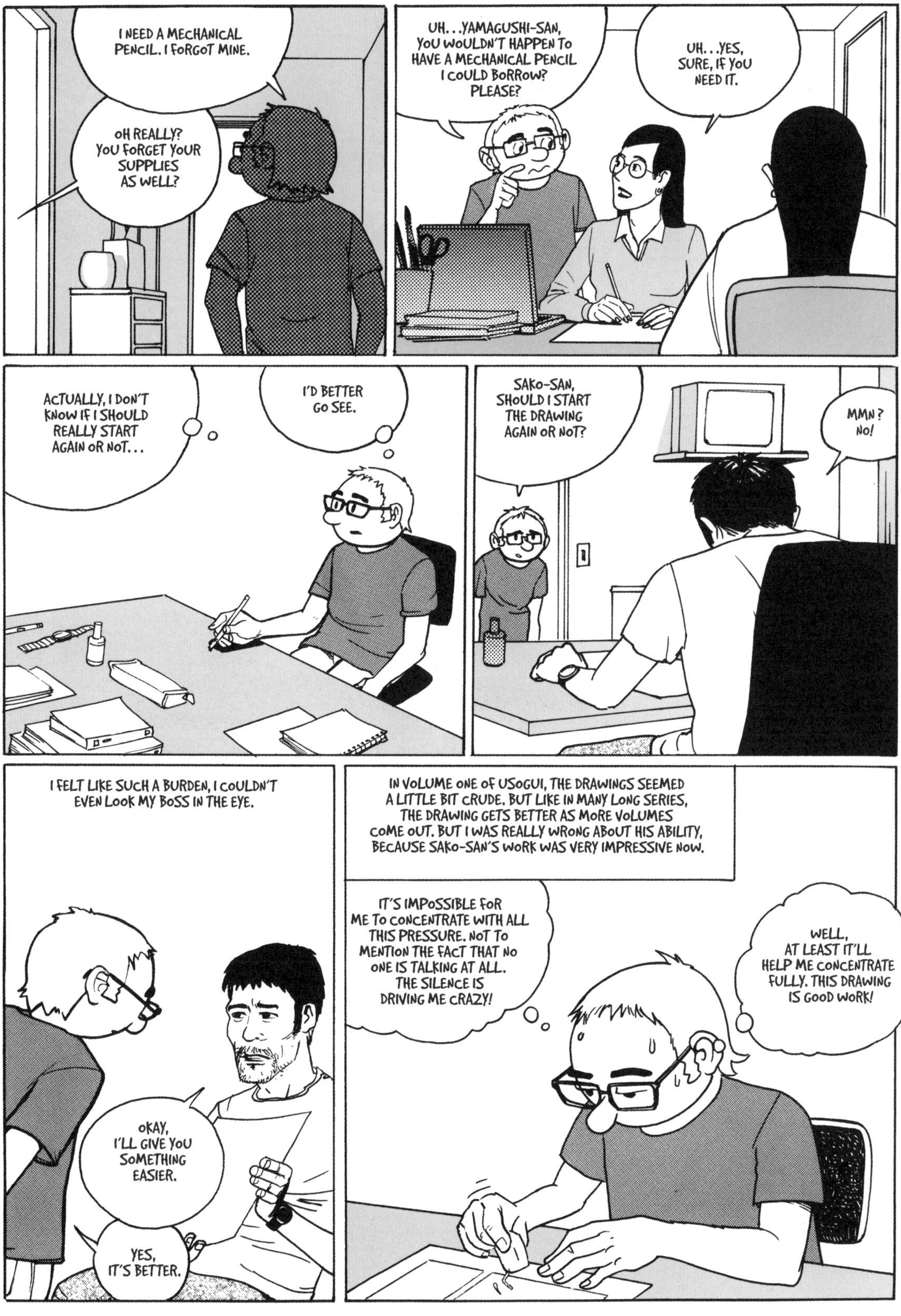

I NEED A MECHANICAL PENCIL. I FORGOT MINE.
OH REALLY? YOU FORGET YOUR SUPPLIES AS WELL?
UH...YAMAGUSHI-SAN, YOU WOULDN'T HAPPEN TO HAVE A MECHANICAL PENCIL I COULD BORROW? PLEASE?
UH...YES, SURE, IF YOU NEED IT.
ACTUALLY, I DON'T KNOW IF I SHOULD REALLY START AGAIN OR NOT...
I'D BETTER GO SEE.
SAKO-SAN, SHOULD I START THE DRAWING AGAIN OR NOT?
MMN? NO!
I FELT LIKE SUCH A BURDEN, I COULDN'T EVEN LOOK MY BOSS IN THE EYE.
OKAY, I'LL GIVE YOU SOMETHING EASIER.
YES, IT'S BETTER.
IN VOLUME ONE OF USOGUI, THE DRAWINGS SEEMED A LITTLE BIT CRUDE. BUT LIKE IN MANY LONG SERIES, THE DRAWING GETS BETTER AS MORE VOLUMES COME OUT. BUT I WAS REALLY WRONG ABOUT HIS ABILITY, BECAUSE SAKO-SAN'S WORK WAS VERY IMPRESSIVE NOW.
IT'S IMPOSSIBLE FOR ME TO CONCENTRATE WITH ALL THIS PRESSURE. NOT TO MENTION THE FACT THAT NO ONE IS TALKING AT ALL. THE SILENCE IS DRIVING ME CRAZY!
WELL, AT LEAST IT'LL HELP ME CONCENTRATE FULLY. THIS DRAWING IS GOOD WORK!

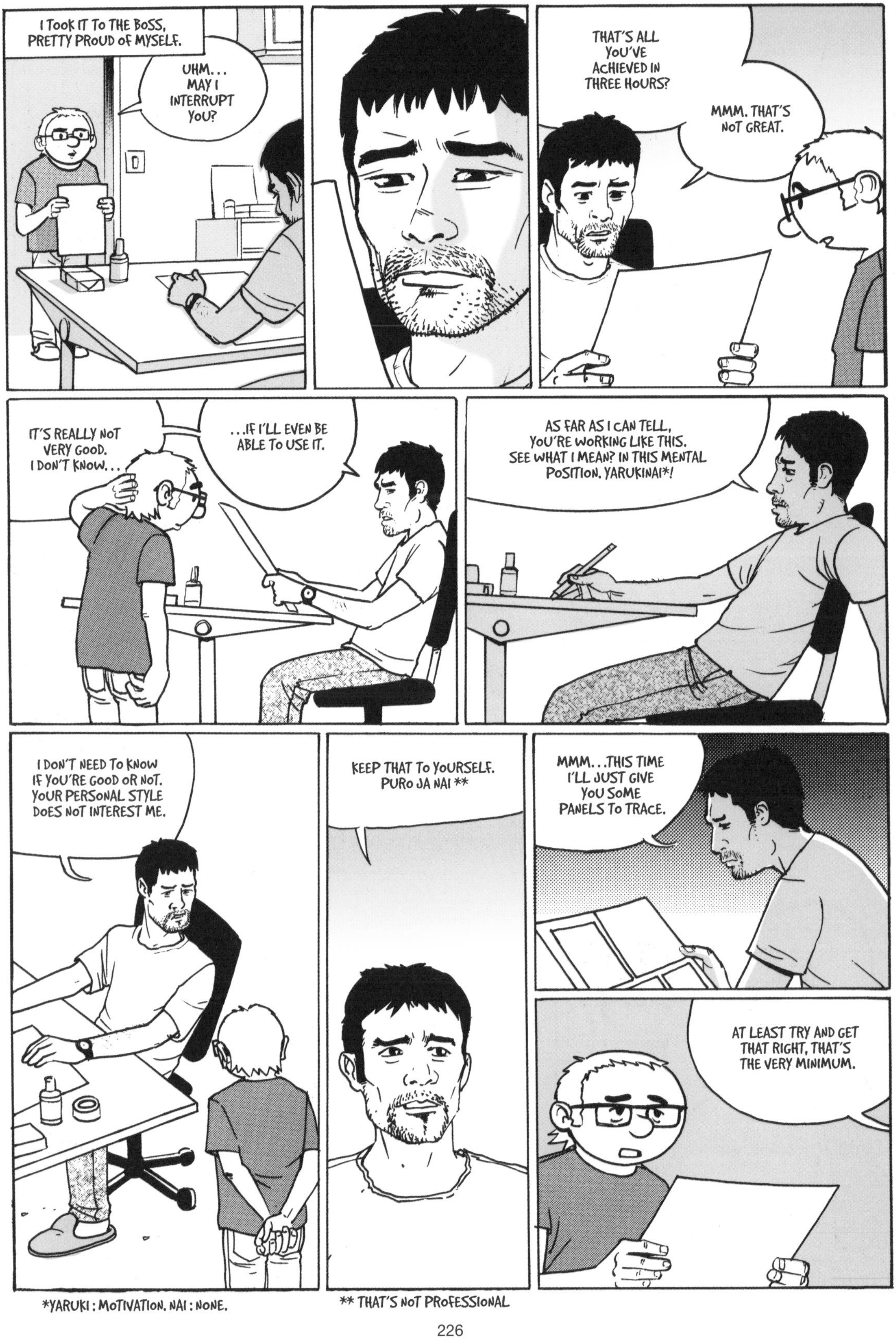
I TOOK IT TO THE BOSS, PRETTY PROUD OF MYSELF.
UHM... MAY I INTERRUPT YOU?
THAT'S ALL YOU'VE ACHIEVED IN THREE HOURS?
MMM. THAT'S NOT GREAT.
IT'S REALLY NOT VERY GOOD. I DON'T KNOW...
...IF I'LL EVEN BE ABLE TO USE IT.
AS FAR AS I CAN TELL, YOU'RE WORKING LIKE THIS. SEE WHAT I MEAN? IN THIS MENTAL POSITION. YARUKINAI*!
I DON'T NEED TO KNOW IF YOU'RE GOOD OR NOT. YOUR PERSONAL STYLE DOES NOT INTEREST ME.
KEEP THAT TO YOURSELF. PURO JA NAI **
MMM...THIS TIME I'LL JUST GIVE YOU SOME PANELS TO TRACE.
AT LEAST TRY AND GET THAT RIGHT, THAT'S THE VERY MINIMUM.

*YARUKI : MOTIVATION. NAI : NONE.

** THAT'S NOT PROFESSIONAL

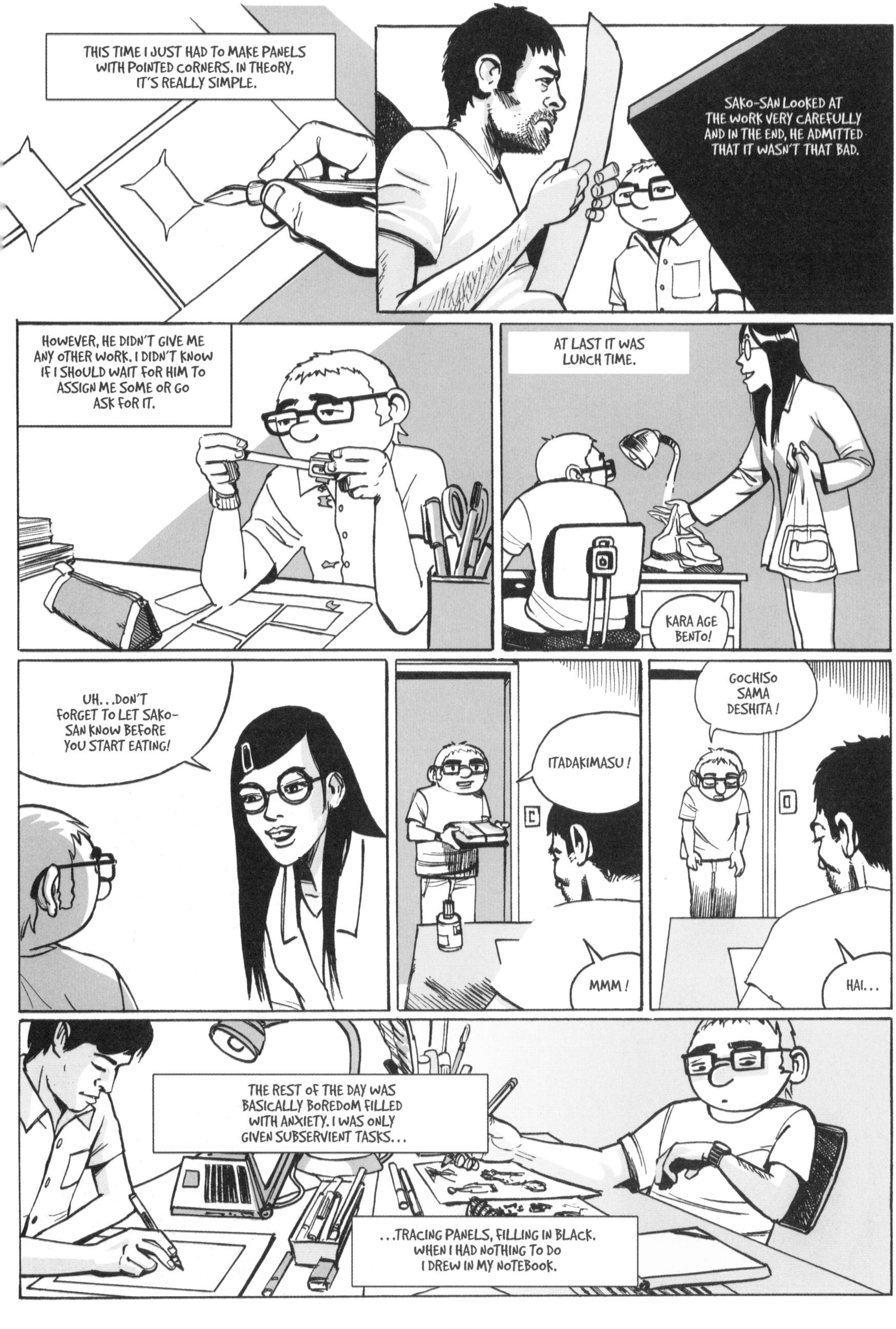

THIS TIME I JUST HAD TO MAKE PANELS WITH POINTED CORNERS. IN THEORY, IT'S REALLY SIMPLE.
SAKO-SAN LOOKED AT THE WORK VERY CAREFULLY AND IN THE END, HE ADMITTED THAT IT WASN'T THAT BAD.
HOWEVER, HE DIDN'T GIVE ME ANY OTHER WORK. I DIDN'T KNOW IF I SHOULD WAIT FOR HIM TO ASSIGN ME SOME OR GO ASK FOR IT.
AT LAST IT WAS LUNCH TIME.
KARA AGE BENTO!
UH...DON'T FORGET TO LET SAKO-SAN KNOW BEFORE YOU START EATING!
ITADAKIMASU!
MMM!
GOCHISO SAMA DESHITA!
HAI...
THE REST OF THE DAY WAS BASICALLY BOREDOM FILLED WITH ANXIETY. I WAS ONLY GIVEN SUBSERVIENT TASKS...
...TRACING PANELS, FILLING IN BLACK. WHEN I HAD NOTHING TO DO I DREW IN MY NOTEBOOK.

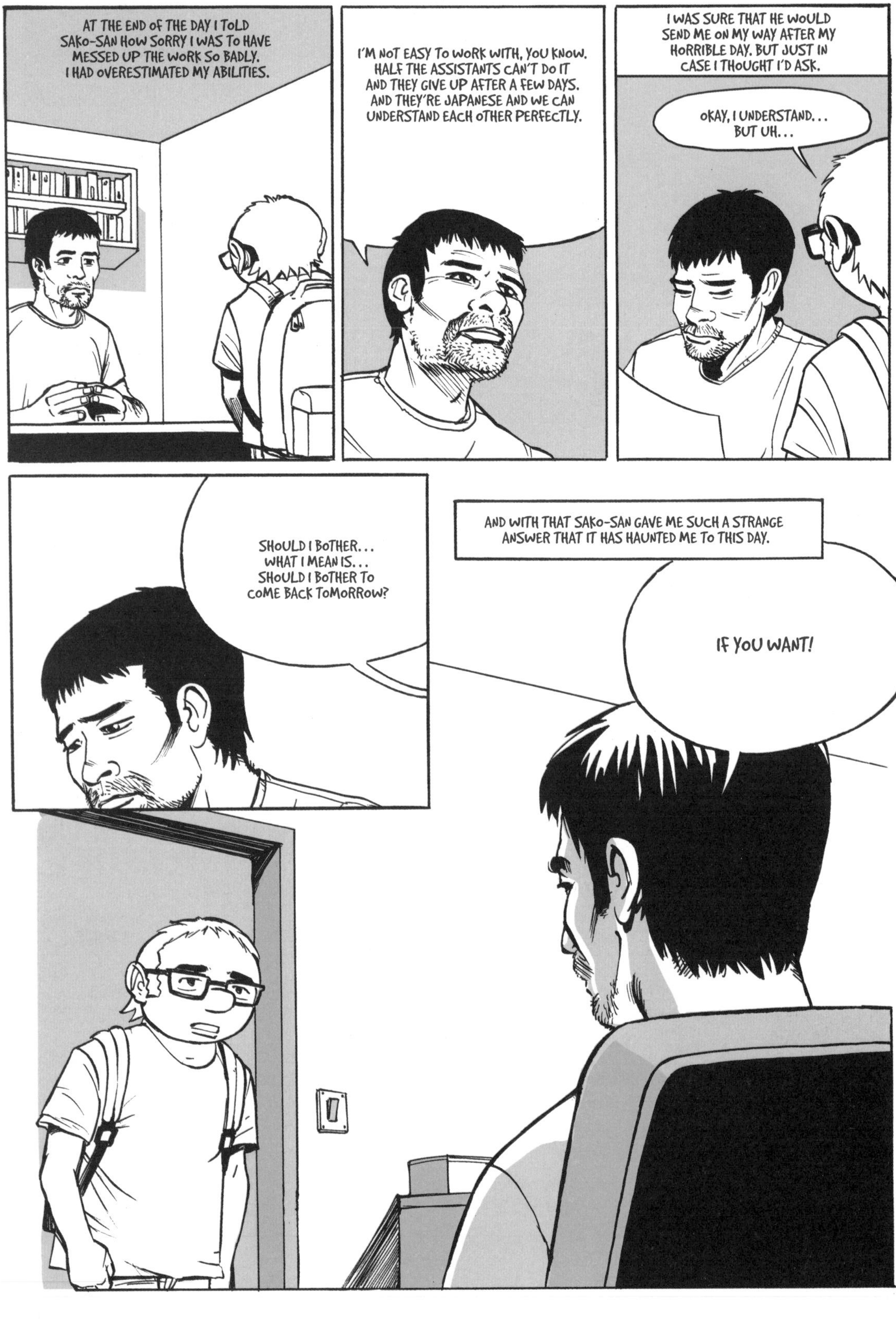
AT THE END OF THE DAY I TOLD SAKO-SAN HOW SORRY I WAS TO HAVE MESSED UP THE WORK SO BADLY. I HAD OVERESTIMATED MY ABILITIES.
I'M NOT EASY TO WORK WITH, YOU KNOW. HALF THE ASSISTANTS CAN'T DO IT AND THEY GIVE UP AFTER A FEW DAYS. AND THEY'RE JAPANESE AND WE CAN UNDERSTAND EACH OTHER PERFECTLY.
I WAS SURE THAT HE WOULD SEND ME ON MY WAY AFTER MY HORRIBLE DAY. BUT JUST IN CASE I THOUGHT I'D ASK.
OKAY, I UNDERSTAND... BUT UH...
SHOULD I BOTHER... WHAT I MEAN IS... SHOULD I BOTHER TO COME BACK TOMORROW?
AND WITH THAT SAKO-SAN GAVE ME SUCH A STRANGE ANSWER THAT IT HAS HAUNTED ME TO THIS DAY.
IF YOU WANT!

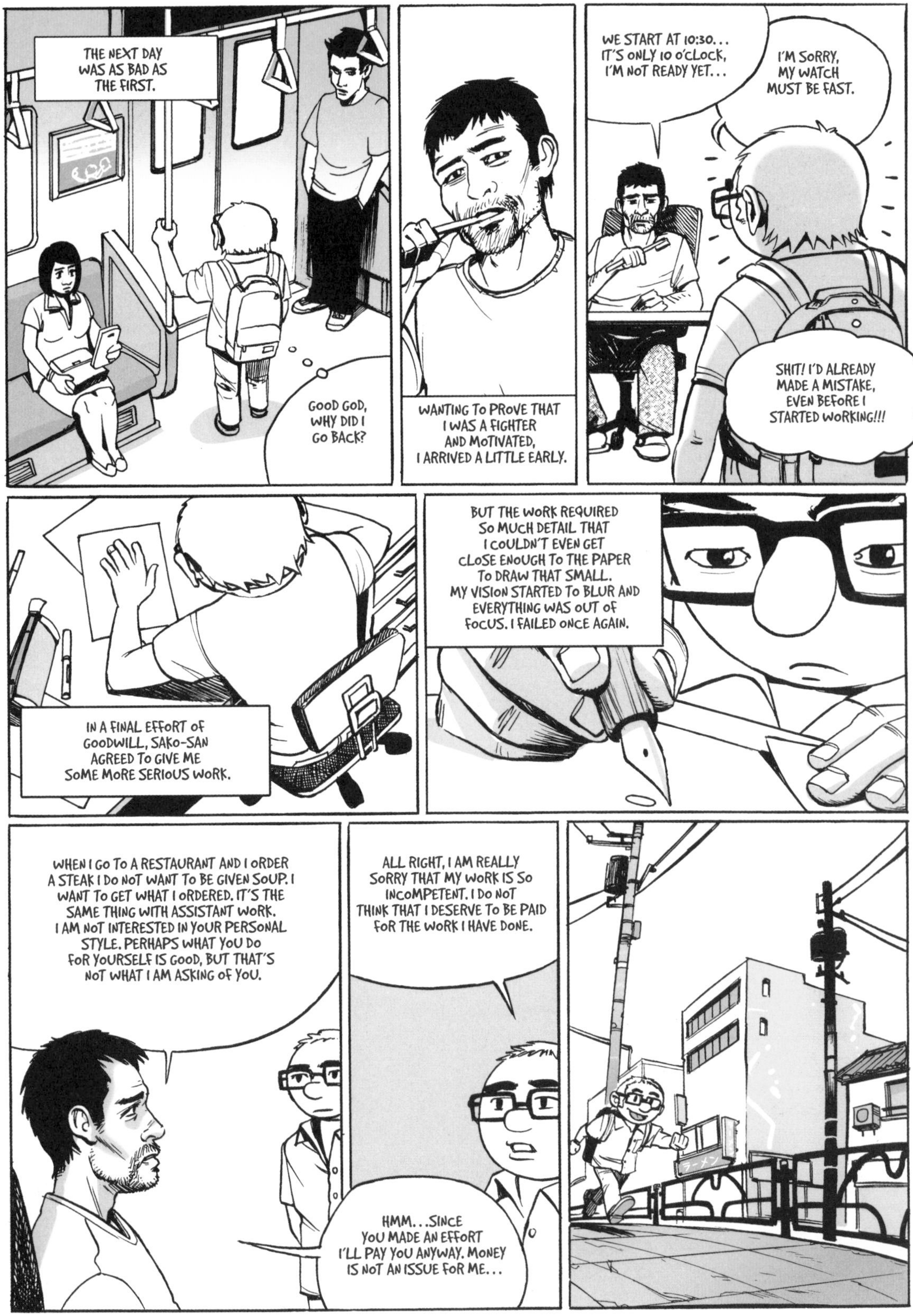
THE NEXT DAY WAS AS BAD AS THE FIRST.
GOOD GOD, WHY DID I GO BACK?
WANTING TO PROVE THAT I WAS A FIGHTER AND MOTIVATED, I ARRIVED A LITTLE EARLY.
WE START AT 10:30... IT'S ONLY 10 O'CLOCK, I'M NOT READY YET...
I'M SORRY, MY WATCH MUST BE FAST.
SHIT! I'D ALREADY MADE A MISTAKE, EVEN BEFORE I STARTED WORKING!!!
IN A FINAL EFFORT OF GOODWILL, SAKO-SAN AGREED TO GIVE ME SOME MORE SERIOUS WORK.
BUT THE WORK REQUIRED SO MUCH DETAIL THAT I COULDN'T EVEN GET CLOSE ENOUGH TO THE PAPER TO DRAW THAT SMALL. MY VISION STARTED TO BLUR AND EVERYTHING WAS OUT OF FOCUS. I FAILED ONCE AGAIN.
WHEN I GO TO A RESTAURANT AND I ORDER A STEAK I DO NOT WANT TO BE GIVEN SOUP. I WANT TO GET WHAT I ORDERED. IT'S THE SAME THING WITH ASSISTANT WORK. I AM NOT INTERESTED IN YOUR PERSONAL STYLE. PERHAPS WHAT YOU DO FOR YOURSELF IS GOOD, BUT THAT'S NOT WHAT I AM ASKING OF YOU.
ALL RIGHT, I AM REALLY SORRY THAT MY WORK IS SO INCOMPETENT. I DO NOT THINK THAT I DESERVE TO BE PAID FOR THE WORK I HAVE DONE.
HMM...SINCE YOU MADE AN EFFORT I'LL PAY YOU ANYWAY. MONEY IS NOT AN ISSUE FOR ME...
ラーメン

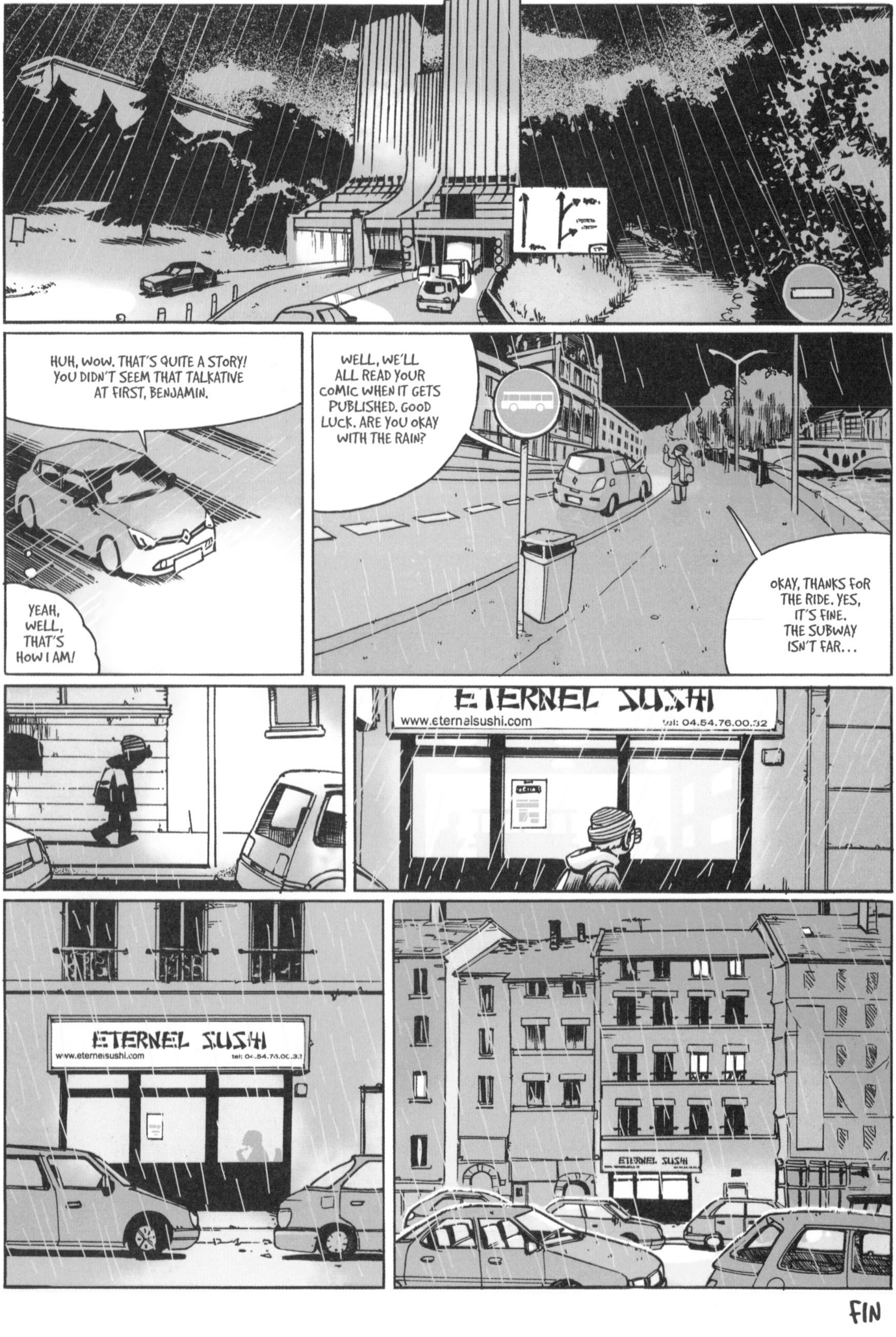
HUH, WOW. THAT'S QUITE A STORY! YOU DIDN'T SEEM THAT TALKATIVE AT FIRST, BENJAMIN.
YEAH, WELL, THAT'S HOW I AM!
WELL, WE'LL ALL READ YOUR COMIC WHEN IT GETS PUBLISHED. GOOD LUCK. ARE YOU OKAY WITH THE RAIN?
OKAY, THANKS FOR THE RIDE. YES, IT'S FINE. THE SUBWAY ISN'T FAR...
ETERNEL SUSHI
www.eternalsushi.com
tel: 04.54.76.00.32
ETERNEL SUSHI
www.eternelsushi.com
ETERNEL SUSHI

FIN